SOUTH AFRICA:
THE PROSPECTS OF PEACEFUL CHANGE
An empirical enquiry into the possibility of democratic conflict regulation

SOUTH AFRICA:
THE PROSPECTS OF PEACEFUL CHANGE

An empirical enquiry into the possibility of democratic
conflict regulation

*THEODOR HANF, HERIBERT WEILAND and
GERDA VIERDAG
in collaboration with
LAWRENCE SCHLEMMER, RAINER HAMPEL and
BURKHARD KRUPP*

REX COLLINGS   London
DAVID PHILIP   Cape Town
INDIANA UNIVERSITY PRESS   Bloomington

Published simultaneously in Great Britain, South Africa, and North America by Rex Collings (6 Paddington Street, London W1M 3LA), David Philip Publisher (Pty) Ltd. (217 Werdmuller Centre, Claremont, Cape), and Indiana University Press (Tenth and Morton Streets, Bloomington, Indiana 47405).

Typesetting by Malvern Typesetting Services, Great Britain
Manufactured in the United States of America
ISBN 086 036 144 6 (Collings)
    0 908396 24 4 (Philip)

Library of Congress Cataloging in Publication Data

Hanf, Theodor.
  South Africa, the prospects of peaceful change.

  Translation of: Südafrika, friedlicher Wandel?
  Bibliography: p.
  Includes indexes.
  1. South Africa—Politics and government—1961-1978.   2. South Africa—Race relations.   I. Weiland, Heribert, 1942-   II. Vierdag, Gerda,   III. Orkin, Mark.   IV. Title.
DT779.9.H3613   1981   960'.327   81-47583
ISBN 0253-35394-7 (Indiana)   AACR2
1 2 3 4 5 85 84 83 82 81

Contents

Preface to the English Edition

The German text of this book was completed in April, 1978 and published in June of the same year. It occasioned a lot of controversy in South Africa. Although relatively few people there could read it in the German, translated accounts of its main conclusions circulated fairly freely. Predictably, it was attacked from both the right and the left, in political and academic circles.

Radical critics of the work argued, inter alia, that the surveys among blacks were biased by the exclusion of Xhosa-speaking people in the Eastern and Western Cape. They considered this group to be relatively militant, and claimed that the effect of excluding it was to inflate support for Chief Gatsha Buthelezi. These critics also questioned the extensive support expressed among blacks for the 'consociational' or 'concordance democracy' options for the country's future political development. They maintained that the results did not reflect what they felt to be the extent of popular enthusiasm for a liberal, unitary democracy. The relatively peaceful stand of blacks revealed in the surveys was also doubted in the light of the critics' expectations that the 1976/77 disturbances in the townships would escalate.

Among conservative critics the assessment of South Africa's policy development as one of 'Scheinkonkordanz' (sham consociation) came under attack. In particular, well-meaning and ever-optimistic verligte Nationalists reacted against having the grand design of separate development described as 'sham' or 'fake'. It was felt that the work was too pessimistic about the prospects for meaningful short-term change. And at the conference in Titisee at which the book was launched, South African government representatives questioned the black samples. They felt the rural black population, which they assumed to be more conservative and contented than the urban populations selected for analysis, was under-represented.

In effect, then, each critic questioned whichever result did not fit into his own picture of social reality. As a prominent person from Soweto told us, 'I completely agree with all the results except one, and there I do

xi

not agree at all.' This seems to be inevitable in empirical social research, and South African reactions to the book have confirmed the experience. On both sides of the political spectrum some findings were questioned, and other—politically acceptable—results welcomed. In short, this is a classic case—itself perhaps a worthwhile subject of further research—of selective perception. This can be expressed in an elementary political maxim: 'If you don't like a finding, attack the sample.'

Criticism of the book in Europe has been directed not so much at the empirical facts and subsequent analysis as at the conjectures on the political future of South Africa in Chapter 15. These 'conjectures' are, indeed, speculative. And it is quite legitimate to advance other conjectures against ours. Of interest is the pattern of these alternative speculations. Conservative critics were delighted with our prediction that the present unilateral regulation of the conflict in South Africa could probably continue for a long time, albeit at increasing cost. From this they concluded that all would be well. On the other hand, liberal and radical critics question precisely this conjecture, for it runs contrary to their respective hopes: the former for rapid and peaceful change, the latter for change that will be equally rapid but revolutionary. Hence, in contrast to criticism in South Africa, that from various quarters in Europe was directed less at our facts and figures, and more at countering our conjectures on the future with different conjectures according to their respective hopes. As a more sophisticated political maxim this might read: 'If you don't like the findings, interpret them to fit your views.'

If one rejects both maxims one is left with conclusions that are sober, even if—like the authors—one finds them unpleasant. We still think, as we did in 1978, that the present unilateral regulation of conflict in South Africa can persist for a long time; and that, like it or not, neither rapid peaceful change nor sudden revolutionary change is likely.

We therefore feel that it is not only inappropriate but also unnecessary to bring the English translation of the original German text up to date. It would be inappropriate because the time-component in empirical research is unalterable. It would be deceptive and misleading to 'update' our data by simply commenting on recent events. It is unnecessary because recent research by Lawrence Schlemmer has confirmed the basic trends revealed in our surveys between 1974 and 1977. He documents this evidence in the Postscript which he prepared for this English edition. Furthermore, as far as our original 'conjectures about the immediate future' are concerned, the reader will be able to convince himself that some of our speculations in that chapter are very close to the mark. Accordingly, having revisited the prospects for peaceful change, the authors have no reason to revise their basic assessments.

Introduction

Even if the prospects for peaceful change are extremely slim, they are worth investigating.

Steve Biko

Do I have any hope? One doesn't need hope to act.

Alan Paton

Our aim in this book is not to tell black or white South Africans what they ought to do. Rather, we try to establish through empirical social research what the various groups would like to do, and what they are in fact able to do.

The overall issue which we consider is whether conflict can be regulated both peacefully *and* democratically.

The events of 1976 and 1977 established beyond doubt that *conflict* exists on a large scale in South Africa. The conflict is both open and latent. Its causes include the distribution of income and wealth between different groups, the enforced social segregation of the groups from each other, and the monopoly of power by one of the groups. This one group has used and continues to use its power to regulate the conflict, and does so unilaterally and towards its own ends.

Now conflict can be regulated in this way for a considerable period of time—longer than the whites dare hope and the blacks concede. But it is unlikely that power can be exercised indefinitely without the consent of the majority. Indeed, the longer a group exercises power without consent, the more likely is violent change.

Given the distribution of power in contemporary South Africa, violent change would involve enormous sacrifices all round. So we consider the chances of *peaceful change*.

Unfortunately, the chances seem slim. A glance at history shows that minorities tend to cling obstinately to their privileges, and then lose everything in defending them. One is far less likely to find minorities who have made timely sacrifices of some things in order to hold onto others. Similarly, once the tables are turned, the majorities that have been exploited and maltreated more often give vent to their long-suppressed

xiii

feelings of hate and revenge than explore the possibilities for a peaceful take-over of power.

Even so, however likely such developments may be when seen from a historical perspective, there is no 'iron law of history' which categorically excludes the possibility of peaceful change under the conditions obtaining in South Africa. And the 'social costs'—a euphemism in social science for human suffering—of violent change are so high that one is surely justified in exploring the constraints, however narrow they might be, within which the current system of conflict regulation in South Africa might be peacefully transformed. This consideration is even more important in the present global political situation; for change by violent means will not only endanger the parties directly concerned, but may also endanger the peace of the African continent and perhaps that of the rest of the world.

We also want to know whether conflict can be regulated *democratically*. We assume that the rule of law, social justice, and democratic rights are not the prerogatives of wealthy Western states. We believe that all the members of a society should be able to decide freely on how they want to shape their economic, cultural, and political co-existence.

This study is thus motivated by a specific interest: we want to ascertain what scope there is in contemporary South Africa for changing the existing system of domination, so as to allow the democratic regulation of conflict, more social justice, a greater diversity of cultural expression, and wider freedom for all South Africans.

We stress that we are concerned with the democratic *regulation* of conflict. For this purpose, the context in which conflict originated in South Africa is only relevant to the extent that it may still influence the present situation. Similarly, explanations of the phenomenon of conflict will be relevant only if they let us formulate more precisely the problem of how conflict may be peacefully and democratically regulated. This problem is important not because it contributes to the progress of social science—that contribution may be modest—but because it bears on the fate of many human beings.

We have tried to offer answers which can be supported by empirical inquiry. Although the literature on conflict regulation in South Africa has expanded rapidly in recent years, it is characterized by a lack of empirical data on the attitudes and opinions of the groups and individuals involved in the political process. We felt it would be useful if we lessened these gaps in our knowledge by empirical means.

But data on the attitudes and opinions of black and white South Africans are hardly a sufficient basis for reliable predictions about South Africa's future. Events in South Africa will not only be determined by the opinions and wishes of its inhabitants but also, as is becoming increasingly evident, by forces and influences outside the country. However, the latter have been expressly excluded from the present study; it is concerned, *ceteris paribus*, with internal South African developments.

But even with respect to internal developments, what actually happens in a society is only partly determined by what the members of the society think and want. It would thus be foolhardy to base a comprehensive prognostication on opinion surveys alone.

On the other hand, empirical surveys may facilitate a precise answer to the overall problem we have set ourselves. Empirical research can indicate how far white South Africans are prepared for peaceful change and democratic conflict regulation, and similarly, what change black South Africans expect and what means of conflict regulation they are prepared to accept. Does the preparedness of the whites match or fall far short of the expectations of the blacks? The question is crucial to change without violence. Thus, in respect of our motivation and of the limitations we have set on the nature of our inquiry, this study must be seen as *an empirical contribution to research into conflict and peace*.

Acknowledgements

A number of people collaborated with the authors in preparing this book. Although all of these were involved in varying degrees in the basic research, the authors alone bear responsibility for the evaluations and conclusions and, of course, for all mistakes that may have occurred.

Professor Lawrence Schlemmer, Director of the Centre for Applied Social Sciences at the University of Natal, is co-author of Part Three. The authors are especially indebted to him for his willingness to put his enormous experience in social research in South Africa at their disposal in the construction of the empirical surveys.

Rainer Hampel and Burkhard Krupp collaborated on the construction of the questionnaires and helped supervise the separate stages of the field-work. They processed and statistically analysed the data from the surveys of the white South Africans. Besides the permanent collaborators, mention must be made of Tania Vergnani-Rütschlin who assisted in the preparation of the surveys of the electorate. She and Doris Simon also conducted some of the interviews with members of the white leadership groups. Dr F. van Zyl Slabbert was kind enough to read and criticize parts of the manuscript.

The authors must also extend their thanks to the many colleagues, politicians, businessmen, and journalists who gave encouragement and support, and who readily granted interviews. They are too numerous to be thanked individually. A special debt is owed to Professor Nic Rhoodie, Otto Krause, and Dr Gerhard Tötemeyer, who prepared the preliminary 'brain-storming' sessions for the study and who opened many doors for the authors.

For insights into the political thinking of black South Africa gratitude is expressed to the late Robert Sobukwe and the late Steve Biko, both in their personal capacities and as representatives of those whose names cannot for obvious reasons be mentioned. Through their contact with the above-mentioned the authors not only learnt much but, above all, grew to esteem two men dedicated to peace.

Hennie Serfontein, a tenacious journalist and friend, requires special acknowledgement. It was he who, years ago, first awakened and then stimulated the authors' curiosity in South Africa. Without his comprehensive knowledge of the background and workings of South African politics the study in its present form would have been almost impossible. In particular, he and his friends served as a living caution against the danger of generalizing on the basis of statistical evidence. They, Afrikaners through and through, yet outspoken opponents of the government's policy, are responsible for the understanding and sympathy this book shows for the Afrikaner people.

The authors wish to express their gratitude to Countess Strachwitz, Mrs Marion Fraser, and Mrs Pam Thornley, who under trying conditions kindly and efficiently handled the English manuscript.

Finally, special thanks are due to John Richardson, who provided the translation, and Mark Orkin, who edited it. With great effort and skill they have made an English text out of a German one—and in the process convincingly refuted the hoary saying, 'traduttore-tradittore'.

PART ONE

Conflict and Conflict Regulation in South Africa:
Conditions for a Peaceful Change from Unilateral to
Democratic Conflict Regulation

CHAPTER 1

Conflict in Plural Societies: On the Possibility of Democratic Regulation

Few states in the world today are liberal democracies. Also in the minority are states with culturally homogeneous populations, i.e., with no cleavages or only minor cleavages between ethnic, linguistic or religious groups. Is there a correlation between cultural homogeneity and democracy on the one hand, and between cultural cleavages and undemocratic forms of government on the other?

This question explains the concern of social scientists with 'plural societies', i.e., societies characterized not only by cleavages between 'upper' and 'lower' classes, but also and more importantly by the juxtaposition and opposition of social segments. In plural societies people are not only or not chiefly classified by class, but by group: racial, ethnic, linguistic, and religious.[1] South Africa is without doubt a prime example of a plural society.[2]

[1] The concept 'plural society' is not uniformly employed in the literature. It is variously used as a synonym for 'fragmented', 'segmented' or 'composite societies'. However, Pierre L. van den Berghe has established a certain consensus on its content: 'Pluralism . . . refers to a property, or set of properties, of societies wherein several distinct social and/or cultural groups coexist within the boundaries of a single polity and share a common economic system that makes them interdependent, yet maintain a greater or lesser degree of autonomy and a set of discrete institutional structures in other spheres of social life . . .' Cf. idem, 'Pluralism', in John J. Honigmann (ed.) *Handbook of Social and Cultural Anthropology* (Chicago, 1973), p. 961.

In his book *Democracy in Plural Societies: A Comparative Exploration* (New Haven and London, 1977), p. 3, Arend Lijphart defines a plural society as one divided by 'segmental cleavages'. In this he has borrowed Harry Eckstein's definition of segmental cleavage; cf. Harry Eckstein, *Division and Cohesion in Democracy: A Study of Norway* (Princeton, 1966), p. 34: 'This exists where political divisions follow very closely, and especially concern, lines of objective social differentiation, especially those particularly salient in a society.'

[2] John Rex, 'The Plural Society: The South African Case', *Race*, 12:4 (1971), pp. 401–13; Ben Magubane, 'A Critical Look on Indices used in the Study of Social Change in Colonial Africa', *Current Anthropology*, 12:4 (1971), pp. 419–45; Leo Kuper, 'Political Change in White Settler Societies: The Possibility of Peaceful Democratization', in Leo Kuper and M. G. Smith (eds), *Pluralism in Africa* (Berkeley &

3

Clearly then, the general question of whether democracy is possible in plural societies is important for a study concerned with the particular case of South Africa. But as is often the case, social scientists have not been able to agree on an answer. Depending on their point of view, they can be divided into 'democratic pessimists' and 'democratic optimists'.[3]

Among the democratic pessimists are the Americans Alvin Rabushka and Kenneth A. Shepsle. After analysing a number of plural societies, they concluded:

> Instead we ask, is the resolution of intense but conflicting preferences in the plural society manageable in a democratic framework? We think not.[4]

Among the democratic optimists is the Dutch political scientist, Arend Lijphart. After a similar analysis—which included some of the societies selected by the Americans—he concluded:

> . . . it may be difficult, but it is not at all impossible to achieve and maintain stable democratic government in a plural society.[5]

1. *Democratic pessimists and democratic optimists: a clash of academic opinion*

Democratic pessimism among social scientists has two roots. The one root derives from the discussion in political science of the stability and instability of democracy in Western industrial states. The discussion distinguishes between what are defined as 'pluralistic' and 'plural' societies.[6] We consider the former case first. In pluralistic societies, there are numerous cleavages between different groups—be they strata or classes, parties, interest groups, and ethnic or religious groups. The important thing is that these cleavages do not coincide, but are cross-cutting. Various members of a given segment, for instance a linguistic or a religious community, will belong to different strata or classes and may support different political movements or opposing interest groups. The different kinds of social cleavage do not reinforce but counteract each

Los Angeles, 1969), pp. 169–93; Pierre L. van den Berghe, *South Africa: A Study in Conflict*, (Middletown, 1965); P. Randall (ed.), *South Africa's Political Alternatives, Report of the Political Commission of the Study Project on Christianity in Apartheid Society, SPRO-CAS No. 10* (Johannesburg, 1973).

Lawrence Schlemmer, 'Theories of the Plural Society and Change in South Africa', *Social Dynamics*, 3:1 (1977), pp. 3–16, includes an excellent survey of recent discussion.

[3] This term was coined by Arend Lijphart, who regards his work as a 'challenge to democratic pessimists'; cf. idem *op cit*, p. 2.

[4] Alvin Rabushka and Kenneth A. Shepsle, *Politics in Plural Societies, A Theory of Democratic Instability* (Columbus, Ohio, 1972), p. 217.

[5] Arend Lijphart, *op cit*, p. 1.

[6] On this distinction cf. Pierre L. van den Berghe, 'Pluralism', *loc cit*, pp. 959f., and Alvin Rabushka and Kenneth A. Shepsle, *op cit*, pp. 20f.

other, thereby creating an interlocking equilibrium.[7] The result is a homogeneous political culture despite all its pluralistic variety; and this is regarded as a prerequisite of stable democracy.[8]

By contrast, plural societies are characterized by a fragmented political culture. The various social cleavages are not cross-cutting but coincide, and therefore reinforce one another. When economic cleavages between strata or classes coincide with cleavages in language and outlook, i.e., when 'horizontal' are simultaneously 'vertical' cleavages, and particularly when political struggles are primarily struggles between different segments, then democracy is regarded as unstable and threatened.

On this argument, then, the Anglo-Saxon democracies are good examples of pluralistic societies with homogeneous political cultures.[9] On the other hand, most countries on the Continent are in varying degrees plural societies with fragmented political cultures, and are consequently precarious and unstable democracies.[10] And as many states in the Third World exhibit even more marked vertical cleavages than in Western Europe, the prospects for democracy in these countries are, on this view, gloomy.

We may now turn to the second root of the pessimism concerning democracy in plural societies. It derives from studies of Asian, African, and Latin American societies. From colonial times cultural anthropologists and economists have noticed deep cleavages between different ethnic and religious groups, and a lack of any unifying consensus. They established that in many of these societies the most important frame of reference for the individual was a vertically determined 'community',[11]

[7] E.g. Seymour Martin Lipset, *Political Man: The Social Bases of Politics* (Garden City, 1963), pp. 77f.; cf. Lewis Coser, *The Functions of Social Conflict* (Glencoe, 1956), pp. 78f.

[8] Karl W. Deutsch, *Nationalism and Social Communication* (Cambridge, Mass., 1953), p. 13, shows that a close relationship exists between cultural homogeneity, homogenous political culture, and political integration. On political integration cf. James S. Coleman and Carl G. Rosberg (eds), *Politial Parties and National Integration in Tropical Africa* (Berkeley, 1964); Leonard Binder, 'National Integration and Political Development', *American Political Science Review*, 58:3 (1964), pp. 630f.

[9] Cf. e.g., William T. Bluhm, *Theories of the Political System: Classics of Political Thought and Modern Political Analysis* (Englewood Cliffs, 1965).

[10] Cf. Gabriel A. Almond, 'Comparative Political Systems', *Journal of Politics,* 18:3 (1956), pp. 391–409; idem and Sidney Verba, *The Civic Culture: Political Attitudes and Democracy in Five Nations* (Princeton, 1963).

[11] This concept was defined by the permanent International Court of Justice as follows: 'Le criterium de la notion de la communauté . . . est l'existence d'une collectivité de personnes vivant dans un pays ou une localité donnée, ayant une race, une religion, une langue et des traditions qui leur sont propres, et unis par l'identité de cette race, de cette religion, de cette langue et de cette tradition dans un sentiment de solidarité à l'effet de conserver leur tradition, de maintenir leur culte, d'assurer l'instruction et l'éducation de leurs enfants conformément au génie de leur race et de

characterized by language, religion, region, ethnicity, or race. This community enjoyed the primordial, if not the exclusive, loyalty of the individual. [12] In most of the political entities created by the colonial powers these social segments now live side by side, but quite separately from one another. [13] The cleavages between them are necessarily worsened when, as often happens, the economic standing of the individual segments differs, i.e., when the horizontal and vertical cleavages coincide.

Thus, in societies such as these where pluralism has been colonially imposed, political conflict is endemic; the democratic regulation of conflict is explicitly or implicitly precluded. Such societies were held together in the past by highly undemocratic colonial rule; when this ceases to apply, one group becomes dominant and regulates group conflict unilaterally—unless the plural society disintegrates into separate political entities for each of the different segments. Indeed, the leading representative of this school of thought, M. G. Smith, regards the undemocratic regulation of conflict as integral to the definition of the concept of a plural society. [14]

Democratic pessimism in one or other form prevailed in the social sciences for a long time, especially during the 1940s and 1950s. And it seemed to be confirmed during the 1960s by the collapse of democratic government in the majority of newly independent former colonies.

During this time, what little optimism there was about the democratic future for plural societies in the Third World was essentially based on the assumption that existing vertical cleavages could be 'depoliticized' [15] and

s'assister mutuellement'. Cf. *Résumé Mensuel des Travaux de la Société des Nations*, 10:7 (1930), p. 219.

[12] Clifford Geertz, 'The Integrative Revolution: Primordial Sentiments and Civil Politics in the New States', in idem (ed.), *Old Societies and New States: The Quest for Modernity in Asia and Africa* (New York, 1963), pp. 105–57, regards as 'communities' such groups defined by language, religion, tradition, race, or kinship as command the primordial loyalty of their members.

[13] Some authors reserve the concept 'plural societies' solely for a specific historical type of society, viz. the multiracial colonial society; cf. especially J. B. Furnivall, *Netherlands India: A Study of Plural Economy* (Cambridge, 1939, repr. 1967); idem, *Colonial Policy and Practice: A Comparative Study of Burma and Netherlands India* (Cambridge, 1948, repr. 1956). By contrast, others do not regard pluralism as a form of society by any means restricted to tropical or colonial situations; cf. M. G. Smith, 'Some Developments in the Analytic Framework of Pluralism', in Leo Kuper and M. G. Smith (eds), *op cit*, pp. 415–58.

[14] M. G. Smith, 'Social and Cultural Pluralism', *Annals of the New York Academy of Sciences*, 83 (1960), pp. 763–77. Smith creates a further limitation by defining the politically dominant group as a minority. In later works Smith speaks of 'differential incorporation' as the basic criterion of plural societies, i.e. the political domination of one cultural group over the others. Cf. idem, 'Institutional and Political Conditions of Pluralism', in Leo Kuper and M. G. Smith (eds), *op cit*, pp. 27–66; idem, 'Some Developments in the Analytic Framework of Pluralism', *loc cit*, pp. 415–58.

[15] A. Etzioni, *Political Unification: A Comparative Study of Leaders and Forces* (New York, 1965), pp. 35f., supports the view that the depoliticization of cultural

thereby dismantled. The hope was that 'political modernization'[16] would weaken traditional political loyalties of a cultural, ethnic, or religious kind. A single national authority would then replace a variety of political authorities in the individual social segments. On this view, the key to stable democracy lay in 'nation building',[17] which ultimately required that the plural character of the society be blurred, if not disappear altogether. In effect the adherents of this school of thought—in their reliance on the concepts of political modernization, political development, and nation building—were optimistic about homogenizing plural societies, but not about the prospects for democracy in societies which remain plural. In retrospect it is clear that this school vastly underestimated the resistance to social integration in these societies.

Only in the mid-1960s did academics start to surmise that democracy might be able to take root even in plural societies. They based their considerations on several plural societies in Europe which were deeply divided by language, religion and outlook, but were nevertheless democracies of considerable stability: Switzerland, the Netherlands, Belgium, Austria, and—outside Europe—the Lebanon (at least until 1975).[18]

On the pessimistic view, these democracies 'in theory should not exist'—as an American political scientist put it to a Dutch colleague—or were classified as 'exceptional cases'.[19]

The democratic optimists argued instead that democracy exists in these plural societies precisely because they have developed patterns of conflict regulation which are particularly well adapted to the requirements of a plural society. Gerhard Lehmbruch refers to these specific patterns of conflict regulation as *Konkordanzdemokratie* ('concordance democracy'), while Arend Lijphart uses the term 'consociational democracy'.[20] The basic tenet of consociational democracy is that

cleavages can defuse them and thereby render cultural pluralism compatible with stable democracy.

[16] Cf. Dankwart A. Rustow, 'Modernization and Comparative Politics. Prospects in Research and Theory', *Comparative Politics*, 1 (1968), pp. 37–51; Samuel P. Huntington, 'The Change to Change: Modernization, Development and Politics', *Comparative Politics*, 3 (1971), pp. 283–322; idem, *Political Order in Changing Societies* (New Haven, 1969). Cf. Szymon Chodak, *Societal Development, Five Approaches with Conclusions from Comparative Analysis* (New York, 1973), pp. 252f.

[17] Cf. the survey of the literature in Stein Rokkan, *Citizens, Elections, Parties: Approaches to the Comparative Study of the Processes of Development* (Oslo, 1970). Cf. also Franz Wilhelm Heimer, 'Begriffe und Theorien der politischen Entwicklung', in Dieter Oberndörfer (ed.), *Systemtheorie, Systemanalyse und Entwicklungsländerforschung* (Berlin, 1971), pp. 449–515.

[18] Cf. the survey of the literature in Hans Daalder, 'The Consociational Democracy Theme', *World Politics*, 26 (1973/74), pp. 604–21.

[19] *Ibid*, p. 607.

[20] The authors developed their concepts independently of each other. Prior to using 'Konkordanzdemokratie', Lehmbruch spoke of 'Proporzdemokratie'. Cf. idem,

conflicts between social segments must not be regulated by majority decision. For, in a plural society, this would always mean a unilateral decision in favour of the largest or strongest group. Conflict must rather be regulated by amicable agreement among the various groups. This presumes that they all participate in the exercise of power, and requires continual compromise. Consociational democracy means that the various groups in a plural society have their cultural as well as their political autonomy recognized. Consociation is achieved and maintained through constantly adjusted compromises, for which the political élites or the leadership of the different segments are responsible.[21]

Thus, the supporters of this school qualify their optimism. They do not claim that any form of democracy can be practised in plural society. But they are convinced that in such contexts, consociational democracy does provide a suitable model of conflict resolution.[22]

This view has a further implication. In 1969, apropos an investigation of the Lebanese political system, one of the authors of our present study argued that the failure of democracy in numerous plural societies of the Third World could be better explained in terms of 'the wrong model of democracy' rather than in terms of a general 'incapacity for democracy'.[23] He contended that the model of democracy, viz., the centralized national state, which had been exported to the Third World in the train of decolonization, was for plural societies the most unimaginative and least suitable model conceivable.

In a comprehensive work published in 1977 Lijphart emphatically

Proporzdemokratie: Politisches System und politische Kultur in der Schweiz und in Österreich (Tübingen, 1967); idem, 'Konkordanzdemokratie im politischen System der Schweiz', Politische Vierteljahresschrift, 9:4 (1968), pp. 443–59. Lijphart based his use of the term 'consociational democracy' on Johannes Althusius' concept of the consociatio. Cf. Arend Lijphart, 'Typologies of Democratic Systems', Comparative Political Studies, 1:1 (1968), pp. 3–44; idem, 'Consociational Democracy', World Politics, 21:1 (1969), pp. 207–25.

Lehmbruch employs the concepts of Konkordanzdemokratie and consociational democracy as synonyms. Cf. idem, 'Consociational Democracy in the International System', European Journal of Political Research, 3 (1975), p. 378.

[21] For a broad overview of works using the approach of consociational democracy see Kenneth McRae's anthology, Consociational Democracy: Political Accommodation in Segmented Societies (Toronto, 1974). Lijphart's most recent book, Democracy in Plural Societies, op cit, provides the most comprehensive and thorough study.

In Chapter 12 below the literature on consociational democracy will be discussed in greater detail.

[22] Arend Lijphart, ibid, p. 238: 'For many of the plural societies of the non-Western world . . . the realistic choice is not between the British normative model of democracy and the consociational model, but between consociational democracy and no democracy at all.'

[23] Cf. Theodor Hanf, Erziehungswesen in Gesellschaft und Politik des Libanon (Bielefeld, 1969); idem, 'Liberale Demokratie in einem Entwicklungsland: Libanon' (Working paper for the study group on 'Übertragbarkeit westlicher Demokratievorstellungen auf Entwicklungsländer', Conference of the Deutsche Vereinigung für Politische Wissenschaft, Berlin, October 1969).

confirmed this contention. In his view consociational democracy is not only an empirical model which convincingly explains the political stability of some plural societies, but also a *normative model* for other plural societies.[24]

Lijphart formulates the normative aspect of consociational democracy as a direct challenge to democratic pessimists. He identifies three crucial errors in their thinking. The first is that they draw a comparison between oversimplified ideal types: homogeneous Western societies and heterogeneous Third World societies. The comparison is based on an idealized view of Anglo-Saxon societies in which their homogeneity is greatly overestimated. Secondly, the democratic pessimists totally disregard the successful experiences of the European consociational democracies. The third and fatal error is to assume that the society has to be reshaped, i.e., its plural character weakened or eradicated, as a prerequisite for democracy. They fail to see that segmental loyalties in plural societies are so strong that attempts to tamper with them are not only likely to fail, but may actually reinforce cohesion within groups and deepen conflict between them. Lijphart maintains that consociational democracy avoids this danger, and can both engender a considerable degree of national unity and promote democracy.[25] Finally, Lijphart warns that democratic pessimism may become a self-fulfilling prophecy:

> If politicians and political scientists are convinced that democracy cannot work in the plural societies of the Third World, they will not even try to introduce it or make it work.[26]

Clearly, democratic pessimism and democratic optimism are diametrically and irreconcilably opposed. And each theory is supported by analysis of material favourable to its own thesis. The pessimistic school bases its analysis partly on functioning non-plural democracies and partly on clearly undemocratic conflict regulation in plural societies, while the democratic optimists draw upon examples of successful consociational democracies. In neither case does 'theory' help us guess at the outcome of an actual study of the feasibility of democratic conflict regulation in South Africa.

On the contrary, such a study would probably contribute to the better understanding of the issue which divides the theories, the problem of democracy in plural societies. For the study would raise the question of democracy in a particularly difficult plural context. Suppose one could show that democratic conflict regulation in South Africa is, while not necessarily easy, at least not impossible. This would strongly support the case of democratic optimism. The opposite conclusion would not contri-

[24] Arend Lijphart, *op cit*, pp. 1f.
[25] *Ibid*, pp. 21f.
[26] *Ibid*, p. 3.

9

bute much to the theoretical debate however, for even the optimists do not rate the prospects of democratic solutions in South Africa very highly. Lijphart, for example, notes that the conflicts within South African society are particularly severe.[27]

In any case, an empirical study on South Africa would be superfluous if one accepted the theses of the pessimists. A measure of optimism is initially a *sine qua non* of this study, if it is to have any point. We thus assume as a *working hypothesis* that *democratic conflict regulation in South Africa is not excluded*. This hypothesis will have to be substantiated—or disproved.

2. *The dimensions, pattern and severity of conflict*

Social science, we have found, cannot predict the prospects for democratic conflict regulation. Do the theories of plural society at least provide us with any pertinent tools for conflict analysis?

It is beyond the scope of this study to review the literature on this topic in detail. However, it is generally agreed that conflict in plural society assumes a variety of forms.[28] These can be subsumed under three major dimensions of conflict, viz., the economic, the socio-cultural, and the political. While the dimensions may be distinguished conceptually in this way for analytical purposes, they are of course closely interrelated. The precise nature of the interrelationship, however, is a matter of some dispute.

One school of thought emphasizes the priority of the economic dimension. Conflict is caused by cleavages between classes which have opposing economic interests. On this view, the cleavages between segments in a society are in themselves unimportant; they only become conflict when the segments pursue diverging and contradictory economic interests.[29] In other words this school holds that conflicts in plural

[27] *Ibid*, p. 236: 'In the extreme cases of plural societies such as South Africa, the outlook for democracy of any kind is poor . . .'

[28] Lawrence Schlemmer, 'Theories of the Plural Society and Change in South Africa', *loc cit*, p. 4.

[29] In particular J. S. Furnivall, *op cit,* attaches great importance to the economic conflict. Many neoMarxist writers simplify the issue by adopting an exclusively economic approach or by making the implicit assumption of an exclusively economic causality.

Cf. i.a., Frederick A. Johnstone, *Class, Race and Gold: A Study of Class Relations and Racial Discrimination in South Africa* (London, 1976); Martin Legassick, 'South Africa: Capital Accumulation and Violence', *Economy and Society*, 3 (1974), pp. 253–91; Stanley Trapido, 'The South African Republic: Class Formation and the State 1850–1900', in *Institute of Commonwealth Studies*, No. 16 (1971–2), pp. 53–65; idem, 'South Africa in a Comparative Study of Industrialization', *Journal of Development Studies*, 7:4 (1971), pp. 309–20; Harold Wolpe, 'Industrialism and Race in South Africa, in S. Zubaida (ed.), *Race and Racialism* (London, 1970), pp. 151–79; idem, 'Class, Race and the Occupational Structure', *ICS* No. 12 (1970–1), pp. 98–119.

societies are in the final analysis class struggles, even if they manifest themselves as ethnic, racial, linguistic, or religious conflicts.

By contrast, it is precisely to these socio-cultural conflicts that a second school attaches prime importance. Individuals are held to have a primordial loyalty not to strata or classes, but to the basic social groups of a plural society: ethnic, racial, linguistic, or religious. [30] This view is supported by the observation that the most serious conflicts in plural societies are often those between people who belong to the same or similar social classes, but to different cultural groups. [31] This fact cannot simply be defined away as 'false consciousness'. [32]

A third school regards as crucial not economic or cultural conflicts, but political conflicts. [33] The reason advanced is that groups and group cleavages, be they economic or cultural, do not exist in a vacuum; they are politically manipulated. Political systems can either intensify or reduce economic and socio-cultural antagonism, either engender unilateral conflict regulation or encourage group compromise.

The first and second schools are generally pessimistic about the

Recent discussion has concentrated on overcoming such economistic restrictions. On the one hand, attention is being paid to the significance of the ideological and political aspects (L. Althusser, N. Poulantzas), and on the other, the theory of the mode of production is being developed further, with special attention being given to the societies of the Third World. Such studies make a point of stressing the fact that although the capitalist mode of production has penetrated 'peripheral societies', this has not destroyed pre-capitalistic modes of production. Accordingly, any attempt to reduce analysis to purely economic contradictions is rejected out of hand in respect of such 'structurally heterogeneous' social formations. The recent discussion is touched upon in the *Review of African Political Economy*, 7 (1976), which deals exclusively with South Africa.

[30] M. G. Smith attaches supreme importance to cultural cleavages. In his view, a plural society is characterized by the juxtaposition of irreconcilable institutional systems. Cf. idem, 'Social and Cultural Pluralism', *loc cit*. Later, he distinguishes between 'cultural pluralism', i.e. purely institutional differences between groups, 'social pluralism', i.e. the coincidence of institutional differences and corporate groups, and, finally, 'structural pluralism', i.e. where institutional and corporate cleavages coincide with the differing degrees of economic and political power held by individual groups (differential incorporation). Cf. M. G. Smith's chapters in Leo Kuper and M. G. Smith, *op cit*. However, the cultural dimension of conflict remains fundamental, because 'structural pluralism' presupposes both 'social' and 'cultural' pluralism, and 'social' in its turn 'cultural' pluralism.

[31] For Ceylon and Malaysia, cf. James Jupp, 'Ceylon and Malaysia', in Adrian Leftwich (ed.), *South Africa: Economic Growth and Political Change* (London, 1974), pp. 187–211.

[32] Cf. Paul Rich, 'Ideology in a Plural Society: The Case of South African Segregation', *Social Dynamics* (1975), pp. 167–80; Adrian Leftwich, 'The Constitution and Continuity of South African Inequality: Some Conceptual Questions', in idem (ed.), *South Africa: Economic Growth and Political Change, op cit*, pp. 125–85.

[33] E.g., Schermerhorn emphasizes the importance of domination and coercion in plural societies, in R. A. Schermerhorn, *Comparative Ethnic Relations* (New York, 1970). In his introduction to Leo Kuper and M. G. Smith, *op cit*, Kuper points out that pluralism must be seen in part as a consequence, and not only a cause, of political domination. Different political systems can shape plural societies in different ways.

possibility of democratic conflict regulation; the former on the basis of economic assumptions and the latter on the basis of cultural assumptions about the inevitability of struggle between classes or cultural groups— struggle in which the possibility of violence cannot be excluded. By contrast, the third school has a voluntaristic strain. In its view, conflict resolution is no less possible than conflict; for both can be influenced or directed by political action.

From the position of the first or second school, it would be pointless to make an empirical study of the possibility of democratic conflict regulation in South Africa. Does doing such a study therefore commit one to the third, the voluntaristic position?

A fourth position is conceivable. There are many plural societies, and the severity of conflict within them varies widely. None of the three schools outlined above can convincingly explain this variation in the degree of conflict. [34] For example, differences between economic interests in plural societies may or may not develop into conflicts *within* cultural groups, or *between* them. Moreover, cultural group conflict can arise irrespective of the economic situation. Finally, economic and cultural conflicts may or may not determine the pattern of political conflict in plural societies. In sum, the economic, cultural, and political dimensions of conflict may coincide in some plural societies, and run counter to one another in others. It is quite possible that in a given plural society one group is economically dominant, another culturally and a third politically. Furthermore, cleavages may cross-cut in some dimensions and coincide in others. So it is surely implausible to stipulate in principle that one dimension of conflict will be primary. And the context of conflict itself may change: the cause of conflict in some previous situation may be different from that in the current context.

Thus, one should treat the relative importance of the dimensions of conflict and the relationship between them in a given society as *empirical questions* [35] rather than a matter of definition.

Suppose then that one wants to determine the potential for conflict and how severe it may be. The first step is to get objective data on just what differences there are between groups. These will include differences in property and income; in the ethnic, linguistic, religious and cultural characteristics of the groups; and in their exercise of political power. For each of these three dimensions, the differences can be smaller or larger: for example, 'objective' economic differences between groups are less important in Switzerland than in South Africa; cultural differences are

---

[34] Cf. Lawrence Schlemmer, *op cit*, p. 5: '. . . the broad concept of pluralism or corporate group organization is unable to explain variation in the degree of conflict among different plural societies.'

[35] I.a., Lawrence Schlemmer, *ibid*, and Sammy Smooha, 'Pluralism and Conflict: A Theoretical Exploration', *Plural Societies*, 6:3 (1975), pp. 69–89, share this point of view.

less important between the various Christian denominations in the Netherlands than between Christians and Moslems in Lebanon; and differences in the way groups exercise power are less important in Austria than in Rhodesia.

One may then derive the aggregate severity of conflict by determining the relationship between the differences in the various dimensions. For example, if a given cultural group has both economic and political power the conflict potential will be high.[36]

In other words, it is only once differences between groups have actually been investigated and the relationship between these differences established for the various dimensions that one is in a position to draw conclusions about the severity of conflict.

3. *How groups view themselves and how they view conflict: the significance of perceptions for conflict regulation in plural societies*

'Objective' differences between groups, i.e., differences that in fact obtain, provide the potential for conflict. But they do not in themselves guarantee that conflict will occur; this depends on 'subjective' factors, i.e., how the parties involved perceive these differences, what they understand by conflict, how they regard it, and how seriously they take it. This question of how conflict is perceived is particularly important for the problem of *regulating* it.

The perceptions of political action have been shown to be crucial to the conflicts between states. Simulation games used in the Stanford study of the causes of World War I have shown that a different perception of hostility might have prevented the outbreak of the war.[37] It is plausible that the perception of conflict may be even more decisive for the regulation of conflict within societies, especially plural societies.

It is probably true in general that objective cleavages and opposing economic interests only develop into conflicts when they are so perceived. The Marxist distinction between a 'class in itself' and a 'class for itself' expresses this precisely. A 'class for itself' has the 'correct consciousness' for class struggle, i.e., it is not only aware of the cleavages and clashes of interest that objectively exist, but also sees them 'in their

[36] Sammy Smooha, *op cit*, p. 82: 'It is clear that superimposition between inequality on the one hand and social and cultural pluralism on the other is bound to exacerbate conflict.' He bases this conclusion on the results of quantitative comparisons analysed by Christopher Bagley, 'Racialism and Pluralism: A Dimensional Analysis of Forty-Eight Countries', *Race*, 13:3 (1972), pp. 347–54.

[37] O. R. Holsti, 'The 1914 Case', *American Political Science Review*, 59:2 (1965), pp. 365–78; idem, 'Comparative Data from Content Analysis: Perceptions of Hostility and Economic Variables in the 1914 Crisis', in R. L. Merritt *et al.* (eds), *Comparing Nations: The Use of Quantitative Data in Cross-National Research* (New Haven, 1966), pp. 169–90; R. C. North, 'Perception and Action in the 1914 Crisis', *Journal of International Affairs*, 21:1 (1967), pp. 103–22.

proper light'. A 'false consciousness' cannot prevent the class struggle but it might delay it. Thus even Marxist social doctrine, which gives precedence to economic cleavages, holds that they must first be perceived as conflicts before they develop into actual conflicts.

In non-Marxist theory the perception of economic conflict is dealt with by the concept of 'relative deprivation'.[38] More important than 'absolute' economic levels is whether a group regards itself as comparatively better or worse off than another. If a group regards itself as relatively disadvantaged a situation of economic conflict exists.

Subjective perceptions are even more important for socio-cultural cleavages than for economic cleavages. Socio-cultural groups in a society are not only differentiated by the characteristics they in fact possess. How such characteristics are assessed and interpreted by members of the society is equally important. Cultural groups[39] can be distinguished by skin colour, language, religion, way of life, customs, or any combination of these and numerous other criteria. But it is only when these characteristics are used by groups to identify themselves or other groups that they become relevant to social processes and conflicts. In other words, these criteria are important to the extent that they shape a group's perception of itself or of alien groups.[40] Thus, the criterion of skin colour is more important in the U.S.A. than in Brazil, language is more important in Belgium than in Switzerland, and religious denomination is more important in Northern Ireland than in the Netherlands.

Now whether or not such criteria of differentiation in fact coincide seems to be less important for group cleavages than how one or other criterion of differentiation is evaluated by the groups concerned. As many examples show, even a single criterion may be enough for differences to develop into conflicts. We thus contend that whether or not there are 'objective' criteria of differentiation, if a specific socio-cultural group perceives itself as different from other groups, then it is in effect a distinct group. In short, a cultural difference is what a sufficiently large

[38] Cf. S. A. Stauffer et al, 'The American Soldier: Adjustment during Army Life', in *Studies in Social Psychology in World War II*, Vol. 1 (Princeton, N.J., 1949).

[39] Here the concept of 'cultural groups' is used in its widest sense: a cultural group is a societal segment defined in terms of non-economic criteria. In Anglo-saxon usage it is more or less synonymous with 'ethnic group'. 'Ethnicity' in this sense may refer to race, origin, religion, or language.

[40] Cf. F. R. Westie in Robert E. L. Faris (ed.), *Handbook of Modern Sociology* (Skokie, Ill., 1964), p. 580: 'It makes no sense sociologically to define race relations as relations between biologically different groups or individuals. The relations between objectively quite different biological groupings may be, in particular times and places, unaffected by such differences; whereas interactions between groupings the world over are shaped by believed differences which do not in fact exist. W. I. Thomas' phenomenological view refers to the most important element in any conceptualization of race relations: "A situation defined as real is real in its consequences." By the same token, in Brazil, to the degree that people do not emphasize the "reality" of skin colour differences, such differences, may be said, sociologically, not to exist.'

14

group in a society regards as a cultural difference, and likewise the conflict between cultural groups is what is regarded as such.[41]

Clearly, the same will apply to political groups and political conflicts; for political groups can be based on innumerable criteria, which may or may not be 'objective'.

As one might expect, therefore, the cardinal feature of plural societies is the forming of political groups, usually on the basis of perceived differences between cultural groups. Political conflicts thus find expression as conflicts in varying degrees between racial, ethnic, linguistic, or religious groups.

A further important question for the analysis of the political dimensions of conflict in plural societies is whether differences arise from a group's actual self-awareness, or from the perception of the group by others. Group self-awareness is an essential element of what in historical and political terminology is called a 'volk' or 'community'. But even when such a self-awareness is lacking, relevant differences can be effected by imposing an identification on a group—especially if this is done by another group in power.

A particularly callous example of the latter was during the Third Reich, when Jews were identified as aliens. The ruling National Socialists defined who counted as Jewish, irrespective of whether the person perceived himself as Jewish or not. An identity imposed in this way can certainly generate a group self-awareness on the part of the affected group. Nevertheless, such self-awareness does not confirm the existence of external criteria, but develops out of a solidarity in being discriminated against, in both senses of the word—'differentiated' and 'oppressed'.[42]

Thus, how groups are perceived is important for the analysis of economic, socio-cultural, and political dimensions of conflict. And just as these dimensions of conflict are interrelated so are the perceptions of them. But it is quite possible that relationships between the perceptions do not coincide with the 'objective' relationships, whatever the criteria for the latter may be taken to be. Indeed, it is likely that the perceptions of these relationships will vary from group to group.[43]

[41] Pierre L. van den Berghe, 'Pluralism', *op cit*, p. 968: 'As ethnicity, however, is not only a function of objective cultural differences, it is also important to take into account the subjective perceptions of cultural differences by members of various groups.'

[42] Similar reactions have also been manifested by American negroes who are searching for a new identity—at times under great inner stress. Cf. George E. Simpson and J. Milton Yinger, *Racial and Cultural Minorities: An Analysis of Prejudice and Discrimination* (New York, 1965), Ch. 6: 'The Consequences of Prejudice and Discrimination: The Responses of Minority-Group Members', pp. 130ff; W. Simon, 'Schwarzer Nationalismus in den USA', *Kölner Zeitschrift für Soziologie und Sozialpsychologie*, 15 (1963), pp. 605–42.

[43] Pierre L. van den Berghe, 'Pluralism', *op cit*, p. 969: 'One must also allow for the complication that the subjective perceptions of various groups are not necessarily congruent with each other.'

Thus, a comprehensive analysis of conflict will take into account the objective realities of group conflict, but will accord decisive weight to the various perceptions of the conflict on the part of the groups involved in assessing the severity of conflict in the economic, cultural, and political dimensions. And when we are dealing with the *regulation* of conflict, how groups view themselves and how they view the conflict are even more central to the analysis.

These introductory thoughts on the possibilities of democratic conflict regulation in plural societies may be summarized as follows. The theoretical debate is unresolved, so we cannot reach any conclusions in advance. We have therefore assumed as a working hypothesis that democratic conflict regulation in South Africa is not impossible. We shall have to test this assumption. For analytical purposes we have distinguished between economic, socio-cultural, and political dimensions of conflict. The relative weight of each will have to be established empirically. How conflict is perceived by the groups involved is taken to be the central factor in conflict regulation, and is therefore the chief concern of our present study.

CHAPTER 2

Unilateral Conflict Regulation: The Present South African System and its Dimensions of Conflict

The inequalities of property and income in South Africa are comparable to those in numerous class societies in the early stages of their industrialization; yet there is less labour strife than in, for instance, Argentina or Italy, and fewer manifestations of class cleavage. The population comprises different race groups; yet clashes between them were fewer than in the United States in the late '60s and early '70s. There is even further fragmentation, on the basis of ethnicity, religion, and language; yet this has never given rise to group conflict as intense as that in the Lebanon, Northern Ireland, or Cyprus.

It strikes foreign visitors that government buildings are less heavily guarded in Pretoria and Cape Town than in Washington, Paris, and Bonn. On internal flights, hand luggage is not even inspected. One wonders whether the Prime Minister, Mr Vorster, was really so mistaken when at a congress of the ruling party he declared to thundering applause that 'South Africa is one of the most peaceful and safe countries in the world'.

On the other hand, representative surveys of urban black opinion revealed as early as 1972 that there was 'enormous resentment towards the whites'. Less than 2 per cent of those interviewed defended the existing system. More than 75 per cent were 'embittered' and 'angry'. And whereas in 1972 almost half the respondents believed their situation was improving, in similar surveys in 1976 only 26 per cent still shared this opinion.[1]

[1] Cf. L. Schlemmer, 'Research Analysis of Principal Problems and Development Priorities in Black Urban Communities' (Address delivered at the Businessmen's Conference on the Quality of Life in Urban Communities, Johannesburg, November 1976). Schlemmer bases his conclusions on his own studies done in the townships of Durban in 1971/72. In 1975 and 1976 he conducted further studies in KwaMashu and Soweto. As early as the beginning of the 1960s E. A. Brett established that animosity

17

As for white South Africans, in 1974 more than half of them felt that most blacks regarded whites with increasing bitterness. Sixty per cent of whites thought a black uprising was probable some time in the future.[2]

Both perspectives are aspects of the present reality of the South African system: on the one hand, open conflict is relatively absent, and on the other hand the groups hate and fear each other. Within the system, there are massive conflicts between the groups. But up to now they have been *regulated unilaterally*, i.e., *by the domination of one group*, which holds and exercises power without the consent of the majority of the population.

1. *Enforced inequality: the economic dimension of conflict*

In no other country in Africa is the contrast between wealth and poverty, development and under-development, as stark as in South Africa. Not far from the highly industrialized Witwatersrand with its dense communications-network lie poor 'homelands' in which few roads are even tarred. In Johannesburg, wealthy residential suburbs are only a few minutes' drive from bleak and overpopulated Soweto, which is still for the most part without electricity. In the farming areas of the 'platteland' propertyless and dependent rural labourers live in humble huts not far from the comfortable homesteads of prosperous farmers.

Property and income differentials as enormous as these may exist in other societies. Peculiar to South Africa is the extent to which these differentials occur along racial lines.

The under-developed part of South Africa is populated almost exclusively by blacks. Approximately one-third of the population live in the bantustans—that 13.7 per cent of the total territory which, in terms of government policy, constitutes the 'homelands' of the blacks.[3] Self-subsistence agriculture predominates in these areas. But yields are so low that the majority of their adult male population is forced to seek a living as migrant labour in the urban industrial areas.

The urban and industrialized regions of the country have been declared to be white preserves, together with the large tracts of the rural areas where market-oriented agriculture predominates. Even in these 'white' areas blacks are in the majority. In the large cities, blacks are at

towards the whites was already widespread among members of the black middle class. Cf. E. A. Brett, *African Attitudes—A Study of the Social, Racial, and Political Attitudes of some Middle-Class Africans* (SAIRR, Johannesburg, 1963).

[2] Based on the authors' own studies; cf. Chapter 4 below.

[3] On the position, size, and economic potential of the homelands cf. Axel J. Halbach, *Die südafrikanischen Bantu-Homelands: Konzeption—Stuktur—Entwicklungsperspektiven* (Munich, 1976), pp. 25ff. For a very critical discussion of the homeland question cf. Gottfried Wellmer, *Südafrikas Bantustans: Geschichte, Ideologie und Wirklichkeit* (Bonn, 1976).

least as numerous as whites; in the 'white' rural areas they are in the overwhelming majority.[4] Yet blacks may only own or control the means of production, including land, inside the homelands. Outside the homelands these privileges are reserved for whites and, to a minimal extent, coloureds and Indians.[5]

Differences in income* correspond to the differences in property ownership. Whites constitute not quite 20 per cent of the economically active population, and receive two-thirds of all wages and salaries in South Africa. By contrast, blacks constitute 70 per cent of the economically active population, but only receive one-quarter of all income.[6] In 1975, the average monthly earnings of a black were R105, of a white R458.[7]

On average, whites earn between four and five times as much as blacks. But the figures vary considerably from sector to sector. Whites earn 5.1 times as much as blacks in the public sector, 4.8 in manufacturing, 4.6 in the wholesale trade, and 3.5 in banking and insurance.[8] The greatest inequality is in the mining sector, which employs predominantly foreign labour from other African states:[9] the ratio here is 8.4 to 1.

*As mentioned in the preface to the English edition, the authors have decided not to adjust the statistical data according to the changes which have taken place in the meantime. The wages and income figures have to be seen in relation to the opinion survey data collected between 1974 and 1977. But even taking into account that the relative income increases over recent years have favoured blacks more than whites, the fundamental economic inequalities still exist.

[4] On the basis of the 1970 census approx. 3.65m blacks live in the rural areas of 'white' South Africa alone, i.e., one-fourth of all South African blacks. Republic of South Africa, Bureau of Census and Statistics, *Population Census* (Pretoria, 1970).

[5] The South African Government employs the following classification: whites, Asians, coloureds, and blacks. Black South Africans were formerly designated Bantu, and before that Natives, both thoroughly repugnant to those affected. In the meantime the Black Consciousness movement has used the term 'black' for all South African race groups dominated by the whites, i.e., also for the Indians and the coloureds. The collective label 'non-whites' frequently employed by whites is also rejected for reasons of political identity. The terms 'Bantu' and 'non-white' are used in this text only insofar as they occur in direct quotations.

We have retained the term 'coloureds', although it has a far wider embrace in many countries beyond South Africa, e.g. Great Britain. In this text the terms 'Asian' and 'Indian' are used as synonyms. Among the whites—formerly officially termed 'Europeans'—we distinguish between English speakers and Afrikaners.

[6] Cf. South African Institute of Race Relations (SAIRR): *A Survey of Race Relations in South Africa, 1976* (Johannesburg, 1977), p. 280, as well as SAIRR, *A Survey . . . , 1975*, pp. 173f. The figures are based upon statistics of the South African Reserve Bank.

[7] Calculations based on figures taken from Arnt Spandau, 'Einkommensverteilung in Südafrika', in Heinz Dietrich Ortlieb and Arnt Spandau (eds), *Südafrika: Revolution oder Evolution?* (Hamburg, 1977), pp. 133f. The figures are based upon data of the Dept of Statistics, Pretoria, 1975. As the latter do not take the income of farm labourers or domestic servants into account, our average monthly wage for blacks may well be on the high side.

[8] Cf. *ibid*, p. 134.

[9] Labour is drawn primarily from Mozambique, Lesotho, and the Transkei

It must be granted that between 1970 and 1975 black incomes grew faster than white, by 103 per cent and 56 per cent respectively.[10] The percentage increase in black income is calculated on a smaller amount to begin with. So it has not been enough to close the income-gap; on the contrary, in absolute terms the gulf between black and white incomes widened in most sectors.[11]

The economic inequalities between the race groups are seen to be even more pronounced when additional data on living standards are included. Dystrophy and malnutrition are unknown among whites, but affect over 60 per cent of all blacks of school-going age.[12] The average life expectancy at birth of a white is about 68 years; of a black, 45 years.[13] The state spends an average of R605 per annum on the education of a white child, and R40 per annum on a black child.[14]

These few facts illustrate the enormous economic inequalities which exist between blacks and whites, inequalities not only in income and property but also in living conditions. The whites enjoy one of the highest standards of living in the world. A large section of the black population lives in poverty—by which we mean that minimum level of existence defined by criteria used in official South African statistics.[15]

Hence, economic differences between strata in South Africa generally

(previously also Malawi). The low wages include accommodation and meals in hostels provided by the mining corporations, medical care, etc. On the controversial question of migrant labour in South Africa cf. particularly Francis Wilson, *Migrant Labour* (Johannesburg, 1972), and Peter Ripken and Gottfried Wellmer (eds), *Wanderarbeit im südlichen Afrika*, ISSA, Vol. 5 (Bonn, 1976).

[10] Cf. SAIRR, *A Survey of Race Relations . . . , 1976, op cit*, p. 276, and Arnt Spandau, 'Einkommensverteilung in Südafrika', *loc cit*, pp. 132ff.

[11] Notwithstanding wage increases for black mine workers of approx. 333 per cent between 1970 and 1975, the absolute wage-gap between blacks and whites rose from R 4040 to R 6850 over the same period. Although the difference in real terms was lower, the absolute wage difference in 1975 was still higher than in 1970. In real terms the wage-gap has been reduced only in the insurance and building society sectors. Cf. A. Spandau, 'Einkommensverteilung . . .', *loc cit*, pp. 134f.

[12] SAIRR, *A Survey of Race Relations . . . , 1976, op cit*, p. 381.

[13] Cf. Sheila van der Horst, *Progress and Retrogression in South Africa: A Personal Appraisal* (SAIRR, Johannesburg, 1971), pp. 22f.

[14] SAIRR, *A Survey of Race Relations . . . , 1976, op cit*, p. 321.

[15] In South Africa a 'physical existence minimum' is calculated on the basis of the individual household—the Household Subsistence Level. The Institute for Planning Research at the University of Port Elizabeth calculated a minimum of R 127 for a 'black' household of six persons for October 1976. This was an average for 20 black townships in South Africa. Cf. SAIRR, *A Survey of Race Relations . . . , 1976*, pp. 275f. The minimum for the larger cities—Johannesburg, Durban, Pretoria—was R 131. This figure makes no allowance for educational, medical, travel, and cultural expenses, i.e. expenses included in a 'cultural existence minimum', called the Household Effective Level. For a definition and calculation of the Household Effective Level cf. A. Spandau, 'Einkommensverteilung in Südafrika', *loc cit*, pp. 138f.

South African statistics work on the basis that the household income—the counterpart of the 'Subsistence Level'—is earned by an average of 1.7 members of the household. Accordingly, the average monthly family income would be approx. R 179.

coincide with differences between the segments characteristic of a plural society; the 'races' are for the most part also 'classes'.[16] However, this statement needs qualification. Comparisons between the average wages of specific race groups tend to obscure the stratification within each race group and especially the fact that the distributions of income partially overlap racial divisions.

In recent years blacks have increasingly been employed in more senior positions, where they work on the same level as whites. They then earn more than whites in the lower income groups. In the public sector blacks are still paid less than whites in comparable positions, but in the private sector equal pay for equal work is fast becoming the rule.[17] In other words, stratum and segment, 'class' and 'race', do not always coincide. Although there are enormous differences of property and income between the ethnic groups, the lines of economic stratification cut across these groups to some extent.

This feature has given rise to the thesis that economic inequality in South Africa is not specifically the result of racial discrimination, but a 'normal' consequence of the country's capitalist economic development. The degree of economic inequality in South Africa is said not to be exceptional, but comparable to that in other semi-industrialized countries.

Thus, Michael O'Dowd[18] uses various indicators to show that South Africa is not a highly developed industrial state. Per capita income, urbanization, and the percentage of the work force in agriculture place South Africa on a similar economic level to Spain—higher than Brazil, but lower than Italy or the Soviet Union. The distribution of income in South Africa is found to be no more unequal than in comparable countries. Skilled workers in South Africa, who happen to be predominantly white, earn about the same as their counterparts in Western Europe and other industrial countries, because technicians are scarce everywhere. Conversely, there is a world-wide surplus of unskilled labour.[19] Indeed, South Africa is only peculiar in the relatively high pay

[16] For a convincing presentation of the thesis of overlapping classes and races see L. Schlemmer, 'Social Forces and Social Change in South Africa', in P. Randall (ed.), *Towards Social Change, SPRO-CAS Publication no. 6* (Johannesburg, 1971), pp. 5–16.

[17] Wage equality has not been fully implemented in the private sector either, though discriminatory measures are being steadily dismantled. An illustration of this process was the statement of 641 members of the Cape Town Chamber of Commerce in April 1977. Cf. *Sunday Times*, Johannesburg, 24.4.1977. For the time being the differentials in the Civil Service are officially prescribed. Cf. below, pp. 30f.

[18] Michael C. O'Dowd, 'South Africa in the Light of the Stages of Economic Growth', in Adrian Leftwich (ed.), *South Africa: Economic Growth and Political Change* (New York, 1974), pp. 29–43; idem, 'Stufen wirtschaftlichen Wachstums', in Heinz D. Ortlieb and Arnt Spandau (eds), *Südafrika—Revolution oder Evolution?, op cit*, pp. 63–79.

[19] According to O'Dowd, the oversupply of unskilled labour in the industrial states is

received by unskilled labour—for the most part black—in comparison with other African and Asian countries.

According to O'Dowd, then, economic inequality in South Africa is less the consequence of arbitrary racial discrimination than of the specific market conditions of a semi-industrialized country.[20] That race and class went hand in hand until the end of the 1950s was a consequence of free economic competition. In short, economic inequality in South Africa has not been enforced, but has evolved 'normally'.[21]

Now it cannot be denied that, for historical reasons, technological development has been slower in some segments of the population than in others. This disadvantage would account in part for the inequality. But it is equally undeniable that throughout South Africa's history racial inequality in the free market has continually been reinforced by political and administrative intervention. As a result, attempts to close the socio-economic gap have had at best marginal success. Inequality has been maintained by imposing limitations on the right of ownership, by regulating the labour market, and by restricting education. Each of these measures has substantially affected the economic interests of the blacks. We consider them in turn.

The most severe restrictions apply to *rights of ownership*. Only in the so-called 'homelands' may blacks acquire rights in immovable property, and only there is black economic activity unimpeded. These areas have a

a consequence of a surplus of migrant labour. Stricter controls on immigration would have prevented wages from falling.

[20] In O'Dowd's opinion racial discrimination has only a marginal effect. He believes that industrial progress will promote a trend towards economic and social equality. He feels that the noticeable improvement in black wages in the last two decades confirms his view. Cf. M. C. O'Dowd, 'Stufen wirtschaftlichen Wachstums', *loc cit*, pp. 74ff.

[21] The neo-Marxist interpretation of South Africa's capitalist development is in sharp contrast to O'Dowd's liberal capitalist approach. In grossly simplified terms, the neo-Marxist view holds that the fundamental class cleavages in South Africa are the result of transferring European capitalist methods of production to South Africa with a corresponding class structure. In view of capital depreciation, the ruling class is prepared to employ any means to keep the cost of the labour factor of production as low as possible and profits as high as possible. Nor are the capitalists afraid to go beyond the market mechanism, and adopt methods of political and administrative manipulation and discrimination. Thus, racial discrimination should be seen as a function of capitalism. By and large, classes coincide with races. Minor deviations are easily explicable: the 'poor whites' are the 'petty bourgeoisie', their conflict with the up-and-coming blacks a strategic manipulation on the part of the owners of capital. The differing interests of the English speakers and the Afrikaners are explained as secondary contradictions within the ruling class.

The leading exponents of the neo-Marxist view are Martin Legassick, Shula Marks, Stanley Trepido, F. A. Johnstone, Charles van Onselen, and Harold Wolpe. A useful survey of the scientific controversy between liberal and neo-Marxist social scientists may be found in Harrison M. Wright, *The Burden of the Present: Liberal—Radical Controversy over Southern African History* (Cape Town, 1977). Cf. also Joel C. Edelstein, 'Pluralist and Marxist Perspectives on Ethnicity and Nation-Building', in Wendell Bell and Walter E. Freeman (eds), *Ethnicity and Nation-Building: Comparative, International and Historical Perspectives* (London, 1974), pp.45–58.

relatively good agricultural potential.[22] But this cannot obscure the institutionalized inequality whereby 70 per cent of the population owns 13 per cent of the land. Moreover, the homelands have few mineral resources and no significant industrial centres. They will be able to support at most half of the total black population for the foreseeable future. As a result, blacks are compelled to work as contract labourers in the 'white' cities, without the hope of ever being allowed to establish themselves there freely.[23]

The second area of control involves the *labour market*. In South Africa it is characterized by discriminatory measures such as job reservation, wage settlements on the basis of racial criteria, controls on the movement of labour, and the refusal to recognize black trade-unions and the right of black labour to strike.

Job reservation is the policy which, outside the homelands, reserves certain qualified occupations for whites. The various regulations date mainly from the 1920s and the 1930s, when less-skilled white labourers feared competition from members of other race groups.[24] Today, job reservation is applied pragmatically. To meet the increasing demand for skilled labour, the list of exceptions to the regulations is continuously extended, in a process of tripartite negotiations between employers, white trade-unions, and the government.[25] The government plays the role of a broker between the employers, who want to open the labour market to black labour, and the trade-unions, which want to preserve their

[22] Approx. 27 per cent of the total territory of South Africa is desert or semi-desert; of this only 0.5 cent lies within the bantustans. Only 35 per cent of the total territory has an annual average rainfall of over 500mm; 67 per cent of the territory allotted to the homelands lies within this rainfall area. The agricultural potential of the homelands is correspondingly high. Cf. Axel J. Halbach, *Die südafrikanischen Bantu-Homelands*, *op cit*, p. 29.

[23] There are two opposing views on the homeland question. Conservative thought regards the homelands as a form of protection for the blacks, who are unable to hold their own in a system of free competition; critics of the South African system see in the homelands a deliberate attempt to create reservoirs of labour for the 'white' industry. By creating bantustans, and thereby artificially creating migratory labour, white agriculture has been ridded of an unwelcome competitor. Cf. Jeffrey Butler, Robert I. Rotberg, and John Adams, *The Black Homelands of South Africa—The Political and Economic Development of Bophuthatswana and KwaZulu* (Berkeley and London, 1977), pp. 9ff. For a deeper analysis on a very theoretical plane see M. Legassick and Harold Wolpe, 'The Bantustans and Capital Accumulation in South Africa', in *Review of African Political Economy*, 7 (1976), pp. 87–107.

[24] The first legal measures were created by the Mines and Works Acts of 1911 and 1921. In terms of these pieces of legislation, blacks and Asians could not be promoted to skilled jobs in the mines. For a good account of job reservation see G. V. Doxey, *The Industrial Colour Bar in South Africa* (Cape Town, 1961).

[25] As a result of the scarcity of skilled labour, the number of positions reserved exclusively for whites has been reduced to a minimum; e.g. while blacks may do the undercoating, the final coat of paint must be applied by a white. Black masons may not lay facing bricks on the facade of buildings; if the building is to be plastered, however, blacks may lay all the bricks. Cf. *Sunday Times*, 'The Silly Farce that Protects only One Job in Fifty', 14.11.1976.

monopoly on skilled jobs.[26] On the one hand, the government has an interest in a well-functioning economy, but on the other hand it cannot ignore the voting power of the white workers. The result is often 'job-splitting', i.e., racially separate labour hierarchies are created, while white labour is compensated with wage increases or additional social benefits.

The provisions governing the exceptions to the regulations can be reversed at any time. Job reservation could be reinstituted in all its force,[27] especially at a time of recession. At present the policy only affects a few occupations.[28] But it remains an effective barrier to the upward mobility of blacks, retarding their advancement into the commercial and industrial middle-class. For the occupations affected are precisely those which attract ambitious blacks intent upon advancing themselves socially and economically.

There are also legal quotas which set the maximum number of black workers which a firm under white management may employ.[29] These quotas constitute an indirect barrier to black mobility. They are intended to induce white businessmen to remove their firms to the borders of the homeland areas; their labour force would then work in 'white South Africa', but live in the black reserves.[30]

One of the most blatantly discriminatory methods of regulating the labour market is by a wage policy based on racial criteria. The maxim of 'equal pay for equal work' is most evidently abused in the public sector and in state-owned industries. A black doctor in a state hospital receives a salary of R5300 p.a., compared to the R7740 p.a. of his white colleague. The salaries of black teachers and nurses can be as much as 50

[26] For a detailed description of the procedure for the regulation of wage conflicts see P. J. van der Merwe, 'Labour Policy', in J. A. Lombard (ed.), *Economic Policy in South Africa* (Cape Town, n.d.), pp. 158–99.

[27] Cf. Robert Kraft, 'Labour: South Africa's Challenge of the Seventies', *Optima*, 20:1 (1970), pp. 2–11.

[28] At present legal job reservation affects only about 2 per cent of registered jobs. In recent years the Minister for Labour, S. P. Botha, has lifted reservations on numerous jobs, in the hotel and catering industry, iron and steel, the automobile and the furniture industries, construction, etc. When job reservation is lifted in a certain sector it is common practice to promote all whites affected to a higher job category. Cf. *Rand Daily Mail*, 'Another Fourteen Jobs are opened to Black Labour', 31.12.1977.

[29] Cf. Sect. 31 of the Physical Planning and Utilization of Resources Act. On the various restrictions applied to the labour market, cf. Benjamin Pogrund, 'Constraints on Black Workers and White Employers in South Africa', Study Project Paper no. 14, in *Foreign Investment in South Africa: The Conditions of the Black Worker* (Uppsala, 1975), pp. 127–60.

[30] For reasons of cost many firms are not prepared to leave the industrial centres, preferring to employ black labour illegally; if the law were strictly observed approx. 50,000 black workers would have to be dismissed. Cf. A. Spandau, *op cit*, pp. 147f. Cf. also W. Beinart, 'The Policy of Industrial Decentralisation in South Africa', Study Project Paper no. 12, in *Foreign Investment in South Africa, op cit*, pp. 85–125.

per cent less than those of their white counterparts.[31]

The 'free play of market forces' is further obstructed by legal restrictions on collective wage bargaining and strikes. Blacks are debarred from freely negotiating their income and working conditions. Black trade-unions are not prohibited. But they are not recognized as legal persons and so have no standing in collective bargaining.[32] White trade-unions, acting in a 'representative capacity', negotiate black wages. The only official voice granted to blacks is in the form of 'works or liaison committees'. However, these are no substitute for proper trade-unions, for they may not negotiate wages. The right of black labour to strike is also severely restricted.[33]

Over and above these restrictions, there is a plethora of regulations which effectively prevent black South Africans from improving their work situation by changing jobs, negotiating with employers, and so on. Blacks may not remain in a white urban area for longer than seventy-two hours without a permit.[34] To obtain a permanent residence permit, a black must prove that he has worked for one employer for an uninterrupted period of ten years, or if for more than one employer, for a period of fifteen years. He can only get work in 'white' South Africa through the state labour bureaux; and then his contract is valid for only one year, and his employer must apply for it to be extended.

This system of control on non-white labour has with justification been called the most perfect system of labour control in the world.[35] Its role in

[31] Another example: the salary of a black teacher holding a doctorate was, in 1976, R 210 less than the starting salary of a white teacher without any further qualifications. Cf. *Sunday Times*, 'The Darker the Skin the Lighter the Pay Packet', 10.10.1976.

[32] For an excellent presentation of examples of wage conflicts in South Africa and the influence of black trade-unions see L. Douwes Dekker, D. Hemson, J. S. Kane-Berman, J. Lever, and L. Schlemmer, 'Case Studies in African Labour Action in South and South West Africa', *The African Review*, 2 (1974), pp. 205–36.

[33] For a survey of the problems of the South African labour market see J. A. Grey Coetzee, *Industrial Relations in South Africa* (Cape Town, 1976), pp. 46f. and 123f. Cf. also L. C. G. Douwes Dekker, 'Principles of Negotiation and Grievance Procedure: With Reference to Migrant Workers on the Mines', *loc cit*, pp. 206–12. The history and present position of the black trade-unions is presented in Edward Feit, *Workers without Weapons: The South African Congress of Trade Unions and the Organization of the African Workers* (Hamden, Connecticut, 1975).

[34] This regulation is based on a regulation dating back to the 1923 Native Urban Areas Act, today widely known—particularly with respect to the pass laws—as Section Ten. Cf. B. Pogrund, *op cit*, pp. 131ff.

[35] John Rex has described the South African system of labour controls as more exploitative than slavery; as a rule, slave-owners accepted responsibility for their slaves in old age as well as for the care of their families, whereas the South African system of migrant labour tries to shift the social responsibility for the workers on to the reserves. Cf. John Rex, 'The Plural Society', *loc cit*, p. 405; idem, 'The Compound, Reserves and Urban Location', *South African Labour Bulletin*, Vol. 1, No. 2, pp. 19ff. Although South African firms have certainly accepted greater social responsibilities in recent years, the basic attitude is still that the homelands are responsible for social welfare.

maintaining inequality is complemented by a third means, an *educational policy* which draws a strict distinction between the races. The educational system for blacks receives less state finance than that for whites, it is tailored to the needs of the homelands, and it provides relatively few facilities for secondary and tertiary education. This is inequality by decree. The outcome is that certificates awarded to blacks—even in the field of technical education—are not generally recognized as equivalent to 'white' diplomas.[36]

It is obvious that this system of control will generate conflict between government and business in a growing economy. In general, businessmen would welcome the increased employment of blacks in higher positions, to relieve the notorious scarcity of skilled labour. However, the government acquiesces only when the interests of white labour are not endangered.

At the same time, employers have a clear interest in the system of control as a whole; for it guarantees them a stable and cheap supply of labour,[37] and costly labour unrest is virtually impossible. Thus, there may be an undeniable conflict of interests between business and the government over the question of job reservation; but superimposed on it is the crucial interest they have in common in the continuation of this system of control.

By now it should be quite clear that there is no free interplay of economic forces on the labour market. As far as blacks are concerned— the predominant part of all South African labour—the South African economy is based on 'forced labour'. The argument of liberal economists that the inequalities of distribution in South Africa are the more or less normal result of fundamental determinants of the supply of labour may well receive support from international comparisons. It is possible that even without the system of racial labour control, property and income in South Africa would be distributed as unequally as at present. It is also possible that even if there were no racial discrimination in the right of ownership and the market for labour, the white population would retain a privileged position—at least for a while—on account of its historically given technological advantage. But it is probable that in that case the

---

[36] Without a doubt, the South African government has greatly expanded the educational facilities over the past decades. Cf. *Official Yearbook of the Republic of South Africa* (Pretoria, 1976), Ch. 42, pp. 665ff. However, the quality of education did not keep pace with this expansion. Moreover, the gap between the standard of education of the blacks and that of the ruling white minority was only slightly closed. Cf. Freda Troup, *Forbidden Pastures—Education under Apartheid* (London, 1976).

[37] As long as only unskilled workers are affected the pass laws and other regulations are effective instruments of control. Unskilled labour can be replaced easily because of the surplus supply. However, once a firm has invested in the training and further education of its labour it is interested in keeping its labour turnover as low as possible. Hence, firms will apply the pass laws as disciplinary measures only in extreme cases. On the ambivalent attitudes of the business world see Chapter 7 below.

26

divisions between classes and strata would not coincide as closely with the divisions between racial groups as they do today.

To summarize: going by the most important objective data, there is large-scale economic inequality in South Africa. A minority has a virtual monopoly on the ownership of the means of production, receives the largest share of the national income, and enjoys a much higher standard of living. The majority is at a disadvantage. By and large, the minority and the majority can be identified with respective population segments, i.e., groups distinguished on the basis of racial criteria. Numerous political and administrative obstacles impede the economic advancement of members of the majority group. These obstacles are directed not at strata but at segments, i.e., racial groups. Thus, class conflict and racial conflict coincide.

The nature and extent of this inequality indicates a situation of potentially serious conflict. However, how serious the economic dimension of conflict will be depends on just how the participants perceive it. Do they regard economic equality as the outcome of their historically determined unequal origins, or of conscious manipulation on the part of the dominant group? Is it perceived as 'class conflict', 'racial conflict', or as a combination of both?

2. *Enforced differentiation: the socio-cultural dimension of conflict*

The several socio-cultural groups in South Africa can be distinguished, as they have been hitherto, on the basis of a number of objective criteria: skin colour, language, religion, and tradition. The experience of cultural differentiation has undoubtedly been important in the formation of South African society.[38]

The European colonists and their descendants encountered in South Africa peoples from whom they differed socio-culturally in virtually every respect: race, language, family and social structure, way of life, economic organization, and level of technological development. Skin colour was the most simple and obvious criterion of differentiation, and was soon identified with all the others. Whoever was different in colour was held to be different in everything else as well.

This experience by the various racial groups of the differences between

---

[38] The authors assume that the reader is acquainted with the basic elements of South African history. For those interested in further reading there are numerous works available. The most important consulted by the authors are Monica Wilson and Leonard Thompson (eds), *The Oxford History of South Africa*, Vols 1 and 2 (Oxford, 1969 and 1971); T. R. H. Davenport, *South Africa: A Modern History* (London and Basingstoke, 1977); C. W. de Kiewiet, *A History of South Africa—Social and Economic* (London, 1957); Harold R. Bilger, *Südafrika in Geschichte und Gegenwart* (Konstanz, 1976).

An excellent history of the Afrikaners is W. A. de Klerk, *The Puritans in Africa: A Story of Afrikanerdom* (London, 1975).

them was bound up with another fundamental experience in South African colonial history, viz., the technical and military superiority of the whites.

A group that has discovered the wheel and possesses gunpowder will enjoy a considerable superiority over a group that has not, on technological grounds alone. In South Africa this superiority led in turn to domination and economic privilege, both of which were then held to be justified by it.

A third formative experience must be added to those of racial differentiation and white technological superiority. The black groups never accepted the whites' claim to dominance. They offered military resistance until as recently as this century, and after white rule became established over the territory comprising the present Republic, continued to resist through various political channels. This experience has had consequences for both parties. The whites' sense of superiority is mingled with fear and animosity; the blacks, notwithstanding their sense of defeat and fear, are conscious of their own might and of their refusal to regard white rule as permanent.

That cultural differences have existed is a historical fact; that they persist cannot however be explained simply in terms of 'historical inevitability'.

Historically, socio-cultural differences were associated with immutable differences in origin and skin colour. But socio-cultural differences are of course subject to social and cultural change. The question then arises of whether such change has in fact occurred.

Empirical studies show that urban society, both black and white, has indeed undergone a social change.[39] Both groups increasingly show a lifestyle typical of a 'Western', urban, industrial and bureaucratic environment. The differences between urban blacks and urban whites seem nowadays to be based more on socio-economic status than ethnocultural origins. It has been noted that the cultural patterns of urban blacks amount to a subculture of poverty similar to that exhibited by urban groups of a similar economic status in other countries. Similarly, there is much evidence that urban whites exhibit socio-cultural characteristics typical of the prosperous middle class in most industrial societies.

Significant change can also be established in respect of another objective criterion, viz., religion. Fully 80 per cent of black South Africans

---

[39] Cf. Lawrence Schlemmer, 'Social Forces and Social Change', *loc cit*, p. 11. Schlemmer bases his study above all on the work of B. A. Pauw, *The Second Generation* (Cape Town, 1963), and Monica Wilson and Archie Mafeje, *Langa: A Study of Social Groups in an African Township* (Cape Town, 1965). On this point cf. also an anthology of conference papers, John Barratt *et al* (eds), *Accelerated Development in Southern Africa* (London and Basingstoke, 1974). The authors' own studies provided clear evidence of change; cf. Parts Two and Three below.

belong to Christian Churches.[40] Thus, a cultural boundary important in many societies has been blurred in South Africa. But many an objective difference still persists—above all, that of language.[41] Even among urbanized blacks, only a small minority speak one of the European languages as their mother tongue.[42] Moreover, in the 'homelands' the whole process of 'modernization' is only in its infancy.

There are many indications that white perceptions of black South Africans are strongly influenced by the continued existence of the 'homeland' enclaves, in which culture is still shaped by ethnic traditions. The average white still sees the black as a tribesman, not a city dweller.[43] This image of the so-called 'non-white' groups seems to be a consequence of cultural lag. It has not kept pace with social changes among these groups; instead of observing their current social practices, the whites evoke a historical stereotype. In other words, their perceptions of blacks are both incomplete and obsolete. They overlook the occurrence of change, and over-emphasize real or imaginary differences.

Various empirical studies on the attitudes of different groups of white South Africans have established that each group places itself first in

[40] Church membership of the black population by percentage, based on the 1970 census data (compared with the percentages for the white population):

	blacks (%)	whites (%)
Dutch Reformed	6.2	49.0
Anglicans	6.2	10.7
Presbyterians	2.2	3.1
Congregationalists	1.2	0.6
Methodists	11.2	9.6
Lutherans	5.1	1.1
Roman Catholics	8.8	8.2
Independent black Churches	18.4	—
Other Christian groupings	10.0	11.6
Other religions	30.8	—

[41] The Bantu languages in South Africa belong to four groups (the constituent languages are given in parentheses):

Nguni (Zulu, Xhosa, Ndebele, Swazi)	58.6%
Sotho (South Sotho, Pedi, Tswana)	30.9%
Venda	2.4%
Tsonga	4.3%
other	3.8%

Republic of South Africa, *Population Census*, 1970.

[42] Even among the urban blacks English is not generally spoken; in the interviews of the urban blacks (see Chapter 11) only 50 per cent chose to conduct the interview in English.

[43] It must be pointed out that the predominant stereotype of the 'tribesman' is to no small extent a consequence of the workings of the apartheid system. The consistent policy of limiting social contact as far as possible, including education, has restricted contact to the work and professional spheres. In these spheres the average white has contact only with less-educated blacks whose way of life is closer to traditional patterns. The educated blacks, who are generally either self-employed or employed by the civil service, find jobs for the most part in the bantustans or the townships.

29

order of preference, and non-white groups last.[44] Afrikaners distance themselves socially from non-whites to the greatest extent; English speakers do so to a lesser extent; and Jews do so least of all.[45] Afrikaners identify more strongly with their own group than do English speakers. Furthermore, group differences carry more weight with whites of lower economic or social standing than with whites who are economically or socially better-off.[46]

Conversely, the available data show that ethnocentricity is not peculiar to white South Africans.[47] All non-white groups display a negative and hostile attitude towards white South Africans in general, though they are more averse to Afrikaners than to English-speaking South Africans.[48] But it is not yet clear whether this general hostility has already given rise to a common 'black' identity embracing black Africans, Indians, and coloureds. This identity certainly exists among a small, well-educated black political élite.[49] However, among the less-educated, the values and institutions of specific ethnic groups still seem to exercise a strong hold. An example of the hold of ethnocentricity among subgroups in South African society is found in attitudes towards the Indian group: most groups find Indians less acceptable than any others, and all groups show the greatest social distance from the Indian group.[50]

In summary, it seems that most South Africans regard South African society as a society of groups, and give their first loyalty to their own

[44] T. Vergnani, 'A Survey of Empirical Attitude Studies Conducted in South Africa' (Duplicated manuscript, Arnold-Bergstraesser-Institut, Freiburg, 1971), provides an excellent survey of empirical studies on attitudes conducted since the 1930s. Cf. also Stanley J. Morse and Christopher Orpen (eds), *Contemporary South Africa: Social Psychological Perspectives* (Cape Town, 1975).

[45] The most important empirical studies on this aspect are those of T. F. Pettigrew, 'Social Distance Attitudes of South African Students', *Social Forces*, 38 (1960), pp. 246–53; H. Lever, 'Ethnic Preferences of White Residents in Johannesburg', *Sociology and Social Research*, 52 (1968), pp. 157–73; and H. Lever and O. J. M. Wagner, 'Ethnic Preferences of Jewish Youth in Johannesburg', *Jewish Journal of Sociology*, 9 (1967), pp. 34–47.

[46] Cf. I. D. MacCrone, *Race Attitudes in South Africa* (Johannesburg, 1937), and Pierre L. van den Berghe, 'Race Attitudes in Durban, South Africa', *Journal of Social Psychology*, 57 (1962), pp. 55–72.

[47] Cf. I. D. MacCrone, 'A Comparative Study of European and Non-European Differences in Race Preferences', *South African Journal of Science*, 35 (1938), pp. 412–16; S. Biesheuvel, 'The Influence of Social Circumstances on the Attitudes of Educated Africans', *South African Journal of Science*, 12 (1953), pp. 309–14; M. L. Edelstein, *What do Young Africans Think?* (Johannesburg, 1972).

[48] Cf. i. a. E. A. Brett, *African Attitudes—A Study of the Social, Racial and Political Attitudes of Some Middle-Class Africans, op cit*; also A. G. J. Crijns, *Race Relations and Race Attitudes in South Africa* (Nijmegen, 1959).

[49] Although Crijns and MacCrone established growing solidarity and awareness of identity among black Africans, there was at the time of those studies no talk of a transcending solidarity between all 'non-white' groups. On the acceptance of the Black Consciousness movement cf. the studies of the authors, Chapter 11 below.

[50] Cf. Pettigrew, Lever, and Van den Berghe, *op cit.*

group—albeit for different reasons and in different ways. It seems that the society still submits to the laws which governed its formation, even though the historical conditions which prevailed then now apply only partially or not at all.

It is incontestable that group differences exist, and that all groups are aware of and emphasize these differences, be they real or imaginary. How are these cultural differences to be accounted for? Have they simply 'evolved' in the normal, historical course of events, or have they been deliberately enforced? It should already be clear that a purely historical explanation is inadequate; for, although the differences between the groups are no longer 'objectively' as great as they were, the perception of these differences remains as strong as ever. On the other hand, we face the same difficulty with cultural differences between groups as we faced with economic differences: one cannot establish with any precision to what extent their existence is 'intended' or 'unintended'.

Even in the absence of barriers to cultural and social interrelations, group differences in South Africa might well still be considerable. After all, there is unrestricted freedom of socio-cultural interaction between the two white groups, yet Afrikaans- and English-speaking South Africans have largely preserved their group identities. This phenomenon can also be observed in other group societies where there are no impediments to group interaction, e.g., the Lebanon, Mauritius, and Switzerland.

However, this speculation can be neither proved nor disproved; for cultural and social relations between groups in South Africa are not in general unhindered. Likewise, we cannot say whether a given cultural distinction was deliberately introduced. But what has been established beyond all doubt is that differentiation is deliberately maintained and indeed sharpened.

We have seen that South Africa possesses the most perfect system of labour controls in the world.[51] The same is true of its controls on social relations. The only appropriate analogy is the Indian caste-system.[52] But whereas in India the modern state is trying to dismantle this antiquated system of social control, in South Africa the modern state has extended it, refined it, and anchored it in law and administration.

Numerous accounts are available of the way different groups are restricted in South Africa, and social relations between them controlled. We shall thus dispense with a detailed description. An outline of the most

[51] Cf. Chapter 2.1, n. 35.

[52] By analogy some writers treat the South African apartheid system as a 'caste system'. Cf. e.g. Pierre L. van den Berghe, *Race and Racism. A Comparative Perspective* (New York, 1967), and J. Butler, 'The Significance of Recent Changes within the White Ruling Caste', in Leonard Thompson and Jeffrey Butler (eds), *Change in Contemporary South Africa* (Berkeley and Los Angeles, 1975), pp. 79–103.

31

important aspects of the system will be sufficient for our analysis.

The corner-stone of the system is so-called 'race classification'. Every citizen of the Republic of South Africa is assigned to one of the following groups: 'white', 'coloured', 'Indian', or 'black'.[53] The essential point is that the classification is racial. The criteria used are not those of culture or group awareness; they are biological or pseudo-biological. Afrikaners and English speakers are both 'white'. 'Coloureds' include Afrikaans-speaking members of the Dutch Reformed Churches, as well as Moslem Malays, descendants of mulatto Mauritians, and Griquas.[54] 'Indians' may be either Christian, Hindu, or Moslem. And the term 'black' covers members of all the black African ethnic groups in South Africa: the Zulus and Xhosas, Shangaans and Vendas, Swazis and Tswanas, among others. In short, what is involved is not the separation of socio-cultural groups but 'racial segregation'. This is made abundantly clear by the frequent, and administrative, practice of distinguishing broadly between 'white' and 'non-white'.

The numerous measures by which segregation is achieved can be divided into three broad groups:[55] those pertaining to
—lawful and unlawful personal relationships;
—residential areas; and
—public and private services and amenities.

Both marriage and sexual intercourse between whites and members of other racial groups are prohibited and punishable by law. This is the crux of social segregation. It confirms the racial nature of the social controls: the distinction is drawn between 'white' and 'non-white', not between different cultural or identity groups. Thus, a coloured, Afrikaans-speaking member of the Dutch Reformed Church may marry a black animist or an Indian Moslem; and a white Afrikaans-speaking member of the Dutch Reformed Church may marry the child of a Moslem immigrant from Syria; yet in spite of a mother tongue and religion in common, the two may not marry each other! In other words, socio-cultural segregation is enforced between the two 'races', 'white' and 'non-white', but not within them.

Residential segregation is more strictly applied. There are prescribed areas for whites, Indians, coloureds and blacks—and in the larger cities, even for different black groups.

[53] On race classification and the use of terms in the present study cf. Chapter 2.1, n. 5.

[54] The Griquas are Hottentots who originally occupied the region around the Cape Peninsula; they interbred primarily with Bushmen and whites, and towards the middle of the eighteenth century withdrew to the Eastern Cape.

[55] Muriel Horrell, *Legislation and Race Relations* (SAIRR, Johannesburg, 1971), provides a good survey of the most important segregation legislation. The annual surveys, *A Survey of Race Relations in South Africa*, edited by M. Horrell, record all changes to existing legislation as well as new laws and regulations.

Segregation of services and amenities is also enforced, with separate facilities being provided either on a two-way basis for whites and non-whites, or on a three-way basis for whites, coloureds and/or Indians, and blacks. Countless aspects of daily life are affected: trains, buses, taxis, ambulances, railway stations, public toilets, restaurants, hospitals, schools, and until recently, even Post Offices and certain churches.[56] Many of these measures have a tradition as long as it is unworthy, beginning in some cases in the days when farmers in the young colony owned slaves.[57] Whereas in the rural areas a benign paternalism may often still prevail, in urban areas segregation is stringently implemented with cold, bureaucratic logic. The actual measures to enforce segregation in the socio-cultural dimension take various forms: some are laid down by law, others in local ordinances, and still others reflect custom and tradition.

The foundations of official discrimination were laid long before the term 'apartheid' became current. Although the practice of apartheid may have been less stringent, the principle was as acceptable to British administrators and English-speaking politicians as it was to the Afrikaners.[58] Nevertheless, the concept itself was crucial to the victory of the National Party in the 1948 elections, and that year is a turning point in the formation of group relations, especially the 'intentional' forms of segregation.[59]

[56] On the other hand, shops and supermarkets, many financial institutions, post office counters, and Anglican, Methodist, Presbyterian, and Roman Catholic churches are not segregated. In recent years—at least in some cities—parks, lifts, museums, first-class hotels, and theatres have been de-segregated. Since March 1978 Dutch Reformed ministers have also been free to hold multiracial services in their churches.

[57] The following statement, printed in *De Express* (a newspaper in the Orange Free State) in 1880, is typical of the discussion in the Reformed Churches on the question of equality for the 'non-whites'; 'The state does not need any "brothers". The farmers and townsmen derive no benefit from it. We do not want servants who can dress as gentlemen and ladies on Sunday to go to church to learn that they are just as good as we are.' Quotation from J. J. van Aswegen, 'Die Verhouding tussen Blank en Nie-Blank in die Oranje-Vrystaat' (Unpublished doctoral thesis, 1968); further examples of the discussion on segregatory measures are included in C. F. J. Muller, *Die Oorsprong van die Groot Trek* (Cape Town, 1974), pp. 197f.

[58] Cf. the thorough, albeit apologetic study by N. J. Rhoodie, *Apartheid and Racial Partnership in Southern Africa* (Pretoria and Cape Town, 1969). Remarkable though it may seem, it was in fact the English who introduced the regulation requiring coloureds to carry passes—in 1809. Racial segregation took on stricter forms in the Boer Republics. The 1854 Constitution of the Transvaal Republic debarred 'non-whites' from holding a seat in parliament. Neither the Transvaal nor the Orange Free State granted civil rights to 'non-whites', nor would they permit equality between whites and 'non-whites' under any circumstances whatsoever.

[59] In a National Party Manifesto for the elections in 1938 Malan set down his thoughts on apartheid which were to form the basis of National Party policy after 1948. '. . . the party intends to apply the principle of segregation to all non-whites; for, this is in the best interests of both the whites and the non-whites. To this aim laws will be passed segregating residential areas, labour organizations, and place of work; the party

33

Until 1948, segregation and discrimination were used pragmatically, as instruments of white minority rule. Separation was applied if it was 'practical', i.e., where it served the interests of the minority and when it was convenient. However, when clothed in the concept of apartheid, racial segregation became an official ideology. Principles prevailed over pragmatic considerations of public interest; they were applied without regard for the immediate benefits, rather than opportunistically. The ruling minority was expected to stand by these principles, regardless of the sacrifices this might demand.

At the heart of this ideology is the Afrikaner idea of ethnic nationalism. Throughout their history, the Afrikaners have been determined to lead their own lives and to preserve their group identity.[60] This unbending will was originally expressed in opposition to the Dutch East India Company; then in the constant struggles against the various black peoples, and in the wars against the might of the British Empire; and finally in the political confrontation with the English-speaking group over control of the political institutions of the Union of South Africa and later the Republic. There are dissimilarities between the epic account of this history by Afrikaner historians and the more sober, at times malicious, commentaries in English.[61] But one point is undisputed: the Afrikaners' will to win has never been broken. This has been a constant and pre-eminent factor, in times of oppression and of domination.[62]

The year 1948 was a historic turning point for the Afrikaners. For the first time since the defeat and collapse of the Boer Republics in 1902, the Afrikaner parties gained power without having to share it. After decades

intends to introduce "job reservation", to prohibit marriage between the races, and will not allow whites to be employed by non-whites.'

Once the National Party had come to power in 1948 it was Verwoerd who developed the idea of apartheid into an ideology. Cf. the most important speeches of Verwoerd in W. Landman, *A Plea for Understanding* (Cape Town, 1968), pp. 111–18 and 134–9.

[60] Cf. in particular W. A. de Klerk, *The Puritans in Africa, op cit*; David Welsh, 'The Political Economy of Afrikaner Nationalism', in A. Leftwich, *South Africa: Economic Growth and Political Change, op cit*, pp. 249–85; René de Villiers, 'Afrikaner Nationalism', in Monica Wilson and Leonard Thompson (eds), *The Oxford History of South Africa*, Vol. II, *op cit*, pp. 365–423; and Hermann Giliomee, 'Die Ontwikkeling van die Afrikaner se Selfkonsepsies' (Working-paper for the conference, 'Die Afrikaner Vandag', March 1974, in Cape Town).

[61] F. A. van Jaarsveld, *The Afrikaner's Interpretation of South African History* (Cape Town, 1964), provides an excellent survey of the various interpretations of the history of the Afrikaner people; cf. in particular the article 'Interpretations and Trends in South African Historical Writing', pp. 116–165.

[62] The historical self-awareness of the ethnic struggle is of paramount importance for an understanding of the Afrikaners' concept of ethnicity today, regardless of whether this is based on precise historiography or on a projection of the present self-awareness onto the past. It is concretely expressed in a cult of monuments to and symbols of the Afrikaner volk and—perhaps of even greater import—in a political language strewn with historical analogies and references. There is hardly a political meeting or speech which does not make some reference to the past. The Afrikaners regard themselves as a community with an historical destiny, and as a people fighting for their existence.

of being completely or partially subjugated to foreigners, they were once again masters of their own destiny. By withdrawing from the Commonwealth and instituting the Republic, the Afrikaners set the seal on their liberation.

The Afrikaner concept of nationhood springs from a variety of sources. There is an important and close connection between nationhood and the specifically South African interpretation of Calvinist teachings. Afrikanerdom is virtually identical with the Dutch Reformed Churches. One finds a considerable literature on theology and the Afrikaner mind, devoted to the causal relationship between South African Calvinism and current South African race policies. [63]

But the theological origin of racial policies may well be less important than the social congruence of the Afrikaner people with the Reformed Churches. The spirit of the Old Testament pervades Church doctrine. The multiplicity of peoples is held to express Divine Will. Accordingly, various churches assume concrete form in God's ordained peoples; and the Dutch Reformed Churches see themselves as specifically incarnate in the Afrikaner people. Their deep piety and the stress they lay on the Old

[63] In 1950 the Churches took an official stand on the apartheid ideology for the first time: 'It is the Will of God that races and people live separately, each with its own language, own culture, etc.; in the light of this, racial segregation in the Church is not only permitted but a Christian duty'. In 1966 the General Synod of the Dutch Reformed Church published a report with the title 'Human Relations in South Africa', in which racial segregation in the Church was unequivocally justified. The General Synod which met in Cape Town in 1974 pursued the discussion further, but no fundamental changes were made. On this point cf. A. B. du Preez, *Die skriftuurlike Grondslag vir Rasseverhoudinge* (Pretoria, 1955); idem, *Eiesoortige Ontwikkeling tot Volksdiens* (Cape Town, 1959); J. C. G. Kotzé, *Principle and Practice in Race Relations* (Stellenbosch, 1962); S. du Toit, *Holy Scripture and Race Relations* (Potchefstroom, 1960); J. D. Vorster, 'Etniese Verskeidenheid, Kerklike Pluriformiteit en die Ekumene', in *Grense, 'n Simposium oor Rasse en ander Verhoudinge* (Stellenbosch, 1961), pp. 65–80.

However, one should treat a direct causal relationship with caution. Although there have been strong trends in the Reformed Churches to justify racial discrimination on theological grounds—interviews conducted within the framework of this study indicate that this group comprises about one-third of all ministers in the Reformed Churches today—there has always been a small group of Calvinist theologians who have rejected the policy of racial segregation as contrary to the teachings of Christ. In 1960, a group of clergymen from different churches—including the Reformed Churches—met in Cottesloe and passed a resolution which stated, i.a.: '. . . we recognize that all race groups living permanently in our country are part of the whole population, and we regard them all as natives of South Africa . . .' Among those who signed were C. F. Beyers Naudé, the founder of the Christian Institute (declared a prohibited organization in October 1977), B. B. Keet (*Die Etiek van Apartheid* (Johannesburg, 1957)), and Ben Marais (*Colour—Unsolved Problem of the West* (Cape Town, 1952)). See also the Koinonia Declaration published by approx. sixty Calvinist academics in Potchefstroom in November 1977 (cf. *Rand Daily Mail*, 26.11.1977).

For a balanced presentation of the relationship between the Church and the ideology of race cf. Peter Randall (ed.), *Apartheid and the Church* (Johannesburg, 1972). Today it would seem that the majority of Afrikaner theologians and ministers take the view that the Bible cannot be used to support or oppose apartheid; the question is essentially a political one, not a religious one.

Testament suggests an analogy between the Afrikaners and the Israelites: each is a people chosen and led by God, and persecuted by strangers and heathens, but a people that will triumph in the end if it unfailingly submits to the will of God.[64] The Reformed Churches have a far greater influence upon the morals, norms, and daily behaviour of their members than do most other Christian denominations. These rigorous attitudes are mirrored in official morals and norms, as well as in public life—from laws governing Sunday observance to the censorship of what, by European standards, is harmless erotica.[65]

The crucial point here is that the Afrikaner is simultaneously aware of himself as an Afrikaner and as a member of a religious group. This imparts an extraordinary emotional depth to his concept of ethnic nationhood.

Language is another important component of the Afrikaners' ethnic consciousness. Their drift away from High Dutch went hand in hand with the emergence of a national consciousness. Recognition of Afrikaans as a language in its own right and as a literary medium was a goal of the Afrikaners' political emancipation, and also a measure of their success. For a long time the struggle against British rule was primarily waged as a struggle for the recognition of the Afrikaans mother-tongue,[66] a struggle which was, as in Flanders or Quebec, intrinsic to ethnic consciousness.[67]

The defence of their religious and their cultural heritage are just two of the elements in the Afrikaners' idea of ethnic nationhood. Another is racial differentiation. They share their language and religion with the majority of coloureds. Yet they exclude the coloureds from their community solely on the ground of skin colour. This reveals in all its callousness the racist element in the Afrikaners' ethnic awareness.[68] It

[64] Cf. F. A. van Jaarsveld, 'Beskou Afrikaner hom steeds as God se Volk?', *Hoofstad*, 7.2.1977.

[65] A study conducted in 1952 testifies to the strong religious habits of the Afrikaner, e.g. Bible-reading and church attendance. Cf. G. Cronjé, *Kerk en Huisgesin. Die Huidige Kerklike en Godsdienstige Lewe van die Afrikaner* (Cape Town, 1958). That these habits have hardly changed in more than two decades is borne out by the authors' own empirical studies, and this notwithstanding the rapid industrialization of the country over this period. Cf. the empirical results in Chapter 6 below.

[66] Most of the present generation of Afrikaner politicians experienced as pupils attempts to enforce Anglicization; the older generation still recount how pupils caught speaking Afrikaans were forced to wear a sign around their necks which read: 'I am a Dutch swine.' The present generation experiences the language struggle through the dislike of or refusal to speak the Afrikaans language on the part of many English speakers, as well as the latter's arrogant belittling of the language as 'kitchen Dutch'. Cf. the survey results in Chapter 7.

[67] Although many English-speakers made the occasion the butt of numerous jokes, most Afrikaners approved the erection of a monument to the Afrikaans language in Paarl in 1975. A delegation of coloureds was also admitted to the unveiling—but seated apart from the whites.

[68] The coloureds share the fate of Germans of Jewish descent in the Third Reich: the

36

was quite clearly expressed in the election slogan of the radical right-wing Herstigte Nasionale Party in 1974: 'My volk, bly wit'.

In addition, the Afrikaners' ethnic awareness has been shaped by the historical experience of group solidarity in the protection of their economic interests,[69] notably in the case of the 'poor whites' during the Great Depression. In the main, poor whites were poor Afrikaners. They had become superfluous in the still largely traditional agricultural system. Being less skilled than other whites, and therefore forced to compete with 'non-white' labour in industrial sectors, the poor whites seemed destined to become a lumpenproletariat. This development was arrested in part by the self-help organizations which the Afrikaners themselves set up. But it was halted primarily by the success of Afrikaner politicians in having legislation enacted which gave white labour a privileged position, to the detriment of 'non-white' labour. To this day, the lower classes of the Afrikaner community remain particularly aware that they owe their social status and relative prosperity to the system of job reservation. This is also true to a lesser though still significant extent for whole sections of the Afrikaner population. For the attainment of political power opened the Civil Service to the Afrikaners, and enabled them to establish and promote semi-public industrial enterprises. Both avenues have offered new opportunities of social and economic advancement to the group as a whole.

But the key issue is struggle—be it political, for language rights, or for economic advancement. The Afrikaners see themselves as a people involved in a constant battle for their identity and well-being. So their conception of nationhood is virtually identical with the struggle of the 'volk'. Because the ethnic group is so closely identified with the religious group, this almost social-Darwinistic view acquires a divine perspective. The struggle for nationhood is a question of dominance: history is viewed in terms of 'rule or be ruled'. One may infer from this that fear, whether overtly expressed or not, is an essential element of the Afrikaners' idea of nationhood. Above all, it is a fear that the past might repeat itself: that they might lose their hard-won prosperity, their political self-determination, and in the last instance their existence as a separate language group and ethnic community. It may well be that this many-layered fear is the driving force behind the policies of discrimination, segregation, and apartheid. For the Afrikaners have always preferred to distinguish themselves from others, both by keeping their linguistic, cultural, and political distance from other whites, and by practising apartheid towards 'non-whites' in virtually every sphere of life.

dominant group has excluded them from the 'volk', and defined them as a separate group, regardless of their own feelings on the question.

[69] Cf. David Welsh, 'The Political Economy of Afrikaner Nationalism', *loc cit.*

The relative importance of these various factors will be discussed in the empirical analysis below. For the moment we stress that one cannot over-estimate the combined importance which these factors have for the Afrikaners' ethnic awareness. And as the Afrikaners are the dominant group in South Africa, the effect on the whole society is extremely far-reaching. As long as South Africans of British descent were still active in politics, racial discrimination was not an ideology. It was practised pragmatically, to serve the economic interests and convenience of the colonizers and their descendants. The distinction they drew was between the 'civilized' and the 'not yet civilized', in effect between 'Europeans' and 'Africans'.

Over recent decades, however, the segregatory labels 'white' and 'non-white' have gained currency. On achieving domination, the Afrikaners sought to extend the British pattern of segregation into a more compre-hensive system of ethnic separation. The system was reconceived, at least in theory. Segregation was no longer only to relieve the 'civilized' from disagreeable contact with the 'uncivilized', but was to be the means to an end, viz., the total segregation of racial and ethnic groups, to the extent of dividing the country into separate ethnic states. Segregation in everyday life, so-called 'petty apartheid', would serve to avoid friction during the transition to 'grand apartheid', i.e., territorial separation. And apartheid would be the means of achieving the new goal of 'separate development'.

Thus the change of government in 1948 did not lead to a dismantling of the existing structures of segregation. Instead, the system was per-fected and systematically extended. The Afrikaners adopted the colonial form of racism and reinforced it with the racist elements peculiar to their own ethnic awareness. But it would be misleading to interpret the Afrikaners' policy of group relations solely in terms of racism. Many of its aspects can only be understood in terms of the more comprehensive concept of nationhood which the Afrikaners were seeking to apply. The education policy towards the 'non-whites' is a typical example. After 1948 segregation was enforced in all educational institutions, including the English-medium universities, which until then had been racially integrated. The concept of 'Bantu Education' provided for the in-struction of each ethnic group in its respective mother-tongue. For 'mother-tongue' education was to be instrumental in promoting the 'sentiment of ethnic patriotism' among the members of each black group.[70]

[70] Many observers regard this solely as a cultural instrument of a policy of 'divide et impera'. However, a more balanced view must take the cultural-political experiences of the Afrikaners into account. The Afrikaners had to fight against cultural alienation for decades, and struggle for the recognition of their language as a medium of school-instruction.

This policy of cultural independence, with the preservation and development of the various languages, is held by the Afrikaner to be indispensable to the individuality and independence of the South African ethnic groups, at least as the Afrikaners perceive and want to perceive them. It would be a mistake to deny outright that the intentions behind this cultural policy might have been subjectively honest. But it would also be short-sighted to overlook the fundamental contradiction inherent in the policy. Mother-tongue instruction is not the instrument of cultural self-discovery for those black South Africans affected by Bantu Education, but an obstacle to their social and economic advancement. For under the prevailing circumstances, a knowledge of English is a *sine qua non* for black advancement.[71]

This contradiction in its cultural policy illuminates the basic dilemma in the policy of apartheid at large. Extrapolating from their own group awareness, the Afrikaners have sought to impose a group awareness on every other group. And they have succeeded, but not quite as they hoped. Decades of emphasis on group differentiation have borne fruit. Nowadays, politically and culturally active black Africans do seek their own identity—but not within the framework of the traditional tribal or ethnic groups, not a Zulu or Xhosa identity. The identity they are seeking is shaped by the concept of 'black consciousness'. The crux of this concept is the blacks' recognition that their hope in the power struggle between the different groups in South Africa lies in forming their own power group. This power will not derive from the separate ethnic groups, but from their common consciousness of being blacks as such,[72] members of a group that is discriminated against socially, economically, and politically. Hence, the aim of 'black consciousness' is to create a sense of group solidarity among all South African 'non-whites', be they black, coloured or Indian.

This opens new possibilities in the future of group relations in South Africa. Ethnic particularism continues to command considerable loyalty among blacks. Yet a single transcending black loyalty, grounded in the consciousness of common suffering, is undoubtedly emerging.

In summary, contemporary South African society is a society of groups. The differentiation of these groups has not only evolved, but has

[71] By analogy: an independent Tanzania may well have chosen Kiswahili as the official language; in colonial Tanganyika a command of English was a sine qua non for Africans.

[72] On the concept of the Black Consciousness movement cf. Steve Biko, 'White Racism and Black Consciousness', in Hendrik W. van der Merwe and David Welsh (eds), *Student Perspectives on South Africa* (Cape Town, 1972), pp. 190–202; idem, 'Black Consciousness and the Quest for a True Humanity', in Basil Moore (ed.), *Black Theology: the South African Voice* (London, 1973), pp. 36–47; Nyameko Pityana, 'What is Black Consciousness?', in Basil Moore (ed.), *op cit*, pp. 58–63. The role of the Black Consciousness movement and its significance in the current black-white conflict is dealt with in greater detail in Chapter 9 below.

also been deliberately imposed. The present situation in respect of groups is not the result of a free interplay of socio-cultural forces, but of a system of administrative control deriving from the colonial tradition and perfected in accordance with the Afrikaners' conception of ethnic awareness. But the system of social compulsion, with its ideological foundations, has a dialectic of its own. Blacks were assigned an identity in accordance with this peculiar ideology. But the identity actually taking shape in the blacks' self-awareness is quite different, and potentially far more embracing and powerful than the one conceived for them. The 'white' concept of ethnic struggle is in the process of generating 'black consciousness'.

3. Between enforced dependence and enforced 'independence': the political dimension of conflict

To all intents and purposes, white South Africans live in a free-market economy and black South Africans in a controlled economy. In their social and cultural relationships, whites are unfettered but relations between whites and other races are strictly regulated. The same asymmetries apply in the political system. The whites enjoy the privileges of a parliamentary democracy, from which all other South Africans are debarred. The political system is one of minority rule, and the minority is constituted on racial criteria. Yet it practises democracy according to the Westminster Rules.

The South African Parliament is elected in free general elections by a majority vote system.[73] But only whites may vote, or refrain from voting. Several parties compete for their favour. The internal structures of these parties accord with democratic principles, but only whites may be members. The government must be drawn from Members of Parliament; hence it too is exclusively white.

All political activity and administrative action in South Africa is strictly in accordance with the law. But the law, having been made by whites, is often to the disadvantage of blacks.[74]

Civil liberties do have some real content, notwithstanding numerous restrictions. Elections are not rigged; political parties do offer alternative

[73] For a well-written account of the formal structure and the functioning of the South African political system cf. D. Worrall (ed.), *South Africa—Government and Politics* (Pretoria, 1971), and in particular the contribution of B. Roux, 'Parliament and Executive', pp. 29–74.

[74] Discrimination and apartheid towards the blacks is legally prescribed in detail. Over and above this, the administrative and security bodies which deal with blacks have inordinate scope. Cf. the United Nations brochure, *Apartheid in Practice* (UNO, 1971); it lists approx. 300 examples of law and procedural ordinances. Cf. further the publications of the Apartheid Commission of the United Nations, 'Notes and Documents', an irregular series of documents and reports on discriminatory practices in South Africa.

programmes; government actions are closely scrutinized by parliament, and severely criticized in a powerful and fairly independent press. It cannot be denied that citizens of the country do enjoy these liberties— but only whites are full citizens.

Blacks do benefit to some extent from civil liberties, including protection by the relatively independent judiciary[75] and by the freedom of the press.[76] But they are denied any part in political decision-making.

The peculiar nature of the South African system derives from this unique dichotomy: constitutional democracy and elements of the rule of law on the one hand, political tutelage and minority rule on the other. Heribert Adam appositely describes the system as a democratically organized racial oligarchy,[77] while Pierre van den Berghe calls it a 'Herrenvolk-democracy'.[78]

Van den Berghe and others[79] have tried to compare the South African system to the Third Reich. However, the analogy is not particularly instructive. There certainly are some similarities between the racist elements in the Afrikaner ideology of ethnic nationhood and the fascist ideology of race; and some Afrikaner politicians did harbour sympathies for the Third Reich, though often in common opposition to Great

[75] Blacks enjoy the protection of the law to a certain degree, as proven by the many judgements which have found whites guilty of discrimination against blacks, and the subsequent sentences. Whites are not always in the right. However, with respect to 'political crimes', i.e. those which affect the security or the existence of the state, one can no longer speak of the rule of law. This is illustrated, on the one hand, by political trials—a blatant example was the court case following the still unexplained death of the Black Consciousness leader, Steve Biko, under suspicious circumstances; and on the other hand, by the growing number of revelations of practices involving the torture of political detainees. On the latter, cf. Christian Institute of Southern Africa, *Torture in South Africa* (Cape Town, 1977), and Amnesty International, *Politische Inhaftierung in Südafrika* (Baden-Baden, 1978), Chs. 5, 6 and 7.

[76] The South African press is highly controversial, and engages in weighty political discussion. Notwithstanding some criticism, the International Press Institute judged the South African press to be relatively free by international standards. In recent years, however, the government has frequently threatened to censor the opposition press. As a result of these threats the press has decided to practise some self-censorship, which has already included some leading journalists among the casualties. That the government will not hesitate to carry out its threats is borne out by the banning of the black newspaper *The World*, and the arrest and brief detention of the editor-in-chief, Percy Qoboza (cf. *Rand Daily Mail*, 20.10.1977: 'The End of Percy's World'), as well as the banning order issued on the editor-in-chief of the East London *Daily Dispatch*.

[77] 'The term "racial oligarchy" (may well) best describe the situation of domination in South Africa. A racially defined minority of privileged caste members rules autocratically over the rest of the caste hierarchy.' Heribert Adam, *Südafrika— Soziologie einer Rassengesellschaft* (Frankfurt, 1969), p. 43.

[78] 'South Africa was "launched" on its career as a racist "Herrenvolk-Democracy", that is, as a state in which a white minority of 20 per cent ruled itself democratically but imposed its tyranny over a non-white majority of 80 per cent.' Pierre L. van den Berghe, *Race and Racism: A Comparative Perspective, op cit*, p. 101.

[79] Cf. in particular Brian Bunting, *The Rise of the South African Reich* (Harmondsworth, 1969).

41

Britain as much as anything else. But these similarities should not be allowed to obscure the fundamental differences between the two systems. Firstly, the National Socialist regime carried arbitrary rule to an extreme, whereas the South African system is extremely legalistic.[80] Secondly, the logical consequence of the National Socialist ideology of race was genocide, whereas apartheid, even in its harsh and paternalistic domination of out-groups, has never denied them the right to exist. Thirdly, the Nazi leaders were ruthless men driven by a lust for power. The Afrikaner leaders are cast in a mould of old-fashioned honour—notwithstanding their severity and extraordinary insensitivity to the feelings and sufferings of those they govern.[81]

Adam[82] has shown that the classical theory of totalitarianism is inapplicable to the South African political system. The attributes which characterize totalitarian rule are absent in South Africa. Firstly, there is no official ideology which all people must openly profess, as in a totalitarian state. Secondly, there is no attempt to impose an ideological conformity upon all the groups in the society. Indeed, the contrary is the case. The cultural, religious, and ideological differences between the groups are not only countenanced but actively cultivated in the hope of generating separate forms of group consciousness. Thirdly, under totalitarianism, one would expect a single, monolithic party with a monopoly on political activity. In South Africa, party pluralism thrives, and the lively opposition press ensures that neither the state nor any one party has a monopoly on information. Fourthly, although the state in South Africa does, in common with totalitarian regimes, try to extend its control even to the private lives of individuals, the motivation is segregation and not the total integration and full mobilization of all citizens. Fifthly, the South African state prescribes what citizens must not do, the totalitarian state what citizens must do. Finally, there is no evidence in South Africa of that irrational terror which threatens supporter and opponent alike, and which in the opinion of many scholars is a significant element of totalitarian practice.

In view of these discrepancies, Adam has proposed that the concept of totalitarianism be extended, to take account of the realities of the South African political system. He describes as 'totalitarian' any system which suppresses all attempts to change it, excludes all alternatives to it, and

---

[80] There is much evidence that the comparisons with National Socialism beloved of the English-speaking press in South Africa achieve just the opposite of their intended effect. The Afrikaners know they are not Nazis, and, accordingly, feel wrongly attacked, and, therefore, strengthened in their attitudes.

[81] Adam also draws a distinction between the South African system and National Socialism, though his argument is different: National Socialism aimed at aggressive expansion, whereas the South African system serves primarily to defend the status quo. Cf. H. Adam, *Südafrika—Soziologie einer Rassengesellschaft, op cit*, pp. 45f.

[82] *Ibid*, pp. 49ff.

persecutes any person or outlaws any organization that promotes change. The South African system is then totalitarian in this sense. In contrast to the classical totalitarian state, which employs irrational terror to prevent any change in the system, the South African state on Adam's view employs a carefully contrived, rational form of terror. Those who are not politically active in the cause of change need have no fear. But those who work to change the system must reckon with calculated repression on a large scale. [83]

This approach offers an insight into the extent and nature of the state's potential for repressing change, which is vital to an understanding of contemporary South African reality. Black political organizations intent on changing the system have been banned, including the two major black parties—the African National Congress and the Pan African Congress—and, more recently, Black Consciousness organizations. The government has also set up some legal measures for strictly controlling organizations which stop short of outright prohibition. [84] But above all, it has at its disposal an arsenal of legal and administrative measures aimed at the individual. Security laws, particularly the Suppression of Communism and the Terrorism Acts, arm the authorities with extraordinarily wide-ranging powers. Individuals may be detained for 180 days without any recourse to law, and without reasons being stated. Another arbitrary measure is the 'banning order', which the authorities are empowered to issue without court authorization. The restrictions which a banning order places on the freedom of the individual may vary greatly. He can be forbidden to travel, leave his house, or be in the company of more than one other person at any one time. Banned persons may neither publish nor be quoted in South Africa. In short, a banning order can turn an individual into a social and political non-person.

The authorities put these repressive measures into effect whenever the political activities of black opponents elicit a response from the population, i.e., whenever there is a chance that they will be effective.

[83] The question repeatedly asked is just how considered and calculated repression in South Africa actually is. Are all steps taken against opponents of the system really precisely planned, are the effects estimated in advance; or are the measures in part unco-ordinated, hastily conceived, and coincidental? There is evidence that the most important acts of repression are indeed planned by the political leaders to achieve specific effects; however, it cannot be denied that Ministers have repeatedly taken steps precipitately, which have been implemented by means of irrational and indiscriminate acts of terror. As proof of this one may take the exaggerated measures against children during the Soweto disturbances, as well as the arbitrary behaviour of the police and the administration in respect of political prisoners and political suspects.

[84] These include warnings and threats by the government against unwelcome critics of the system, e.g., the threat of press censorship. Of a more serious nature are the restrictions placed on institutions critical of the system, e.g., the prohibition on foreign aid for organizations listed in terms of the Affected Organizations Act of 1974—including, among others, the Christian Institute of Southern Africa (before its prohibition in 1977).

These measures are also used against whites who actively support the interests of the black population and co-operate closely with them. [85]

Until now, these measures have not been used against persons whose political activities occur within the framework of the 'white' political system. White dissidents and opposition parties may be as scathing about the system as they like, provided they do not transgress the political 'colour bar'.

In other words, 'totalitarian' measures in the broadest sense of the concept do not affect the democratic rights of the minority. They are applied only when one criticizes and opposes the system in ways which go beyond what is sanctioned for the white minority group. When Adam speaks of a 'democratic police state'[86] he is correct, in that a police state has been erected in South Africa by democratic processes. This police state acts against anyone outside the racially limited democracy who questions the limits of this democracy.

Whatever influence the racial majority of the population may have had on the minority democracy has been removed over the past three decades. This accomplishment is primarily an expression of the Afrikaner political will. Under British colonial rule, politics was de facto the preserve of the white group, but not de iure. In accordance with the British tradition of 'civilized government', democratic rights were extended to those non-whites who fulfilled certain criteria of education and ownership, i.e., who were 'civilized'. Hence, in the Cape Colony the coloureds and a tiny minority of blacks had the vote. There were also a few blacks on the voters' roll in Natal. On the other hand, the suffrage was never extended to blacks in the Boer Republics of the Transvaal and the Orange Free State. And when in 1910 the former colonies and republics were united as provinces of the Union of South Africa, the electoral laws and provisions applying in each case were retained without amendment.

Although the Afrikaners accepted this compromise in 1910, they categorically rejected the British conception of gradually extending democratic rights to all 'civilized' inhabitants of the country. As their political influence grew, so did their efforts to exclude 'non-whites' from the democratic process altogether. In 1936 they succeeded in having the blacks removed from the common voters' roll.

Thereafter, those blacks who had been entitled to vote could send three—white—representatives to Parliament. In 1956, not quite a decade after the Afrikaners had returned the National Party to power, the coloureds were also removed from the common roll. They were placed

---

[85] White victims of the repressive measures of October 1977 include Donald Woods, editor-in-chief of the *Daily Dispatch*, C. F. Beyers Naudé, and Theo Kotze, both directors of the Christian Institute.

[86] H. Adam, *Südafrika: Soziologie einer Rassengesellschaft, op cit*, p. 57.

44

on a separate roll, with the right to elect four—white—Members of Parliament. Black representation in Parliament was finally abolished in 1959, and coloured representation in 1969. The passing of a law against 'improper interference' completed the political separation of the racial groups: whites were prohibited from participating in 'non-white' politics and vice versa. From then on, multiracial parties were illegal. The Progressive Party chose to acquiesce, and split into 'white' and 'non-white' parties; the small Liberal Party chose to disband.

Total separation was thereby achieved. The white minority lives in a democracy, the black majority in a police state.

The political dimension of unilateral conflict regulation can usefully be considered in the light of the model of internal colonialism. The model has been variously applied to South Africa, usually by way of a loose analogy.[87] It is inadequate for the analysis of complex multidimensional relationships within a society. But when applied to the political dimension, it provides a fruitful comparison between the situation within South Africa and the patterns of constitutional and political relations between former colonial metropoles and their colonies. In other words, the South African political system—democracy for

[87] Parallel to the theoretical discussion on plural societies, the model of internal colonialism has been used to show that in a society with ethnic group differences patterns of domination and exploitation can arise within a country analogous to those of external colonization. This concept has attracted a lot of attention, particularly in the discussion in the USA and Latin America, as a means of explaining the underprivileging of ethnic minorities (cf. R. Blauner, 'Internal Colonialism and Ghetto Revolt', *Social Problems*, 16:4 (1969), pp. 393–408, and P. Gonzales Casanova, 'Internal Colonialism and National Development', *Studies in Comparative and National Development*, 1:4 (1965), pp. 27–37).

Considerations based on the dependence theory use the term 'internal colonialism' to denote the processes whereby the masses on the periphery are exploited by the bourgeoisie of the metropoles. Cf. the survey by T. Evers and P. Wogau, 'Dependencia: Lateinamerikanische Beiträge zur Theorie der Unterentwicklung', *Das Argument*, 79 (1973), pp. 404–574. In an historical analysis Michael Hechter has applied the concept to the British Isles (*Internal Colonialism—The Celtic Fringe in British National Development, 1536–1966*, (London, 1975)). The concept was introduced into the South African discussion by Leo Marquard (*South Africa's Colonial Policy* (Johannesburg, 1957)). Heribert Adam then adopted it, defining it as follows: '. . . a complex system of interwoven coercive, economic, and ideological controls, which have been labeled domestic or internal colonialism.' (H. Adam, *Modernizing Racial Domination. The Dynamics of South African Politics* (Berkeley, 1971), p. 2). It has also been applied by G. M. Carter, P. Karis, and N. M. Stultz, *South Africa's Transkei, The Politics of Domestic Colonialism* (London, 1967). Recently, Harold Wolpe has subjected the concept to a critical analysis within the theory of the mode of production. According to Wolpe, internal colonialism in South Africa is an expression of the fact that by means of the mechanisms of apartheid and enforced migratory labour the dominant capitalistic mode of production is destroying the non-capitalistic mode of production in the black reserves; this results in a situation in which these reserves continually grow poorer. Cf. Harold Wolpe, 'The Theory of Internal Colonialism: The South African Case', in Ivar Oxaal, Tony Barnett, and David Booth (eds), *Beyond the Sociology of Development—Economy and Society in Latin America and Africa* (London and Boston, 1975), pp. 229–52.

one category of citizens and authoritarian rule for the rest—is held to correspond to the basic political pattern which prevailed in the colonial empires of Western democracies. At the height of colonialism, all the powers—Britain, France, Belgium, the Netherlands—maintained basically the same political systems in their colonies. While the white inhabitants of the mother-country enjoyed full political rights, the local populations in the colonies were ruled by an authoritarian administration. And colonial peoples were as a rule not granted a voice in decision-making, although they did enjoy certain benefits such as the rule of law and freedom of information. The situation of blacks in present-day South Africa is comparable in both respects. There is a further similarity: liberals in the mother-country could attack the political system, just as they do in white South Africa today—with, in both cases, police state methods preventing the people actually affected by the system from expressing themselves.

The difference is that in the case of external colonialism, the minority under democracy and the majority under authoritarian colonial rule were in different countries on different continents. In the case of internal colonialism, the two political structures co-exist in one and the same country.

Taken in conjunction with the concept of national struggle, the model of internal colonialism provides a particularly compelling interpretation of contemporary South African society. The minority enjoy democratic government and the majority are subjected to authoritarian domination, in accordance with the ethnic differences between them. This situation is potentially far more disruptive within the boundaries of one country than in the case of external colonialism.

The inhabitants of the colonial mother-countries could avoid being dominated by the majority groups formerly under their sway; they simply acceded to the latter's demands for political self-determination, and relinquished their colonial empires.[88] Great Britain, Belgium, and the Netherlands never seriously considered whether to grant democratic rights in the respective mother-countries to the inhabitants of the former colonies. In the case of the French West African empire the issue was debated for a number of years, but finally settled in the same way. The Europeans in France preferred to grant their colonies independence rather than be outnumbered by Frenchmen from Africa.[89] In short, there

[88] On the question of decolonization and the ambivalent attitudes prevalent in the mother-countries towards the future role of the colonies, cf. particularly Rudolf von Albertini, *Dekolonisation: Die Diskussion über Verwaltung und Zukunft der Kolonien 1919–1960* (Cologne and Opladen, 1966), as well as Franz Ansprenger, *Politik im schwarzen Afrika* (Cologne and Opladen, 1961).

[89] R. von Albertini, *Dekolonisation, op cit*, pp. 464–538; F. Ansprenger, *Auflösung der Kolonialreiche* (Munich, 1966), particularly Part II; A. Bleckmann, *Das französische Kolonialreich und die Gründung neuer Staaten* (Cologne and Berlin, 1969).

was a conflict in external colonialism between the colonizers, who wanted to retain their dominance, and the colonized, who wanted a say in political matters. In all major instances, the conflict was solved not by integrating the subjected majority into the political system of the imperial power, but by secession. The peoples of the respective mother-countries retained their autonomy by relinquishing political control over their colonies.

But when colonizer and colonized share the same country, the conflict becomes more bitter and intractable. After 1948, South Africa's rulers rejected any solution to the conflict which would have granted the majority a voice in political matters. But they too have realized that the present dispensation cannot last indefinitely. And, as in the decolonization process, the theoretical solution they have devised is secession. In the South African version, it is known as 'grand apartheid'.

The principal architect of the policy was Hendrik Verwoerd, the Prime Minister who was assassinated in 1966. It has been progressively implemented since 1959.[90] The fundamental idea behind grand apartheid is a partition of the present Republic, by carving out a number of independent states for the various black ethnic groups on the one hand, and by retaining the remainder of the territory as one state for the white ethnic group on the other hand. In terms of the recommendations of a commission in 1936, certain areas of what was then the Union were to be set aside as black reserves. These reserves, now known as black homelands or bantustans, are supposed to form the territories of the new black states. They constitute approximately 13 per cent of the area of the Republic, and contain about one-third of the overall black population.[91] The intention of the policy is that the homelands advance to full independence as sovereign national states. Their citizens will not only be those blacks effectively resident in them, but also all black citizens of the Republic who are members of one of the respective ethnic groups. Blacks who continue to live in the white Republic would thus acquire the status of 'foreign' workers. To keep the number of these foreign workers down, the policy provides for the development of 'border areas', i.e., industrial areas adjoining the new states. In the 'ideal case' the foreign worker would commute between his home in an independent black state and his place of work in the white Republic.

In October 1976 the Transkei was granted 'independence', and became the first of these new black states. A second 'homeland', Bophuthat-

---

[90] Besides Verwoerd, the creator of the apartheid ideology was his close confidant, the German Werner Eiselen. Cf. Werner Eiselen, 'Das Regierungsprogramm der getrennten Entwicklung' (1959), in Freimut Duve (ed.), *Kap ohne Hoffnung oder Die Politik der Apartheid* (Hamburg, 1965), pp. 12–24.

[91] For exact figures on the population of the homelands—both de facto and de iure—cf. A. J. Halbach, *Die südafrikanischen Bantu-Homelands, op cit*, pp. 45ff.

swana, followed suit in December 1977.[92] A further five territories have been granted local autonomy to varying extents, including political executives with limited powers and parliaments constituted of elected members and appointed traditional chiefs. Black politicians have different motives for working within the framework of the bantustan policy. Some of them take advantage of a legal platform from which to express their basic opposition to the policy without running foul of the police state. Others see the policy as a lesser evil than the status quo, and hope that formal independence will improve the living conditions of their respective peoples. Thus, before seriously considering independence, all bantustan leaders have tried to wring territorial and economic concessions from the South African government. However, the majority of urban black Africans have grave reservations about the whole bantustan policy.[93]

Whether or not the bantustan institutions enjoy support among black Africans, the fact remains that the concept of grand apartheid has already been partially implemented. This has had some impact on the South African political system. Areas and institutions have been created which afford blacks legal possibilities of political activity and expression. Whether they use these possibilities to support or oppose the concept of grand apartheid does not affect the fact that by using them at all they are contributing to the realization of the concept.[94]

Internal colonialism in South Africa has now reached the stage of imminent decolonization. But the dominant group will for the most part set the conditions and prescribe the form in which decolonization will occur. These are such that one may speak of a transition from internal colonialism to external neo-colonialism, i.e., from a relationship of direct domination within the confines of a single state to a relationship in which small and poor black states are dependent on a large and wealthy white state.

Whether they are formally independent or not, the black areas remain geographically and economically on the periphery of the white-controlled industrial and military metropole. They have little hope of ever becoming economically viable. With the exception of the Transkei and possibly the Ciskei, the bantustans are geographically fragmented; they are already over-populated; few of them have significant mineral

[92] Vendaland intends to become the third homeland to accept independence. On the independence of the Transkei, cf. P. Laurence, *South Africa's Politics of Partition* (Johannesburg, 1976). On the independence of Bophuthatswana cf. the critical reports of P. Laurence, 'How Valid is a Homeland Election?' *Rand Daily Mail*, 9.8.1977, and B. Hitchcock, 'Which Way Mafeking?', *Rand Daily Mail*, 6.12.1977.

[93] Cf. the results of the interviews conducted by the authors, Chapter 11 below.

[94] Christopher R. Hill, 'The Future of Separate Development in South Africa', in Christian P. Potholm and Richard Dale (eds), *Southern Africa in Perspective* (New York and London, 1972), pp. 59–68, pays special attention to this aspect.

deposits; and most of their adult male populations have long had to seek work in 'white' industrial centres. The bantustans are thus enclaves of traditional subsistence agriculture and reservoirs of labour for 'white' industry. They seem destined to a future of economic dependence.[95]

The supporters of the bantustan philosophy within the ruling group are by no means unaware of this state of affairs. But some welcome it on the grounds that dependent neighbours are less troublesome, and others accept it as the consequence of decolonization. The former view may well prove mistaken, but the latter is borne out by numerous examples. Many African states are smaller, poorer, and scarcely less dependent than the Transkei. However, what the leaders of white South Africa overlook, or are determined to overlook, is the fundamental difference between the dissolution of the European colonial empires and a seeming decolonization within the framework of grand apartheid. In the European colonial case, independence resolved the conflict between the rulers and the ruled, at least with respect to political control within the metropolitan state. But independence for the bantustans does not resolve the dilemma of political control within white South Africa. Independent bantustans do not alter the fact that the majority of South African blacks neither live in the bantustans nor can be removed there. Even if the bantustan philosophy were to be implemented in its entirety, there would be more black 'foreign workers' in 'white' South Africa than whites.

4. *Unilateral conflict regulation: the common denominator*

In the foregoing sections we outlined the most important structural characteristics and peculiarities of the South African system and discussed the economic, socio-cultural, and political dimensions of conflict. We established that within this system there are open and latent group conflicts on a large scale, and that one group has constantly exploited its dominance to effect unilateral conflict regulation.

The economic discussions showed South African society to be a highly stratified class society, in which the classes and the 'racially' defined population segments by and large coincide. Economic conflict is generally experienced as racial conflict. The socio-cultural discussion showed that ethnic, religious, and linguistic heterogeneity have resulted in an extremely fragmented society, in which the differentiating characteristics again largely coincide. The ruling group's concept of ethnic nationhood, and the reaction of the dominated groups to this, are crucial

---

[95] The relationship between the bantustans and the 'white Republic' can be illustrated by the dependence theory, based on the situation in Latin America, which provides an explanation of the unbalanced relationship between the metropole and the periphery. There is an exhaustive body of Spanish and English literature on the subject. Cf. n.87 above.

determinants of a self-awareness of each group. The political discussion showed that the South African system of minority rule is quasi-colonial in nature. The Afrikaner core of the white group has shaped the socio-cultural structure of the country. At the same time, the whites exercise political power, which they use to preserve their economic privileges and to entrench socio-cultural differences.

To maintain its position, the ruling group has erected a police state vested with extensive powers of repression. To obviate the growing potential for conflict, the ruling group has embarked upon a policy of transforming its quasi-colonial dominance within the existing state into a neo-imperialist domination of formally independent states. An enforced dependence is being replaced by an equally enforced mock 'independence'.

The economic, socio-cultural, and political dimensions of conflict discussed above have a common denominator. Regardless of the nature of the conflict, it is regulated *unilaterally* by means of those instruments of power which enable the minority to dominate the majority.

In this way, the minority will be able for the foreseeable future to regulate conflict as it sees fit, and to dispense with the consent of the majority. As matters stand at present, power without majority consent is the most significant feature of the South African political and economic system.

CHAPTER 3

Peaceful Change and Democratic Conflict Regulation: Prerequisites and Normative Stipulations

As things stand, only the ruling white minority can *initiate* peaceful change. The black majority have systematically been deprived of the means of doing so themselves. By and large, any form of black political activity—peaceful or otherwise—which questions the existing system is unlawful; all black individuals and organizations who engage in political activity beyond mere rhetoric lay themselves open to repressive counter-measures. If all black attempts to initiate change elicit a violent reaction from the dominant group, it will eventually become apparent that peaceful methods are futile, and violence will then be resorted to. But that is beyond the scope of this study.

Hence, if peaceful change in South Africa is to be at all possible, the prerequisites for it must be met within the white political system, the locus of power in South Africa. This is a necessary condition for peaceful change, but not a sufficient one. For even if it is fulfilled, the black majority may not be prepared to respond to white initiative. And if they were, what requirements might they attach to their co-operation? In this chapter, we shall firstly consider general conditions for peaceful change, then specify more closely the content of this notion, and finally discuss it from the normative viewpoint of democratic conflict regulation.

1. General conditions for peaceful change

Is peaceful change possible? This depends on whether the whites are prepared to initiate it, and the blacks to respond to the whites' initiative.

Two factors are particularly important in the *white* political system: the role of the political leaders; and the attitudes of the electorate, especially how far they are prepared to be loyal to the leaders.

The political leadership is particularly important because the ethno-political structure of the white party system in South Africa promotes stable party formations and voting behaviour. As a rule, political change in South Africa results less often from elections than from changes of opinion within the parties or their groups of leaders.

At the same time, government within the minority in South Africa takes the form of a parliamentary democracy. Now the history of political parties shows that the position of party leaders is endangered when their views shift too far from the political consensus among their supporters, or vice versa. In South Africa, such shifts have until now occurred gradually; accordingly, parties have usually remained in power for one or more decades. The current political leadership, both in the government and in the opposition, contrasts with that of earlier times in its lack of decisive and pertinacious personalities. Unlike Smuts, Hertzog, or Verwoerd, the present leaders are careful not to lose touch with what they, rightly or wrongly, take to be the general political outlook of their voters.

Under these circumstances, political innovations aimed at peaceful change will have to fulfil two conditions if they are to meet with success within the *white* political system:

First condition: The white political leadership must be convinced of the necessity for peaceful change, and must believe that the opinions and attitudes of the electorate are not inconsistent with such change.

Second condition: The *actual* opinions and attitudes of the electorate must show a trend compatible with peaceful change, or at least not overwhelmingly opposed to it.

Leadership groups also assume decisive political importance among the black population.[1] Strong personalities have played a leading part in the political history of black South Africa,[2] from men such as the Reverend Dube, Professor Jabavu, and Doctor Xuma in the first half of this century, through Chief Albert Luthuli, to Steve Biko and the current leaders. Certainly, the government's repressive measures over the past decade and a half have severely curtailed the effectiveness of the black political leadership. Charismatic leaders such as Nelson Mandela have been imprisoned, while others have been banned or exiled. Yet despite these difficult conditions, a powerful black leadership has emerged: 'homeland' leaders who refuse to accept the system, clergymen, trade-unionists, student leaders, and the leaders of the recently banned Black Consciousness movement. Although their leadership has often been

[1] In this chapter 'black population' refers exclusively to black Africans; no account is taken of the coloureds and Indians, for the power struggle in South Africa is essentially one between the black Africans and the whites. The coloureds and the Indians play only a marginal role.

[2] On the political history of black South Africa cf. Chapter 9.

limited to specific groups or regions, their influence has been considerable. It is hardly possible to conceive of peaceful change without the consent of at least the influential portions of these black leadership groups.

The black leadership groups are as dependent as their white counterparts on a broad consensus among the relevant portions of the population. Now blacks do have the franchise in the homelands, and a limited franchise in certain black urban residential areas. But those blacks who are politically most aware scorn participation in the elections for councils which they regard as politically irrelevant;[3] and the rural population is, as may be expected under the circumstances, scarcely educated or mobilized politically. Consequently, the 'voters' are at most only a marginal political factor in black South Africa. Real political clout lies with the inhabitants of the urban conglomerations, those who are involved in the process of industrial production. They have been politicized by their own living conditions and the mass media and their interest in the country's development is strongly political. The urban blacks are politically the 'critical mass' of black South Africa. Whoever earns their support becomes an effective political force—as is clear in the efforts of homeland leaders to build up an urban following.

These considerations imply that there are two further conditions for peaceful change, viz., those necessary for the consent of *black* South Africa to any peaceful conflict regulation:

Third condition: The black leadership groups must agree to the terms and guidelines governing peaceful change.

Fourth condition: The urban blacks must show by their attitudes and behaviour that they are at least not opposed to the proposed course of peaceful change.

2. *Democratic conflict regulation as the goal of peaceful change: a normative and substantive definition*

'Peaceful change' as it stands expresses little more than an interest in

[3] Their argument runs basically as follows: whoever participates in the homeland elections also accepts the unilateral conflict regulation which the whites are striving for—let alone the numerous possibilities the whites still have of intervening in homeland politics. Cf. J. Butler, R. I. Rotberg, and J. Adams, *The Black Homelands of South Africa, op cit*, pp. 50ff, as well as G. Wellmer, *Südafrikas Bantustans, op cit*, Ch. 10. In the past only a small minority of those entitled to vote have participated in the elections for the so-called Urban Bantu Councils, advisory bodies for the black townships with very limited powers. These Councils have been replaced by the so-called Community Councils, whose powers are somewhat greater. The elections to these in November 1977 and April 1978 were also boycotted by the majority of blacks. For the arguments for and against the Community Councils cf. *Rand Daily Mail*, 15.11.1977, 'Speaking in the "Vacuum" of Soweto'.

53

changing the existing system without the use of violence. But mere change is not enough. We need to define some substantive goals, against which to test the possibilities and prospects of peaceful change.

For the purposes of this study of the South African system, our definition is as follows:

'Peaceful change' is any transformation of the existing system, without the use of violence, which facilitates the democratic regulation of existing conflicts; where regulation may take any form that both
—satisfies the value requirement of a social order founded on the rule of law, social justice, and constitutional democracy, and
—is acceptable to the significant political forces in white *and* black South Africa.

We have deliberately not made our goals more specific than a democratic state based on the rule of law, social justice, and constitutional government. This allows for a variety of political, social, and economic orders. One cannot realistically define the goals of peaceful change more precisely. Naturally, it is worth enquiring empirically into the various conceptions South Africans may have of a desirable future society— whether they prefer one state or several, a federation or a commonwealth, and a socialist or a mixed or a free market economy. But we do not think it is useful to build specific conceptions of the constitutional, social, or economic order into our normative concept of peaceful change.

In summary, our definition of peaceful change leaves it open for all South Africans to decide freely on how they want to live. Details of how they conceive the rule of law, social justice, and democracy is an empirical question, not a matter for normative stipulation.

Our definition of the goals of peaceful change avoids being too narrow. It also avoids being too broad. Changes which do little more than modify the existing system, i.e., do not essentially alter the pattern of unilateral conflict regulation, would not help to avert a violent eruption of conflict any more than the present system does. Conversely, simply to replace one form of unilateral conflict regulation by another would equally inevitably involve violence. It is thus difficult to conceive of any peaceful change on a large scale which would not conform with our normative postulate. *If change in South Africa is to be peaceful, it must lead to more justice and liberty.*

Granted this conception of the goals of peaceful change, we must now operationalize it in terms of the dimensions of conflict identified in the previous chapter, viz., the economic, socio-cultural, and political.

In the *economic sphere* the highest priority is the repeal of discriminatory laws and administrative restrictions, especially job reservation and racially based pay differentials. Peaceful change also requires that the right of association be extended to all South Africans, that trade-unions and the right to strike be recognized, and that equal rights of ownership be granted to all. All of this amounts to no more than recognizing legal equality among South Africans of all population groups.

Legal equality in respect of labour and economic rights is important, but not enough. Actual economic relations will have to change. To accord with the postulate of social justice there must be guarantees to ensure that legal equality has real implications for all segments of the population, and that they are in a position to take advantage of them. This will require a redistribution of public expenditure to reduce inequalities between population groups, above all in education and infrastructural development. The majority of the population presently suffers under structural disadvantages; the principle of social justice requires that they be dismantled.

Our normative stipulation can legitimately be interpreted in various ways—involving for instance the question of co-determination. However, such considerations will only affect the socio-political organization of individual communities, and thus by definition do not concern our conception of peaceful change. What certainly will concern us, however, is a broad political agreement to replace the current, skew distribution of economic gain with some new pattern of redistribution.

In the sphere of social relations between the population groups, the crux of peaceful change is again the abolition of legal and administrative discrimination. Discriminatory measures include the enforced segregation of public and private services and amenities, residential segregation, and the illegality of personal relationships between people of different races. On the other hand, whether the state should aspire to effective social integration, or the extent to which it should force different groups to engage in it, is a question for each community to settle within the limits of our normative stipulation. What peaceful change will minimally require is that there be no obstacles to social integration. Whether social integration should itself be a goal is a question partly of what individuals and groups choose to do, and partly of political expediency. As such, it may be left open.

The *political* sphere is most contentious as regards our goals for peaceful change. In principle, the minimal requirement is that the domination of the political system by one group be replaced by dispensation which will give all South Africans an equal say in determining their political order. This basic postulative political equality can be satisfied by a wide variety of constitutional arrangements.

There are three distinct bodies of opinion on the future system of government in South Africa. One proposal is that the country be partitioned into two or more states, in which the different population groups will be able to exercise their right of self-determination separately. Another proposal is that there be a unitary state under one central government embracing all South Africans irrespective of their ethnic group. And a third proposal favours some form of constitutional power sharing between the different population groups. This proposal includes a range of options, from a federal state with a strong executive, through a very loose federation, to a commonwealth of nations; from a federation based on race groups rather than geographic units, through a federal arrangement incorporating states demarcated geographically but de facto along racial lines, to a purely geographic 'colour-blind' federation.

The complexity of these options is increased by the eclectic approach of some political groupings which, for example, advocate a general partition within which one or other part may subscribe to federation or integration.

Each body of opinion is associated, though far from exclusively, with one political grouping. Thus, the governing party officially favours partition, viz., the separating off of the 'independent' bantustans. But other forms of division are also propounded within the party, including a radical partitioning of the country into two roughly equal states. There are also minority groups within the party which favour the federal incorporation, and perhaps the political integration, of the coloureds and Indians. A small group would even like to include the urban blacks.

Black political forces in South Africa tend to support the concept of a unitary multiracial state, as do some small political groupings of white South Africans.

The third proposal finds most of its support in the white opposition, which is seeking acceptable forms of power sharing. 'Race federation' had long been a policy of the former United Party; and in recent years the Progressive Party and its successor, the Progressive Federal Party, have propounded various federal schemes. Some black politicians have also favoured forms of federation.[4]

The related concept of consociational democracy was first developed in the South African context in 1973, by the Political Commission of the 'Study Project on Christianity in an Apartheid Society', a project initiated by the Christian Institute.[5] A solution along these lines has

[4] Special mention must be made of Gatsha Buthelezi's speech which he delivered as Hoernlé Memorial Lecture in Cape Town on 16.1.1974: *White and Black Nationalism, Ethnicity and the Future of the Homelands.*

[5] Peter Randall (ed.), *South Africa's Political Alternatives, SPRO-CAS Report No. 10* (Johannesburg, 1973), in particular Chs 10 and 11. Of historic significance is the so-called Bulugha Conference (named after the locality near East London where it was held). For the first time representatives of all racial groups in South Africa gathered to discuss a federal concept. Cf. the minutes to the conference: D. Woods (ed.), *Conference at Bulugha, 9–11 November 1973* (*Daily Dispatch*, East London).

lately gained support among influential circles of National Party academics.

Just who supports which proposal, and to what degree, will be analysed empirically below.[6] For the moment, what is important is that there are three fundamentally different conceptions of the goals of political change, each supported by different political groupings.

We now need to assess these conceptions in the light of our stipulations.

It is impossible to evaluate them against each other, since each in principle allows for a democratic settlement of conflict. The confederation of Switzerland or any one of the Benelux states meets the requirement of a liberal constitutional democracy as adequately as the French 'république une et indivisible'. So we cannot tell in advance how far any one conception *per se* would conduce to the goals we have prescribed.

The only meaningful way of comparing them is by seeing how far each can be put into practice, so as not only to accord with the normative postulate, but also to help bring it about within the South African context.

If one is aiming at peaceful change, it is only legitimate to divide up the country if the states so created are genuinely sovereign and potentially democratic in geographic, demographic, and economic respects. It is quite obvious that bantustans in their present form do not meet this requirement; Basuto QwaQwa is not Luxembourg. On the other hand, a partition of South Africa along the lines proposed by Blenck and Von der Ropp[7] would meet the requirement. Each state would be allotted an area with an economic potential corresponding to its share of the population. The conditions of partition, to be acceptable in terms of the goals of peaceful change, would in the final instance have to be worked out and freely agreed to by all the parties concerned.

Similarly, a unitary state within the existing borders may or may not comply with our normative ideal. But it could be as unacceptable as partition into bantustans, or a federation which discriminates against groups or regions, on a number of counts—if it lacked elementary social justice, if it simply substituted class privilege for racial privilege, if it perpetuated the existence of an underdeveloped periphery dependent on the industrialized heart of the country, or if it did not prevent discrimination against cultural and ethnic minorities.

A federation or a consociational democracy does not necessarily accord with democratic principles. Neither would do so within the South African case if it were constructed to perpetuate inequality between

6 Cf. below, Chapters 7 and 8.

7 Jürgen Blenck and Klaus von der Ropp, 'Republik Südafrika: Teilung als Ausweg?', *Außenpolitik*, 27:3 (1976), pp. 308–24.

population groups and regions. But various conceivable forms of a federal state or a consociational democracy would be fully acceptable from our normative point of view if they guaranteed to all groups and regions an appropriate degree of both power and social justice—the latter by means of, say, the sort of transfers that are made between the Länder of the Federal Republic of Germany.

So all three conceptions of the political system are in principle compatible with the goal of peacefully realizing social justice in a liberal democracy. If pursued with determination, each could lead to more justice and liberty.

We can now formulate an operational definition of peaceful change:

A 'peaceful change' is one which occurs in accordance with the following intentions:
—to abolish discrimination in labour and economic relations, and promote social justice by means of transfers in favour of disadvantaged groups;
—to abolish discrimination in social relations, and facilitate voluntary social integration;
—to end political domination by one group, and establish a political order in which all South Africans will have an equal say in determining their future, whether
  —within the framework of several states created by partition, where each has an economic potential corresponding to its share of the population; or
  —within the framework of a unitary state; or
  —within the framework of a federal state or a consociational democracy.

From now on, the term 'peaceful change' will thus denote both the way change occurs as well as the goals towards which it is directed.

CHAPTER 4

White Readiness for Change—Black Perceptions and Expectations of Change: The Construction and Conduct of the Empirical Surveys

1. Available material

Not much has been published on the opinions and attitudes of whites and blacks in South Africa.

Most of the available material deals with the *white leadership groups*. Leaders in every field tend to express their opinions and intentions in government statements, speeches, interviews, articles, political pamphlets, etc. When these are carefully compiled and analysed, they certainly give an indication of the leaders' openness to peaceful change as defined above. H. O. Staub, J. Hoagland, K. Stephen, E. Runge[1] and other journalists have produced excellent articles and books on South Africa in this way. But their works are inherently impressionistic; although they include some acute analyses of the situation, they lack the data and representativeness of a systematic survey.

Special mention must be made of two scientific studies of South African élites. In 1966/67 H. Adam[2] received 349 replies to a questionnaire he sent to members of the power-élite. And in 1972, H. W. van der Merwe et al.[3] published a study of 925 incumbents of top positions in

[1] Hans O. Staub, *Südafrikareport: Rassentrennung—Wunschtraum, Wahn und Wirklichkeit* (Vienna, 1975). Jim Hoagland, *South Africa—Civilizations in Conflict* (London, 1973). Klaus Stephan, *Südafrika—Weg in die Tragödie* (Munich, 1977). Erika Runge, *Südafrika—Rassendiktatur zwischen Elend und Widerstand: Protokolle und Dokumente zur Apartheid* (Reinbek, 1974).

[2] Heribert Adam, 'The South African Power-Élite: A Survey of Ideological Commitment', in Heribert Adam (ed.), *South Africa—Sociological Perspectives* (London, 1971), pp. 73–102.

[3] Hendrik W. van der Merwe *et al*, *White South African Élites—A Study of Incumbents of Top Positions in the Republic of South Africa* (Duplicated manuscript, Cape Town, 1972); published in an abbreviated version in book-form (Cape Town, 1974).

South Africa. Both studies included active politicians[4] as well as large samples of South African leaders in various fields. Adam concentrates on attitudes to racism and apartheid, while the van der Merwe study provides an insight into the structure and recruitment of the South African élite;[5] but as yet, no study has specifically concentrated on the attitudes of the white leadership groups, and particularly the power-élite, towards the problems of peaceful change.

It is far more difficult to establish the attitudes of the *black political élite*, mainly because of the problems one encounters in collecting data. Firstly, while blacks do have access to the press, it is restricted. On the one hand, the leading white newspapers do not always report the opinions of black opposition leaders, and on the other hand, black newspapers have repeatedly been financially muzzled or even banned. Secondly, some of the most influential black political leaders are themselves banned, and are forbidden to express in writing any opinions whatsoever.[6] So the only opinions which are freely available are either those of politicians living in exile—who are often out of touch with developments in South Africa—or those of politicians within the country whose freedom of speech and expression has not been restricted.[7] This body of material has not yet been systematically analysed.[8]

Contrary to a widely held belief, very little is reliably known about the attitudes of the *white electorate* to peaceful change. Analyses of election results are not very helpful. Voters supporting a specific party do not always agree with its programme. And South African voting patterns are extraordinarily stable, and so throw little light on why people actually vote as they do. Research on political opinions in South Africa is limited. A few newspapers, notably *Rapport* and *The Star*, have com-

[4] The actual power-élite has thus far not been properly analysed; in the Van der Merwe study economists and politicians are under-represented. Cf. H. W. van der Merwe, *op cit*, pp. 5 and 14. In the Adam study only 25 per cent of the politicians approached by letter participated in the survey. Cf. H. Adam, 'The South African Power-Élite', *loc cit*, p. 75.

[5] Besides a socio-demographic description of the South African élite, the second part of the Van der Merwe study deals with the white élite's expectations of the future and some of their political attitudes, e.g. towards democracy, the various political parties in South Africa, and political tolerance. Cf. in particular Chs. 8 and 9 of the study.

[6] Statements and opinions of the people in this circle up to the time the banning-order was served are freely available—at least abroad—and may be included in analyses.

[7] Including the speeches of, e.g., the homeland leaders; those of Gatsha Buthelezi in particular are well worth reading.

[8] References to the opinions and attitudes of the black leadership abound in the literature on South Africa, either in the form of short biographical accounts or within the framework of more general analyses. Besides the published speeches of the various leaders, cf. the journalistic literature mentioned in n. 1 above, to which may be added Gisela Albrecht, *Soweto oder der Aufstand der Vorstädte—Gespräche mit Südafrikanern* (Reinbek, 1977). On the attitudes of the homeland leaders Buthelezi and Mangope cf. J. Butler, R. I. Rotberg, and J. Adams, *The Black Homelands of South Africa, op cit*, Ch. 5.

60

missioned opinion polls at various intervals before elections; but these have emphasized a few points of immediate political relevance.[9] More comprehensive polls of voter attitudes have occasionally been commissioned by the political parties, but the results are never published.

South African social scientists have paid relatively little attention to the South African electorate. What material there is on voting behaviour is the work of H. Lever[10] and W. A. Kleynhans,[11] who base their research on the methods established by E. F. Lazarsfeld.[12] By contrast, sociopsychological research into white perceptions of other race groups and attitudes towards them have been conducted in South Africa for a number of decades. As early as 1937 I. D. MacCrone[13] published a study on the attitudes of whites towards other race groups. Since then, Malherbe, Pettigrew, Van den Berghe, Lever, Du Plessis, and Orpen have produced empirical studies of the attitudes and prejudices of South African whites, notably schoolchildren and students.[14] Studies which go beyond student groups include those which E. G. Malherbe conducted among members of the army in 1946,[15] and H. Lever among white adults in Johannesburg in 1964.[16]

Finally, there are the investigations into attitudes and opinions which count as political sociology. Pioneers in this field were W. Hudson, G. F. Jacobs, and S. Biesheuvel.[17] Special mention must be made of L. Schlemmer's studies[18] of the political attitudes of white voters, and the

[9] *Rapport* commissions the market research institute, Mark- en Meningopnames (Edms) Beperk, to conduct opinion polls on current topics at irregular intervals; *The Star* commissions the institute Pegasus to conduct opinion polls on voting trends.

[10] H. Lever, *The South African Voter—Some Aspects of Voting Behaviour* (Cape Town, 1972).

[11] W. A. Kleynhans, 'Political Parties in South Africa', *Politikon*, 2 (1975), pp. 6–32; cf. as well the commentary and reports on voting trends in the South African press.

[12] E. F. Lazarsfeld, B. Berelson, and H. Gaudet, *The People's Choice* (New York, 1944).

[13] I. D. MacCrone, *Race Attitudes in South Africa* (Johannesburg, 1957).

[14] E. G. Malherbe, *The Bilingual School* (Johannesburg, 1943); T. F. Pettigrew, 'Social Distance Attitudes of South African Students', *loc cit*; P. L. van den Berghe, 'Race Attitudes in Durban, South Africa', *loc cit*; H. Lever, 'A Comparative Study of Social Distance among Various Groups in the White High School Population of Johannesburg' (Doctoral thesis, Johannesburg, 1966); idem, *Ethnic Attitudes of Johannesburg Youth* (Johannesburg, 1968), and H. Lever and O. J. M. Wagner, 'Ethnic Preferences of Jewish Youth in Johannesburg', *loc cit*; A. P. du Plessis, ''n Sosiologiese Studie van die Houding van die Afrikaanssprekende Student teenoor die Naturel in Suid-Afrika' (M.A. thesis, Bloemfontein, 1950); C. Orpen, 'Authoritarian and Racial Attitudes among English-Speaking South Africans', *Journal of Social Psychology*, 84 (1971), pp. 301–2; for further publications by Orpen cf. *Journal of Psychology*, 77/78 (1971).

[15] E. G. Malherbe, *Race Attitudes and Education* (Johannesburg, 1946).

[16] H. Lever, 'Ethnic Preferences of White Residents in Johannesburg', *loc cit*.

[17] W. Hudson, G. F. Jacobs, and S. Biesheuvel, *Anatomy of South Africa. A Scientific Study of Present-Day Attitudes* (Cape Town, 1966).

[18] L. Schlemmer, *Privilege, Prejudice and Parties—A Study of Patterns of Political*

thorough study by C. J. van der Merwe and B. Piek[19] of white voters' attitudes towards the coloureds. These studies are valuable, but are inconclusive on the question of peaceful change in South Africa, mainly because they are not representative of attitudes on a national level.[20]

The *political attitudes of the blacks* are least studied and understood. Commendable work in this field includes M. L. Edelstein's[21] sociological study of schoolchildren in Soweto, and the political and sociological studies by E. A. Brett,[22] P. Mayer,[23] and L. Schlemmer[24] of black attitudes in Johannesburg and Durban. However, they are of limited relevance to the present study.

In view of the scarcity of material, we had to undertake comprehensive empirical surveys if we were to attain our objectives. We conducted four surveys:

—in-depth interviews with white political leaders;
—interviews among the white electorate;
—in-depth interviews with black political leaders; and
—interviews among urban blacks.

We describe below our sample construction and interviewing methods in each case.

2. *In-depth interviews with white political leaders*

What constitutes political leadership or a political élite is one of the oldest and most contentious questions in political sociology. Every definition of a leadership group is thus somewhat arbitrary.[25] Our study

Motivation among White Voters in Durban (Johannesburg, 1973); idem, 'The Afrikaners: Youth and Change', *Optima*, 24 (1974), pp. 56–65.

[19] C. J. van der Merwe and Ben Piek, *Die Houding van Blanke Kiesers Jeens die Kleurlinge* (Johannesburg, 1976).

[20] An exception is the study by C. J. van der Merwe and B. Piek, which is based on a random sample of the whole white population. As their study is concerned with attitudes towards coloureds, it is of little help in the present study.

[21] M. L. Edelstein, *What do Young Africans Think?, op cit.*

[22] E. A. Brett, *African Attitudes: A Study of the Social, Racial and Political Attitudes of Some Middle-Class Africans, op cit.*

[23] Philip Mayer, 'Class, Status, and Ethnicity as perceived by Johannesburg Africans', in L. Thompson and J. Butler (eds), *Change in Contemporary South Africa, op cit*, pp. 138–67.

[24] L. Schlemmer, 'Black Attitudes: Reaction and Adaptation' (Centre for Applied Social Sciences, Durban, 1975).

For the purposes of comparison older studies may be mentioned: I. D. MacCrone, 'Reaction to Domination in a Colour-Caste Society; A Preliminary Study of the Race Attitudes of a Dominated Group', *Journal of Social Psychology*, 26 (1947), pp. 69–98, and P. L. van den Berghe, 'Race Attitudes in Durban, South Africa', *loc cit.*

[25] R. A. Dahl gives a very wide definition of élites in that he includes all those who either exercise or can exercise influence. A person possesses influence if that person is able to bring another person to some act of commission or omission. Cf. R. A. Dahl, *Who Governs? Democracy and Power in an American City,*(New Haven and London,

required that we establish who exert the greatest influence on political activity in white South Africa, within both the government and the opposition. So we decided to select the 200 politically most influential white South Africans. We interpreted 'political leadership' widely, to include not only active politicians but also senior civil servants and military personnel, prominent businessmen, trade-unionists, churchmen, academics, and political commentators insofar as they had any direct political influence on a party or political organization.

We chose individuals on the basis of their reputations.[26] The first step was to ask several leading journalists each to compile a list of the 200 people whom they thought were most influential in South Africa. Quotas were specified for the different political groupings on the basis of their parliamentary strength. The smaller groupings were slightly over-represented, to provide an adequate reflection of the range of opinions they encompassed. This does not affect the results, for the investigation is concerned not with political leadership as a whole but with each individual subgroup. We then presented the lists—which were remarkably similar—to leading members of all parties and intra-party groups. We asked them to delete or add names in both their own groups and those of their political opponents. In this way we were able to compile a list of political leaders whose influence was attested to, both by experts and by representatives from their own ranks. The final list contained the names of 207 people, each of whom was asked for an interview.[27] Only two refused our request.

Interviews were conducted with 74 politicians, 59 leading businessmen and economists, and 72 leading representatives of the civil service, the scientific field, the churches, and the media.[28] The sample included nine Cabinet Ministers, four Ministerial Secretaries, the chairman of the

1961). Paul Drewe, *Methoden zur Identifizierung von Eliten* (Duplicated manuscript, Rotterdam, 1970), provides a good survey of the concept 'élite' and theories of élites. On the discussion of types of élites cf. also H. W. van der Merwe *et al, op cit.*

[26] Three techniques are primarily used to identify élites: the decision technique, which includes those people who have successfully participated in important decision-making processes; the position technique, which includes incumbents of leading positions in public life; and the reputation technique, which includes those people who are thought to exercise influence, irrespective of whether they are incumbents of top positions or not. Although the approaches of the three techniques differ, this does not exclude the possibility that the élite groups individually identified may, by and large, overlap. Cf. P. Drewe, *op cit*, pp. 3ff, and H. W. van der Merwe *et al, op cit*, Ch. 1.

[27] All respondents were initially approached by letter. It was explained to them what the purpose and the intention of the interview were. The time and place of the interview were arranged later by telephone. The interviews took place for the most part in the office of the respondent.

[28] Sixty-five of the 74 politicians interviewed are or were members of Parliament; 49 of the businessmen interviewed are either self-employed or leading managers; other respondents included 10 trade-unionists, 14 top officials in the government administration and the security forces, 21 academics, 18 representatives of the press, and 19 church leaders.

largest South African business corporation, the most important trade-union leaders, six editors-in-chief, and the heads of five churches. One hundred and forty-two interviewees were Afrikaans-speaking, a slight over-representation relative to the population ratio of 2:1. But as Afrikaners predominate in all fields except the business sector, this figure may well be a true reflection of the actual division of power within white South African society.[29]

The interviews were partly structured. Specific questions dealt with the respondent's assessment of the electorate, the main features of his political stance, and finally personal attitudes to peaceful change. Once these questions had been covered, the interview ranged freely over subjects with which the respondent was well acquainted or in which he took a particular interest. The interviews lasted between one and two hours, and were conducted by one or usually two of the authors themselves.[30]

The interviews were done between March and September 1974. In late 1976 and early 1977, 64 people were interviewed again, to establish possible trends in how their political orientation had developed or changed.

3. Interviews with white voters

Fully a tenth of the adult white population is not registered on the voters' roll. Many whites are not South African nationals, while others entitled to vote failed to register before elections for reasons of apathy or resignation. We were concerned with the openness to change of those whites who take an active interest in the political life of the country. So in taking a representative sample of the electorate we deliberately excluded those who would or could not exercise any influence on political processes in the country.

The interviews had several aims: firstly, to establish the political preferences and voting behaviour of white South Africans; secondly, to enquire into those opinions and attitudes towards economic, social, and political relations between the race groups which are relevant to peaceful change; and thirdly, to identify the factors which might influence political attitudes, such as religious beliefs, fear, openness to innovation,

[29] This may provide an illustration of the difference between the reputation and decision techniques of identifying élites on the one hand, and the position technique on the other; had the authors used the position technique—as Van der Merwe did—the distribution would have been different; for English speakers dominate in the business sector, Afrikaners in the political sector.

[30] It was agreed that the names of the respondents would not be mentioned, but that their professional positions and political leanings could be, provided this would not immediately identify the respondent concerned. Thus, the interviews were strictly confidential. This probably accounts for the fact that the discussions were extremely open, as will become apparent in Chapter 7 below.

political participation, and group identification. We also hoped that the results would indicate whether the opinions and likely behaviour of the electorate altered in time. To this end, we carried out four polls of the white electorate, viz., in June 1974, June 1976, November 1976, and July 1977. The first of these was conceived of as a basic survey. The sample was accordingly representative of the South African electorate as a whole. Certain of the questions in this survey concerned with peaceful change proved to be particularly significant; so subsequent surveys concentrated on these.

All the interviews were conducted by South African firms specializing in opinion polls.[31] The authors and their colleagues constructed the questionnaires[32] and analysed the data.

The basic survey consisted of fully structured interviews which were conducted by professional interviewers, lasting an average of 50 minutes. The sample is representative of the white electorate in South Africa. It is a stratified random sample of the voters' rolls used for the 1974 parliamentary elections. It comprised 1,800 persons, out of a total electorate of 2,141,354 in 1974. In accordance with the distribution of the electorate, 1,566 interviews were conducted in urban areas and 234 (13 per cent) in rural areas.[33]

Stratified random samples were also used in the follow-up surveys. But white South African voters are highly mobile, and the 1974 voters' rolls had become somewhat dated. So it was necessary to base the sample on the statistics of white South African households.[34] To ensure complete comparability with the basic survey, non-voters were excluded when the data were processed. The sample in each of the follow-up surveys

[31] The first survey was conducted by Intercontinental Marketing Services Africa (IMSA), Johannesburg; the follow-up surveys by Market Research Africa (MRA), Johannesburg.

[32] The questionnaires are reprinted in the Appendix.

[33] Stratification characteristics were distribution by province and urban/rural. Of the 165 constituencies in South Africa, every second one was randomly selected at the provincial level. Accordingly, the survey included 38 constituencies in the Transvaal, 28 in the Cape Province, 10 in Natal, and 7 in the Orange Free State. These constituencies were divided into urban and rural constituencies on the basis of their location. In the urban constituencies every n-th voter on the voters' roll was selected (in the Transvaal every 20th, in the Cape Province every 18th, in Natal every 19th, in the Orange Free State every 16th); this provided 1566 potential respondents. In principle the same method was applied to the rural constituencies; however, a further criterion, viz. sex, was applied to prevent the possibility of distortion on the basis of sex in the relatively small sample of 234 respondents. If a person selected could not be reached at home, he was replaced after the third unsuccessful attempt by another person chosen by the same process of random selection.

[34] The random samples each include 500 males and 500 females. The random sample of households is representative of 86 per cent of the adult white South African population. All inhabitants of the large and medium-sized cities and of towns with a population exceeding 200 inhabitants were included; only inhabitants of towns with a population of less than 200 and farm-dwellers—the so-called 'deep rurals'—were excluded.

comprised 1,000 persons, and the interviews lasted 20 minutes on average. Although there were fewer questions, the questions themselves were not altered; so attitudes over the period from 1974 to 1977 are directly comparable.[35]

4. In-depth interviews with black political leaders

Although there is a lot of theoretical discussion about black political leadership, the problem is finally a practical one. There is no democratic machinery for black South Africa which could express the relative strengths of political trends. Elections for the 'homeland parliaments' and the black urban advisory councils cannot be accepted as reliable indicators. In this situation, we had to find out which persons were regarded as representative of the relevant trends in black political thinking.

Our method was similar to that used in sampling the white leadership. A list of 67 personalities was drawn up on the basis of their reputations. We included homeland politicians, church leaders, labour leaders, supporters of the banned ANC and PAC, and leaders of the subsequently prohibited Black Consciousness movement. In terms of their banning orders a number of the interviewees may not be quoted, while others would not allow themselves to be quoted under any circumstances, or even included in a list of names. We feel obliged to respect this request for anonymity, and have chosen to keep all the identities secret. The interviewing techniques and methods employed are the same as those used in the survey of white political leaders.

5. Interviews with urban blacks

At the same time as we interviewed white voters, we sought to determine urban black attitudes to peaceful change. We hoped that the interview schedule would throw some light on blacks' opinions of the society in which they live, and the state which by and large regulates their lives. We were especially interested in their fears, hopes, and expectations for the future.

The empirical survey was limited to blacks living in the urban conglomerations of Johannesburg (Soweto), Pretoria and Durban.[36] These are the most important, though by no means the only, major urban black centres. We included Soweto because, with its population of

[35] To ensure comparability in longitudinal comparisons the 'deep rurals' in the 1974 survey were omitted.

[36] Naturally, the authors would have preferred to have had a representative study of all blacks, i.e. both rural and urban blacks. For various reasons it was impossible to conduct such a study. An additional survey of the rural blacks would have involved extremely high costs on account of the enormous size of the country alone; moreover, it

almost a million, it epitomizes the situation of non-homeland blacks. Its population is a cross-section of all linguistic groups in black South Africa; for this as well as for geographic reasons, it would be well-nigh impossible to incorporate the city into one or other homeland. Soweto is thus a melting pot which poses a major problem for the official ideology of 'separate development'.

Durban and Pretoria are different. Black township areas around Durban are almost fully urbanized. But in contrast with Soweto they either fall within the boundaries of the homeland of KwaZulu, or are closely associated with it.[37] So ethnicity is far stronger there. And the Pretoria townships were included in the sample because, in contrast to both Soweto and Durban, they house a range of non-homeland urban blacks who live and work in a predominantly Afrikaans-speaking milieu. We could thus test whether blacks in such a milieu have attitudes different from blacks in an English-speaking environment.[38]

The interview schedule was designed in 1975 and successfully pretested in the same year. However, the actual survey had to be interrupted in the spring of 1976. On the one hand, several respondents were apprehensive during the interviews, and on the other hand many of the black interviewers themselves became fearful of the openly radical opinions that were sometimes expressed.[39] These reactions are quite understandable if one recalls that this was only a few months before the outbreak of the disturbances in Soweto, and the mood in the townships was unusually tense.

We succeeded with a fresh attempt in April and May of 1977. Surprisingly, the events in Soweto had produced a climate more conducive to opinion surveys among urban blacks. Although the interviewers

would have been well-nigh impossible to have obtained a representative sample of the rural blacks in view of the lack of adequate statistics on rural blacks in South Africa; finally, the level of education of the homeland inhabitants and farm labourers would have necessitated a totally different range of interviewing techniques.

[37] The two largest townships of Durban, Umlazi and KwaMashu, lie within the borders of the homeland KwaZulu. Although the two smaller townships included in the sample, Lamontville and Chesterville, are so-called residential areas outside the homelands, they are closely tied to KwaZulu.

[38] The attitudes of the blacks in Pretoria may to a certain extent be taken as typical of blacks living in smaller Afrikaans-speaking cities and towns in the Transvaal and the Orange Free State.

[39] In view of these difficulties the market research institute applied to the then Minister of Bantu Administration without the knowledge of the authors, for official permission to conduct the survey. It was hoped that this would remove the fear on the part of the interviewers and the respondents that they might be dealing with police-informers, which could involve retaliatory measures at a later date. In a letter of the Department of 26.3.1976 it was stated: '. . . the questionnaire does not cover the normal field of social research.' As interviews of blacks by blacks are not illegal under South African law, the authors decided to conduct the survey without the official permission of the government. Another leading market research institute was prepared to conduct the survey even under these difficult conditions.

occasionally met with the same distrust as before, most respondents articulated frank and outspoken opinions. Seventy-seven per cent of respondents expressed their satisfaction at being able to take an open stand on issues of vital interest to themselves. As the result makes quite clear[40] urban blacks have overcome their fear of expressing their views on political matters. Moreover, the interviewers' previous apprehension had now been replaced by great interest and enthusiasm.[41]

The sample used was of the 'quota' type. It was composed exclusively of adult male urban blacks[42] controlled by the following characteristics: residential area, age, linguistic group, and socio-economic status.[43] The total sample size was 1,020: 600 in Soweto, and 210 in the black townships of Durban and Pretoria respectively.[44] The interviews were fully structured and lasted 55 minutes on average. They were conducted by professional black interviewers in the language chosen by the respondent. To guarantee anonymity, the interviews took place on quiet street corners, in parks and railway stations, at places of work, or whenever possible at the respondent's home.

[40] This is particularly clear in the replies to the open questions on the Soweto demonstrations and on the most important needs and desires of the blacks. Cf. the questionnaire reprinted in the Appendix, especially Q. 28 and Q. 64.

[41] At this point the authors would like to thank the market research institute IMSA and in particular the black interviewers for their courageous and untiring effort.

[42] In restricting the sample to black males the authors do not wish to imply that they under-estimate the important role played by women in creating black political attitudes and influencing political behaviour. To keep the number of characteristics as small as possible—so as to avoid working with subgroups too small to be statistically significant—the authors decided to interview only males. The motivation for this decision was not only methodological but also political: many women reside illegally in the urban areas, and, hence, are not prepared to grant political interviews. Consequently, it would have been difficult to have obtained a representative sample.

[43] The quota sample was controlled by the following characteristics:

City:	Soweto/Pretoria/Durban
Age:	18–24/25–34/35–49/50 +
Status:	Upper and upper-middle/lower-middle/lower
Language group:	Nguni/Sotho/other

The characteristic socio-economic status was measured primarily by income, which, however, correlated highly with education. The upper and upper-middle groups were deliberately over-represented by a factor of 2.8 in Soweto, 2.4 in Durban, and 2.3 in Pretoria. This was done because it was considered advantageous to have a substantial number of better-educated—and presumably most informed and active—higher status people in the sample to better enable statistical analysis. In the computer-processing of the results, however, the groups were re-weighted to rectify the distributions and ensure complete representativeness.

[44] The surveys included the most important areas within each city:

Soweto:	Chiawelo, Diepkloof, Dube, Emdeni, White City/Jabavu, Jabulani, Klipspruit, Mapetla, Meadowlands, Mofolo, Molapo, Moletsane, Moroka, Naledi, Orlando, Pimville, Phiri, Senaoane, Tladi, Zola
Pretoria:	Attridgeville, Mamelodi, Saulsville, Vlakfontein
Durban:	Chesterville, KwaMashu, Lamontville, Umlazi

The survey was supplemented by a series of semi-structured interviews.[45] Each discussion involved eight to ten people from some specific group: young blacks with a high standard of education in Johannesburg and Durban; industrial workers in Johannesburg and Durban; clerks and workers from the service sector in Johannesburg; and a group of older, better-educated blacks in Soweto. The tape-recordings of these conversations will be used below to clarify the representative interviews.

[45] With the assistance of a market research institute the participants in the townships were brought together to form *ad hoc* groups, and interviewed either in the townships or in the offices of the market research institute.

CHAPTER 5

South Africa 1974–1977: a State
of Flux During the Empirical Surveys

Every empirical study records a specific historical moment, a snapshot of
attitudes at a specific point in time. In evaluating the attitudes captured,
one must therefore take account of the circumstances of the respondents'
lives at the time of the interviews. In our case, it is necessary to sketch the
general economic, cultural, and political situation obtaining in South
Africa over the period of the survey.

Social science has not yet resolved the effects of a changing environment on the behaviour and especially the attitudes of people. Some
contend that patterns of opinion, especially basic political and socio-
cultural orientations, remain relatively constant.[1] Others have
established during research into segregation in the United States that
when general conditions change, attitudes follow suit.[2] In view of the
momentous changes which occurred in South Africa in the mid-1970s
this problem has a special significance for us, and we shall return to it
below.[3]

Our study of the possibilities of peaceful change in South Africa was
conducted in the period from 1974 to 1977. The first interviews with
white voters were conducted in June 1974, shortly after the
parliamentary elections which had returned the ruling National Party to
power with its second-largest mandate until then.[4] At that time leading

[1] For an instructive survey of the state of attitude research cf. the anthology compiled
by Neil Warren and Maria Jahoda (eds), *Attitudes* (Harmondsworth, 1973), as well as
J. Bem, *Meinungen, Einstellungen, Vorurteile* (Frankfurt, 1964).

[2] In this context mention must be made of the studies by T. F. Pettigrew and P. B.
Sheatsley. Cf. T. F. Pettigrew, 'Racially Separate or Together?', *Journal of Social
Issues*, 25 (1969), pp. 43–69; P. B. Sheatsley, 'White Attitudes toward the Negro',
Daedalus, 95 (1966), 217–38.

[3] An answer is given below in Chapter 8.

[4] Compared to the tremendous victory of 1966 the National Party suffered a clear
setback; it lost nine seats. However, in the elections of 1974 the NP recovered some of
the lost ground.

white politicians and businessmen assessed the country's position in the following terms:

'South Africa is in an enviable position. We have a flourishing economy and a stable government.'

'We can solve our problems on our own. We don't need anyone to tell us what to do.'

'In South Africa we are not afraid of international threats. As a volk we depend only on ourselves and don't pay any attention to the opinions of outsiders. We don't even take the U.S.A. seriously.'

The South African *economy* was growing rapidly, riding on the wave of a rising gold price.[5] *Race relations* between black and white within the country did not seem to give much cause for concern. Indeed, it seemed to many observers that the seeds of 'separate development' had finally taken root, thirteen years after Sharpeville. Some of the South African politicians we interviewed gloated about the racial discontent in the USA, declaring that it could not happen in South Africa. As to *international relations*, the 1970s had seen South Africa breaking out of the self-imposed isolation which had accompanied the implementation of apartheid. There was a policy of 'dialogue' with Africa, which initially bore fruit with certain states[6] and encouraged South Africa to prepare for a continental role as Africa's military and economic giant.

But the confident visions of a 'golden age' soon turned out to be illusory. Within a few years, the country was to be in the throes of a severe economic recession, shaken by racial unrest, and an international pariah more than ever before.

1. *External pressures: South Africa's changing position in international politics*

Within the space of a few years, Southern Africa has become the centre

---

[5] In 1974 the gold price was rising daily. Optimists were speculating on the possibility of a gold price of $300 per fine oz; in fact, in January 1975 the price stood at just under $200 per fine oz.

[6] Observers provide widely differing assessments of South Africa's 'détente policy'. The policy was initially conceived in terms of economic and technical co-operation with neighbouring black African states, but later took on increasingly political overtones. However, it cannot be denied that it did produce some tangible results. Relatively intensive relations were established by means of secret diplomacy with Zambia, Zaire, Liberia, Gabon, and the Ivory Coast. The outward manifestation of this policy was the signing of the Lusaka Manifesto in 1969, which was, however, soon qualified by the Mogadishu and Dar-es-Salaam Declarations. At any rate, in 1974 and 1975 the Organization for African Unity was unable to agree on a common policy towards South Africa. Cf. John Seiler, 'South African Perspectives and Responses to External Pressures', *Journal of Modern African Studies*, 13:3 (1975), pp. 447–68, and David Hirschmann, 'Southern Africa: Détente?', *Journal of Modern African Studies*, 14:1 (1976), pp. 107–26.

of major political storms. The end of the war in Indo-China and the developing peace in the Middle East have focused international attention on the question of decolonization in Southern Africa. The first major development was the collapse of the Portuguese colonial empire. Observers were surprised that the balance of power in the buffer-zone around South Africa could shift so quickly.[7]

When Mozambique received independence in September 1974 the South African government adopted a very reserved stance. It faced pressure from Mozambican Portuguese and the radical right wing in South Africa who, toying with the notion of a unilateral declaration of independence on the Rhodesian pattern, demanded that South Africa immediately invade Mozambique.[8]

The South African government, however, held to its policy of détente and to the principle of non-intervention. It accepted the advent of the socialist FRELIMO Government without comment.[9] As in its ambivalent policy towards Rhodesia, South Africa sought effectively to safeguard its own territory rather than expand its sphere of influence. This calculation paid off with Mozambique; although relations between the two countries are not cordial, their reciprocal dependence has necessitated a policy of pragmatic co-operation with each other.[10]

By contrast, the principle of non-intervention was blatantly disregarded in the course of Angola's decolonization. The South African

The different viewpoints on South Africa's détente policy are stated in the report on the 46th Annual Conference of the Institute of Race Relations, 1976, *South Africa in Africa, An Evaluation of Détente*, SAIRR Papers (Johannesburg, 1976).

[7] Representative of the many publications is the anthology compiled by Ch. P. Potholm and R. Dale, *Southern Africa in Perspective: Essays in Regional Politics* (New York, 1972), in particular, C. W. Petersen, 'The Military Balance in Southern Africa', pp. 298–320, and Ch. P. Potholm, 'Toward the Millenium', pp. 321–31. Even renowned experts were reckoning with a lengthy Portuguese presence in Africa.

[8] In Lourenço Marques (Maputo) an attempted putsch took place in September 1974, with the aim of preventing FRELIMO from taking power. The expected South African assistance did not materialize. In South Africa itself the very conservative Herstigte Nasionale Party (HNP) openly advocated an invasion of Mozambique.

[9] In this connection the Minister of Defence, P. W. Botha, stated: 'We do not believe it is in the interests of the Republic to interfere in the affairs of other countries, because we do not want other countries to poke their noses into our affairs.' House of Assembly *Debates*, 9.9.1974, col. 2537, quoted in John Seiler, *op cit*, p. 459.
FRELIMO = Frente de Libertação de Mosambique.

[10] The interdependence can be illustrated by the following examples. South Africa meets a large part of its energy requirements with electricity supplied from the Cabora Bassa Dam. However, the electricity conversion plant is on South African territory. If supplies were disrupted South Africa could cut off the supply of electricity to Maputo. Over 80,000 Mozambican workers are employed in South African gold mines; if they were all withdrawn at one go this would have consequences for the South African gold industry. But in such a case Mozambique would lose an important source of foreign exchange. Finally, a large percentage of South Africa's imports and exports pass through the port of Maputo; however, without South African technicians and experts it would be impossible to maintain the turnover of the port at its current high volume.

government launched an invasion of Angola to back up the pro-Western liberation movements—FNLA and UNITA—in their war with the pro-Soviet MPLA.[11] The aim, to see a government in power which would adopt an accommodating approach towards South Africa, was in keeping with the basic tenets of the détente policy.[12] Regardless of whether, or to what extent, South Africa was misled and then abandoned by Zambia, Zaire, and above all the USA,[13] her invasion of Angola proved to be a military and political miscalculation. South African troops initially had the better of the MPLA forces. But when Cuban reinforcements armed with heavy Soviet weaponry were flown in, the South African front broke, though without being decisively defeated.[14] Instead of sending reinforcements the South African government decided on retreat, evidently for political rather than military reasons.

On one interpretation of the invasion, the South African army was seizing an ideal opportunity for military manoeuvres. This elated view does not detract from the damage dealt to the army's reputation of invincibility.

The political consequences were even more serious. A pro-South African government did not come to power in Luanda, nor—as was hoped at one time—a secessionist government in Huambo.[15] Moreover, the entire détente policy suffered a serious setback. Zambia and other states which had supported the détente policy with secret diplomacy in the past now found themselves obliged to follow a strongly anti-South African line.[16]

Finally, South Africa's intervention rendered more likely an escalation of the Southern African conflict, with all its international consequences.

[11] FNLA = Frente Nacional de Libertação de Angola.
UNITA = União Nacional para a Independêndia Total de Angola.
MPLA = Movimento Popular de Libertação de Angola.

[12] To all appearances it seems that the desires of the partners in dialogue, Zambia and Zaire, played no small part in the decision to give UNITA and the FNLA strong support. Cf. F.-W. Heimer, 'The Decolonisation Conflict in Angola, 1974–1976, An Essay in Political Sociology' (Mimeograph, Arnold-Bergstraesser-Institut, Freiburg, 1977), p. 60, in particular n. 271.

[13] A comprehensive account of the background to the South African intervention in Angola is provided in R. W. Johnson, *How Long will South Africa Survive?* London, 1977), in particular chs. 7 and 8. Special emphasis is placed on the key-role of the American Secretary of State, Henry Kissinger.

[14] Robert Moss did some research into the South African invasion. Cf. *The Sunday Telegraph*, 31.1.1977, 6.2.1977, and 13.2.1977. He quotes the South African Minister of Defence, P. W. Botha: 'South Africa has no answers to some of the weapons being ued by Cubans in Angola.' (*Rand Daily Mail*, 12.2.1976). Cf. also Heribert Adam, 'Three Perspectives on the Future of South Africa', *op cit*, p. 5. Cf. F.-W. Heimer, 'The Decolonisation Conflict', *op cit*, p. 62.

[15] The UNITA Government formed in Huambo lasted only two months.

[16] Cf. R. W. Johnson, *op cit*, pp. 124ff and 162f. For an evaluation of Zambia's role in the polity of détente cf. Timothy M. Shaw, 'The Foreign Policy of Zambia: Ideology and Interests', *The Journal of Modern African Studies*, 14:1 (1976), pp. 102ff.

Before then, the Soviet Union and the United States had largely restricted their involvement to financial support for the respective sides. South Africa's invasion of Angola and the impending destruction of the MPLA led Cuba to enter the war with extensive Soviet support. This support took the form of human and material resources. Its role in the MPLA's victory, and subsequently, induced the USA—after some initial hesitation—to revise its policy towards South Africa.

The revised policy was just the opposite of what the South African government had hoped for. It had counted on white South Africa's receiving recognition and support as an 'outpost of Western civilization' and a 'bulwark against Communism' but it became clear after President Carter took office that the United States did not consider white minority government as politically stable in the long run. The new administration judged that the USA's long-term geopolitical and military interests in a supply of raw materials from Southern Africa would be far better served if a pro-Western, multiracial or black government came to power as soon as possible.

Consequently, since 1976 South Africa has been criticized with increasing vehemence by the West. Increasing pressure is being exerted on her to accelerate the process of decolonization in Rhodesia and Namibia. And demands that the apartheid system be dismantled are becoming more vocal. Faced with international isolation, the government has chosen to follow the lessons of Afrikaner history, and undertake the 'struggle' alone. It has made drastic preparations for an economic and military emergency. The severe tax increases, the sharp rise in military expenditure, [17] and the frequent references to the possibility of war or a national emergency [18] should be seen in this light.

2. *Internal pressures: the revolt of the silent majority*

Although the South African government has taken pains since the Angolan episode to demonstrate its military might and invincibility, the black majority in South Africa sees the withdrawal from Angola and the progress of decolonization in neighbouring states as signs that black rule will eventually be established over the whole of Southern Africa. Growing self-confidence on the part of the blacks, and the hope of change in the near future, were undoubtedly important in contributing to the wave of protest by black youth in June and subsequent months of 1976.

[17] In the 1975/76 Budget the Defence Appropriation was increased by 36 per cent in comparison with the previous year. The 1976/77 Budget included a further increase of 50 per cent. Cf. *Internationales Afrika Forum*, 12:1 (1976), p. 36.

[18] Cf. *Sunday Times*, Johannesburg, 13.3.1977: 'It's Total War: General Malan Speaks with Brutal Frankness.'

The immediate cause of the unrest was the introduction of Afrikaans as an official medium of instruction in black high schools. But this was only the spark that ignited the powder keg.[19] The demonstrators soon voiced substantial political demands, from the abolition of the Bantu Education system—created specifically for the blacks—through a general dismantling of petty apartheid, to demands for equal political rights and 'one man, one vote'.[20] The state's security forces were caught unaware by protest on this scale, and they reacted with inordinate severity. Afterwards, the state blamed the protest on Communist infiltration. But this alone could not explain the unexpectedly widespread participation of urban blacks in the protest, the repeated outbreaks of disturbance, and the broad solidarity of the coloureds. The protest potential was hardly diminished by massive police intimidation and the arrest or flight of hundreds of young blacks.[21]

The racial unrest came as a shock to the majority of white South Africans. Few whites had reckoned on such a vociferous demonstration of discontent, after fifteen years of apparently untroubled co-existence with blacks. It took some time for many whites to realize that this was not simply a short-lived outburst from a dissatisfied or ungrateful minority, but possibly the expression of a widespread rejection of the whites' apartheid system in all its ramifications.[22]

These initial reactions to the protests of the youth were intensified and reinforced by the reactions of the world at large. The foreign press devoted a lot of space to the causes and likely consequences of the protests. Coverage of conditions within South Africa had not been so extensive and detailed—and critical—since the Sharpeville riots. South Africa's image in the rest of the world became increasingly tarnished.[23]

3. *Economic pressures: the economic consequences of political developments*

Throughout its history, South Africa has always tried to follow its own

[19] The student protests since 16.6.1976 will be dealt with in greater detail in Chapter 9 below.

[20] The range of demands and the nature of the protests exceeded everything that had happened since the early 1960s. In the *Sunday Times* of 9.1.1977 Stanley Uys wrote: 'There is an almost unbridgeable gulf between the aspirations of young black militants and the concessions the government can make.' (Quoted in H. Adam: 'Three Perspectives on the Future of South Africa', *op cit*, p. 6.)

[21] The clearest illustration of this is the fact that the protests hardly let up in 1977. After the death of the Black Consciousness leader, Steve Biko, demonstrations involving over 10,000 persons at a time took place.

[22] Evidence of this is provided in the interviews with leading South Africans conducted at the end of 1976 and early 1977; cf. Chapter 7 below.

[23] The South African government reacted angrily; it saw the worsening of South Africa's international reputation less as a consequence of the events themselves than of

75

course, in defiance even of far more powerful adversaries. It could have faced the growing internal and external criticisms with far less concern had the economic situation not deteriorated rapidly in the mid-1970s: the growth rate declined, the rate of inflation reached double figures, the number of bankruptcies grew alarmingly, and unemployment among urban blacks rose to 20 per cent.[24]

One of the causes of this development was the *world-wide economic recession*, an aftermath of the oil crisis which affected virtually every industrial state and most developing countries. South Africa, with its highly developed industrial sector and heavy dependence on trade, could hardly remain untouched. At first she was able to hold her own on the international market, because of relatively low wage levels and the soaring price of gold. But as the rate of inflation started to rise and export markets to shrink, South Africa was also sucked into the vortex of world-wide 'stagflation'.

Internal factors must also be apportioned a share of responsibility for the crisis, especially the *overheating of the domestic economy* and inflationary practices and policies. South Africa had been encouraged to embark on an ambitious investment programme by the lengthy boom at the beginning of the 1970s, and by the steady rise in the price of gold when the fixed gold price was abandoned. The public and para-statal sectors required enormous amounts of capital and credit to finance the government's programme. Priority had also been given to various extravagant projects which were deemed necessary for the realization of separate development. And there was an almost insatiable demand for credit in the private sector. So when the gold price started falling in 1975,[25] the whole economy ran into liquidity and balance-of-payments difficulties. It was patently overstretched. Businessmen and consumers bore the brunt; despite rising output, real incomes fell by 10 per cent over a period of two years.[26]

The fall in the gold price was only temporary; but even when it started to rise again, liquidity remained very tight—evidence that the fluctuation in the price of gold cannot be regarded as the fundamental cause of the credit squeeze. The loss of foreign confidence in the South African economy was far more serious. The smouldering racial unrest had sown doubt about the political stability of the country.[27] This was reflected in

slanted press coverage thereof, by which is meant the coverage by the English-speaking pro-opposition press, which the government is placing under increasing pressure.

[24] Cf. the press coverage, in particular *Internationales Afrika Forum*, 12:1 (1976), and the *Financial Mail*, 8.9.1975, 16.7.1976, and 10.7.1977.

[25] Between January 1975 and September 1976 the gold price fell from $195.50 to $104.20 per fine oz. on the London market.

[26] *Financial Mail*, 11.2.1977, p. 363: 'In fact, real per capita income is now about 10 per cent lower than two years ago, while unemployment has doubled.'

[27] *Standard Bank Review* (November 1976): 'Attitudes towards South Africa as a

the reluctance of foreign firms to invest capital in the country.[28] The pattern of foreign credits was quite clear: with increasing frequency, short-term credits replaced long-term loans. It became almost impossible to rely on foreign capital when planning to finance new capital investment over a number of years.

Finally, the loss of confidence in the economy and the general political uncertainty have manifested themselves in the collapse of the property market, and the volume of capital being exported in contravention of the stringent regulations. Not only foreigners but a growing number of South Africans are trying to move money out of the country. Even if the amount involved is still comparatively small, it is in itself a sign of the growing loss of confidence in the future political stability of the country.[29]

To summarize, South Africa has been under strong political pressure both internally and externally since the mid-1970s. In the following chapters we shall present the findings of our empirical survey from 1974 to 1977. They will reveal whether or to what extent the attitudes of white South Africans changed over this period.

credit risk were adversely affected by social unrest in major urban areas and the increasing internationalization of South African problems.' Quoted from H. Adam, 'Three Perspectives on the Future of South Africa', *op cit*, p. 8.

[28] Restraints would possibly have been greater if many investment projects had not been financially guaranteed by foreign state credits—e.g. by the American Eximbank, the ECGD in Great Britain, and the Kreditanstalt für Wiederaufbau (KfW) in the Federal Republic of Germany. Cf. *Financial Mail*, 10.6.1977.

[29] Moreover, immigration has declined rapidly since 1976, while at the same time emigration—particularly of the self-employed—has increased.

PART TWO

The White Power-Centre and its
Openness to Change

The White Power-Centre and its Openness to Change

Not only South African society but also its white power-centre is fragmented. The politics of this power-centre can be properly understood only if one gives due consideration to the deep split within it, between two very different and largely opposed political cultures.

White politics in South Africa is a struggle between ethno-linguistic groups within the framework of a parliamentary democracy. Two ethnic groups—which differ in their conceptions of themselves, have diverging interests and disparate political styles, and seek to attain different goals—are kept together by the common institutional framework of Westminster democracy. At the same time, this institutional framework ensures a constant struggle for ascendency between the two groups. The Westminster model evolved in a homogeneous political culture; if transplanted to a fragmented society, it almost inevitably precipitates a struggle. It becomes likely that political formations will develop within each societal segment. The political struggle then takes place between these segments. This tendency is enhanced by the simple majority electoral system, based on the principle of 'the winner takes all'. If the winners and losers are ethnic groups rather than parties with different political policies, this procedure can facilitate the permanent ascendency of one ethnic group.

This is precisely what has occurred within the political system of white South Africa. The Afrikaner ethnic group came to power in 1948; within the framework of the present parliamentary system, there is little prospect of its ever losing power. *However, the struggle between the white ethnic groups continues to stamp its mark on all aspects of South African politics, not least the racial conflict.*

This split at the centre of white power in South Africa constitutes the most important reality of the system when one is considering the possibilities of peaceful change. For whatever the political leaders and the electorate might think about peaceful change, their actions are largely governed by their ethnic group membership. This part of our study will deal with this phenomenon. Chapter 6 deals with the political cultures and structures of the white power-centre. In Chapter 7 we analyse the attitudes of the white leaders, and in Chapter 8 the attitudes of the white electorate, in respect of their openness to peaceful change.

'Laager' and 'Club': the Divided Political Culture and the Fragmented Political Structure of White South Africa

As in many bilingual societies, bilingualism in South Africa means quite different things in everyday life and in politics. Many English-speaking South Africans generally avoid speaking Afrikaans, often because of their weak command of the language. Afrikaners speak English more frequently, not by choice but because it is often unavoidable in professional life.

In politics the situation is quite different. During election campaigns Afrikaans-speaking candidates make a point of delivering part of every speech in English. Their English-speaking rivals reciprocate, even if it entails reading the Afrikaans section with a bad accent.

The nuances of political statements vary with the choice of language. The key concepts used in a speech are a clear indication of whether it has been translated or not. It is no accident that political reports and commentaries in the English-speaking press are strewn with Afrikaans words. Sometimes this is deliberate, for polemical effect—'swart gevaar' is put in inverted commas to imply that an English speaker would never invoke the words 'black peril'. At other times Afrikaans is used to circumvent the difficulties of translation, or to impart the emotional connotations which translation cannot capture, e.g., in words such as 'volk', 'volkseenheid', and 'ware Afrikaner'.

This is not mere semantics. Afrikaners call themselves Afrikaners, feel themselves to be a 'volk', aspire to 'volkseenheid' (unity of the people), and have a very precise conception of just what constitutes a 'ware Afrikaner' (true Afrikaner). They constitute one of the political cultures of white South Africa. The other political culture is that of the 'English-speaking South Africans'. This somewhat clumsy label reflects its complex content. English-speaking South Africans are neither simply British, nor 'Engelse' as the Afrikaners often call them for simplicity's sake. They are not a volk but a comparatively heterogeneous society: descendants of old British settler families and recent immigrants, Christians and Jews, bearers of German, Polish, and Portuguese as well as English surnames. Notwithstanding all this diversity, especially by contrast with the Afrikaners, all sections of this society do have one thing in common—the British element. This is predominant not only numerically but also in respect of tradition, values, and morals. Groups of non-British origin are no less characterized by it. English-speaking South Africans thus constitute a society that is not only heterogeneous but also more open than Afrikaans society. One might say that one can only be born an Afrikaner, but one can become an English-speaking South African.

The different origins and languages of the two societies of white South Africa[1] form the foundation of the differences in their political cultures and types of political organization.

1. *Africa's 'first new nation' and 'last settler community': profiles of their political awareness*

The *Afrikaners* regard themselves as the 'first new nation' in Africa, a nation which was formed in the struggle against foreign domination and had to throw off the yoke of imperialism.[2] The traditional enemy of this nation was the mighty British Empire. Through their policy of successive annexations the British tried to deny the Boers an independent existence, and are therefore regarded as the historical oppressors and the enemies of freedom.

After they had lost the Second War of Independence the Afrikaners had to accept a future in which they shared a single state with people of British descent. From the point of view of the victors the creation of the Union of South Africa in 1910 represented a generous compromise. The colonies of Natal and the Cape of Good Hope were joined with the former republics of the Transvaal and the Orange Free State to form one state, in which Afrikaners and people of British origin had equal rights. This state soon achieved de facto independence as a Dominion within the framework of the British Empire. However, as far as the majority of Afrikaners were concerned, this affected the circumstances but not the nature of the struggle for nationhood. Henceforth it would be pursued within the framework of parliamentary democracy. In the minds of the Afrikaners, South Africans of British descent owed their loyalty in the last instance not to South Africa but to a far-off mother-country. They might be here today but gone tomorrow, to England or Canada or Australia. It was not they but the Afrikaners who constituted the real

[1] Besides the two sub-societies characterized here there is a third group, the so-called 'bilinguals', i.e. those who identify themselves with neither of the other language or ethnic groups. For the most part, these people belong to the better-educated, upper income strata, or are recent immigrants. As this group comprises only 5 per cent of the white South African population they are not treated separately in the following analysis.

[2] On the historical interpretation of the fragmented political cultures and the different self-awarenesses of the two language groups cf. i.a. W. A. de Klerk, *The Puritans in Africa*, op cit, T. D. Moodie, *The Rise of Afrikanerdom: Power, Apartheid, and the Afrikaner Civil Religion* (Berkeley and Los Angeles, 1975), and D. Welsh, 'The Politics of White Supremacy', in L. Thompson and J. Butler (eds), *Change in Contemporary South Africa*, op cit, pp. 51–78, and J. Butler, 'The Significance of Recent Changes Within the White Ruling Caste', loc cit, pp. 79–103.

South African nation, who were the true 'Africans'. As a nation, they saw their historic task as defending or re-establishing their freedom from oppression—whether in the form of imperialistic aggression and concentration camps, or in the subtler forms of cultural alienation and economic dependency.

From this point of view one can understand the obvious sympathy of many Afrikaners for the independence movements in former black African colonies, and also the remarkable love-hate relationship with black nationalism within South Africa itself. Despite the conflict of interests between Afrikaner nationalism and black nationalism, on account of their claims to the same country, the Afrikaners are well aware of the fundamental similarities between the two movements. Black nationalism may be the adversary of the future; the enemy of the past was British imperialism in all its manifestations.

The self-awareness of *English-speaking South Africans* takes a radically different form. Seen from a historical perspective, this self-awareness was first that of a colony, a part of the British Empire, and later that of a self-governing and self-confident Dominion. In both cases English-speaking South Africans regarded themselves as an integral part of the British tradition, and the idea of nationhood remained foreign to them. Although the belief in an Anglo-Saxon mission did play a central role in imperialism, this was conceived in universalistic rather than ethnically exclusive terms. British rule throughout the world certainly meant domination, but at the same time it meant liberal and enlightened rule. Inherent in the concept of 'civilized government' was the idea of spreading democracy. Even 'uncivilized peoples' should be given the benefits of just and fair governance. Above all, British rule purported to offer its subject peoples the future possibility of becoming 'civilized'. In practice, of course, the timing of this possibility was extremely flexible, and depending on the situation might require from decades to centuries. The criteria of 'civilization' were also flexible. They were devised and implemented in a highly pragmatic—or one might say opportunistic—manner, taking the interests of both the imperial power and the settler colony into account. The smaller the colony of settlers the more quickly a certificate of civilization could be earned, e.g., in British West Africa. If the number of settlers was larger, e.g., in Kenya or Rhodesia, the process took far longer. In Kenya the interests of the settlers were sacrificed to the more global interests of the mother-country; in Rhodesia the settlers were able to maintain their position by rebelling against the mother-country. Because of the early independence of the Union, the descendants of the British in South Africa were spared the Rhodesian dilemma of having to choose between a sacrifice of their political privileges and open rebellion. But they have not been spared a crisis of conscience similar to that of the white Rhodesian settlers—the dilemma between preserving their economic and political privileges, and laying claim to the liberal British heritage.

The line separating the preservation of privilege from the liberal heritage cuts right across English-speaking South Africa, and it is anything but clear. To be sure, there is a relatively small, clearly distinguishable group on either side. On the one hand there are the 'dyed-in-the-wool' colonials, who reject any talk of change, even for generations into the future. In spirit they are close to the right-wing extremists in Rhodesia; they do not allow themselves to be outdone even by conservative Afrikaners in the depth of their racial feeling. On the other hand, there are the genuine liberals—actually radicals in the South African context—who actively support the ideal of a single, socially and politically multiracial society with equal rights for all citizens. The former group includes a relatively large number of comparatively recent arrivals in South Africa, immigrants who have elected to settle there largely because of the privileges which they would never have been able to enjoy in their countries of origin, and who have identified themselves with the English-speaking group. Prominent among the latter, the liberal group, is the relatively large proportion of Jewish South Africans, i.e., members of a group which has itself experienced the excesses of discrimination and has by and large become immune to racism.

However, the large majority of English-speaking South Africans fall somewhere between these extremes. One finds an uncompromising stand on the preservation of white domination combined with genuinely liberal practices in the field of social relations between the racial groups. And declamations of liberalism and democracy are at times belied by crude racial behaviour.

Because the Afrikaners have held power since 1948, the ambiguous self-awareness of English-speaking South Africans has not yet been put to the test. In the shadow of Afrikaner rule it has been possible for the old colonial settler outlook to exist alongside visions of a future egalitarian utopia for South Africans of all races.

Common to the whole group of English speakers is a dislike of their Afrikaans-speaking counterparts. Admittedly, the contempt in which the British of the early colonial period held the 'uncivilized' and 'unruly' Boers has given way to a reluctant respect for them in power. With the decline of British imperial might, English-speaking South Africans have had to come to terms with a situation in which they can no longer turn to the former mother-country for support. Thrown upon South Africa alone, they have been forced to accept that the two white groups have a community of political interest. But opinions among the English speakers differ widely on the manner in which the Afrikaners represent these interests. That they efficiently preserve white privilege is beyond doubt. Whereas the liberals oppose the preservation of privilege as such, the conservatives object only to the manner in which it is done, which they feel to be unnecessarily harsh and above all unrefined. However, irrespective of their political stance, most English speakers have a sense of cultural superiority towards the Afrikaners. English-speaking South Africa considers itself to be upholding Greek culture within an Afrikaner Roman Empire.

2. *Power and wealth: shifting economic profiles and their political consequences*

At the end of the Anglo-Boer wars, Briton and Boer respectively were not only conqueror and conquered in South Africa but also rich man and poor man. The outcome had sealed the political defeat of the independent Boer republics at the hands of British imperialism and also the economic defeat of the 'Boerenasie', a nation of farmers, at the hands of British capital. The Afrikaner view of the enemy as 'capitalist Jingoism' contained both economic and political elements.

In the 1880s less than one-half of one per cent of all Afrikaners, as against an overwhelming majority of English speakers, lived in the cities. The economic position of the Afrikaners was already precarious before the turn of the century. In the cities British capital was creating a flourishing mining industry, and English-speaking artisans and tradesmen enjoyed growing prosperity. But traditional agriculture was in a crisis. The Afrikaner population was growing, but the fixing of colonial boundaries had removed the possibility of further treks in search of land. Young men increasingly found themselves compelled to leave the countryside. The Anglo-Boer wars brought destruction and vast movements of population, which heightened this development. Growing numbers of Afrikaners were forced to find a livelihood in the cities as unqualified and badly-paid workers. The English speakers were already entrenched in trade and industry; the outcome of the wars now gave them control of public administration as well. Thus, there was on the one hand a nation of impoverished farmers and proletariat workers, and on the other a nation of prosperous artisans, traders, skilled workers, and qualified bureaucrats, whose economic advantages were reinforced by political power. Over the subsequent eighty years the economic standing of the groups has changed drastically. But one feature has remained— English-speaking South Africa has retained its economic superiority, although it is less conspicuous.[3]

[3] On changes in the economic profiles of the groups, particularly the rise of the Afrikaners, cf. D. Welsh, 'The Political Economy of Afrikaner Nationalism', in A. Leftwich (ed.), *South Africa: Economic Growth and Political Change, op cit*, pp. 249–85, and J. L. Sadie, 'The Economic Factor in Afrikaner Society' (Duplicated manuscript, Geneva, 1975).

The Afrikaners are no longer an agricultural nation. Although over 80 per cent of all white farmers are Afrikaans, well over 80 per cent of all Afrikaners live in the cities. And farmers are no longer poor, thanks to their over-representation in parliament[4] and their consequent influence on the government's agricultural policies.

Political factors were thus important for the economic advancement of what is today the relatively small group of farmers. This was even more the case in *the Afrikaners' rise within the civil service*. The process began some decades ago when bilingualism was laid down as a requirement of employment, a requirement which Afrikaners fulfilled more often than English speakers. The victory of the National Party in 1948 greatly accelerated this trend. Until then, the English-speaking community had held a quasi-monopoly on the top posts in the civil service. Not only was this broken, but has been replaced by a similar quasi-monopoly of Afrikaners. Thus, in both the political leadership and the civil administration—which, as in all modern countries, has expanded enormously in recent decades—the Afrikaner group has gained control of the 'offices of power'.

A parallel development of equal importance has taken place in the *para-statal sphere*. In the past four decades a comprehensive range of semi-state industries has been established with public funds by a public body, the Industrial Development Corporation. These semi-state enterprises have given the government considerable direct influence on the economy, and have provided a large number of employment opportunities, not least in management. In contrast to the private sector— which is still largely in the hands of the English-speaking group— Afrikaners have not only had an equal opportunity in these industries but have de facto been given preference.

But the economic advancement of the Afrikaners has by no means been limited to public and semi-public fields.[5] It began long before they gained political power, and was manifested both in the field of organized labour and in co-operative self-help organizations, as well as in the *private sector*.

At the beginning of the century the trade-unions were for the most part organizations of English-speaking artisans, which the unskilled Afrikaans labourers were hesitant to join. However, by the start of the First World War the Afrikaners were already in a majority among the white miners. Today, Afrikaners dominate most of the white trade-

---

[4] On the over-representation of rural constituencies in South Africa cf. Chapter 6.7 below.

[5] An excellent account of Afrikaner penetration into all aspects of public life, and the concomitant bureaucratization of Afrikanerdom, is presented in F. van Zyl Slabbert, 'Afrikaner Nationalism, White Politics and Political Change in South Africa', in L. Thompson and J. Butler (eds), *Change in Contemporary South Africa, op cit*, pp. 3–18.

unions. Most English-speaking workers have accepted Afrikaner leadership, which—with the co-operation of the government—has ensured a position of privilege for white labour, and above all protected it from all non-white competition.

Even more remarkable has been the growth of Afrikaner business since the beginning of the 1920s: publishing houses, insurance companies, wine co-operatives, credit co-operatives, construction companies, savings banks, and commercial banks. An Afrikaans Chamber of Commerce was founded, as well as an institution to promote investment in Afrikaner firms.

All these institutions and enterprises essentially owe their success to the solidarity of the Afrikaner people, who always gave them preference over 'foreign' institutions. This success was the basis of the tremendous increase in the Afrikaners' share of economic wealth. Between 1939 and 1964 this grew from 3 per cent to 10 per cent in mining, from 1 per cent to 10 per cent in industry, from 5 per cent to 21 per cent in banking, and from 8 per cent to 31 per cent in commerce.[6]

The average income of the Afrikaners in relation to that of English speakers has also increased spectacularly. Taking the average Afrikaner income as 100, the average English speaker earned 180 in 1946, 120 in 1960, and 115–120 in 1969.[7] At present the ratio is about 100:110.[8]

Despite this rapid progress, the domination of the private sector by English speakers has remained largely intact. Excluding agriculture, 81 per cent of total income in the private sector accrues to English-speaking South Africans. Even including agriculture, the figure is 74 per cent.[9] These figures clearly illustrate the extent to which the closing of the income differential between these two ethnic groups has been a function of development in the civil service and the para-statal sphere. The large private firms are still mainly in the hands of the English-speaking population.[10]

[6] Quoted from D. Welsh, 'Political Economy of Afrikaner Nationalism', *loc cit*, p. 263, who, in turn, bases his figures on H. Adam, *Modernizing Racial Domination*, *op cit*, whose data are based on the calculations of J. L. Sadie, 'The Afrikaner in the South African Economy' (Mimeograph, 1966), later published in *Stats* (December 1968), pp. 874–5.

[7] D. Welsh, *op cit*, p. 262, based on Sadie's figures.

[8] These figures are based on two representative surveys by the authors conducted in 1976.

[9] The figures—also based on Sadie's data—do not include the parastatal industries such as ISCOR, SASOL, etc., which are, in effect, controlled by Afrikaners. In that case the English-speaking share of income might well be lower. Sadie's 1974 estimates indicate that the relative shares of the language groups in the private sector have been more or less constant for decades. He estimates that the Afrikaner share of income in the year 2000 will be 34 per cent.

[10] Of the approx. 500 companies listed on the Johannesburg Stock Exchange at the end of the 1960s less than 10 per cent were controlled by Afrikaners.

To summarize, English-speaking South Africa has lost its political power, but is still economically dominant. Its most talented members are not particularly interested in careers in politics or public administration, which offer them few prospects. They prefer commercial and financial success: 'If one has no hope of governing anyway, it is much more fun making money.' Afrikaans South Africa has left far behind it the era of impoverished farmers and industrial workers. And while the prosperity of English-speaking South Africans was not prejudiced by their loss of political control, for the Afrikaners their rise to prosperity was closely linked to the rise to the power.

3. 'Boer' and 'Brit': an empirical perspective on the socio-economic and cultural contrasts between the ethnic groups

Some empirical data will let us characterize the two white language groups more precisely. Each has its own political culture, with distinct demographic and socio-economic features and fundamental value orientations.[11]

The demographic distribution of the two white ethnic groups varies from province to province. The white population of the Orange Free State is almost exclusively Afrikaans, with the English-speaking minority constituting only 10 per cent of the white population. Natal, by contrast, is the most English of all the provinces—here only one-third of the population speaks Afrikaans. In the Transvaal and the Cape the Afrikaners constitute two-thirds of all whites. Half the total white South African population lives in the Transvaal, and about one-third in the Cape. These data are summarized in Figure 6.1.

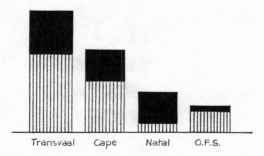

Transvaal   Cape   Natal   O.F.S.

Approximately 87 per cent of all whites live in urban areas. The remainder, living on farms and in small towns, comprise 16.5 per cent of Afrikaners and only 7 per cent of English speakers. The ethnic groups

[11] The following account is based on the interviews of white South Africans described in Chapter 4. As there were no significant changes in the data over the period covered by the surveys, the account in this section is based primarily on the interviews of 1974. Cf. the questionnaires reprinted in the Appendix.

also differ considerably in their degree of urbanization. Only one-third of the Afrikaners, as against two-thirds of the English speakers, grew up in a city. Moreover, over 10 per cent of English speakers grew up abroad. In short, they are overwhelmingly city-dwellers, whereas Afrikaners tend to be townsmen and have, or had when they were young, strong links with the countryside.

In the main, the members of the two ethnic groups belong to different *religious denominations*. Ninety-one per cent of the Afrikaners are members of the Dutch Reformed Churches, the rest being divided among various pentecostal movements and other religious denominations. Among English speakers, Anglicans constitute about 30 per cent; Methodists and Baptists, about 25 per cent each; Presbyterians and Catholics, about 10 per cent each; and Jews 7 per cent. Three per cent of the English speakers and only 0.5 per cent of the Afrikaners call themselves atheists.

We can draw further distinctions in respect· of *education*,[12] *occupation, and social status*. Twelve per cent of English speakers, compared to 19 per cent of Afrikaans speakers, are less-educated (Std 5–6). The reverse holds for university education: 11 per cent of English speakers and 8 per cent of Afrikaans speakers have degrees. There are interesting differences of occupation: the Afrikaners are over-represented in the primary sector, transport, and the civil service, and the English speakers in industry, commerce and banking.

Figure 6.2 contrasts the two ethnic groups according to an index of social stratification constructed out of household income, occupation, and education.[13] The English speakers are more heavily represented in the upper strata, and the Afrikaners in the lower strata.

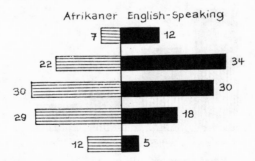

Afrikaner   English-Speaking

7 — 12
22 — 34
30 — 30
29 — 18
12 — 5

[12] For computer processing the data on the educational level of the respondents (cf. Q. 23 of the questionnaire) were divided into five groups: Standard 5/6 or below; Standard 7/8; Standard 9/10; technical college or other post-school diploma; university graduates.

[13] The stratification index was constructed on the basis of a Ridit analysis (Relative to an Identified Distribution analysis). The indicators included in the index were: monthly household income, education of the respondent, and occupation of the head of the household. The Ridit-values were then classified into five groups.

These broad distinctions with respect to established social indicators provide an initial characterization of the two political cultures. The data on the differences in *value orientations* reveal more fundamental dissimilarities between the ethnic groups.

To begin with, they differ fundamentally in their attitudes towards religion. We constructed an index of how far the groups agree with the teachings of their respective religions, out of questions dealing with belief in God, life after death, and the basic tenets of the doctrines.[14] The results are shown in Figure 6.3.

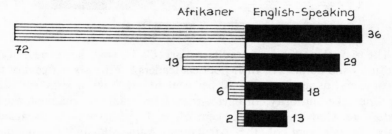

The results for religious activity[15] such as church-attendance and Bible-reading provide a similar picture (Figure 6.4).

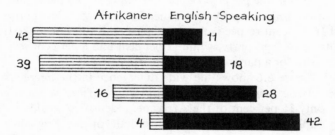

The Afrikaners reveal themselves to be an extraordinarily religious group, in terms of their agreement with doctrine and their attendance at church. This is particularly clear from the data on Bible-reading. Three-quarters of the Afrikaners maintain that they read the Bible daily, a further 12 per cent at least once a week, and only 6 per cent seldom or not at all. It may not be far-fetched to suggest some connection between the religiousness of the Afrikaners and their comparatively high birth rate: 27 per cent have four to six children, as against only 16 per cent of the English speakers.

[14] On the basis of Q. 16J, 16E, 16FF, and 16W a summative index of 'religiousness' was constructed. Each agreement was allotted one point, which results in an index 0–4. The scale values correspond, i.e. agree = 4 points; disagree = 1 or 0 points.

[15] The index 'religious activity' is a summation of the frequency of bible-reading (8 grades) and the frequency of church attendance (8 grades) to four classes; cf. questionnaire Q. 22.

The value conceptions of the two ethnic groups also differ with respect to their readiness for or resistance to change, and their attitudes towards authority and order and towards tolerance, flexibility, and openness.

As Figure 6.5 shows, the Afrikaners are far more conservative than the English speakers, and regard any change with far greater reserve.[16]

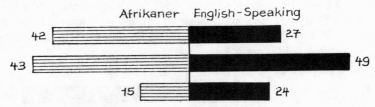

The two ethnic groups also differ markedly in what they expect of the attitudes and abilities of their political leaders.[17] Fifty-six per cent of the Afrikaners, as against only 30 per cent of the English speakers value qualities like authority, firmness, regard for tradition, maintenance of order, etc. Conversely, 63 per cent of the English speakers, as against only 43 per cent of the Afrikaners, value flexibility, tolerance, enlightenment, and affability.

The two ethnic groups also differ sharply in respect of their political activity.[18] Forty-three per cent of the Afrikaner respondents and only 11 per cent of the English speakers are members of a political party, 29 per cent and 16 per cent respectively attend party meetings or make financial contributions to their party, while 12 per cent and 8 per cent respectively do active work for a party or hold some office in one.

Finally, Figure 6.6 shows the wide divergence in the *degree to which members of the respective ethnic groups identify with their group.*[19] Whereas only 15 per cent of the Afrikaners identified weakly with their ethnic group, this was true for almost half of the English-speaking group.

Thus, the Afrikaners are largely urbanized although still strongly influenced by the rural milieu. They are comparatively over-represented

[16] The index 'conservatism' was compiled by summing Q. 16 and 16AA.

[17] Cf. questionnaire Q. 15. The quality 'honesty' was valued equally highly by both groups, and placed above all others.

[18] Cf. questionnaire Q. 34 and 35.

[19] The index 'group identification' was compiled by summing Q. 3, 3A, C, D, and E, and 160.

in agriculture, transport, the civil service, and the white lower strata. They are very religious, have large families, are conservative, place a high value on authority, firmness, and law and order, are politically very active, and regard themselves as a volk.

The English-speaking South Africans are almost entirely urbanized, and are over-represented in commerce, industry, and in the upper white strata. They are less religious and conservative than Afrikaners, and approve of adaptability and tolerance. They do not regard themselves as a volk, and their group identification is limited.

4. *A national movement versus political parties: profiles of political structures*

The above differences in the self-awareness of the two ethnic groups and in their socio-cultural and economic characteristics provide the framework for their differing political cultures and structures, as manifested in different political doctrines, systems, and leadership structures and styles.

Each of these differences can be illustrated by an ideal-type contrast. Firstly there is the contrast between the concepts of 'ethnic nationalism' and 'South Africanism'. Secondly there is the contrast between party structures. That of the Afrikaners is essentially a 'national movement', struggling for its ethnic unity; whereas that of the English speakers exhibits a party pluralism based on competing interpretations of 'South Africanism'. Indeed, one could well simplify the contrast even further and speak of an Afrikaans one-party system and an English-speaking multi-party system. Thirdly, there is a strong contrast between the political styles of the two groups. On the Afrikaner side there is a single party with a mass membership which can be easily and effectively mobilized; on the English-speaking side party organization is characterized by small committees of officials and dignitaries, while the membership is mobilized only around election time. One might label the difference by drawing analogies with the Afrikaner 'laager' and the English 'club' respectively.

Two political doctrines

The *ethnic nationalism* of the Afrikaners seeks to reverse their defeat in the Anglo-Boer wars by parliamentary means, whereas *South Africanism* seeks to reconcile and politically unite the former adversaries under the banner of the common interests of the white minority.

The political rationale of ethnic nationalism is self-evident. If all Afrikaners are united in one political party, their numerical superiority is enough to assure them of political power. The political rationale of white

South Africanism is based on precisely the opposite calculation. As an exclusively English-speaking party can never command an absolute majority, a doctrine must be found to which a substantial portion of the Afrikaner population can subscribe. So 'white' South Africanism tries to bridge the barriers of culture and language by appealing to a transcending South African loyalty. A liberal variant of South Africanism seeks to bridge not only the ethnic but also the racial barriers. It stands for civil rights for both white and black South Africans.[20]

These are essentially the political tenets which have determined the history of the political parties in South Africa since Union. Ethnic nationalism fights for the unification of the Afrikaner people within a 'national movement'; white South Africanism seeks the support of Afrikaners to add to its English-speaking adherents; liberal South Africanism looks for multiracial opportunities, and also tries to recruit Afrikaners to augment its overwhelmingly English-speaking following. Finally, just as both forms of South Africanism aim to attract Afrikaner support, so the ethnic nationalism of the Afrikaners increasingly aims at canvassing English-speaking votes—but not necessarily members—by representing itself as the most effective guardian of the interests of not only Afrikaners but all white South Africans.

However, until very recently the efforts of Afrikaner nationalism to attract English-speaking support have been incidental; and the struggle between the conservative and liberal variants of South Africanism has in effect taken place on the sidelines of South African politics. For the real struggle since the founding of the Union has been for the Afrikaner vote. This largely explains one obvious phenomenon of South African politics: practically all the leading white politicians of this century have been Afrikaners, even the leaders of parties with overwhelmingly English-speaking support. Only parties with credible Afrikaans leaders are potentially attractive to Afrikaner voters, and hence capable of commanding a majority.

In other words, Afrikaners have formulated the doctrine of South Africanism as well as that of Afrikaner nationalism, and have influenced the shape of the English-speaking parties as well as those of their own people.

Two party systems

The history of South African political parties between 1911 and 1948 is dominated by the struggle between political factions each headed by

---

[20] On this point there are two opposing views: a moderate group favours a qualified franchise based on criteria of education and property; a radical-liberal group favours the general franchise for blacks (one man one vote).

Afrikaner generals of the Anglo-Boer wars. This twice led to victories for Afrikaner nationalism.

In 1914 General Hertzog broke away from the South African Party, which he had founded with Generals Smuts and Botha in 1911, and formed the *National Party.* In the 1915 general elections the NP won one-fifth of the seats, and after the elections in 1920 held even more seats than the South African Party. Smuts was only able to remain in power by forming a coalition, and soon thereafter by fusing with the exclusively English-speaking Unionist Party, which identified itself with the aims of British imperialism. This enabled Smuts to win the elections in 1921. But his alliance with the 'Jingoes' had discredited him in the eyes of the majority of Afrikaners. His open support for the mining companies and thereby for British capital during the miners' strikes in 1922 convinced many Afrikaners that he had turned against his people and become a pawn of the British.

After the 1924 general elections Hertzog's NP, in alliance with the Labour Party, commanded a majority. The Labour Party represented the interests of the English-speaking workers, and could thus have its demands satisfied by laws which discriminated against non-white labour in industry. At the same time, this 'marriage of convenience' enabled the NP to achieve some of its fundamental nationalist goals. In 1925 Afrikaans replaced Dutch as one of the two official languages of the Union; in 1926 the full constitutional equality of the Dominions was accepted in principle by Britain, and incorporated in the Statute of Westminster in 1931. And in 1929 the National Party won an absolute majority for the first time.

South Africa suffered severely during the Great Depression of the early 1930s. Hertzog felt that the situation called for a government with as broad a base as possible. So in 1933 he and Smuts formed a 'national coalition', and in 1934 they fused their parties to form the United South African National Party, known in short as the *United Party.* The fusion met with immediate resistance from some NP supporters. The NP in the Cape Province under the leadership of Dr Malan rejected fusion by a large majority and went into opposition. Once again the two basic doctrines in South African politics were consolidated in parties with contrasting institutional frameworks. Dr Malan's party did not agree with Hertzog's view that the fundamental goals of Afrikaner nationalism had been achieved with the signing of the Statute of Westminster. The new party revived the fear that Afrikanerdom might be crushed in the British embrace. It set as its political goals the right of South Africa to remain neutral if Britain went to war, and ultimately the creation of a republic.

The 'long march' of the new NP had begun. In the general elections of 1938 it won almost one-fifth of the seats, like the NP under Hertzog in

1915. In 1939 Hertzog resigned from the government and broke with the UP over the issue of South Africa's entry into the Second World War as an ally of Great Britain. In 1943 Smuts and his UP, in coalition with two smaller parties, won a general election for the last time. Five years later the situation had changed considerably. The war helped Smuts in 1943— the tide had turned in the Allies' favour, and South Africans were generally proud of the part played by their troops. But post-war difficulties worked against him, as did the electoral system.[21] The outcome was that in the 1948 general election the alliance between the NP and the Afrikaner Party achieved a majority of eight seats in parliament, although the governing parties together had a majority at the polls of approximately 100,000 votes.

However, the decisive factor was Smuts's loss of Afrikaner mass support for the second time. The NP and the Afrikaner Party (which fused in 1951) had attracted approximately two-thirds of the Afrikaner vote. Afrikaner nationalism had again come to power, and was not to relinquish it thereafter. The NP won increased majorities in all subsequent elections, except for a slight setback in 1970. Today it has the support of more than 80 per cent of the Afrikaners.[22]

The NP derives its basic strength from its complete identity with the Afrikaner people: 'Die party is die volk en die volk is die party.' The party is the political aspect of a far more comprehensive social mobilization of the whole ethnic group. As was shown above, Afrikaner nationalism was born in the struggle to preserve the cultural identity of the people, and above all their language. Before an Afrikaner party existed, the *Afrikaans Churches* provided the social structure of the Afrikaner people. So it is not coincidental that the National Party represents not only an Afrikaner nationalism but a 'Christian Nationalism', where the word 'Christian' in this context denotes the peculiarly South African form of Calvinism. The caustic aphorism, 'The Dutch Reformed Churches are the National Party at prayer', is hardly an exaggeration. However, the subsequent social organization of Afrikanerdom has not been limited to the churches. The cultural life of the national group is governed by the *Federasie van Afrikaanse Kultuurverenigings* (FAK), which links artistic, literary, and social activities. The FAK promotes pride in the language and the development of an Afrikaans literature. It founded the Institute for Christian National Education, which has had a decisive influence on the government's educational policies. It was the moving force behind the Afrikaner youth organization, the Voortrekkers, and also the Noodhulpliga, a kind of Afrikaner Red Cross; and it was on the initiative

[21] On the functioning of the majority vote system in South Africa cf. Chapter 6.7 below.

[22] Cf. the results of the authors' empirical surveys, Chapter 6.5 and 6.6 below.

of the FAK that the Afrikaner economic organizations described earlier were founded.

The umbrella organization of these manifold religious, cultural, and economic organizations is a numerically small but incredibly influential organization—the *Afrikaner Broederbond*. In theory, the Broederbond is a secret organization. But much is now known about it, both from statements by the organization itself and through revelations in the press. So its political significance can be assessed.[23]

The aim of the Broederbond is to promote Afrikaner interests in every conceivable field. New members are recruited solely by co-option. Only influential people in important social positions are invited to become members, and are admitted only after a trial period of several years in the so-called Ruiterwag. Members must be male Afrikaners over the age of 25 years, belong to one of the three Reformed Churches, have led a blameless life, and unreservedly support Afrikaner nationalism. As a rule, the most prominent people in any given area belong to the Broederbond: the minister of the church, the magistrate, the school principal, the police commander, the editor of the Afrikaans newspaper, doctors, and people in responsible positions in other Afrikaner organizations. The organization of the Broederbond is highly disciplined. The national executive consists of twelve members, including the Chairman and Secretary. Regular circulars keep the lower echelons informed of opinion at the top, and also serve to canvass the views of members on specific issues. Each Broeder is sworn to secrecy in matters relating to the membership and activities of the organization. The influence of such an organization on appointments in all branches of public life and especially in Afrikaner institutions is obvious.

It is often suggested that the Broederbond is the power behind the Afrikaner throne, to the extent of dictating government decisions. This allegation is unproven, and the personalities of the Prime Ministers since 1948 hardly support it. It is now widely assumed that the Broederbond has passed the zenith of its political power; and that it is today an instrument of the government, most of whose members belong to it as a matter of course, rather than the reverse. However, one may accept that the Broederbond played a crucial role in the rise of the NP to power, presently identifies completely with the NP, and continues to be an extremely effective link between the party and all the other institutions of the Afrikaner ethnic group.

Dr Verwoerd once contended that 'the National Party was never an ordinary political party, nor is it one now. It is a national movement.'

[23] Following on his series of articles about the Broederbond in the Johannesburg *Sunday Times* in 1973 and 1974, J. H. P. Serfontein has published a book, *Brotherhood of Power: An Exposé of the Secret Afrikaner Broederbond* (London, 1979), which describes the structure, goals and membership of the organization in great detail.

This is evidently not the wishful thinking of a party leader but a pretty accurate description of the situation.

As the party of an ethnic group the NP is far from being as monolithic as is often assumed. It embraces a considerable range of political opinions and is subject to a variety of influences.[24] The organization of the party in the four provinces clearly diverges. During the early years of the NP under Hertzog the Orange Free State stipulated the party line. After the split in 1934 the NP in the Cape Province assumed the leadership under Dr Malan. After Malan's death the leadership of the party shifted to the north, reflecting the growing demographic and political importance of the Transvaal. The tension between the National Party of the Transvaal and of the Cape is reflected in the bitter competition between the two press empires which the respective sections control: Perskor in the Transvaal and Nasionale Pers in the Cape. Differences of political opinion have resulted in two marginal groups breaking away from the NP. In 1960 a group under the leadership of a Member of Parliament, Japie Basson, broke with the party over Verwoerd's proposal to remove the coloureds from the voters' roll. They founded the 'National Union', which joined the United Party after unsuccessfully contesting the 1961 general elections. And in 1969 a group of right-wing radicals under the leadership of a former Cabinet Minister, Dr Albert Hertzog, also broke away. Calling itself the Herstigte (reconstituted) Nasionale Party (HNP), this group collected Afrikaner protest votes with a programme of uncompromising racism and popularist anti-capitalism.[25]

The NP itself has two wings. The one comprises the so-called 'verligtes', who adopt a relatively liberal stance; the other, the so-called 'verkramptes', whose opinions are hardly distinguishable from those of the HNP.[26] They are kept together by their shared fundamental concern for preserving the 'unity of the volk'. What shocked nationalistic Afrikaners was not the political stance as such of a Basson or a Hertzog, but their flouting of this unity. Unity has brought the Afrikaners success and power; it is beyond question; it is a dogma.

After the electoral victory of 1948, the crowning triumph of Afrikaner nationalism was its realization of the old republican dream. In October

[24] On the party structure of the NP and other parties cf. D. Worrall, 'Politics and Parties', in idem, *South Africa: Government and Politics, op cit*, pp. 246ff.

[25] Cf. J. H. P. Serfontein, *Die Verkrampte Aanslag* (Cape Town and Pretoria, 1970).

[26] The concepts of verlig and verkramp were coined by W. J. de Klerk. Cf. 'The Concepts "verkramp" and "verlig"', in N. Rhoodie (ed.), *South African Dialogue— Contrasts in South African Thinking on Basic Race Issues* (Johannesburg, 1972), pp. 519-31. The ambivalent position between openness to change and party loyalty, in which verligte supporters of the NP find themselves, is excellently described by F. van Zyl Slabbert, 'Afrikaner Nationalism, White Politics and Political Change in South Africa', *loc cit*, pp. 12ff.

1960 Verwoerd called a referendum on the question of a republic: 830,520 votes were cast in favour, 733,861 votes against. Six months later, Verwoerd took South Africa out of the Commonwealth in the face of growing criticism of her racial policies by other member states. With that move the National Party fulfilled the ideals of the Afrikaners: complete independence from Britain, a definitive reversal of the defeat in the Wars of Independence, and the total victory of Afrikanerdom.

The political development of Afrikaans South Africa has thus culminated in a remarkable degree of political unity, in victory, and in the unquestionable supremacy of the ethnic-nationalist party. English-speaking South Africa, and the Afrikaner minority which sides with it, have taken quite a different course.

The defeat of the UP in 1948 marked the beginning of an era of increasingly ineffective *opposition*. The death of General Smuts in 1950 deprived white South Africanism of its most respected leader and main unifying figure. Since then there has not been a politician or a political programme able to attract a large enough body of Afrikaners away from the NP. The opposition has been unable to devise a policy which could command a majority of votes. On the contrary: it has itself developed into a quasi-autonomous multi-party system. A lot of energy is expended in earnestly debating alternative programmes of opposition—all quite removed from the real power struggle—while the possibility of a change of government recedes into an ever more distant future.

Initially the overwhelming majority of English-speaking South Africans and the much reduced but still significant group of Afrikaner adherents to the Smuts and Botha tradition—the so-called 'bloedsappe'—regrouped in the only remaining opposition party, the *United Party*.[27] But Smuts's successors, Strauss and after 1956 Sir de Villiers Graaff, were unable to contain the heterogeneous English traditions within one party. At the end of the 1940s, convinced liberals such as the Member of Parliament, Margaret Ballinger, the author, Alan Paton, and the educationalist, Edgar Brooks, founded the *Liberal Party*. At its party congress in 1954, the Liberal Party adopted a programme which called for equal rights for all South Africans, irrespective of colour, within a common multiracial society.[28] The Liberal Party did not find much support among white South Africans, but nonetheless represented an important position of principle. For as long as non-white voters sent representatives to the House of Assembly and the Senate, they voted

[27] The other, primarily English-speaking parties disappeared one after the other. The remaining convinced jingoes found a political home in the United Party. On the party programme of the United Party during the 1960s cf. 'United Party: Handbook for Better Race Relations', in E. H. Brookes, *Apartheid, A Documentary Study of Modern South Africa* (London, 1968), pp. 27ff.

[28] On the programme of the Liberal Party, cf. 'Statement by Alan Paton, National President of the Liberal Party', in E. H. Brookes, *Apartheid, op cit*, pp. 37ff.

Liberal. When the government passed legislation prohibiting multiracial parties in 1968, the Liberal Party decided to disband rather than sacrifice its principles. But its policy of 'one man one vote' remains the political standpoint of a small but significant group of mainly English-speaking intellectuals.

More important for the political scene in South Africa was the founding of another party: the *Progressive Party* (PP). It was founded in 1959 by a group which broke away from the UP. It also aimed at a liberal multiracial democracy for South Africa. It proposed to attain this by a more gradual approach than the Liberal Party, and rejected immediate universal suffrage.[29] The PP settled instead for a franchise qualified according to educational criteria, which would apply to all South Africans irrespective of race. In this conception the PP was heir to the classical British tradition of 'civilized government'. Party support was drawn particularly from the wealthier English-speaking section of the white population, including much of the Jewish community. The PP received considerable financial and organizational support from the mining magnate, Harry Oppenheimer. For two decades the most prominent personality in the party was its sole MP, Helen Suzman. She became by far the most effective champion of civil and human rights in parliament, and in effect assumed the functions of an 'ombudsman' to the Republic at large.

Even after the PP broke away, the UP was by no means a homogeneous political force. Sir de Villiers Graaff held the party together for twenty years, but was unable either to give it a consistent political image or to develop a clear alternative to the government's policies. The Afrikaner minority in the party consisted of members of a small, anglicized Afrikaner upper class, and 'bloedsappe' who stood by the party of Botha and Smuts for reasons of family tradition—both very conservative groups. The right wing of the party also included the political heirs of the 'Jingo tradition'; their hold over the country districts of Natal gave them control of the Natal caucus, enabling them to form a strong pressure-group within the party. At the same time there were also strong liberal forces at work within the party, especially in the Transvaal and the Cape Province. Although their stance was closer to the PP than to the right wing of their own party, they felt it was politic to pursue their aims within the framework of a larger organization. The binding force in the United Party was above all an aversion to the ethnic nationalism of the National Party and to apartheid ideology, which was considered too doctrinaire.

From the beginning of the 1970s the tensions within the UP increased. The right wing pursued strategy of 'overtaking the Nationalists on the

[29] Cf. the party programme of the PP: 'Safeguard Your Future, The Principles of the Progressive Party of South Africa', in E. H. Brookes, *Apartheid*, *op cit*, pp. 34ff.

right', by emphasizing the benefits of a pragmatic form of white rule in contrast to the 'ideological' politics of the NP. The left wing of the party aimed to be a 'moderately liberal' opposition to the NP, and thereby to prod the government in the direction of more moderate race policies. During 1973 and 1974 the conflict between the 'Old Guard' and the 'Young Turks' in the party gradually heightened, and a rift seemed imminent.

In the general elections of 1974 a considerable section of the opposition vote switched its allegiance from the UP to the PP. For the first time the PP won six seats, all of them in constituencies where an English-speaking upper-class electorate hoped that the PP would provide more effective opposition.[30] And within the UP the 'Young Turks' did better than the 'Old Guard', and saw in their own and the Progressives' success the beginning of a fundamental change in the voting patterns of the opposition. After the elections, this group tried to get its proposals adopted as official party policy. When it failed, four of its MPs under the leadership of Harry Schwarz, Chairman of the Transvaal section of the United Party, resigned and founded the Reform Party. Its policies were similar to those of the Progressive Party. As expected, the two merged a few months later to form the *Progressive Reform Party* (PRP). In 1976 the new party managed to win a further seat from the UP in a by-election in Durban,[31] giving it twelve seats in Parliament against the UP's thirty-six.

1977 saw the end of the UP. Sir de Villiers Graaff took the initiative in proposing a new party, which he hoped would unite the opposition. After months of negotiations the talks between the opposition parties broke down over the PRP's insistence that the programme of the new party include an unambiguous commitment to abolish racial discrimination in any form whatsoever. The proposed programme was in any case too liberal for a number of UP MPs. When six of them, under the leadership of Myburgh Streicher and John Wiley, objected to the programme, they were expelled from the UP. They then formed their own party, the *South African Party* (SAP), which seems to find support particularly among the 'bloedsappe'. Sir de Villiers Graaff could muster support beyond the ranks of his own party only from the small Democratic Party, led by Dr Gerdener, which was not represented in Parliament. On 1 July 1977 the UP and the DP together founded the *New Republican Party* (NRP).

A group of liberal MPs in the UP, who had been close to the reformist group around Harry Schwarz but had not joined him in resigning, refused to follow Sir de Villiers Graaff in the NRP. They followed the

[30] The party gained a seventh seat in a by-election in Pinelands in June 1974.
[31] By-election in Durban North in May 1976.

example of the Reformers instead, and joined the PRP, which then became known as the *Progressive Federal Party* (PFP).[32]

So the opposition now consists of three groups. On the right there is the splinter party, the SAP, which will probably join the NP or come to terms with the NRP in due course. The NRP is in effect the former UP, stripped of its left and right wings and its previous, once illustrious, name. The PFP, augmented by the remainder of the UP reformists around Japie Basson, has substantially increased its parliamentary representation. In contrast to the rather vague political images of the NRP and the SAP, the 'Progressives' present a picture of determination and growing strength. The party is much stronger, and its programme has also changed: a unitary South African state and the qualified franchise are no longer election slogans. The PFP now advocates a constitutional dispensation which will give political rights to all South Africans without any one group being in a position to dominate another.[33] In the general elections held on 30 November 1977 the PFP gained seventeen seats as against the NRP's ten and the SAP's three. It thus became the official opposition. The liberal tendency within the South African opposition is no longer clearly in a minority. English-speaking South Africa is now more divided than ever before. It now indisputably has a multi-party system, within the political subculture of an ethnic and linguistic minority. It seems less likely than ever, after the election results of 1977, that the English-speaking opposition will be able to win significant support from the Afrikaner ethnic group in the foreseeable future. In the fragmented political system in South Africa the opposition's prospects of commanding a majority are more remote than ever.

We would have done scant justice to the political culture of Afrikaans-speaking South Africa if we had confined our account to the party-political scene. The same is true of English-speaking South Africa, which also has a number of *politically relevant institutions outside the party.* But in contrast to the Afrikaans case, the structural framework of the predominantly English-speaking institutions is less coherent; it is characterized by considerable heterogeneity.

The Afrikaans-language press, although it has become more critical in recent years, still has very close ties with the NP. This is much less true of the *English-language press.* The English-language press is effectively an extra-parliamentary opposition in its own right. The large dailies and weeklies in the Transvaal, the Cape, and Natal have opposed the government far more consistently than the UP over the past decades,

[32] For a summary of the programme and goals of the new parties cf. *The Star*, Johannesburg, 18.11.1977.

[33] Cf. 'What Progfeds stand for: The Seven Eglin-Basson Principles', *Rand Daily Mail*, 6.9.1977.

though without identifying themselves with the Progressives. They have defended civil liberties uncompromisingly and courageously, and have been far more outspoken on the government's race policies than the MPs of the official opposition. It should be noted, however, that in recent years some of the English-language newspapers seem to have been currying favour with the government—whether because of government or financial pressure—and have lost their critical edge.[34]

Two important institutions which have taken a liberal line on political issues are the *Institute of Race Relations* and the *Christian Institute*. Both of them have conscientiously compiled information on the state of race relations and have actively promoted contact and dialogue between the racial groups. For years the Christian Institute provided the religious and moral backbone of consistent opposition to the whole apartheid policy. In 1974 the government declared it an 'affected organization' and finally prohibited it at the end of 1977.[35] Although the Institute of Race Relations is equally annoying to the government, it has been spared legal harassment so far on account of the unimpeachable nature of its information and documentation.

It is significant that Afrikaners play a leading role in both the English-language press and these two Institutes. The Director of the Institute of Race Relations, Fred van Wyk, and the Director of the Christian Institute, Dr Beyers Naudé—who was served with a banning order in 1977—are both thoroughgoing Afrikaners.

There is no counterpart in English-speaking South Africa to the political role played by the Afrikaner Churches. The Anglican, Presbyterian, Methodist, and Catholic Churches have remained aloof from party politics. But they have all taken an unequivocal stand against racial discrimination, both individually and, where applicable, collectively as members of the South African Council of Churches. So their significance in respect of race policies cannot be neglected. These *Churches*, together with the Council of Churches, are the most important social institutions in South Africa today which still bridge the colour-bar.

A political picture of English-speaking South Africa would not be complete without a mention of the *National Union of South African Students* (NUSAS). Apart from the disbanded Liberal Party, NUSAS

[34] This has been most noticeable in the case of the *Sunday Times*, which has become less and less critical of the government since 1975, in part due to changes in ownership and in some of the principal political commentators.

[35] An organization which has been declared an 'affected organization' may not receive any financial support from abroad. The aim of the Affected Organizations Act of 1974, an act passed after the publication of the report of the so-called Schlebusch Commission, is to deprive organizations critical of the government of their foreign financial support, and, thereby, force them to curb their activities. Cf. M. Horrell *et al*, *A Survey of Race Relations in South Africa, 1974* , *op cit*, pp. 25ff.

has maintained the most consistent line of opposition to the government's policies. In particular, it has fought a long though unsuccessful battle against the segregation of the universities. NUSAS rejects the policies of all the parties represented in parliament on the grounds that they promote unjustified privileges for the white minority.

The press, the Institutes, the Churches, and the student movement together still constitute the most important forums for the articulation and organization of liberal opinion in South Africa today. Apart from the press, they are supported by very small minorities in the white population. But the government takes their opposition very seriously, even more seriously than it does the parliamentary opposition. Although they are continually subjected to the repressive measures of the state—such as house-searches by the police, and banning orders—they have so far refused to be silenced. Taken as a whole, the political institutions of English-speaking South Africa span a broad spectrum of opinions and positions. The structural patterns of this group evidence an open society willing to tolerate a great deal of dissent, in contrast to the more closed structures of the Afrikaner ethnic group, whose purpose is to maintain unity and avoid intra-group conflict. In general, the political structure of English-speaking white South Africa resembles the system of a homogeneous majority, in which opinions and parties compete for influence; in actual fact it is the political subculture of a more or less powerless minority. By contrast, the political structure of Afrikaner South Africa resembles that of a numerical minority for whom political unity is the prime concern; in actual fact it is the political subculture of a powerful white majority.

Two political styles and structures of leadership

These opposed political structures are reflected in very different political styles, and accordingly in different kinds of party leadership. If one were to seek European analogies, the opposition parties in South Africa could be compared to the British Whigs and Tories of the previous century. (There is no counterpart to Labour in white South African politics.) The NP, however, resembles in style and character the ethnic and religious parties in Europe, such as the Flemish Christian People's Party, the German Centre Party, or the South Tyrol People's Party.

Like most ethnic parties, the NP is a *mass membership party*. It is superbly organized from grass roots to executive, in accordance, moreover, with well-respected rules of internal party democracy. Party officials at all levels are elected, in elections which are by no means a pure formality. Grass roots participation at party meetings is regular and intensive. On the 'platteland', with the great distances between farms, party meetings are also social gatherings, where relatives, friends, and neighbours meet. In the cities, especially the metropolitan conurbations where predominantly Afrikaner suburbs have developed in recent years, the party is the most important institutional framework next to the Church by which Afrikaners meet and get to know one another in what is still very much an English-speaking urban and business world.

The regional party organizations regularly hold 'stryddae', which blend training, debate, and mobilization. The four provincial congresses provide the annual high points of party life, and are attended by hundreds of delegates and supporters.

Party meetings follow a fixed pattern and have a distinctive ritual atmosphere. There is a lot of singing—folk songs before the actual meeting, and religious and patriotic hymns afterwards. The actual meeting is opened with a reading from the Bible and a prayer by a minister of religion. Larger meetings close with the national anthem.

The superb organization of the party manifests itself most clearly at election time. In each constituency many volunteers place themselves at the disposal of the party. The voters' rolls are used to canvass the electorate systematically. Party members call on each voter and note his party preference on a card. Uncommitted voters are then visited, sometimes by the candidate personally. Postal votes are arranged for those unable to get to the polling-booths on election-day, as well as transport facilities for elderly, ailing and otherwise incapacitated voters. [36]

Characteristic of the NP is the high degree of permanent mobilization, even when there is no election in the offing. This is rendered possible by the thorough integration of the party into the whole structure of Afrikaner society, as discussed above. Attendance at party meetings is as much an element of normal social intercourse for an Afrikaner as attendance at church; it is a self-evident duty.

The *structure of the NP leadership* is equally clearly shaped by this integration of the party into the life of the whole community. As we have already seen in connection with the Broederbond, there are very close links between the Afrikaner élites in all walks of life; there is also frequent exchange of personnel among them. Political leaders are recruited from the ministry, Afrikaans journalism, the academic world, the permanent party organization, and the business sector. Leading Afrikaners in the various fields frequently are politically influential, even if they do not exercise political functions *per se*. This constant contact and extensive mobility between the Afrikaner élite groups and the political leadership produces an unusual conjunction of two structural features—functioning intra-party democracy and a concomitant diversity of opinion on the one hand, and on the other a party leadership

[36] Election propaganda such as described here is practised by all parties, though not with anything approaching the intensity of the NP.

which enjoys great authority and the almost unquestioning allegiance of party members. The authority of the leaders derives from the Afrikaners' pride in men who are the living embodiment of the rise of Afrikanerdom; professors and bank directors, editors-in-chief and ministers, are admired as a reflection of the Afrikaners and their advancement. At the same time, the party base plays a large role in the selection of party officials. The selection mechanism is egalitarian, rooted in the tradition of the settler community. This strengthens the identification of the people with their leaders. And the success of the leaders is in turn taken as proof of their competence.

This structure can of course only be effective if the party leaders work in close harmony. Like any other ethnic party, the NP embraces a broad spectrum of opinions, inevitably leading to controversy. So two mechanisms operate to reconcile dissension with the general principle of collective harmony. The one mechanism is the practice of reducing all conflicts to questions of method rather than of goals; the other is the enforcement of strict discipline once decisions have been taken and officially endorsed. No matter how intensive a struggle within the NP may be, basic agreement on the aims of party policy is always emphasized, and the conflict is explained as a difference of opinion over the best way of realizing these aims. Each of the conflicting groups usually tries to present its point of view as the correct interpretation of a position which the party has always held. Struggles within the NP therefore often assume a sort of scholastic character: the 'original teachings' are never questioned, only their interpretation. Even drastic changes of party policy are presented as nothing more than the logical development of an unchanged and unchanging party doctrine. Harmony within the party is then further preserved by the formal discipline among the leaders: 'The party caucus discusses everything heatedly, until the Prime Minister has his say.' The Prime Minister usually speaks only when he feels assured of broad agreement; but then he can count on strict discipline.

In summary, the postulate of 'the unity of the Afrikaner volk' has shaped the style of the NP leadership. Despite all the in-fighting, the Afrikaner élite is always at pains to avoid giving any impression of violating this basic principle. If the élite is sufficiently united in itself it can then count on broad mass support. An appropriate analogy is often drawn between the political culture and party of the Afrikaners and a 'laager', which was the defence tactic practised by the Boers during the Great Trek. The wagons were drawn into a circular wall to protect against outsiders; its effectiveness depended on strict discipline and the maintenance of unity.

The appropriate analogy for the *political culture of the white South African opposition* is the English 'club'. The style of the opposition has been shaped by British tradition, although—or perhaps precisely because—Afrikaners are made especially welcome in the opposition clubs. The Afrikaners of the opposition have left the 'laager' of their people to converse at the English fireside.

A delight in discussion and an aura of exclusiveness characterize the opposition clubs. Unlike the NP, neither the UP nor the PP has ever pursued an essentially unchanging, supposedly infallible party doctrine. New concepts, programmes, and blueprints are accorded due attention. The frequent controversies within the parties are aired in public, and vigorously debated in the English-language press. Where NP politicians always make a point of demonstrating their complete agreement with the party line, politicians of the opposition try to improve their political standing by having an impact on their respective party policies. In debates in Parliament, Nationalist MPs delight in pointing out inconsistencies within the opposition platform—which admittedly does not particularly bother the opposition politicians, for unlike the Nationalists, they regard different points of view within the party as quite normal. The splits within the UP were precipitated less by the incompatibility of the various viewpoints than by clashes over their respective prospects. The former UP had a far more authoritarian structure than the NP, with the leaders having far greater powers in matters of party policy and appointments at both provincial and national levels. Important decisions in the UP were usually taken by small backroom committees.

In contrast to the NP, both opposition parties tend to resemble electioneering agencies, each led by a small circle of professional politicians.[37] As in the NP, the policies of the opposition parties are also much influenced by leaders in other fields, particularly in the business world. But unlike the ruling party, the opposition parties used not to attract many prominent personalities from other fields as parliamentary candidates. Until recently, a managerial post in the business world, a university chair, or the editorship of a large newspaper were considered more attractive than the role of an MP condemned to the opposition benches for the foreseeable future. Only since 1974 has the opposition succeeded in persuading well-known businessmen, academics, and church leaders to stand for parliament. And the political opinions of opposition élites are articulated less through the parties than directly through the respective organs of the press, chambers of commerce, business associations, churches, and institutes.

The political structures of white South Africa thus differ as much in their leadership structures and political styles as they do in their party systems and political doctrines.

[37] D. Worrall terms the South African opposition parties 'cadre parties', and the NP a party of the masses. D. Worrall, 'Politics and Parties', *loc cit*, pp. 250f.

5. *Ethnic groups and party preferences: political subcultures from an empirical perspective*

Ethnic group membership is by far the most important determinant of party preference. Nevertheless, ethnic group membership and party preference do not fully coincide. Although the National Party is the party of the Afrikaners, it does have some English-speaking supporters. And although both the conservative and the liberal opposition draw nearly all their support from English-speaking South Africans, they do have some Afrikaans adherents. We shall now investigate the features of these political subcultures more closely.

We shall first determine the most important factors in party preference. This can be done with the aid of the 'automatic interaction detector'. It assesses the explanatory power of each of the characteristics and grades them in descending order.[38] We included both socio-economic and attitudinal characteristics.[39] Then we shall present the profiles of the political subcultures.

The analysis is based on data from the 1974 questionnaire for two reasons. Firstly, the party structures which had shaped the political subcultures for almost twenty years still existed at that time. Secondly, these data were more comprehensive and so made possible a detailed analysis of the smaller subgroups as well. The reaction of the various subcultures to changes within the party structures of the white opposition will be dealt with later.

Thus, what we analyse below are the white parties as they existed in 1974, viz., the National Party (NP), the United Party (UP), and the Progressive Party (PP).

The break-down of respondents who supported one of these parties is:

NP	70%
UP	22%
PP	8%

The first and most important characteristic distinguishing the parties is

[38] The Automatic Interaction Detector is a multi-variable analysis which, to 'explain' a dependent variable, chooses those variables from a list of potentially independent variables which are best able to explain the dependent variable. To facilitate this, the sample is broken down step by step into groups in which the mean value of the variable being explained is, on the one hand, the highest value, and, on the other hand, the lowest. In this way one can determine which of the variables exercise the greatest influence on the forming of political attitudes. On the statistical methods cf. J. A. Sonquist, E. L. Baker, and J. N. Morgan, *Searching for Structure* (Ann Arbor, 1973).

[39] Information was gathered on a large number of variables, 34 of which were used in the final analysis. These included, on the one hand, characteristics of status such as language group, age, education, descent, etc., and on the other hand, criteria of behaviour such as voting behaviour, religious activity, political activity, etc., and, finally, personality characteristics such as conservatism, racism, etc.

membership of the respective ethnic or linguistic groups. Among Afrikaners the vote was:

NP	91%
UP	7%
PP	1%

Among English speakers, the voting was:

NP	27%
UP	52%
PP	21%

The second most important characteristic which distinguished the Afrikaners was the strength of their identification with their ethnic group. Those who identified more strongly had a greater preference for the National Party: 94 per cent of these respondents supported it, with 5 per cent for the UP and 1 per cent for the PP. Where group identification was weak, the share of support for the NP dropped and that for the UP rose, to 20 per cent.

For Afrikaners with a strong group awareness, the third most important distinguishing characteristic was their degree of trust in the leadership; for those with a weak group awareness, it was their professional status. Thus, among respondents with a strong group awareness and a large degree of trust in the political leadership, the share of NP supporters rose to 96 per cent. And in the group with a weak awareness, the share of NP supporters is higher among civil servants and people employed in transport and industry, and lower among farmers, businessmen, and senior employees.

Among the English speakers, the second most important distinguishing characteristic was their identification with the party, i.e., how consistently they voted. Of those who identified most strongly with any one party by consistently voting for it, 64 per cent supported the UP. The third most important distinguishing characteristic among regular English-speaking voters is church membership: 70 per cent of Anglicans, Presbyterians, and Methodists support the UP, and only 10 per cent the PP; whereas 42 per cent of Catholics, Jews, and atheists regularly voted for the UP, and 32 per cent for the PP.

Among the English-speaking floating vote, i.e., voters who identify much less strongly with their party, one may distinguish party preference on the basis of education. Among the less-educated the proportion of NP voters is 47 per cent, but among the better-educated the PP receives most support, 46 per cent.

The automatic interaction detector thus reveals the extent to which ethnic group membership and party structure are related. By far the most important *criterion of differentiation* is *ethnic group membership.*

Figure 6.7

Automatic interaction detector on
party preference

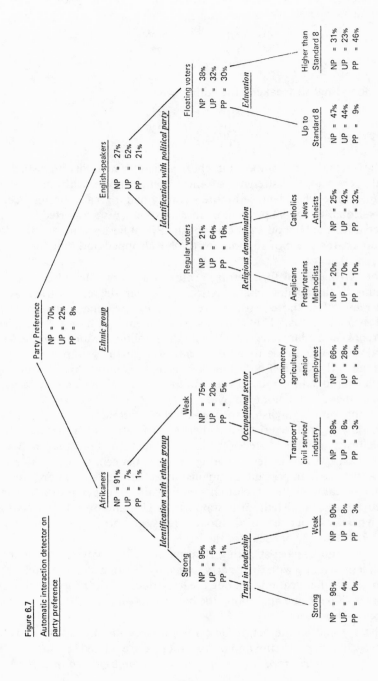

Secondary differentiating criteria are only variants of it: among the Afrikaners, stronger or weaker group awareness; among the English speakers, more or less consistent support of one of the opposition parties. Two of the effective criteria on a tertiary level are, once again, variants of the ethnic group criterion: trust in the leadership among Afrikaners with strong group awareness, or religious affiliation among the English speakers. Among the Afrikaners, trust in the leadership indicates a greater degree of group identification. Among the English speakers, church membership indicates differences in ethnic origin: Anglican, Presbyterian, and Methodist are the denominations of people of largely British origin, whereas Catholics and Jews are far less homogeneous and in any case less 'British' groups.

Socio-economic factors which are independent of ethnic origin, group membership, or both, also play a role at the tertiary level of differentiation, i.e., when the Afrikaners' group awareness or the English speakers' party identification is weak. People of a higher professional status or level of education in both these groups have a greater tendency to support the opposition, whereas those of a lower status or level of education tend to support the government.

The ethnic factor is evidently of varying significance for the three parties. It is most unambiguous in the case of the NP, which is supported by 91 per cent of Afrikaners and by 96 per cent among those with the strongest ethnic group awareness. The UP enjoys the support of 52 per cent of all English speakers, and the figure rises to 70 per cent among people of British descent in a narrow sense. Clearly, although its British core has a strong group or party awareness, the English-speaking population as a whole is far less homogeneous than the Afrikaans population.

Finally, there is also a 'group factor' in the case of the Progressive Party. While it is in any case a predominantly English-speaking party, its support is most considerable among the members of one composite subgroup, viz., the Catholics, Jews and atheists. At the same time, it is the one party where social status plays an important role. Its share of the votes among highly-educated English-speaking floating voters is twice as high as among English speakers in general, and its share among upper-class Afrikaners with a weak group awareness is six times as high as among Afrikaners in general.

Social status is also an important factor for another subgroup, the English-speaking NP supporters. The NP support among English-speaking floating voters with a low level of education is almost twice as high as among English speakers in general.

To summarize: party preferences as a whole can be almost entirely explained by ethnic or language group membership. This holds most strongly for Afrikaner supporters of the National Party, and somewhat

111

less strongly for United Party supporters of British descent and for the Progressive Party. High socio-economic status plays its greatest role in support for the PP, and low status in English-speaking support for the NP.

The analysis thus confirms the existence of *political subcultures which differ significantly from each other* within the two major political cultures of South Africa.

Table 6.1 shows how, on the basis of the 1974 questionnaire, the supporters of the white South African parties are distributed among the ethnic groups.[40]

Table 6.1

Ethnic group	NP	UP	PP	HNP	DP/Others	
Afrikaners	90	7	1	1	1	
English speakers	27	50	20	—	3	(N = 1663)

For the purposes of the following analysis we may neglect the splinter groups, the HNP and the DP. The majority of HNP supporters are socially very similar to the conservative wing of the NP, although it is significant that approximately one-third of their support derives not from Afrikaners but from naturalized immigrants, such as Germans, Greeks, and Italians, especially with a low standard of education and professional status. And voters who sympathize with the DP are similar to PP supporters—primarily members of the better-educated and higher-income strata.

We must now turn to the social profiles of the political subcultures which diverge from the respective majority groups—Afrikaners who support the UP and the PP, and the English speakers who support the NP and the PP. The first point to note is that in quantitative terms the 'deviants' form small minorities among the Afrikaners, whereas among the English-speaking group there are—beside the conservative UP majority—a liberal minority and also a significant minority which supports the governing party.

From which groups are these minorities drawn?

The Afrikaners who vote for the United Party fit the familiar image of the *bloedsappe*, the voters who support the party of Botha and Smuts for reasons of family tradition. They are mainly found in the Cape Province and in the Orange Free State, almost exclusively in rural areas. More than 25 per cent of them have never lived in a city. Academics are under-represented in this group, and farmers twice as strongly represented as the national average.

[40] The percentages refer only to party supporters; 120 respondents either expressed no party preference or did not answer the question.

Progressive Afrikaners, by contrast, have almost all moved to the cities, have enjoyed rapid social advancement, have the highest standard of education of all the political subcultures—more than half of them are university graduates—and hold senior positions.

The *English-speaking supporters of the National Party* are particularly numerous in Natal, seldom belong to the typically British religious denominations—many have converted to the Dutch Reformed Church—and include a slightly above-average proportion of socially unsuccessful people. As many as 15 per cent are naturalized immigrants.

Members of religious minorities are strongly represented among the *Progressives*—Jews, Catholics, and atheists give three times as much support to the Progressive Party as to any other party—and socially they are drawn from the highest education and income strata. Ninety-five per cent of them live in the city.

How do the 'deviant groups' differ from the respective majority groups in their values and political behaviour?

We have seen that, on the whole, Afrikaners differ from English speakers in their particularly strong *religiousness*. This also applies to the subgroups. Among Afrikaners, 83 per cent of NP supporters, 77 per cent of UP supporters, and 53 per cent of PP supporters are very religious. By contrast, among English speakers 37 per cent of NP supporters, 31 per cent of UP supporters, and only 20 per cent of PP supporters are very religious. In other words, even politically progressive Afrikaners are far more religious than the most conservative English speakers.

The ethnic groups also differ fundamentally with respect to the value of *conservatism*. Only 15 per cent of the Afrikaner supporters of the NP are not conservative. The figure for the bloedsappe of the UP is even smaller—only 9 per cent are not conservative. The PP Afrikaners are the most progressive of all groups of voters, including the English speakers—58 per cent are not conservative.

Among English speakers, 18 per cent of NP supporters are not conservative, a proportion barely higher than the Afrikaner supporters of the NP. And UP supporters distrust change almost as much as the supporters of the governing party—only 17 per cent are not conservative. Among English-speaking Progressives, almost 50 per cent are not conservative—fewer than their Afrikaans colleagues in the party.

The differences between the subcultures with respect to *contacts of a social and political nature* with members of the other ethnic and linguistic groups are most revealing. Taking the most important groups of Afrikaans and English-speaking South Africans—NP Afrikaners, and English-speaking UP and PP supporters—one finds that 40–50 per cent have distant contacts, and 35 per cent have no such contact at all. In other words, the major white political groupings, including both the conservative and liberal English speakers, practise a form of voluntary apartheid among themselves. On the other hand, the bloedsappe—in keeping with their tradition—and especially the Afrikaner supporters of the PP, try to cultivate close contacts with the other ethnic groups; fully 47 per cent of the latter have close intergroup contacts, reflecting their minority status within their own economic, social, and political environment.

There are also strong differences between the subgroups with respect to their *identification with one party.* Only one-tenth of the Afrikaner supporters of the NP are potential floating voters, compared to 14 per cent of English and 13 per cent of Afrikaner UP supporters. On the other hand, 43 per cent of English-speaking NP supporters are floating voters, compared to 46 per cent of English-speaking and 75 per cent of Afrikaans-speaking Progressives. However, PP supporters are often floating voters for 'technical' reasons, because in many constituencies the PP does not put up a candidate.[41]

The most important floating voters are thus the group which comprises almost half of the English-speaking supporters of the NP.

Differences in *identification with an ethnic group* are as strong as differences in identification with a party. Ethnic group awareness is particularly strong among Afrikaner supporters of the NP; only 12 per cent do not identify strongly with their group. On the other hand, 39 per cent and 41 per cent, respectively, of Afrikaans and English-speaking UP supporters have only a weak awareness of their ethnic group, whereas the figures for the PP are 53 per cent and 51 per cent, respectively. The ethnic or language group awareness of the English-speaking supporters of the NP is equally weak; 53 per cent do not identify strongly with the English-speaking group.

Finally, as far as *political involvement* is concerned, although there are differences between the subcultures, the differences between the two major political cultures are even greater. Whether in the NP, the UP, or the PP, Afrikaners are more often and more intensely politically active than English speakers. The figures for Afrikaners who actually belong to the party they support are 45 per cent for the NP, 31 per cent for the UP, and as much as 36 per cent for the PP. For the English speakers, the figures are 13 per cent, 11 per cent, and 15 per cent respectively. This confirms our previous observation: politics in white South Africa, whether in the ruling or the opposition camp, is largely an Afrikaner affair.

By way of a summary, we can depict membership of the white South African parties, as well as of the subcultures which arise from an overlapping of the boundaries of the ethnic and political cultures, as

[41] Under a majority vote system candidates are put up only in constituencies in which they stand some chance of winning; until 1974 this was the case in very few constituencies.

follows: Afrikaners who vote for the NP form the overwhelming majority of Afrikaners *per se* and thus share the same social characteristics: strongly rurally oriented, under-represented in the upper strata, highly religious, conservative, and with a strong ethnic awareness; in short, they are 'ware Afrikaners'.

The English-speaking voters for the NP consist of 'untypical' English speakers, immigrants, and supporters of smaller religious groups and sects. They have a low level of education, belong to the lower-income strata, are just as conservative as their Afrikaans colleagues, but in contrast to them are lacking in group awareness. They are a subgroup which has adapted to the dominating group.

English-speaking UP voters are the core of previously British South Africa. They are also conservative, and, except for Natal, overwhelmingly urban. Their group awareness is weak, but their actual social contacts are as restricted to their own group as those of the NP Afrikaners.

The Afrikaner supporters of the UP are the tradition-minded bloedsappe, the most rural and conservative of all subgroups, and very religious; but in contrast to the Afrikaner supporters of the NP and their English-speaking fellow supporters of the UP, they do cultivate contacts across the ethnic and language group barriers. They are the voters who favour conservative 'white South Africanism'.

English-speaking Progressives are like the English-speaking supporters of the NP in being drawn largely from religious minority groups, but are unlike them in coming from the upper strata. They are the most urbanized and the least religious of the subgroups.

Finally, there are the Afrikaner supporters of the PP, who are less numerous but politically more active than their English-speaking counterparts. They are better-educated and more progressive than all the other subgroups, and like all Afrikaners are relatively strongly religious and politically involved.

Overall, the empirical analysis of the electorate confirms the concept of a dichotomous political culture in which the ethnic factor is predominant. However, it also provides some elements for a more differentiated analysis: where parties and ethnic groups partially overlap, specific ethno-political subcultures emerge.

6. *The growing 'laager' and the unsettled 'club': changes in the party preferences of the ethnic groups, 1974–1977*

By the mid-seventies, the party scene was in a state of flux, especially among the opposition. Individuals switched between parties, and parties split and fused. The outcome is that the UP is no longer 'united', having split to form the New Republican Party (NRP) and the (new) South

African Party (SAP); and two groupings from within the UP joined forces with the Progressive Party, forming the Progressive Reform Party (PRP), and then, in 1977, the Progressive Federal Party (PFP). We must now consider whether these changes in the party structure have been accompanied by changes in voters' party preferences. Table 6.2 compares voters' attitudes as polled between 1974 and 1977.

Table 6.2

	NP	UP (NRP/SAP)	PP (PRP/PFP)	HNP	Others	Undecided
April 1974	62	20	7	1	5	6
Oct. 1976	62	14	5	1	5	13
July 1977	63	4	6	0.5	11	16

We may draw three conclusions from the comparison:

—Voters' preferences for the National Party and the Progressive Party have remained largely constant over the period.
—The United Party has gradually disintegrated. Its offshoots have failed to retain about three-quarters of its previous following.
—The number of 'undecided' voters and voters with no party preference has risen dramatically over the period. In 1977 more than one-quarter of all white voters did not declare support for any of the official political parties.

What has happened? Do the most important structures of white South African politics no longer exist? Have the socio-cultural characteristics of South African voters changed? The changes have in fact been minimal. Our analysis of the 1977 electorate indicates that the characteristics of the supporters of the various parties have remained much the same.

Table 6.3

	NP	UP		PP	HNP	No preference	Others/ Undecided
April 1974							
Afrikaners	86	7		1	2	1	3
English speakers	23	45		18	—	5	9
October 1976				*PRP*			
Afrikaners	82	6		—	2	2	8
English speakers	29	26		14	—	9	23
July 1977		*NRP*	*SAP*	*PFP*			
Afrikaners	84	—	2	—	1	4	8
English speakers	26	4	4	15	—	21	30

As Table 6.3 shows, the most important factor in party preference is still membership of one or other language group. The NP is still an Afrikaner party, and English speakers still predominate in the opposition. The HNP is an exception.

About 85 per cent of all NP sympathizers belong to the Afrikaans ethnic group, as in 1974 and 1977. More than four-fifths are members of the Dutch Reformed Churches. The typical NP Afrikaner of 1977 continues to be economically active in agriculture, the civil service, or semi-state enterprises, to come from the middle or lower income groups, and to have a relatively low level of education.

Also as before, the English-speaking minority in the NP has a lower standard of education than the Afrikaner majority, and so is to be found in the lower socio-economic strata. English-speaking support of the NP occurs particularly in the Transvaal and Natal, mainly among artisans and industrial workers in the former and among owners of small or medium properties in the latter.

The composition of the PFP following has also not changed substantially since 1974. Despite the prominent proportion of Afrikaans names in the party leadership—Slabbert, de Beer, Basson, etc.—over 90 per cent of its supporters speak English. And despite its own active membership campaigns, and the collapse of the UP, it has been unable to achieve a significant increase of support from the Afrikaans population group. The typical PFP supporter lives, as before, in the urban centres of the Cape and the Transvaal; is better educated, very likely to have attended university, and a member of the upper social strata. The self-employed are over-represented in the party, as are Jews, Catholics, and atheists.

Until the early sixties the United Party won most of the opposition votes and was able to rally the majority of the English-speaking population behind it. What kind of following do its two successors now have? The NRP, the larger of the two, has become an entirely English-speaking party. Its strongholds are exclusively in Natal and the Eastern Cape; it appears to have become the party of old British immigrant stock, and rather resembles the Dominion Party of the 1930s. Its supporters are chiefly Anglicans, who belong to the upper-middle class in respect of education and income.

The other successor to the UP is the SAP. Its supporters, unlike those of the NRP, tend to live in the Cape, and approximately 50 per cent of them speak Afrikaans. The remaining bloedsappe are evidently to be found in this group; they are now mainly older, single Afrikaners living in the country who are staunch members of the Dutch Reformed Church. The English-speaking supporters of the SAP are found among the lower-middle class, live in Natal or the Cape, and are employed as artisans or industrial workers.

117

In general, then, one may say that the typical features of the supporters of the various established parties have hardly changed over the period. This even applies, with some qualifications, to former UP supporters. One question of particular interest remains: what kind of people are included in the dramatically increased proportion of undecided and 'party-less' voters, a group which increased almost fourfold between 1974 and 1977? Interestingly, more than three-quarters of them are English-speaking South Africans. They are chiefly Anglicans, Baptists, Methodists, and Jews; belong to the middle class and have a high standard of education; and are mostly over 40, although some of the very young, the new voters, also fall into this category.

The characteristics of the undecided voters almost exactly match those of the old UP supporters. Evidently, a broad group of UP voters have been made politically homeless by the erosion and collapse of the party. Whereas the NP and PRP/PFP have been able to maintain their traditional electoral base and their characteristic kinds of voters, typical UP voters may now be found in its offshoots and above all among the undecided. The results of the survey thus establish that *the political subcultures have persisted. It is not the voters who have changed but the parties—more precisely, the opposition parties.* There is no longer any one opposition party which transcends subcultural boundaries to any significant extent. The NRP and the SAP have in effect become 'subculture parties', catering for the Victorian British and the bloedsappe respectively. Finally, a considerable section of the electorate has no place in the new party scene.

The survey of voters' preferences on which the above analysis is based was conducted four months before the 1977 parliamentary elections. The elections produced an increased NP majority, and the PFP was also able to increase its representation. Did the voters who were undecided in July vote after all for one of the official parties in November? The NRP and, especially, the SAP failed to win the 'don't knows'. But the PFP also did not realize its high expectations. On the basis of the election results, the party that gained from the situation seems to have been the NP.

What really happened? An analysis of the results confirms what the prominent electoral researcher, W. Kleynhans,[42] had predicted a day before the election: a large number of eligible voters did not go to the polls. Although the importance of the election as an answer to the international pressures on South Africa had been repeatedly stressed, the turn-out of 65 per cent was about 5 per cent below the 1974 level. A more detailed analysis of the election results in conjunction with the survey data reveals that it was indeed the voters who had been undecided who stayed away. The results in the individual constituencies suggest that the

[42] Cf. 'Tomorrow: The Big Stay-Away?', in *The Star*, Johannesburg, 29.11.1977.

118

NP succeeded in mobilizing the Afrikaner electorate to an even greater extent. This would account for most of the increase in NP votes. By contrast, there was clearly a smaller turn-out among the English-speaking South Africans, who comprised three-quarters of the 'don't knows' in the survey.[43] Although the election data are not broken down by language groups, the situation was probably as follows: almost two-thirds of the previously undecided voters abstained on polling day, and the remaining one-third voted for the NP and the PFP in a ratio of 2:1.

It follows that neither the NP nor the PFP managed to gain much electoral ground from the collapse of the old UP. Their parliamentary representation rose not so much because they increased their share of the votes cast, but because of the way votes count in the Westminster model. Relatively speaking, the NP gained and the PFP, which had had hopes before the election of winning about thirty seats, lost. It failed to attract the old UP voters, who for the most part stayed home on polling day instead.

7. A 'built-in majority': the Westminster model in a fragmented political culture

Major factors in the NP's assumption of political power in 1948 were its appeal to ethnic nationalism, and the constitution of the party as an ethnically oriented collective movement. The decisive contribution however was made by the electoral system, which the country had inherited from Britain. In this system, the candidate in each constituency who gains the most votes is declared elected. In other words, it is victory in the individual constituencies which counts, by contrast with the system of proportional representation, in which parliamentary seats are allocated to each party according to the fraction it receives of the total number of votes cast in the country as a whole. The British system can lead to large discrepancies between the party preferences of the electorate as a whole and the respective numbers of MPs in parliament. As a rule, majorities— no matter how narrow—tend to be over-represented in parliament and minorities under-represented, in comparison with the respective numbers of votes they receive.

Table 6.4 compares the number of votes cast for the NP with the number of parliamentary seats it won between 1948 and 1977. This clearly illustrates how much the governing party gained from the electoral system alone over this period.

As the official opposition, the UP was never able to translate its real strength into parliamentary seats—its voting power was 'wasted' in its own strongholds. A numerical example makes this clear: in the 1970

[43] This conclusion is based on an analysis of the participation in individual constituencies compared with 1974.

Table 6.4

Election year	1948	1953	1958	1961	1966	1970	1974	1977
Votes cast*	1,075,328	1,195,109	1,135,402	785,156	1,278,235	1,478,769	1,128,299	1,059,992
NP votes	443,278**	585,052	625,616	360,468	737,985	803,012	638,424	688,740
Seats in parliament	150	150	150	150	160	160	165	165
NP seats	79	88	97	99	120	112	117	134***
% of votes	41.2	48.9	55.1	45.9	57.7	54.3	55.8	64.9
% of seats	52.7	58.6	64.7	66.0	75.0	70.0	70.9	81.2

Sources: South Africa, *1976 Official Year Book*, p. 184 and Kenneth A. Heard, *General Elections in South Africa, 1943–1970*, (London, 1974), passim.

*Calculations do not include South West Africa, for which six seats have been allotted in parliament since 1950. They have all been held by the NP.

**Including the 41,885 votes for the Afrikaner Party (9 seats), which fused with the NP in 1951.

***The election in the Springs (Transvaal) constituency was postponed because of the murder of the NP candidate. So a total of 164 MPs were elected in 1977.

elections the NP needed, on average, 7,535 votes to win one parliamentary seat, the UP 13,495, and the PP—the smallest opposition party—51,760 votes, i.e., almost seven times as many as the NP.

In an electoral system like this, which rewards narrow majorities and 'penalizes' strongholds, the delimitation of the constituencies is particularly important. The total number of parliamentary seats has been increased three times since 1948;[44] thirteen new constituencies were created in 1974 alone.[45] In addition, most of the constituencies' boundaries were redrawn to take into account demographic shifts and changed residential patterns. These changes, which are supervised by a judicial commission, the 'Delimitation Commission', are not always uncontroversial; in many cases—whether intentionally or not—one or

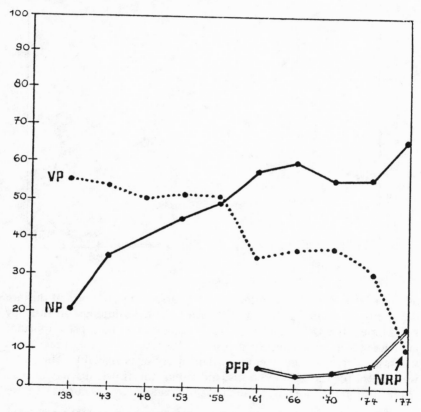

percentage of votes cast

[44] In 1952, 1965, and 1974. Cf. Electoral Laws Amendment Act, 1952; Twelfth Delimitation Commission, 1965; *Government Gazette Extraordinary*, Vol. 19, No. 1364 (February 1966) and *Government Gazette*, Vol. 104, No. 4161 (February 1974).

[45] At the same time eight constituencies or constituency designations were abolished.

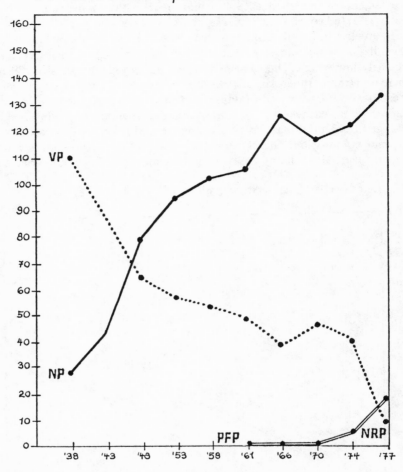

number of seats in parliament

other party is given an advantage. Particularly good examples of this are the thinly populated rural constituencies. In determining constituency boundaries, the Delimitation Commission takes as its most important guideline the average constituency size or 'quota'—the total of registered voters divided by the number of parliamentary seats available. The quota was 12,974 for the 1974 elections. Individual constituencies may deviate from this quota,[46] i.e., be 'loaded' or 'unloaded', by as much as 15 per

[46] Over and above this, there are another seven criteria which should be considered by the delimitation of constituencies: (a) mutual or clashing interests; (b) communications system; (c) physical features; (d) existing boundaries of constituencies; (e) population density; (f) likelihood of a population increase or decrease in the constituency; (g) existing boundaries of the local authorities. *Government Gazette* (February 1974), p. 5.

cent. In very sparsely populated areas the unloading may even reach 30 per cent.[47]

As a result of this process, a constituency in the Karoo with 9,500 eligible voters carries the same weight in parliament as a Johannesburg constituency with approximately 15,000 voters. On average, three rural constituencies correspond to about two urban constituencies. Rural voters are thus comparatively over-represented in parliament.

This would not be a problem if the supporters of each of the parties were similarly distributed between town and country. But this is not the case. The British electoral system is highly controversial in South Africa precisely because the opposition strongholds lie in the urban areas, which are comparatively under-represented in parliament, while the NP predominates in the rural areas. The 1977 elections were typical: the opposition was able to win only two of the sixty-eight constituencies with less than 13,000 eligible voters, whereas in the large cities with con-stituencies of more than 13,000 voters its success rate was much higher.[48]

It would be simplistic, however, to make the clear-cut distinction that country-dwellers vote NP and city-dwellers vote for the opposition parties. The NP advances of the last three decades have taken place less on the 'platteland' than in the cities. The number of urban seats they hold has risen from sixteen in 1948 to over sixty in 1977. This increase roughly corresponds with the enormous post-war exodus of the Afrikaners from the rural areas.

If one relates increasing urbanization in South Africa to simultaneous increases in the number of urban NP constituencies, it seems to follow that city life does not necessarily change voting behaviour. This con-clusion is supported by empirical data. There is only a tenuous con-nection between the degree of urbanization of a constituency and its support for opposition parties.[49] By comparison, voting behaviour correlates very closely with membership of a particular language group. This is particularly true for the relation between the proportion of the Afrikaner population per constituency and the NP's share of the vote.[50] The identity of party and ethnic group is once again confirmed. Even processes that accompany urbanization, such as social advancement and

[47] 'Provided in the case of an electoral division with an area of 25,000 square kilometres or more, the commission may reduce the number of voters to a number equal to 70 per cent of the quota.' *Government Gazette* (February 1974), p. 5.

[48] Whereas the opposition was able to win only 3 per cent of the smaller con-stituencies (under 13,000 voters), it was successful in about 30 per cent of the larger constituencies.

[49] The correlation coefficient for the relationship between the degree of urbanization and voting preference for one or other party was only .21.

[50] The share of Afrikaners per constituency population explains 59 per cent of the total variance of the variable 'voting share of the NP'. The correlation coefficient is .77.

changes in occupation, hardly influence voting behaviour.[51] This can be chiefly attributed to the standard residential patterns in South Africa; Afrikaners prefer 'to be among themselves'. People who move from the country to the city seek their own kind; English-speaking and Afrikaans suburbs can be found side by side in all the larger cities. This means that the determination of constituency boundaries can also decide the election results in urban areas. The inclusion of a single street in which one of the two language groups predominates can cause the victory or defeat of one or other party.

The answer to the question of why the Afrikaners are so firmly in power is thus that the NP can be doubly sure of remaining the majority party. Firstly, *the high degree of identification between the volk and the party guarantees the NP a decisive majority* for the foreseeable future.[52] Secondly, the *British electoral system* used in South Africa disadvantages the opposition in its urban strongholds and *strengthens the Afrikaners' hold* on political power.

Yet despite the almost unchallengeable position of the governing party, the elections are hotly contested. Indeed, the National Party fights the election battles far more fiercely than the opposition parties. At every election the NP tries to link fears for the Afrikaners' survival with the need for them to retain power. The opposition thus has to contend less with economic or 'bread and butter' issues than with catch-phrases like 'Afrikaanse identiteit' and 'swart gevaar', which have become highly emotive election slogans. The set-back in the parliamentary elections of 1970 was the first in the long rise of Afrikanerdom and the NP. It was traumatic for the Afrikaner leadership. Since then, every political measure is evaluated in terms of whether it might impair the NP's political dominance, no matter how unlikely this might seem.

A change of government within the existing parliamentary system hardly seems possible at the moment. This is evident not only in the results of the 1977 elections but also in our empirical data on the electoral basis of the parties and voting behaviour.

The election results of 1974 and 1977 speak for themselves. In 1974 the NP gained 117 and in 1977 fully 134 of the 165 parliamentary seats.[53] The respective majorities were as follows:

[51] Although there are signfiicant differences between the voting behaviour of different social strata, the factor of social stratification is far less important than language group affiliation. The correlation coefficient is only .22.

[52] In view of the demographic preponderance of Afrikaners, this statement would hold even in the event of proportional representation being introduced.

[53] Excluding the Springs constituency, which the NP later won in a by-election. The total of 165 does not include the parliamentary seats reserved to South West Africa/Namibia.

	1974	1977
Uncontested seats[54]	29	42
Constituency majorities of over 80%	25	68
Constituency majorities of 70–80%	23	10
	77	120

In other words, the ruling party won 77 and 120 constituencies respectively, either against no opposition or with an overwhelming majority. It needs only 83 seats for an absolute majority in parliament. If one evaluates opposition seats by the same criterion, the opposition parties together held 24 safe constituencies in 1974, only six of which were still safe in 1977.[55]

So the position of the NP is more secure than ever. But can it trust its voters and rely on retaining a majority, despite dissatisfaction and disaffection among the electorate over government policy?

Voters were asked whether differences of opinion with their party's political line would let them change their allegiance. They answered as follows:

— Of NP supporters
  17% would vote for another party,
  29% would abstain;

— Of opposition supporters
  44% would vote for another party,
  25% would abstain.[56]

The proportion of potential floating voters is evidently considerably higher among supporters of the opposition parties than among supporters of the governing party—a further indication of the fragmentation of political cultures in South Africa. The findings on party allegiance we obtained in 1974 have thus found remarkably accurate confirmation in the collapse of the former United Party, which lost about two-thirds of its supporters between 1974 and 1977.

If the above figures on party allegiance and on abstention are applied to the National Party of 1978, one finds that its position might be weakened in an extreme situation, but even then it would not lose its

[54] Under the majority vote system, no election is held in constituencies in which no opposing candidate is put up; the single candidate is returned 'uncontested'.

[55] This calculation of safe opposition seats is hypothetical to the extent that the opposition has been treated as a single party. If the individual parties are taken into account, in 1974 there were only 10 safe opposition seats, in 1977 only 3. In approx. 10 seats the struggle between the opposition parties produced in 1977 a situation in which they 'neutralized' each other—to the benefit of the NP as third party.

[56] Cf. the appended questionnaires, Q. 30 and 31.

parliamentary majority if its followers behaved in accordance with the survey results. Even if all the opposition parties from the HNP to the PFP were to band together, and there were a system of proportional representation, the National Party would not be toppled from its majority.[57] In the prevailing political circumstances, such assumptions are quite fanciful. Given the present electoral system, the NP will remain the decisive force at the centre of white power for the foreseeable future. *Peaceful change will only occur in South Africa through and with the consent of the National Party.*

[57] Given the existing voting system the NP could not lose more than 22 seats. In the case of proportional representation, even under the most unfavourable conditions—a 17 per cent swing to the opposition, 29 per cent of the voters do not vote, and the opposition unites—the NP would still have a 5-8 per cent majority of the votes.

CHAPTER 7

Between Intransigence and Openness to Change: Opinions and Attitudes of White Leadership Groups between 1974 and 1977

For years now 'verkramp' and 'verlig' have been key concepts in the South African political vocabulary. Since Willem de Klerk, the editor-in-chief of the 'Transvaler', coined the concepts, vast amounts of time and ink have been spent on interpreting and defining them.[1] Initially the concepts were applied to different groups within Afrikaner nationalism. Then they were used to label the conservative and relatively liberal wings of the United Party. And subsequently the concepts have occasionally been inverted: for instance supporters of a multiracial unitary state who reject all compromise with ethnic nationalism have been termed 'verkrampte Progs'.

Are such diffuse concepts of any use for political analysis?

A point in their favour is that they are expressive. On the other hand, the ambiguous way they are used in the press and in political discourse makes them difficult to operationalize. They are really meaningful only when applied to tendencies within the National Party. A 'verkrampte' Nationalist is generally oriented towards the status quo; a 'verligte' takes a more enlightened view of the interests of his group, and is more open to change. We shall apply the concepts only to Afrikaner Nationalists: 'verkramp' will denote 'less open to change' and 'verlig' will denote 'more open to change'. In addition, 'verkramp' can also be usefully applied to the HNP.

---

[1] W. J. de Klerk himself provides a brief explanation of the concepts: 'The Concepts "Verkramp" and "Verlig",' in N. Rhoodie (ed.), *South African Dialogue—Contrasts in South African Thinking on Basic Race Issues, op cit*. This account is complemented by another article in the anthology: O. Krause, 'Trends in Afrikaner Race Attitudes', *op cit*, pp. 532–9.

But to classify political positions more precisely, we choose other yardsticks.

Within the framework of the present study we define as 'oriented to the status quo' those who

— approve of 'job reservation', i.e., the principle on which black labour is subordinate to white labour, and race is a basis of pay differentials;
— support petty apartheid, or are in favour of only marginal changes; and
— wish to pursue the present bantustan policy without modification, or would like a federal state in which the whites retain their dominant position, or would accept a multiracial unitary state with a qualified franchise only in the very distant future.

We define as 'open to change' those who

— want to abolish all racial discrimination in the field of social relations;
— want to remove all discrimination in the economy and the labour market, and want to close the wage-gap between the race groups as quickly as possible; and
— are in favour of a radical and economically 'just' partition of the country, or a federal state in which all citizens have an effective share of power, or a unitary state in which universal franchise will obtain after a brief transition period.

Although a number of the respondents fitted one or other of the ideal types, most were spread across the wide spectrum between an orientation towards the status quo and an openness to change as defined above. Their views on each of the three dimensions of change, viz., economic, social, and political, will be analysed in detail below. However, we can get a general picture and distinguish the most important trends among the various leadership groups by constructing a scale for the different standpoints out of the three dimensions of change. The scale provides a preliminary break-down in terms of the most important characteristics of openness to change.

The sample comprises 205 people, and is thus of limited statistical value. The qualitative differences between the statements are more important than the quantitative ones. Even so, the frequencies with which the various opinions occur have some use: they are an approximate indication of specific trends within the different leadership groups. In this chapter we shall not cite significance tests or absolute frequencies; this would only detract from the general view, and might create an unwarranted impression of statistical precision. The figures are given as percentages. Their value lies in their illustrative character.

The opinions expressed speak for themselves, so comment on them will be kept to a minimum.

128

1. *Intransigence and openness to change: basic trends in the general sample*

Tables 7.1 to 7.3 show the clear distinctions that can be drawn between the different attitudes to peaceful change, according to ethnic group, religious affiliation, political office, occupation and party membership respectively.

Table 7.1

Attitude to change		Afrikaners	English speakers
		%	%
intransigent	1	21	—
	2	31	6
	3	34	36
open to change	4	14	58

Table 7.2

Attitude to change		Dutch Reformed Churches	Anglicans	Catholics, Lutherans & Jews
		%	%	%
intransigent	1	23	—	—
	2	34	4	4
	3	32	41	40
open to change	4	11	50	54

Table 7.3

Attitude to change		Ministers	MPs	Other political office-bearers	Party supporters
		%	%	%	%
intransigent	1	31	18	37	9
	2	69	36	—	19
	3	—	22	16	46
open to change	4	—	24	47	26

The higher the political office, the lower the openness to change. Of course one must allow that members of the Cabinet tend not to express disagreement with official party policy, even in confidential interviews. But the range of opinions among parliamentarians, even of the governing party, is very much broader. 'Other political office-bearers' chiefly include party functionaries, whose attitudes towards change are sharply divided. Prominent persons who exercise political influence without actually holding political office reveal, by contrast, a much greater openness to change. This becomes even more apparent when one analyses the élite groups by occupation, as in Table 7.4.

Table 7.4

Attitude to change		Professional %	Academics %	Churchmen %	Business-men %	Media figures %
intransigent	1	19	21	18	12	4
	2	36	11	9	22	13
	3	18	58	36	47	35
open to change	4	27	10	36	19	48

To summarize so far, openness to change is higher among English speakers than Afrikaners, among those without political office than political incumbents, and among businessmen and other opinion leaders than politicians.

These basic trends vary across a spectrum, according to party membership (see Table 7.5).

Table 7.5

Attitude to change		HNP %	NP %	NRP %	PFP %
intransigent	1	100	22	—	—
	2	—	44	4	—
	3	—	34	60	25
open to change	4	—	—	36	75

Adherents of the Herstigte Nasionale Party (HNP) are without exception verkramp. Among members of the élite group supporting the National Party (NP), politically influential academics are the most verlig, followed by NP journalists and businessmen, while holders of political office within the party are the most verkramp. By contrast, political leaders are more verlig than their supporters in the business world in the cases of the New Republican Party (NRP) and the Progressive Federal Party (PFP).

The Afrikaners are less open to change than the English speakers in all these groups, with one important exception: in the elite group of PFP supporters, the Afrikaners are considerably more open to change than their English-speaking counterparts. In other words, the strongest proponents and opponents of peaceful change are both to be found among the Afrikaners.

The following sections will provide a more detailed analysis of the opinions of élite groups concerning the different dimensions of peaceful change. They will deal respectively with politicians; with opinion-makers, i.e., politically influential academics, church leaders, and journalists; with business leaders; with politicians' opinions of their supporters; and finally, with the attitudes of the main power-élite—that small circle of the most influential political personalities, the so-called 'inner circle'.

2. *Politicians and peaceful change in 1974*

Our approach in this section is deliberately a-historical; we base our analysis of interviews in 1974 and 1977 on the party membership of the respondents in 1977. This is immaterial as far as the NP leadership is concerned, since none of these respondents changed their party membership. We shall describe as 'NRP' those respondents who were members of the UP in 1974 and of the NRP in 1977. And 'PFP' denotes those politicians who belonged to the party in 1977, but in 1974 belonged either to the PP or to the 'Young Turks' in the UP.[2] We have to go by current party membership if we are to establish whether the opinions of specific élite groups changed between 1974 and 1977.

As we have seen, the attitudes of the respondents differ most according to party membership. This is particularly true of professional politicians, as Table 7.6 shows.

Table 7.6

Politicians' attitude to change		HNP	NP	NRP	PFP
		%	%	%	%
intransigent	1	100	29	—	—
	2	—	62	24	—
	3	—	9	58	12
open to change	4	—	—	18	88

The table makes clear where each of the four parties stands on the question of change. It also shows that there is a range of opinion within three of the parties. These various differences of opinion must now be

[2] In comparing the results of the 1974 and 1977 surveys, the NP remains unchanged. The NRP (1977) comprises the 1974 members of the UP *without* the Schwarz and Basson groups. The PFP extrapolated back to 1974 comprises the PP members of 1974 *together with* the Schwarz and Basson groups. Cf. above.

analysed more closely. This will be done for each of the dimensions of peaceful change, namely the economic, social, and political relations between the race groups.

Politicians on race relations in the economy

Politicians in the political parties of white South Africa have very diverse views on *job reservation*. Representatives of the right-wing splinter party, the HNP, unanimously approve of it, while politicians in the NRP and PFP accorded it little significance. Within the governing party, the NP, there are divergent opinions: 9 per cent regard job reservation as necessary to protect the white worker, 68 per cent think that it is unimportant in practice but politically significant, and 23 per cent— almost a quarter—think that it is not important.

The strongest support for job reservation is expressed by members of the HNP:

> *It is scandalous to create loopholes in job reservation. It is being done at the expense of the white man. The legal regulations are being disregarded. It is unacceptable that blacks infiltrate whites' jobs. The trend must be reversed by reducing our economic growth.* [3]

Similar opinions are expressed by the right wing of the NP:

> *Even if job reservation is rarely enforced, it is still necessary for the protection of the white worker. In the white areas there will be no change in this respect.*

A large majority of NP politicians take a different view, based solely on political pragmatism:

> *Job reservation only affects a small part of the labour force, but it is very important in psychological terms. It gives a feeling of security to our poor whites, those who can't help it that they're made that way. That's why we need it.*

> *For political reasons we can't do without it. It may be unimportant in numerical terms, but it hangs like the sword of Damocles over all our labour relations. We can only keep the white workers on our side if we give them security.*

But, as Table 7.7 shows, NP politicians come to very different conclusions about the future of job reservation.

More than a third of the NP are in favour of retaining the status quo. The majority are in favour of a more flexible application of the policy, which would take the requirements of the economy into account without depriving the whites of their privileges.

[3] For reasons of confidence—cf. Ch. 4.2, n. 30 above—respondents' political affiliation, but not their names are mentioned.

Table 7.7

	NP Politicians %
job reservation must be retained	35
job reservation can be relaxed if economically desirable	53
job reservation must be abolished	12

A Minister explained this pragmatic, flexible approach as follows:

The trade-unions are showing ever less resistance to the gradual abolition of job reservation. We have developed a method of overcoming their resistance in a rational manner. Once we have ascertained that there is a scarcity of labour in a specific field, we inform the trade-unions, and together we stipulate a period of several months during which time they can try and find white workers. If they cannot find them the job is then thrown open to non-whites. In this way we will gradually eradicate the problem. Naturally, this assumes that whites will become better trained and better qualified. But as a rule this can be arranged without difficulty.

The verligte wing of the NP is very critical of job reservation:

It must be abolished step by step. It is impossible in the long run to hold a job for a man just because he's got a white skin.

To summarize, the majority of NP politicians are in favour of compromising between economic necessity and the retention of privileges for their working-class supporters. Approximately one-tenth regard the economic disadvantages as more important than the political advantages, and hence are in favour of abolishing job reservation directly.

NRP politicians also base their unequivocal rejection of job reservation on economic reasoning:

Job reservation has no value and should disappear completely. It is only of psychological importance as long as it gives white workers a stronger sense of security. And that was the greatest mistake that the government could make; for this kind of security can only be maintained in the short term, and it makes the whites lazy.

It's a scandal: there are thousands of people who want to work, and there is enough work for them, but these people are legally prevented from doing it. That is unforgivable.

The arguments of the NRP explicitly or implicitly assume that whites should retain privileges in the labour market. But they regard job reservation as a superfluous means to this end.

Job reservation is even more strongly rejected by the PFP politicians:

Job reservation is collapsing. The whites are so occupied in governing this country that there are more and more job opportunities which they themselves cannot fill. All attempts to conceal the collapse by re-classifying jobs are in vain.

To get a more concrete idea of whether politicians were really ready to abolish job reservation, we asked about the standing of the races in the *labour hierarchy*. If one is consistent, the abolition of job reservation directly implies that blacks and whites will work together on an equal footing, and by the same token that whites could have black superiors. However, many politicians have not drawn this conclusion, as Table 7.8 illustrates.

Table 7.8

	NP	NRP	PFP
	%	%	%
Blacks may only be subordinate to whites or work in separate labour hierarchies	49	—	—
Blacks may work with whites at the same level	39	38	—
Blacks may also be in charge of whites	12	62	100

One-third of NP politicians took a verkramp position on our previous, abstract question. The figure on this concrete question rises to one-half, while 40 per cent are open to partial change. The 12 per cent who were previously in favour of abolishing job reservation are consistent in their replies to the question about the labour hierarchy. Almost 40 per cent of the NRP politicians are inconsistent in not being prepared to accept blacks in charge of whites. The PFP politicians are consistent without exception, as are the representatives of the HNP at the other end of the political spectrum.

The leaders of the HNP are not in any doubt:

Blacks should only be used as assistants. 'Baasskap' is undoubtedly a paternalistic concept. But blacks accept it because they are prepared to be led by whites.

Once again, there is little to distinguish the opinions on the right wing of the NP from those of the HNP:

We will never accept that whites and blacks can work together as equals. And under no circumstances will a white ever have to work under a black.

Just imagine what friction would arise if we allowed both races to work on the same job and the black turned out to be better than the white. In that case one would have to make him the foreman on the basis of his qualifications, and no white man would ever accept that.

An important variant of this verkrampte position seeks to defer to economic necessity by establishing parallel labour hierarchies for members of the different races:

Blacks and whites can only do the same work if they are in separate hierarchies, that is, if a firm has different divisions for the different races.

We would let a whole sector go black, like the building and construction industry, rather than have the races mixing too closely.

A centre group in the NP accepts blacks and whites working together on the same level:

Even if the whites don't like it, economic development forces us to let more and more blacks advance to higher positions. Whites will have to work more closely with blacks out of necessity. But they will never accept working under blacks.

One Cabinet Minister was even of this opinion:

To let whites work under blacks would cause a revolution.

One part of this centre group is quite aware of the inevitable:

We have always tried to protect the white worker. But we know that we can't do this for ever. We are trying to train and educate whites so well that possibly they will never find themselves in this situation.

A small group of verligte NP politicians think that they can make more exacting demands of their supporters:

People do anything for money. For a higher standard of living whites are quite prepared to accept some unpleasantness and also to work with blacks. It will even be possible to put blacks in charge of them.

A white won't like a non-white as his superior, but will accept him. A qualified black manager will be accepted, and by the Afrikaners more easily than by the English-speakers.

Almost 40 per cent of the NRP are quite clearly less open to change than the verligtes in the NP. Although they are in favour of abolishing legal job reservation, they rely on the efficacy of other mechanisms to maintain the whites' occupational privileges:

I believe that even without legal regulations the market will solve most problems.

Businessmen will make sure that only the people who have what it takes will get into managerial positions.

135

In the economy most whites will remain on top, like corks floating on water.

In short, NRP politicians are against legal discrimination but hope that white privileges 'established in the free market' will replace it.

PFP politicians also regard the question of blacks in charge as a 'sensitive' point, and one which will cause more problems in the lower than in the upper social strata. Even so, their position is unequivocal:

The abolition of job reservation is not enough, although it is a necessary first step. What must disappear is the whole industrial colour-bar which, quite apart from legal and administrative regulations, is sustained by trade-unions and also by businessmen.

The politicians of the white parties thus differ considerably on the question of job reservation and the labour hierarchy. Table 7.9 shows that the same applies to the question of *reducing or closing the wage-gap.*

Table 7.9

	NP	NRP	PFP
	%	%	%
No wage increases for blacks or only in step with inflation	19	—	—
Wage increases to improve the standard of living	39	—	—
The wage-gap should gradually be closed	42	61	13
The wage-gap should be closed as a matter of orgency	—	39	87

There are also big differences in the reasons given for the existence of the wage-gap (see Table 7.10).

Table 7.10

	NP	NRP	PFP
	%	%	%
Non-whites live more cheaply	19	—	—
Different levels of productivity	51		7
Over-supply of cheap labour	12	23	27
Political reasons	18	54	66

Once again, the attitude of the HNP leaders is clear and unambiguous:

Lower wages for blacks are fully justified. They have a lower productivity and must therefore also be paid less. Moreover, the blacks have far fewer expenses than the whites because their standard of living is far lower.

One-fifth of the NP politicians take the same view:

Blacks will not be paid the same wage as whites, whether they work on the same level or even a higher level. If there is to be wage equality then the non-whites' privileges such as housing assistance and cheaper transport must also be abolished. Although it is difficult to measure productivity, it has been generally established that the productivity of blacks is lower.

One Minister is of this opinion:

Most of our voters would support a gradual closing of the wage-gap, with the emphasis on 'gradual'. If we proceeded too quickly there would be a great deal of anger.

One of his Cabinet colleagues states:

The wage-gap has been reduced over the last ten years. We aim to reduce these differences by the economic advancement of the whole country and all its groups. We shall not broadcast it, but we are continuing to work in this direction.

In contrast to the NP politicians, those of the NRP are without exception in favour of closing the wage-gap. But a large majority of them also emphasize that it can only take place slowly:

In principle the wage-gap is a bad thing and we should therefore close it. But there are some factors to take into account. Our voters, for instance, have nothing against equal wages for the coloureds, provided that they pay the same taxes, rents, school fees, and medical rates. And they also demand that productivity be the same.

An NRP MP succinctly formulated the ambivalent attitude of the NRP:

Equal pay for equal work. That also disadvantages the non-whites, but by fair means.

Some of the PFP politicians draw a clear distinction between the wage-gap which is a consequence of political policy and the wage-gap resulting from the workings of the labour-market:

In considering the question of the wage-gap, one must distinguish between the unequal remuneration of members of different race groups holding down the same qualified positions on the one hand, and income differences between wage groups as a whole on the other. In the former instance, the wage-gap can be closed without great difficulty, and this will soon come about. The wage-gap in the latter instance is quite another matter. Firstly, there are the questions of productivity and differences in economic behaviour, particularly the disposition to save. Secondly, and this is the decisive point, this wage-gap is a gap between the payment of skilled and unskilled labour.

137

This kind of disparity exists in all economies. In Western industrial societies it has been reduced mainly because unskilled work has become unpopular in those societies. No-one wants to do it, and this has resulted in a general shortage of labour. So unskilled work is better paid; yet foreign workers still have to be used because the local workers refuse to take such jobs in spite of the higher rates. In most developing countries, however, the gap between skilled and unskilled rates has widened. People now earn a lot on the higher rungs of the social ladder, whereas at the bottom an immense supply of labour keeps wages down. South Africa is somewhere between these two stages. Unskilled labour is not scarce, so its pay remains low. It will only be possible to do something about this wage-gap when South African blacks are educated in far greater numbers. Hence, for both economic and political reasons, we advocate a comprehensive educational programme for blacks.

The left wing within the PFP stresses the political urgency of this problem:

Disparities in wealth must be reduced by radical means, and quickly. This will require various measures—in education, wage policy, and taxation; and if there is no other way, by nationalisation. Only when a reasonable degree of equality has been established between the groups in this country will friction decrease and peaceful co-existence become possible.

This group does not spare its own party from criticism:

The wage-gap is not only a consequence of government policy. The government must indeed be held responsible when black doctors do not receive the same salary as white doctors. But when a foreman on a mine receives ten or twenty times as much as the people who do the work, not only the government is to blame. It is curious, to put it mildly, that Harry Oppenheimer finances the PFP with money which he earns by means of black mine-workers.

In conclusion, we may summarize the potential for change in the field of economic relations as follows.

The politicians of the PFP are predominantly and consistently open to change. The majority of the NRP politicians are also in favour of dismantling at least the discriminatory legislation affecting the economic relations between the racial groups. So the parliamentary opposition raises no obstacle to peaceful change in this dimension.

The extra-parliamentary right-wing HNP does not merely want to maintain the status quo but advocates reverting to an even more discriminatory situation. As we have shown above, the HNP's electoral prospects are hopeless. However, within the governing party there is a broad body of verkrampte opinion which expresses sympathy for a position very similar to that of the HNP; whereas the group which

138

supports fundamental economic change comprises only one-fifth of all NP politicians.

The majority of NP politicians occupy a position in the centre, characterized by immobility on the one hand and a growing awareness of the need for economic and political change on the other. These politicians are prepared to accept pragmatic revisions in their political and economic outlook. Although they are not keen, they are not prepared—like the verkramptes—to allow considerations of 'principle' to obstruct any revisions deemed to be necessary. In other words, although they are not in favour of change, they don't oppose it when it appears opportune. These 'pragmatic revisionists' are less an active group than a 'critical mass' within the leadership of the governing party, swaying decisions in one instance or another in favour of intransigence or change.

Politicians on social relations between the race groups

The central issue in the field of social relations is 'petty apartheid'. This denotes all forms of racial segregation from services and amenities to the most private matters. There are far greater differences of opinion between the different political forces on this question than on the question of economic relations. At the same time, the degree of openness to change—even within each party grouping—is far more variable than in the field of economic relations.

The most openly verkrampte attitudes are expressed by leaders of the HNP:

Any departure from the tenets of strict apartheid is treason. If blacks are treated and accepted like whites this will gradually lead to revolution, and the whites will have to leave the country. In actual fact blacks are quite different from whites, and want to remain so. If one lets them be and does not draw them into white affairs they are quite happy. It is even a mistake to try and dress them in European clothes, or acquaint them with European culture. They are becoming more and more alienated, and this will eventually cause an explosion.

A large group within the NP adopts a stand on social relations between the races similar to that of the HNP. Whereas only one-fifth of NP politicians unequivocally support the status quo in the economic sphere, in this sphere almost one-half do:

I don't draw a distinction between grand and petty apartheid. Apartheid is and will continue to be the way of life in South Africa.

I am against social contacts, even in trivial matters. I don't want my daughter even to speak to male Bantu.

139

A Minister stated his views quite clearly:

I am afraid that what you call 'petty apartheid' will always exist in this country. We want neither social nor biological integration. And we don't want anything that could lead to them.

Many statements revealed fears of 'going soft':

Apartheid must be maintained in its entirety; it is the basis of our whole system. One must not concede them an inch, or offer them any prospects, otherwise we will become soft.

The verkrampte position is rationalized in various ways, e.g., the need to protect the lower white strata, or the bad experiences which other countries have apparently had with integration:

One must think above all of the man in the street. He would have to sit next to blacks in the bus, lie next to them at the swimming-pool, and so on, while the rich with their own cars and swimming-pools would be able to afford their own private apartheid.

The strict regulations help to prevent personal humiliation and suffering. Take the Immorality Act. What happened to German coloureds after 1945? Most of them ended up in orphanages. Equality does not necessarily reduce tension; whereas we want to avoid friction.

Over one-fifth of the NP politicians we interviewed—especially back-benchers—invoked crude justifications:

It is simply a fact that blacks are different, both in their nature—they smell different—and in their habits—they eat differently and live differently.

You can see the difference in civilisation. Blacks eat with their hands, leave everything lying around dirty, and relieve themselves openly in the streets.

Although we have already taken a lot of trouble to teach the blacks to be civilised, they will never reach our level of development.

The basic argument of the verkrampte position may be summarized as follows:

We want to retain our identity, and to achieve this we must be separate in every sphere.

A back-bencher was more straightforward:

The whites in this country want to stay white.

For this group, the opinions of blacks or of the rest of the world are no reason to change:

140

If the blacks don't like our attitude they can leave. They don't have to stay here.

We know that we are unpopular abroad. But we are not going to change our views because of outside criticism.

The group of intransigent NP politicians is matched by an equally strong group of pragmatists, who favour in varying degrees the lessening and gradual abolition of racial segregation in social relations. These politicians realize that in many aspects of daily life segregation is costly and cumbersome. Therefore they feel that

much of petty apartheid can be dispensed with.

This applies above all to apartheid regulations in the petty sense:

Residential areas, schools, and marriage are the essential issues. The rest are all practicalities.

The hard core of petty apartheid must stay, namely, the rejection of mixed marriages. This concerns the survival of the white group.

This group of NP politicians is thus, in principle, prepared to abolish racial segregation in lifts, parks, buses, theatres, museums, restaurants, and so on, albeit gradually and cautiously. There is considerable anxiety about unpleasant consequences:

The abolition of petty apartheid presents practical problems in the first instance. When lifts were de-segregated in Johannesburg, they were suddenly all full. Why? Previously most non-whites—messenger boys, delivery boys, and so on—had had to go up and down the stairs on foot. As a rule we used to have two lifts for whites, one for non-whites, and one for goods. If we had done the right thing, there would have been one for whites and five for non-whites. Now we suddenly realise that we have far too few services at our disposal. We are becoming aware of our mistakes. But what do you think it will be like when the buses are open to all? In future we must avoid friction at all costs. It could cause problems very quickly in a country like ours. If two whites fight one another, or two blacks, it is simply a fight. If a white and a black fight, it is a racial incident.

Hence gradual progress becomes a principle. A Minister defined it as follows:

There will be a lot of changes in the coming years. It is crucial that they take place very gradually. Our policy is change with a low profile. The more quietly something happens the easier it is to implement it, and the easier it is for us to go even further. The economic advancement of the non-whites will make most things much easier.

Turning now to the NRP politicians, we find that pragmatism and gradualism also characterize their attitudes to change in social relations between the racial groups. None of them accepts racial segregation as a principle, but many of their statements show that a de facto separation between the racial groups is regarded as preferable among the whites. Although the NRP accepts the need to dismantle the legal framework of apartheid, only a small minority show any haste in the matter.

It is obvious that for many supporters of the conservative opposition the NP policy is a not unwelcome alibi:

> *The years of indoctrination by the NP have had their effect. People are very afraid that the dam will burst once one starts to make concessions. We must take this into account, and proceed very carefully. There will be trouble where poorer whites come into contact with blacks.*

> *The habits of segregation must be broken slowly. In this respect, the basic consideration is that people of all colours can work together without difficulty, but they want to live apart and spend their leisure time separately.*

In actual fact, the majority of the NRP politicians do not really want to go much further than the pragmatists of the NP in dismantling segregation:

> *Many petty apartheid regulations are simply impractical and ludicrous. Segregation will certainly have to disappear in parks, in some cinemas, in exhibitions, etc. Where it will remain is in residential areas, beaches, swimming-pools, etc.*

The crux of the NRP policy is that decisions pertaining to social relations should be decentralized, rather than regulated across the whole country:

> *One should as far as possible allow the local authorities to decide in these matters.*

NRP politicians apparently do not expect the local authorities to be much concerned:

> *The segregation of residential areas could be abolished very soon. Why shouldn't a wealthy Indian doctor not buy a house in Bishopscourt?*

As in the area of economic relations, NRP politicians hope that 'the market' will solve the problems in this area:

> *The NP made a great mistake in legislating for petty apartheid. Previously, much the same was achieved by routine separation, far more reasonably.*

In the words of a leading MP:

> *The easiest way of abolishing petty apartheid is to replace racial segregation by social segregation.*

PFP politicians as a whole take a much clearer stand in favour of greater freedom in the sphere of social relations. They also see substantial problems in dismantling the existing barriers, and qualified or elaborated many of their statements. They also cannot conceal their anxiety that a blunt demand for changes in social relations would not be well received by their voters:

Many supporters of the opposition are opposed to discrimination in theory, but find it very difficult to stand by this in practice. They support the abolition of segregation on moral grounds, but are loath to face the consequences for themselves. Living as a white in South Africa is like belonging to a club. The facilities in the club are there, in the first place, for the members. This does not imply any hostility towards any outsiders. But to throw the club open to everyone would be unthinkable, to begin with.

A gradual opening of the 'white club' to others also finds some favour among a number of PFP politicians:

Everyone would like to see petty apartheid disappear, as long as he is not affected personally. But in concrete terms, there is a lot of resistance. We support the principle that segregation must be abolished. But in implementing this we must be very careful to prevent a backlash, which even the blacks are afraid of. It is important to note the differences between the reactions of the English and the Afrikaners. For the Afrikaners it is a question of principle. They need a doctrine, and so proceed logically according to how close the contacts are. As far as the English are concerned, this is immaterial. They are only interested in comfortable buses, clean toilets, and maintaining property values. If we can guarantee these they could not care less about segregation. So it must be dismantled piece by piece in close and constant consultation with the blacks.

Notwithstanding these 'gradualistic' considerations, most PFP politicians clearly accept as their goal complete freedom of social relations between the racial groups:

I regard the sphere of social relations as crucial. For it is here that, in the last instance, our credibility is at stake.

However, PFP politicians are divided on the question of how fast and how far to go. Some leading figures from the old Progressive Party are past masters in the art of terminological interpretation:

Petty apartheid must disappear. This includes separate parks and counters, cinemas, entertainment, entrances, etc. On the other hand, schools, residential areas, and political power are aspects of grand apartheid. The 'Progs' are against petty apartheid, but most do not support integrated schools; this would be the borderline. Admittedly, the question of residential areas is undefined in our policy. Decisions

143

in this regard would be left to the relevant authorities at the local level.

Others express themselves without such semantic contortions:

The residential suburbs will remain a sensitive issue. We will have to reckon with an outcry at any attempt to de-segregate them.

Economic considerations also play a role:

Our supporters would hardly accept integrated residential areas—less for racial than for economic reasons. As in the USA, the kind of neighbourhood would probably affect property prices in South Africa.

Allowing a choice between separated and integrated residential areas is recommended as a way out of this dilemma:

There is no point in forcing social integration upon our society. So what we should do is plan all new property developments as mixed residential areas.

Finally, one-quarter of the PFP politicians we interviewed rejected this sort of compromise and gradualism as half-hearted and problematical:

Petty apartheid must be completely abandoned, including the separation of residential areas. The only solution is the complete abolition of discrimination.

Thus, the potential for change among South African politicians is far less in respect of social relations between the racial groups than of economic relations between them. One-quarter of the politicians in the liberal opposition party are in favour of radical change, whereas more than half of them, although supporting rapid change, want it to be implemented step by step. Among the conservative opposition a majority are in favour of abolishing the legal restrictions, but there is obviously a strong group which hopes that social mechanisms will replace administrative segregation in various respects. Even so, the opposition parties in general are in favour of abolishing enforced segregation.

Within the governing party, no group is committed to fundamental change. NP politicians can be divided into two roughly equal groups in respect of their attitudes to social relations. On the one hand, there is a group which—like the HNP—supports the status quo without reservation; it consists largely, but by no means exclusively, of back-benchers. On the other hand, there is a group which is prepared to accept a partial and pragmatic dismantling of petty apartheid in the narrow sense of the term. Once again, as in the case of economic relations, it would seem that the pragmatic wing of the NP is the crucial political power group. Emotionally, the politicians within this group also incline towards the status quo in respect of social relations. However, judging by their

144

comments, considerations of 'principle' will not prevent them from accepting substantial changes in the status quo in the interests of practical requirements. They are not active agents for change, but under certain circumstances they could be mobilized towards it.

Politicians on the political relations between the racial groups

Although the three major 'blueprints' for a future political dispensation in South Africa each draw their main support from one of the political parties in parliament, these conceptions are not only interpreted differently within the three parties, but also transcend party boundaries. Above all, a state based on group co-existence and one or other federal solution is an idea that attracts the attention of politicians in all three political formations.

In these respects the HNP plays the role of an outsider:

> *We are opposed to all the political conceptions current in South Africa: separate development, federation, and of course integration. The non-whites should not be given any power or sovereignty at all.*

> *Vorster has no right to give away white land. South Africa belongs to the whites; they were the first ones here. The homelands for blacks are those which the English created: Lesotho, Botswana, and Swaziland. If they don't want to live under white rule they should go there.*

While, as we have seen, some of the NP politicians shared the HNP's views on economic and social relations, none of them took this stand. The vast majority of the NP leadership supports the official bantustan policy, that the so-called homelands should be granted independence within the boundaries laid down in 1936. Four-fifths of the NP politicians we interviewed want to see this goal realized, but are not prepared to go beyond it:

> *More than half of the best agricultural land in South Africa already belongs to bantustans. We'll gladly give them half the Karoo, but no more fertile land. That would be too risky. Agricultural production in Southern African would then fall.*

> *Israel has less land than the Transkei and much less fertile land, and it gets along quite well on that.*

> *We will not give up the cities or the industrial areas under any circumstances. It will never go that far.*

> *Germany doesn't give any land to Holland, simply because more people live there.*

On the other hand, one-fifth of the NP politicians interviewed were prepared to extend the present bantustan policy if this would ensure the success of the idea of territorial separate development:

145

Our sovereignty comes first. So we would rather pay more and give away more land than accept any restrictions on our self-determination.

We shall have to give up more land than was decided in 1936. Although it cannot yet be said aloud, the Land Act of 1936 cannot be the end of the story.

Further sacrifices of land are necessary and also possible. We need a fair and just solution.

It is basically quite clear that one must not create any enclaves. That always causes trouble. Port St. Johns can remain white as little as Simonstown could remain British. We shall have to be more consistent in the future.

There is no alternative to the policy of separate development. If it fails we lose everything. So we shall have to be very bold in dividing the country. We are prepared to cede half of South Africa rather than give up our political principles.

The four-fifths of NP politicians who support the bantustan policy in its present form also regard the 'problem' of the urban blacks as solved for the most part within the framework of this policy. The blacks should become citizens of the homelands, and thus foreign workers in the Republic. Over 50 per cent of the NP politicians are prepared to accept them purely as migrant workers, without any political rights at all. A further one-third would even like to remove them from 'white' South Africa, fully in accordance with the HNP's view:

The urban Bantu must be sent home as quickly as possible.

A little under one-fifth of the NP politicians are prepared to grant the urban blacks certain improvements in their situation, such as better infrastructural development in the black residential areas or the right to own property. And only a few isolated individuals are in favour of granting the urban blacks the right to establish their own political organizations. In short, the overwhelming majority of the NP politicians support the official stand, that the 'problem' of the urban blacks will be solved by the independence of the bantustans.

In 1974 the so-called 'coloured problem' was still regarded as the 'unsolved problem' of the policy of self-development. Even Ministers made the admission:

What will happen with the coloureds? In all honesty, we don't have the answer.

The next generation will have to solve the coloured question.

The HNP takes a clear stand:

146

The coloureds are the only group which warrant a homeland solution in present-day South Africa.

Sixteen per cent of the NP politicians we interviewed shared this feeling:

The secret wish of all South Africans is that the coloureds should finally have their own homeland.

At some stage or other they are going to have to be given the Cape.

A broad majority within the party do not want a homeland for the coloureds, but also reject integrating them with the whites. Some of the NP politicians base this rejection on the 'otherness' of the coloureds:

Compared to us they are too different, too under-developed, too addicted to alcohol.

Of course they are a problem. It is true that they don't have their own language and religion. But it is true above all that until now they have not wanted a separate identity. They want to be white. I'm sorry; we can give them money and buildings and institutions, but not an identity.

To be frank, there is no real difference between Bantu and coloureds. I don't believe in the often-quoted biological and cultural relationship to the Afrikaner. If we are not consistent in our policy towards the coloureds, no-one will take us seriously.

The majority of the NP politicians who are undecided on this question reject integration for directly political reasons:

Their numbers are now growing at a frightening rate. So one cannot afford to integrate them politically.

If they were given the vote they would be decisive in thirty per cent of the constituencies. This would be political lunacy; for previous experience has shown that the coloureds vote for the UP. They would naturally also vote for the opposition today.

In short, in the eyes of the majority of NP politicians the greatest defect of the coloureds is that they do not vote for the NP.

But there are also many NP politicians who are deeply concerned and unhappy about the issue:

The question of the coloureds is the weakest point in the theory of separate development. There are practical reasons: if there were a homeland for them, it would have to include Cape Town, Paarl, and Stellenbosch, and who wants that? It is also the weakest point because, culturally, they are part of us. Think of opera and ballet, music and poetry. A community of two million people, which is growing faster than any other section of humanity, which for the most part speaks Afrikaans and belongs to the Reformed Churches, could

147

be a valuable ally of the whites. Their culture is Western and they feel that they are a part of us. We must find an appropriate solution to this issue.

Finally, there is a minority that takes an unequivocal stand:

In the last instance, the coloured question must be solved by some or other form of integration. No other solution is realistic.

In general, then, the majority of NP politicians support the government's bantustan policy without modification. One-fifth of the politicians interviewed are prepared to go beyond this policy. They favour a partition which accords better with the demographic strength and the economic needs of the blacks. Concerning the questions of the urban blacks and the coloureds, the group of NP politicians reasonably open to change is a few per cent smaller.

The overwhelming majority of NP politicians only think in terms of the bantustan policy or a more extended partition. They reject any other political solutions, whether a federal arrangement or a multiracial, unitary, and integrated state:

A federal solution would mean that a single central body would exercise power, i.e., in effect government by the black majority. That is no solution at all.

A majority government would mean the end of the white man's self-determination. Developments throughout Africa have shown that the best we can hope for under black majority rule is an enlightened dictatorship. At present we have racial domination; we would simply have a different race in power. Clear separation is preferable.

We will never share political power over ourselves.

By contrast, the opposition takes the view that the policy of the government and the governing party is totally unrealistic:

The bantustan policy can never solve South Africa's problems, especially in view of demographic developments. One can manipulate the figures as one likes: there can never be a white majority, and arithmetic won't help.

The old UP, now the NRP, came to this conclusion:

The only way out is a policy which does not count heads. There will be possibilities for bargaining if we move towards a federal state.

However, the conservative opposition party only wants to follow this path with extreme caution:

Our version of federation is a pragmatic blend of territorial and communal federation: territorial representation for the homelands

148

and urban black areas, and representation for the coloureds and Indians as communities. The goal is that all groups participate in the central legislature. During the period of transition, the final say will remain where it is now—in the white parliament. This may be a brake, but it can also be an accelerator. The transition must take place step by step, and peacefully.

It is felt that the realization of a federation will be and should be a very lengthy process. One of the leading representatives of the NRP thinks it will take decades to achieve a federal state with a genuine and equal sharing of power.

An NRP MP emphasizes that the policy is politically advantageous precisely because of the long period of time involved in arriving at a federal state:

We can simply reassure our voters that absolutely nothing will change in the foreseeable future.

These statements reveal that for a substantial proportion of the NRP a federal state is little more than a new name for the status quo.

The NRP thus offers no real political alternative to the policy of the NP. A genuine alternative has to be sought in the PFP. In contrast to the prevalent view in the NP, PFP politicians believe that a democratic state is possible within a multiracial South Africa; or they at least hope it is possible:

We must, together with the blacks, try to create a liberal political system as quickly as possible. There are three factors in favour of the possible success of such an attempt: firstly, South African blacks are much more strongly modernized than any other African people; secondly, they have a very moderate, reasonable, and judicious political leadership; and thirdly, South Africa is an industrialized country.

Within the PFP there are considerable differences of opinion on just how a liberal political system is to be set up. The official party policy at the time of the survey was very complex, including elements of both a unitary and a federal state as well as the idea of a qualified franchise. Although all PFP politicians support the policy in principle, they almost always express reservations. Some ensure to emphasize the gradualism of a qualified franchise; others—mainly supporters of the old Liberal Party—would prefer a multiracial unitary state with equal voting rights for all; and finally there is also a strong federal and/or consociational tendency within the PFP.

Representatives of the first approach take this view:

The consequences of a universal franchise would be the same as in the rest of Africa. The underlying idea of the qualified franchise is

149

Rhodes' formula of 'equal rights for all civilized men'. A civilized man was defined for practical purposes as one who could read and write and who earned his living in a monetary economic system, in other words, someone who was no longer 'tribal'. One can grant that South Africa's blacks are more advanced than others on the continent—a longer period of contact with Europeans, more organisation and industrialization. But is that enough reason to settle on 'one man, one vote'? For my part, I would rather place my fate in the hands of educated people.

Other PFP politicians think the formula of the qualified franchise creates problems:

This formula is almost impossible to put into practice. The NP has popularised the idea of a universal franchise, even though the parliaments concerned have only limited powers. It will be well-nigh impossible to deprive anyone of the vote once he has been granted it.

The third approach supports the inclusion of federal elements in the political structure:

I now favour a federation. Any other solution will mean violence.

There are two things which are important: effective political participation for the non-whites, and a guarantee of rights of the white minority. There would be no sense in replacing white domination by black domination. Therefore, all in all the idea of a federal state seems to me to be along the right lines. But it can only be created in consultation with all other groups.

However, the differing approaches within the PFP are not obviously contradictory. PFP politicians are generally agreed that it is more important to initiate political change as such—only then would detailed policies come into their own:

The question of a definitive political formula is less pressing at present than the task of bringing the different groups closer together.

I personally am prepared to support all attempts at liberalization, irrespective of the formula or the precise direction.

The PFP is quite aware that in the future whites will not be able to draw up political blueprints on their own:

The most pressing problem is the creation of structures which allow for effective negotiation between the different groups. The details of the political programme for the future, in other words, the form of the 'new deal', can only be worked out in agreement with black leaders.

A more contentious problem among PFP politicians is the importance of the future economic dispensation, whatever the nature of the political solution. The majority accept, either consciously or without reflection, the model of a free enterprise system. However, there are also some politicians who would be classed as moderate social democrats or left-wing liberals in a European context:

Economic redistribution is as important for a future South Africa as the redistribution of power.

The variety of opinions among the PFP politicians illustrates the peculiar dilemma of this party. Whereas the NP accepts the status quo of the bantustan policy and the NRP aims to make this status quo more acceptable, the PFP seriously aspires to peaceful political change. Within the party at least two of the possible goals of such change have been thought through to their logical conclusion: the federal democratic state and the unitary democratic state. The discussion on the possible socio-political forms which such solutions might take has at least started. In terms of peaceful change, the PFP is a force to be reckoned with. This party wants peaceful change in a liberal direction. But it does not have the means to implement such change; it can only try to persuade the government to adopt its policies.

It is doubtful whether the NRP has the potential to promote political change, but on the other hand it presents no serious obstacle to change. Taken as a whole, the question of initiating peaceful change is subject to developments within the governing party. It has distanced itself from the 'arch-conservative' position of the HNP more clearly in the political sphere than in the economic and social spheres. But the great majority within this party cling to a policy which can in no way satisfy the goals conceived for peaceful change. On the other hand, almost one-fifth of the NP politicians interviewed adopted positions which differ from the official policy and which at least point towards peaceful change. Consequently, special attention will have to be paid to these politicians' prospects for having their views accepted within the NP.

3. *Political opinion-makers and peaceful change*

In most parliamentary systems, leading academics, churchmen, and people in the media do exercise some influence upon the formation of political opinions. However, it would be wrong to include members of these groups in the political leadership as such. Accordingly, the sample for the present study included only those academics, churchmen, journalists, etc. who are generally thought to exercise influence within their respective political groupings, in other words, those who may be accepted as political opinion-makers.

These shapers of opinion occupy an unusually important position within the various political leadership groups in South Africa, both in the

151

governing party as well as in the parties of the opposition.

As discussed above, there is a considerable internal exchange between the different segments of the political leadership within NP Afrikanerdom. Professors become editors-in-chief of party newspapers, clergymen become Members of Parliament and Ministers, publishers become party leaders. Eminent political personalities who are not bound by Cabinet or caucus discipline fulfil a special function in the development of political thought within the framework of the NP. They take the lead in debates within the party, are the spokesmen on various tendencies, and try to point out the direction which the party and the government should take. So their opinions are not always representative of the actual disposition of power within the political institutions. But such opinions are often indicative of future developments within these institutions. Occasionally the statements made by these opinion-makers may be denied by the government and the party; but as a rule, they express in public what the politicians discuss behind closed doors. They frequently play a decisive role in shaping new political developments. Besides their function as precursors, these opinion-makers fulfil another significant role: they are responsible for the political and ideological interpretation of decisions taken by the NP. Their task ranges from interpretation of the Bible to interpretation of the party programme; hence, the opinion-makers of the NP may be regarded as the 'high-priests' of apartheid policy in its 'late scholastic stage':

> *The crux of the problem is this: whereas one man may change his opinion, the party can hardly do so. The NP may not admit to mistakes. Thus, we have to engage in intellectual acrobatics to prove that any meaningful changes within the policy do not actually run counter to the Grand Principle.*

As will be shown below, the 'scholastics' of the NP do not confine their activities to apologetic interpretations of the actual policy; they have rather become the spokesmen of what is at least a partial political reformation.

The opinion-makers within the opposition fulfil a different function. These academics, churchmen, and journalists do not regard the formulation and interpretation of the political tenets of one or other party as their responsibility: they instead form a kind of 'extra-parliamentary opposition'. This is especially true of the opinion-makers in the churches and the press. The English-speaking churches in South Africa are the most important social institutions still bridging the racial barriers. Their representatives, more than any other white leaders, are in constant contact with the black population, and in recent years they have increasingly taken the stand on social and political questions that their religious convictions have demanded. The English-language newspapers are not tied to specific parties, but by and large express independent opinions and are far more consistent in their support of liberal political positions than the opposition parties. Thus, they too are a strong and independent force in the formation of public opinion.

In the following brief analysis of the opinions of the opinion-makers in both political camps on the question of political change, we do not attempt to discuss the whole range of different opinions, but rather concentrate on those points where the opinion-makers clearly differ from the politicians.

As far as the government camp is concerned, the opinion-makers are clearly more verlig than the full-time politicians on all important issues.

Table 7.11

Potential for change in the NP		Politicians	Church leaders	Media figures	Academics
		%	%	%	%
intransigent	1	29	29	9	23
	2	62	14	27	12
	3	9	57	64	65
open to change	4	—	—	—	—

Those relatively open to change are a majority in each of the three subgroups of opinion-makers, whereas among the politicians they form only a small minority. Among churchmen and academics one-quarter are clearly opposed to change, and among the journalists only one-tenth. These differences are manifested on all questions of peaceful change.

Only 12 per cent of the politicians as against 44 per cent of the opinion-makers are in favour of abolishing job reservation. And one-third of the former as against only 11 per cent of the latter are in favour of retaining job reservation.

Almost half of the opinion-makers think that blacks should be able to be put in charge of whites, but only 10 per cent of the NP politicians share this view. Sixty-one per cent of the opinion-makers think it necessary slowly to close the wage-gap between black and white, by contrast with 42 per cent of the politicians. And 17 per cent of the NP opinion-makers were in favour of closing the wage-gap quickly, whereas no NP politicians were.

The following statement is typical of the opinions on the verligte wing on the question of change in economic relations:

Job reservation is little more than a ridiculous verbal exercise. Enormous economic redistribution is necessary for stable political development. Income-tax must be more progressive, firms should recognize the black trade-unions as negotiating partners so that their

153

legitimate demands can be dealt with on a sensible basis, and then we need a sort of Marshall Plan for the black areas in South Africa.

NP opinion-makers are similarly verlig in respect of social relations. Twenty-five per cent of the Nationalist opinion-makers as against 2 per cent of the politicians are in favour of immediately dismantling petty apartheid measures in the narrow sense. Fourteen per cent are also in favour of providing a choice between segregated and integrated residential areas, and 6 per cent would like to see all residential segregation abolished:

As a Christian and a Nationalist Afrikaner, I totally reject petty apartheid. These regulations only serve to make blacks bitter and unhappy, and finally to make them our enemies. There can be no justification for this.

Several leading theologians, journalists, and academics in the NP do not regard interracial marriage as taboo:

All petty apartheid regulations must disappear, including the prohibition of interracial marriages. Our verkramptes still talk a lot about the need for protecting black and coloured girls from prostitution. But we don't need the Immorality Act for that; a law prohibiting prostitution would have the same effect.

As regards political change, all opinion-makers within the NP support the policy of separate development. They share the opinion of the majority of the politicians that there would be no hope for democracy in an undivided South Africa:

There is little reason to assume that the blacks will obey the rules in a liberal parliamentary democracy. Black Africa is dominated by one-party states. That is why we believe in separate development.

But whereas 81 per cent of the NP politicians want to implement the policy in terms of the areas laid down in 1936, only one-third of the opinion-makers are in favour of abiding by this territorial arrangement. A clear majority (61 per cent) regard the Land Act of 1936 as utterly inadequate for a genuine policy of partition:

The bantustans should be consolidated on generous terms and given independence as quickly as possible. Some form of umbrella body could be formed on the basis of financial redistribution among these independent states. Consolidation, independence, and redistribution must be negotiated.

If the idea of separate development is to be successfully implemented the blacks must be offered at least half of the Republic of South Africa. There must be an equitable division of both the agricultural and the mineral wealth of the country.

154

The views of NP opinion-makers also differ with respect to the future position of the coloureds and the urban blacks. Only 14 per cent of the politicians, as against 61 per cent of the churchmen, journalists, and academics, want integration with the coloureds:

The coloureds should be recognised as members of our nation. However, this cannot be done on the basis of Westminster democracy. Under no circumstances must the situation arise in which the coloureds hold the balance between the English speakers and the Afrikaners.

The integration of the coloureds is the only possible solution. The politicans know this; but they refuse to admit it, and try to get out of it by making small concessions.

With respect to the urban blacks only little less than one-third of the opinion-makers think they should be 'sent back' or treated purely as migrant workers, as opposed to 81 per cent of the politicians. One-third of the opinion-makers as opposed to 16 per cent of the politicans would accord them at least the same rights as are enjoyed by foreign workers in European countries:

The blacks in the rest of the white Republic must become foreigners. As such they should have all rights except the right to vote, including the right to own land—perhaps with a few restrictions such as practised in Switzerland.

And the largest group (36 per cent) of the NP opinion-makers favour the remaining option, the formation of separate political bodies for the urban blacks, which would then be incorporated—the details are still rather vague—into the political institutions of 'white' South Africa:

We have lost 25 years by trying, in vain, to solve the race-group problem with the homeland policy. Even if the policy were implemented in its totality there would still be millions of blacks in the white areas. We will have to find a political dispensation in which the urban blacks will share power.

To my mind the only possible political solution is the independence of consolidated bantustans and the political integration of the coloureds, Indians, and urban blacks.

The leading academics, churchmen, and media people within the NP thus firmly support the idea of 'separate development'. At the same time, the majority do not think it can be realized in terms of the present official government policy. Their opinions incline to a far more radical division of the country, in which the black population would be granted a greater share of the land and the mineral wealth. A majority of the NP opinion-makers are in favour of integrating the coloureds. Also in contrast to official government policy, a majority are in favour of

155

considerably improving the position of the urban blacks and granting them more rights; and they are at least entertaining the thought of integrating them 'in some way or other'. Thus, as a whole, the opinion-makers within the NP are far more open to change than the politicians. The important point in this connection is that within the NP leadership of South Africa there is a dynamic group, a majority of whom are in favour of at least partial changes. They stand in contrast to the group of relatively verligte politicians, whom circumstances have brought to accept peaceful change rather against their will. The verligte opinion-makers rather adopt a more positive approach to change, seeing it as a challenge as well as a possibility. So their influence upon the governing party as a whole must be seen as a decisive factor promoting openness to change within it.

The position of the opinion-makers within the opposition can be presented very briefly; for their views hardly differ from those of the opposition politicians who are open to change. The only difference is one of how fast to move.

Without exception the opposition opinion-makers are in favour of immediately abolishing job reservation. Four-fifths of them think a rapid closing of the wage-gap between black and white is necessary—as do the PFP politicians. They are also in favour of rapid and radical change in the sphere of social relations. Whereas even among the PFP politicians only one-quarter are in favour of an immediate and total abolition of petty apartheid, this is the view of over three-quarters of the opposition opinion-makers:

> *The whole of petty apartheid could be abolished between one day and the next. The politicians' fears that the voters would not allow this are excessive; the voters are not nearly as conservative as the politicians think.*

All the opinion-makers in the opposition are in favour of a complete integration of the coloureds, and two-thirds of them are for the integration of the urban blacks as well. On this point as well they are considerably more open to peaceful change than the PFP politicians.

The majority of the opinion-makers in the opposition would support an integrated multiracial unitary state or a federal state. They go much further than the politicians in accepting universal franchise: 45 per cent are in favour of 'one man one vote', in contrast to 13 per cent of the PFP politicians. Furthermore, one-quarter think that an active policy of economic redistribution is necessary.

Thirty-nine per cent of the group are opposed to the idea of a federal state. The majority would accept a federation more out of realism than conviction:

> *I have abandoned the idea of a unitary state because I am now con-*

vinced that it would only be achieved in South Africa by a revolution, sustained by a one-man or one-party dictatorship. I am convinced that the Westminster model cannot function in fragmented societies. I thus think that in our situation we have to look for other forms of liberal democracy. I believe in a common society, but within a federal rather than a unitary framework.

To summarize: the opinion-makers in the opposition form the group within the overall white South African leadership which is most unequivocally open to peaceful change.

In both the government and the opposition camps the politically influential academics, churchmen, and figures in the media are more open to change than the politicians. However, the opinion-makers on both sides doubt whether the politicians will move quickly enough in accepting their views on the required changes.

Many of them are anxious about the consequences of maintaining the status quo for too long:

Most whites in this country are afraid. So am I. I am afraid because there are many people here who are prepared to resort to revolutionary means; and they are prepared to do so because they have been excluded from participating in the exercise of power. We must try to reduce this revolutionary potential. The best guarantee against the revolution in this country is a large black middle class. What these people want above all is education and progress for their children. That is the social equivalent of the vote.

A leading NP journalist goes even further:

I fear that we are heading for a war. We don't have the friendship of the blacks, and the coloureds have been pushed aside and are starting to hit back. And our politicians are not prepared to integrate them.

Both sides expect the impetus towards peaceful change to come from outside. A leading opposition opinion-maker stated:

South Africa will react to pressure. If the politicians and the voters had their way, they would simply go on as they have until now.

4. *The economic élite and peaceful change*

One does not have to be a political economist to realize that in modern industrial societies economics and politics are closely linked by innumerable formal and informal contacts. It follows that the businessmen and economists, as well as leading office-bearers in labour and employer organizations, also exert considerable influence on decision-making and the formation of political opinion in South Africa.

Of course, South Africa is in a special situation compared to other

157

industrial states. Although the South African economy is essentially capitalist, the principles of free enterprise come into conflict in many ways with both the postulates and the realities of the policy of separate development. The roots of this conflict, between the desire to allow the free play of market forces and the apparently inevitable socio-political practice of state intervention, lie in the struggle for power between the two white ethnic groups, Afrikaners and people of the British descent. The economic solidarity of the Afrikaners plays an important part in this struggle. They were successful not only in organizing white labour under their aegis, but also in laying the foundation during the first half of this century for 'the volk's own industrial sector'. Even so, the continuing dominance of English-speaking South Africans in major industries is, as it were, a Trojan horse in the Afrikaner laager:

> *Equality between the ethnic groups will only be achieved when the Afrikaners draw level with the English speakers. For money is power. It was this insight which stimulated the economic activity of the Afrikaners in the twenties and thirties. Although we have had political power since 1948, the goal of the Afrikaners is still far from attained. We still don't have economic power.*

However, the Afrikaners' attempt to beat 'British imperialism' at its own game by building up their own industrial empire has produced an unintended result. The more the Afrikaners 'undermined' the English-dominated economic apparatus and expanded their own corporations, the more Afrikaner businessmen felt themselves bound by the laws of the free enterprise economy and ran into conflict with the goals of their own ethnic group:

> *It is impossible to beat English imperialism and preserve apartheid at the same time. Every time Afrikaners gain ground on the English in the political and economic spheres, contradictions in the apartheid programme automatically become apparent.*

For one businessman close to the HNP, the economic development of recent years amounts to a betrayal of the interests of the Afrikaner people:

> *The verligte Afrikaner is highly profit-oriented. His outlook is very dangerous to the Afrikaner community and the state. Following the ways of big business and the English will probably lead to the downfall of apartheid. More and more Afrikaners are being swallowed by Anglo American, that English-dominated economic monster which is interested only in profit and not in our country.*

This statement elicits angry denials from the people involved. But there can be no doubt that Afrikaner businessmen are indeed urging that the rigid structures of apartheid be adapted to 'economic necessities':

158

Note that it is precisely the Afrikaners in the economic field who are becoming more and more critical, despite their fundamental loyalty to the government, and who have realized the urgent need for change.

As we shall see below, when one compares the differences in attitude between the leaders of the two language groups, they are smallest among the economic élite: 'Money speaks its own language'.

Obviously businessmen have a common interest, based on the criterion of profitability, in changing the existing legislation. Two-thirds are in favour of the immediate abolition of job reservation:

In the business world job reservation is basically a nuisance. It involves separation on the basis on racial criteria, not rational economic criteria. In terms of economic criteria productive blacks should be given precedence over unproductive whites.

A further 25 per cent of primarily pro-government Afrikaners do not want to see the legislation changed, but are in favour of disregarding it in practice. The only voices strongly opposed to the abolition of job reservation come from the exclusively white trade-unions:

If we abolish job reservation, white trades will be swamped by the other races. Blacks will readily accept lower wages and force us out of the trades.

It is obvious that businessmen are not opposed to this readiness on the part of the non-whites, or at least to a functioning free labour market. But it is almost impossible to shake the politically guaranteed position of power of the exclusively white trade-unions. According to a leading Afrikaner manager:

Job reservation does not take economic rationality and productivity into account. In the gold mines, with their ratio of whites to blacks of 1:10, you can find a white foreman relaxing on a bed during the day while the blacks do the work. No one can do anything about it because the white mine-workers' unions are too strong.

By and large, both Afrikaans and English-speaking businessmen express support for giving blacks the chance to rise whenever they show the ability. Three-quarters of the respondents thought there would be little problem in blacks working next to whites on an equal footing. But there is a great deal of scepticism about blacks being put in charge of whites. Only about one-quarter of pro-government businessmen and one-half of businessmen who support the opposition think this is possible. But their doubt is due less to ideological and political reasons than their belief that for the foreseeable future few blacks would be in a position to exercise executive functions in responsible economic positions:

159

There are enormous differences between the races. Blacks don't have the same degree of economic understanding as whites and so are unable, for example, to distinguish between cause and effect. Therefore they are clearly less successful than whites in the technical and economic occupations. As a rule blacks are good speakers, but not thoughtful managers with a talent for organisation. For these reasons the management in our economy will remain European for quite some time.

On the question of closing the wage-gap the opinions of businessmen are naturally much more detailed than those of other leadership groups. In their perspective the wage-gap is primarily a problem of costing. The most important criterion for determining a worker's wage—be he black or white—is his productivity:

Economic and wage policy should be based not on race but on performance. Whites are by and large better trained and educated than blacks and therefore receive higher wages. But there is one critical area. The intelligent blacks work far better than many of our lower-class whites and therefore should also be better paid. But if we do that we run into trouble with the trade-unions.

In general, hardly any of the businessmen think that the wage-gap will be closed soon. Another argument is often raised in addition to the question of productivity:

How can one pay higher wages when profit-levels are generally low? Economic laws have to be obeyed. Naturally, unskilled labour is the first to go.

This statement clearly illustrates just how strongly the openness to change in the business world is governed by economic self-interest. Job reservation causes an artificial scarcity in urgently needed labour and hence excessively high wage costs. There is a surplus of black labour; businessmen can produce far more profitably if they take advantage of this surplus to pay exploitative wages:

White businessmen practise a deliberate policy of low wages and exploitation. Frame [a businessman in Natal] does basically the same thing when he recruits his labour from the Transkei rather than on the local market. He attracts the Xhosas with promises of high wages, but which are still lower than the 'minimum existence level' for blacks in Durban.

It is thus not surprising that white businessmen respond very coolly to the idea of negotiating with black trade-unions as equals.

Almost three-quarters of respondents were satisfied with the regulations made under the existing labour laws. They think that the

160

liaison- or works-committees which operate at the level of individual firms are satisfactory mechanisms of communication and conflict regulation between employers and employees. Besides the economic reasons, political reasons are also given:

> *Black trade-unions could become a serious political danger in our country. They could only function responsibly with a fairly educated membership. The works-committees which we have at present are quite adequate and function perfectly. I must add that in our firm we have spies among the workers who immediately report any dissatisfaction and warn us in advance of any planned collective action. In this way we are able to handle all difficulties before they surface and avoid serious confrontation between the employees and ourselves.*

A progressive trade-unionist formulated the opposite argument:

> *In principle we have nothing against works-committees. But the system has not worked so far; for black employees have not been accepted as equal negotiating partners. Above all, there have not been any proper negotiations of wages. In terms of the Industrial Conciliation Act wage agreements can only be worked out between the government or the employers and the registered trade-unions, in which blacks are not represented. Negotiations in the works-committees thus only deal with the general atmosphere in the firm, the canteen food, and better toilets, and nothing else.*

Notwithstanding the general satisfaction with the regulations made under the existing labour legislation approximately one-third of the businessmen, primarily critics of the government, do not exclude the possibility that blacks will receive full trade-union representation in the future. But then the trade-unions should not be exclusively black but, as far as possible, mixed:

> *In the long run one will not be able to prevent trade-union representation for blacks. But if possible it should occur within the framework of multiracial trade-unions. Otherwise we shall lapse into the old pattern of black-white conflict.*

When the attitude of businessmen towards change in the sphere of social relations between black and white is analysed, it becomes apparent that party-political and ethnic group considerations predominate. Businessmen who support the opposition are evidently more open to change than their pro-government colleagues. Thus, half the latter regard so-called petty apartheid as discriminatory and would like to see it gradually abolished. But only 36 per cent would favour its immediate abolition in theatres, public transport, and restaurants.

By contrast, businessmen who support the opposition go considerably further. About half of them demand that the petty apartheid regulations

161

be dismantled immediately, while a further third—as against 5 per cent among government supporters—would be prepared to open white residential areas to non-whites. More or less implicit in these considerations is 'money-apartheid', i.e., separation by class rather than race:

> The whole petty apartheid edifice is quite unnecessary. Promoting capitalism will ensure that segregation occurs naturally.

Businessmen's attitudes to petty apartheid are also strongly influenced by economic factors:

> I regard petty apartheid as a luxury which we cannot afford. Separate facilities for the different racial groups at railway-stations, in post-offices, in public transport, etc., obviously cost a lot of money. One can hardly over-estimate the negative effect on the productivity of our economy which arises from segregation at work and from the long journeys required by segregated residential areas.

Although the business community may strongly criticize the government's openness to change in the economic sphere, it finds little fault with the official homelands policy. The opposition's proposals for a multiracial unitary state or a federation enjoy limited support, even among businessmen critical of the government. A unitary state on the basis of 'one man one vote' is almost unanimously rejected, while the concept of power-sharing on a federal basis is approved by about one-third of the government critics. Besides separate development the only proposal which enjoys a relatively high degree of support is a qualified franchise. Implicit in this is the vision of a capitalist society in which racial segregation would be abolished and a stable black middle-class created:

> Our principal concern should be to create a black middle-class. It would divide the excessively powerful Bantu bloc and help differentiate the social structure.

All pro-government businessmen, together with one-third of those critical of the government, are in favour of the principle of separate development. The arguments they use to support this view are, once again, largely economic: that investments in the homelands are profitable, that the homelands are economically viable, and that Southern Africa needs political stability if the economy is to flourish.

It partly follows from this economic approach that only a small majority favour the homeland policy in its present form, based upon the Land Act of 1936:

> Although the economic development of the homelands will be very slow, it is possible in principle. But the territorial boundaries will have to be adjusted if the policy of separate development is to be realized.

But consolidation of the homelands would not be enough on its own; new industrial centres would have to be created in the homelands, if only to take account of the need to decentralize South Africa's economic potential. But there is little chance of so fundamental a change from the present form of economic development occurring via the Homeland Development Corporation:

Political policy is over-emphasized and economic sense neglected. This is typical of the Afrikaners. Verwoerd was an anthropologist and a psychologist, not an economist. He thought that the Bantu would be able to develop by themselves. Consequently, no white capital was allowed in the homelands. But this is nonsense if development is to take place within the foreseeable future.

This view is sceptical, but ultimately still optimistic. It may be contrasted with the view of the minority who oppose the government's policy:

Grand apartheid is too costly and therefore cannot be realized. To achieve economic take-off or even partial economic independence requires mineral resources, an infrastructure, and a certain level of education among the local population. None of these exists in the homelands, nor can increased investment simply take their place. To my mind the homeland policy is a fantastic waste of money.

A pro-government Afrikaans-speaking manager remarked laconically:

The problem with the policy of homeland development is that a good political idea will unfortunately never become an economic reality.

The pragmatic rather than dogmatic approach of the business world is illustrated particularly well in its attitudes to the future of the coloureds and Indians. Two-thirds of the government supporters and three-quarters of the pro-opposition businessmen are in favour of fully integrating these groups:

The NP acted quite shamelessly when it deprived the coloureds of their political rights. This was probably the government's greatest mistake. The coloureds are half Afrikaners and must be integrated, come what may.

It is taken as axiomatic by the whole business world that the urban blacks will always remain in 'white' South Africa. The reason is simply that they provide skilled black labour, without which the South African economy could not survive:

Even a costly programme of rationalization would not let us dispense with the blacks. The more sophisticated our economy becomes, the less we can rely on migratory labour. We need increasing numbers of better-educated blacks, who must be granted the right to reside in the cities.

Nevertheless, there is widespread perplexity about the role of urban blacks in a future South African society. The majority of pro-government businessmen would prefer only to grant their economic advancement and the right to own land in the black townships. Only 20 per cent would be prepared to grant them political rights as well. By contrast, the overwhelming majority of businessmen who support the opposition are in favour of granting the blacks self-administration, but even 90 per cent of this group reject full integration:

We cannot grant the blacks political rights because this would mean that eventually the whites would lose their right of self-determination. It is almost impossible to separate the two. The greatest problem is the birth-rate—we are being outnumbered.

To summarize, South Africa's economic leadership, be it English- or Afrikaans-speaking, pro- or anti-government, is in favour of moderate and controlled change. The businessmen's openness to reform is largely governed by their economic self-interest. In their view, a capitalist social order is most likely to promote peaceful change; for rising prosperity has the potential to overcome racial conflict without violence.

5. *The leadership's view of the electorate*

It is often the case in a parliamentary system that the voters' actual thoughts and desires are less important in shaping decisions than what the political leadership thinks are the voters' attitudes and voting behaviour.

This section will accordingly deal with the South African leadership's view of its voters. The statistics refer only to the views of politicians in the narrowest sense of the term. But in the commentary, which is based on quotations from the interviews, the politicians' views are supplemented by the statements of representatives of other leadership groups.

The significance of social strata

Over three-quarters of the politicians in all the parties are convinced that the white lower classes tend to be conservative and the upper classes liberal.

A leading verkrampte NP parliamentarian gave the following reason:

The opposition voters . . . have their private apartheid, the apartheid of money. The NP, by contrast, enjoys strong support from the less well-off whites; they, and not the wealthy, have to live and work in close contact with the non-whites.

A verligte NP journalist emphasized another aspect:

164

Our lower classes are naturally far more conservative, especially those on the fringes of society who have little more to sell than their white skin.

An opposition MP emphasized the close connection between class and political awareness:

One social stratum differs from another primarily in how politically informed it is. The average voter knows very little about party programmes; his actions are influenced by personalities and very general impressions. That is where the NP has the advantage. Its notion of segregation is devastatingly simple.

The opposition places its hopes for increased support on the economic advancement of the whites:

Among those advancing up the social scale there is an especially high proportion of verligtes, whom one may call economically emancipated Afrikaners. Whoever is involved in business or overseas travel begins to think. Although this group is numerically small, it may be politically influential.

The significance of urbanization

Almost half of the opposition politicians hope that increasing urbanization will promote liberal tendencies among the electorate. But even they feel that if urbanization works in their favour at all—about which they are not convinced—it will only do so in the long run:

One must draw some distinctions in considering urbanization. If Afrikaners who migrate to the cities move into exclusively Afrikaner suburbs they remain in a closed society and, reacting against the impression of an overwhelmingly English-speaking city, may even draw together more closely. If on the other hand they move into linguistically mixed suburbs the situation may be quite different.
Urbanization may take a generation to have political effects.

As for NP politicians, almost 80 per cent think that urbanization will affect the political orientation of voters only slightly, if at all. A Minister explained:

Even when Afrikaners move to the city, they largely keep their traditional attitudes. In the country their closed social contacts are stabilized by the family structure, isolation, the lack of communication, religion, etc. In the city these factors are replaced by the contrast between Afrikaners and other groups, and this also creates social cohesion.
Consequently the political effects of urbanization on the Afrikaners are limited.

165

A leading NP journalist gave a similar analysis:

Afrikaners who have recently moved to the city often feel afraid of the strange and unknown environment. They are then especially susceptible to ideologies which offer simple explanations and orientations. There have been similar phenomena in other countries: in Nazi Germany, and in California, where the John Birch Society has had a remarkable success. In South Africa verkramptheid is particularly prevalent in the urban areas. It is manifested, for example, in the excessive emphasis placed on rural values. Farm life is regarded as idyllic. The phenomenon of rural revivalism is very strong among the urban population. There are enormous numbers of small plots and pseudo-farms around Pretoria and Bloemfontein. And when an Afrikaner makes a lot of money the first thing he does is buy himself a real farm. As a rule, it is only the children of those who move to the cities who become properly urbanized.

The significance of religion

Politicians in the various parties have very different beliefs about the influence of religion on the political attitudes of voters. Sixty-five per cent of the NP politicians think that religion has a strong influence, and 70 per cent that the church possesses considerable political power. Far fewer opposition politicians share these views.

This reflects the fact that religion is far more important for the Afrikaner population—the main source of NP votes—than for the largely English-speaking supporters of the opposition parties. A Minister emphasized the special character of the Reformed Churches:

Our Church is a church of the volk, but not in the European sense of an established church, implying the automatic membership of every citizen. Rather, we want individual and active church membership. But we believe that the church is realised in human communities, i.e., manifests itself concretely in different peoples. This idea is not derived from the Bible, but is, we believe, justified by it. We are convinced that in no way does separate development run counter to holy writ. Thus, we have different churches for the different peoples.

A conservative church leader emphasized the connection between church and political orientation:

The policy of separate development is the political expression of our religiously based respect for the particularity and independence of all peoples.

A church leader on the verligte wing of the NP took this view:

There is more political flexibility today in the NP than in the Church. In our Church, the HNP is still strongly represented. From my ex-

166

perience I fear that the Church will be the last institution to open itself to change.

Other church leaders who are open to change, while also active in the NP, emphasize instead the changing trend in the Reformed Churches:

Over the last ten years Reformed theologians have tended to stop using the Bible to justify apartheid. Among students there is hardly anyone who will support the old view. There are simply no arguments in the Bible which justify excluding people from the church.

Certain people who feel they have a 'direct line' to Heaven find the imperative for racial segregation in Calvin's teachings. Others come to opposite conclusions on the same teachings. My own struggle against apartheid has its cultural motivation in the Calvinist tradition of publicly stating and promoting one's convictions.

Leadership groups in the NP, whether open to change or not, think that secularization has had little effect on the Afrikaners:

South African Calvinism has had an unbroken tradition. There is far less secularization than in Europe. Surveys indicate that 600,000 people listen to the daily Bible-reading on the radio; indeed, it is the programme with the highest rating. There is almost nothing like it in any other country.

In recent years an enormous number of churches have been built in the suburbs of the cities. The church occupies a central place in the social values of rural life, and this has been maintained in the cities. On Sundays some people attend services twice. The effects of secularization will probably only become evident in the next generation.

One Cabinet Minister made the interesting point that political convictions can shape religious attitudes as much as the other way round:

Religious and political cohesion strengthen each other. It is quite possible that a desire for political stability may promote religious stability.

A church leader on the verligte wing of the NP made a similar observation:

The church is the most important institutional symbol of Afrikanerdom. Many people attend church for cultural, social, or political reasons, even if they are no longer religious.

An opposition MP defined these developments as 'hidden secularization' and emphasized that they were irrelevant to political change:

There is a double morality in the religious attitudes of many people. Their deeds are very different from their words. Urbanized Afrikaners

167

retain a superficial contact with their church; but behind this facade a process of secularization is undoubtedly taking place, and making rapid progress. One might speak of a 'hidden secularization'. But it has no immediate political effect. If it were true that everyone who no longer attends church had also left the NP, then the opposition would already be in power.

For the average NP politician, the connection between religion and politics is quite simple. The argument runs as follows:

We believe that God has given us this country, and that it is our right and our duty to use it and keep it.

There is clearly observable evidence of this belief:

As a politician I cultivate a very close relationship with the church. In my view apartheid has a religious motivation, and at election meetings I always appear with a predikant.

Many Nationalists see a direct connection between religion and party-political preference:

Afrikaners who are no longer religious leave us and join the other parties. Although they still speak Afrikaans, they are no longer 'ware Afrikaners'.

A Cabinet Minister stated laconically:

When the party is no longer on a good standing with our churches, it will be finished.

An opposition MP was of this opinion:

The philosophy of Calvinism runs counter to change. It provides the Afrikaners with a messianic dream: 'Let others form a plural society, not us'.

A particularly significant factor is that religion is important for the verligtes as well as the verkramptes in the NP. Where the latter believe that Reformed theology gives its blessing to the status quo, the former are motivated to investigate new directions in religious thought. On this point a Nationalist MP stated:

People are re-thinking their political ideas because of their intensely religious life-style, and the new theology. This is a particularly interesting development. Our theologians are now pointing out that, in keeping with Christian doctrine, every person, black or white, must be regarded as a human being with equal needs and rights. The Christian concepts of humanity and justice are requiring us to demand that politics provide more human rights for all in South Africa.

Similarly, a leading figure in the media emphasized:

Strong religiousness can engender enlightened as well as verkrampte attitudes. The developments in Potchefstroom show that fundamental religious thought can lead to the recognition of the dignity of all men, and therefore to more open-minded political views.

Most respondents thought that the English churches had a far smaller influence on the political attitudes of white voters than the Afrikaans churches.

A verkrampte NP journalist disapproved of the attitude of these churches, and was pleased that they were of so little consequence:

One often finds the most remarkable things in the non-Calvinist churches. There is the theology of revolution, a God of social change, and the permanently revolutionary Christian. That anything of the present could be valuable never even occurs to these people. These churches are continually interfering in politics. How arrogant are their clergymen, always wanting to be the only ones who know God's will! Thank God that they have so few followers!

A leading NRP MP expressed roughly the same view:

For the average white voter the churches belong in that small part of his world where he expects tranquillity and not unrest. If the church does not accord with these expectations, it is by no means certain that he will follow it.

Liberal PFP politicians agree with this analysis, although they give it a quite different interpretation:

One should have no illusions about the Christianity of whites in South Africa. White church members do not oppose what the bishops say, but still cling to their privileges. They interpret their religion to accord with their own interests.

To the extent that opposition politicians hope that religion will work in favour of change, they look more to the Afrikaans than the English churches:

Changes in religious attitudes have the most marked political effects among Afrikaners. A group of people who take their Christianity seriously suddenly discover that it is not necessarily compatible with Nationalist ideology. Christianity is for all men while Nationalism implies exclusion and group-centredness. So there is increasing doubt about the concept of Christian Nationalism, which makes political capital out of people's religious attitudes and feelings.

The significance of ethnic groups

Our assessment of religion as a political factor has already shown that there was considerable variation in how the political leaders assessed the

169

evident differences between the churches of the two ethnic or language groups. The extent of this variation depended on party affiliation. There was even greater variation in the perceived significance of the ethnic groups.

Afrikaans-speaking respondents, whatever their party affiliation, answered these questions in depth and with enthusiasm, whereas English speakers tended to dismiss them.

Three-quarters of the NP politicians thought that ethnic group affiliation was the most important factor in voting behaviour. And only one-third of them thought that the significance of ethnic groups for political orientation was decreasing. Three-quarters were also convinced that verligte Afrikaners would remain loyal to the NP in all circumstances.

By contrast, less than half of the opposition politicians thought that one's ethnic group was the most important determinant of one's political affiliation. And about half of them thought it was possible that verligte Afrikaners would join their party. The hopes of these respondents have evidently influenced their analysis.

The clearest difference lies in the respective estimations of the present political significance of the 'Boer-Brit' divide. Half of the NP politicians thought that this cleavage was very strong, or even unbridgeable, as against only one-fifth of the NRP and the PFP politicians. The way in which the political leadership groups judge this issue is extremely important for an understanding of present-day white South Africa. We accordingly analyse its most important facets.

Firstly, historical perceptions still play a major role:

We Afrikaners are unable to forget the past, and above all the injustices we suffered at the hands of the English. All of us can still remember our fathers' and grandfathers' accounts of the cruelties of the English, and we ourselves experienced a lot of discrimination when we were young. Even now we still find that the English in general are arrogant towards us. To some extent we are still fighting for our identity.

Many Afrikaner political leaders still doubt how South African the English speakers are:

One still cannot accept the English as full South Africans. They sit perched on their suitcases and can return to England at any time. Their whole way of thinking and attitude to life is still Anglo-Saxon.

Each group thinks in terms of highly stylized stereotypes:

The fight for survival has shaped our Afrikaner character: we are honest, militant, religious, and have strong ties to our fatherland. This is our identity, and we are not prepared to give it up.
The typical Englishman believes that he belongs to the upper class,

170

fancies that he is superior, and without doubt is not as dogmatic as we are. Afrikaners by contrast are stubborn, but also logical and consistent, honest and religious. This attitude is incompatible with the Englishman's inclination to compromise.

A Minister holds the English-language press mainly responsible for these caricatures:

The English-language press has terribly stereotyped prejudices about the Afrikaner: it presents us as coarse, uncivilized, racist, harsh, authoritarian, and fascist. This description naturally demands a reply: we see the English as dishonest, hypocritical, arrogant, unrealistic, unpatriotic, unchristian, colonial, and mendacious.

An English-speaking opposition MP put the opposite view:

There is still an enormous amount of prejudice. The Afrikaners still regard the English as people with one foot in Britain. On the other hand, the English regard the Afrikaners as 'hairybacks'. English-speaking South Africans gave up in 1948, when Smuts lost. They confined themselves to making money. What else could they do?

Leading representatives of both language groups located the traditional differences in the mentalities of the ethnic groups. A top NP journalist was of this opinion:

The English are still rooted in their Jingoism and the Victorian past. The Afrikaners were strongly affected by the Boer War.

These historical experiences have given rise to very different attitudes. English-speaking politicians express these views:

The English have a different way of life and feel that it is threatened by the Afrikaners.

The Afrikaner is fighting for the survival of his group. The Englishman wants freedom of the individual.

By contrast, a Cabinet Minister took this view:

People get worked up and quarrel about small things. But these are symptomatic of different attitudes. For the Afrikaner it is natural to go to church on Sunday, not to tennis. He has his own opinions on education, censorship, decorum and tact, pornography, etc. No one is prepared to give way on such issues.

This view was expressed in a startling manner by a conservative church leader:

You can see the real difference by comparing what students from Stellenbosch and from Cape Town do on a Sunday. The former do social work among the poor, the latter seduce coloured girls.

171

At a more abstract level, many respondents contrasted the principled and legalistic Afrikaner way of thinking with English pragmatism. An NP journalist thought this contrast was rooted in historical differences:

> *The Dutch inheritance has had a great influence. The Dutch are surrounded by water, so they surrounded themselves with dykes and lived in constant fear that these would start to leak. A corresponding fear among South African Afrikaners produced the apartheid laws and the idea of the homelands. Afrikaners are typically not prepared to make small compromises because they fear that the dykes will break with the first crack. Much of our politics can be explained by this attitude. By contrast, the English are far less fundamental and consistent. They try to proceed in a pragmatic way, one step after another.*

A Minister further underlined the political fundamentalism of the Afrikaners:

> *On most questions the Afrikaner is systematic and logical rather than pragmatic. This is the cause of his conspicuous legalism. Everything must have its own order, and be logically and consistently regulated to the last detail. However, this logic does have a goal—the preservation of identity. This identity is a complex reality with social, cultural, religious, and ethnic elements—and also skin-colour—which has been formed over the centuries. Thus, in the matter of petty apartheid the Afrikaners emphasize the systematic aspect and the English the question of practical convenience. The Afrikaner always wants to know where what one has started will end.*

Notwithstanding the official policy of bilingualism, the language struggle continues to be of great importance for the cleavage between the ethnic groups. In this instance, the differences of opinion run along linguistic and not political lines. A PFP politician, an Afrikaner, argues:

> *The language problem plays a crucial role. It is also the chief basis of the strength of the NP. The crux of the problem is that the English do not speak Afrikaans, out of either laziness or arrogance.*

A statement by one of his party colleagues indirectly confirms his analysis:

> *I speak English on principle. I find it difficult enough to say anything sensible in my own language. In a bilingual country it should be quite enough for everyone to understand the other language, without having to be able to express oneself in it. The Nationalists play on the language problem, and thereby impress mainly the elderly and the economically worse-off Afrikaners. For it is mainly these groups who have an inferiority complex towards the English speakers.*

However, there are no signs of an inferiority complex among the

Afrikaner leadership groups, least of all in the political sphere. An NP politician evinced the pride of his group in almost poetical terms:

> *The Afrikaners rule the country. Everything that is politically sound comes from the Afrikaners. All our Prime Ministers have been Afrikaners. And the real men in the opposition are Afrikaners—like Nic Olivier, Van Zyl Slabbert, and Beyers Naudé. The Afrikaners and the English live in completely different traditions. The Afrikaner culture is based on Calvinism, the English culture on a loose theism. Calvinists believe that God watches over everything and rules the world. The English believe that God created the world but then left it to them to ensure that everything works. The Afrikaner stands alone today. The English have left to him the task of preserving the standards of civilization, while they make money under his protection. The English make every crisis so complicated, and they take the blacks as their allies. They cannot forgive us for finally having won the civil war.*

In the government camp the cleavage we are outlining undoubtedly plays an enormous role in politics and particularly in elections. An NP journalist made this statement, not without cynicism:

> *The Boer-Brit contrast is surely more important for voting behaviour than actual political questions. For example, the HNP supporters hate the English even more than the blacks. All verkramptes tend to support conspiracy theories. The English are always given a leading role in them, together with the Jews, the Catholics, and the Communists. There is no doubt that the division between Boer and Brit cements NP unity.*

An opposition MP came to the same conclusion, though with some bitterness:

> *The NP artificially sustains the Afrikaners' fear of English domination. It serves the interests of the establishment, especially the leadership. With two-thirds of the seats in parliament there is no valid reason for any such fear. It is the—admittedly effective—tactic of a mediocre leadership which is clinging to power, and therefore does not baulk at irresponsible propaganda.*

Politicians' views on voters' reactions to changes in party programmes

The views which politicians take of how their voters may react to changes in party policies can have considerable significance for political change.

However, we must first ask whether the politicians themselves believe that the policies of their respective parties have altered. The situation is clear in both opposition parties: NRP politicians have no doubt that the old UP underwent a decisive change in adopting a conception of

173

federation. On the other hand, the PFP politicians feel that only the accent has shifted in their party programme.

The most interesting differences of opinion occur between NP politicians. Almost one-third insist that the party line has not changed at all; a little more than one-third maintain that policies have been developed and in part altered; and the remaining third speak of fundamental changes.

It is mainly the verkrampte politicians who believe that nothing has changed in the NP:

> We still use the concept of 'white baasskap'. At every meeting we talk about baasskap, leadership, and apartheid. The whites will always rule this country. We won't share our power with the natives. Separate development is only a different name for the same thing, and that is total segregation.

> In the course of time 'apartheid' acquired a pejorative connotation, and we therefore no longer use the word officially. But we still use it among ourselves.

The 'further development' of the NP programme is described as follows:

> Previously we only favoured white baasskap. Today we are for white baasskap in the white areas and black baasskap in the black areas.

By contrast, the verligte wing stresses:

> The political philosophy of our party has indeed changed. The emphasis is now placed upon developing the non-white population, and we mean this seriously.

About half of the NP politicians assume that their voters either have not noticed the changes in policy or have only gone along with them in part. Only one-fifth think that the voters have kept up with the party:

> Our voters have caught up with the changes in the party's programme, even though it may have taken some time. For example, the idea of bantustan independence was initially taken seriously only by a few, and one spoke of 'in a thousand years at the soonest'. It is quite different now.

Among the opposition, only some of the NRP politicians feel that their voters have followed the changes in their party policy. One member was sceptical:

> What the voters know about the party programme is nil. Opposition voters basically vote against the NP, not for a programme. If we were to believe anything else we would be kidding ourselves.

Another was a little more optimistic:

> What we have been able to hammer home is that we do offer an

174

alternative to the NP, and it sounds good. Where previously we had no trademark, now we have one.

The PFP politicians, on the other hand, reckon that their voters have a good knowledge of the party programme. In any case their followers are by comparison politically interested and well informed.

Politicians' views on the voters' expectations of leadership

A clear majority of NP politicians, half of the NRP politicians, and only a minority of the leadership group of the PFP, believe that the electorate is strongly orientated towards the political leaders in its attitudes and follows them closely.

An MP of the ruling party makes no secret of his élitist outlook:

In South Africa the people are overwhelmingly uncritical of the leadership. We politicians subscribe to the maxim: act, then talk. We first proceed, and then we explain.

A majority of the politicians we interviewed in all parties—88 per cent of the NP, 77 per cent of the NRP, and 73 per cent of the PFP—are of course of the view that deference towards the leadership is most prevalent among the Afrikaners, and considerably less among the English speakers.

A leading figure in the NP nevertheless perceives limits in the readiness of the Afrikaners to follow their leaders unthinkingly:

The Afrikaners do follow their leaders. In general, the political leadership gives the line and the voters accept it. But there are limits. The loyalty of the electorate is not boundless, as history has shown in the cases of Hertzog, Smuts, and also Beyers Naudé. If the leadership gets too distant, deviates neither right nor left, or seems intractable, then its followers may cease to go along. That is typically Afrikaans.

Similarly, a Cabinet Minister drew this distinction:

The Afrikaner wants a strong leader. But he is at the same time very critical. It is not unusual at campaign meetings for a simple farmer to get up and without respect for rank tell the Prime Minister what he thinks. This was the tradition in the Afrikaner republics—the people are very democratic and very self-assured. But once they have been persuaded by some idea or approach they support it unconditionally.

Similarly, another Minister felt this:

Our main problem is to find out how fast to go: not to move too far ahead of the masses, but not to let them tread on our heels.

But at least one part of the NP leadership is more confident:

The NP has built up such reserves of loyalty that we can take controversial decisions without electoral support.

The politicians' assessment of the voters' capacity for change

South African politicians, depending on their party affiliation, take very different views of the resistance or openness to change of the electorate:

Table 7.12

	NP	NRP	PFP
	%	%	%
Voters' opinions lag behind those of the leaders	91	69	40
Voters keep up with the leaders	9	23	20
Voters are ahead of the leaders; the leaders are irresolute	—	8	40

NP politicians think that their voters are uninformed. In the opinion of one Minister:

The voters lag behind the leaders. Everything takes time. We have to explain each innovation to the voters step by step. Most of them don't read newspapers, don't listen to the radio, and are largely isolated from other sources of political information.

A Cabinet colleague drew the following conclusion:

As a party we have the task of continually educating our voters.

A back-bencher in the NP blandly expressed his low opinion of the electorate:

By and large the voters are far behind the political leadership. The leaders have to take the decisions and drag the voters along behind them. The voters don't want everything explained to them, either. If we told them too much they wouldn't vote for us.

Contempt for the electorate is also evident in the following statement of an NRP MP:

Party supporters are like a herd of sheep. One has continually to prod them and lead them, and take care not to lose them in one's haste. There have to be leaders on the right and the left of the herd, and also bringing up the rear, so that no one escapes and flees. For we can only win with the whole herd.

By contrast, the opinion-makers of the NP would certainly not agree with this view of the electorate. They regard the voters as far less verkramp than do the politicians:

176

In my view the NP is not moving fast enough. It pays too much attention to the verkramptes. This is not the time to look backwards. Besides, the average Afrikaner votes neither for the far left nor for the far right.

For this reason they are very critical of the party politicians:

One can demand quite a lot from the voters. In the final instance, it all depends on the party. The NP shouldn't try to keep the voters happy. It should practise politics.

The opinion-makers accordingly place the onus on the political leadership:

The Afrikaners will follow a strong leader, a 'blood, sweat, and tears' speech, even if it involves a change of course. They want clear leadership.

Finally, there is a small group of NP politicians who share the same view:

By and large, the people follow their leader. South Africa's history provides many examples of leaders who had great success with unpopular proposals and actions, and received support for them.

6. *Peaceful change in the inner circle*

One of the most important questions in the analysis of political systems is who makes the top decisions. But it is often the most difficult question to answer with convincing empirical data. In many governments the legal office-bearers are not necessarily the people who actually take the decisions. Kennedy's 'kitchen Cabinet' and 'the Reich President's son, not foreseen in the Constitution' during the last stages of the Weimar Republic are only two notable examples of the difference between the Constitution and constitutional reality at the highest level of political activity. In most cases, a correct understanding of how top-level decisions were reached is confined to the actors themselves, or to historians who later make a thorough study of the relevant papers. The former seldom intend to be scientific and analytical; the latter can only do their job thirty or fifty years later. Therefore contemporary political analysis must necessarily be based on statements that are only partly verified at best.

In South Africa active politicians and political observers alike frequently mention the *inner circle*. This refers to a small circle of politically influential men whose opinions are assumed to carry a great deal of weight with the Prime Minister when he makes his decisions.

All observers agree that the Prime Minister is the central figure in the white South African system, and that his decisions are most important.

177

Nor does anyone doubt that the Prime Minister greatly respects the opinions of a small leadership group.

One is on fairly firm ground so far, but one runs into problems as soon as one starts considering the composition of the inner circle. It is almost certain that this small leadership group is not identical with the Cabinet. Clear statements by leading politicians support this view:

> *Precisely speaking, the Government as a whole does not take decisions. Given the way the present Cabinet works . . . . decisions are taken in smaller groups; at least the more important decisions.*

Many observations of our own also support this view, indicating considerable differences in the power and influence of individual Cabinet members. There is also a lot of evidence that a few prominent people outside the Cabinet are members of the inner circle.

The way in which decisions are actually reached within this circle is undoubtedly very interesting. But it is not particularly relevant to our study. What is important is whether in fact this group does take decisions, and who belongs to it.

The first question, whether the circle actually takes decisions, was answered with an unequivocal 'yes' by all the politicians we interviewed. A small number of politicians in the governing party were asked who these influential men were. There was widespread agreement on between ten and fourteen names: some Ministers, one or two leading civil servants, figures in the media, military men, academics, and businessmen. Of the fourteen names mentioned, twelve could be interviewed.

Now it might be objected that one or other of these interviewees did not belong to the circle, or that some people's views were canvassed only on specific issues, or that a couple of members of the circle were omitted. But the fact remains that the opinions of these twelve leading politicians are of utmost significance when it comes to key issues in government policy. It is thus both necessary and extremely interesting to devote a separate analysis to this élite group's views on the question of peaceful change.

As a whole, the opinions of the inner circle provide a pretty fair reflection of the range of opinions found among NP politicians. In other words, the members of the inner circle are not drawn from one or other particular tendency within the party, but embrace the leading representatives of all the tendencies.

Nevertheless, their opinions did diverge at some points from the general view of NP politicians as a whole; most surprisingly in that they showed greater pragmatism and flexibility. This is the more remarkable in that prominent personalities occupying important positions tend to express their views with great caution. This section will deal with these divergences of opinion in detail.

178

On the question of economic relations between the racial groups the inner circle is more verlig than the governing party as a whole. For example, one-quarter of its members are not averse to whites' working under black superiors, whereas only one-tenth of NP politicians as a whole share this opinion.

And where more than one-fifth of all NP politicians support the verkrampte position on the wage-gap—that increases in black wages and salaries should at best only keep pace with the rate of inflation—no one at all takes this position in the inner circle. The majority are in favour of slowly closing the wage-gap, and the minority think it is necessary to take immediate measures aiming at economic equality.

One of the Ministers was quite forthright:

Of course the black workers are frustrated. They are paid too little. That must change, and will change. In an integrated economy—and there can be no doubt that we have and will continue to have one—a wage-gap cannot be allowed to persist.

He emphasized the political significance of changes in economic relationships:

Economic advancement is the prime goal of the non-whites, quite understandably. Their advancement is a requirement if our system is to function without friction—a requirement which must be met without fail.

There is no hesitation about black economic advancement:

This is undoubtedly possible in South Africa. The welfare of all the people can be guaranteed because the prospects for economic development are unbelievably good—also good enough for many more than the present population.

On the question of change in social relations between the racial groups, the opinions of the inner circle are far more polarized than in the party as a whole.

The verkrampte wing regards the maintenance of petty apartheid as a ·question of principle:

There will always be segregatory measures. We will never have the same social relations with the black peoples of Africa as with the British, Germans, French, and Americans. For our views on identity include not only language and culture but also ethnicity—we want to continue to be a white volk.

Another verkrampte member of the inner circle sees a close connection between identity and the preservation of privilege:

We will hold on to everything that whites regard as a guarantee of their identity—plus certain privileges in the service sector as well.

179

By contrast, the verligte wing holds radically different views:

Residential segregation would persist even without legal provision. But in the near future the whole question of interracial marriage will have to be dealt with seriously.

Lifts, park-benches, hotels—this is all nonsense. It can all vanish, and it should vanish soon. The only thing that counts is that the political power structures be soundly managed.

Within the inner power-centre of white South Africa one will find widely differing attitudes on co-existence between the races. Segregation is a question of principle for some; for others, it is an annoying hindrance in the search for an appropriate resolution of the only important question, that of the political relations between the racial groups.

Support for separate development as prescribed by the official policy is significantly lower within the inner circle than among NP politicians as a whole. One-third of the inner circle dismiss bantustans according to the 1936 boundaries:

If we want them independent, extensive consolidation will have to take place. A KwaZulu which consists of nine parts is not viable.

The boundaries have to be completely redrawn. We must be prepared to cede up to half of the country.

One-third of the inner circle also deviate from the official party and government line on the question of the urban blacks:

The urban blacks have to be given economic rights as quickly as possible—for example, the right to own land and settle permanently. In the long run there is no chance of co-existence unless we create a black middle class.

The urban blacks have to get some form or other of political representation. In my opinion this will finally involve representation in parliament.

Attitudes to the question of the coloureds are strongly polarized. The verkrampte wing sees them as a separate group:

A common language, religion, and history do not create a common identity.
One should not deceive oneself—colour plays a role here.

For the majority of the inner circle this does not constitute a 'fundamental' problem, but only a pragmatic and political one. But even at this level of political decision-making, there is an evident fear that, given political integration, the coloureds will as before align themselves with the English-speaking group and try to drive the Afrikaners from power. Some very verligte members of the inner circle take the view that

coloureds are half Afrikaners and must be integrated.

But even they would like political integration to take a form

which will prevent the coloureds from holding the balance.

A majority of the inner circle are therefore searching for a way to allow coloureds to share political power, but to prevent them from aligning with the English speakers.

The verligte opinions of the inner circle are thus far clearer than those of less influential verligte politicians.

The bantustan boundaries of 1936 are more widely subjected to criticism in the inner circle. And it is taken for granted by almost half of the inner circle that the urban blacks cannot simply be treated as migrant labour. The case of the coloureds also shows that a significant group within the inner circle are seriously considering non-white participation in political power—they hesitate for reasons of political practicality, not principle. And a small group are not afraid to consider ways of drawing the urban blacks into the political system, though their ideas are still very vague.

A particularly influential and respected member of the latter group argues to the following conclusion, which is logical even though it would surprise many observers:

Separate development is not a dogma, although many people regard it as such. The policy of the NP is open as to whether the ultimate solution will be the maintenance of separate development or the participation of other groups in the political life of the country. We are not adamant about this.

The range of positions in the inner circle is particularly evident here: about one-third of its members regard separate development as given, whereas for the other leading politicians anything can change

if the interests of the Afrikaner volk require it.

This is what finally distinguishes the inner circle from the mass of NP politicians—its considerations are not guided by principles and policies, but only by the *interests of the Afrikaner volk:*

If the interests of the volk should change, then our ideas and our policies will have to change.

In other words, the most powerful men in South Africa would be prepared to accept change if they think it is to the advantage of their own group. But just what is involved is hotly contested within this top group. We shall have to examine below how far perceptions of what is involved have changed in recent years as a result of changing external and internal circumstances; and therefore how far political opinions within the inner circle have changed.

181

7. *Polarization, adaptation, and intransigence: trends of opinion in the white leadership groups in 1976/77*

However one may interpret the events in and around the country between 1974 and 1977, the fact remains that the political leaders of white South Africa have hardly changed their basic opinions. Indeed, the different political groups tend to feel that events have confirmed their respective views.

One common element in most statements from 1977 cannot be over-looked: people believe that

the pace of events has somehow or other accelerated,

and

we have to respond more quickly and more suitably than before.

But opinions differ widely on how quickly, let alone in which way, to respond.

What has happened to the opinions of the political leadership groups can be succinctly summarized as follows: a further polarization of the political tendencies in white South Africa, including a polarization within the tendencies; a cautious but noticeable adaptation to changing circumstances in the way the respective political programmes are interpreted and defined; and a persistence of the respective basic orientations.

In this section we shall first describe how recent events are perceived, and relate the differences to the various groups. Then we shall analyse changes in attitude towards the basic problems of peaceful change amongst the opposition, business leaders, the politicians of the governing party, and finally the members of the inner circle.

The leadership groups' views of the events of recent years

Different events assume a significance for different groups. The majority of the opposition leaders emphasize the disturbances among the black population; the business leaders place less emphasis on the disturbances themselves than on their effects on business prospects; while the politicians in the governing party have not been particularly impressed by internal and external political events, but rather by the growing attention paid to South Africa by the Western states—attention which these politicians regard as interference. The inner circle has been particularly irritated by the policy of the West towards South Africa.

The Soweto uprising and political developments in black South Africa have made a very strong impression on leading representatives of extra-parliamentary opposition organizations and institutions. They have the

182

strongest contact of all white political groups with the black political scene. They regard the unrest in 1976/77 as

a turning point in South African politics; the tip of the iceberg of black dissatisfaction; a mobilization of wider, hitherto a-political circles among urban blacks; a growing perception among blacks of the black-white conflict as a class struggle; and the rapid radicalization of black youth.

They fear that the cleavages will widen and that violent clashes will become more frequent. They think that these processes will be intensified by the attitude of the government, and also by the readiness of the black youth to over-estimate their chances:

The government reacts brutally to the symptoms instead of treating the causes.

They continually arrest and beat up suspected ring-leaders, and thereby increase the radicals' support.

Many young black activists completely misjudge the power situation in the country. They live in a fool's paradise, lose themselves in verbal radicalism, and confuse their desires with reality. They will probably become extremely frustrated within a short time. This can only become a new source of violence.

The leaders of the parliamentary opposition have more diverse opinions on these events, but by and large regard them as significant.

The conservative opposition regards the internal unrest as a confirmation of their earlier warnings. As an NRP MP declared:

These events have not changed my political views at all. I always thought that something like this would happen. We have always believed that blacks must become citizens of the Republic and that we must ensure them a suitable situation.

However, this group tends to minimize the importance of the unrest:

The black movement in 1960 was far more dangerous. Black labour played a leading part at that time. This time it was only the students.

They are more concerned about the economic situation:

As a result of events in Angola, Mozambique, and Rhodesia, the outside world has little confidence in our future. People are investing less. Unfortunately, we need overseas capital as we are not in a position to raise enough locally. But I must concede that I would think twice about investing in Northern Ireland or the Near East, for example.

The PFP politicians are far more concerned about the internal situation, while at the same time seeing some hope in the West's policy

183

towards South Africa. Like the majority of the extra-parliamentary opposition, they are aware of the growing radicalization of the blacks:

> *The Black Consciousness movement is gaining enormous support, and on the way to winning over the whole younger generation. These people have assumed a clear and simple position, and are extremely militant. Despite all the repression, their self-confidence is still fully intact. They may have some illusions about how far things will change. But that will have no effect at all on the dynamism of the movement.*

> *Most whites are only faintly aware of how far the politicization of the blacks has advanced. All the gentleness and subservience has been driven out of a whole generation. They are not interested in compromise.*

Leading PFP politicians stress the change in Western interests in South Africa:

> *The South African government has the wrong idea about Western intentions. The Western powers want to stop the advance of Communism in Africa. But they can only do this if they are on the side of the blacks, not on the side of white minority regimes.*

Of course, they say that Western pressure on South Africa will only be beneficial subject to certain conditions:

> *The West should state clearly what it actually wants: to support the blacks on the one hand, and on the other to help white South Africans if they agree to a peaceful compromise solution. It would be no good if the Western powers aimed to have all the changes implemented immediately. Whites would only react by thinking that the demands of the West are irrelevant, for they could not satisfy them in any case.*

For business leaders, the prime effects have been the dramatic worsening of the climate for investment, growing unemployment, and increasing state interference:

> *There is no joy in running a war economy, let alone an economy in a civil war.*

NP politicians make a point of seeming relaxed, and practising 'politics as usual'. They stress that South Africa still attracts a lot of immigrants:

> *The immigration figures are no different before and after Soweto. By comparison with Australia and New Zealand we are doing well. That is probably the best indicator of fear: evidently, we have none.*

Their confidence in the government's and the party's ability to deal with any problems is still unbroken:

Fear has undoubtedly increased a little among the population at large. But the leaders know that they can control the situation. Constructive solutions will be found.

The internal unrest is regarded as unfortunate, but by no means a serious threat. NP politicians are convinced that they have handled more serious situations:

I don't see any reason for panic. The unrest at Sharpeville was far more difficult. At that time the blacks had genuine leaders, and broad sections of the population supported them. And we were far less ready than we are today. We were able to deal with the situation then. The Soweto disturbances and those which are still continuing are rather like the student unrest in Europe in the late sixties. They are troublesome but not really dangerous.

NP politicians only see the disturbances as a threat if they are taken in conjunction with external events:

Soweto is a problem above all because it has occurred at the same time as the deteriorating situation on the borders, in Angola, and Mozambique, and with growing pressure from the West.

Finally, a number of the respondents regarded international influences as the most important cause of the disturbances in the country:

The urban blacks have been strongly influenced by the ideas of the American Black Power movement. And they are strongly motivated by the changing international scene. By contrast, there has hardly been any trouble in the rural areas.

Over the last year we have been experiencing an organized Marxist influence.

Some politicians on the verligte wing of the NP share the view that the internal unrest, unlike the growing foreign pressure, does not constitute a serious threat. On the other hand they regard the unrest as an indication of black dissatisfaction with urban living conditions:

There is certainly no cause for panic. But we should take these events as a warning to implement the requisite changes more quickly.

Finally, there are widely different assessments of the events of recent years in the inner circle. Representatives of the verkramptes treat the internal unrest as insignificant, but emphasize future foreign threats:

Neither Sharpeville nor Soweto constituted a serious threat to white South Africa. We do have some internal problems—what countries don't? However, most South Africans are law-abiding citizens. The events of last year were played up by the gutter press. We always had the situation under control. The police were able to handle the whole affair, and we did not have to call in the army once.

185

> *A conventional war against foreign Marxist forces is a real danger. But we shall also be able to deal with that. We shall take strong action against any threat, whether in the North or in South West Africa.*

The internal events were assessed quite differently by a leading verligte:

> *I take the disturbances in Soweto and so on very seriously. They could have been avoided. The signs were there for a long time, and appropriate measures could have been taken. What happened was utterly unnecessary. There were undoubtedly Communist agitators. But only a small spark was needed to ignite the powder-keg of existing problems.*

One Minister, a member of the pragmatic centre group of the inner circle, took a similar view:

> *A deep-rooted problem suddenly surfaced. A survey of the causes of the Soweto disturbances has shown that over 85% of the complaints concerned problems which could have been solved without further ado—buses, trains, trading monopolies, licences. But the people at Bantu Administration always maintain that they knew it all. They insisted that they were in regular contact with the blacks and spoke with them daily—but if there is anyone to whom the blacks weren't speaking, it was the officials of this Department. No, the situation can be kept well under control; but it is serious, especially against the background of Angola, Mozambique, and Western interference.*

To summarize: perceptions of the recent events in and around South Africa are basically determined by the respective political standpoints of the perceivers. What seemed to the opposition to be the writing on the wall, and to the business world a serious drawback, made far less impression on the politicians in the NP. However, within the small inner circle of leaders, the best informed and most powerful men in South Africa, assessments also differed extremely widely.

What we must now investigate are the implications for their future political activities which the leadership groups have drawn from these events.

The opposition's search for a new role

A Cassandra seldom receives thanks for her warnings. South Africa's white opposition has been condemned to this task for three decades, and since the events of the past years it has become more thankless. The number of whites who are prepared to listen to the opposition has decreased steadily and continues to do so. The blacks are also ever less interested in the white opposition. The only whites who count as far as they are concerned, both in the bad as well as in the—still hoped for—good sense, are the Prime Minister and his National Party.

186

Thus, the people who are most strongly affected by the increasing polarization between black and white are those who have always tried to oppose it. The leadership groups of the liberal minority among the whites—who have worked for the betterment of the black population in churches, institutes, social welfare and education for many years, and who have supported the cause of a multiracial South Africa—find themselves in a particularly difficult situation. For years they have been despised, obstructed, and persecuted by the government; now they are increasingly being rejected by the blacks, especially the black youth. What began before 1972 with the withdrawal of black students from the liberal National Union of South African Students (NUSAS) has led, particularly over the last three years, to a growing rejection of white liberals in the churches, associations, and institutions in which they have played a leading role until now:

> *Organizations which are still run by whites are being increasingly rejected by blacks. Blacks are no longer satisfied with the nomination of a few 'honorary chiefs' if the effective control remains with the whites. Everything that smacks of white liberalism is emphatically rejected. The argument that there are not enough qualified blacks available for particular duties is no longer acceptable. Young blacks think that any activity which is not led and carried out by blacks is pointless. It is better to have nothing to do with it. Here we see how strongly the ideas of the Black Consciousness movement have taken hold.*

This was the experience of a leading white churchman. Many other leaders of the extra-parliamentary opposition have had similar experiences. Basically, most of them approve of the determination of black leaders to take responsibility in social, educational, and political affairs:

> *But it is not easy to accept that the idea of a working partnership is being crushed in the confrontation between white power and black power, that one is treated with growing distrust not because of what one does but because of one's white skin. I understand the reactions of the young blacks. Nevertheless, it hurts when one is directly affected.*

Most of the whites who are active in these areas are prepared to continue under the new conditions, to accept the resulting technical and organizational difficulties, and to work under black leadership:

> *What we can do is create miniature versions of the future South Africa within our domains, even at the cost of some self-denial and a lack of personal growth in what we do. When a new start is finally made, there should be at least some whites who have previously and without coercion accepted the consequences of equality and majority rule.*

The leading liberals who for the most part work for or with organizations dealing with blacks are faced by another problem. They cannot, or can only partly, keep up with the ideological development of the young black élite:

For many young blacks political equality is only the beginning. They want socialism. For them political rights are only an instrument to overthrow existing class differences. Even now, many of them would be prepared to accept a one-party state on an African pattern.

Very few leading whites in the opposition are convinced supporters of a socialist economic order, and only a few more would be prepared to accept a majority decision in favour of socialism:

How could the blacks in this country have ever learnt to appreciate the advantages of free-market enterprise? The government and its policy are the most successful propagators of socialism among the majority of the population. The longer the present policy is continued the more likely is socialism in the future. Whites can count themselves lucky if blacks continue to support the idea of a multiracial society and a parliamentary democracy.

Thus, the leaders of the white liberals stick to their basic convictions, and also regard it as their duty to provide an example for a multiracial society, at least in those areas in which they have any influence. The events of the past years have made their work much more difficult, and their pessimism has grown. But they are remarkably determined to resist the growing repression by the government, and not to be cowed:

We have in any case been watched and spied upon for years. Terror and assaults by right-wing radicals are on the increase. Every one of us must reckon with a banning order. But every banning order is also a chance to win the trust of the majority—and that is what we need for the future.

'Prophetic politics'—pointing the way, and demanding real alternatives to the present system—remains the task which the extra-parliamentary liberal opposition sets itself.

By contrast, the parliamentary opposition has always claimed to offer an alternative to the present government within the white system. An increasing awareness of the futility of traditional opposition politics may well have been even more important than the events of recent years in causing the break-up of the former official Opposition, the United Party, and the laborious attempts to form new groups by means of splits and fusions. However, the disturbances in South Africa, political developments among the blacks, and changes on the international scene have also contributed considerably to thought and discussion about the role of the white opposition in South Africa. The right wing of the old United Party presents the clearest option. It first called itself the In-

188

dependent United Party, and then the South African Party (SAP). Its leaders decided to accept the broad framework of the racial policy of the NP:

We accept the homelands. The racial question should not be the main criterion which distinguishes our party from others. There should be more unity on the racial question. What are needed are normal contrasts between political parties, as in other countries. There is no reason to join the governing party—it is strong enough in any case. We need an opposition which accepts the homelands policy.

The leaders of the NRP continue to stand by their earlier convictions:

All the events of recent years have proved that our political analysis of the situation has been correct since the sixties.

The voters who support the opposition are generally conservative; although they dislike ideological rigidity and ethnic terminology, they are by no means ready to accept a policy which would result in black majority rule:

The PFP therefore has only limited prospects in the South African political system. They will be able to win a maximum of eighteen to twenty seats. Over and above that, only the NP can win what we [the UP] lose. Even if the NRP disappears, the PFP will not win more than twenty seats. The rest of our voters would support the NP.

The main weakness of the old opposition was not their programme but the infighting among their leaders. It was this which destroyed their organization. The leaders of the NRP have no illusions about the prospects of a conservative opposition party when they place their hopes on a 'centrist policy':

Many people dislike the present polarization. They find themselves today in a political no-man's-land. They range from disillusioned Nats to cautious Progs. What they want is a party of the centre.

Between 1974 and 1977 the greatest changes in the white political system were within the liberal parliamentary opposition. They started with the PP breakthrough in the 1974 parliamentary elections; for the first time the PP was able to form a caucus. In 1975 it joined with the Reformed Party to form the PRP. And finally, in 1977, after the disintegration of the UP, the Basson group and PRP together formed the PFP. They came out of the 1977 elections as the strongest opposition party.

The PP started as a small minority group which had only one seat in parliament—Helen Suzman's—and which concentrated mainly on questions of principle and human rights. It has become the official opposition, embracing a wide range of powerful personalities and with

189

extensive parliamentary responsibilities. This transition has given rise to a disciplined but intense discussion on the future role of the party in South African politics:

There are two clearly distinct approaches. One favours a role in white politics, the other looks to a multiracial political system of the future. Both approaches cut right across the boundary between former Progs and former Reformists.

The former approach starts from the assumption that there are opposition voters

who want to be represented. And that can only be done by a political party, not a protest movement. It would be dangerous to reach a situation in which—as in Rhodesia—there is practically no white opposition. Some of our members want to give the party an extra-clean liberal image. That is only feasible for people who can go back to England at any time. But we must also be concerned with future Afrikaans voters who don't have a secure future abroad.

Advocates of the latter approach fear that an opposition which is content to be only a 'white opposition' will

provide an alibi for the government. We can't simply act as though we were the opposition in Australia or Canada. The pleasures of traditional parliamentary debate should not blind us to the fact that in South Africa the situation is quite different.

However, these two approaches differ in emphasis rather than direction. There are signs that agreement will be reached on a kind of 'double strategy':

On the one hand we have to try and express the concerns of the white population fairly convincingly, and on the other represent the liberal section of the white electorate adequately. At the same time, two things must be avoided: on the one hand, we must not be exclusively concerned with the white political system, for then we would be no more than another UP; and on the other we must not only be an agency concerned with human rights and aid, as Helen Suzman was for so many years—that function is indeed necessary, but insufficient. In other words, we must try to find a position that would situate us in the middle of the political spectrum of South Africa as a whole.

According to the PFP politicians, the main change in the overall South African scene in recent years has been the socio-political reorientation of important black groups:

The black movements are becoming increasingly inclined to socialism. Our reaction to this—especially from that section of the party with a big business background—has been partly nervous. For a long time we enjoyed having the blacks as, so to speak, the members-in-waiting of a

190

liberal white tradition. These times are past. All opposition politicians are beginning to realize that South Africa's problems do not have a political solution. The need for an economic solution has moved into the foreground.

They therefore take a very critical view of the white opposition's relationship to black politics:

Given the developments in the black community, the white opposition can no longer pretend to use its vote in parliament in the interest of the black majority. The blacks don't want others to speak for them, they want to speak for themselves. Moreover, there are hardly any whites who would go as far as the blacks want them to. No white politician can be more progressive than black politics.

This view has led the PFP to seek to intensify dialogue with black political forces, while at the same time effectively representing the white liberal position:

When the day of the great conference between blacks and whites finally arrives, the white opposition must also have a place at the table. We don't want to make all the preparations just so that the NP and the blacks can settle the final business between themselves.

PFP politicians believe more strongly than ever that a precondition for such negotiations is the total abolition of all forms of racial discrimination, whether in the social or the economic sphere:

On this issue the PFP have taken a clear and unmistakable stand. We have finally abandoned our previous reservations, which were formulated to take account of the voters' feelings. We reject all forms of discrimination and also, naturally, all forms of compulsory social integration. Our new policy for schools illustrates what we mean: we demand that state schools accept children of all races, but those who want to open a private school for specific groups should not be prevented from doing so. There is no turning back on the issue of non-discrimination. This was where the negotiations with the UP broke down; they wanted to retain some legalized privileges for the whites, and we didn't.

The official position of the PFP on the question of social and economic relationships has thus been a genuinely liberal one since 1977. And on the question of political relationships their policy has been developed and made more precise. The fundamental concept of federation is more strongly emphasized than before, not least in the party's new name:

We believe that decentralization and the division of powers in a federal state would be the most suitable constitutional dispensation for a future South Africa. But we view the detailed plan we have drawn up as no more than a basis for discussion. The time when whites could present their own blueprints is past. The future constitution, whatever its form, can only be drawn up on the basis of free negotiations between all the people involved.

Hence the PFP has in fact abandoned its previous concept of a qualified franchise; it is not even considered as a possibility for future negotiation.

PFP leaders have no illusions about the immediate prospects of their policy. They accept that for the moment their potential electoral support is limited:

There will be a further scattering of old UP supporters, some to us, some to the NP. Polarization among English speakers will increase, with the bloedsappe either joining the SAP, or the NP or HNP. We shall gain more support, though not significantly. We are not yet an alternative to the government; but we have become a better opposition than before. That in itself is something.

They fear that the internal political situation will deteriorate in the coming years:

The government is tending to become more repressive. It is quite likely that the country will become even more of a police state. The 'Nats' reject all compromises. But the longer we postpone compromising with the blacks, the more radical will become the people with whom we will eventually have to deal. The cost in terms of human life and material destruction will then be greater too.

In their view, the chief role of the opposition lies in presenting clear policy alternatives which

those Nats who are not totally verkramp can adopt when internal unrest and external pressure force them to abandon their present inactivity.

In short, the white opposition has changed considerably in the past three years. The conservative element sticks to its traditional positions, condemning itself to irrelevance. The leaders of the radical opposition forces not represented in parliament find themselves in a far more delicate position than before; their scope for action is increasingly restricted by the authorities on the one hand, and on the other they face growing distrust from the blacks and a declining readiness to co-operate. The liberal opposition in parliament is faced with a similar dilemma, albeit to a lesser degree. It is trying to represent the interests of that part of the white population which rejects the existing system, while at the same time holding a meaningful dialogue with moderate black political forces. On the crucial question of peaceful change its views have become more specific, involving the total abolition of discrimination in social and economic relations, as well as negotiations between all population groups to find a generally acceptable solution in the field of political relations. This programme implies that the new official opposition is a party of peaceful change in the terms of our definition. But it does not have any prospect of initiating peaceful change. As one of its leaders pointed out:

> *The National Party still holds the key to peaceful change, even more so than before.*

Concern in the business community

The business community has expressed its concern at the far-reaching changes of recent years more strongly than almost any other group in white South Africa. Without exception leaders in the economic field who were interviewed again at the end of 1976 or the beginning of 1977[4] expressed their anxiety:

> *The economic climate has deteriorated rapidly. A German banker told me only a fortnight ago that for the moment he has to advise his clients against investing in South Africa.*

Further:

> *In my experience the primary interest of foreign businessmen is not the abolition of apartheid. They are interested only in political and economic stability, not in how this stability is guaranteed.*

These two statements by Afrikaners of different political convictions reflect the general concern which members of the business community feel about their prospects of retaining their share of the market against international competition. They accordingly demand immediate steps to restore political stability and economic confidence. All the respondents—irrespective of their political viewpoints—forcefully accuse the government of apathy:

> *The cause of the disastrous economic situation is the lack of a future-oriented policy. The government must immediately take the necessary steps to initiate long-overdue changes.*

The changes which the business community demand[5] are not radical.

[4] Of the 59 leading personalities in the economic sector interviewed in 1974, 16 were interviewed again in 1976/77, including three trade-unionists.

[5] To rebut the accusation that people simply blame the politicians without being prepared to do anything themselves, leading businessmen of all political persuasions agreed at a conference in December 1976 to set up a 'Foundation for Urban Development'. The first major project this Foundation will undertake is the electrification of Soweto.

However, work has been very slow in getting underway. The *Financial Mail* of 9.9.1977 wrote that work on the project itself had not yet begun. Representatives of the Foundation blame delays on the part of the public authorities and deliberate delaying tactics on the part of the administration.

They are asking for hardly more than in 1974. But the demands have become more urgent and impatient.

This is particularly clear in the economic sphere. No one has a kind word for job reservation or restrictions on non-white advancement:

> *The best way of changing the South African economy is by creating a liberal capitalist society. This implies not only equal pay for equal work, but the complete abolition of job reservation and other forms of discrimination.*

But despite all the lip-service paid to a free enterprise system, they have as many reservations as in 1974 about the freedom to organize trade-unions and to bargain wages:

> *I simply don't understand the issue of trade-unions. In South Africa the black trade-unions don't have any power because most black workers can be replaced at any time. As far as I am concerned the existing works- and liaison-committees in the individual firms are quite adequate. The blacks would exploit trade-union recognition for other purposes, like political pressure.*

The business community was far more ready in 1976 than in 1974 to fight the existing petty apartheid regulations. About half of the respondents, as against 12 per cent in 1974, would even accept the abolition of the Group Areas Act or a repeal of the Mixed Marriages Act. But they still make no secret of their hope that legal apartheid would be replaced by 'financial apartheid':

> *Petty apartheid must be abolished completely, not excluding the schools and residential areas. This would hardly change the present situation; for even within white society the different classes don't mix. Similarly, if the prohibitions were lifted only a few members of the black middle and upper class would move into white areas.*

Finally, the economic leaders are also impatient with the political situation:

> *As far as politics is concerned, after the events of recent years there is hardly anyone who wants to maintain the status quo.*

However, two political perspectives are excluded at the outset: integration,

> *which would lead to absolute chaos;*

and a radical partition of the country

> *because in that situation the non-whites would hardly be able to feed themselves on their own.*

By contrast, they all accept that it is politically possible, indeed

194

urgently necessary, to extend full civil rights to Indians and coloureds immediately. But a great deal of confusion still surrounds the future status of the urban blacks. It is accepted that they are permanent residents of the cities. But at the same time only a small minority accept their integration into white society. Most respondents hope that the problem can be circumvented; for example, that an active and generous homeland policy would be attractive to the blacks and perhaps facilitate a solution to the problem at some later time:

> *If the black-white ratio could be drastically reduced by a consistent application of the homelands policy, it might be possible to integrate the urban blacks on the same pattern as the coloureds and the Indians.*

It is interesting that since 1974 the concept of the homelands has gained ground, even among business leaders who support the opposition. It does not necessarily exclude the different concept of a qualified franchise for educated and propertied blacks. Many business leaders believe that the successful creation of consolidated bantustans would give a policy of partial integration or federation a much greater chance of success. They are convinced that economic improvement will necessarily lead the blacks to demand a political say. As the blacks are not only an indispensable source of labour but also invaluable consumers, the question of their future political status demands urgent consideration:

> *What we need is a responsible and able black middle class. Our economy is so strong that we can meet most of the blacks' aspirations. They should have some say in political matters, if not through integration then by means of separate voters' rolls.*

The governing party: the slow progress of pragmatism

Neither black unrest nor the changing international scene has had much impact on the NP politicians, still less let them question the basic correctness of their policy. But it would be wrong to conclude that the attitudes of these politicians to peaceful change have not altered at all. We proved above that the idea of a monolithic NP is a myth; the idea that they are totally unable to change is similarly false. If one compares the surveys of 1977 with those of 1974 one does notice shifts in the opinions of the leaders and their governing party. The shifts are not dramatic, but taken together they show that the 'pragmatic' position has gained some ground. There have been small changes in basic orientation, and some adaptation to changing circumstances. The pragmatists have made their gains at the expense of the doctrinaire verkrampte wing of the party.

In 1977 more than 60 per cent of the respondents approved the gradual abolition of petty apartheid, compared to 45 per cent in 1974. And approximately one-tenth now take the view that petty apartheid could and should be abolished immediately.

In 1974 an MP declared:

I support segregation in all spheres of life. I even think it is right to segregate parks. Only by segregation can we avoid friction.

In 1977 the same MP was of this opinion:

Petty apartheid should disappear, with the exception of segregated schools, residential areas, and public transport. Serious friction is especially a possibility in public transport. But even in respect of these remaining areas of segregation it should be possible to come to some agreement with the blacks.

In 1974 almost half of the respondents felt that job reservation should be maintained under all circumstances; in 1977 only 10 per cent still shared this view. And conversely, the group in favour of totally abolishing job reservation rose from 20 per cent to 50 per cent.

In 1974 one parliamentarian took this view:

It is wise to keep the different racial groups apart, even economically. Under no circumstances should there be any direct contact.

In 1977 the same politician said:

Job reservation can be abolished. The party will do this gradually, not spectacularly. But we need more blacks in the economy, even if some whites run away.

In 1974 about half the respondents felt that the wage-gap should be closed; in 1977 the figure was over 80 per cent.

Scepticism about the official bantustan policy has increased. One-quarter of the respondents believed that the division of land laid down in the 1936 Act could not be adhered to.

In 1974 an MP declared:

We are not prepared to give up industrial areas or cities under any circumstances. It will never go that far. The 1936 Act is the limit on concessions.

In 1977 he said:

Even if there is an outcry, the homelands must be consolidated so as to create viable territories.

In 1974 one-quarter of the NP politicians thought that black migrant labourers should be sent back to the homelands; in 1977 none supported this view. In 1974 only one-tenth of the respondents were prepared to grant a degree of self-administration to urban blacks; in 1977 the proportion had increased to 40 per cent:

196

The civil rights of blacks in the cities must be given more actual content. Homeland governments must have a say as well. Urban blacks should be given political rights over their communal affairs, particularly education.

It is evident that the Soweto events have made their mark.

Interestingly, support for the political integration of the coloureds into the white system fell from one-quarter of respondents to one-fifth. Instead of integration, there was a great deal of support for a constitutional dispensation which would include the coloureds and the Indians in a kind of umbrella body; and shortly after the survey had been completed the new constitutional proposals were published.

As a whole, therefore, there has been a clear trend towards undertaking pragmatic modifications and further developments of the policy, while in principle sticking to the concept of 'separate development':

The party is now aware that change must come, come quickly, and be clearly defined. Although the verkrampte wing is still fairly strong, it doesn't dare speak as openly as before.

By 1977 NP politicians were even more certain than in 1974 that the majority of voters would follow them. But the number who felt that the voters were 'still a long way behind developments within the party' had decreased. By contrast, one-tenth of the respondents felt for the first time that voters were 'ahead of the party' on the question of 'necessary changes':

We must change or die. We can no longer get away with some pretence or other.

These words were not spoken by a verligte but by one of the pragmatists. Perhaps the most important change in the NP is the new internal debate about what is 'pretence' and what is 'change':

A wide-open discussion on our particular political re-orientation has begun in the NP.

For the moment, the fact that this debate is taking place at all is more important than its outcome. For the first time in many years the party and the government have admitted that they do not have a definitive and complete doctrine answering all problems which may arise. This implies that the principle of the unalterability of NP politics—held high for so many decades—has implicitly been abandoned.

Polarization and agreement in the inner circle

Such problems with doctrine as may arise are, admittedly, expressed

197

more clearly by members of the inner circle of the party and Cabinet than in the parliamentary caucus or party organs. So it is within the inner circle that the changes between 1974 and 1977 are most noticeable.

There has been a further polarization of views since 1974. At first sight it seems unlikely that such divergent opinions can be held within the same party and government. However, the polarization is offset by the will of all concerned to hold the party and the inner leadership together. In cases of doubt all differences of opinion are subordinated to the unity of the volk and the party; for,

> *without unity the basis of our power would vanish. Unity is the supreme commandment for Afrikaners—otherwise we endanger our self-determination. So everyone has to make sacrifices, whether he likes it or not. Naturally, this means that our progress is slow, even when more haste would be appropriate.*

These are the words of one of the leading verligte Ministers. They imply that speculations about a split in the inner circle are unrealistic. The contrasting positions on individual questions which will be discussed below should therefore be understood as standpoints of debate within the inner circle and the party. The actual policy is then the outcome of complex compromises.

The conservative wing of the inner circle is the bastion of traditional opinion. It doesn't see any reason to change its views:

> *We have been here for three hundred years and we shall remain here for even longer. We have been right for three hundred years and the future will show that we are still right.*

The attitudes of this wing are shaped more than ever before by the belief that only strength and an uncompromising position will guarantee the survival of the Afrikaner volk:

> *We live in Africa. Africa has remained dark and uncivilized. One must deal properly with these people, otherwise they will overrun us. South Africa is white, and we shall keep it that way.*

Fundamental changes in social relations between the races are accordingly still rejected:

> *Of course we must get rid of unnecessary discrimination based on colour and race. For example, racial segregation in theatres is unnecessary. But we are in favour of any discrimination which is necessary to protect our volk from others who do not have the same traditions.*

This includes

> *constitutional guarantees for the identity of the whites, and the prevention of any social situation which could undermine white*

198

identity. Families, residential areas, schools, and churches will not be integrated.

These segregatory measures are necessary because there are people in South Africa who are not prepared to accept their responsibility—they are not the people of my volk. But because they are there, the state has to assume responsibility for them.

Nor is the right wing of the inner circle prepared to make any concessions in respect of political relations:

Consolidation beyond the boundaries laid down in 1936? Forget it. We hardly have enough money to implement the promised consolidation. Everything else is academic gossip.

What gives the non-whites the right to rule the whole of South Africa? We have as much right as they. Why doesn't Holland want to integrate with Germany, then? Because of historical reasons. So why aren't these historical reasons valid here? The Xhosas will never accept a state in which the Zulus are in the majority. The peoples of South Africa all differ: in language, history, and customs.

In 1977, the representatives of the pragmatic centre group in the inner circle expressed themselves far more cautiously than three years before. Certain modifications of the current policy are conceivable to them. But they don't take a stand and prefer to keep in the background.

On the question of economic relations they think that measures to improve the lot of the black population are necessary

to reduce revolutionary potential.

They still take a very cautious stand on the question of job reservation:

We have to take the interests of our workers into account, especially during the current recession.

The wage-gap should be reduced, but

high wages must be tied to performance and higher productivity.

Although they do not oppose changes in social relations on principle, they are extremely reticent for party-political reasons:

If the segregation laws had never been passed we would probably be better off. But they do exist now, and are the symbol of white identity. The voters would certainly not accept their abolition yet, and we are therefore still holding back. It will take a lot of courage to abolish petty apartheid.

A leading Cabinet Minister was extraordinarily ambivalent on the question of political relations. To begin with, he declared:

We still maintain that the homelands offer the political solution.

But he was prepared to make this concession:

199

We don't—for the present—want to include urban blacks in the structure of Cabinet committees.

In other words, the pragmatists have adopted National Party orthodoxy for the present, but in contrast to the conservative wing do not exclude further changes in the future.

The liberal wing of the inner circle, by contrast, would like to see such changes introduced as soon as possible. Their policies have gained in breadth and detail since 1974. But even the representatives of this group hardly spoke with enthusiasm about what they take to be the correct policy:

My heart and my emotions have been shaped by my background and education. So I should like to see South Africa remain as it is. But someone in my position must not only have a heart, but must more importantly be able to use his head. And my head tells me that change must come.

The liberal wing of the inner circle places great emphasis on economic relations. The economic development of the homelands should be advanced far more quickly:

Unfortunately, in this area the spirit of Verwoerd still reigns. People are afraid of miniature Japans, which would take advantage of their cheap labour to produce goods more cheaply. If we are not prepared to accept such possibilities, the homeland policy is nonsense.

The problem of the urban blacks is also seen in the first instance as an economic one:

We have to offer the blacks a meaningful existence, and an improved quality of life. This is primarily a socio-economic problem, not a problem of race relations. It is the problem of the urban masses during an industrial revolution. Soweto is not all that different from the workers' quarters in Europe during the industrialisation there. If all the inhabitants of Soweto were white the problem would be the same. In that case we probably already have had a revolution. The most important changes are those needed in the economic field. Naturally man doesn't live by bread alone, but he does live on bread to begin with.

Such considerations have encouraged the verligte wing to support not only the abolition of discrimination in economic relations, but also a drastic improvement in the infrastructure and a proper social policy:

England avoided a revolution by creating a welfare state. We must learn from that experience.

On the issue of social relations between the race groups, the verligte group would like to see enforced segregation abandoned as soon as possible:

Most of these methods can disappear without any song and dance. There should not be any problem in allowing private schools to admit all races. The Immorality Act and the Mixed Marriages Act are unnecessary and should be abolished. They are particularly humiliating to the non-whites and serve no political purpose.

In respect of political relations, the leading verligtes would like to see a number of measures, which would amount to

a completely modified form of the policy of separate development.

The political goal of this group remains

the preservation of cultural and national identity, and the maintenance of political control over our own destiny.

But they are convinced that this goal has not been taken seriously so far, nor pursued by the appropriate means:

We must face the facts. In this country there are different ethnic groups, and we have made their segregation the cornerstone of our policy. But for twenty-five years separate development and multinationalism were little more than slogans. Only in recent years has anything really been done about 'development'. Separate development will fail as long as it is seen as discrimination and we cannot offer a better quality of life. Nor can we simply continue to overlook the fact that separation can succeed so far but no further. It is simply not true to say that South Africa will no longer be black when the homelands become independent. The urban blacks are here, and they won't simply vanish if we don't think of them.

These were the words of a leading Cabinet Minister. For the verligtes, evidently, there are two aspects of the problem: on the one hand, to devise a practicable and credible homeland policy; and on the other hand, to find a new way of co-existence with the urban blacks which, although recognizing the existence of ethnic groups, doesn't aim at segregation at all costs.

The homeland policy should

be radically changed in geopolitical terms. We must get used to the idea that if we try to hold on to everything, we shall lose everything. It is quite obvious that a creation like Bophuthatswana does not make sense in its present form. Instead of founding a new capital in the bush, Mafeking should have been the capital. The homelands policy only makes sense if these countries are governable political units.

In the view of this group, radical consolidation must take place quickly. So it cannot be done by the slow and expensive procedure of buying up land:

The practice of obligatory resettlement must be stopped. Whoever

201

wants to sell up and settle elsewhere must do so at his own cost; otherwise he can remain as a citizen of the homeland. Naturally, we should have to guarantee these people financially against nationalization. Only under such conditions will radical consolidation be possible.

A consistent homeland policy of this kind is seen as meeting a precondition for a new deal with the urban blacks:

We must admit that there will always be blacks in the urban areas. Soweto simply cannot be included in a homeland solution. The orthodox view, that blacks should never be given political rights in the white areas, has become insupportable.

The leading verligtes thus accept that the urban blacks should be given political rights. But their ideas vary on what these rights would involve.

As a minimum, the blacks should be given

effective political autonomy in their local urban areas. In doing this, we have to take certain risks, and also accept political decisions which we don't like—as in the homeland policy, when for example the Transkei changed its policy on the medium of instruction in schools in a way which we did not like. [6] *Our policy can be taken seriously only if we genuinely undertake to transfer power.*

Local autonomy of this kind is as far as some verligtes in the inner circle are prepared to go; however others go further and consider black 'city states' with full and sovereign independence, which could be linked to the remainder of the Republic in some form of confederation.

But for the most important representatives of the liberal wing, local autonomy is only a temporary measure. In the last instance, they regard it necessary

to include the blacks in our political system within the framework of a pluralistic solution.

In terms of this policy the Cabinet Council in the new constitutional proposals should include the urban blacks as a fourth group, together with the whites, the coloureds, and the Indians. This would fully incorporate the urban blacks into the political system. This system would, however, no longer correspond to the unitary Westminster model, but to a plural model based on ethnic groups. This policy thus preserves the basic group-orientation of the Nationalists but allows for all groups to

[6] In Bantu Education the government had implemented the principle of 'mother-tongue instruction': in primary schools the medium of instruction was to be the respective mother-tongue. One of the first measures of the Transkei Government upon achieving internal autonomy—i.e. long before the so-called 'independence'—was to restore English as the medium of instruction. Cf. Th. Hanf *et al*, 'Education—An Obstacle to Development?', *Comparative Education Review*, 19:1 (1975), pp. 68–88.

participate in the exercise of power—once the numerical superiority of the blacks in 'white' South Africa has been substantially reduced by granting independence to considerably enlarged homelands:

Segregation would then be replaced by constitutionally organised co-operation. Discrimination would no longer exist. But each group would retain its cultural and also its political identity.

Thus, within the inner circle those open to change hold views on the economic, social, and political relations between the races that are radically different from the views of those who resist change. But the two groups are still united by the basic conviction that society and state in South Africa must be shaped by the principle that ethnic group identity be preserved. In the final analysis, their motive is their identification with the Afrikaner volk, the volk which they keep, and want to keep, in power.

They differ on how best to attain this goal. In recent years the difference has widened. Whereas one group clings to the orthodox teachings of the Verwoerd era—and a centre group vacillates and is prepared to grant only marginal changes—the verligte group aspires to a fundamental renewal of the policy of preserving ethnic group identity, and aims to eradicate the most blatant aspects of discrimination. The dream of the liberal opposition, a multiracial society in a unitary state, is as foreign to leading verligtes as it is unacceptable to leading verkramptes. This rejection of a multiracial society in a unitary state is basically why the entire Afrikaner leadership unanimously rejects what it perceives as the Western states' new policy toward South Africa. Leading South African politicians have since 1977 adopted an emotional and pronounced anti-Western, and particularly anti-American, stance. This may be regarded as the most spectacular change in South African politics in recent years. The reaction reached its peak in the campaign leading up to the parliamentary elections on 30 November 1977; the NP campaigned primarily against the policy of the Western states, and only then against the opposition, whom it claimed was their agent.

Without doubt an election campaign about 'patriotism' was an excellent way of striking at the already divided opposition. But the anti-Western stance of the South African government was not only an effective instrument in internal politics. It should also be seen as an expression of a deep-rooted fear that the basic political orientation of the NP may be threatened from without. Politicians oriented towards the status quo, as well as those open to change, were equally determined to reject the United States' demand for majority rule in South Africa on the basis of one man one vote. The conservative wing of the inner circle framed its rejection in highly emotional terms:

White South Africa is a fact. The West cannot simply sweep us away. People want us to sacrifice ourselves and simply give up. But we will stick to our right of self-determination, just as we did previously when we fought against the British. We were far weaker seventy years ago. Nevertheless we fought well in the two Wars of Independence, and in both World Wars. And now that the fight is about our own country, we will fight much more fiercely. South Africa will win through. The Western countries are paralysed; they argue among themselves and feel inferior towards Russia. The West will have to face up to historic facts.

A leading pragmatist was as emotional:

Unfortunately, the Western world is ruled at the moment by a bunch of cowards—I have never seen so many cowards in my life. So we cannot afford to resist the will of our people simply to please the West. For example, we have achieved quite a lot in the field of sport, but no-one in the West has publicly acknowledged this. Had this been forthcoming it would have been far easier for me to go to my voters and point out to them that the policy had been a success. The world applies double standards. Since Carter took over, American policy has turned upside down. He wants to apply divine standards here on earth. Reality will bring him to reason, even if it takes a little while.

The leaders of the verligtes agree that Western demands for a multi-racial unitary state are quite out of place. They also fear that their own prospects in the party may be diminished by the reaction to the policies of the West:

The new American policy poses great dangers for verligte politics in South Africa. Ambassador Young's demands for majority rule, and Mondale's declaration that this means 'one man one vote' has produced an unmistakable shift to the right in the parliamentary caucus. We have always argued that discrimination must disappear if the West is to accept our policy. Now we are told that the West is demanding not only the abolition of discrimination but our un-conditional surrender—which is what 'one man one vote' amounts to. So the verkramptes can now easily say that it is pointless to make any concessions at all if they will not satisfy the West in any case.

This explains precisely why some leading verligtes—as well as the leaders of the parliamentary opposition, for similar reasons—have criticized the West's policy towards South Africa in the strongest terms. They do this as much because they need to preserve their credibility in their own ranks as because they believe the policy is wrong.

Do the leaders of the verligtes think their views have any prospects within the NP?

Our people will accept all necessary steps if they are explained to them in enough detail; this applies to the most convinced racists. For our policy offers the only real prospect for the survival of our people.

A Cabinet Minister shares this opinion. He added:

We are still following each other nose to tail, like donkeys. We must break this circle at all costs.

This analysis has on the whole confirmed our introductory outline of the changes of opinion among the white political leadership groups: polarization has increased. Whereas the opposition has adopted a clear liberal stance that makes their chance of success even slimmer than before, and politically influential businessmen watch the worsening economic situation with increasing concern, the government party still stands its ground—although pragmatism has gained ground at the expense of doctrinaire attitudes, thereby increasing the likelihood of modifications in the official policy. In the leadership circles of the NP and the state there is a growing division between the supporters of orthodox apartheid on the one hand, and on the other the representatives of a new conception of government based on ethnic groups, in which latent discrimination has no place and the position of the whites and especially the Afrikaners will be effectively guaranteed.

In other words, while there have been no fundamental changes, there are signs that at least part of the power-élite has been set to thinking.

CHAPTER 8

Between Concessions and Control: Opinions and Attitudes of White Voters, 1974–1977

South Africa's white voters are afraid. They are also prepared to fight for their existence. The great majority are both afraid and ready to fight. Two-thirds of the white voting population think there will be a black uprising in the future. They also fear that their children will not be as well off as they themselves are now. More than three-quarters of them expect that the position of the whites will be seriously threatened. But three-quarters are also determined to resist all external and internal threats, whatever the risk involved.

Their fear on the one hand, and readiness to fight on the other, are loosely and partly inconsistently linked with their attitudes towards peaceful change. The white voters vacillate between an occasionally pronounced readiness to make concessions, and a strong desire to control the nature and pace of change.

The following sections examine these matters more closely: firstly, the fears of the white voters; secondly, their readiness to fight; thirdly, their openness to change in 1974; fourthly, changes in this openness between 1974 and 1977; and finally, whether or not South African politicians have correctly assessed their constituents' openness to change.

1. *The voters' fear of the future*

It is unusual for a white South African to admit he is afraid. Social esteem more often attaches to expressions of confidence and self-assurance. Official speeches always emphasize how calm and secure South Africa is, especially by comparison with other African states, or even with the United States and Great Britain, where racial unrest continually flares up. But the observer may be suspicious of the thunderous applause which such statements usually receive. Does a person who really feels secure and unthreatened constantly seek this kind of assurance? Is this not perhaps a mechanism of group reassurance in the face of threats?

Our empirical findings confirm this suspicion. Respondents overwhelmingly agree with statements which express a socially desirable optimism. Thus, 89 per cent of respondents agreed with this statement:

No matter what the future holds, I feel we will manage.

And 85 per cent affirmed:

I can look forward to my future with confidence.

When the same persons in the same year were asked other questions on fear, they reacted completely differently. Eighty-one per cent held this view:

It seems that threats to our position will become serious in the future.

However, this answer could be interpreted to mean that while the respondents do in fact foresee threats, they believe they can handle them. However, the analysis of answers to questions which referred directly and specifically to fear present a quite different picture.

I feel uncertain and fearful about my future. —37% agreed.
I am afraid that our children might never enjoy as high a standard of living as we have now. —67% agreed.
The chances are that eventually there will be a Black uprising in South Africa. —65% agreed.

The answers to these questions are closely related. So they have been subsumed in an index of 'fear about the future'. Persons who answered all three questions in the negative are regarded as having 'no fear'; whereas one, two, and three answers in the affirmative signify 'slight', 'pronounced', and 'very strong' fear respectively.

In 1974, the fear of 27 per cent of the respondents was 'pronounced', and of 18 per cent 'very strong'.

Clearly, a considerable number of those who agreed with statements expressing the socially desirable confidence simultaneously display clear indications of fear. We may illustrate this with a slightly exaggerated analogy: confidence about the future is like whistling in the dark to keep one's courage up.

Our follow-up survey confirmed this conclusion (see Table 8.1).

These figures allow us to trace the impact of the Soweto demonstrations. In 1976, fear increases substantially, and in 1977 it again decreases a little. But even after the back-swing of the pendulum, the percentage of white South Africans displaying strong fear is much higher than in 1974, and the percentage of those who show no fear has continued to decrease, even in 1977.

How are these figures distributed among the white population groups? In 1974, the Afrikaners were somewhat less afraid than the English-speaking group; by 1977 the position was reversed: 59 per cent of the Afrikaners expressed pronounced or very strong fear, as against only 53 per cent of the English speakers. It is worth noting that the differences between the two groups are smaller on this issue than in respect of most other attitudes; Afrikaans- and English-speaking South Africans are most alike in their shared apprehensions.

Table 8.1

	June 1974	June 1976	Oct. 1976	July 1977
	%	%	%	%
No fear	25	22	18	17
Slight fear	30	28	22	26
Pronounced fear	27	26	29	30
Very strong fear	18	23	31	27

In 1974 there were marked differences by party affiliation, but by 1977 these had almost disappeared. Supporters of the National Party were much less frightened than supporters of the opposition in 1974. But they caught up quickly: in 1974, 43 per cent of the NP supporters showed pronounced or very strong fear, whereas in 1977 the figure had reached already 57 per cent.

All the interviews revealed a close relationship between the level of education and the degree of fear: the less educated, the more fearful.

The greatest differences were by province. Although fear increased over the period in all four provinces, the interviews proved this effect to be strongest in the Transvaal and Natal, whereas in the Cape and in the Orange Free State it was noticeably weaker. For the Transvaal and Natal include very large numbers of blacks, who are also conspicuous in the densely populated conurbations. They are also the two provinces which border on the states to the north.

These differences by province reveal that the fears of white South Africans are based on what they perceive to be very real dangers.

What are these perceived dangers? They are afraid, as has been pointed out, of a black uprising in the future. But above all they are afraid of having to live under black rule. We asked the following question:

What would life be like for Whites in some country or another where Bantu have the main say in government? Here is a list of words. Please read through this list quickly and pick any number of words: Words you feel *could fit life in a country under a mainly Bantu government* in the long run.[1]

Words with positive connotations were selected by hardly any English-speaking or Afrikaans respondents; and their frequency decreased from 1974 to 1977. The following sets of figures are percentage data from the surveys conducted in June 1974, 1976 and 1977 respectively. Twenty-two per cent—11 per cent—6 per cent of the English-speaking respondents and 9 per cent—6 per cent—2 per cent of the Afrikaners expect black government to be constitutional. Sixteen per cent—17 per cent—12 per cent and 10 per cent—5 per cent—7 per cent, respectively are hopeful about co-operation between the different race groups. Seventeen per cent—18 per cent—14 per cent and 6 per cent—5 per cent—5 per cent respectively expect such a state. And between 4 per cent and 7 per cent of both language groups choose the terms 'fair', 'peaceful', 'safe' and 'prosperous'. The net result is clear: white South Africans expect very little good of a state governed by blacks.

A large majority of the white voters regard the future of such a country as 'uncertain'. Between 70 per cent and 80 per cent of both language groups share this view. Almost half (44 per cent—46 per cent—42 per cent) of the English-speaking voters and a majority (57 per cent—67 per cent—62 per cent) of Afrikaners believe that life would be 'chaotic'. And the idea of a state governed by blacks is 'terrifying' for one-third of the English speakers, and for one-half of the Afrikaners.

At the same time, fears of a black state going communist have diminished: 69 per cent—64 per cent—52 per cent among the Afrikaners, 53 per cent—47 per cent—29 per cent among the English speakers. Similarly, fears that a state governed by blacks would be 'undemocratic' have also decreased: from one-half to just less than one-third among Afrikaners and from one-third to one-quarter among the English speakers.

These findings are necessarily somewhat inconsistent in their substance; for the procedure of choosing from a list of emotive words taps the respondents' feelings on an issue rather than their opinions. However, they do provide an illuminating pattern of hopes and fears.

To summarize, the majority of white South Africans are quite fearful for their future: afraid that they might lose power, and afraid of what might happen then.

2. *The voters' readiness to fight*

As much as it is 'socially undesirable' to admit fear in South Africa, it is

[1] Vide Q. 17 in Appendix 1. Concepts with positive connotations were, e.g.: prosperous, peaceful, safe future, hopeful; those with negative connotations: uncertain, chaotic, terrifying, communistic, undemocratic, etc.

'socially desirable' to be prepared to fight. The Afrikaner government places a premium on militant patriotism. In the same way, representatives of the opposition—many of them highly decorated veterans of the Second World War—do not want to let themselves be outdone in patriotic matters. In parliament they delight in pointing out that leading members of the National Party were not 'there'. But the opposition constantly warns against rampant militancy, on the argument that the only good war is one that doesn't happen.

What do the voters feel about armed confrontation? In 1977 we asked the following questions:

> *Many people believe these days that South Africa might face war from outside and unrest from inside in the future. Assuming things like that would happen, which of the following opinions come closest to your own views?*
> *—We should fight to maintain South Africa as it is, whatever the risks may be.*
> *—If we cannot maintain things as they are we should rather leave the country.*
> *—We should adapt to the situation and accept urban Blacks in our political system in order to avoid serious confrontation.*

Almost three-quarters of the respondents were in favour of fighting. Only one-fifth opted to avoid conflict by making political concessions. And only 2 per cent considered the possibility of emigrating.

The differences between the language groups are considerable. Only one-tenth of Afrikaners are in favour of adapting, as against a good third among the English speakers.

The differences by party affiliation are even greater. Eighty-five per cent of NP supporters declare that they are ready to fight; the majority of the small group of NP supporters prepared to make concessions are English-speaking.

The supporters of the conservative opposition parties, the NRP and SAP, are divided almost equally between those prepared to fight and those prepared to make concessions; most Afrikaner supporters of the opposition take the former stand.

Three-quarters of the liberal opposition, the PFP, are against fighting regardless of the consequences; they would prefer political adaptation.

The more educated respondents are less prepared to fight. About 70 per cent of the English speakers with eight years' schooling or less are ready to fight, as against only one-third of those with more education. Among university graduates the figure drops to one-fifth. There are similar differences among the Afrikaners: almost 90 per cent of the least-educated are prepared to fight, as against three-quarters of those who have completed their schooling and 64 per cent of university graduates.

But even taking education as the criterion, the preparedness to fight remains essentially an ethnic phenomenon: the least-educated English speakers are hardly more prepared to fight than the best-educated Afrikaners.

An analysis of the respondents by age-group shows this even more clearly. Among the Afrikaners the readiness to fight is almost constant in all age-groups.[2] The English speakers are quite another matter: readiness is highest (59 per cent) among those over 50 years of age, and decreases towards the age-group 16–24, only one-third of whom opt for fighting. English speakers who are liable for military service obviously look forward to an armed confrontation with little enthusiasm.

These cleavages between the ethnic groups are also reflected in the respondents' answers to an open question on the reasons for their choice. The replies of the Afrikaners accord with classical stereotypes. One-quarter gave a version of the Latin 'dulce et decorum est'—it is an honour to die for one's country. Almost one-fifth referred to the Afrikaners' history: 'We should fight for our country as did our forefathers.' And one-tenth felt there was no other way out: 'We have nowhere else to go.'

Seventeen per cent of the English-speaking voters also felt it was honourable to fight. But the most popular choices were, in contrast to the Afrikaners, for negotiation: 'Racial confrontation should be avoided; peace should be preserved at all cost' (14 per cent) and 'South Africa belongs to all of its inhabitants; everyone must be given a fair chance' (12 per cent). In sum, one may say that a readiness to fight is unambiguously and overwhelmingly an attitude of the Afrikaners. It is primarily older English-speaking South Africans who express a readiness to fight—the memories of their own army days probably play a role—whereas the younger generation by and large feel that the prospective war is not their war.

The Afrikaners' attitude is rooted in deep patriotic convictions, a historical consciousness dominated by the idea of struggle, and the belief that there is no alternative. Clearly, even though some of the replies may have been prompted by social desirability our findings reveal that the Afrikaners at least will answer a call to arms.

3. The voters' openness to change in 1974

The Afrikaners are undoubtedly determined to fight, and there is a lot of speculation in South Africa about the possibility of war. But it should not be forgotten that military confrontation is not the first means of settling disputes, but the last. It is a ritual of conflict regulation that one of the parties involved tries to force the other to capitulate by threatening

[2] It lies between 80 and 90 per cent for all age-groups.

to go to extremes. But it is also tacitly accepted that not every controversial issue warrants the taking up of arms. Beneath the threshold of violent confrontation are many possibilities for peaceful conflict settlement. One requirement, however, is that all the parties involved in the conflict are prepared to compromise.

The key to peaceful change in South Africa is thus the white voters' preparedness to make concessions and renounce their privileges. This is all the more important given the fact [3] that the political leaders—who are in a position to initiate change—regard the voters as predominantly conservative and intransigent. Is this assessment right or wrong? Are the voters in fact obstructing change, or is the political leadership using the ostensible orientation towards the status quo of its constituents to justify its own intransigence?

In the 1974 survey 52 per cent of respondents agreed with the following statement:

> *Any concessions to the non-Whites will endanger the Whites' position in the long run.*

And 75 per cent agreed that:

> *We can make many concessions to non-Whites as long as Whites have the main say in politics.*

Evidently, the readiness to make concessions depends on the circumstances in which concessions will be made. About half of the respondents realize that concessions of any kind are irreconcilable with the preservation of white privilege indefinitely. On the other hand, almost three-quarters are ready to make concessions if they do not infringe on the political power of the white minority. These results, however, do not indicate the proportion of voters actually ready to accept fundamental changes—i.e., including political changes—and the proportion not prepared to make any concessions at all. These will be examined in greater detail below. But it is already clear that openness to change varies by ethnic group: 60 per cent of the Afrikaners regard concessions as dangerous, as against only one-third of English-speaking South Africans. The attitude of the Afrikaners is governed by principle, in sharp contrast to the rather pragmatic approach of the English speakers. However, there is remarkably little difference between the opinions of the two language groups in their willingness to make concessions provided that the political status quo is preserved: 79 per cent of English-speaking voters, and 71 per cent of Afrikaners. From this it would seem that the majority of white South Africans regard their unrestricted hold on political power as a *sine qua non*.

Thus, despite their indubitable fighting spirit, the whites in South

[3] Cf. Chapter 7.5.

212

Africa have not generally taken up an 'all or nothing' position. They show varying degrees of willingness to make concessions. In the following subsections we will consider the nature and the extent of the concessions which the whites are willing to make in the economic, social, and political dimensions.[4]

Openness to change in the economic dimension

Race relations in the work-place are characterized by privileges for the whites and disadvantages for the blacks. The latter include job reservation, the subordination of black workers to whites, different payment of the races for the same work, and finally the non-recognition of black trade-unions. The question scale was designed to measure whether whites were more or less open to change in each of these respects.[5] Regarding *job reservation* and *the professional hierarchy* we asked:

Which professional positions should the Blacks in South Africa be able to reach? Should official policy allow that:[6]

	Agree
— *Blacks should be allowed in skilled jobs if White workers' jobs are not threatened by it?*[7]	78%
— *Blacks should be allowed in clerical jobs and to work together with Whites in offices?*	44%
— *Blacks should be allowed in skilled jobs if economically necessary, even if some White workers' jobs are threatened?*	43%
— *Blacks should be allowed in all occupations in White areas?*	41%
— *Blacks should be allowed in jobs of great importance and high prestige, like senior officials in companies?*	40%
— *Blacks should be allowed in jobs where they may be in charge of Whites?*	25%

The percentages illustrate the extent to which whites are prepared to make concessions. More than three-quarters of the respondents are in favour of blacks filling jobs for which no whites can be found. Just under half accept the professional advancement of blacks, and even their

[4] Cf. Chapter 3.2.

[5] In designing the questionnaire hypothetical scales which appeared to be valid were first constructed. These were then statistically tested on the data using factor analysis and other methods such as scalogram analysis. The term 'scale' in the following denotes one-dimensional scales.

[6] For easier reference, the order of the questions in this and all following scales reflects the answer frequency. The actual order of questions adhered to in the interview can be seen from the questionnaire included in the Appendix.

[7] This question has not been included in the scale on openness to change—cf. the scale below. Using the principal-component solution this statement does not correlate with other statements on job reservation, i.e. the respondents understood it not as a step leading to change but as an affirmation of the status quo. Accordingly, it does not reflect openness to change.

213

equal occupational status.[8] A minority of voters, but constituting as many as 25 per cent, are prepared to work under a black superior, an attitude which an outside observer would hardly expect to find in South Africa.

The respondents' openness to change with respect to job reservation can be summarized on a three-part scale:[9]

Oriented towards the status quo	40%
Open to some change	41%
Open to fundamental change	19%

Which people fit into which categories?[10] Those with little education—largely Afrikaners—are mostly in favour of job reservation. Fifty-seven per cent of those with the lowest level of education (5-6 years of schooling) and 52 per cent of the Afrikaners want to preserve the status quo. This attitude is clearly manifested in the policies of the conservative trade-unions, whose members are for the most part Afrikaans-speaking. To relax or abolish job reservation would eliminate the current practice of artificially screening job-applicants; some people would lose their jobs to qualified 'non-whites'. Apart from this equality of occupational status, co-operation with a black colleague or even a black superior is hardly compatible with the conventional 'baasskap' way of thinking, which is prevalent among the lower classes.[11] It is less common—apart from a minority of lower-class members with little education—among English-speaking South Africans. English-speaking upper-middle and upper classes are particularly in favour of abolishing all restrictions on the mobility of labour—an appropriately rational attitude for a group that is chiefly active in private enterprise, and would profit from an absence of restrictions on free competition.

[8] A postal survey conducted by the Cape Town opinion research institute, Mark-en Meningsopnames (Edms) Bpk, in November 1974 produced similar results, which, however, are not directly comparable due to the different question formulation and sample selection: 'non-whites should be trained as skilled workers and receive the same pay as whites'—48 per cent were in agreement.

[9] The scale refers to five questions on job reservation and was constructed as follows: one point was allotted for each positive response. The score indicates a greater or lesser openness to change. For the scale with three grades, one or no positive response was labelled 'oriented towards the status quo'; two to four, 'open to some change'; and five positive answers 'open to fundamental change'.

[10] The Automatic Interaction Detector (AID) was used to investigate the most important explanatory variables for the opinions expressed. (Cf. Chapter 6, n.38 for details.) The evaluation showed that variables such as language group, party preference, level of education, social class, and residential area are consistently the most important explanatory characteristics. The variables age and sex, on the other hand, exercise hardly any significant influence; while membership of a religious denomination generally coincides with membership of a particular language group—particularly in respect of the Afrikaners and members of the Dutch Reformed Church.

[11] This becomes particularly evident when attitudes to job reservation are considered in conjunction with opinions on petty apartheid. The correlation for members of the lower strata is very strong.

What are the views of the supporters of the various political parties? Followers of the NP hold opinions which largely coincide with those of the Afrikaans-speaking group; English-speaking Nationalists, however, are somewhat more open to change. The impact of ethnic group membership on the attitudes of respondents is particularly evident among the 'bloedsappe' of the UP. Approximately half of them support the status quo, a result more in line with that of the NP than for the UP, only 27 per cent of whom are in favour of retaining all restrictions. Finally, the Progressives, whose supporters are drawn mostly from the English-speaking middle and upper classes, are prepared to agree to change across the board. Seventy-six per cent of them would accept a black superior—though possibly with the implicit reservation that the situation would probably never come to that.

Any prospects of equal status and occupational advancement are of small consolation to the blacks, however, if they are not accompanied by material equality, i.e., *equal pay for equal work*. There have been large wage increases since the beginning of the seventies and some equalization. But flagrant differences in wages and salaries still exist. The following questions tried to establish the extent to which the white population at large would agree to closing the wage-gap:

Do you agree or disagree with the following statements:

	Agree
—*Bantu wages should be increased to allow them a higher standard of living.*	81%
—*Bantu wages should be increased to gradually close the wage-gap between Blacks and Whites.*	65%
—*Whites and non-Whites should get equal pay for equal work.*	60%
—*The wage-gap between Blacks and Whites should be closed even if it leads to increased prices.*	37%

A summary scale[12] shows the following:

Oriented towards the status quo	28%
Open to some change	44%
Open to fundamental change	29%

Once again, it is primarily English-speaking and better-educated voters, Progressives, and to some extent UP supporters who plead for the closing of the wage-gap.[13] Followers of the HNP, 36 per cent of NP supporters, and also 32 per cent of the bloedsappe are not prepared to make any concessions. Nevertheless, two-thirds of the Afrikaners and 88

[12] The scale is composed as follows: 0–1 positive answers = oriented towards the status quo; 2–3 = open to some change; 4 = open to fundamental change.

[13] Forty-eight per cent of English speakers, 51 per cent of university graduates, 67 per cent of Progressives and 41 per cent of UP supporters were in favour of closing the wage-gap as soon as possible.

per cent of the English speakers are in favour of a gradual—and in many cases, a more rapid—closing of the wage-gap.

Thus, in general, there seems to be a greater readiness to grant wage increases to the blacks than to open all occupations to them. The empirical findings confirm this surmise: openness to change is almost one-third higher with respect to wages than occupation.[14] The explanation is obvious: in several sectors job reservation is still enforced by 'statutory provisions'. The Afrikaners in particular, who passed and implemented these laws, are reluctant to tinker with them. By contrast, there are far fewer regulations governing wages. The possibility of change is greater here. Moreover, the attitudes involved are common to all societies at times of thorough-going redistribution—the privileged are more willing to accept the betterment of the underprivileged if it is not directly at their expense.

A final indication of openness to economic concessions can be inferred from the answers to the following question:

Blacks should be allowed trade-unions to push for higher wages even if it means White wage increases are slower.

We have already seen that leading politicians and businessmen have many reservations about black trade-unions on account of their unpredictable political effect. Despite this, and despite the fact that the question pointed out the inherent economic disadvantages for whites—especially slower wage increases—34 per cent of the respondents agreed with this statement: 27 per cent of the Afrikaners and 47 per cent of the English speakers. There is thus a general readiness to make concessions in the economic field which should not be under-estimated. While fully a third of the respondents are oriented towards the status quo, approximately 40 per cent are prepared to accept change with reservations and about one-quarter are open to fundamental change.

Openness to change in social relations

'Apartheid is the South African way of life.' Many white South Africans use this claim to rationalize or play down the importance of racial discrimination in everyday life.

How do white voters feel about petty apartheid? Is it as important to them as some leading politicians claim? Do they support it because it is more pleasant and comfortable to ride in reserved railway carriages and live in demarcated residential areas? Or do they want segregation because they fear their identity would be threatened by closer contact with other

---

[14] This is deduced from a correlation of the scale values on job reservation with those on wage adjustment. The exact percentage, which may vary slightly due to the formulation of the question and the scaling, is less important than the fact that there is a difference of attitude on these two issues.

race groups? The voters were given different sets of questions to establish on the one hand the extent of their agreement or disagreement with the official policy of petty apartheid, and on the other their personal readiness—notwithstanding official regulations—to cultivate contact with 'non-whites'.

Do you think official policy should separate the races or not in each of the following:

	For separation
—*lifts in public buildings*	56%
—*churches*	57%
—*buses and trains*	76%
—*intimate friendship between the sexes*	89%
—*residential areas*	91%
—*marriage*	91%

In general, the majority of the voters in 1974 agreed with the existing petty apartheid regulations. But the importance of the individual measures was variously assessed. Separate residential areas and the prohibition of mixed marriages are 'intangible goods', which may not be brought into question. Segregated public transport was favoured by three-quarters of the whites, and segregated lifts[15] and churches by approximately one-half.

Does the openness of whites as individuals to contact with members of other racial groups differ from their attitude towards the official apartheid policy? We obtained our answers by means of a 'social distance scale',[16] presented to the voters in question form. It contains virtually the same questions as on official apartheid policy; but the respondent is only asked to consider persons of the same social class and occupation as himself. Then, to ascertain whether whites distinguish between racial groups in their desire for segregation, we tested for their social distance from black Africans as well as from coloureds.[17] The

[15] In 1974 racial segregation was still widely practised in public lifts.

[16] The Social Distance Scale used here was constructed following E. S. Bogardus. Social Distance Scales have also proved applicable on an intercultural basis; cf. e.g. H. C. Triandis and M. L. Triandis, 'A Cross-Cultural Study of Social Distance', *Psychological Monographs*, 76: 540 (1962). H. Lever, following the earlier studies of MacCrone, transposed the method to the South African context: 'Ethnic Preferences of White Residents in Johannesburg', *loc cit*, p. 157–73; idem, *Ethnic Attitudes of Johannesburg Youth, op cit*.

[17] Two questions (Q. 13a and Q.13b) are reproduced here in combination:

People have different personal feelings about contact with non-whites. Think of Coloureds/Blacks in a similar position in life as yourself. What kind of contact would you personally accept with Coloureds/Blacks? Give me just your personal feeling about each of the following types of contact:

following scale summarizes the results:[18]

Table 8.2

	Official apartheid policy	Social distance from: Blacks	Social distance from: Coloureds
	%	%	%
status quo-oriented/ large distance	59	59	47
open to some change/ middle distance	31	32	41
open to basic change/ small distance	10	9	13

White social distance from the lighter-skinned, predominantly Afrikaans-speaking, better-educated coloureds is notably less than from black Africans. However, this distance increases in sensitive areas of contact. White voters who are more open to contact with coloureds than black Africans in many areas of everyday life are not necessarily so when it comes to residential areas, let alone close personal relationships. In the latter areas the respondents clearly perceive a threat to their identity, especially the Afrikaners, who almost totally reject this kind of contact.[19]

There is a striking correlation between social distance from blacks and basic approval of petty apartheid legislation.[20] We found the following significant differences between those who support and those who oppose petty apartheid. The supporters are primarily oriented towards their party and group. And people from the Transvaal and the Free State who come into daily contact with blacks display a far greater social distance than inhabitants of the Cape.

The attitudes of the whites differ mainly by class and by *level of education*. One-third of the better-educated are in favour of abolishing

	Coloureds yes %	Blacks yes %
—would shake hands with such a Coloured/Black	73	65
—would sit next to such a Coloured/Black on a bus	63	52
—would accept such a Coloured/Black worshipping at my church	59	49
—would accept such a Coloured/Black as my neighbour	28	18
—would invite such a Coloured/Black to dine in my house	27	19
—would dance with such a Coloured/Black at a party	16	12
—would marry such a Coloured/Black if allowed	5	3

[18] The three levels were composed as follows: 0–2 positive responses = large distance; 3–5 = medium distance; 6 and more = small distance.

[19] The Afrikaners' readiness to have contact lies between two and three per cent, that of English speakers, by contrast, around 23 per cent.

[20] The correlation of the scale values on social distance and on attitudes to petty apartheid is $r = .75$.

218

all forms of segregation, as compared with only 2 per cent of the least-educated. Social distance also decreases with rising levels of education. An interesting point in this respect is that whites are far more prepared to cultivate relationships across the colour-bar than to reject apartheid laws. This could quite possibly result from the way in which the questions were posed: those on social distance referred to people of equal social standing, whereas those on apartheid legislation referred to all 'non-whites'. So it is not surprising that class-specific orientations assume greater importance than racial barriers. In other words, a white doctor objects less to contact with a black colleague than with an unqualified black worker, and might well prefer it to contact with a white assistant. This class-specific orientation across racial boundaries does not hold to the same extent for all classes. Members of the white lower classes are far more racialist. As the behaviour of some white trade-unions bears out, these whites are concerned with preserving their privileges, and their attitudes do not reflect the characteristics of a specific class or stratum. Seventy-nine per cent of all white members of the lower classes reject any form of social contact with black South Africans.

The correlation between attitudes and *ethnic affiliation* is even stronger. Seventy-eight per cent of the Afrikaners support a consistent policy of apartheid compared to only 25 per cent of the English speakers. Three per cent of the Afrikaners as opposed to 24 per cent of the English speakers favour its abolition. Social distance varies similarly by ethnic affiliation, as shown in Table 8.3.

Table 8.3

| | Official petty apartheid policy | | Social distance from: | | | |
| | | | Blacks | | Coloureds | |
	Afrik.	Engl.	Afrik.	Engl.	Afrik.	Engl.
	%	%	%	%	%	%
status quo-oriented/ large distance	78	26	78	28	65	17
open to some change/ medium distance	19	51	20	49	30	53
open to basic change/ small distance	3	23	3	23	4	30

The figures confirm that apartheid is, above all, an Afrikaner conception—it is in keeping with Afrikaner thought, it is the Afrikaners' preferred policy, and it is supported chiefly by Afrikaners. Almost 90 per cent of Afrikaners who identify strongly with their own ethnic group are oriented towards the status quo.[21] This is equally true of the supporters

[21] AID indicates group identification to be the most important explanatory variable amongst the Afrikaners.

219

of the HNP and the right wing of the NP. Party loyalty is also a factor: although social distance among educated Afrikaners is only slightly greater than among English-speaking South Africans, more than one-third of the former are in favour of retaining most of the apartheid laws. Thus, Afrikaners who in private are quite prepared to accept contact with other race groups are not prepared to question the official framework of apartheid.

English-speaking South Africans, in keeping with their tradition, are relatively liberal. Many of them do not support social segregation, but they do not completely reject it either. They want integration in many spheres of daily life, but are more reticent when it comes to the private sphere. The supporters of the former UP are typical of this approach: more than half of them are open to some change, a third—predominantly the less-educated and the bloedsappe—support the status quo, and only 10 per cent favour the abolition of all apartheid regulations. Finally, two-thirds of the Progressives call for total abolition.[22]

All in all, one may say that the voters' readiness to abolish petty apartheid is minimal. More than half are in favour of strict maintenance of the status quo, and only one-tenth are in favour of complete abolition. Those who incline towards change are chiefly English-speaking South Africans, supporters of the opposition parties, and the better-educated in all groups. Though the whites were considerably more open to social contact with coloureds than with black Africans, there were few in-dications in 1974 that the majority of voters were ready to abolish the racial barriers between the groups.

Openness to political change

Most ordinary blacks do not want political rights, only better wages and living conditions.

This kind of comment is commonly heard from white South Africans, who, having declared that the blacks lack political interest, then conclude that any form of franchise for the black majority—let alone equitable political representation—is superfluous. Almost 85 per cent of the whites agree with the above statement. It would be a mistake, however, to conclude that only 15 per cent are prepared to grant the blacks any

[22] Attitudes towards the petty apartheid policy differ according to party and language groups as follows (in per cent):

	Afrikaners			English speakers		
	NP	UP	PP	NP	UP	PP
—oriented towards the status quo	80	68	5	48	32	3
—open to some change	19	25	47	45	56	36
—open to fundamental change	2	8	48	7	13	61

political rights. Since political awareness and the expression of political aspirations are known to be dependent on the level of education, whites who are open to change may have been contending that as a matter of fact ordinary blacks prefer economic improvement. Whether this is indeed a matter of fact will have to be examined below.

Public discussion among the whites on the need for political change essentially revolves around the political conceptions already discussed: separate development, integration in a unitary state, and the political participation of all groups in a federal system.

Which of these conceptions do the voters prefer? What kind of political representation for blacks are they ready to accept? Each of the three conceptions was treated by similar procedures to the economic and social dimensions. The voters were presented with a set of questions, and whoever accepted political equality for all South Africans and was prepared to relinquish the political privileges of the white minority is regarded as open to change.[23]

The voters were posed the following set of questions on *separate development:*

The policy of separate development is supposed to lead eventually to the independence of the homelands. Do you agree or disagree with the following statements?

	Agree
—*There should be independent homelands as they are planned at the moment.*	77%
—*We should be prepared to give a great deal of collateral aid to independent homelands to make separate development succeed.*	55%
—*We should be prepared to pay more taxes for homeland development.*	36%
—*There should be independent homelands with more land and some of our industrial areas.*	25%
—*We should be prepared to give up half of South Africa to make separate development succeed.*	15%

The concept of separate development in its current form was approved by a clear three-quarters of all respondents. The figure for Afrikaners was almost 90 per cent. However, the more whites have to sacrifice for the homelands policy to be realized, the more their support decreases. This is particularly evident when it comes to handing over land, resources, industry and the like, in order to make the black areas into economically viable states. Only a small minority agree to the radical division of South Africa into two halves—12 per cent of the Afrikaners and 20 per cent of the English speakers. It is inconceivable, at least for

[23] Cf. Chapter 3.2 on the subject of the normative content of the various political conceptions.

the residents of the Transvaal and the Orange Free State, that they should have to leave the land which their grandparents settled on and repeatedly fought for. They give the lowest support to this proposal.

The differences between the language groups are particularly interesting. Table 8.4 summarizes the results.[24]

Table 8.4

Separate development	Afrikaners	English speakers
	%	%
status quo-oriented	53	44
open to some change	38	40
open to basic change	9	17

It becomes clear that although separate development is a chiefly Afrikaner policy, English-speaking South Africans are not wholly opposed to it. Approximately one-third of them can be expected to support it, although only 26 per cent of them sympathize with the National Party. In other words, a substantial section of opposition supporters at the same time support the government's bantustan policy, notably a majority of the bloedsappe.

Who are the people who favour consolidating the homelands to the extent of radical partition? Among the Afrikaners it is the verligtes: predominantly members of the National Party and some of the former Democratic Party, well-educated and from the upper middle class. They either work in private industry or are self-employed.

English-speaking South Africans are more open to change than the Afrikaners. It is above all the supporters of the Progressive Party—and especially its Afrikaans-speaking supporters—who accept a far-reaching consolidation of the homelands. They obviously assume that the effects of a decade of separate development are largely irreversible, and therefore support a policy of forced consolidation now. An additional consideration may motivate the Progressives, who are the chief supporters of political integration—partition on geeral terms could facilitate the transition to a multiracial political system in the remainder of 'white' South Africa.

The voters were given the following series of questions on the idea of *political integration:*

Some political leaders suggest that non-Whites take part in our politics, not only in the homelands. Do you agree or disagree with the following statements?

[24] The status quo statement (independence within the present boundaries) is not contained in the short scale. The individual scale values are obtained as follows: no positive responses = status quo or complete rejection of separate development; 1–2 positive responses = open to some change; 3–4 = open to fundamental change.

222

	Agree
—No non-White should vote in our White political system.	53%
—Coloureds should be accepted as equal citizens. [25]	42%
—Well-educated non-Whites with decent jobs should vote in our country no matter what their numbers.	34%
—Non-Whites should be allowed to be elected as members of our parliament.	24%
—All Whites and non-Whites should have the right to an equal vote in our country. [26]	13%

These results show that more than half of all white South Africans are not prepared to grant 'non-whites' a place in the white political system. Only 13 per cent support a multiracial system based on the principle of 'one man one vote'. Approximately one-third want a qualified franchise for the blacks.

Who supports political integration and who opposes it?

Table 8.5

Integration/ universal franchise	Afrikaners	English-speakers	Afrikaans NP- UP- PP- supporters			English speaking NP- UP- PP- supporters		
status quo-oriented	63	26	66	44	5	37	13	3
open to some change	31	43	30	43	32	51	54	14
open to basic change	6	31	4	13	63	12	33	83

If separate development is a typically Afrikaner policy, then integration—at least on the basis of a qualified franchise—is the policy of English-speaking South Africa, in the tradition of 'civilized government'. It is therefore not surprising that it meets with considerable opposition from the Afrikaners. Whereas 31 per cent of English-speaking South Africans advocate complete equality for all races in an integrated South Africa, the corresponding figure for Afrikaners is only 6 per cent. Party preference is an important factor in this respect: NP supporters are most opposed to this idea, PP supporters least. The NP supporters who display some readiness to accept change do so primarily in respect of the coloureds and, to a limited extent, the urban blacks, to both of whom they would grant a qualified franchise. Supporters of the former UP take a middle course—as they do on practically every issue—

[25] This statement is listed on the questionnaire as a separate item (Q. 16M) but has been included in the presentation of this question because of its high correlation with the overall franchise scale.

[26] Forty-one per cent of NP supporters potentially open to change are prepared to integrate with the Coloureds, but only a maximum of eight per cent are in favour of integration with black Africans.

223

between the NP and the PP. One must not forget, however, that the majority of UP Afrikaners are bloedsappe, with opinions closer to those of the NP than those of the majority in the UP.

Finally, we established voters' opinions on *the conception of a federal state* with the following statements:

> *Some political leaders want South Africa to become a federal state, i.e., a state with some sharing of power between White and non-White groups and areas. Do you agree or disagree with the following statements?*
>
> | | Agree |
> |---|---|
> | —*There should be a federal state in which non-White groups and areas should not take part at all in nation-wide government decisions but just run their own group affairs under a central White government.* | 70% |
> | —*There should be a federal state in which non-White groups and areas take some part in nation-wide government decisions but the White group has the final say in government.* | 65% |
> | —*There should be a federal state in which power should be shared equally between White and non-White groups and areas so that no one group dominates.* | 21% |

Our familiar spectrum—of support for the status quo, some change, or fundamental change—is again repeated here.[27] White South Africans are prepared to make concessions provided that their political supremacy is not challenged. Only one-fifth would accept genuine power-sharing. Again, it is primarily the Afrikaners who oppose power-sharing: almost 90 per cent of them reject it, as compared to 60 per cent of English speakers.

The opposition of the NP Afrikaners, which is even stronger than that among NP supporters as a whole, is understandable, for power-sharing is diametrically opposed to the policy of separate development. But the strong opposition to it among English-speaking voters is surprising, especially since it was the UP—a predominantly English-speaking party—which adopted 'federation' as its official platform in the early 1970s, and fought the 1974 election campaign on it. Even so, only 30 per cent of its supporters agreed to a federal state with an equal division of power, whereas 60 per cent preferred a federal arrangement which granted the blacs little more than a marginal say in decision-making. However, one has to take account of the UP supporters. Their party never managed to formulate a clear federal policy, so they were never

[27] A scale showing change cannot be constructed for the federation solution. Factor analysis has shown that the first two items, in which lasting political privileges are accorded to the whites ('. . . under a central white government'; or '. . . white group has the final say'), were evidently taken as status quo items. Thus, the questions must be interpreted individually.

sure what federal constitution they wanted for a future South Africa. Given our survey data, it was only logical that the so-called Young Turks in the UP should have coalesced with the Progressives in 1975. Two-thirds of the Progressives, more than any other group of voters, support a federation with genuine power-sharing.[28]

In summary, we may say that *the status quo orientation predominates* in respect of each *of the three political options.* The majority of the Afrikaners and almost half of the English speakers supported the existing political system in 1974, and were not prepared to relinquish their privileges.

Openness to change and the need for control—an overview

How ready to make concessions is the white electorate as a whole? Is it open to peaceful change?

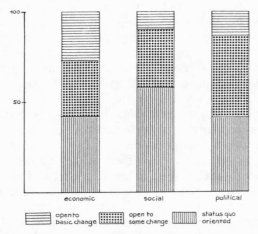

Figure 8.1 summarizes the attitudes of the white voters in 1974 as discussed above.[29] In general, voters are prepared to accept change only

[28] In 1974 the following percentages were in favour of a real division of power on a consociational basis:

	Afrikaners			*English speakers*		
	NP	UP	PP	NP	UP	PP
	10	13	62	14	36	69

[29] A direct comparison of the scale values or percentage values is problematic in so far as questions of a varying degree of 'difficulty' form the basis of the scales. Thus, for example, it may be asked whether the question on interracial marriages was felt by the respondents to be as difficult as the question on 'a black as a superior', or a question on the 'one man one vote' issue or on another form of political equality. A certain normative evaluation doubtless underlies the interpretation of the individual questions. This evaluation refers to the privileges of the ruling minority laid down by law. Nevertheless, by comparing the three areas of investigation it is possible to judge readiness for change, in which the exact percentages are less significant than the tendencies.

225

up to a point. They are conservative on the whole, with about half of the whites preferring the status quo.

Readiness to accept change is strongest in the economic field. About one-quarter of the voters support the full equality of blacks and whites, while approximately 40 per cent want to retain all their privileges—job reservation, higher wages, restrictions on black trade-unions, etc.

In the social field the majority of voters would like to maintain strict segregation within the legally institutionalized framework of apartheid. Less than 10 per cent favour the abolition of all discriminatory privileges.

Similarly, there is little openness to change in the field of politics. Some 10 per cent of the voters agree to equal political representation for the black majority. One-third are willing to grant them some voice in politics, but about one-half are not prepared to make any concessions at all.

There are similarities as well as differences among these attitudes: one may detect both intransigence and flexibility in all three fields. At the one extreme there are the upholders of the status quo, comprising almost half of the South African voting population. At the other extreme there are the 10 per cent of voters who champion the cause of fundamental change and the abolition of all forms of discrimination. Between the two extremes there is a group which supports change to varying degrees. It can be shown by means of correlation and factor analysis that those who are open to change are open to it in all three dimensions: supporters of social change also support economic and political change. (Similarly, supporters of the status quo are opposed to making concessions in any dimension.) Interestingly enough, this is even true of attitudes towards different political policies: supporters of a universal franchise would also accept a genuine sharing of power in a federal state, and even—in two out of three cases—a consistently implemented homelands policy giving the proposed states a real prospect of autonomy. In other words, the small nucleus of those who are truly open to change want change at any price, and support any measure to overcome the status quo. This may be a consequence of their resignation; having accepted that the radical changes they hope for are hardly feasible in South Africa under the present circumstances, they regard any move against white privilege as better than nothing.

Our statistical analysis shows that language-group affiliation and education are the most important variables in shaping socio-political attitudes. The polarization of white South Africa into two political cultures is manifested in different socio-cultural profiles and political structures, and to an equal extent in different sets of attitudes.

According to Figure 8.2, the English-speaking ethnic group is more open to change, more conciliatory, and more pragmatic in all three of the fields investigated. But even in this group, no more than 30 per cent are open to fundamental change in the non-economic dimensions. By comparison, the Afrikaners are consistently more oriented to the status quo, less flexible, and more strongly bound by principle. They support the policies and the laws introduced by the leaders of their ethnic group.

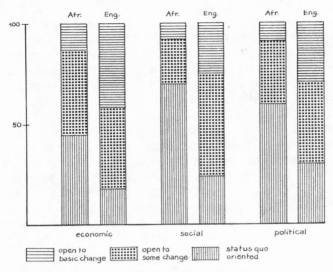

Other socio-cultural and political characteristics help to delineate more clearly the political cultures of those oriented to the status quo and those open to change. Statistically speaking, South Africans who want to preserve the status quo are predominantly Afrikaans, are members of the National Party, and in many cases grew up in rural areas. They usually belong to one of the Dutch Reformed Churches, and are practising Christians. They identify strongly with their ethnic group and their party, and have a fundamentally conservative and ethnocentric view of life. South Africans more open to change tend to be English-speaking, inclined towards the opposition parties, typical city-dwellers, and Anglican, Jewish, Methodist, Catholic or atheist. Their religious activity is minimal or else very intense. They are critical of the government's policies, have overseas contacts, and largely disassociate themselves from a policy of 'law and order'.

Within each ethnic group there are subgroups which cannot be ignored which do not fit into this rough categorization—verligtes or Progressives among the Afrikaners, or arch-conservatives among the English speakers, like the traditionalist British Jingoes or Portuguese and Greek immigrants.

The overriding significance of ethnic group membership is modulated by only one factor: education. Regardless of language and party af-

227

filiation, the better-educated are found to be consistently more liberal and open to change than the less-educated. Verligtes or Progressives are typically highly educated, belong to the upper social strata, and are more tolerant and open-minded. But the ethnic group identity which the Afrikaners value so highly demands a good deal of discipline from members of the group, and thus from the educated as well. So it is the educated Afrikaner who is continually torn between his own desire for change and the influence of the party's commitment to the status quo. Since he is usually subject to strong social constraints by his peers and by the party, he often aligns himself willy-nilly with official policy. It is thus not surprising that an English-speaking South African with more than eight years of schooling is twice as ready to accept change as his Afrikaans-speaking compatriot.

Between the arch-conservative proponents of the status quo and the radical supporters of fundamental change, there is the group of white South Africans who are 'open to some change'. How can this group be more clearly defined? Factor analysis shows that the opinions expressed in the interviews cannot simply be arranged along a continuum from change to status quo. There is a second factor, *'the desire to retain control'*. The replies to the following statements clearly show that voters can be classified by their desire for more or less political control: [30]

	Agree
What we need is strong action to keep order.	89%
We can make concessions to non-Whites as long as Whites have the main say in politics.	75%
The Bantu groups should remain under the control of a White government.	75%
The basis of any policy should be the interests of the ordinary White voter.	74%
Well-educated non-Whites should be allowed to vote in our country, but the Whites should retain control.	50%

The desire to retain control is very strong. But this is not necessarily inconsistent with openness to change. The empirical data show that those who are ready for some change desire it subject to varying degrees of control. They apparently cannot rid themselves of a paternalistic attitude: change yes, but only under white control.

How do the profiles of those open to fundamental change and those in favour of preserving the status quo differ in respect of their orientation towards control? It is remarkable that Afrikaners and English-speaking South Africans hardly differ at all in this regard (Table 8.6)—or at least the contrast is much less marked than in regard to other attitudes.

Only in the small minority which places practically no value on control

[30] Further items expressing the need for control are Q. 11,4; Q. 14a,1; and Q.14a,2.

228

Table 8.6

Desire to retain control[31]	Afrikaners	English speakers
	%	%
Strong control	41	36
Limited control	56	50
No control	3	15

are there differences between the ethnic groups. This minority can be exactly defined: it consists almost entirely of supporters of the Progressive Party, together with the better-educated, i.e., it is comparable to the group which displays a 'genuine openness to change'. All other South Africans, whatever their language or party, want control.

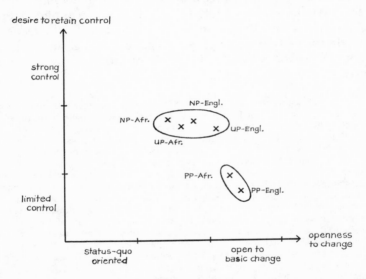

The situation is illustrated in Figure 8.3. The differences between the language and party groups in respect of openness or resistance to change (the horizontal axis) are substantial; in respect of desire to retain control (the vertical axis) the groups take on a similar value. In other words, although the UP English speaker is much less oriented towards the status quo than the NP Afrikaner, he desires much the same degree of political control. Thus, regardless of the degree of change they are prepared to accept, *the majority of white voters do not want to give up the final say in political matters.* The exceptions to this are the mostly well-educated English- and Afrikaans-speaking supporters of the PP, who truly want

[31] The scales were compiled as follows: 4–5 positive responses = strong control; 1–3 positive responses = limited control; and no agreement whatsoever = no control.

229

to introduce fundamental changes and also reject the paternalism of insisting on controlling them.

4. *The attitudes of the voters over time*

Having analysed the voters' attitudes in 1974, we now turn to the period for 1974 to 1977. We pointed out above that white voters' fears increased in this period. Did they also change their political opinions? And if so, what change was involved? How did the whites react to the threat they perceived: rigorously, uncompromisingly, and with increased intransigence? Or has the impression of events on them been such that they have become more thoughtful and open to compromise?

We may get some answers from a comparison of the earlier results with those of the three follow-up surveys of June/July 1976, October/November 1976, and July 1977.[32] The same areas of opinion were examined in all four surveys; however, in the follow-up interviews the comprehensive sets of questions were replaced by single questions which in substance were especially illustrative of attitudes towards peaceful change.

[32] The follow-up interviews also proved very interesting for the authors from the point of view of research into attitudes and prejudice. A single study does without doubt provide important information about the attitudes of the ethnic group questioned—in particular about the distribution of attitudes within the various sub-groups such as, for example, classes, language and age groups, etc. But statements about the extent of the openness to change must remain necessarily subjective due to the authors' assessments—for example when formulating questions or drawing up an index—as long as there is no suitable basis for comparison. Comparative statements can be made, however, by utilizing longitudinal studies with the same interview schemes. Consider in this respect the methodological remarks of Roger Jowell: 'Prejudice is a relative concept. It is of little value to know that 50 per cent of the population is prejudiced, unless we intend to monitor the level over time and, if we do, then it does not really matter whether we call the percentage 50 per cent or 25 per cent as long as we use the same basis for calculating the percentage on the next occasion. So a series of surveys can be invaluable for looking at changes in the population over time, and they enable us to search for patterns which may emerge in response to external stimuli—such as legislation against discrimination, immigration controls, race riots, and so on.' (R. Jowell, 'The Measurement of Prejudice', in Peter Watson (ed.), *Psychology and Race* (Harmondsworth, 1973), p. 48).

It is only possible to gain reliable information about the absolute level of the distribution of attitudes—e.g. that white South Africans have especially great prejudices about blacks—with the help of a *tertium comparationis*, such as comparable surveys in other countries. The authors thus questioned German, Dutch and British people about their attitudes towards 'guest workers', Surinamese, and people of colour (West Indians, Pakistanis, etc.) respectively. For the results cf. Deutsches Institut für Internationale Pädagogische Forschung/Arnold-Bergstraesser-Institut: Projektgruppe Vorurteilsforschung, 'Einstellungen zu Fremdgruppen im internationalen Vergleich, Ergebnisse repräsentativer Befragungen in der Bundesrepublik Deutschland, Großbritannien, den Niederlanden and Südafrika' (Frankfurt/Freiburg 1976, mimeographed manuscript); and R. Hampel and B. Krupp, 'The Cultural and Political Framework of Prejudice in South Africa and Great Britain', *Journal of Social Psychology*, 103 (1977), pp. 193–202.

We first consider opinions on race relations in the *economic and occupational fields*. There is a clear trend.

Whites and non-Whites should get equal pay for equal work.

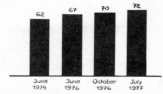

Blacks should be allowed in all occupations in White areas.

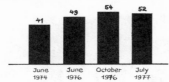

Blacks should be allowed in jobs where Blacks may be in charge of Whites.

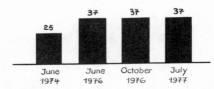

In 1974 the white voters already displayed considerable openness to change in the economic field. This openness continued to increase, even though South Africa was severely affected by the international economic crisis during these years.

By 1977, more than two-thirds of white South Africans accepted the principle of equal pay for equal work. But even more important, a majority of voters also accepted free and equal job opportunities for South Africans of all races. Three-quarters of the English-speaking voters and approximately half of the Afrikaners seem to have realized that traditional group privileges and economic controls are not necessarily beneficial to South African industrial society.

There was a particularly important change of opinion on one point: whites have clearly become more willing to work under a black superior. This is especially noticeable among Afrikaners. In 1977 one-quarter of them were prepared to work under a black 'baas'.[33] This is higher than the percentage of Germans prepared to work under a 'Gastarbeiter'.[34] If

[33] In 1974 it was only 13 per cent.

[34] In Germany in 1976 the comparative figure was only 22 per cent; in South Africa at the same time, however, the figure for all whites was 36 per cent. Cf. DIPF/ABI; Projektgruppe Vorurteilsforschung, *op cit*, p. 2.

one considers the deeply rooted 'master-servant mentality' of the Afrikaners—a mentality internalized over centuries—this result indicates a fundamental change in attitude.[35]

Can similar changes in attitude be established for *social contacts* between blacks and whites? It seems not, when one examines opinions on whether the official policy of racial segregation is necessary. We asked the following question:

In what area do you think official policy should separate the races?

The percentages of respondents in favour of abolishing segregation in the various areas were as follows:

—in lifts in public buildings

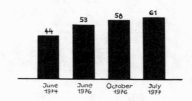

—in churches

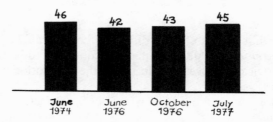

—in public transport

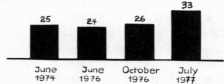

[35] In a survey conducted by the opinion research institute Mark-en-Meningsopnames in October 1976, the result was even higher. Thirty-four per cent of Afrikaners were prepared 'to work under a non-white if he has risen to a superior position as a result of proven ability'. This greater readiness may probably be attributed above all to the different formulation of the question. Firstly, the concept 'non-white' includes coloureds and Indians as well as black Africans, i.e. groups that have already moved up into higher professional positions. Secondly, a rationalization for the professional advancement of the 'non-white superior' is included in the question. Both aspects facilitate a positive response.

—in residential areas

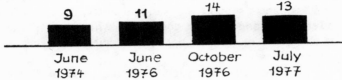

9	11	14	13
June 1974	June 1976	October 1976	July 1977

—in marriage

9	11	14	13
June 1974	June 1976	October 1976	July 1977

All in all, the attitudes of whites towards segregation in the social sphere hardly changed between 1974 and 1977.[36] Afrikaners in particular were as unready to abolish restrictions on interracial social contact in 1977 as they had been in 1974. On the other hand, a verkrampte backlash did not occur;[37] and English-speaking South Africans, who had already been more open to change than the Afrikaners in 1974, were somewhat more liberal in a number of areas. The percentage of those in favour of abolishing apartheid in public transport and in residential areas increased slightly.[38]

Although in general the wish for segregation of the races remained unchanged, there was one notable exception: the demand for racial segregation in lifts steadily diminished. In 1974, when there were still segregated lifts in most public buildings, only 28 per cent of the Afrikaners supported the abolition of this practice. Then, as the 'whites only' signs began to disappear and segregated lifts became a rarity, increasing numbers of white South Africans apparently became accustomed or resigned to the fact; for the demand for official segregation diminished thereafter. By July 1977 fully half of all Afrikaners agreed with abolition. This might be taken as supporting the thesis derived from research into prejudice, viz., that an effect of abolishing discriminatory

[36] Percentage shifts of up to 5 per cent are not regarded as statistically significant changes.

[37] Mark-en-Meningsopnames obtained higher agreement rates in October 1976 both for mixed church attendance (54 per cent) and for the abolition of the 'Mixed Marriages Act' (30 per cent). But here too reservations are in order with regard to the feasibility of comparisons for the reasons given above (n. 35). Nevertheless, here is further evidence that the verkrampte backlash has not set in.

[38] The readiness of English speakers to abolish separation in public transport has risen from 44 to 59 per cent, and from 18 to 25 per cent regarding segregation of residential areas. Amongst the Afrikaners, a change only as regards public transport is discernible, a rise from 11 to 19 per cent.

laws and ordinances is that the attitudes of the population concerned will change. The experience of the United States in enforcing civil rights would also support this thesis.[39] There was thus a spectacular change in attitude, though hardly in a spectacular area.

In general, however, the intransigence in the social dimension stands in sharp contrast to the openness to change in the economic dimension. The pattern of attitudes becomes clearer when other relevant factors such as party preference are taken into account.

We shall deal with *party preference* first. Since more than three-quarters of Afrikaners support the National Party, the opinions of the NP followers correspond almost completely with those of the ethnic group as a whole. Among the opposition parties, however, there are interesting variations.

How did the thoughts of UP supporters change, as the party slowly disintegrated between 1975 and 1977? The comparison shows that they became somewhat more conservative. The increased openness to change which English speakers exhibited in some areas is thus less attributable to the UP supporters than to the Progressives and the group of 'undecided' voters who were rendered politically homeless by the demise of the UP. This trend was particularly evident among UP Afrikaners, who still comprised almost 30 per cent of the UP voters in 1974. By 1976, this group was noticeably more verkramp in respect of all the areas discussed here—to some extent even more so than the NP Afrikaners. It is thus quite conceivable that in this period the UP Afrikaners open to change either followed the 'Young Turks' into the PRP or drifted over to the NP. Lastly, a section of the UP Afrikaners probably chose not to join either party, at least for the while.

Finally, the English-speaking supporters of the National Party are a group of considerable interest. They display typically English pragmatism on the question of social contact between the racial groups. In this respect they are about twice as liberal as their Afrikaans-speaking party colleagues. But their attitude towards economic change is different: after a noticeable liberalization between 1974 and October 1976, their openness to change diminished in the subsequent period.[40] This subgroup's change of opinion, therefore, did not last very long. While prepared to accept change under the impact of dramatic events, they remembered their privileges when the situation calmed down.

The members of the different *educational strata* also revealed varying

[39] Cf. P. D. Sheatsley, 'White Attitudes Towards the Negro', *loc cit*, pp. 217–38.

[40] This applies above all in the economic sphere. This group's openness to change fell by more than 10 per cent between October 1976 and July 1977 on all three questions concerning race-relations in economic life. Whereas, for example, 50 per cent of English-speaking NP supporters were ready to accept a black as a superior in 1976, the figure was only 36 per cent in 1977.

changes in attitude. The voter survey in 1974 showed that the better-educated were about twice as open to change as the less-educated. A comparison between 1974 and 1977 further establishes that those with more education became more liberal, faster than those with less. This is especially true for the Afrikaners: better-educated Afrikaners from the upper middle class underwent a comparatively greater change in attitude over this period than their English-speaking counterparts.[41] This may partly reflect the higher level of education of the English-speaking group as a whole, and the fact that already in 1974 this group was in general more open to change than the Afrikaners. The point of this result is that although the Afrikaner ethnic group as a whole did not change its outlook to any remarkable extent, within the group—particularly among the better-educated—a significant change of opinion did occur.

The question of *political power-sharing* is far more decisive than job reservation or petty apartheid for the South Africa of the future. How do the whites react to the increasingly vociferous calls of the black majority for just political representation in their country? Have the growing political pressures from within and without induced a change in the voters' opinions on the political future of the country? In the follow-up surveys questions were once again put about the three main political conceptions—partition, integration, and federation.

The chances of realizing a policy of separate development were evaluated very differently from before:

There should be independent Bantustans as they are planned at the moment.

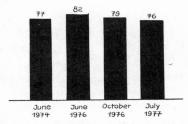

There should be independent Bantustans with more land and some of our industrial areas.

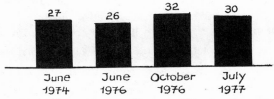

[41] Here, too, the changes have mainly occurred in the economic sphere (blacks as superiors: from 41 to 54 per cent), with only minimal changes taking place in the social area.

We should be prepared to give up half of South Africa to make separate development succeed.

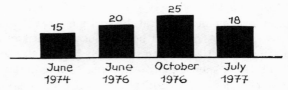

The diagrams show that the overwhelming majority of white South Africans still stand firmly behind the government's policy of separate development. The events of 1976 have perhaps given them some food for thought, but a fundamental change of opinion has not occurred. However, support for the government's programme among English-speaking South Africans is diminishing, a trend which cuts across all party groupings.[42] Corresponding to this development is a growing readiness to grant consolidated, viable homelands to the black population. In 1977 42 per cent of English speakers agreed with this policy;[43] among the Afrikaners only about one-quarter seriously considered the idea of generously consolidating the homelands. The idea received a temporary upsurge of support (28 per cent) in October 1976, shortly after the disturbances, but this soon faded away. The only group which have consistently set as their goal a genuine consolidation, and which remain true to their convictions, are the educated and verligte Afrikaners. They can be found in the NP and, above all, in the Afrikaans-speaking wing of the PFP.[44]

Finally, there has been a particularly noticeable fluctuation of attitude towards the proposal that South Africa be radically divided into two halves. Between April 1974 and October 1976 the proportion agreeing to a radical partition rose to one-quarter of the population. The Afrikaners in particular changed their attitude.[45] And among the Afrikaans-speaking adherents of the UP, the proportion of supporters of a radical partition rose to more than one-third. The basic motive for this dramatic change of opinion seems to have been a fear of lasting disturbances, or even of an eventual, violent upheaval. This assumption is confirmed by the results of the 1977 survey. The level of support for a radical partition dropped significantly once the government had firmly stifled the unrest and shown itself to be master of the situation again. The whites are apparently not prepared to give up half the country without massive,

[42] Within three years support for the official homeland policy fell from 65 per cent to 55 per cent.

[43] In 1974 the figure was only 33 per cent.

[44] In the period from 1974 to 1977 support among university graduates (who make up, however, only 6 per cent of the Afrikaners) for the consolidated homeland concept remained unchanged at approx. 40 per cent.

[45] Their agreement rose from 12 to 24 per cent.

probably violent pressure; the prospects of peaceful change in this direction are thus small.

Attitudes towards the option of *integrating black and white* within a unitary Republic of South Africa were examined by means of the following questions:

No non-White should vote in our White political system.

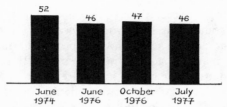

Well-educated non-Whites with decent jobs should vote in our country no matter what their numbers.

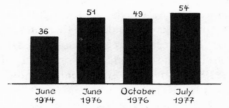

All Whites and non-Whites should have the right to an equal vote in our country.

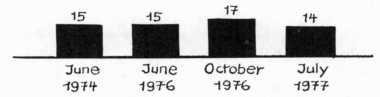

It is immediately apparent that integration on the basis of a universal franchise is as firmly rejected as before. This of course applies to the Afrikaners or the supporters of the National Party, who reject such a solution almost unanimously.[46] But it also applies to the English speakers, among whom fully a quarter consistently oppose 'one man one vote'. The changing circumstances of 1976 have evidently failed to produce a readiness to compromise. This holds true for speakers of both English and Afrikaans, for the less well- and the better-educated. Only among the adherents of the PFP is there much sympathy for a universal franchise (40–50 per cent). However, in view of its small following in the population at large, the PFP constitutes an insignificant minority. No

[46] Only 6–8 per cent of the Afrikaners accepted this concept over the whole period.

237

matter how often the world at large may demand 'one man one vote' for all South Africans in a unitary state, there is not the faintest chance that the white minority will accede peacefully to such an arrangement.

Allied with this uncompromising rejection of total political integration is the insistence of a majority of Afrikaners (although in decreasing numbers with the passage of time) that the blacks be granted no voting rights at all in 'white' South Africa.

But between these two extremes there is a vaguely defined body of opinion open to some forms of *political concession*. It draws distinctions between different degrees and kinds of power-sharing. To reject the formula of 'one man one vote' is not necessarily to reject all forms of political representation for blacks in the Republic of South Africa. In actual fact, white South Africans are giving more and more thought to an 'interim solution'. They would prefer separate development, but at the same time recognize the difficulties involved in implementing the official government policy. On the other hand, they shrink from the thought of full integration, which—in the light of the demographic preponderance of the blacks—would place them in a powerless minority position. Many of them seem to regard a qualified franchise for non-whites as one such 'interim solution'. This proposal gained considerable support between 1974 and 1977, particularly among the Afrikaners, whose support for it rose from 18 per cent to 40 per cent. Since more than two-thirds of the English speakers had originally endorsed the proposal,[47] it may be assumed that it already enjoys majority support among the white South African electorate.

The voters' readiness to make concessions can go beyond a qualified franchise which extends political rights to property-holders or the educated; but for the moment only one non-white population group comes into consideration—the coloureds:

We should consider strengthening our position by accepting Coloureds as equal citizens.

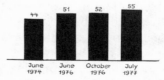

By 1977, 55 per cent of the voters were prepared to accept coloureds as equal citizens. More than two-thirds of the English speakers agreed with this statement over the whole period. More interesting is the change of opinion amongst the Afrikaners, who until very recently resisted all demands for integration, and who as recently as 1956 deprived the coloureds in the Cape of their entrenched political rights. Even if—as the

[47] Agreement rose from 66 per cent to 77 per cent amongst English speakers.

238

reaction to the Erika Theron report showed—the political leadership could not go so far as to reverse this decision, it does seem that the electorate at least is increasingly prepared to approve such a step. Thus, the readiness of the Afrikaners to accept integration of the coloureds rose from 31 per cent in 1974 to 45 per cent in 1977,[48] and to as much as 60 per cent among verligte Afrikaners and those with more education. These findings confirm the trend detected as early as 1975/76 by the South African sociologists C. J. van der Merwe and B. Piek in their study of the attitudes of white voters.[49] In other words the white population is, despite various reservations, inclined to accept the coloureds into the white political system.

Finally, the increasing readiness to make concessions towards political alternatives to official government policy is evident in the growing support for the idea of a consociational federation:

South Africa should become a federal state in which power should be shared equally between White and non-White groups and areas so that no one group dominates.

Twenty-three per cent of the whites agreed in 1974, and 33 per cent in 1977. Again, most support is found in the English-speaking population, irrespective of party affiliation.[50] The change in attitude amongst Afrikaners is noteworthy, especially supporters of the National Party. Their acceptance of the idea rose from 13 per cent to 21 per cent within a three-year period. The largest increase is found among the educated, and in the Cape:[51] perhaps people here see an opportunity to enable the coloureds to enjoy adequate and equitable political representation.

In conclusion, we may state that the fundamental political orientation of voters has remained largely stable. On the whole, no spectacular changes in attitude have occurred in the political sphere. But there has certainly not been a backlash either. On the contrary; between 1974 and 1977 the readiness of the whites to consider a just political representation

[48] The rising trend is confirmed by comparison with a study conducted by L. Schlemmer in Durban in 1971/72. At that time only 28 per cent of voters were prepared to accept a similar statement. Between 1971 and 1977 a steady increase can thus be noted. Cf. L. Schlemmer, *Privilege, Prejudice and Parties, A Study of Patterns of Political Motivation among White Voters in Durban, op cit*, pp. 24ff.

[49] C. J. van der Merwe and B. Piek, *Die Houding van Blanke Kiesers Jeens die Kleurlinge, op cit*, pp. 33ff.

[50] Their support rose from 39 per cent to 55 per cent between 1974 and 1977.

[51] From 14 per cent to 42 per cent.

of the black majority in the Republic has increased. And this readiness is no longer confined to the English-speaking opposition. It is also occurring to an increasing extent among Afrikaners and even within the National Party. At present only a minority are in favour of integrating at least some of the 'non-white' ethnic groups and of a more equitable distribution of political power. But it is a growing minority, and one which the party leadership can no longer afford to ignore. The results speak for themselves: by 1977, 20 per cent favoured the representation of all racial groups according to a principle of equal rights, 40 per cent supported a qualified franchise, and 45 per cent approved granting full civil rights to the coloureds. No-one could have predicted these results in 1974.

5. *Leadership and electorate—a misunderstanding?*

The general consensus of opinion among political leadership groups is that the white electorate is uninformed, deeply conservative, and reluctant to change. On this view, the electorate can only be nudged very gently in the direction of necessary changes if the politicians are not to occasion the wrath of their supporters.[52] Our empirical study has established that the politicians' image of the electorate is largely false. The voters' opinions on important political questions are as clearly defined as those of the politicians. The former are undoubtedly conservative, but less so than the latter would like to think; and in a number of areas, the voters are more open to change than their leaders.

This is especially true in the economic dimension: a clear majority are in favour of increasing black wages. Similarly, a majority of the electorate would agree to the abolition of job reservation. There is even evidence of a growing trend to accept blacks as supervisors.

The voters are more resistant to change in the social dimension, but again less so than the politicians believe. The abolition of separate lifts and the subsequent clear change in attitudes shows that once political decisions are taken the electorate is prepared to accept them. There is undoubtedly a predominant orientation towards the status quo in the political realm as well; the voters are afraid of surrendering political control over their own destiny. But a vague readiness to make concessions does exist in the political field, and it has grown considerably during the period covered by our study. A majority of the electorate are today in favour of a qualified franchise for all South Africans. There is also majority support for full political integration of the coloureds. And substantial minorities support the idea of consociational democracy.

[52] Cf. Chapter 7.5.

This openness to change obviously does not amount to a political movement able to compel politicians to embark upon a particular course of action. But the fact remains that the electorate is much more amenable to change than the politicians believe, or claim they believe. And there is substantial evidence that the voters would be even readier for change if they were encouraged by their leaders.

PART THREE

The Black Majority's Expectations of Change

Blacks in South Africa are not a silent majority, but they are a majority which has often been silenced. For almost two decades, leading spokesmen have been arrested, served with banning orders, or died in detention—to prevent them from expressing the majority's expectations of change.

This majority has nevertheless continued to express its desires and will, for over half a century, with astonishing continuity. What is expressed, however, is not uniform. There has long been a diversity of opinion on just how the majority should attain its goals. Chapter 9 will deal with this diversity of political cultures and structures in the black opposition.

Despite all the repression, black South Africa continues to have political leaders of exceptional quality, most of whom are still remarkably moderate. The different groups of leaders represent a wide spectrum of competing social and political interests. These aspects will be discussed in Chapter 10.

In Chapter 11 we shall try to establish how far the inhabitants of the black cities support the various political tendencies. For the political line which the black opposition takes on the present system is decided by the wishes of urban blacks. Their opinions and attitudes will determine whether peaceful change can be implemented in South Africa or not.

CHAPTER 9

Unity and Fragmentation in Black Politics: the Political Cultures and Structures of Black Opposition

Black politics in South Africa means opposition to white domination. The black opposition is unified in its rejection of this domination. But beyond this, black politics is hardly less fragmented than white politics. This fragmentation originates in a number of differences: differences in the historical experiences and traditions of black South Africans, in how they conceive of a future society and what they want of it, in their reactions to the white government's attempts to split them up, and in the strategies of opposition which have ensued. These differences have given rise to clearly *distinguishable* political cultures in black South Africa. Out of these have grown the different *political* trends and organizations which are already competing for roles in the future struggle for power; a political system in the wings.

The political trend which the black population will follow in the long run will be determined in the black cities, which form the social and geographic centre of black political struggle. Will this trend be towards a *political melting pot* furthering black unity, or will it be towards *black fragmentation*?

In the following sections, we shall briefly consider the political culture and structures of the black opposition. We intend to provide no more than an outline, as with our sketch of the political culture of the locus of white power. We have selected and stressed those features which seem to have a particular bearing on the possibilities of peaceful change.

1. *Continuity and rivalry: The historical experiences, main ideas, and strategies of black opposition*

Black opposition in South Africa has a long history. It is a history of remarkable continuity in the struggle for liberty and equality, but also of

244

competition and rivalry between the aspirations of different groups and movements. Both continuity and rivalry have contributed decisively to the present black political scene.

The historical roots[1]

The origins of the current political system in South Africa—whites entrenched in domination over blacks—go back more than 300 years, to the beginning of settler colonialism. But white domination was only finally established within living memory, a time which the oldest living South Africans can still recall.

Contemporary black opposition is part of a tradition of black resistance. Different historical experiences, especially during the last hundred years, have made an important contribution to the emergence of clearly distinguishable political cultures in black South Africa.

White domination had already been firmly established over large areas of the present Republic more than a century ago. In the Boer republics the blacks had become vassals of the white settlers. They had been driven from their fertile land, been forced to work for the white farmers, found their freedom of movement restricted, and had no political rights. And in the southern part of present-day Zululand, British policies had created an early form of grand apartheid.[2] Certain chiefdoms had been granted a degree of autonomy within clearly demarcated reserves, but had to pay a hut tax and provide labour for the settlers in Natal.

But in other parts of the country there had been a *gradual move towards political equality.* Already by the middle of the last century the franchise had been extended to 'civilized' blacks and coloureds in the former Cape Colony. Whoever possessed a certain level of education and a certain amount of property was recognized as 'civilized'; though, as the influence of the black voters grew, the criteria were stiffened. Nevertheless, the qualified franchise imparted to those blacks who gained it a sense of civil equality, and to those who did not, at least the hope of becoming citizens. At the turn of the century black voters accounted for 6 per cent of the total registration in the Cape Colony. But in some constituencies in the Eastern Cape this figure reached almost 50 per cent; black votes here decided the result of the election. In this way, blacks became acquainted with the advantages of the British democratic tradition. The conceptions of political goals which blacks throughout

[1] A number of excellent histories are available, among which Monica Wilson and Leonard Thompson (eds), *The Oxford History of South Africa*, 2 Vols, *op cit*, deserves special mention. The following presentation is based largely on this work.

[2] Cf. David Welsh, *The Roots of Segregation: Native Policy in Colonial Natal, 1845-1910* (Cape Town and London, 1971); cf. also Leonard Thompson, 'The Subjection of the African Chiefdoms', in Monica Wilson and Leonard Thompson (eds), *The Oxford History of South Africa, op cit*, Vol. II, pp. 245-85.

245

South Africa now have, were decisively influenced by the experiences in the Cape and, in particular, in the Eastern Cape.

Thirdly, there was an experience of a quite different nature: the creation of powerful *black nations and states which resisted by force of arms* the whites' claims to domination, and which were only defeated in certain cases after decades of struggle.

The Pedis in the Eastern Transvaal bitterly resisted both the Afrikaners and the English between 1870 and 1882. The Vendas were only defeated finally in 1898, by a united expeditionary force of Afrikaners, Swazis and Shangaans. And the Zulu empire offered even more dramatic resistance. King Shaka is judged by historians to have been a man of extraordinary will-power and exceptional military and political gifts. Out of a number of tribes of the Northern Nguni, he created in the north-eastern part of the country a highly centralized and powerful monarchy, which on any account must be regarded as a nation. Shaka's expansionary policies led to the establishment of other black states, while thousands of people fled from the 'Mfecane' (the diaspora) to Basutoland, Pondoland, and present-day Zimbabwe-Rhodesia. Thus, a black African tradition of centralized nation states developed here quite independently of similar traditions in Europe. In 1877, the English tried to break the power of the Zulu empire. But the Zulus, led by King Keteswayo, a successor of Shaka, inflicted on them their greatest defeat since the Crimean War; 1,600 British soldiers fell at Isandlwana. The British forces were considerably reinforced thereafter, and at the battle of Ulundi in 1879 they managed to break the power of the Zulus. England then set about systematically destroying the Zulu nation, creating thirteen different chiefdoms and prohibiting a Zulu standing army.

Despite the many cleavages which such measures created among the Zulus, the English could not destroy their pride and solidarity. As late as 1906, Chief Bambata was able to mobilize thousands of Zulu warriors against the settler domination. The uprising was bloodily suppressed. It was above all the fear of the Zulus which decided whether or not Natal would join in the Union of South Africa in 1910.

The struggle between black and white is, therefore, a historical experience which has shaped the political consciousness of many blacks. This is also true of the struggle between black and black. Many black groups still have unhappy memories of Shaka's Mfecane. The Mfengu fought on the side of the whites against Xhosa-speaking groups, and Swazis and Shangaans helped the Afrikaners to defeat the Vendas and the Pedis. Many of these old conflicts have not been forgotten. Even today, one can hear the opinion expressed in the Transvaal that Zulu migrant labourers are arrogant, and still regard themselves as warriors of Shaka.

246

Finally, the variety of the urban blacks' historical experiences and traditions can be illustrated in a somewhat simplistic way. There are some people whose fathers, grandfathers, and great-grandfathers lived like serfs on Afrikaner farms in the Transvaal or the Orange Free State for over a century and a half. There are families from the Eastern Cape who have been Christians for over two hundred years, who enjoyed a long period of political equality, and once had the vote. And there are others whose fathers or grandfathers survived the sieges of the Afrikaners and the British in the mountains of Sekhukhuneland or in the Soutpansberg, or fought against the British in Zulu regiments.

The clearly distinguishable political cultures of the present are based on different social and political traditions such as these.

Conflict between the main political ideas

Black political thought has been influenced by a wide variety of political teachings and value systems: traditional African values and Victorian liberalism, Afrikaner ethnic teachings and imperial colonialism, Christianity and Marxism.

For the half-century after the founding of the Union of South Africa, the central political vision of the black opposition[3] was a single South African nation with equal rights and duties for all inhabitants of the country, regardless of birth, colour, language, and creed. Only after the white government smashed the black opposition organizations in 1960 and forced through the homelands policy did black politics crystallize around three juxtaposed and opposing political ideas. The first is that the homelands policy must be accepted, whether voluntarily or involuntarily. The second is that a united South Africa with equal rights for all must be uncompromisingly pursued. The third has the same end as the second, but differs on the means—it supports a partial exploitation of legal possibilities offered by the bantustan system for attaining this goal. We consider the three ideas in turn.

At the end of the 1960s, a group of black political leaders began to *accept the homelands policy*. Before then, no homeland leader had opted for 'independence'—not even the leaders of the Transkei or Bophuthatswana, who have since gone the whole way. Despite these leaders' assurances, the concept of homeland independence was neither

---

[3] On what follows cf. i.a. Peter Walshe, *The Rise of African Nationalism in South Africa* (Berkeley, 1971); Mary Benson, *South Africa: The Struggle for a Birthright* (Harmondsworth, 1966); Gwendolen M. Carter, 'African Concepts of Nationalism in South Africa', in Heribert Adam (ed.), *South Africa: Sociological Perspectives, op cit*, pp. 103–20; Fatima Meer, 'African Nationalism: Some Inhibiting Factors', in Heribert Adam (ed.), *South Africa: Sociological Perspectives, op cit*, pp. 121–57; Edward Feit, *African Opposition in South Africa—the Failure of Passive Resistance* (Stanford, 1967).

initiated nor developed by black politicians. It was accepted by them in the face of both Afrikaner power and the hopelessly inferior position of the blacks.

Based on the persuasive force of political reality, this idea has indubitably become very influential in black politics.

The second idea, *of a united, multiracial South Africa*, is as dominant in black politics today as it was at the beginning of the century. It has been expressed in various ways during the history of black opposition, resulting in competing tendencies and different organizations. The fundamental idea has nevertheless displayed a remarkable continuity.

We can distinguish three tendencies: liberal democratic, influenced by Christian principles; Marxist; and African Nationalist. Right up until the present, the Christian, liberal democratic tendency has had the strongest influence. Marxism was very important at certain times, but was never able to oust the other two. And at times, curious ideologies were created from elements of all three.

Between 1912 and 1959 these three schools of thought confronted each other within one organization, the African National Congress (ANC)—the first, and for decades the major, organization of black opposition. The ANC was formed in protest against the constitution of the Union of South Africa, which, although retaining the qualified franchise for blacks in the Cape Province, left blacks in all other parts of the country without any political rights at all. The initial aims of the ANC were the winning of political rights, the abolition of the colour bar in the workplace, and the overcoming of tribal differences between blacks. These aims clearly reflected the values and political culture of the black middle class. In the early years of the ANC, lawyers and clergymen who had been educated in England and the USA played a large role. Christian teachings strongly influenced the content and the structure of the main political ideas. The unity and equality of all men, irrespective of skin colour, language, and ethnic origin, were derived from the concept of equality in the sight of God. Contact with black American church leaders led to the use of the Scriptures as a basis for rejecting racialism. The language of ANC protest had a clear Christian and biblical tone. Non-racialism was regarded as morally superior to the restricted ethnic nationalism of the Afrikaners. The tradition of the qualified franchise in the Cape was largely compatible with these values, and was conceived of as the starting point for black rights in the whole of South Africa. Any thoughts of dividing the country or geographic separation were rejected in principle. Only in the last twenty years have a few ANC leaders given some thought to partition as a possible second-best solution, but the idea has never enjoyed wide support.

In 1936 black interests were dealt a heavy blow by the Hertzog government. The blacks were deprived of the common vote they had in the Cape Province, and a new Land Act enlarged the 1912 boundaries of the black reserves and affirmed the policy of geographic separation. As a result, some attention was given to new ideas within the black opposition. Marcus Garvey's Pan-African slogan 'Africa for the Africans' gained popularity. And the South African Communist Party decided to give the *national* liberation of the indigenous peoples preference over the class struggle.

Under these influences the political demands of the ANC became less 'moderate'. The goal was no longer a qualified franchise, but full political equality on the basis of 'one man one vote'. The ANC also demanded the recognition of trade-unions, the abolition of the pass laws, the right to own property anywhere in the country, the abolition of job discrimination, equal per capita expenditure on education for pupils of all races, and a programme for drastically improved welfare institutions.

In the late 1940s, both the Marxist and the African Nationalist trends gained ground within the ANC, through the South African Communist Party and the Youth League of the ANC respectively. The Youth League emphasized the necessity of spiritually emancipating the blacks, and honoured black heroes of the past such as Shaka and Moshoeshoe. At the same time, it stressed the 'socialist' elements of traditional African society. In the second half of the 1950s the conflict between the two schools deepened. The 'Freedom Charter' of the ANC, adopted in 1955, showed the growing influence of the left wing. New goals were included alongside the traditional demands for liberal democracy: the nationalization of industry, the redistribution of wealth, and a non-racial re-allocation of land. The Youth League opposed the last demand—it was in favour of allocating land to blacks only.

There was also disagreement about whether blacks should work with other population groups. The Youth League rejected co-operation with the South African Indian Congress, with some white radical groups, and with the Coloured People's Organization. It split away from the ANC in 1959, and called itself the Pan African Congress (PAC). In 1960, both the ANC and the PAC were prohibited. However, their respective policies survive, though for many years they have only been able to be freely expressed by the members in exile. The ANC-in-exile in London has maintained its close links with the South African Communist Party: its goal is a multiracial, socialist South Africa. The PAC-in-exile maintains the African Nationalist line of the old PAC in an even stronger form: in its view South Africa is a paradigm case of colonialism. There are also the ANC African Nationalists, non-Marxists, who split away from the London ANC and have their headquarters in Dar-Es-Salaam. This wing feels that discussions of the future social order in South Africa are premature—the liberation struggle must take precedence. Its political goals are quite close to those of the PAC. In South Africa itself, no black

249

organization of any significance articulated the principles of a multiracial unitary state during the 1960s. But they were kept alive by numerous individuals, black writers, church leaders, teachers, and business—and above all, by black students.

Towards the end of the 1960s a series of new organizations arose which share these principles: the Black Consciousness movement. Through these organizations a new generation, which had no personal connection with the ANC and the PAC, adopted these principles in a form somewhere between the positions of the two older movements. The African Nationalist component of Black Consciousness relates the movement to the PAC: blacks should reflect on their own culture, shed any feelings of inferiority with respect to whites, and regain their pride and dignity. On the other hand, the broad connotation of the concept 'black' relates the movement to the old ANC: Black Consciousness regards as black all those against whom the existing system discriminates—coloureds and Indians as well as Africans. The economic programme of Black Consciousness contains elements of both the ANC's socialism in its demand for the nationalization of major industries, and the PAC's socialism in its conception of 'black communalism',[4] which is based on African traditions. We shall return to this point later. Finally, in rejecting Marxism and accepting Tanzania as its model, Black Consciousness is related to the PAC and ANC African Nationalists.

The movement is further linked to the older tradition of black opposition, in having been strongly influenced by both American black theology and Christianity in general.

Thus, from the outset right until the present, black political thought has adhered with remarkable continuity to the idea of a multiracial South Africa. In having adopted this idea the black opposition—whether in its Christian and liberal democratic, its Marxist or its African Nationalist form—has never displayed a particularist nationalism. Even the African Nationalist form was always pan-national. First the Youth League, then the PAC, and now the Black Consciousness movement have been accused of being black racists. But the PAC has always insisted that non-Africans who are prepared to identify themselves with the Africans' interests will be accepted. And Black Consciousness includes coloureds and Indians, and espouses full and equal rights for whites in a future society, while rejecting group exclusiveness and political privileges. For the vast majority of the black opposition, nationalism always meant a comprehensive, non-racial 'South Africanism'. In line with this central theme, the political goal since the 1930s has been universal franchise.

[4] Cf. the 'Declaration of Principles of the Black People's Convention', in *Pro Veritate* (June 1976), pp. 6–7; cf. also Reinhard Brückner, *Südafrikas schwarze Zukunft* (Frankfurt, 1977), pp. 103–6.

Partition or the qualified franchise have always been less popular or compromise options, and of even less import after the fifties.

Since the beginning of the 1970s, a *third major idea* had made tremendous advances, viz., that a new South Africa can be created through the *exploitation of the legal possibilities of the homeland system.*

The old parties, and the Black Consciousness movement, reject any compromises with 'separate development'. But the new opposition movement takes the view that every opportunity to promote black interests must be exploited—and even the bantustan system offers such possibilities. This approach is represented, above all, by Gatsha Buthelezi and his Inkatha movement. It rejects homeland independence out of hand, in contrast to those who accept the homelands policy. Rather, it shares the political aims of those who support a unitary multiracial South Africa. But it differs from them in turn in not rejecting the institutions of the homelands policy as tools for attaining this goal. The second and third schools of thought, therefore, differ less in their goals than in their methods. This difference has, however, been widened by differences of strategy within the black opposition.

Conflicts over strategies

The political cultures of black South Africa differ even more in their strategies of opposition towards white domination than they do in their main political ideas. Once again, we can make a three-fold distinction, which corresponds—though not completely—to that outlined above: between the strategy of co-operation with white policies, the strategy of activist protest and struggle against these policies, and the strategy which seeks to create a political power base through an organized mobilization of the masses—a power base which is by the very fact of its existence in a position to force the white government to change its current policies.

The *strategy of co-operation* has been adopted by most of the homeland leaders. The co-operation is, in the current situation, necessarily very one-sided. The homelands depend on the goodwill of the South African government: they need budget subsidies and South African 'development aid', and they have to remember that their citizens take jobs as migrant labourers in the 'white republic'. Only with the support of the white government are they in a position to keep their population at all satisfied, and to offer their intelligentsia attractive job opportunities. All the homelands want to consolidate their territories, within boundaries in excess of those laid down in the Land Act of 1936. But their negotiating position is extremely weak. All they can offer in return is to accept the independence on which the white government is keen. Most of the homeland leaders therefore try to exact as high a price

251

as possible, knowing very well that once they accept independence they will have no more call on the government of the Republic. In short, this strategy involves capitulating to the intentions of the white government under the most favourable conditions available.

The *strategy of protest* has the longest history in the black opposition movement. In the early years of the ANC, protest took peaceful and dignified forms: petitions, delegations and deputations, and resolutions passed at conferences. These forms of protest assumed that white South African liberals could co-operate with Britain to influence the situation in favour of black interests.

Methods which would have led to direct confrontation with the government were thus deliberately avoided. More active forms of protest were only adopted much later, when 'moderate protest' had proved to be utterly ineffective, and when the National Party government showed its intransigence. In 1949 the ANC accepted a 'programme of action', in which passive resistance and the downing of tools were regarded as means necessary for attaining its goals. In the first half of the 1950s, the ANC started its 'defiance campaign' under the influence of the Youth League. There were strikes and successful boycotts. Thousands of blacks demonstrated their disregard of the pass laws. This activism initially strengthened the black opposition, and the membership of the ANC increased dramatically. But there were also unsuccessful campaigns—for example, a boycott of the Bantu Education system began with great enthusiasm, but could not be sustained.

In the second half of the 1950s, the government increasingly suppressed all attempts at passive resistance: mass gatherings were prohibited, and ANC leaders were immobilized by banning orders and other measures.

Activist protest quickly reached its peak when the PAC split away from the ANC. PAC activities openly challenged white power, and threw the country into a state of crisis. In Cape Town, 30,000 blacks marched on Parliament. Smaller demonstrations, bus boycotts, and anti-pass campaigns were conducted in many other centres. And then came the Sharpeville massacre. More than 20,000 blacks marched to a police station in protest against the pass laws. The police opened fire. Sixty-nine blacks were killed and 180 injured. The government hesitated for a day or two, during which time the pass laws were suspended. Then it acted quickly and decisively: 18,000 people were rounded up by the police in black residential areas throughout the country. The ANC called for a new struggle against the pass laws. It also demanded a national convention which would work out a new political dispensation for the country. These were its last legal activities. On 8 April 1960 both the PAC and the ANC were banned. The leader of the PAC, Robert Sobukwe, was sentenced to three years' imprisonment, afterwards regularly extended by a special Act of Parliament. From that time on-wards, parts of the black opposition went underground. ANC members and white Communists founded Umkonto we Sizwe (Spear of the Nation), and the PAC began to commit acts of violence under the name of Poqo ('pure'). The organization managed to organize a number of demonstrations, and some attacks on electricity pylons, post offices, and railway property. But the effects were negligible. Thousands of blacks were arrested in connection with clandestine activities. Nelson Mandela, one of the top men in the ANC, was sentenced to life imprisonment in 1962 for being a leader of Umkonto we Sizwe. He delivered a speech in the courtroom which made him a hero of the black resistance—a reputation still unbroken. However, by the mid-1960s at latest, the Government had completely quelled organized resistance.

For as long as black protest was legal, it was remarkably peaceful in both tone and style. Fatima Meer analysed the speeches made during the years of the 'Defiance Campaign', 1952 to 1956. She found that only 11 per cent could be regarded as violent and hostile, while about 20 per cent expressed animosity towards whites. But the majority consisted of protests, demands for change, and sermons of hope.[5] For about a decade after the mid-1960s, there was no further active protest. In 1974, the South African Students' Organization (SASO)—the student section of the Black Consciousness movement—organized some mass meetings in solidarity with the recently victorious Frelimo in Mozambique. The government cracked down immediately: all gatherings were forbidden, and many students were arrested or served with banning orders.

On balance, the protest strategy has achieved very little. White power is well organized, determined, and bent on preserving interests in-compatible with even the most moderate of black demands. Against this, neither peaceful proclamations and demonstrations, nor active protests in the usual forms of passive resistance and boycotts, nor even civil disobedience, ever had any prospects of success. Black opposition had to choose between ineffectiveness and subversion, and when it chose subversion this was broken without difficulty by the state security system.

There is a *third strategy, mass mobilization*. This has thus far not really been tested. It was proposed for the first time at the beginning of the 1940s by A. X. Xuma, then President of the ANC. Xuma con-centrated on organizational discipline, founding local organizations and improving co-ordination at provincial level. He believed that before any action could be undertaken one had to mobilize the masses efficiently; premature confrontation should be avoided. His opponents in the ANC, however, thought that mobilization could best be achieved through

[5] Fatima Meer, 'African Nationalism: Some Inhibiting Factors', *op cit.*

253

confrontation, or at least through dramatic activism. In 1949 Xuma was defeated in the elections for the Presidency of the ANC. Black organizations have without a doubt paid dearly for discarding his proposals. There is evidence that the political aims of the ANC were too abstract for many blacks, especially compared to the constant problems of daily life. Albert Luthuli referred to this weakness in his memoirs: he warned the activists in the movement against disregarding the small man's level of awareness. The readiness to fight to the bitter end is, as a rule, found more often among the better-educated and the young than among those whose lives are a daily struggle to support themselves and their families. Apparently the supporters of the protest strategy also persistently under-estimated the strength of the white government and its repressive apparatus. For example, when the government sent in the police, this was interpreted as a sign of white panic and therefore a 'moral victory for the black opposition'. The fact was overlooked that the state apparatus never once came near to mobilizing its full strength.

Dr Xuma's alternative of patient organizational work and mass mobilization was only adopted again in the mid-1970s, when Buthelezi reconstituted the Inkatha movement. By carefully exploiting the scope legally allowed to him by the bantustan policy he laid the foundation for a mass organization which already has more members and is far better organized than the ANC at the height of its popularity. We shall return to this point below.

In summary, then, we have established that clearly differing political subcultures can be distinguished within the black opposition in respect of their historical experiences, main political ideas, and basic strategies. The historical experience of oppression and subjection has left a deep mark on many black South Africans, and at the present time has led a section of the blacks to accept the basic tenets of the bantustan policy, and to co-operate with the white government in realizing it.

On the other hand, the historical experience of a relatively liberal British policy in the old Cape Colony gave birth to the important idea of a non-racial South Africa. For half a century the majority of people involved in the black opposition movement tried to realize this goal by means of peaceful protest, and then resorted to non-violent activism. The smashing of the organizations of the protest movement—from the ANC through to Black Consciousness—has not dissuaded the many blacks who continue to support this idea and reject all compromise with government policies. This political culture has exhibited a remarkable continuity even in its variants—the Christian and liberal democratic, the Marxist, and the African Nationalist—and despite the long period without any proper organization.

Another variant of the same political idea has in the meantime developed into an important subculture in its own right. This political movement, Buthelezi's Inkatha, has adopted the older strategy of mass mobilization. It has tried to learn from the defeat of the protest movement and, for the meantime, wants to avoid confrontation with the white powers without accepting their policies. This political culture has its organizational strength in Zululand, where the historical memories of a strong black nation and military resistance to foreign domination are still very much alive. This may well foreshadow its strength.

For half a century the black opposition has been characterized by the continuity both of its conceptions and of the rivalry between the different political cultures and tendencies. The same is true of contemporary black opposition.

2. *The struggle for future power: political organizations and tendencies in black South Africa today*

The present black opposition differs from that of the past mainly in that various *organized* tendencies now compete with each other for influence. Until the PAC split away from the ANC in 1959, rivalries had been played out within one organization; and after that date, there was only a short period until both organizations were prohibited, during which they could compete for support.

Today, however, a number of organizations and tendencies are competing for the support and co-operation of the black population: various homeland leaders are trying to build up their own political bases; the old parties, although prohibited, still command the sympathies of many black South Africans; the Black Consciousness movement has, in the course of a decade, become an important political phenomenon; and Inkatha has, for the past few years, been making the most comprehensive attempt at political organization in the history of black opposition.

It would thus appear that the struggle for future power has already begun in the black political system. We shall now attempt to characterize the above organizations and tendencies, to define their goals more precisely, and to estimate their significance.

The homeland leaders and their organizations

All homeland leaders have levelled criticism of some kind or other at the policy of separate development. But only Gatsha Buthelezi, in founding an organization on a national level, has laid claim to political leadership transcending a bantustan or ethnic group. The others are no more than homeland leaders. They are the subject of this section. Each of them has tried to form his own political party, and in most homelands there are also opposition parties. But none of these parties has a significant

255

membership, and as a rule they are active only during election campaigns. The general political policy of the homeland leaders, and the strategy open to them, have already been outlined. Notwithstanding their criticism of the white government, the leaders of two homelands, Kaiser Matanzima and Lukas Mangope, have opted for 'independence'. Their homelands, the Transkei and Bophuthatswana respectively, have become autonomous regions. Present indications are that two other homelands, the Ciskei and Vendaland, will agree to become independent in the near future. This seems less likely for Lebowa, Gazankulu, Ndebele and Basuto QwaQwa. The leaders of some of these regions have declared that they will only consider independence seriously when their territories have been considerably enlarged. Cedric Phatudi and Hudson Ntsanwisi, the heads of government in Lebowa and Gazankulu, have allied themselves politically with Buthelezi. The alliance was formalized in the 'Black Unity front', which is stronger symbolically than organizationally. Homeland leaders, especially those who have opted for independence, are widely rejected by urban blacks. This is hardly surprising, since city dwellers, as a result of this 'independence', automatically become expatriates in white South Africa.[6] But it cannot be overlooked that the homeland structures offer better-educated blacks some quite attractive possibilities, especially in the civil service and also in the educational system. These possibilities compete quite favourably with those in urban areas.

Hence, one can assume that homeland leaders do have some support: among ordinary people with strong ethnic bonds, and among those educated people who look to their own interests.

The ANC and PAC

One reads repeatedly in the South African press of arrests made in connection with the actual or alleged subversive activities of these two organizations.[7] It is difficult to judge just how well organized the underground is. Of greater political import is the fact that both the ANC and the PAC are still very active, even as unorganized movements. Many blacks continue to identify themselves with their goals, and their leaders still enjoy much prestige among the black population, regardless of whether they have been banned or are in prison or exile.

It seems that many would agree with the following statement by the Chairman of Inkatha's Strategy Commission: 'History will show that the ANC has and will have its legitimate place in South Africa's future. Not

[6] On the attitudes of the urban blacks to the homeland policy cf. Philip Mayer, *Urban Africans and the Bantustans* (Johannesburg, South African Institute of Race Relations, 1972).

[7] Cf. e.g., *Rand Daily Mail*, March 1978.

to recognize the legitimacy of the ANC in the liberation struggle is to deny reality. We cannot wish away the ANC, and then act as though it did not exist. For seventeen years it has worked in exile for freedom in South Africa. It is recognized by the OAU and many other states, and we can be sure that its efforts will receive widespread support.'[8] Evidently, the ANC and PAC will, whether organized or not, continue to represent important bodies of political opinion in black South Africa.

The Black Consciousness movement

In 1968 representatives of black students withdrew from the University Christian Movement and from NUSAS (the National Union of South African Students) and founded SASO, the South African Students' Organization. SASO was an exclusively black students' union. By 'black' was understood not a racial group, but all people oppressed by the existing system. SASO was very soon established at all black universities, and within a short time had founded pupil groups in many high schools. In 1972, former members of SASO with various other black organizations founded the Black People's Convention (BPC), the adult organization of the Black Consciousness movement.

The political goal of Black Consciousness is a democratic and non-racial South Africa. The precondition for this is that blacks must be spiritually liberated from the sense of inferiority which centuries of white domination and paternalism have engendered. Blacks must regain their self-confidence and pride. Black solidarity will be created through black self-help. Co-operation with white liberals and radicals is rejected, as blunting black élan and independence. Members of the movement initiated a number of self-help community projects, and above all undertook a comprehensive campaign to create awareness among blacks. In 1976, they attempted for the first time to develop an economic and socio-political conception of a future South Africa. In terms of the doctrine of 'black communalism', the different levels of the economy would be differently organized. Agricultural production would be organized in co-operatives—all land would belong to the people, but would be parcelled out to families, with the state controlling the distribution and transfer. Local retail trade would be run by the local administration. Heavy industry, the mines, and the banks would be taken over by the state. Wholesale trade, as well as 'less important' branches of industry would remain in private hands.

This conception had obviously not been carefully considered, as leaders in the movement admitted. In trying to find a genuinely African solution, it drew on elements of both a free market and a state economy.

[8] Cf. Gibson Thula, *The Process of Power Sharing* (South African Institute of Race Relations, Doc. RR 178/77, 20.12.1977), p. 6.

It obviously clashed with certain vested interests in the black population: on the one hand, with the interests of farmers, who are granted far-reaching powers in respect of their land by traditional law; and on the other hand with the interests of the numerous traders and small businessmen. At the same time, it left the business interests of the white middle class unscathed. The economic programme of Black Consciousness was clearly drawn up by intellectuals. Indeed, the movement draws most of its support from intellectuals, above all from young people in schools and universities. Many observers connect the emergence of Black Consciousness with the system of Bantu Education. Black Consciousness is the product of black schools and black universities, i.e., of a totally segregated educational system.[9] Its adherents are the pupils and students of the last decade, who grew up under a system of 'hermetically' perfect apartheid. Unlike earlier generations, they do not know individual whites, nor do they have any white friends—they know only the system. In this system, whites are administrators, policemen, and functionaries. The leaders of Black Consciousness deliberately do not seek support among older blacks. In their view, their elders had been broken or softened by the system, or had built up unrealistic hopes from unrepresentative contacts with 'whites who are different'.

Like so many attempts at deliberate political socialization, the system of Bantu Education failed. 'Young people are not formed only by what they are told in school—precisely the opposite is often the case. Even the training of slaves can produce bad slaves.'[10] Similarly, an education designed to produce homeland inhabitants with a strong tribal awareness produced instead a generation of uncompromising and hard young radicals, who reject the system forced upon them.

SASO and the BPC constitute the organizational structures of the Black Consciousness movement. But it is more than these organizations; it is a broad, largely spontaneous movement articulating itself in different forms at different times and places. The leaders and structures change quickly. Some observers have spoken of 'instant leadership', as during the unrest in 1976/77. Although the government arrested hundreds of 'ringleaders', new demonstrations kept occurring under a 'leadership' which remained unknown mainly because it was not organized.

Black Consciousness reveals the strengths and weaknesses typical of a movement which draws most of its support from students. Its strengths include great flexibility, rapid communication, and the ability to disperse and reform in no time at all, all of which make repressing it exceedingly

---

[9] Cf. Theodor Hanf and Gerda Vierdag, *'People's College'—'The World''s Education Supplement'* (Deutsches Institut für Internationale Pädagogische Forschung, Frankfurt, 1977), pp. 42ff.

[10] *Ibid*, p. 46.

difficult. When an individual is arrested, several others are ready to take his place, all hitherto unknown. Many youths regard it as an honour to have been arrested—the 'graduates of John Vorster Square', who have been detained in the notorious police headquarters, are held to be trustworthy. Seen from this point of view, it is probably correct that 'the movement can only grow' as one of its earlier leaders calmly and self-confidently stated. But these strengths are simultaneously its weaknesses. It is in essence a 'superstructural movement',[11] which can produce spectacular demonstrations at any time without, however, affecting the system's real power-base. On the other hand, as a superstructural movement is is also more difficult to suppress. In October 1977 the South African government prohibited a total of seventeen organizations which belonged to the Black Consciousness movement. But many of them were not particularly efficiently organized. Even before the unrest, informal groupings were often more important to Black Consciousness than formal ones. So although the government has prohibited the organizations, the currency of their political ideas is scarcely affected.

Inkatha—The National Cultural Liberation Movement

In 1928, the Zulu King Dinizulu founded an organization named Inkatha yeNkululeko yeSizwe, the 'National Cultural Liberation Movement'. It aimed to promote Zulu culture and solidarity *and* simultaneously to further black unity in South Africa.

Almost fifty years later Gatsha Buthelezi began to turn this traditional association into a modern mobilizing organization with a clear political image. At the beginning of 1978 it had approximately 175,000 members[12] and over a thousand local cells in Natal, the Transvaal, and the Orange Free State. The flags, songs, symbols and slogans of Inkatha are those of the ANC. Buthelezi was an active member of the ANC Youth League and was expelled from the University of Fort Hare because of his ANC activities. He was a close associate of Albert Luthuli, President of the ANC for many years. It was with the consent of Luthuli and other ANC leaders that Buthelezi became active in Zulu homeland politics, and finally Chief Minister of KwaZulu. Inkatha undoubtedly stands in the tradition of the ANC—admittedly, as we have noted, following a strategy which could not command a majority when it was first proposed in the ANC.

Inkatha's goal is 'cultural liberation', i.e., the overcoming of inferiority, and the re-awakening of pride and spiritual independence among blacks. 'If you want to, you can also call it "black con-

[11] Cf. Gisela Albrecht's outstanding description, 'Der Aufstand in der Köpfen', in idem, *Soweto oder der Aufstand der Vorstädte, op cit*, pp. 228ff.

[12] Figure given by the Secretary-General of Inkatha, Prof. Bengu, on 22.1.1978.

sciousness"'', said a prominent Inkatha leader.[13] Inkatha strongly emphasizes the role of self-help in overcoming under-development. The movement demands the abolition of all racial discrimination, a new system of education, and 'the full inclusion of blacks in the political decision-making processes as well as majority rule'.[14]

Of crucial importance is its strategy of mobilizing and building up the solidarity of ordinary members before any specific political action is undertaken. To quote Buthelezi, 'Before we do anything, we must organize ourselves in a disciplined manner. We must learn to support each other, to plan together, and to act together.'[15] 'If Inkatha grows, we shall become a tidal wave which will bring change in South Africa.'[16] 'We are a movement of normal men and women from everyday life.'[17] What does Inkatha hope to gain from this strategy? 'If we can create discipline, we could paralyse the whole country in a few days.'[18]

Inkatha has so far not produced any systematic political conceptions of the future. However, there are some indications of what would be involved. On the one hand, the interests of ordinary people are given great importance. 'It is not the function of political leaders to impose their ideal system on the people.'[19] On the other hand, at least as far as KwaZulu is concerned, a 'one party democracy' is held to be desirable. Buthelezi's reasons are partly that in a poor and under-developed society the opposition would tend to exploit poverty for demagogic reasons; but above all that a multi-party system in the homelands would invite manipulation by the white government. 'Political leadership in the Westminster model only makes sense in situations in which there are several options.'[20] It is still unclear whether Buthelezi thinks that in a multiracial South Africa there would be 'several options'. The former General Secretary of Inkatha, S. M. Bengu, doubts whether a multi-party system would work even in a non-racial South Africa. However, totalitarian one-party systems in Africa have proved themselves equally unacceptable. A new constitution should take into account the interests of all sections of society, and should be based on African cultural values.[21] Thus far, however, Buthelezi has deliberately refused to be tied to one political conception. 'There is no blueprint for the society which

[13] Gibson Thula, Chairman of Inkatha's Strategy Commission.

[14] Cf. Gibson Thula, *op cit*, p. 7.

[15] Gatsha Buthelezi, speech made in Soweto on 14.3.1976.

[16] Idem, speech made on Shaka's Day, 24.10.1977.

[17] Idem, speech made on 14.3.1976.

[18] Idem, speech made on 24.10.1977.

[19] Idem, speech made in Windhoek on Namibia Day, 25.9.1976.

[20] Idem, speech made at the University of Cape Town, 8.9.1976.

[21] Sibusico M. E. Bengu, *Cultural Liberation, Principles and Practices* (University of Natal, May 1977), Lecture 4, p. 5.

we want to construct.' 'What we urgently need is a general conference of blacks at which the future of South Africa would be discussed.'[22] In recent years his readiness to make concessions to the whites has markedly declined. As recently as 1974 he proposed a plan for a federal form of transitional government.[23] Although this aroused great interest in pro-government newspapers,[24] the government itself did not react at all. Two years later he remarked, 'I must emphasize that in future it will be increasingly difficult to make conciliatory proposals such as I made in my federation plan.'[25] 'Whether we like it or not, whether we think it is good or bad, South Africa is clearly moving towards majority rule. If one rejects that, it means that one has decided to accept violence'[26] Majority rule is thus the unambiguous goal. On the other hand, Inkatha's declaration of principles proposes that in the future South African society the political rights of all 'national groups' should be guaranteed.[27] Thus the formulation of 'majority rule' is made in conjunction with that of 'power-sharing'.[28] This is further evidence of a readiness to make concessions and to compromise. The political options are being kept open.

By contrast, the economic goals of Inkatha are more precisely formulated. Buthelezi regards 'a radical redistribution of wealth' and 'increased productivity' as simultaneous preconditions for any political system in a period of transition.[29] According to Bengu,[30] some kind of 'African socialism' will be necessary. For 'no capitalist system in Southern Africa has been able to distribute wealth and power in a way that would guarantee political stability.'[31] Therefore industry should be placed under state control, and trade-unions as well, since '. . . black trade-unions could become the tool of an élitist artisan class interested in maintaining the status quo'.[32]

Buthelezi accordingly thinks that a mixed economy with strong state

[22] Gatsha Buthelezi, speech made at the University of Portland, Oregon, USA, 1.3.1977.

[23] Idem, *White and Black Nationalism, Ethnicity and the Future of the Homelands* (Johannesburg, Institute of Race Relations, 1974).

[24] Cf. Lawrence Schlemmer and Tim Muil, 'Social and Political Change in the African Areas: A Case Study of KwaZulu', in Leonard Thompson and Jeffrey Butler (eds), *Change in Contemporary South Africa, op cit*, pp. 132f.

[25] Gatsha Buthelezi, speech made in Soweto, 14.3.1976.

[26] Idem, speech made at the University of Cape Town, 8.9.1976.

[27] 'We believe that the political rights of all *national groups* should be protected within a constitutional framework which outlaws discrimination based on colour, sex or creed'. 'Inkatha: Statement of Beliefs', quoted from Gibson Thula, *op cit*, p. 8.

[28] Gibson Thula, *op cit*, passim.

[29] Gatsha Buthelezi, speech made in Windhoek, 25.9.1976.

[30] S. M. Bengu, *op cit*, cf. as well contributions to the discussion, *loc cit*.

[31] Gatsha Buthelezi, speech made in Portland, 1.3.1977.

[32] Ibid.

control would be the most appropriate model: state control over the most important resources in particular, and otherwise the encouragement of private business. Buthelezi's attitude to the question of private foreign investment also reveals considerable pragmatism: 'In the present circumstances, I cannot afford to be an ideological puritan.'[33]

In Inkatha's view, whites are South Africans entitled to full rights. 'I don't regard the whites as superfluous foreigners. They belong to Africa. South Africa is their fatherland; they have the right to live here. There can be no political solution in which they are not active partners.'[34] Pragmatic considerations are again important. 'If one realistically aspires to a better society, then one must realize that this is impossible without the whites. Trade and industry cannot stand still, even for a short period.'[35]

Inkatha thus reveals considerable pragmatic flexibility, in both its political and its economic goals. In aiming for majority rule and economic redistribution it allows that the modalities of these goals can be negotiated later. Finally, pragmatism is also a fundamental characteristic of the political strategy of Inkatha. It exploits the political institutions of the bantustan policy to suit its purpose. By functioning within these institutions it gains a legal basis. The white government can deprive it of this only by changing the rules, i.e., at the price of discarding the entire policy of 'separate development'.[36] This strategy provides a political immunity which can be used to pursue goals running completely counter to government policies. Set against this is the government's strategy that even an unwilling acceptance of bantustan structures will, in the last instance, legitimate the bantustan policy. Which strategy succeeds will depend to a considerable degree on the political effectiveness of Inkatha. It was pragmatically logical, after the protest strategy of the old opposition failed, to adopt the remaining strategy of mass mobilization based on the relative security of a homeland institution. Without such security, it is doubtful whether the movement could have attained even its present levels of organization.

This strategy inevitably drew heavy criticism from other political quarters among the blacks. Whatever its reasons, Inkatha is accused of serving the government's policy of separation in general, and of

[33] Idem, speech made at the University of Williamete, Salem, USA, 23.2.1977; cf. also *Natal Mercury*, 30.1.1978.

[34] Gatsha Buthelezi, speech made in Johannesburg at the Conference on Racial Discrimination, 3–4.12.1976.

[35] Idem, speech made in Portland, 1.3.1977; cf. as well Gibson Thula, *op cit*, p. 8: 'We have to recognize that our country does not belong to a single race group. We also have to admit that the various groups are interdependent in virtually all facts of life, viz. social, political and economic.'

[36] Cf. the considerations of Colin Legum, 'Political Leadership in the Bantustans', *Third World*, 2 (1973), p. 17.

promoting Zulu tribalism in particular. There are two answers to this accusation, a pragmatic one and a more fundamental one. The pragmatic argument claims that 'There are many different ways of pursuing black nationalism . . . there are ethnic groups, tribes, trade-unions . . . and many others.' 'Nothing can prevent us from creating a number of Inkathas. With similar structures and constitutions, they can form a joint movement of liberation.'[37] The more fundamental argument is that 'There is a unity in the black society which is based on a deeply rooted black nationalism, and which transcends all differences within the society.' 'There is no Zulu freedom which would be different from the freedom of each and every black man.'[38]

Obviously, Inkatha hopes that other groups will join it, or at least co-operate with it. In any case, it hopes to lead the black movement, and win further support through its success. The pragmatic argument will probably be particularly important in the immediate future. The Zulus are the largest of all black groups. They cannot be regarded simply as a tribe, nor can their sense of solidarity be characterized as simple tribalism.[39] The evidence is that, as mentioned above, Shaka's Mfecane was in fact an early example of 'nation-building'. Smaller tribal units were absorbed into one larger group which—like the Swazis and the Basutos under similar circumstances—then developed a sense of solidarity very like that of a nation.[40] However, as Schlemmer has found, this Zulu identity does not prevent Zulus from identifying with a broader black nationalism—on the contrary, the two seem to be related.[41] And conversely, there are indications that Inkatha enjoys considerable support among the other black groups.[42] Should this be supported by empirical study, the fundamental argument would also hold. A movement has good prospects of developing into the strongest force in the black opposition if it enjoys the support of the strongest group, and succeeds in gaining support beyond this group by being based on a sense of quasi-nationalism which is in turn compatible with a more comprehensive nationalism.

Buthelezi is therefore trying, as has been mentioned, to strengthen his organization through alliances. These include, on the one hand, the 'Black Unity Front', an alliance with those homeland leaders who, like

[37] Gatsha Buthelezi, speech made in Soweto, 14.3.1976.

[38] Ibid.

[39] The authors have gained some valuable insights on this point from the doctoral thesis of Joost Hensen, to be published shortly.

[40] Cf. David Hammond-Tooke, 'Tribal Cohesion and the Incorporative Process in the Transkei, South Africa', in R. Cohen and J. Middleton (eds), *From Tribe to Nation in Africa* (Philadelphia, 1970).

[41] Lawrence Schlemmer, 'Black Attitudes: Reaction and Adaptation' (Centre for Applied Social Sciences, University of Natal, Durban, 1975).

[42] Cf. Tom Duff, 'A Huge Zulu Force on the Move', *The Star*, 6.8.1977.

him, reject the bantustan system; and on the other hand, a pact with the Coloured Labour Party and the Indian Reform Party. This keeps Inkatha in line with the tradition of the old Congress alliance, and even more importantly, evidences a broad support for its strategy of transgressing the barriers of a 'racial group'.

3. *Rebellion or organization? On the social and political background of the opposition in the black cities*

Black opposition at the time of the Congress movement was almost exclusively urban; the old organizations had almost no support in the reserves. By contrast, the present opposition is by no means confined to the cities. One can speak of a 'dialectic of the homelands policy', one aspect of which is the growing politicization of the rural areas. 'Black' universities have been set up far from the urban centres, and children born in the cities are parted from their parents and sent to the homelands because it is easier to get a place in school there. These schoolchildren, students, and teachers brought the ideas of Black Consciousness to the black 'platteland'. This is even more true for the Inkatha movement, for which the rural areas are not a political diaspora, but the foundation of its organizational strength.

Be that as it may, the struggle for influence between the different tendencies of the black opposition continues to be played out in the cities. For it is here that one-third of all blacks live, from all parts of the country and all ethnic groups; and here that they are most important for the economy of the country and in closest daily contact with whites. The urban blacks are living proof that the basic intention of apartheid policy has failed, and the greatest problem for the architects presently reconstructing 'separate development'. Whether peaceful change is possible depends significantly on which political trends prevail among the urban blacks, and above all on their desires and goals and on how they hope to have their expectations realized. The black cities remain at the centre of black politics, and of black-white political relations. In the following section, we shall outline the pattern behind the political attitudes and the political behaviour of urban blacks.[43] What are the black cities like, and who lives there? How can one explain the unrest which has occurred there in recent years, and continued for so long? And how effective is this unrest?

Black cities—Black city-dwellers

The black cities are situated on the edge of the major white cities,

[43] Cf. The Urban Foundation, *Proceedings of the Businessmen's Conference on the Quality of Urban Life* (Johannesburg, November 1976).

separated from them by hills and often by a broad belt of uncultivated countryside. They don't feature on many tourist maps, and no street signs point them out. White South Africa has been very careful to put them as far out of sight as possible.

Nevertheless, on the basis of population alone, they are themselves major cities with hundreds of thousands of inhabitants. In the case of Soweto, the figure is probably more than a million. Black cities of over one million inhabitants are also found in other African countries. In Kinshasa, Nairobi, and Abidjan there are enormous slums next to the modern city centres and the well-kept, wealthy areas. Despite the poverty, these slums are extraordinarily colourful, imaginatively constructed and vibrantly alive. By contrast, South Africa's black cities give the impression of carefully planned and administered shabbiness, of overwhelming sadness. They are dormitories rather than residential cities. Straight roads of small, unattractive grey or brown houses stretch from horizon to horizon, each roofed with corrugated iron and set in a tiny garden. Except on the few tarred streets, every passing car raises a cloud of dust in the dry season, or a shower of mud when it has rained. The houses are all alike: the inhabitants call them 'match-boxes'. As we established in the course of this survey, each accommodates an average of six to seven people, in two bedrooms. Water taps and toilets are outside the house, and only about a fifth of all houses have electricity. There are few services and amenities in the black areas. As a rule, in each quarter there are a few general dealers and bottle stores, a beer hall, a couple of football fields and churches and community buildings. Only in rare instances are there children's playgrounds and parks.

Everything that makes a real city is situated in the 'white city', where blacks may only work and shop. The quality of life in South Africa's black cities, however measured, cannot be very high. It must be conceded that the living conditions satisfy the basic necessities of life. One is at least 'properly housed'. But the unrelieved shabbiness and monotony of a black city can hardly be conducive to a joyful existence. In fact, the disadvantages that tell most on the inhabitants are different again. The black cities are situated far from where they work, so they spend a large part of every day in overcrowded trains and buses. They have to leave their homes very early and return very late. Transport facilities within the black areas themselves are poor. So workers returning home in the evening are frequently robbed by young gangsters. The crime rate in black residential areas is generally high, so there is a constant fear of burglary and attack. But urban blacks are afflicted by another, even more unsettling insecurity. They don't know whether they will be allowed to stay in the city. In terms of government policy, they are only temporary sojourners in a 'white area'. This especially affects the migrant workers, who are only allowed to live in the cities for a limited period, and are housed without their families in separate, barrack-like hostels. But even those inhabitants of the black cities who have gained the right to live there permanently in terms of the existing laws are faced with uncertainty: for they too are classed as citizens of the respective homelands. Though it often happens that widows, the unemployed, or children who have reached their majority are deported by the white authorities to one of the homelands—even if they have never been there in their lives and have no relations there. Although the number of blacks in the urban areas is continuously increasing, the threat remains of their losing their rights of residency. This uncertainty does not exist for the inhabitants of the black cities around Durban, however, for these fall in the KwaZulu homeland.

This important difference among urban blacks is certainly not the only one. Despite the similarity in external conditions and constraints, the various cities differ markedly in their inhabitants' origins, group membership, standard of education, social status, and degree of politicization. The three urban areas which we have studied accordingly have quite different social profiles. Since these profiles may have some bearing on political attitudes, they are briefly outlined here.

The clearest differentiation is in the *ethnic composition* of the three cities (Table 9.1).

Table 9.1

Ethnic groups	Soweto N = 600	Durban N = 210	Pretoria N = 210
	%	%	%
Zulu	31	91	4
Xhosa	10	5	1
Pedi	9	—	36
South Sotho	14	—	6
Tswana	17	1	16
Venda	5	—	4
Swazi	6	2	7
Ndebele	2	0.5	10
Shangaan	5	—	17
Other	1	0.5	—

Soweto's inhabitants have the most varied origin, including Nguni-speaking blacks from the East Coast (Zulu, Xhosa and Swazi), as well as large groups which originally came from the interior of the country (Sotho, Tswana, and Venda). Black Pretoria is equally varied. Here there are hardly any Nguni speakers at all; the largest groups speak North Sotho, Tswana and Shangaan, and the vast majority come from the Northern and Eastern Transvaal and from Mozambique. The black population of Durban is the most homogeneous: 91 per cent Zulus. But the Zulus are also the largest group in Soweto, where they constitute almost a third of all inhabitants.

The distributions of education and social status differ by city and by ethnic group.

The *standard of education* is highest in Durban and lowest by far in Pretoria (Figure 9.1).

The differences in *socio-economic status* between the cities are similar (Figure 9.2): the greatest proportion of blacks with a relatively high income is found in Durban, and with a relatively low income, in Pretoria.

There are also clear differences in these respects between the members of different ethnic groups.

Table 9.2

Ethnic groups	Soweto		Durban		Pretoria	
	Up to 8 years' schooling	More than 8 years' schooling	Up to 8 years' schooling	More than 8 years' schooling	Up to 8 years' schooling	More than 8 years' schooling
	%	%	%	%	%	%
Zulu	34	27	92	90	5	2
Xhosa	7	14	4	6	1	—
Pedi	8	9	—	—	39	24
South Sotho	15	12	—	—	5	8
Tswana	15	19	2	1	10	37
Venda	5	4	—	—	5	2
Swazi	5	6	3	2	7	7
Ndebele	2	3	—	—	9	13
Shangaan	7	4	—	—	19	7
Other	1	1	—	1	—	—

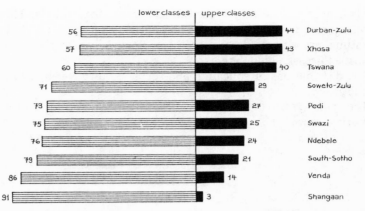

	lower classes	upper classes	
56		44	Durban-Zulu
57		43	Xhosa
60		40	Tswana
71		29	Soweto-Zulu
73		27	Pedi
75		25	Swazi
76		24	Ndebele
79		21	South-Sotho
86		14	Venda
91		3	Shangaan

As Table 9.2 and Figure 9.3 show, in Soweto the Xhosas and the Tswanas have both a relatively high standard of education and status. In Durban the Xhosas are relatively better off, whereas in Pretoria Tswanas in particular, but also the Pedi and the Ndebele, are better educated. The Vendas and Shangaans are far worse off in both respects. These differences reflect primarily the varying extent to which the ethnic groups are urbanized. Those who settled in the cities first have had a more favourable chance of both receiving a modern education and entering better occupations.

The areas also differ in the *religious* affiliation of their inhabitants (Table 9.3).

Table 9.3

Religious affiliation	Soweto	Durban	Pretoria
	%	%	%
'Official' Christian churches	59	70	63
Traditional African religions	30	24	27
No religious affiliation	11	6	10

Durban has the highest representation of 'official' Christian churches, and the lowest of traditional African religions. The number of religious groups which have separated from the official Christian churches and exhibit various forms of African Christianity or religious syncretism is highest in Soweto. The official Christian churches are represented most strongly among the better-educated (Figure 9.4). On the other hand, contemporary atheistic humanism is almost unknown among urban blacks. Those who have not become Christians have apparently remained animists.

There are also considerable differences between the three cities, set out in Table 9.4, in the extent to which people are *politically informed*, as

268

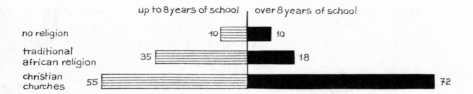

up to 8 years of school | over 8 years of school

no religion	10	10
traditional african religion	35	18
christian churches	55	72

assessed on the basis of newspaper readership. Most newspaper readers live in Durban and Soweto, and fewer in Pretoria. The *Rand Daily Mail*, the white newspaper most critical of the government, has a large readership among better-educated blacks, especially in the Transvaal. The black *World*, which was banned late in 1977, had a very large readership in all three cities, including Durban, and especially among those with a lower standard of education. *Ilanga*, a Zulu newspaper with pro-Buthelezi sympathies, and critical of the government, also caters for the less-educated strata. In Durban, practically all better-educated blacks read white opposition newspapers, and the less-educated, *Ilanga*. Only in Pretoria is there a significant group of less-educated blacks who hardly read a newspaper at all.

Table 9.4

Newspaper	Soweto		Durban		Pretoria	
	Up to 8 years' schooling	More than 8 years' schooling	Up to 8 years' schooling	More than 8 years' schooling	Up to 8 years' schooling	More than 8 years' schooling
	%	%	%	%	%	%
Rand Daily Mail	44	85	2	14	26	84
Other English newspapers in the Transvaal	27	64	—	4	20	71
English daily newspapers in Natal	—	—	65	99	—	—
English weekly newspapers	12	36	4	44	10	34
The World	72	70	17	39	48	61
Ilanga	8	—	79	36	1	—
Other newspapers*	2	3	10	2	4	5
Read no newspapers	11	1	11	2	40	7

*Including African newspapers and the Inkatha paper, 'The Nation'.

Finally, a few differences between the cities emerge in respect of membership of social, cultural and political organizations (Table 9.5). In

269

all areas, approximately a third of the respondents were members of some or other organization—usually a sports club. Only in Durban do political organizations have a substantial membership—12 per cent of all respondents, for the most part members of Inkatha.

Table 9.5

Organization	Soweto	Durban	Pretoria
	%	%	%
Church organizations	1	—	2
Sports clubs	15	9	20
Cultural associations	5	6	1
Trade-unions	1	2	1
Political organizations	2	12	1
Welfare organizations	4	2	5
Professional and occupational associations	2	4	1
Citizens' associations	1	1	—
No organizational affiliations	71	69	70

The figures outlined above display markedly different profiles for the inhabitants of the three urban areas. We analyse below how far these differences influence political attitudes.

The youth rebellion in the black cities[44]

Since 1976, the political climate in most black cities has been determined by the continuing unrest and repeated demonstrations of young blacks.

The unrest began on 16 June 1976. Its immediate cause was a march of black scholars in protest against the introduction of Afrikaans as a medium of instruction in black schools. In 1955, the government had decided that instruction ought to be given equally in English and Afrikaans. Although twenty years had elapsed since the decision was taken, at the beginning of 1976 preparations were made to implement it. Long before the start of the unrest there had been attempts—by black school principals, parents' associations, clergymen, and the Institute of Race Relations—to tell the authorities that such a step would be resisted by black schoolchildren.[45] The schoolchildren were opposed to Afrikaans for both practical and political reasons. Neither the children nor most of the teachers has a command of the language. As a medium of instruction

[44] Cf. the comprehensive account by Gisela Albrecht, *Soweto oder der Aufstand der Vorstädte, op cit*, and Reinhard Brückner, *Südafrikas schwarze Zukunft, op cit*.

[45] As early as 27.9.1974 a black church leader had stated in an interview with the authors: 'If the Afrikaners want to enforce Afrikaans as a medium of instruction this will lead to a clash. In their own interests they should not go too far.'

270

it would simply have made the material more difficult to understand, and reduced the pupils' chances in the examinations. The other objection was that the language is a symbol of Afrikaner domination and apartheid.

The scholars' resistance initially took the form of a boycott of schools in Soweto. The white authorities, however, remained adamant that their ordinance be implemented. On 16 June 1976 over a thousand secondary school students in Soweto went on a protest march. They carried placards with slogans such as 'To hell with Afrikaans', 'Afrikaans stinks', 'Afrikaans is a tribal language', and so on. In other words, it was hardly a demonstration to appeal to language-conscious Afrikaners—but it was most certainly not a revolutionary uprising.

The demonstrators were in a cheerful and noisy mood. The schoolchildren were obviously enjoying for once showing the authorities what they thought. When cars drove past they raised their fists in the Black Power salute and shouted: 'Power', but without hostility. The younger generation in Soweto had by 1976 long been acquainted with the symbols and basic ideas of the Black Consciousness movement.

The protest march continued on its way without incident, until it was stopped by two armed policemen. The policemen were uncertain about the intentions of the demonstrators, and ordered them to disperse. When they did not, the police fired shots into the air. The students, as much shocked as enraged, stoned and injured two policemen. The police thereupon shot into the crowd. Four schoolchildren were killed.

The demonstrators fled, and unrest broke out throughout the black residential areas. Administration offices were attacked, and two white officials murdered. Buses and cars belonging to white firms were set alight, and beer halls and liquor stores destroyed. The demonstrators shouted slogans such as 'Less beer, more education', and 'Schools, not spirits'.[46]

As the unrest continued, political themes gained increasing prominence. The schoolchildren called on the adults to join them. There was an attempt to march on Johannesburg, and a demonstration in the centre of the 'white' city—both of which were quickly suppressed. The schoolchildren then called on black workers to come out on a general strike. Groups of schoolchildren tried to prevent workers from boarding trains at the railway stations, and workers returning home in the evening were harried. People were threatened with arson if they went to work, and some houses were set alight. Seventy-five per cent of workers responded to the first call for a one-day strike. Further calls were less successful, mainly because police were protecting the railway stations. However, a proportion of the workers continued to support the strikes.

[46] A large part of the budget for the administration of the black cities derives from the revenues of the tax on alcohol. For this reason the authorities promote the consumption of alcohol. The demonstrators were well aware of this fact.

271

Demonstrations took place in other parts of the country: in Pretoria, several towns on the Witwatersrand, the Northern Transvaal, the Eastern Cape, as well as in Cape Town, where coloured youths braved massive police cordons to march into the centre of the city.

The demonstrations seem to have been extended in a well-co-ordinated fashion, with the Soweto Students' Representative Council playing a leading role. However, there did not seem to be any key leaders. The police arrested members of the Students' Council, but the demonstrations continued with new and unknown youths at their head.

Although the police were able to prevent demonstrations taking place elsewhere, within the black cities the disturbances continued intermittently for some months, broken by periods of calm.

Hundreds of demonstrators lost their lives in clashes with the police.

The group interviews with Soweto schoolchildren, which Schlemmer conducted in October and November 1976,[47] reveal a frightening readiness for struggle and sacrifice:

We have no future besides this struggle.

I am no longer afraid of guns. When there is shooting, I shout 'Happy', for that is the slogan of the day . . . The police have brought Christmas to Soweto—their shots sound like Christmas rockets!
We are showing the whites that the day of the obedient Bantu is past.
Long-suffering people are now prepared to fight, and also to die if necessary.

The idea of struggle acquired an almost mythical quality:

We shall be free. If we are killed, there will be stronger people to continue the fight until we are free.

We alone have no future in any case.
Struggle is man's life—victory or defeat is in God's hands.
We will give all we have for the struggle.
The police will exterminate us. But we will fight to the last. We succeed or we die.

Clearly, the struggle was no longer only concerned with questions of education, or the frustrations of life in Soweto:

We live not for Soweto, but for a better humanity.

Our blood will feed the soil of freedom.

The group interviews suggest that the demonstrations were motivated more by an inner sense of duty than by practical strategy. Some respondents interpreted the police action as responses of fear and panic:

[47] The interviews were constructed by Lawrence Schlemmer and conducted by experienced black interviewers. Fifty youths participated.

What gives us hope is precisely that the Boers resort to violence. That is the sign that they have lost their nerve. We will cause them to lose other things too, and then we will attain what we want.

However, the majority expressed the belief that the struggle would continue and grow of its own momentum, and that in the long run it would necessarily be successful.

What were the consequences of the disturbances?

We must state at the outset that at no time was there a serious threat to 'law and order'. Many people died, but the South African police never had to deploy more than a fraction of their strength. Had the police felt seriously threatened, the number of deaths would most certainly have been far higher. If the mass demonstrations are regarded as an attempt at immediate liberation or the violent overthrow of the system, they were undoubtedly a tragic failure. In his study of Black Consciousness, Noel Manganyi refers to them as a 'dustbin revolution'—brave, idealistic, but tragically incapable of shaking the edifice of state security and white power.

Nevertheless, the white government did react. The economic consequences were dealt with above. And on the question of the medium of instruction, the government yielded. It announced improvements in the educational system, including the scrapping of the hated term 'Bantu' in educational contexts. Leasehold was also made easier for urban blacks. Previously only those who had opted for homeland citizenship were allowed to lease a house; this was now extended to every person entitled to reside in the city. The government also introduced some marginal political and administrative changes in the black cities: the 'Urban Bantu Councils'—which had had purely advisory functions—would be replaced by 'Community Councils', which would be granted some administrative powers.[48]

Typically, however, these concessions were only marginal. Full property rights in the cities were not granted, nor full communal self-administration. The black population reacted with contempt. The Community Council elections were a complete failure. In a number of seats candidates were not even nominated, and where there was voting the percentage poll was extremely low.

By contrast, a council of political leaders was formed in Soweto which received extensive recognition from the population—the 'Committee of Ten'. It consisted of respected spokesmen from different black organizations, and was also recognized by the school principals. But the government refused to talk to the Committee on the grounds that it was influenced by the Black Consciousness movement. When the Black

[48] The Urban Bantu Councils had only advisory functions. Their standing among the blacks was never very high. In council elections the percentage poll was usually between 15 and 25 per cent.

Consciousness organizations were prohibited, the most important members of the Committee of Ten were arrested at the same time.

The result thus far has been a complete deadlock. The white government refuses to recognize the spokesmen of the most viable black movements: while the population refuses to participate in elections which the government hopes will provide leaders who are prepared to be accommodating. The young continued to resist for a long time. Violent demonstrations were succeeded by a boycott in a number of schools, especially in Johannesburg and Pretoria. Isolated demonstrations continue to occur regularly. The unrest certainly tailed off, but not before it had decisively determined the political climate in the black cities.

What is the significance of the unrest and its aftermath?

It is patently obvious that the language question was only the spark which ignited a huge keg of discontent. Firstly, there was immense dissatisfaction with the whole system of Bantu Education. Blacks regard this education as second class, deliberately designed to give them an inferior training. And in the eyes of the young, the educational system is not only an evil in itself, but also a symbol of the whole hated system of apartheid.[49] The social milieu of young urban blacks is effectively segregated from any other. Black parents at least have contact at work with people of other groups and races. But schoolchildren and unemployed youths spend all their time in the ghetto world of the black cities. Their only contact with the outside world is at points where the restrictions on the ghetto are imposed: with white authorities and with an educational system devised by whites. These contacts are frustrating, so it is at these points that they concentrate their aggression. The educational system is supremely important; it ordains whether or not they will be able to escape via a satisfactory career from the poverty and sadness of a ghetto existence. Yet the realities of the school system only increase the tension. For years all the schools have been overcrowded. In 1975 alone, the number of pupils attending secondary schools jumped by 52 per cent. This necessarily lowered the quality of the teaching, and increased the pupils' fears for the future.

Unemployment is a further reason for the unrest, explaining why the demonstrations drew their main support from youths and young adults. Unemployment, particularly among the black youth, had risen dramatically by mid-1976. The youths' expectations of the future were the more strongly influenced because this followed a long period of economic prosperity. Between 1970 and 1975, job opportunities open to blacks had improved markedly, and their wages and salaries had risen

[49] Cf Theodor Hanf and Gerda Vierdag, *'People's College'—'The World''s Educational Supplement, op cit*, Ch. 3.1.

as never before. The stark contrast between that period and the increasing unemployment was very disillusioning. As discussed above, setbacks after periods of rapid progress typically precede unrest in a society.[50]

Unemployment among the youth was particularly hard-hitting in the cities because the poor community structures offered hardly any appealing diversions, such as sport or other leisure activities, which in other societies moderate politicization.

There were also other factors. Compulsory homeland citizenship must have been particularly infuriating to young people who, born and bred in the cities, have never even seen a homeland. And the political revolutions in Mozambique and Angola, as well as the first concessions by whites in Rhodesia and Namibia, must have generated a certain optimism. For many young people, the time for change seemed at hand.

In summary, we have established that the youth in the black cities were subjected to the same frustrations as adults, plus a few more. Yet they did not feel the pull of work and family duties which breaks political activism among adults. The Black Consciousness movement undoubtedly provided them with the concepts and slogans to express their political discontent and their desires. In particular, many young people had been so strongly motivated by the Black Consciousness scholar organizations that, even after repeated arrests, there were always new leaders to take the initiative. The demonstrations showed that a large proportion of the young had become almost puritanically militant and ready to accept sacrifice, and were not decisively discouraged when the movement was not an immediate success.

The implication for the present is that *a whole generation has undergone an inordinately strong politicization.* Even if many youths were not very motivated politically at the time of the first demonstrations, confrontations with the police and experience of solidarity has strongly shaped their political consciousness.

The social and political limits of the disturbances

For decades there have been frequent predictions that a bloody revolution is imminent in South Africa. The unrest in the black cities in 1976 and 1977 gave rise to a new wave of such pronouncements. However, although the unrest was important in the formation of black political consciousness, it would be quite mistaken to interpret it as a serious blow to white power.

For, although the unrest was widespread and long-lasting, it had clear social and political limits. It mainly involved the youth, especially pupils

[50] Cf., for instance, T. D. Gurr, *Why Men Rebel* (Princeton, 1970).

275

and students. Adults—particularly the workers, who form the backbone of the South African economy—at most participated partially. This is the most important *social limit* to the unrest.

Many observers have spoken of a political generation gap. Adults of fixed occupation and family responsibilities tend, especially in times of recession and unemployment, to be politically cautious. They may also have remembered earlier failures: the 'Defiance Campaigns' of the ANC in the 1950s and the suppression of the black protest movement after Sharpeville were bitter experiences for many older black South Africans. There is a very realistic and simple economic reason for political caution: most families need regular salaries and wages simply to survive. In other words, they can maintain a strike or survive a lock-out for a few days at most. It is also realistic to acknowledge the great strength of white power: state controls are strict, the means for repression are considerable, and blacks are specifically concentrated and isolated in areas where they are easy to control.

We must nevertheless ask whether the frustrations of apartheid society might not drive the entire black population to act in desperation, as the youth have done in recent years, despite their relative powerlessness.[51] This has not happened so far. It has been argued that the reason, apart from economic restraints and the actual power structure, is a particular outlook or set of attitudes among the black population.

In this connection, a member of the Black Consciousness movement, now in exile, speaks of 'a psychological yoke of despondency'.[52] Fatima Meer points out another dimension: 'The strength of the state is not based on sheer brute force. . . . It holds the people in its sway by a mixture of conviction and open violence . . . so that the average non-white believes that he, in South Africa, is happier than people elsewhere, and that his economic security is worth more than a pipe-dream of freedom.'[53] Feit develops this view with the idea that blacks have a perception of 'reciprocal usefulness': they see their economic security and progress as closely bound up with the economic interests and activity of the whites.[54] This view of mutual dependence damps political activism in times of rising economic prosperity.

Schlemmer's study of the urban blacks, carried out in 1971–72 in Durban,[55] has empirically established the presence of certain perceptions

[51] Cf. Heribert Adam, *Modernizing Racial Discrimination, op cit*, p. 183.

[52] Ranwedzi Nengwekhulu, 'The Meaning of Black Consciousness in the Struggle for Liberation in South Africa', *Notes and Documents of the United Nations Centre against Apartheid*, No. 16/76 (July 1976), p. 3.

[53] Fatima Meer, 'African Nationalism: Some Inhibiting Factors', *loc cit*, p. 122.

[54] Edward Feit, *African Opposition in South Africa—The Failure of Passive Resistance, op cit*, Ch. 1.

[55] Lawrence Schlemmer, 'Political Adaptation and Reaction among Urban Africans in South Africa', *Social Dynamics*, 2:1 (1976), pp. 3–19.

which help explain their lack of revolutionary activity. Only 6 per cent of respondents could be classified as satisfied, and most thought that their poor situation was unjustified. But despite this overwhelming dissatisfaction and their perception of 'relative deprivation', and despite also a total rejection of apartheid, only 30–40 per cent could be classified as 'activists'. The blacks who were interviewed, including a number of activists, doubted that confrontation would have any point, for a number of reasons. A considerable proportion of respondents expected change through reform, which they thought would occur in time without the system being put under pressure. Only a little over half thought that majority rule would lead to a better society. About a third were prepared to accept rationalization of white domination—there was frequent agreement with the contention that blacks did not yet have the knowledge, ability and experience necessary to take over the reins of government. About half of the respondents were prepared to accept the homeland policy, if only to escape the frustrations of urban society under apartheid. Finally, half the respondents saw white domination as so strongly entrenched that there was no possibility of overthrowing it.

These various perceptions however were never put forward jointly by individual respondents, but were widely distributed. Schlemmer accordingly concluded that only a small minority of blacks in Durban either were prepared to involve themselves in active resistance to apartheid, or were in a position to do so.

These facts help explain why working adults were not involved in the recent urban unrest. It is possible, as some spokesmen of the older generation have claimed, that there is no 'political generation gap'. For example, David Thebahali, former Chairman of the Soweto Urban Bantu Council, stated before resigning under pressure from the youth, that their actions had the full support of parents.[56] And Bishop Manas Buthelezi, former chairman of the Black Parents' Association of Soweto, explained: 'It is not a generation gap . . . it is a question of different methods'.[57] The generation gap may thus exist precisely in the different methods. Both younger and older blacks, schoolchildren and workers, are united in their rejection of the present system and the frustration they share. But there are very wide disagreements on how to change the system and how to end the frustration. So, while the older generation undoubtedly has tremendous sympathy for the young and for what they have done, it has joined in their rebellion.

These, then, are the social limits of the urban unrest. The *political limits* are similar. Representatives of all political tendencies, including some homeland leaders, have shown sympathy for the young people's

[56] *Rand Daily Mail*, 17.12.1976.

[57] Thomas Ross, 'Erst müssen wir wie Löwen werden', *Frankfurter Allgemeine Zeitung*, 16.4.1977.

rebellion, and understanding of their cause. But only the leaders of the Black Consciousness movement identify themselves with the rebellion. As one of them stated, it was actually their own movement which sustained the protest, even if 'it started much earlier than we ourselves had expected'. The old Congress organizations also expressed their approval, and then even tried to claim responsibility for having started the unrest—which the leaders of the Black Consciousness movement regarded as an attempt to 'steal the credit'. *Inkatha*, however, disapproved of the unrest. Given their choice of strategy, its leaders could not see the sense of a political confrontation which was doomed to fail. It cannot have been purely coincidental that, apart from a few incidents at the University of KwaZulu, there was no unrest in Natal. Part of the reason may have been that two of the most important factors in the schoolchildren's protest did not apply in Natal: firstly, the KwaZulu Ministry of Education, not Pretoria, is responsible for nearly all the schools; and secondly, the whole question of homeland citizenship, so pressing in Pretoria and Soweto, has no real substance in Natal where most of the black urban areas fall within KwaZulu. But the main reason for the absence of unrest in Natal was probably Inkatha's influence on the youth there.

Finally, it is worth noting that the *black trade-unions* kept a very low profile throughout the unrest. Black trade-unions in South Africa have waxed and waned.[58] In the early 1960s, a strong tendency to politicize the labour movement developed within the non-racial South African Council of Trade Unions, particularly among the black trade-unions which belonged to this federation. This was obviously because the predicament of the black workers largely derives from their lack of political rights. The reaction of the white government to this development was to serve banning orders on a large number of trade-union leaders. The organization was hit so hard that it slowly collapsed. By the end of the 1960s, only two black trade-unions survived.

Since 1972, trade-unionism has been regaining support. For example, the Urban Training Project, a moderate and non-political organization, has had some success in the Transvaal and Natal with its aim of training labour leaders. In 1973, there was a wave of strikes in and around Durban which paralysed industry for a fortnight.[59] Over 70,000 black workers went on strike, with some support from Indian workers. Employers were forced to make substantial concessions, and the government raised the minimum wages for unskilled labour.

[58] For a brief account cf. M. A. du Toit, *South African Trade Unions: History, Legislation, Policy* (Johannesburg, 1976); cf. as well Edward Feit, *Workers Without Weapons, op cit.*

[59] Cf. Institute for Industrial Education, *The Durban Strikes 1973* (Johannesburg, 1974).

The reasons for the strike in Natal were clearly economic, not political. There was a remarkable solidarity and discipline among the workers. The strike was able to continue for a relatively long time because, as Heribert Adam pointed out, the workers received support in their daily subsistence from the surrounding rural areas.[60]

Both the ANC-in-exile and the Black Consciousness movement claimed to have had some influence on the strike, but this was denied by the labour leaders in Natal.

The success of the strike invigorated the black trade-union movement. By 1974 there were twenty trade-unions, with about 40,000 members. Their situation became more difficult with the onset of the recession. The organization of the Urban Training Project was weakened by the banning orders served on its leaders. A labour organization, the Black and Allied Workers' Union, was founded within the Black Consciousness movement. Its success has been limited so far. The majority of unionized black workers belong to non-political organizations.

These organizations obviously did not want to participate in the unrest. On the one hand, they remembered the failure of the political general strike in 1960 and the demise of the political trade-union movement in the following years. On the other hand, the workers achieved their economic goals in the 1973 strike. So in 1976 and 1977 they were not prepared to risk years of patient organizing towards their own longer-term goals.

The labour movement is like Inkatha, then, in being interested in organization rather than rebellion. We saw earlier that there is a division between the generations over political methods. There is the same division over methods between the student movement and Black Consciousness on the one hand, and organized labour and Inkatha on the other—or to be more precise, it is a *division over strategy. The black opposition is divided in the cities—notwithstanding the unity of its basic aspirations.*

The different attitudes towards the recent unrest clearly demonstrate that the political cultures of the various tendencies in the black opposition are determined by different historical traditions, guiding principles, and contrasting strategies; and these result, in the last instance, in completely different ideas about the form the struggle with white power is to take.

Thus, the homeland leaders by and large co-operate with the white government; the dynamic of Black Consciousness, fuelled by the young students of Soweto, is directed at a strategy of protest and 'the great refusal', and hopes to achieve change by rejecting any co-operation with

---

[60] Heribert Adam, 'When the Chips Are Down: Confrontation and Accommodation in South Africa', *Contemporary Crises*, 1 (1977), pp. 417–35.

279

the system; and Inkatha seeks to exploit the full scope allowed by the present situation to construct a powerful and well-organized political machine, able bit by bit to wring concessions from the regime.

The prospect which each of these tendencies has of playing the major role in black opposition has to be established empirically.

CHAPTER 10

Different Approaches to the Same Goal: Opinions and Attitudes of Black Political Leadership Groups in 1977

As far as our goals are concerned, we are all radicals. Could one expect anything else under the prevailing circumstances in this country? Everybody accepts that these circumstances will have to change; but what is the best way? On this point we disagree considerably.

This is the view of one of the most powerful and most contentious black politicians, on the thorny question of how the leadership groups of black South Africa are united and divided. They are united in their political goal, that the existing social, economic, and political power relationships must be fundamentally changed. But as soon as one touches on the form which a future society should take, their conceptions differ. And the disagreement is even greater about the ways and means of achieving the necessary change.

The first section of this chapter deals with what black leadership groups think about change in race relations. The second section analyses how the spokesmen of the various tendencies view their own and the other approaches. The third section deals with their views on the possibilities and prospects of achieving the desired changes by peaceful means.

1. *Opinions of black leadership groups on the goals of change*

All the black leaders interviewed agree on two points. They reject apartheid, and they are prepared to live together and co-operate with whites. Representatives of very different political tendencies stress the latter; but despite their substantial agreement, the emphasis differs.

As a former leader of the ANC explained:

We do not accept apartheid. This land belongs to us. Whites are very welcome to live with us, but not as masters over servants.

A homeland leader states:

The ideology of separate development does not work anywhere. There is hardly any field in which blacks or whites can do anything alone. What we need is not separate but co-operative development.

The abolition of discrimination in all walks of life is a goal shared by all black politicians. Even a homeland leader who is generally regarded as conservative makes this demand:

There must be an end to the artificial fostering of group consciousness. People may not marry whom they want. Skin colour is abused as part of the power struggle, not to mention as a criterion for wealth. Whoever favours this is not a Christian but a hypocrite. People must be regarded as people, not as members of groups.

We shall begin with an analysis of race relations in the *economic sphere*. The various political tendencies differ widely in their views on this point.

One homeland leader demands the abolition of discriminatory labour legislation:

These laws only serve white interests. When blacks try to look after their interests they are fired. They have to do the same work as whites for less pay. This is the first thing that will have to change.

A leading spokesman of the Indian community underlined the political importance of a non-discriminatory economic policy:

The government is right that Communism is a threat to Southern Africa. But they use the wrong means to fight it. The less-educated black thinks that Communism will liberate him, because he has no idea of what Communism is. In my view, the best defence against Communism would be a policy of economic emancipation. This would offer the mass of the population more than merely the loss of their chains.

An influential black businessman fears that the government's policy will discredit the free enterprise system:

What we have at present is a free-market economy restricted to whites, and something quite different for blacks. Can one then hope that this economic and social order will survive into the future?

Black trade-unionists emphasize the importance of the right of association:

Whites regard us not as people but as units of labour, to be obtained as cheaply as possible. Look at those English-speaking socialites who like to be known for their social work, but treat their servants badly and pay them miserable wages. In this sphere, as in all others, we cannot put an end to exploitation without genuine trade-union rights.

A leading representative of the Inkatha movement espouses a policy of pragmatically changing economic relations:

Without the whites our economy would collapse; but it would also collapse without an appropriate participation of the blacks. We should share the fruits of the country—then we would be able to get on well with each other. The blacks themselves have to play a part in their economic liberation. We can help to build up our own consumer goods industry, and do a lot to promote our agricultural development. The question of a free market or a planned economy is secondary— everything that helps black development is good.

The leaders of the Black Consciousness movement do not think that repealing the discriminatory economic legislation will be enough to achieve the desired degree of change in the economic relations between the race groups. They propose an economic and socio-political alternative:

Our conception is of African communalism, which has much in common with the Tanzanian conception. We must begin with our African way of life, and try to adapt it to the realities of industrial society. We cannot simply accept capitalism in its present form—for we would then not escape from racism, but simply replace whites by blacks. But we also reject Marxism.

They are quite aware that this conception needs to be developed:

Our doctrine is naturally not yet clear, given the situation in which we find ourselves. A few years ago one couldn't even mention socialism.

They also realize that in certain circumstances practical considerations outweigh more far-reaching socio-political changes:

Naturally, white liberals like the PFP people only want to abolish discrimination and institute a normal capitalist system. That would suit them and all the Western countries, as well as many members of our black middle class. One mustn't forget how conservative many blacks are. We ourselves, of course, don't want to stop there. But for the moment any kind of liberalisation suits us.

There were two distinct trends among the ANC leaders interviewed. A representative of the Nationalist wing refused to commit himself in advance to a socio-political order:

I think it is premature to take ideological decisions on the future economic order. Let there first be freedom, and for that we need all our strength; then the people can decide.

283

A supporter of the left wing of the ANC took a different view:

Everyone speaks of socialism, from Kaunda to Buthelezi. They want a moderate socialism; but there is no such thing. South Africa will be socialist.

These statements make clear that the socio-political struggle over South Africa's future economic order has already begun.

As far as attitudes to *social relations* between the race groups are concerned, there are hardly any differences between the various political tendencies. All black leaders take for granted that petty apartheid must disappear. But the question of social relations is still important for some coloured politicians:

The crux of the problem is petty apartheid. A society which institutionalises discrimination breeds resentment. Petty apartheid is an insult to human dignity. We want to be accepted as people.

However, for many black politicians the material disadvantages of petty apartheid are more important—less pay, lower quality services, etc. Thus, an Inkatha leader treated the white fear of social contact with amusement:

The whites need the Immorality Act to protect them against their own weaknesses. It is almost always Afrikaners who contravene this law, especially policemen. It is whites who creep around at night looking for black women . . .

And an ANC leader commented contemptuously:

I am pretty indifferent about social relations—their park benches, their white girls . . . The crucial struggle is economic. Our people want a better life.

The Black Consciousness movement is also unconcerned about petty apartheid. What counts for them is that blacks become self-aware:

We have had our most thorough-going success in consciousness-raising among ordinary people. You can see it among domestic servants. They stop using lipstick and imitating European hairstyles. Our women are beginning to dress as Africans. The younger generation no longer has any complexes.

When Inkatha leaders insist upon the abolition of petty apartheid, it is primarily for political reasons. They stress the importance of human contact if peaceful change is to be possible:

I still think that co-existence is valuable. People must get used to each other, live with each other, get to know each other, become friends. At present human relations are cold. That is why this petty apartheid nonsense must first disappear.

The opinions of the black political groups on the *political relations* between the race groups are ambivalent. All respondents agree that South Africa should be a single country, and not divided among its inhabitants. But beyond this the different political tendencies diverge, about how far they should be prepared to make constitutional compromises with the white minority in the interests of peaceful change, and about the future role of the whites.

A 'moderate' homeland leader took this view:

This country, South Africa, belongs to all who live here. It is high time that people stopped talking nonsense about South Africa's being empty before the whites arrived. That's ideology, not history. The NP wants to split South African society, and artificially segregate the groups. We must resist this attempt.

A coloured politician emphasized:

I reject a special solution for the coloureds. I refuse to support measures of this kind. I don't want to be a collaborator. As long as the blacks are kept in slavery, we are not free either. We want a multiracial state for everyone. I believe that the white man also has a place in this country. His future depends on how he behaves.

A leader of the Black Consciousness movement expressed himself more forcefully:

We regard South Africa as our country, the country of those who have the right to call themselves 'natives'. It is the blacks' country, given them by God—if God really exists.

An ANC leader used similar terms:

South Africa—let's not deceive ourselves—belongs to the blacks. What is all this nonsense about 300 years of white history? The Portuguese were in Africa for 500 years, and they have had to leave. We will accept the whites, but not in a position of domination.

Thus, the conceptions of the ideal political situation are quite similar. But reactions to the current dispensation differ widely.

A minority of homeland politicians are prepared to accept territorial independence. They justify their view as follows:

Today, as a homeland leader, I can do everything for which others were deported to Robben Island a few years ago. If my country were independent, I might be able to do far more. For our hands are tied by Pretoria in many respects, especially the practical implementation of development projects. We can't even make use of foreign aid. In this respect it is almost better to be independent, and to develop the country.

Another reason for considering independence is the constant humiliation which we have to endure from white South Africans. This

285

is why we prefer freedom and poverty to continued oppression with a
higher standard of living.

However, most homeland politicians reject the policy of independence:

The Land Act of 1936 would have to be radically revised before one
could talk properly about homelands. There should not only be talk
about consolidation and territorial enlargement; something should
finally be done about it. Independence is out of the question, given the
present borders.

Numerous 'moderate' politicians emphasize that the official bantustan
policy cannot be genuine:

Take KwaZulu for example. Four and a half million Zulus, more than
the total white population, live on forty-four patches of land without
an outlet to the sea. Could anyone believe that such a situation is
viable?

The black leaders of various tendencies see a danger that a section of the
black élite could be tempted by the prospects that 'independence' offers.
An ANC leader observes:

A number of people say they agree with the homelands concept
because the homelands offer good jobs and reasonable salaries.

A trade-union leader took a similar view:

The Transkei is playing a dangerous game at the moment. Many well-
educated people are going back there because they are offered well-
paid jobs and in this way are lulled into satisfaction of a sort.

On the whole, however, independence for the bantustans is rejected,
whether within their present borders or as territorially consolidated
states. Even conservative politicians do not believe that the white
government is prepared to give any serious consideration to consolidation:

One could imagine viable homelands—for instance, a KwaZulu which
included Durban and Richard's Bay. There would have to be sensible
borders and an appropriate distribution of the wealth of the land. But
the whites know exactly what they are going to give up and what not;
certainly, no areas with mineral resources. The whole policy is a
fraud.

The government's policy is considered dishonest, so many respondents
think it pointless even to regard it as an alternative. The attitudes
towards partition are much the same. An Inkatha politician states:

Partition is born of fear. And fear leads to false conclusions. The
partition of the country on the basis of (the) 1936 (Land Act) is in any
case utterly absurd. A genuine partition of the country into two equal

parts, sharing its wealth, might be more plausible. In at least giving us a power base, that would be a step in the right direction. But this government is too obstinate, too afraid, and too petty even to consider a genuine partition.

A leader of the Black Consciousness movement commented on this point:

A partition of South Africa would serve absolutely no purpose. If the Leistner Plan or similar proposals were implemented, the present problems between the race groups would still exist in the southern part of the country. If on the other hand whites fundamentally changed their attitudes, partition would be quite superfluous. This is why we favour one country, from Cape Point to the Limpopo.

The reasons for rejecting partition are not only rational. An ANC leader expressed the emotional side:

Radical partition is both wrong and ungodly, just as wrong and ungodly as apartheid and the bantustans. There is only one solution, a really Christian solution: brotherhood. Blacks and whites must regard each other as brothers. Partition won't work. A divided South Africa would be weak, or no South Africa at all. If this country is to be saved, it must be saved by blacks and whites together.

The idea of a qualified franchise is rejected even more strongly and clearly by black political leaders than the policy of partition. An Inkatha leader stated:

No black politician can accept a qualified vote. The government gave us 'one man, one vote' in the homelands. How can I go and tell my people that this would no longer apply in a common country? The proposals of the Progressives perhaps made some sense fifteen years ago. But how can we accept them today?

A coloured politician is of this opinion:

Qualified franchise is unacceptable; it is an invitation to manipulation.

For an ANC leader, the qualified franchise was

. . . not worth discussing. A few years ago one might have considered it as a transitional measure. Today, universal franchise is the only solution. And that is how it should be. For what we are finally after is precisely a united, multiracial society.

The views of black leadership groups on federation are more diverse. None of the respondents was a convinced federalist. However, some of them are prepared to think about it, because of the group awareness and fear that they recognize on the part of whites.

A homeland politician explained:

287

Of course I am in favour of majority rule—if it can be implemented. In my mind, that could be the best solution. But even though one aims at it, one should not lose sight of the possibility of meaningful compromise.

Another took the view:

I believe in a federal solution in which no one group is dominant. It could prevent any one group from trying to exclude others from power or destroy them. A constitution which allowed for an extensive devolution of power might be one way of lessening white fears. In a society like ours compromise is the only way.

A labour leader came to a similar conclusion:

Because the whites are afraid, a federation is probably the only peaceful solution that is plausible for the time being.

Other labour leaders, however, were far more sceptical:

We'll accept a federation if we have to; but only if it's like the U.S.A., where blacks and whites can live wherever they want. But when whites talk about federation, it is precisely because they want to restrict our freedom of movement. We don't believe they are prepared to accept a genuine federal state.

This distrust of white intentions leads most black political leaders to reject the idea of a federal state. In the main, they see it as perpetuating apartheid by other means.

As a coloured politician explained:

I reject all forms of group representation. As long as groups remain institutionalized, racism has not been abolished— and we have had enough of that. Given the distrust at present, any form of group representation would only make matters worse.

A 'moderate' black politician shared this view:

A federal state can only work if there are equal opportunities for all citizens in all parts of the country. This is not a radical stance; I simply believe that nothing else would work. The crux of the problem is freedom throughout the country. Political solutions in terms of ethnicity don't help at all. I am convinced that national awareness must transcend regional, ethnic, and racial points of view. Our leaders must be chosen for their competence, not their skin colour. Ethnic nations make no sense to me. The idea of ethnicity runs counter to all developments on our continent; it would be disastrous to promote tribalism and entrench it constitutionally as well.

An Inkatha leader was ambivalent:

A federal plan for South Africa would be unacceptable on a foun-

288

dation of the bantustan philosophy. If it is to make any sense at all, it must be linked to a new and fair distribution of land and wealth. The federation could then be a plausible transitional solution.

A respondent from the Black Consciousness movement explained:

We are in favour of cultural pluralism in South Africa. But to entrench these differences in the constitution can only lead to catastrophe. We cannot accept that.

As a representative of the nationalist wing of the ANC put it:

A federal state has no hope in South Africa. It would not only smell of apartheid, but effectively reinforce it. The Swiss system works among equals; but among unequals a federal state only entrenches inequality.

In the rejection of the federal concept by the left wing of the ANC, there are unmistakably totalitarian tones:

In South African conditions, federalism is a swear-word. We want to maintain the unity of the country, and reject everything which detracts from it. We must eradicate tribalism. Federalism in this country must be rejected entirely. We must bring everyone together and re-educate them in the understanding of a unitary state.

Finally, there are different views about which of the goals we have mentioned should be given priority. For the leaders of the labour organizations, their members' aspirations set a clear priority:

What are the real problems facing black workers? The first is the high cost of living: inflation particularly affects the black lower class. The second problem is transport: blacks have to go extremely long distances to work, and many spend two to four hours a day travelling. Over and above this, the cost of transport takes a considerable part of black incomes. Thirdly, there are the appallingly bad living conditions. Workers living in compounds or factory quarters lead a life unworthy of human beings. Our highest priority must be to abolish these situations.

Another labour leader came to a similar conclusion, but also referred to a growing politicization:

Above all, people want to work where they choose. Secondly, they demand equal pay for equal work, and then education and training appropriate to their abilities. While these three concrete and immediate labour demands are top priority, political desires and demands are not quite so clearly put. Yet it is evident that in the last three years workers have become increasingly politically aware.

Most political leaders give priority to economic reforms and improvements in the general living conditions of the black population. But they do not expect that these goals could be achieved before political changes have taken place:

> *The most pressing aspirations are clearly for a secure place to live, a secure job, and equal education. If the government did something about these problems, a lot of tension would be relieved. But things will probably work differently. Only when we have won the struggle for political rights will we be able to make improvements in other areas.*

Or as a leader of the Black Consciousness movement tersely put it:

> *Political rights are crucial; everything else depends on them.*

The debate in the black leadership groups about which goals should take priority is by no means restricted to the question of economic improvements on the one hand and political rights on the other. In 1976 and 1977 the question of a different and better *education* received a lot of attention. The Soweto demonstrations began with questions of education, and they continue to take first place for a significant proportion of the black protest movement. Moreover, we may draw important conclusions about the different priorities and strategies of the various political tendencies from the attitudes of their leadership groups to educational problems. So we shall deal with these problems for a moment in more detail.

All political tendencies are unanimous in rejecting 'Bantu Education', racial segregation, and all other measures which discriminate against the black population in their education.

But there are wide differences of opinion on how important it is to abolish Bantu Education and whether activist measures, including a total school boycott if necessary, should be employed.

The labour movement tends to adopt a 'moderate' stand. They believe that other questions deserve preference, for example wages, working conditions, transport, housing, etc. They are also very sceptical about the prospects of successful political activism in the educational sphere, especially a school boycott. Finally, they fear that the children of workers in particular will suffer from these measures.

As labour leaders put it:

> *The majority of workers could not care less what kind of education they get; they are happy to get any education at all.*
>
> *Workers outnumber the highly politicized youngsters. Most adult workers know full well that there is no point in a short educational boycott. They want their children to have school certificates, however they get them.*
>
> *The boycott of examinations has practically collapsed. I welcome that, for we must also think of tomorrow. And tomorrow will not be achieved by boycott of examinations, but only by a general strike.*

This desire to take whatever opportunities are presently available is also found in 'moderates' outside the labour movement. They do not believe that fundamental changes are imminent, still less that they can be brought about by a school boycott. In that case, the school boycott can only harm the black community. Thus, a 'moderate' politician took the view:

> *Last year's events have undoubtedly raised the level of awareness. But the student organisations are too weak and too unstructured to maintain their demands over a long period. the majority of blacks say, 'For the time being the system will continue. If we want jobs, we need examinations; so we must go to school.'*

A leader of the Inkatha movement came to the following conclusion:

> *I don't think the school boycott is practicable. Bantu Education is bad, but better than no education at all. You should not experiment with your own life. We have to prepare ourselves for when we will be running the country.*

The Inkatha movement is considering how to exploit the partial autonomy of the Zulu homeland to introduce changes in education. They make the point that even the Transkei, which in their view is 'extremely docile', had introduced significant changes to the educational policy prescribed by Pretoria long before its independence, especially regarding the medium of instruction. In Inkatha's view, therefore, it makes sense to work for autonomy in certain political spheres, even if one rejects independence as Inkatha does in contrast to the Transkei. One must exploit whatever scope for action is allowed 'regardless of the government's motives in allowing this scope', but without making any concessions of principle.

There are those who totally reject the current educational system. They have taken a very different stand. A student leader from Soweto formulated it as follows:

> *We totally reject this so-called 'education'. We are simply not prepared to work with the system of exploitation any longer. We refuse to supply it with cheap skilled labour. The revolt has already brought about a lot of changes. The whites are very afraid—and we have lost our fear. Large business concerns will feel the consequences of our boycott; and the riots have caused a sensation in the rest of the world. The drop in foreign investments since last year is already very encouraging. If we can only persevere, we shall get the better of the whites economically.*

But leading representatives of the Black Consciousness movement are more sceptical about the immediate effects of the schoolchildren's demonstrations. They also take a much more sober view of how close the desired political revolution may be. So, like many 'moderates', although for quite different reasons, their educational policy reflects pragmatic considerations. As a leading person in the movement stated:

One can do nothing without some formal education. We must have matriculants and university graduates. If there are no other examinations available, we must take what there is. The only alternative would be no education at all. And that would be stupid.

Another Black Consciousness spokesman voiced a more discriminating pragmatism, and pointed to the need for making possible partial alternatives to the existing educational system:

One's attitude to the educational system in this country naturally depends a lot on one's assumptions about the timing of political change. If one totally rejects education under the present system, one is assuming that change will occur in the very near future. And whoever simply accepts Bantu Education is not counting on change for a very long time.

At any rate, what we need is an education which both promotes change and prepares us for change. When THAT day arrives, we don't want to be in the position of the Congo in 1960. So Bantu Education is better than no education—just as it is better to drink water infected with bilharzia than to die of thirst immediately. Even if we have in this sense to accept the existing educational system, we should nevertheless try to find other and different educational opportunities—which would prepare us for our future roles and promote free and independent thought. In doing this we should always keep in mind what our future society will be like.

To summarize, black political opinion is unanimous in rejecting the existing system of Bantu Education, but there are divergences on the form of protest against the system. Labour organizations give relatively little importance to educational policy. Workers are inclined to take any opportunity for education, in order to improve their situation. In their view the major problem is not the 'how' but the 'whether' of education. A large 'moderate' centre group considers the opportunities pragmatically. An education boycott will not help to change the system—one should try to make the best of what there is. Many others, especially supporters of the Inkatha movement, see possibilities in exploiting the partial autonomy of the homelands, which they otherwise reject, to introduce educational reforms. By contrast, an influential group of highly politicized schoolchildren and students in the large cities support the policy which calls for a total boycott of education as the first step in changing the political system. The leadership of the Black Consciousness movement is sceptical about such rapid change. They thus reject the educational boycott. They hope to counter the distortions of Bantu Education and prepare the younger generation for their future

292

role through additional or alternative educational opportunities.

The leadership of the Black Consciousness movement is already giving a lot of thought to a conception of education which will go beyond simply achieving equality with the 'white' school system.

They fully realize that the future educational system will have to be tailored to the economic needs of the country, and not simply consist in expanding the system of privileged education for the already privileged white population:

We cannot simply adopt the white educational system. It doesn't meet the requirements of a partially under-developed country. Education must be adapted to the needs of economic and social development. Perhaps we can learn something from the Tanzanian experience.

Thus, as in their search for economic and socio-political concepts, the young Black Consciousness leaders look to Tanzania for their educational blueprint.

Yet they take a remarkably realistic approach to the problems of cultural identity, which are part and parcel of any concrete conception of education:

South Africa will not be able simply to forget its past and, like Tanzania or Zaïre, simply choose what it wants to take over from Europe. We have been subjected to European influences far longer and far more thoroughly than any other African country, so we just have to live with the fact that in the future too we will be different from other African countries. South Africa will have a bastardized culture like Brazil. I say that with some sadness, but I can also see that mixing the positive contributions of different cultures may have its advantages.

This statement should make it quite clear just how mistaken it is to interpret the Black Consciousness movement and its goals as 'black racism'.

In conclusion, we may summarize the opinion of black leadership groups on the goals of change as follows. All black leaders agree in demanding an end to economic discrimination. However, conceptions of South Africa's future economic and social order vary widely. The conservative section among the leaders wants a genuine free enterprise economy. Another group inclines towards a social welfare conception, with redistribution, but also stresses—especially in the case of Inkatha—that self-help is important. The Black Consciousness movement aims at a formulation of African socialism based on the Tanzanian example. The Nationalist wing of the ANC regards considerations of the economic and political order as premature for the moment, whereas the Communist wing of the ANC is in no doubt about the only acceptable solution. Thus, black South Africa is agreed on the demand for an end to economic discrimination, but beyond that there are disagreements about economic and socio-political issues that span the entire ideological spectrum—just as in most Western industrial countries.

As far as race relations in the social sphere are concerned, they are seen as a purely political problem, by coloured leaders above all. This is because coloureds do not differ from whites in either language or culture, and so experience petty apartheid as racism in its purest form. Representatives of the African population group emphasize the financial and material disadvantages which result from petty apartheid, but otherwise react with an equanimity born of cultural self-awareness which allows them to treat petty apartheid as essentially a problem for whites. Black Consciousness and Inkatha differ in their chosen emphasis. The former want to strengthen black awareness and turn it into a political force, while the latter also emphasize that close social contact between black and white will make peaceful change more likely.

We may summarize the political goals as follows. Firstly, any policy of partition—whether within the bantustan boundaries prescribed in 1936, in the form of consolidated territories, or even a more radical partition—is rejected by all the black leadership groups, bar a small minority among the homeland politicians. The reasons for this rejection vary. It is inconceivable to many of the respondents that the white government would ever consider an equitable partition. Others note that if a partition is to be just, it would require a change of attitude among whites that would allow other, better solutions to co-existence.

The concept of qualified franchise is rejected out of hand by all black leaders. Black leaders are also opposed to federalism, or at best are ambivalent about it. All federal solutions are suspected to be apartheid in other constitutional guises. Even moderate politial leaders are only prepared to consider a federal state as a compromise solution, when other more preferable solutions seem to be unattainable by peaceful means. But even the politicians who are open to this compromise would prefer a multiracial, unitary state. Despite the strong emotional appeal of this vision, there is a widespread readiness to negotiate should the white leadership offer genuine compromises. But this is something which the black leadership groups are very sceptical about.

2. *The views of black politicians on political trends in black South Africa*

Elections are an invaluable indicator of the relative strengths of political trends and movements. One appreciates this most when they are lacking. In the absence of such quantifiable data, even the leaders of the various political tendencies in black South Africa can only guess at their strength.

In this section we intend to examine the quantitative and qualitative assessments by black political leaders of the political organizations or tendencies they represent, as well as their opinions of the relative strength and political relevance of the others.

Almost all respondents agreed that urban black support is essential to the appeal and success of a political movement. Politicians recognize that urban blacks have the greatest political awareness of all sections of the population:

Initially, the old ANC was active in the rural areas. It was not for nothing that they later concentrated on the cities. In the rural areas blacks still have a relatively tolerable existence. But in the cities oppression is obvious. It is the urban blacks who reach the conclusion that change is necessary.

This is why all political movements try to gain influence in the cities. A homeland politician explained:

My 'legal' power base is the homeland, of course. But how could I not try to represent urban blacks as well? In South Africa both urban and rural blacks suffer discrimination; we are oppressed in the cities as well as in the country.

Most respondents shared the opinion that—apart from Buthelezi—the homeland leaders enjoy very little support in the cities:

It may be that they are influential on the platteland; the blacks there are loyal to them. But in the cities they can hardly count on any followers.

The homeland politicians themselves are more optimistic:

Of course there are a number of city dwellers who support us. Matanzima is the only one who has lost all urban supporters—sold them down the drain. But our people know that we will not do that.

The homeland leaders regard themselves as pragmatists, trying to make the best of a bad situation:

Many people think we are only men of straw. In the initial stages of the bantustan policy we undoubtedly were. But things have changed. What was there before? The ANC has been demanding basic human rights since 1912, yet the whites have retained their privileged position unchallenged. For years there were no spokesmen for the blacks. If we don't stand up and demand our due, nothing will happen in the future either. And what better way is there for us to speak effectively and safely than from the basis of the homelands? The homelands have, against the will of their creators, become a centre of power, a political platform for blacks. This development is irreversible.

A few 'moderate' politicians admit the good intentions of the homeland leaders:

295

One shouldn't call them 'sell-outs'. Many people believe that the bantustan concept can help the blacks. They have achieved something in the field of education, for instance in Lebowa and Gazankulu.

The homeland politicians are acceptable to Inkatha leaders

. . . as long as they don't accept independence. If we accepted the homeland policy we would put the seal on our dependency.

But for the Black Consciousness movement and the supporters of the old ANC and PAC, homeland politicians are

men of straw;
collaborators and traitors;
and
sell-outs to the government.

The so-called 'moderate' black politicians do not form a coherent group. They are prominent personalities who as businessmen, academics, or journalists exercise some personal influence, and whose opinions are respected in the black community. They do not, however, represent an organization:

We are essentially black liberals. Like the Black Consciousness people and the ANC, we also reject the bantustan policy out of hand; but we are not enthusiastic about the socialist tendencies of those organizations.

They continue to hope that whites will adopt a policy of open negotiation and compromise while 'there is still time':

What the whites should do first and foremost is make a clear declaration that they intend to abandon all forms of discrimination. A round-table conference should then be called involving not only the homeland leaders but above all the historic leaders of the blacks, such as Nelson Mandela. That should restore some semblance of national consensus. Then it would be most important to improve the quality of life of black people as soon as possible. In that event, the question of transferring political power could be postponed for a considerable time.

The organized political forces regard the 'moderates' as a group without a future:

They, and for that matter all black intellectuals, have a limited choice. They can back one or other form of the homelands policy, they can support Buthelezi, or they can join the Black Consciousness movement—that is, if we ignore the minority who let themselves be bought by the white establishment. But ultimately they have to choose.

Coloured and Indian politicians are in a similar situation. They vacillate between fearing the black majority and identifying with them. An elderly coloured politician conceded:

We are afraid of identifying with blacks because we don't believe that blacks identify with us. Under a black government we could expect to be treated as a minority. Basically, the blacks hate the coloureds, and hate the Indians even more.

But a student leader held this opinion:

Since 1976 the youth of the so-called coloured population has taken a clear stand. And since the government rejected the Theron Report the older generation has also lost their illusions. Whether one likes to or not, it is rational to align oneself with the likely winners. The future losers don't want anything to do with us in any case. Differences between brown and black have most noticeably vanished in the squatter areas of the Cape, where their shared deprivation is most obvious. The aims of the Black Consciousness movement have already been partly met there.

Black labour organizations, however, have expressed reservations about including coloureds and Indians:

The coloureds and Indians are a tricky issue. The leaders of the Black Consciousness movement count them as black, but the man in the street does not. They are privileged; they identify themselves more with the whites. Besides, Indians are bad employers and exploit us; a lot of blacks who work for them don't want to accept them as blacks.

A 'moderate' politician had similar comments:

I regard the alliance between the blacks and the coloureds as an artificial match. In fact, the vast majority of coloureds would be quite content with white status. In this respect the ideals of the Black Consciousness movement are all well and good, but as far as I am concerned they are unrealistic.

But for the leaders of Black Consciousness the inclusion of coloureds and Indians is quite settled:

They are all oppressed, and we therefore regard them as blacks. Indians hold important positions in SASO and BPC, for example. Certainly, many of our ordinary people are still prejudiced against them; but I am sure that they will all come round soon.

A previous ANC leader stated:

The black urban masses have fully accepted the idea of black unity, including the Indians and coloureds. I think this is one of the most important occurrences in this country. I am convinced that on this issue the Black Consciousness movement has achieved far more by now than the ANC ever did in previous years.

Just how successful the idea of black unity has been among students is illustrated by a homeland leader's report of an event at the (black) University of the North:

You should have seen how van der Ross, the Rector of the University for coloureds, was received at the University of the North. The occasion was the inauguration of the black principal there, whom Minister M. C. Botha referred to as the first black principal. Then van der Ross spoke, and declared that it was he who was the first black principal of a South African university. At this the students gave him a tremendous ovation.

Black labour organizations, apart from one smaller organization and sections of a few others in Natal, largely hold back from political matters:

Workers are still very aware of the failure of the political trade-union movement in the early 60s. The majority of organised labour today doesn't want politics, but clear, unequivocal and non-political trade-unionism.

They are somewhat distrustful of any political tendencies in which students and intellectuals play a leading role:

One should not forget that there are deep class divisions in the black community. It has been found that there are enormous differences of attitude between the workers and the middle class. Almost all students are middle and upper class, the cream of society. There are hardly any working-class children among them. It goes without saying that students can afford to protest. If anything goes wrong, they can always run home to mother. By contrast, the workers are inordinately cautious, because they carry many responsibilities and have a lot to do.

Leaders of the Black Consciousness movement realize that they have not yet broken through to organized labour:

There is still an enormous amount of work to be done in creating awareness. Too many of the present trade-union leaders oppose us. Our own trade-unions have had a very difficult time.

The Inkatha politicians, on the other hand, are very sympathetic towards the labour organizations:

Intellectuals and students do indeed play an important role. But ordinary people are even more important, especially the workers. In the last instance, they alone can achieve change.

A number of former ANC and PAC politicians showed affinities with the labour organizations:

In many cases trade-union activity is more important today than direct political involvement. The workers must be successful in the struggle for higher wages and better working conditions, and so have to gain more self-confidence. Nothing will change in this country until a powerful and well-organized labour movement exists again. I have advised my friends to keep out of the politics for the time being and involve themselves in trade-union activity.

The political perspective of the labour movement is becoming clear:

We have realized that our strength lies in our potential power as workers. We know that the whites can do nothing without us. We will turn the situation to our advantage—not dramatically, but steadily. Eventually, the minority will no longer be able to exploit the majority.

At the centre of the black political spectrum are Gatsha Buthelezi and the Inkatha movement. Inkatha is an organization with considerable self-awareness:

We are the strongest black organization in the country since the ANC was prohibited. We embody the whole tradition of black protest, and black protest now means Inkatha. We reject the apartheid system as totally as anyone else. We don't need any lessons in black consciousness. We ourselves represent this consciousness, but not in the way that SASO does. And we doubt that much can be achieved by the constant excitement of student protest.

The strength of the movement and its leader are extolled thus:

Gatsha can precipitate demonstrations such as Sharpeville or Soweto whenever he wants to. And if anything like that happened in Natal, the rest would seem like child's play. We have certain traditions here, you know. And the government, incidentally, is quite aware of that. For example, during the bus drivers' strike there were more policemen about than strikers. But at the present we don't think such demonstrations would be useful.

It is emphasized that its methods differ from those of other political organizations:

We reject the existing system. But we are determined to exploit it without accepting it. We take advantage of the scope which it allows, and the platform which it offers, to speak for the blacks of this country and to work for their betterment. We take what we can get. That doesn't prevent us from demanding more, and we will not stop doing so.

The possibilities of self-help and of working through black organizations are accorded a lot of importance:

We can do a lot ourselves for the social and economic advancement of our people.

299

An Inkatha leader stressed practical improvements, and a gradual approach:

The quality of life of my people is very important to me. We won't achieve radical change overnight, but steady change from day to day.

Inkatha's strong basis among the Zulus and throughout Natal is regarded as a great advantage. On this point, a young leader of the organization stated:

In the Transvaal, and also in the Cape, political movements are often the concern of specific generations. Here in Natal there is no generation gap, not even in political terms. Natal is full of Zulus, and tradition is unbroken here. We feel like members of a family, in acknowledging and respecting our elders, and we want to keep it that way. We know that our grandparents themselves fought for freedom, and we respect what our parents have done. This creates great solidarity, consciously or unconsciously. This even applies to migrant workers. When they are needed they are there to help. The majority of people in Natal, even the youth, are supporters of Buthelezi. They trust him to lead us well.

They also anticipate success in other parts of the country in future:

Once an organization is on its feet, success breeds success. Our following in the Transvaal is by no means restricted to Zulus. Besides, it doesn't do the movement any harm to have the strongest people in the country behind them. The rest will follow. Gatsha is a national leader—which doesn't contradict the fact that he is also a Zulu leader.

The leaders of the other political tendencies pass a wide variety of judgements on Buthelezi and Inkatha. One homeland leader was of this opinion:

Buthelezi is the one leader who has a large following among all ethnic groups and in all regions. Only Mandela and Sobukwe can compete with him in popularity, especially among the older generation.

The assessment of a 'moderate' politician was ambivalent:

I can accept him as a person, but I reject him as a homeland leader. The homeland policy will always be unacceptable to the majority of the urban population, irrespective of its representatives.

A labour leader reacted with similar ambivalence:

We admire Gatsha Buthelezi as a strong leader. We are aware that he is working within the system in order to oppose it. But we are doubtful of how successful he is going to be.

A black trade-unionist in Natal pointed out that black workers reject neither Buthelezi nor Inkatha, despite what influential, left-wing white trade-union leaders might think:

The workers display their practical realism in matters of political organizations as well. Initially, a lot of them were very distrustful of Inkatha. Since then, however, an overwhelming number of urban workers have decided to join Inkatha. As a result, the character of the organization has naturally changed greatly. Urban workers are playing an increasing role in it.

It is among the leaders of the Black Consciousness movement that the radical rejection of Buthelezi and his organization predominates:

Anyone who works within the framework of the homeland system is finished as far as we are concerned. It doesn't matter what his motivation is. Not even for Buthelezi can we make an exception. On the contrary: we believe that he is supporting the system in a very clever way.

Sure, Gatsha enjoys a lot of support, because our people hunger for freedom and like to hear him talk. But he is a coward. He speaks from his safe platform within the system, and then leaves the young people who actually do something in the lurch. I must admit that he is very intelligent. But he represents the interests of those who are earning well in established and safe positions. He holds Natal firmly in his grip; he prevented people there from joining our movement. But in the rest of the country he doesn't count at all.

Rejection is often mixed with admiration:

Buthelezi is unique among the homeland leaders—he is the great deceiver. A few years ago his popularity rested on the fact that he was the only one who spelt out anything clearly. And then he built up a quasi-ruling party, and uses the symbols of the ANC—a man of different colours, so to speak. But soon he will have to make up his mind where he stands: is he an ANC man, or a socialist, or just another homeland leader? His following among the young is shrinking rapidly. What he still has is an ethnic base—which isn't going to help him at all—just as it hasn't helped anyone in Africa. He has neither a clear policy nor a clear set of principles.

The leaders of the Black Consciousness movement are even more opposed to Inkatha than to Buthelezi:

Buthelezi is so arrogant about his Inkatha approach. It only works on tribal feeling. Opposition to the association is growing. It is a dangerous tool of tribalism. But it is typical of the change of awareness in recent years that Gatsha himself is flirting with the language and ideas of Black Consciousness, and that in Inkatha there is even talk of socialism.

ANC politicians are also in two minds about Buthelezi and Inkatha. A leading ANC man outlined the dilemma:

Buthelezi is a problem. I know him well, he is a friend of mine.

301

Whether one likes it or not, he accepted his homeland role with the approval of the ANC leaders. Zululand was the last homeland to be created. Chief Luthuli agreed at the time, because he thought it was necessary to do something about the problem of Zulu migrant workers. But I have the feeling that Buthelezi is playing his role a little too well.

Another took this view:

The Boers aren't stupid. They grant a person the right to criticize, to speak, to throw stones at them, as long as he serves their policy, in that he fulfils some function in terms of it. Gatsha's politics remind me of a man who boards a train for Cape Town, sticks his head out of the window, and continuously yells, 'I am not travelling to Cape Town!'

An ANC functionary explained that it is especially ANC supporters among the general populace who accept a close connection between Buthelezi and the ANC as a fact:

There can be no doubt that many people, especially in Natal, associate Chief Gatsha Buthelezi with Chief Luthuli. Luthuli played a great role in the mind of the people, not because he was Luthuli, but because of what he stood for, namely, the principles of the ANC. For most people it is quite clear that Buthelezi is carrying on the ANC line.

But a pro-ANC student leader was incensed by this:

Most of our people, and especially the ordinary people, still support the ANC. This is why Buthelezi has gone and adopted the language, symbols, and flag of the ANC. It is all deception. He is paid by the South African government, just like any little policeman. He said he would use his position as a platform. Platform for what? What he is saying, has been said a long time ago. It hasn't changed anything. Buthelezi only gives the system credibility. Unfortunately the majority have been taken in by him.

The most serious accusation levelled against Buthelezi and Inkatha is that of tribalism. While ANC people in Natal do not make this accusation, their silence is countered by voices from other parts of the country:

Inkatha may well be very strong in Natal, but it will always remain a tribal organisation. The way the government exploited the Zulus during the recent disturbances has rewakened all the old feelings among the other blacks about the Zulus' history of aggression and domination. No, Buthelezi has nothing to say outside Zululand.

An old ANC leader in the Transvaal, just back from a trip to Natal, expressed his mixed feelings poignantly:

This Inkatha thing closely resembles the old ANC. But I don't know whether to be suspicious or happy. For over a decade, the ANC was a bit of underground activity, a lot of talk in exile, but a strong feeling among the masses. It seems as if Inkatha can mobilise this feeling. But can one really trust these fellows?

As for the Black Consciousness movement, it, like Inkatha, does not lack self-awareness. But the defensive undertones which one detects when Inkatha leaders speak of their organization is completely foreign to the Black Consciousness leaders. Black Consciousness regards itself as the movement of the youth and the future. With remarkable confidence, state repression is viewed as confirmation rather than hindrance:

The constant repression in fact confirms that we are on the right path. It is precisely this repression which has helped us to expand tremendously, though less as an organization—in this respect they can harass us considerably—than as a body of thought. It was far more uncomfortable a few years ago, when, just as SASO was developing, we were unexpectedly treated as darling children by the Afrikaanse Studentebond (ASB). Such approval from the wrong quarters was a dangerous thing. Today the ASB hardly bothers about us—they have enough on their hands fighting the English.

The Black Consciousness leaders believe that the progress of their movement is inexorable, on account not of themselves but of the forces that they have released in a specific social and historical situation:

The movement continues to grow among the youth, especially the schoolchildren. We can only grow. We ourselves didn't expect that matters would get going so quickly. It all started far sooner than we had planned. We began only a few years ago as a small group in SASO. We were faced with an attractive vision of a multiracial society—such as NUSAS offered us—and we had to come to grips with that first. Our beginnings were very small, but today we control every campus. We should only have reached this stage in some years' time. What is the reason for this? We simply spelt out facts and aspirations clearly, and the youth could do little else but agree. A fundamentally new attitude in a whole generation bears witness to the success of our organization. It is a generation which knows only the Boer state of 1948, and is reacting to it. As long as this situation lasts our movement will continue to gain support from below. Many who hesitated at first have joined us since the events of 1976/77.

Black Consciousness concentrates deliberately and exclusively on the younger generation:

When we started the organization we told ourselves that it would be a waste of time to try to convince the older generation. We should concentrate exclusively on the youth. In any case, in ten years' time we

303

shall be the opinion-makers. The older people play a minor role, and we are the decisive age group. The situation itself will force our elders to take a stand. The Soweto events have borne out this view, and the majority have joined us. When its children or relations are arrested or murdered, a family automatically takes sides. The older generation was always far less militant; someone or other still had a white friend, and hence still had hope. Our generation—let alone the next one— only knows the system. It is much easier for us to be hard.

Black Consciousness has, with self-assurance, established its relationship to other trends and set itself apart from them:

The Black Consciousness movement is a totally new movement of a specific generation. It looks back at what has gone before, but won't allow any ideology to influence its goals and methods. We took of-fence at Mashinini's[1] flirt with the ANC. This young man was led astray for a while by the temptations of exile and the organizations-in-exile. But since his return to Botswana we have accepted him again. We try and minimize friction in our movement between the ANC and the PAC. People such as Mandela and Sobukwe are symbols of our struggle. But they can't do anything, whereas the whole of our generation is prepared to do something.

As one would expect, leaders of other political tendencies have very varied reactions to the Black Consciousness movement. A homeland politician took a positive view:

The Black Consciousness movement is a natural reaction to the stupid and narrow-minded educational policies of the white government. It is the logical result of separate development. I can well understand the students at the black universities, and find their reaction quite natural. The whites wanted separation, and now that they have got it, and the result is perhaps not quite what they had intended, they are em-barrassed. I think that Black Consciousness is justified.

A 'moderate' politician agreed with the basic principles of Black Consciousness. But he continued:

What troubles me, though, is that the subtle and reasonable vision of the leadership often takes the form of black racism at the grass roots. I doubt whether the leaders will be able to prevail.

Another 'moderate' pointed to this problem of a judicious and far-sighted leadership with a far less discriminating policy, and raised the question of the movement's organizational problems:

One must not overlook the weak points of the student movement.

[1] After fleeing South Africa Tsietsi Mashinini went to London, where he participated in a public rally organized by the ANC. However, he subsequently decided against joining one of the established organizations-in-exile and returned to Botswana, where most of the Soweto demonstrators who had fled had sought asylum.

> *There is hardly any contact between the students in the Cape, the North, and Natal; basically, one group knows very little about another. The riots in Soweto and elsewhere showed that there was no leadership structure of any kind, only a kind of 'instant leadership'.*

A labour leader rated the influence of Black Consciousness very highly, especially in the Transvaal:

> *The Black Consciousness movement has gained enormous support among the mass of people in Soweto and other townships since the events of last year. One can say that the masses have now become politically aware. Especially those parents whose children were involved in the events in some or another way are far more politicized than before.*

Another trade-unionist assessed their influence across the country as follows:

> *The movement's support varies. It is mainly active in the cities. It hasn't made a breakthrough in Durban, nor in most of the rural areas. Nevertheless, sporadic incidents in the homelands show that the ideas of Black Consciousness are gaining ground among the younger generation everywhere. For the language of the movement appeals to the younger generation, even if they don't fully understand the ideology.*

Inkatha leaders level this accusation against the Black Consciousness movement:

> *It equates schools and campuses with reality. It is easy to boycott an educational system, but a powerful economic and political system is quite another matter. They under-estimate the power of the system and so choose unsuitable methods. We disagree with them about the methods, but not about the goal.*

Young intellectuals in Inkatha are also annoyed by the claim of Black Consciousness to a 'monopoly on ideology'. A young Inkatha leader explained:

> *Look here, I share the experience of people in my situation—early social involvement, regular arrests among my immediate family circle, constant harassment by the police. It makes me furious when other people constantly want to dictate to me what the correct black awareness should be. They argue wildly, they reject anyone who wants to co-operate with whites—whether or not these whites are reasonable and the co-operation rewarding. They are becoming sectional, and in their own way, racist. In the last analysis, they too are practising the government's policy, though from the other side. I cannot and will not go along.*

The ANC has mixed reactions to Black Consciousness. The left wing in

305

particular, where the influence of white Marxists is still strongly felt, emphasizes

the danger of black racism.

This group also emphasizes the movement's superstructural bias.

However, the Nationalist wing of the ANC and former PAC leaders view Black Consciousness with considerable sympathy:

There is a new generation, which wants to do what we did in their own way.

In conclusion, we examine attitudes towards the 'classical' organizations, the ANC and the PAC. Their former leaders—some of them still under banning orders, all of them under close observation—see the situation of the organization in different ways:

The ANC has been destroyed as a political organization within the country. The underground movement is a special case—it will finally be judged on its military efficiency rather than on its political influence, which must necessarily be small. The movement-in-exile is divided, and a matter of contention among us here. This is a pity, for it could fulfil an important role. But there is still a very strong adherence and loyalty to the ideas and goals of the ANC on the part of a large number of people, especially in the cities.

A younger ANC man also viewed the movement-in-exile with ambivalence:

Our organizations in exile are important. They are located in places where they can speak on our behalf. Unfortunately, they are divided among themselves, often on account of personal ambitions. I would be prepared to fight, but not for the personal ambition of some or other individual.

A former leader of the ANC was sceptical about whether the 'historical' leaders had any role to play in the future:

It is difficult to say how far the men on Robben Island are the political leaders of the future. Their names still exercise a great hold. But they have been imprisoned for a long time and no longer have a clear personal impression of the outside world. They have lost contact with present developments. Sure, the names of Sobukwe, Mandela, and so on still mean a great deal to the black community. But gradually they are losing their impact. A lot has changed in the absence of these leaders, and one should not forget that the politics they practised don't mean very much to us today. Even if they were free, they have been isolated from the problems of the country for so long that this could prevent them from taking leading positions.

A former leader of the PAC shared this view:

We shouldn't have any illusions. There is still strong emotional support among the older generation. But for the younger generation the people on Robben Island or in exile are little more than names. The youth are not quite sure how they should react to them, and so prefer to support leaders of their own generation.

Leaders of the other political tendencies assess the situation similarly. They hotly deny that the movements-in-exile have any influence on current developments within the country. As an Inkatha politician explained:

The politicians in exile have, for the most part, been rejected. Exile has no relevance to life within the country. Mashinini, whose standing was very high during the Soweto disturbances, was rejected by the students here after his flirtation in London with the ANC. His standing improved again only after he had returned to Botswana; but basically he is finished.

A Black Consciousness leader expressed himself even more strongly:

The leaders in exile cannot speak for the people in the country today. They have been away too long, and have had hardly any contact with the younger generation. The goals of the two generations are also quite different. The older generation previously shared the position of white liberalism. In our view, whites have too much influence over the leaders of the exiled movements, especially the ANC in London. Those people almost feel at home in exile—and the whites among them are, as it were, also at home.

By contrast, the imprisoned and banned leaders enjoy a very high standing. In the opinion of one homeland leader:

I believe that Mandela still enjoys the widest support and highest standing. The older generation especially supports him unequivocally.

An Inkatha politician had a more qualified view:

The people on Robben Island are still greatly respected, but rather as symbols than as real leaders. If they were released they would possibly be quickly forgotten. The language they used in their time was far more moderate than that current among blacks.

Both Inkatha and Black Consciousness stand, in their respective ways, in the tradition of the classical organizations. An Inkatha leader explained:

Chief Gatsha was always a member of the ANC. Look at our flag, and listen to what we say, and then you will know where the ANC is.

The attitude of the Black Consciousness movement to the older organizations is more complicated:

The ANC is an intrinsic and historical part of the long struggle of blacks in this country. But it would go too far to speak of a bond of trust between the ANC and ourselves. We hope later to tie up more closely and co-operate more.

We are separated from the ANC less by the generation gap than by a gap of politics at different times. The London ANC with its strong influence of the white Communist party is far to our left, while the African Nationalist ANC (Dar-Es-Salaam) is perhaps a little to the right of us. We have a lot in common with the new PAC and the ANC African Nationalists. We must aim to bring all the organizations closer together—which we admit may be difficult with the older generation because of long-standing personal differences. Largely on account of a historical accident we occupy a pretty central position: we have certain socialist ideas in common with the ANC, but without their Communist approach, and we share black awareness with the ANC African Nationalists and the PAC.

The way the different political tendencies present themselves, and their assessments of one another, provide an extremely complex picture of the black political scene.

Neither homeland leaders nor 'moderate' politicians are very optimistic about their own strength and prospects for the future. The former by and large tend to orient themselves towards Buthelezi; the latter waver between Buthelezi, whose homeland strategy they reject, and the Black Consciousness movement, of whose socialist and radical tone they disapprove.

For political reasons the labour movement wants to retain its a-political stance. Although many labour leaders have personal ties with the 'classical' parties, they sympathize with Buthelezi's strategy, sharing his approach of gradual change and a cautious exploitation of legal possibilities. By contrast, the left wing of the trade-unions, whose support lies mainly in Natal, totally rejects any identification with Inkatha or Black Consciousness.

The leaders of the 'classical' parties have ambivalent attitudes to these new political phenomena, Inkatha and Black Consciousness. A section of the old ANC leadership supports Inkatha, though not without reservations; another section, and the former PAC politicians, are closer to the Black Consciousness movement.

Notwithstanding the complexities of these interrelationships, the essential conflict of the black political scene is that between Buthelezi and the Black Consciousness movement. A 'moderate' politician put it succinctly:

There is increasing polarization, not only between black and white but also between black and black.

However, some leaders both in Inkatha and the Black Consciousness movement take the view that government policy will force both movements ultimately to make common cause. Thus, a BPC leader held this opinion:

> To be frank, one must admit that Gatsha has mobilized and made aware many people whom our students could not have reached. But when Inkatha comes up against the existing restrictions, against the obstinate 'No' of the whites—and that is sure to happen soon—then Gatsha will simply have to choose the same path as Black Consciousness. The South African system will bring Inkatha and Black Consciousness together, whether they like it or not.

Similarly, an Inkatha politician stated:

> I am a convinced pacifist. But I think of the example of Martin Luther King: if non-violence does not achieve anything, then black power automatically gets going. Some day Inkatha and the radical students will march together.

3. *The views of black political leaders on the prospects for peaceful change*

There can be no doubt that the leaders of the most important political tendencies in black South Africa desire peace. A leading member of Inkatha explained:

> I believe that one should use every conceivable opportunity to negotiate, as long as the guns aren't yet talking.

Leaders were asked whether they believe that peaceful change is possible. Regardless of their political line, and the extent of their hopes for peaceful change, all politicians stressed the importance of the time factor in the strongest possible terms.

A homeland leader:

> Time is against a gradual development. We don't have much time left. If the government doesn't take any decisive steps it is impossible to predict what the blacks might do.

A trade-unionist:

> There is still an opportunity for dialogue and compromise in South Africa. But this opportunity should be grasped as quickly as possible. The time factor is tremendously important and becoming increasingly so.

An Inkatha leader:

> Change that comes too late is irrelevant.

An ANC man:

> The time for goodwill is running out. If we don't make use of it, it will soon be too late.

Above all, the decisive changes in the attitudes of black youth, which have been noticed by all political leaders, show that time is running out. It is seen as a bad omen that disturbances have continued since the Soweto events of 1976; the cleavages between the generations are deepening; religion, formerly the strongest factor against violence, is in crisis.

The extent of the Soweto events and subsequent disturbances, their intensity, and the speed with which they spread took almost all black leaders by surprise. Representatives of all black political tendencies rejected the government's contention that the riots were organized from outside.

In the opinion of a homeland leader:

The frustrations had reached a point where they had to find some outlet or other. More and more people were saying that there had been enough talk, and it was time to do something. Nevertheless, most people were surprised at the intensity of the protest after the first incidents had occurred. The schoolchildren protested, the police reacted brutally, and then everything went up in flames. God knows, sophisticated organization was simply unnecessary. The schoolchildren know one another, have the same thoughts and desires, and can reach understanding among themselves in minutes. A whole generation was just sick and tired of everything—a generation which doesn't react in the same way as earlier ones.

Various tendencies differ considerably in their evaluation of the political importance of the disturbances. The 'moderate' politicians, for example, warn against giving them too much significance:

Many of our young people over-estimate the importance of the disturbances. Some of them believe that the revolution is just around the corner. I don't believe that. Since Sharpeville, a far stronger leadership and far better organization have enabled the government to put the blacks where they want them. The apparatus of oppression is far more powerful today than it was fifteen years ago. For this reason I fear that the radical language of SASO and the BPC is largely a sort of escapism.

A trade-unionist explained the cautious attitude of labour towards the unrest:

Our workers are extremely practical and realistic people. During the strikes of 1974 they played an important and disciplined role, whereas they didn't lift a finger in 1976. Why? In 1974 we were concerned with concrete benefits: higher wages and better working conditions. The unrest of 1976 was the schoolchildren's affair, and the students'. Our workers decided to wait and see before they risked themselves. They know that they have a lot to lose. In the beginning most workers didn't approve of the students' unrest. On the other hand, their respect for the young is such that they accept there must be very telling reasons for the students to go as far as they did.

A politician close to the Black Consciousness movement underlines the differences between the unrest at the beginning of the 1960s and the disturbances of 1976/77:

There are many important differences between the events of fifteen years ago and those of 1976. At the earlier time the leaders of the black movement were known. It was possible to hold talks with the government. All the leaders were adults. Today the leadership is largely unknown, and certainly very much younger. No talks have been held with the other side. The student leaders were prepared to take incredible risks. In Soweto alone there are between 200,000 and 250,000 schoolchildren and students. The social pressure they exert amongst themselves is very strong; either one goes along or one is finished as far as the others are concerned.

A student leader expressed the opinion of the radical groups among the urban youth:

The whites have become deeply fearful, while we have lost our fear. If we had had guns the whole matter would have been settled already. Over the coming years we must patiently build up our arsenal. Sabotage will be an important element of the struggle, especially against the large business enterprises and the power supply lines. That way we'll get the better of the whites economically. The drop in foreign investment in the last year is very encouraging.

But a leading representative of the Black Consciousness movement thinks that the radical view is illusory:

No, the Soweto riots and the whole unrest haven't changed the power structures. The system was seriously threatened after Sharpeville; there can be no talk of that being the case now. Yet one should not underestimate the change in awareness that is taking place as a result of the events last year. Young people no longer accept the situation, and they are not prepared to put up with it. A greater break with the past than ever before has taken place in black South Africa. In short, although Soweto has not changed the power structure, it has changed the structures of awareness. And that counts. Students have achieved something. Whatever one does in the future, one will have to work from the assumption that young people today think differently, are prepared to risk more, have less patience, and will not be fobbed off.

Although the disturbances are differently assessed, there is general agreement that the present generation of schoolchildren and students differs radically from the older generation in its political attitude.

A homeland leader felt that he was under pressure from two sides:

311

The young people feel that we older people are too slow, too open to compromise, and too patient. The Black Consciousness movement is gaining influence rapidly, and the pot is about to boil over. On the other hand, members of the government believe that we are demanding too much development, not allowing things to mature properly, and so on. That is the dilemma of the homeland leaders.

A 'moderate' politician confirmed:

My children's generation doesn't want to have anything to do with whites at all. My generation, which is still prepared to talk and to accept the sharing of power, is still alive. If something doesn't happen soon, I predict a long, hard struggle and a local war.

From their point of view, the leaders of the Black Consciousness movement came to the same conclusion:

The older generation is a problem. They want to keep calm. Younger people are far more militant. The most influential organizations are led by very young people. The older people are still suffering from an inferiority complex, which is the cause of their subservience to the government. In the course of the last year a very strong solidarity has materialised in my generation. Many people whom I had already written off sat with me in prison—that is a ray of hope. As far as the boys and girls now at school are concerned, they are far more radical than we are. We have doubt about a peaceful solution, but still hope for one. The very young, however, believe only in fighting.

An older ANC leader clarified the conflict between the generations:

We grew up in an age which accepted white rule and our own inferiority without question. Today that has changed completely. The youth don't accept it any more, nor the discriminatory laws. In 1920 I came to Johannesburg as a young teacher. At that time, if there was a quarrel between a white and a black the majority of the blacks took the part of the white. Today that is a thing of the past. Many elderly blacks do not understand that the youth have lost all respect for the whites. Here in the city all the moral functions of traditional society have been thrown overboard. Industrialization has influenced the change. By finding jobs the young people have emancipated themselves from their families financially. The older generation has lost all effective power. That was the basis of the political conflict between the generations which was so clear in 1976.

Many of the politicians who were interviewed pointed out that in the meantime a different consensus is developing between the generations. Many older blacks are adopting the radical position of their children.

A Black Consciousness leader said:

The differences between young and old are narrowing. When I was a student at Turfloop my parents felt that I should first complete my

312

studies and then become involved in politics. Today the situation is different. Parents now know that their children must take a stand and fight the system. When the police shot at children, the older generation changed their minds.

A student leader gave a similar account:

I believe that the generation gap has begun to close. Parents were so incensed at the reaction of the government and particularly the police that today they listen to their children rather than the other way round. One saw that the over-reaction of the police turned peaceful rallies into violent demonstrations. The police were exceptionally brutal. It was only then that parents started to endorse their children's actions.

(At this point a student leader's mother, who was present at the interview, exlaimed: *'I enjoyed the demonstrations. God, did I enjoy them!'*)

According to political leaders, the change in the political attitudes of the younger generation is illustrated very well by the religious crisis which has arisen as a result of the political situation. Representatives of all political tendencies take more or less the same view of the crisis of religion among the youth.

A 'moderate' politician:

Preachers of the Reformed Churches enter election campaigns and call upon whites to preserve their 'identity', which is actually domination. This makes a travesty of their Christianity. The majority of educated blacks today find it difficult to believe in a church while the government calls itself Christian. The young generation has begun to discard Christianity. It is extremely difficult for us older people to show them the Light of God—and that is the fault of the whites.

A labour leader:

The churches find themselves in a very difficult situation. Many people don't believe in them any more. Many better-educated people take the view that religion softens the blacks, that it offers them the consolation of eternal life and lets them forget how miserable it is here on earth. The whites brought Christianity to the country; but they have proven themselves unchristian. Where is the justice and love that Christians preach? The churches have made our people subservient. They give us the Bible and take away our land. Today we want our freedom, not in a future life but now.

An office-bearer of the Black Consciousness movement:

Our view of Christianity is different today from that of a few years ago. Increasing numbers of black people are asking: 'Is God actually white or black? What is the stand of our Lord Jesus Christ on the

313

events of the moment? Does he side with those who shoot or those who throw stones?'

An ANC man summed up:

When we draw practical conclusions from the Bible, the whites regard us as Communists. The white man rejects the Christian ideals by his actions. This enormous gulf is the crucial problem of Christianity for the blacks.

On the other hand, among the leaders of Inkatha and the members of the Black Consciousness movement there are many personalities whose motivation has a religious element. It is this that lets one bishop see the possibility of a turning point in the youth's crisis of religion:

The young leaders have a new attitude towards the Church. They are extremely active, both in the Church and in politics. Many of the young leaders who have been banned by the government come from Church circles.

A student leader welcomed the growing social and political involvement of the Church:

As long as Christianity is regarded as the symbol of oppression, it will decline. But today the Church is trying to change, and boldly articulate the opinions of the people. For blacks this is a sign of hope in the Church.

Many statements of black leaders mixed a hope for a peaceful future under the banner of Christianity with a distrust of white attitudes.

A leader of the Black Consciousness movement held this opinion:

Whites think they are Christians. But I don't think they regard me as a brother—at most they regard me as a brother kaffir. If whites took their Christianity seriously, if they accepted us as equals, then everything would be different in this country. Most blacks still sing a hymn, the hymn of a community of all men that includes whites. Why then do whites exclude us from this community?

An Inkatha politician came to a similar conclusion:

The majority of our people still take the Christian message seriously. Most blacks want the whites to stay here, and want to live with them, even now. They support peaceful change; and it would still be possible if whites were prepared to accept it.

Of decisive importance to black politicians of all tendencies is whether white South Africans are open to peaceful change. As an ANC politician explained:

The central question is whether white South Africans are prepared to change. There is increasing polarization, fear of a conflict involving the

314

great powers, the possibility of a world conflict . . . white South Africans are the only ones who could prevent an escalation.

But in the view of all the various black politicians, whites show little interest in change and compromise. They thus view the future with deep pessimism.

A homeland leader explained:

What do the politics of the NP and the Afrikaner rulers of this country amount to in practice? They promised us that the policy of separate development would bring equal opportunities, and possibilities as high as the sky. But in reality the sky is no higher than the ceiling of our houses. The Afrikaners want to retain their position of power under all circumstances, and give nothing away. Everything else is simply ideology. If the whites don't undergo a fundamental change in attitudes within a short time I am sceptical whether there will be any peaceful solution. Time is working against it.

A 'moderate' politician from Soweto said:

Young blacks have absolutely nothing in common with the present system. They have reached the stage where nothing matters, where they want to bring down the system by any available means. Although the desire for mutual contact is growing among many whites and blacks—mainly in fear of what is coming—those blacks who seek such contact find themselves increasingly in a dilemma. The constant rejection of black by white is leading to an increasing rejection of whites by blacks. The reaction of our youth to the politics of the white man is quite simple: they reject him as he rejects them. This is why I am not very optimistic about the prospects of peaceful change. The 'moderates' among the blacks are steadily losing their importance and influence. There is growing resistance to the pursuit of peaceful change, and the hope of achieving anything in this way is decreasing. If radical reforms are not introduced shortly—and in view of the government's intransigence I think it unlikely—soon hardly anyone will believe that a peaceful solution is possible.

An Inkatha politician:

The whites must surely see that civil war is just around the corner. Why do they insist on behaving as the Portuguese did in their former colonies? They should understand that South Africa also belongs to them, and look for appropriate solutions. They have become extremely nervous. Instead of thinking about solutions they ban student leaders and arrest journalists. Increasing numbers of our young people perceive the Afrikaners as purely pig-headed. They are prepared to challenge the system, even under suicidal conditions.

Given the present power relationships, it surely would be suicide; yet the young people are no longer afraid of it. What the white side needs today is statesmanship and quick action, to prevent bloodshed.

315

But at the moment the government only gives way when the situation becomes quite untenable.

A student leader reached a similar conclusion:

There is still perhaps a chance, if the whites finally see reason. But the time for compromise is running out. More and more young people believe that bloodshed is inevitable. It is hardly possible to reason and negotiate with the government supporters. They are too extreme. I am afraid that future developments will not be peaceful.

The conclusion of a brilliant analysis by a leader of the Black Consciousness movement is the same:

Unfortunately peaceful change is not very likely. Sure, Vorster probably doesn't doubt that he has the overwhelming majority of the Boers behind him. But he does not want to cause another split in his party. Hence, he pays excessive attention to his right wing. He explains to his people that concessions could satisfy neither the demands of the outside world nor those of the blacks; and therefore one should not even begin to make concessions. The whites' views of the blacks are extremely stereotyped. And, therefore, they have a very narrow view of their own role as well: 'Kragdadigheid', domination, firmness, conservatism. Any change and any concession is sneered at as weakness. The whole Afrikaans culture is oriented towards preserving the past, not towards adaptation, flexibility, and change. This whole syndrome makes change within a reasonable space of time most improbable. The crux of the Afrikaners' problem is that although their ideological propaganda doesn't convince anyone else it does convince them: they are taken in by it and believe it.

And an ANC politician concluded:

I am very sorry to say that I see little likelihood of peaceful change in this country. I truly say this with much sadness. The Afrikaners will not tolerate any changes outside the apartheid system, and we cannot accept this system. I fear that a long and bloody civil war is in the offing. Have no illusion about the length of this war; it will be a grim and hard guerilla war, and carry on for a very long time.

Political leaders of every tendency place the blame for what may come to pass squarely on the shoulders of the white government, because

one cannot hope for the slightest meaningful compromise from this government.

Hence most respondents fear that a calamity can no longer be averted:

We are sitting in a bus which is hurtling towards the edge of a cliff, and we are all going to be dashed to pieces on the rocks below.

Some black leaders already look beyond a violent conflict:

316

I am a convinced supporter of a multiracial society, and I will remain so. I no longer believe in peaceful change because I cannot any more. While I still believe in peaceful co-existence between the races, that will only be achieved after a bloody confrontation.

On the other hand, others still hope that white attitudes will change under the influence of growing pressures:

The whites are becoming more afraid and feel themselves threatened. In the states around us change was also only a dream, a while ago; but by now it has already occurred. One can feel the whites' fear everywhere. Perhaps this fear can become the driving force for change.

CHAPTER 11

Impotent Pacifists and Militant Democrats: the Perceptions, Goals, and Expectations of Change Among Urban Blacks in 1977

1. *Between peaceableness and a readiness for conflict*

> *Violence never solves anything. Struggle won't help us, only peaceful negotiations.*

> *The whites are very powerful—we are helpless against them.*

> *Blacks have no weapons—the whites would kill us all.*

> *We are not yet ready. But our time will come.*

> *We must fight. Blacks have pleaded with whites for centuries. They treat us as slaves—that's all.*

These are answers to an open question on the significance or expediency of violent action: a sense of impotence in one case, the hope of future emancipation in another, and a readiness to engage in immediate struggle in a third.

The feeling of *impotence* is still dominant. Fifty-five per cent of the respondents agreed to the statement:

> *Someone like me can do little to improve the life of blacks in South Africa.*

And 42 per cent agreed with the statement:

> *No matter what Africans try to do to improve their lives, they will not succeed against the power of the whites.*

318

Who feels particularly powerless?[1] The older people, those in the worst paid jobs, the unemployed, or with the least education. They still have strong ties with a homeland and have not been living in the city very long. They are conservative[2] and strongly bound to the tribe, and are mistrustful of other blacks. They are most numerous among the Pedis, Vendas, Shangaans and South Sothos, and also in the black townships of Pretoria.[3]

The feeling of powerlessness is closely bound up with a mistrust of other blacks, as well as a tendency to regard whites as the lesser evil. So 39 per cent held this view:

The whites are strict but also honest and fair—we would not be happier under our own people.

And 42 per cent agreed with the statement:

If Africans governed themselves there would be no improvement because they would fight among themselves.

This mistrust is strongest among those with the lowest level of education, and within this group is especially prevalent in the Pretoria area, where the power of the Afrikaners is most apparent.

The better-educated, no matter where they live, neither share this mistrust nor feel inevitably inferior to the whites. Younger people as a whole have more confidence in themselves and in other blacks. They

[1] The variables have not all been listed individually: instead, scales have been developed for the various aspects considered, and used as new variables in the analysis. The complex variables are explained below. No attempt has been made to give the significance for each relationship examined between variables. The results shown are statistically significant at the 5 per cent level.

[2] Two questions were used to determine the extent to which the respondents were conservative in attitude or open to change:

'*One should know that something really works before taking a chance on it*' (79 per cent agree)
and
'*If you try to change things you usually make them worse*' (31 per cent agree).

The black South Africans appear to be more conservative than respondents from various Asian societies. A random sample of youth leaders from Asian countries gave positive responses to the same questions in 51–68 per cent and in 16–24 per cent of the cases respectively. Cf. G. Vierdag, N. C. Tagaza, and Th. Hanf, *Regionale Jugend-leiterausbildung in Asien* (Frankfurt am Main, 1977), p. 46f; M. Fremerey, Th. Hanf, and G. Vierdag, *Jugendbildung in Indonesien* (Frankfurt am Main, 1976), p. 87.

[3] The two variables concerning the feeling of powerlessness were combined to form one scale. Forty-one per cent felt particularly 'powerless'. There were the following deviations from this group's average: 60-year olds and above (75 per cent); unskilled workers and unemployed (56 per cent and 61 per cent respectively); respondents with four or less years of schooling (58 per cent); those with close ties to a homeland (44 per cent); those who have lived less than 15 years in a city (48 per cent); conservatives (55 per cent); those with close tribal bonds (47 per cent); Pedis, South Sothos, Vendas, Shangaans (54 per cent, 53 per cent, 51 per cent, 49 per cent); Pretoria (59 per cent).

319

generally also have a better education than the older generation.

But there are also some among the older and less-educated who feel less helpless and have less negative opinions about other blacks. These include people who feel at home in the city, have passed off immediate tribal connections and are less conservative. They are found especially frequently in Durban.[4]

On the Soweto disturbances: extracts from group interviews

The whites think we are idiots. They oppress us. If peaceful means achieve nothing, then violence is the only answer.

The Boers no longer believe in peace so we must fight for our freedom.

As the unwanted citizens of South Africa we can do nothing else. Demonstrations are the only answer.

Now the whites and the whole world know that we are unhappy in this country.

It was no good. They didn't so much as harm the hair on a single white man's head. It was our property that was destroyed, not the white man's.

It was crazy to set fire to schools if you're fighting for better education at the same time.

Using violence leads nowhere, only to tears and mourning.

Many people died.

It was right. The fear is gone. Our parents sold us to the whites, our children will free us from slavery.

It was magnificent. Only violence can change South Africa. We are fighting for the country which the whites stole from us.

A clear majority of the respondents regard *caution in politics* as appropriate—hardly a surprising result. Thus, 66 per cent agreed that:

It is wise for Africans in town to be careful in politics and not to lose what they have.

All the same, one-quarter hold the opposite opinion. The members of the lower-paid and less-educated classes in particular proved cautious. Those blacks among the better-off and the educated who were cautious are mainly to be found in the Pretoria region. The least cautious are students and better-educated Soweto residents.[5]

---

[4] Twenty-eight per cent of the respondents agreed to both statements. Those displaying above average 'mistrust' of blacks are thus respondents with up to four years of schooling (44 per cent) and those living in the Pretoria area (37 per cent); less mistrustful, on the other hand, are those who feel at home in the city (23 per cent), those who have no close connection with the homelands (23 per cent), and those living in Durban (17 per cent).

[5] In favour of caution in politics are 79 per cent of those from the lower strata and 78

320

The cautiousness of the majority does not, however, mean that blacks reject protests and demonstrations. The number of urban blacks who approve the Soweto events goes well beyond the number who are not cautious. Thus, in response to this question:

Some say that the demonstrations by young people in Soweto and other places were a good thing for the future of South African people. Others say no good can come out of such actions. What do you feel?

Fifty-seven per cent agreed with the first contention, and 39 per cent with the second. Strongest approval for the Soweto demonstrations is found amongst schoolchildren and students, and this applies all over the country: 71 per cent thought them a good thing. But among adults with nine or more years of schooling, a majority are still in agreement: 55 per cent in Pretoria, 59 per cent in Durban, and no less than 78 per cent in Soweto. In the case of the less-educated strata, however, there are clear differences between the regions: in Pretoria and Durban only 27 per cent and 31 per cent respectively are for the demonstrations while in Soweto the figure is 62 per cent. Thus, the young and better-educated everywhere take a positive view of the Soweto events. A majority of older and less-educated people in Pretoria and Durban are opposed to them. But in Soweto, two-thirds of the respondents overall are in favour.

The picture becomes clearer if one considers the reasons which respondents gave for their choices. These were investigated with the help of an open question.

Among those judgements that were negative, references to the consequences are prominent:

People have been killed; personal tragedies.	7%
People have suffered; imprisonment; unemployment.	7%
Facilities for blacks have been destroyed.	7%

Other criticisms are more concerned with the tactics and circumstances of the demonstrations, without fundamentally rejecting protest:

To fight without weapons is nonsense.	2%
Tsotsis ruined a good cause.	1%
The actions were badly planned; they should have been started everywhere in South Africa at once.	2%

A further group cites the superiority of the whites as a major factor:

Open struggle will only bring us defeat.	3%
The whites are too powerful.	2%

per cent of respondents with less than eight years' schooling, while cautious respondents with more schooling are to be found mainly in Pretoria (81 per cent); cautious to a less than average extent are students (56 per cent) and better educated people in Soweto (55 per cent).

Finally, a not insignificant proportion of 7 per cent is in favour of peaceful change.

Negative judgements of the Soweto demonstrations are chiefly found among respondents who show strong feelings of political impotence, are mistrustful of other blacks, and are highly cautious about political issues: older and poorer people, the conservatives, those with large families, those who identify less with the cities, who are less educated, or who favour peaceful change on principle.[6] Only the last group shows an individuating characteristic—it is highly religious.[7]

Those in favour of the Soweto demonstrations can be divided into two groups according to the reasons they give: in one group the emphasis is on protest, in the other on struggle. The protest group welcomes the Soweto demonstrations because it hopes that they will result in greater understanding on the part of the whites, attract the attention of the outside world, and lead to improved living conditions. Almost one-fifth of all respondents give prominence to concrete objects of protest: above all, improvements in the educational system and in the infrastructure in black residential areas. In other words, the protest group sees the demonstrations not as the beginning of a greater and total conflict, but rather as a warning signal to the whites and the government. There are a number of reasons for protesting:

Abolition of Bantu Education; better conditions in the residential areas; other specific objects of protest.	19%
Whites will respect us more, now that they know what we think; the government will now take notice of us.	10%
No attention would be paid to our affairs without protest.	3%
The outside world will become aware of us.	3%

The protest group comprises 40 per cent of all respondents. The other group, which supports radical protest with an accent on far-reaching political activism and political struggle, comprises 18 per cent of all

---

[6] The Soweto events were rejected by respondents who exhibit feelings of political impotence (49 per cent); are mistrustful (56 per cent), cautious in political questions (48 per cent), older (61 per cent), and poorer (52 per cent); have six or more children (61 per cent); do not identify closely with the city (50 per cent); are conservative (51 per cent); have had four or fewer years of schooling (60 per cent); and are in favour of peaceful changes on principle (60 per cent).

[7] The index for religiousness was constructed from the following questions:

'I believe in Christ, the Son of God;
I believe in a life after death, where good people will be rewarded and bad people will be punished;
I try hard to live my daily life according to the teachings of my religion;
I go to church: yes, regularly; yes, sometimes; no.'

Twenty-three per cent are very religious, 37 per cent religious, 24 per cent somewhat religious, 16 per cent irreligious.

respondents. There is an important distinction within the latter group. The majority emphasize that large-scale protest is necessary to achieve political goals; a minority stress that protest is not enough, and that the use of violence is inevitable:

> Demonstrations are necessary in order to achieve political goals and they must continue; discrimination must be abolished and political rights won; black solidarity is necessary. 10%
>
> We shall achieve nothing without violence; violence is the only language they understand; a pity we had no weapons. 7%

The argument that nothing can be changed in South Africa without the use of force was expressed most frequently in Soweto, where the figure was 8.6 per cent.

It has already been shown that the *image of white power* which urban blacks have has some bearing on the question of whether they are peaceable or ready to engage in conflict. To clarify this point, a question was framed to determine black estimations of white power. To obtain candid answers, the question was projected beyond South Africa:

> *Mozambique used to be ruled by Portugal. After years of fighting, Africans have become leaders in Mozambique—they are called Frelimo. Do you agree with the following statements or not?*
>
> *yes*
>
> —*Frelimo won only because of the help it got from other African countries.* 35%
>
> —*Frelimo won because of its own strength and struggle.* 47%
>
> —*Frelimo won only because of the weakness of the Portuguese.* 11%
>
> —*Frelimo would never have won if the South African whites had been in place of the whites in Mozambique.* 18%

Thus, less than one-fifth of urban blacks expect white South Africa to do any better than the Portuguese did, if faced with an armed liberation movement with the drive of Frelimo.

The minority that did attribute a greater degree of power to the whites of South Africa is found among the less-educated and those with strong tribal bonds.[8]

If the results of the different questions on white power and black powerlessness are compared, one finds remarkable differences depending on what is emphasized:

[8] Respondents with up to eight years' schooling (27 per cent); those with close tribal bonds (30 per cent).

	yes
A feeling of personal powerlessness.[9]	55%
A feeling of the powerlessness of all blacks.	42%
A feeling of the powerlessness of an armed liberation movement.	18%

Clearly, the sense of black powerlessness as well as of white power is internally differentiated. While a majority of respondents feel helpless as individuals, only a minority regard the blacks as a group as without hope and inferior, and only a small minority still believe that a liberation movement has no prospects of success.

On Frelimo: extracts from group interviews

I don't think that Frelimo could have succeeded against the South African whites. They are so heavily armed that to fight them openly would be crazy; if we started a war it would be suicide for us. We only hope that God will help us.

I think Frelimo would have been able to win, even against the South Africans. Their war lasted eleven years; Portugal kept pouring in weapons but Frelimo fought on in the bush. Later on the Boers supported Portugal, but Frelimo won even though the Boers were there too. No, they could have won here as well.

I like Frelimo. They chased out the Portuguese and now rule the country. I think they're just like us: once they were oppressed and now they can fight for their freedom. We too must fight for our freedom; we are still some way behind them.

I'm not for Frelimo. I have a high opinion of them because they have fought and freed themselves. But I don't like the government. People are suffering under the Frelimo government. I work with people from Mozambique. They say there is still a kind of slavery there. You can't decide what you want to do, the government decides for you. Their government has turned its back on God and on the peoples' ancestors. It's forbidden to pray. That's what I have heard.

What, then, are the opinions of urban blacks on the subject of *peaceful and non-peaceful forms of change*?

Aspects of their attitudes become evident in our analysis of the arguments for and against the Soweto demonstrations. A more precise answer is possible with the help of a question which projected the South

[9] Even though the extent to which South Africans feel personally powerless differs by education (students, 53 per cent; respondents with more than eight years' schooling, 45 per cent), the overall percentages are considerably higher than those for corresponding groups in Asia, where less than 20 per cent show feelings of powerlessness. Cf. G. Vierdag, N. C. Tagaza, and Th. Hanf, *Regionale Jugendleiterausbildung in Asien, op cit*, p. 45.

African problem onto Rhodesia, so that respondents would not become anxious in the interview situation.

Now we would like you to think of Rhodesia. Rhodesia is a country with many Africans ruled by a much smaller number of Whites. Africans do not have the same political rights as Whites and they also get lower wages and cannot live where they like.

There are Africans in this country who want to change things, but they have different ideas on how to bring about changes. Here are some of the things that Africans in this country think.

Do you agree with the following statements or not?

	yes
—*Improvements for Africans will come through patient negotiation between White and Black leaders.*	65%
—*The only way of bringing improvements for Africans is by making trouble in public and by strikes.*	10%
—*Africans will never get improvements without fighting and violent action.*	28%
—*Fighting and violence will harm the Africans very much more than the Whites because the Whites are very strong.*	48%
—*Africans should never think of fighting and violence because hurting anybody, even Whites, is very bad.*	61%

In the previous, spontaneous replies to an open question on the Soweto events, 7 per cent had considered fighting and the use of violence to be unavoidable. Here, in a context which, on the one hand facilitates an open answer—one is discussing 'another country'—but which on the other hand puts the question of violence directly, it now appears that more than one-quarter of all respondents believe that no change is possible without violence.

As might be expected from the previous results, this group is drawn from students, the more urbanized blacks, and upper-income and better-educated strata. These people also feel less powerless, have confidence and trust in other blacks, and are least prone to think in ethnic categories. They approve of the Soweto demonstrations and have a high opinion of the strength of Frelimo. This group is represented most strongly in Soweto.[10] One-quarter of all blacks have, thus, already written off the possibility of peaceful change—and they are an influential proportion. Nonetheless, a clear majority are still peacefully disposed. Sixty-one per cent regard the use of violence as bad in principle; once again, there is a high correlation between this attitude and

[10] In favour of struggle and violence are students (41 per cent); those who identify with the city (38 per cent); members of the upper social strata (47 per cent); those with more than eight years of schooling (39 per cent), who do not feel powerless (40 per cent), are not mistrustful (39 per cent), and do not have strong tribal bonds (32 per cent); those in favour of the Soweto demonstrations (45 per cent), who support Frelimo (48 per cent), and who live in Soweto (35 per cent).

religiousness.[11] And 65 per cent, almost two-thirds, still believe in peaceful change through negotiation.

The consequences are obvious: even among the urban black population, in political terms the best informed and most involved section of black South Africa, there is a clear majority in favour of non-violent change. However, the black political leadership groups fear that this situation could quickly change, and their fears are confirmed by the empirical data: disillusionment increases with the degree of urbanization and education, and hopes of peaceful change decrease. The readiness for conflict is growing, especially among urban black youth.[12]

On 'black democrats': extracts from group interviews

We don't want any political leaders like Idi Amin. Amin appointed himself leader; we want to elect our leaders.

If a leader we have elected does something we don't want, then we'll elect a different one.

We don't care whether a leader is a Sotho or a Zulu. As long as he's black, it doesn't matter what group he belongs to.

People who can't read or write should also be allowed to vote. They have their natural abilities, they have the power of reason that they were born with. It isn't their fault that they didn't go to school. Everyone should be able to vote.

(Workers from Soweto)

2. *Black democrats*

What is the stand of urban blacks on democracy? It is a favourite argument among white South Africans that blacks cannot be granted political rights because they are incapable of liberal democracy. The argument points out that authoritarian leadership, intolerance, the suppression of criticism and dissent, and one-party regimes are to be found in most countries of black Africa. And it cannot be assumed that the blacks of South Africa will be better democrats than those in other countries of the continent. Against this view, a liberal minority stress that due to massive social change, South African blacks, especially those living in the big cities, cannot be compared with blacks of central African countries still living in largely traditional social structures. In very simple

[11] The religious reject violence (71 per cent), the irreligious less so (41 per cent).

[12] An index of 'peaceableness' was developed on the basis of responses to the projection on to the Rhodesian situation. Twenty-three per cent are not peaceable in outlook. Fifteen per cent of those who identify with a rural milieu reject peaceful forms of behaviour, while 29 per cent of city-dwellers display this attitude; the percentage of 'not peaceables' rises with increasing education from 10 per cent to 49 per cent. Of the young, 29 per cent reject a peaceful attitude.

terms, the question is thus: are South Africa's blacks 'different' in their attitudes to democracy? The answer is that they are. On the crucial issues of authoritarian or democratic leadership, tolerance of criticism and dissenting opinions, and a one-party versus a multi-party system, a majority of urban blacks showed themselves to be supporters of liberal democracy. In order to obtain frank answers, the questions about democracy were projected onto other African states.

> *Think of an independent African country ruled by Africans—such as Tanzania, Zambia, Botswana or any other independent African country: what do you think is best for such a country?*

On the subject of *desired political leadership*, the choice was unequivocal:

> *Now let us think of what kind of leader would be good for such an African country. Choose between the following leaders:*
> *—A leader who decides, after getting guidance from many assistants and followers, or*
> *—A leader who makes his own decisions and guides his assistants and followers.*

Eighty-nine per cent of all respondents preferred the former leader, and only 9 per cent the latter. The authoritarian political leader, who takes all his decisions on his own is thus in no demand amongst urban blacks.

Their statements on the subject of the *tolerance of criticism* are almost equally unequivocal:

> *What would be the best for such an African country:*
> *—A government which listens to criticisms and tries to satisfy people who disagree with it, or*
> *—A government which does not allow too much criticism for the sake of order and unity?*

Although the latter alternative is rationalized by a very positive principle, only 18 per cent of respondents favoured it. Eighty per cent chose the former alternative. It seems that these replies reflect the experiences of people who have suffered the consequences of the institutionalized deafness of the South African system to black criticism.

The question of whether a *one-party* or a *multi-party system* is preferable received very mixed answers:

> *What do you think is best for such an African country:*
> *—Only one political party, with one single plan for the country's future, or*
> *—More than one party, each with its own plan for the country's future?*

The slightly larger group, 49 per cent, is in favour of the one-party system, while 45 per cent opt for a system with more than one party.

The relatively high vote for a one-party system can probably be attributed to the fact that this question was put immediately after the introductory sentence, i.e. after the citing of Tanzania, Zambia, etc. It can be assumed that some of the respondents still had the named countries in mind, but projected the subsequent questions more decisively onto their own country.

In fact, completely different answers were obtained to a question with very similar content that was put a little later. These answers probably reflect more clearly what the respondents want for South Africa:

What do you think is best for such an African country:
—An opposition party which is able to criticize government plans, or
—No opposition party, because opposition can divide the country?

Although the latter alternative would encourage a negative answer, only 25 per cent rejected an opposition party, while 72 per cent favoured its existence.

The four questions on democracy proved to be closely connected, with the answers reflecting a consistent pattern of opinion. An aggregate index was therefore composed. Only 32 per cent of respondents emerged as consistent non-democrats. Thirty-four per cent are not entirely consistent, but predominantly democratic in attitude. Thirty-three per cent are 'true' democrats. *Thus, as a whole, two-thirds of urban blacks may be regarded as potentially democratic.*

Who, then, is a democrat and who is not?

The non-democrats are recruited mainly from the lower-income and lower-education groups, and from respondents with strong ties to a homeland or ethnic group. They are most frequently to be found in Pretoria.

Democrats are characterized by high professional positions, better jobs, a longer time spent in the city, and looser tribal ties. They are encountered fairly rarely in Pretoria, and much more often in Durban and Johannesburg.[13]

In addition to basic attitudes towards democracy, attitudes towards the political role of other groups are also significant for a plural society:

If the Blacks in South Africa were politically in control, what would they do about the political rights of Indians, Coloureds and White South Africans?

[13] Democrats are 17 per cent of those with four or fewer years of schooling, as opposed to 50 per cent of those with a high-school diploma or higher qualifications; 22 per cent of respondents from the lower strata as opposed to 59 per cent of those in the upper strata; 29 per cent of those who still have strong ties with a homeland, as opposed to 39 per cent of those who fully identify with the city; 22 per cent of those with ethnic bonds, as opposed to 37 per cent of those without; 22 per cent, 36 per cent and 36 per cent of respondents in Pretoria, Soweto and Durban respectively; 30 per cent of those who feel politically powerless, 41 per cent of those who do not share this feeling.

This question is naturally very hypothetical for a group so dependent and powerless at the moment. The use of projection again suggested itself, in order to obtain realistic answers. Respondents were thus asked to consider the situation in another country, which was described so as to permit an identification with their own:

We would like you to think of Kenya which is an independent African country ruled by Africans. Kenya has two big groups of African people and some smaller groups, and also has many Whites and Indians. Kenya is busy deciding on plans for the people of Kenya. We would like you to think of what would be best for Kenya.

The following answers were obtained to questions on the political role of minorities:

	yes
Should Indians be allowed to stay in Kenya?	73%
Should Indians be allowed to vote?	68%
Should Coloureds be allowed to stay in Kenya?	87%
Should Coloureds be allowed to vote?	81%
Should Whites be allowed to stay in Kenya?	79%
Should Whites be allowed to vote?	73%

As a whole, then, a large majority favour the political equality of ethnic minorities—a result which one would not necessarily expect from members of an oppressed majority.

The coloureds receive most frequent acceptance—this again in quite a surprising attitude towards a group which is relatively privileged under the present regime and which, at least until recently, did not by any means identify itself clearly with the blacks but rather sought recognition among the whites.

The greatest reserve is shown towards the Indians—particularly amongst blacks in Durban, where the Indians are most numerous and where there is a long tradition of black-Indian conflict. But even in Durban there is a majority in favour of political rights for Indians.[14] The differences between the answers from Durban and from the other areas show especially clearly that respondents made the desired projection from Kenya onto South Africa.

Finally, the fact that three-quarters of all respondents want whites to have political rights too shows a remarkable potential for political tolerance among urban blacks.

[14] A variable, 'political rights of minorities', was constructed for each group from the two questions on Indians, coloureds and whites. The following differences by region emerge:

	Soweto	*Durban*	*Pretoria*
Indians	75%	57%	72%
Coloureds	84%	84%	79%
Whites	75%	77%	64%

Who recognizes the political rights of minorities and who rejects them? Minority political rights are favoured above all by those blacks previously identified as democrats (see Figure 11.1).

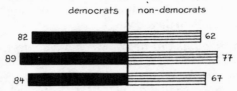

Even among the non-democrats, there is a majority in favour of political rights for minorities. But this majority is much larger among the democrats.

There is a significant deviation regarding attitudes to whites. There were more indications against political rights for whites from younger people than from older people.[15] So it is by no means certain that the high degree of tolerance towards whites at present will continue into the future.

Another question arises here. What is the distribution of peaceful and non-peaceful attitudes between *democrats* and *non-democrats?*

Table 11.1

	Democrats	Non-democrats
	%	%
Peaceably disposed	41	53
Less peaceably disposed	31	26
Not peaceably disposed	28	22

Table 11.1 shows that non-democrats are slightly more peaceably inclined than democrats—but the non-democrats are, as we saw above, those who are poorer, less educated, and with a stronger sense of political powerlessness; in short, those who are peaceable through fear and impotence.

Those who feel less helpless are both more democratic and more ready to fight for political rights. Democrats welcome the Soweto uprisings and tend to be less cautious in political matters.[16] Above all, they are clearly committed to political struggle: whereas 29 per cent of the non-democrats are prepared to fight, no less than 39 per cent of the democrats are.

In other words: *the more democratic a black South African is, the*

[15] Sixty-four per cent of the 18–34-year-olds would accord the whites political rights, compared with the 82 per cent of the respondents of 35 years or older.

[16] Sixty-six per cent of the democrats, as opposed to 50 per cent of the non-democrats approved of the Soweto disturbances. Sixty-six per cent of the democrats and 78 per cent of the non-democrats are inclined to caution in political matters.

stronger his demands for political rights and the readier he is to adopt non-peaceful means to attain them.

3. *Goals of change*

What kind of economic, social, and political order do urban blacks want in South Africa? It has already become abundantly clear that they are highly discontented with existing conditions. The question is now whether their opinions and attitudes allow us to infer what their objectives are for a future society.

Goals of economic change

Firstly, the *feeling of relative deprivation*[17] is overwhelmingly strong, as is the conviction that blacks have a right to economic equality with whites. No less than 94 per cent of the respondents agreed with the following statement, while only 5 per cent disagreed:

> *When I see what the whites have I feel envious and feel that I have a right to have the same.*

An almost equally high proportion, 84 per cent, believe that *solidarity among black workers* would give them a very strong position in economic disputes with employers. The pessimistic minority are found mainly in Pretoria.

On economic change: extracts from group interviews

If a white sweeps the street and I sweep the street why should he get more money for it?

It's unjust that a Boer with only five years' school earns twice as much as a black with a high school diploma.

Since we have to buy in the same shops we want the same wages as whites.

We want to live like them. We are fed up with being beggars. We must get our own businesses.

These houses are matchboxes.

We want bigger houses with electricity and bathrooms. We need more trains for our transport; we don't want to be packed together like sardines all the time. We want to get the lands back that the whites took from us. Then we'll be able to feed ourselves.

We can't find work at present, that's why we are starving.

Many blacks are unemployed simply because they are black. It's the blacks that don't work, the whites get work. Our children are looking for work but they keep getting sent home. Even if they have learnt a lot it doesn't help them.

They must give us our share of the wealth if they want peace.

[17] On the concept of 'relative deprivation' cf. Chapter 1.3.

331

A narrow majority view *trade-unions* favourably. Thus, 53 per cent of the respondents disagreed with the statement:

Africans who support trade-unions cause a lot of trouble and bring no progress.

It was members of the less-educated sections of the population and those with a strong sense of powerlessness [18] who above all spoke deprecatingly of trade-unions.

The strongest support for trade-unions is found among the better-educated strata in Durban. This is probably a reflection of the prestige which the trade-unions won in Natal in the successful strikes of 1974.

That the urban blacks want economic equality with the whites shows clearly that they regard the existing distribution of property and income as a cause of conflict. The emphasis placed on black worker solidarity makes evident a wish for change. And the fact that over half the blacks welcome trade-unionism indicates a considerable readiness for conflict.

Clearly, they want economic change—but what kind?

Seventy-four per cent of the respondents mentioned higher salaries, equal pay for equal work, and greater job opportunities. Thirty-seven per cent want better housing, the right to buy property, and improvements in public transport and in the infrastructure of the black residential areas. Thirty-four per cent mentioned changes and improvements in the educational system. All these items—which were repeatedly mentioned in reply to an open question—evidence the blacks' desire to improve their position in the South African economy. [19]

Do they reject the existing economic system as such? Particular attention was paid to this issue in the present study, as it is very important for the possibility of conflict regulation. A number of questions were drawn up to determine the balance of opinion between a free enterprise economy and socialist economic systems. But during the preliminary testing of the interview schedule, it emerged that the answers were so overwhelmingly in favour of the free enterprise options that a number of questions had to be dropped. Significant differences appeared in the replies to three questions, and these were then included in the main study. A first question tested the *readiness to take personal economic risks*—a requirement of a free enterprise economy. The question was deliberately formulated to make risks seem less attractive than security:

What kind of job would you prefer:
—A job in a factory or an office with a good salary you can rely on, or
—Your own business where you can win a lot or lose a lot?

---

[18] Trade-unions were rejected by 53 per cent of the respondents from the lower social strata, but by only 9 per cent of those from the upper strata; and by 64 per cent of those with feelings of powerlessness.

[19] Cf. Chapter 11.7, below.

Fully 63 per cent of the respondents chose the second possibility, and only 37 per cent the first.

A similar picture emerges from replies to a question dealing with *public or private ownership of the means of production*—the central feature of an economic order:

> *Thinking of an independent African country ruled by Africans such as Tanzania, Zambia, Botswana: what do you think would be best for such an African country?*
> —*Factories and businesses should be owned by private African businessmen who will work hard to make their business grow, or*
> —*Factories and businesses should be owned by the African government so that the representatives of the people decide how the businesses should be run.*

The free enterprise alternative is preferred by 65 per cent of the respondents, the socialist by 32 per cent.

Finally, there was a question intended to determine the strength of *egalitarian ideas about income:*

> *An educated African who has been to university should not earn more than an ordinary African factory worker.*

Only 10 per cent of respondents agreed with this statement, while 83 per cent rejected it.

A majority of the respondents thus express a readiness to take personal economic risks, and a belief that financial reward should be commensurate with individual economic performance. There is also a clear majority in favour of private ownership of the means of production. Finally, an overwhelming majority reject the notion of an equal distribution of income.

As a whole, then, urban blacks do not seem to be at all opposed to a free enterprise economic system; they want a fair place in it, not its abolition.

A closer analysis of the minority that did favour state ownership of the means of production confirms this conclusion. It might be thought that this minority forms the nucleus of a desire for a South African form of socialism. But this does not appear to be so. Rather, it seems that this reply to our question derives from and can be explained by traditional conceptions. Respondents belonging to this group have not lived in town very long. Almost half of them have strong ties with the homeland. They identify with a particular ethnic group much more frequently than the respondents preferring private ownership of factories and businesses. Vendas and Pedis are highly represented in the group. So are inhabitants of the black townships of Pretoria and Durban, whereas their occurrence in Soweto is rare. [20] Moreover, the attitudes of this minority confirm that they are hardly 'socialists' in the modern sense of the term. Almost 40 per cent of them are distrustful of other blacks, compared to only one-quarter of the 'capitalists'. Almost half feel personally powerless, and more than three-quarters think that great caution in politics is necessary, while these attitudes are held to a much lesser extent by 'capitalists'. And more than half the 'socialists' oppose the trade-unions, against less than one-third of the 'capitalists' who share this view. Given these social characteristics and attitudes, it is hardly surprising to find that the proportion of 'socialists' that name conservative homeland politicians as their preferred leaders is double the proportion among the supporters of a free enterprise system.

It is probable that at most only a quarter of the 'socialists' could count as supporters of modern socialism: a maximum of 8 per cent of all respondents combine the option against private ownership of the means of production with a political preference for the ANC, PAC, or BPC.

If one defines a socialist attitude more rigidly as one which favours both state ownership of the means of production and an egalitarian incomes policy, one is left with only 3 per cent of all respondents. This small minority is hardly represented in Soweto. It is distinguished from the minority mainly by the fact that its members tend to disapprove of the Soweto demonstrations, and have a poor opinion of activism in the struggle for black rights. This again points to traditionalism rather than socialism. [21]

In brief: *There is every indication that modern socialism is still completely foreign to the overwhelming majority of blacks, and that expectations of economic change are directed almost exclusively at a greater share of an advancement in the free enterprise system, in that to a remarkable degree respondents are orientated towards performance and ready to take risks in 'entrepreneurial' enterprises.*

This basic orientation is confirmed by our inquiries into the role our black respondents assigned to the Indian and white minorities in economic life. Once again the questions on this topic were framed as a projection onto Kenya:

[20] State ownership of the means of production is approved by 44 per cent of those who have not had much experience of urban life, by 30 per cent of those who have lived in the city for more than 15 years; by 45 per cent of those with strong ties to a homeland; by 32 per cent of those who identify with a particular ethnic group; by 41 per cent of Pedis; 43 per cent of Vendas; by 41 per cent in Durban; by 41 per cent in Pretoria; by 28 per cent in Soweto.

[21] Cf. the answers to the statement: 'A successful and educated African should not live like the whites but follow a true African way of life'; 83 per cent of the 'socialists' agree as compared to 62 per cent of the 'capitalists'. A further indication of traditionalism results from matching the answers to the question on the personal readiness to take economic risks with the answers to the question on private or public ownership of the means of production: 90 per cent of the socialists were in favour of one's own business in which one can win a lot but also lose a lot.

	yes
Should Indians be allowed to have businesses?	73%
Should Whites be allowed to have businesses?	78%

Thus, roughly three-quarters of the respondents think both Indians and whites should be citizens with full economic rights in an independent country ruled by blacks. The Indians did slightly less well than the whites—once again on account of the attitudes prevalent among the black inhabitants of Natal.[22]

However, the answers to a question on land ownership are quite discrepant. Forty-three per cent answered yes, but 54 per cent said no, to this question:

Should Whites be allowed to have big farms?

Those who have not lived in the city for long, and display strong ethnic ties, are most opposed to white ownership of land—less than one-third agreed. Among city dwellers and the 'de-tribalized', however, approximately half agree.

But the greatest difference on this question is regional. While half the respondents in Soweto and Pretoria would allow the whites to retain their farms, in Durban the figure is less than one-quarter. In Soweto, even among the Zulus 52 per cent say yes, as opposed to only 22 per cent of Zulus in Durban. This clearly indicates that the urban blacks in Natal, as was shown earlier, are still much more closely tied to rural areas and to the specific problems of rural life. There are huge white farms in Natal lying right in the middle of the areas which form the KwaZulu homeland—obvious manifestations of the extremely inequitable distribution of land between black and white.

The answers to this question on the ownership of land are evidence of what would, in all probability, be the first economic change desired by non-urban blacks: more land. The replies in Durban make clear that *the issue of a redistribution of agricultural land cannot be excluded from any peaceful settlement of economic conflicts.*

To sum up: urban blacks want equal economic rights and the educational opportunities necessary to exercise them. They do not reject the free enterprise system but want to be given a chance to succeed in it. Most of them want a change in the present distribution of land. They accept the participation of minorities in the economy, but they demand a proper place for the majority.

4. *Change in inter-group relationships*

Is there *black racism* as well as white racism in South Africa? Many

[22] Cf. Durban, 63 per cent; Soweto, 78 per cent; Pretoria, 80 per cent.

supporters of government policy like to think so, since this would justify their own position. On the other hand, many white liberals fear that it might exist: whether it stems from the blacks' own tradition, or is a reaction to the policies of the whites, it could one day be turned against the whites.

The essence of racist convictions is, usually, a belief in the innate superiority or inferiority of groups that have been biologically or pseudobiologically defined. The following question was put to the urban blacks:

Think of Africans, Indians, Coloureds and Whites who have all had exactly the same education, who would be the most intelligent, next intelligent, and who would be the least intelligent?

Thirty-four per cent of the respondents believed all to be equally intelligent. The other replies are categorized in Table 11.2.

Table 11.2

	Most intelligent	Next most intelligent	Least intelligent
	%	%	%
Afrikaners	37	13	5
Whites	23	20	8
Indians	1	17	21
Coloureds	1	10	26
Don't know	5	6	8

Given the fact that the question prompts the existence of differences, it is remarkable that a fully a third of the respondents gave the clearly non-racist answer that all are equally intelligent. A slightly larger group put their own 'race' first. One-fifth are convinced of their own inferiority and hold the whites to be the most intelligent group. The clearest indication of the existence of genuine black racism is the deprecatory evaluation of the Indians and coloureds, who were ranked as the least intelligent groups by one-fifth and one-quarter respectively.

It is above all the better-educated with better-paid jobs and democratic attitudes who are not racist. Those who rate the black group highest are less educated, conservative, and feel powerless. And those who believe the whites to be most intelligent also belong to the lower-income and less-educated strata of the population. They are still strongly bound to the tribe, peaceably disposed, and politically are predominantly cautious. The question of who ranks Indians and coloureds lowest is particularly interesting. They are respondents who know neither Indians nor coloureds very well, for in Durban Indians are regarded as unintelligent much less often than in Soweto. It is members of the lower strata who rank both coloureds and Indians low on the scale especially frequently. [23] This is a classic case of compensatory racial prejudice on the part of those who are at the 'bottom' of their own group—the racism of the little man, in this instance black.

On the social aspects of race relations: extracts from group interviews

We want to be called South Africans, not Bantu.

We want our dignity as people, as human beings. People must have the freedom to get together with anyone they can, with anyone they want to be with.

Whites are most intelligent, not because they are born intelligent but because they get a better education.

Black girlfriends for whites? Out of the question!

We want representatives in Parliament, and we want the same living standards as the whites. It doesn't bother us that we don't live together with them.

Separate residential areas were introduced by the whites. They had this crazy idea of separating us. We hate being separated.

The peoples of South Africa should not live apart. We would like van der Merwe as our neighbour. I'd have anyone as a neighbour — Xhosa, Sotho, Venda, or white.

I don't particularly care whether my children go to school with whites. What I do want is for them to get the same education as white children. Education should have nothing to do with colour.

So the answer to our initial question is that *there are also racial prejudices among blacks.* Among both black and white South Africans prejudice is strongest in the relatively deprived members of the respective

[23] The following answered that all are equally intelligent: 49 per cent of respondents with eight or more years' schooling, 22 per cent with less than eight years' education; 57 per cent of those in higher professional positions, 29 per cent of those in lower jobs; 47 per cent of the democrats, 24 per cent of the non-democrats.

Blacks are rated most intelligent by 40 per cent of the respondents with eight or less years' schooling, 32 per cent with more than eight years' schooling; 43 per cent of conservatives, 34 per cent of non-conservatives; 42 per cent of respondents with feelings of powerlessness, and 33 per cent of those without such feelings.

Whites are rated most intelligent by 27 per cent of respondents with four years' schooling or less, 6 per cent of those with a university diploma; 28 per cent of those belonging to the lower strata, 16 per cent of those from the upper strata; 36 per cent of those with strong tribal bonds, 20 per cent of those with no such bonds; 25 per cent of the peaceable, 15 per cent of the non-peaceable; and 90 per cent of those who are cautious in political matters.

Indians are held to be least intelligent by 28 per cent of respondents with little education in Soweto and 19 per cent of such respondents in Durban; while in the lower social strata 24 per cent and 29 per cent consider the Indians and coloureds respectively to be least intelligent, in the upper strata this is the case among 15 per cent and 19 per cent respectively.

groups, in the educationally and economically underprivileged. A prejudice in favour of one's own group and against other groups is a very 'normal' prejudice. But prejudice against one's own group is highly specific—in this case, an extreme expression of the internalization of apartheid society. However, the most surprising result is that one-third of urban blacks are clearly not racist in their attitudes.

In an international comparative study[24] Germans, Dutch, Britons, and white South Africans were asked to comment on the following statement:

> *The innate qualities and abilities of Germans and of 'guest workers' (or Dutch and Surinamese, Britons and coloureds, whites and Bantu) are basically the same.*

In full agreement were 44 per cent of the Germans, 35 per cent of the Dutch, 49 per cent of the British, and 24 per cent of the white South Africans. In contrast with these figures, the 34 per cent of black South Africans who answered 'all are equally intelligent' to a question which suggested the opposite, must be regarded as a high proportion; the more so if one considers that the blacks, even the better-off among them, are underprivileged as regards education and income in South African society as a whole. For in the three European countries included in the survey and in white South Africa, the less-educated and less well-off strata of the respective populations showed a level of prejudice considerably above the average values given here.

Thus, apartheid society has decreased prejudice among urban blacks with some education: *the blacks are relatively less racist than the whites of South Africa, and even than comparable Europeans.* As in the case of Jews, the experience of discrimination has diminished prejudices. Whatever black racism survives is an inadequate excuse for white racism.

What are *relations between the various black groups* like in urban society?

We showed above that the policy of the government assumes the existence of different black nations and defined homeland states. According to this policy, urban blacks are merely homeland citizens who happen to live in 'white' cities for economic reasons, and—according to the theory of 'separate development'—only on a temporary basis.

Things look quite different from the blacks' point of view. Firstly, their *identification with the city* is of note. When asked the question:

> *What place do you feel in your heart to be your home?*

[24] Cf. Projektgruppe Vorurteilsforschung, Deutsches Institut für Internationale Pädagogische Forschung und Arnold-Bergstraesser-Institut, 'Einstellungen zu Fremdgruppen im internationalen Vergleich', *loc cit*; cf. also Rainer Hampel and Burkhard Krupp, 'The Cultural and the Political Framework of Prejudice in South Africa and Britain', *loc cit*.

no less than 62 per cent name Johannesburg, Soweto, Durban, or Pretoria, or environs of these cities, such as townships. Twenty per cent name a homeland or other place in a city. Thirteen per cent list places in proclaimed white areas as their home.

On group relationships among blacks: extracts from interviews
Blacks are only divided because the white man introduced hatred between the people in the black cities.

Our people don't want anything to do with ethnic groups any more.

In Soweto there are no differences any more between the black groups. In other places, like the East Rand, there are still people who believe in such things. The police try to strengthen the differences. But we don't fall for that any more.

Anyone who has been to school has nothing against marrying someone from another group. Only the illiterate are still against the idea.

Love knows no colour-bar. It's fine if a Zulu marries a Sotho woman or vice versa, as long as they like each other.

There is no apartheid among us blacks; we are all black.

Fifty-four per cent of the respondents have relatives in the homelands. However, a total of 66 per cent have little contact with the homelands: 35 per cent never visiting a homeland, 7 per cent practically never, and a further 25 per cent about once a year. Less than one-third of the respondents have material ties with a homeland: 32 per cent own land there, 22 per cent cattle, and 29 per cent a house.

If the information above is summarized in the form of an index, the following is the result:

Exclusively tied to the city	30%
Strongly tied to the city	34%
Weakly tied to the city	16%
Strongly tied to a homeland	20%

In brief: less than a fifth, or on a generous interpretation, less than a third of the respondents are the ideal-type of the urban black as envisaged by government policy. The great majority identify mainly or entirely with the cities, and the highest degree of identification is found amongst the residents of Soweto. Convinced city-dwellers are above all better educated and in better jobs. They are less conservative, believe less in animistic traditions, as Christians are less religious, and have fewer children. They are also the most convinced democrats and the least peaceably disposed. Finally, since the younger generation identifies with the city to an above average extent, convinced city-dwellers are increasing in number.[25] There is every indication that the urban blacks form a new society which has little in common with the traditional rural society.

This impression is confirmed by examining *urban black attitudes towards blacks from other ethnic groups.* The respondents replied as follows to three questions involving crucial indicators of such relationships:

	yes
An African's child should marry into its own tribal group only.	27%
I prefer to be with people who speak my own language.	19%
I don't care whether my neighbour belongs to my own tribal group or to another.	95%

An index summarizing these three answers gives the following distribution:

Strong tribal ties	15%
Partial tribal ties	22%
No tribal ties	64%

Those with strong tribal ties identify less with the city, have less school education and earn less. They are clearly conservative, feel impotent, and are cautious politically. They are peaceable—and rarely democrats.[26]

The great majority, however, have no tribal ties. The cities are melting-pots, in which individuals do not so much belong to different black peoples, as merge into one black people. One important qualification must be made here, which will be shown later to be politically significant: Durban, as opposed to Soweto and Pretoria, is not a melting-pot. It is not that a new black people is emerging there—one already exists, the Zulus.

In the specific conditions of Durban neither the mechanics of urbanization nor the breaking down of ethnic and linguistic barriers are at

[25] Identification with the city was expressed by 73 per cent of the respondents in Soweto, 42 per cent in Durban, and 60 per cent in Pretoria; 59 per cent of those with eight years' schooling or less, 70 per cent with more than 8 years' education; 58 per cent among the lower strata, 69 per cent among the upper strata; 70 per cent of the non-conservatives; 42 per cent of those who believe in animistic traditions (52 per cent of those with close ties to a homeland believe in animistic traditions); and 28 per cent of younger respondents (compared to 17 per cent with homeland ties).
The following is a profile of those who identify with the city (the figures in brackets are, by contrast, for those with homeland ties): religious, 21 per cent (28 per cent); have four or more children, 31 per cent (43 per cent); are democrats, 39 per cent (29 per cent); are not peaceable 28 per cent (15 per cent).

[26] The following is a profile of those with tribal bonds (the figures in brackets are, by contrast, for those without tribal bonds): identify with the city, 18 per cent (34 per cent); have eight years' schooling or less, 70 per cent (55 per cent); belong to the lower social strata 67 per cent (52 per cent); are conservative, 49 per cent (28 per cent); feel powerless, 47 per cent (38 per cent); are politically cautious, 87 per cent (66 per cent); are not peaceable in outlook, 18 per cent (26 per cent); are democrats, 22 per cent (37 per cent).

work. And relations with the rural areas are completely different there. Most of the black townships of Durban lie in the KwaZulu homeland. Distances are small and contacts with the country much more intensive. Thus, it is not surprising that full identification with the city is found among only 19 per cent of the Zulus in Durban, while the figure for Zulus in Johannesburg is 47 per cent. And limited identification with the city is found among 58 per cent of the Zulus in Durban, while the comparable figure for Soweto is 17 per cent.

On tribalism: extracts from group interviews
What happens if a Sotho marries a Zulu or a Zulu a Sotho? How would that be?
It's not strange. I myself have married a Zulu girl although I am not a Zulu. All that I see is that she has borne me children; that's important.
When people from different groups get married, it's no different from mixing tea and sugar—it tastes good.
People should be able to get married if they love one another, no matter what they are. It's only natural. Any marriage is right as long as the people are right for each other.

(Workers from Soweto)

Since the Zulus form the overwhelming majority in Durban, the question of their contact with other black groups is an entirely different one. Whereas only 21 per cent of Soweto Zulus reject the idea of marriage with members of other groups, almost half the Zulus in Durban do so—but at the same time, they have far less opportunity to make such marriages. While only 15 per cent of Soweto Zulus prefer to talk to members of their own language group, 36 per cent of the Durban Zulus do—but for the most part they speak no other African language. And Zulus with strong tribal ties are three times more numerous in Durban than in Soweto. These comparisons show clearly that what is at work *is not tribalism*, but the effect of very different geographical and social environments. Thus it is not surprising that Zulus who are tied weakly to the city and strongly to their own group do not correlate in other respects with the features which characterize rurally and tribally oriented groups in Johannesburg and Pretoria.

Thus, the rural and tribal Zulus in Durban are actually just as conservative or not conservative, just as politically cautious or not cautious, as the urban and less tribal Zulus in Soweto. The two groups express hostile attitudes, or hold democratic opinions, to the same extent.

However, there are noteworthy differences of attitude among them in two respects: the Zulus in Durban feel considerably less powerless than those in Soweto, and they are only half as mistrustful towards other

341

blacks. Since they feel strong they don't need to be mistrustful.

In Soweto and Pretoria people and groups are breaking their traditional ties and merging to form a new urban society. In Durban, peoples' links with their origins remain intact; in this case an existing society is modernizing itself. In spite of the differences discernible among the urban blacks in the Transvaal, one may still conclude that social relations between the different black groups do not pose a problem for most people. The majority have nothing against marriage between groups, though the minority that reject it may be smaller or larger. Members of different groups are everywhere welcome as neighbours. *There is no apartheid between the black groups in the cities.*

What do urban blacks think about social relations with the minority groups? Two questions were put on the subject, once again by projecting the problem onto Kenya:

	yes
Should Indians be allowed to have African girl-friends?	52%
Should Whites be allowed to have African girl-friends?	51%

Answering yes to these questions requires a high degree of tolerance. Yet in both cases more than half the respondents did so. Once more it is the better-educated and those in better jobs who give positive answers—as well as the democrats.[27] Even when free social relations could disadvantage one's own economically inferior group, as could be expected in this case, the majority still opted for them.

The respondents decisively rejected the continuation of any enforced separation. In the preliminary tests, questions on petty apartheid were rejected so unanimously that it would have been pointless to include them in the main survey. Thus only one question on this topic was put:

Should the Coloureds be allowed to have their own schools?

Seventy per cent of the respondents said no.

Thus, a great tolerance—even concerning awkward questions of social relations—is combined with a decisive rejection of institutionalized and enforced separation.

[27] If the variables of region and education are considered, the following picture emerges:

	Allow African girl-friend to *Indians*		Allow African girl-friend to *whites*	
	8 years' school. or less	over 8 years' schooling	8 years' school. or less	over 8 years' schooling
Soweto	56	72	55	64
Durban	22	43	38	45
Pretoria	54	58	48	57
Together	50	63	51	57

Sixty per cent of the democrats would allow Indians and 59 per cent would allow whites to have African girl-friends; the figures for non-democrats are 48 per cent and 49 per cent respectively.

On the coloureds: extracts from group interviews

The coloureds are children of Africa. They are people like us, we can live with them.

I don't think much of the Transvaal coloureds. They sit around and do nothing, and take the side of the whites. That's why they get better salaries and better houses. The coloureds are a product of the Immorality Act.

Boers like Simon van der Stel didn't bring their wives with them when they came into this country. The coloureds resulted from their contacts with black women. That's why the coloureds belong more to our people than the Indians.

I don't like the coloureds because they don't fight on our side. They are our cousins but they pretend not to know us.

We like the coloureds who join us in the struggles; especially those in Cape Town, who tried to do something, like us.

They are our cousins, they are the children of our sisters. According to our tradition the child of an unmarried sister is my child. When these 'Simon van der Stels' went away, they left their children behind. The children, the coloureds, will stay with us.

On the Indians

The Indians can stay here if they clean the streets like us and work in the sugar-cane plantations.

I don't know what we should do with the Indians. They exploit us even more than the whites do. They suck our blood. They invented the black-market. If they could, they'd try to take over the whole country; South Africa would become another India. No, I have no time for the Indians.

Indians are always trying to push Africans out of a job, so that they can recommend another Indian for it. Whenever you go into an Indian shop you are cheated. They live at our expense, they are all swindlers.

Indians come from India and now they want to be called Baas. They think they are better just because they have long hair and sometimes a lighter skin than ours.

The Boers try to divide us. They give the Indians and the coloureds better chances, and so they succeed in making us hate the Indians and the coloureds.

In reply to an open question on what they thought were the most urgent changes, almost one-third of the respondents listed the abolition of discrimination, the restoration of human rights, the removal of petty apartheid, and the introduction of better race relations. We can conclude that *urban blacks have remarkably few prejudices*, that relations between various black groups are not problematic, and that the majority are *tolerant* towards the 'racial' minorities. They reject the existing separation of the races, and do not want to replace it with another. They want a society such as they had largely realized among themselves, where there are no restrictions on social contact.

5. *Political goals*

What kind of political dispensation do urban blacks want in a future South Africa? What would they prefer, and what would they accept?

Firstly, there is the question of whether the policy of *bantustan independence*, as presently promoted by the government, is acceptable. Secondly, there is the related question of whether *other* and more radical *forms of participation* are acceptable to urban blacks as a possible form of conflict regulation in the political arena.

On the homelands

The homelands? I am completely against them. They have no government, just a kind of fake freedom. It's not a government, it's a cage which they have named a government. They have been ordered to control themselves.

We don't want any homelands because they practise discrimination. The Transkei only wants Xhosas, Bophuthatswana only wants Tswanas. Only in KwaZulu is there a man who will accept any blacks. Mangope throws other people out of his country.

The Transkei isn't an independent state. It is still controlled by Pretoria. The people can't do anything without asking the Baas in Pretoria.

Transkei? That's not a government. If you leave your child alone in a playground, it can do what it wants. But only until you come back and tell it what to do. That's how it is for the Transkei.

In the main survey, no questions at all were asked about the independence of the homelands in their present form; for the preliminary survey had shown that an overwhelming majority of urban blacks do not even regard them as an option.

So we investigated the position regarding an extended version of the homelands. The question was introduced as follows:

About plans for the Africans in the future. Which of the following plans would Africans who live and work around you—Africans like yourself—be happy to accept?

The first possibility was then presented:

Some say: Africans should get independent states for themselves in

344

South Africa—independent states bigger and richer than the present homelands and including some industrial areas.

Fifty-four per cent of the respondents agree with this proposal, while 44 per cent react negatively. Does this count as legitimate support for the idea of extended homelands? Some doubts are in order. It may be that the appeal of words such as 'bigger', 'richer', as well as 'industrial areas', prompted agreement.

These doubts are compounded if the answers to the alternative proposal are considered:

Some say: South Africa should be divided into two halves, one half for Blacks and the other half for Whites, that is, Blacks ruled by Blacks, and Whites ruled by Whites.

Although this proposes a partition far more favourable to the blacks than extended homelands, only 22 per cent of the respondents agreed with it, and 76 per cent, i.e., three-quarters, reject it.

The picture becomes clear when one examines reactions to a third proposal for partition, deliberately formulated to offer blacks an even more favourable dispensation:

South Africa should be divided, but the Blacks should get the bigger part and the Whites the smaller one.

Less than one-third of the respondents, 30 per cent, agreed with this; fully two-thirds, 67 per cent, reject even this form of partition. It thus seems very likely that the first question was misunderstood. Someone who rejects a scheme by which the blacks would receive the larger part of the country is unlikely to accept extended bantustans. The assent of respondents to the first proposal must therefore be interpreted as approval for 'bigger', 'richer', and 'industrial areas' for the blacks.

On partition of the country
A partition of South Africa won't work. The whites will divide the country, give us the dry regions, and keep the rich ones for themselves. No-one has the right to divide our country.
Partition South Africa? That would create even more racial discrimination. We would fight for the other half.

What kinds of people agreed with these proposals? Supporters of partition belong to the less-educated and lower-income strata; identify less with the city and have strong tribal ties; are predominantly conservative and religious; feel powerless and are cautious in political matters; have little regard for trade-unions and political activism; are more strongly racialist and less tolerant towards Indians, coloureds and

345

whites; are frequently in favour of state ownership of the means of production; and, finally, are peaceable but not democrats.

On the unity of South Africa

We should all live together, no matter whether we are black, white or yellow. We should be one people, for all people are equal in the eyes of God. Blacks and whites should share all their knowledge and abilities for a happier future for our country.

The Boers' tactics of 'divide and rule' must disappear completely. Our common goal should be a united South Africa for blacks and whites. God created us equal. We should all be one happy family, irrespective of colour.

Africans, coloureds and Indians shouldn't just be one black people; the whites too should belong to one nation in one country.

All of us, blacks and whites, are South Africans.

> (Former political prisoner, now in Soweto
> after twelve years on Robben Island)

By contrast, those who oppose partition are the better-educated, especially the young people among them, ready for political struggle, and democrats—as illustrated in Table 11.3.

Thus, partition as a means of regulating political conflict is unacceptable to the vast majority of urban blacks. This rejection is the more significant in that it is found among those who are politically active. In brief: the majority of urban blacks do not want any apartheid at all—be it petty, grand, or 'very grand'.

What this majority does want is *one South Africa* for blacks and whites *with equal political rights for all.*

The compromise of qualified franchise, promoted for some time now by the Progressive Party, finds hardly any support among urban blacks. Only 21 per cent of respondents agree and over three-quarters disagree[28] with the idea that

> *South Africa should be one country for Blacks and Whites together, but only those with decent jobs and better education should be allowed to vote.*

By contrast, the undiluted vision of a united and multiracial South Africa enjoys overwhelming support:

> *South Africa should be one place for all people. All people—that is Blacks and Whites, rich and poor, educated and illiterates—should be allowed to vote.*

Eighty-three per cent of respondents agree, and only 16 per cent disagree.

[28] Cf. Table 11.3.

Table 11.3

Characteristics	Partition into two halves 22% = 100		Partition with the bigger part for the blacks 30% = 100		Qualified franchise 21% = 100	
Education: less/more	134*	56	116	79	10	90
Strata: lower/upper	124	46	110	77	101	97
Residents of Soweto		82		81		96
Residents of Durban		98	128			98
Residents of Pretoria	153		126		112	
Identification with the city: weak/strmg	126	69	114	84	108	95
Tribal bonds: strong/weak	144	85	135	86	133	86
Feeling of powerlessness: greatest/least	124	70	113	80	120	77
Mistrust: greatest/least	138	70	118	96	124	80
Conservatism/readiness for change	115	93	101	99	127	86
Religiousness: strong/weak	111	72	111	80	124	75
Political activism: weak/strong	131	67	108	74	113	89
Trade-unions: against/for	132	79			134	79
Cautiousness in politics: more/less	111	73			108	81
Peaceable/not peaceable	124	63	106	95	106	70
State ownership/free entevrise	127	87	125	87	106	97
Tolerant towards minorities: no/yes	171	73	178	71	144	84
Democrats: no/yes	118	57	113	64	111	89

*The figures listed give the deviation from the standard (= 100).

On the division of power: extracts from group interviews

The present system of government must cease. We need a new constitution in which all races get a fair share in government. In Swaziland blacks and whites live together; we want to live together with whites in the same way.

There should be a government in which there are black and white ministers. It would also be good if there were blacks and whites in the opposition. Opposition is important.

A government which is half black and half white is even better than majority rule. That way all people would be involved.

In this majority which desires equal political rights in a unified state, there is a hard core comprising those who accept only this proposal and reject all others. They make up 21 per cent of all respondents. Who are they?

As Table 11.4 shows, they are mostly better educated and more affluent; they are preponderant in Soweto and Durban, and few in

347

Pretoria; identify with the city and do not have many tribal ties; have the least sense of powerlessness, and do not mistrust other blacks; have a high opinion of the Soweto demonstrations, Frelimo, and the trade-unions; are unequivocally in favour of free enterprise and very tolerant towards the Indian, coloured and white minorities; are militant rather than peaceable; and, finally, are the best democrats.

Table 11.4

Characteristics	Supporters of		
	Partition 22% = 100	Consociational Democracy 47% = 100	Unitary State 21% = 100
Upper strata	46*	78	138
Inhabitants of Soweto	82	92	119
Inhabitants of Durban	98	84	113
Inhabitants of Pretoria	153	139	32
Strong identification with city	69	94	120
No tribal bonds	85	95	123
No feeling of powerlessness	70	78	140
Not mistrustful of other blacks	70	81	113
Not conservative	93	89	117
Not religious	72	82	125
In favour of Soweto demonstrations	77	92	139
Pro-Frelimo			139
In favour of trade-unions	79	95	121
Not politically cautious	73	77	136
Not peaceable	63	83	134
In favour of free enterprise	87	96	115
Tolerant towards minorities	73	98	126
Democrats	57	83	158

*The figures give the deviatim from the standard (= 100).

We thus find that respondents are clearly polarized by their reactions to proposals for partition on the one hand, and a unitary multiracial state on the other. About a fifth would be content with some partition of the country into two parts, and those who regard the guarantee of full rights for all South Africans as the only acceptable solution constitute another fifth. These two groups display opposing profiles in nearly all the features examined so far.

However, three-fifths of the respondents fall between these two extremes. Most of them would also prefer the multiracial unitary state, but they are prepared to accept other possibilities of conflict regulation.

Is there any support for *federal or consociational conceptions* in this centre group? Compared with the simple notions of partition and a unitary state, the idea of a federal state and especially of consociational democracy are complex—and both conceptions are relatively unknown in South Africa. So we had to devise formulations which were phrased so as to be comprehensible to respondents with little education, but without detracting from the essence of the terms.

The first question concerned a federal state with majority rule in which the minority has a share in the central government, and in addition exercises a limited form of autonomy in one region:

Blacks should be the strongest in the main government, but Whites should be allowed to run their own affairs in their own areas.

A majority, 65 per cent, rejected this federal solution; 32 per cent, or barely one-third of the respondents, favoured it.

The second question presented a consociational form of geographic federation with power sharing on an equal basis between blacks and whites:

In South Africa there should be Black provinces where Blacks vote for their leaders, and White provinces where Whites vote for their leaders, and Black and White leaders should have equal power in a main South African government.

This proposal had a better reception: 47 per cent approve and 51 per cent disapprove. *Thus, for almost half of all urban blacks a form of consociational democracy is the next-best solution after a multiracial unitary state.*

Who are these potential 'consociational democrats'? [29]

Socially and politically they occupy a position between those in favour of partition and the radical supporters of a unitary state. Consider the characteristics we listed above. They are displayed by an above-average proportion of those exclusively in favour of a unitary state, and a below-average proportion of the supporters of partition. The 'consociational democrats' manifest them to a slightly below-average extent. They form a group which does not rank as highly in terms of income and education as the unitary state supporters, but more highly than the supporters of partition. They are conservative, moderately peaceable, are inclined towards free enterprise, and tolerant of minorities. Finally, they are passably democratic—in short, a compromise group.

It is surprising at first instance that among the proposals rejected by the majority there are two which would seem to advance black interests significantly: a partition, by which the blacks would receive the greater part of the country and the whites only a small 'whitestan'; and a federal solution, which would place even such a 'whitestan' under the authority

[29] Cf. Table 11.4.

of a black-dominated central government. The compromise, the formula of consociational democracy chosen by the majority, allows the whites considerably more competence and power. Why does this formula win a relatively large measure of support, whereas the two 'whitestan' formulas do not?

One possible explanation may be that any kind of 'whitestan' situation, no matter how favourable to black interests, is regarded as perpetuating apartheid policy, and is thus rejected. But that would not explain why white provinces in a black-dominated federal state are unacceptable, whereas such provinces as part of a consociational arrangement are acceptable to almost half of the respondents.

There is another interpretation which may at first seem paradoxical: *there are many urban blacks who want the whites to participate in the future South Africa of their choice, no matter what.*

On the whites: extracts from group interviews
It's not that we don't like the whites. We like them but we don't like at all what they are doing to us. They must share with us what belongs to us all.

If the whites left? I wouldn't feel happy. I would miss them. We have become too used to them being here, to working with them. We need them too. And they still owe us a lot.

If the whites left the country there would be a terrific mess. It would be like being in a bus with no driver. Everyone would try to drive the bus even if they couldn't drive.

If the whites went I would feel as if someone had taken my clothes away from me. We need them because there is much knowledge they have kept from us. They must stay here until we have learned enough from them.

This country is the whites' home as much as it is ours. They have no other home, and there is nowhere else they could go. We should all live in peace together. We blacks should not imitate their bad oppressive ways if one day things are better for us. Our forefathers had pity on them when they first came to this country: they allowed them to stay here. No, it would not be good if the whites had to leave the country. All I want is for them to put aside their badness and behave like normal people.

We need the whites for many things in life, especially for agriculture and food.

I would be very happy if the whites would disappear from this country. Then I would know that the oppressor is gone.

This is shown to be the case by a closer look at those who reject partition with black superiority on the one hand and a federal state with an autonomous white region on the other, but who also do not welcome a unitary state. This group turns out to be drawn from better-educated and higher-income strata. Some of them find qualified franchise acceptable. They are good democrats, not very peaceably disposed, and support strong protest against the present situation.[30] It appears that although these people urgently want political change, they are also prepared to compromise; but in their view compromise is possible only with the whites, not by excluding them.

We may summarize the above as follows. All urban blacks want fundamental political change. Only a minority would settle for a partition of the country, even a partition under which the blacks receive the larger part. A federal state and a qualified franchise are also, in the main, rejected. The overwhelming majority want equal political rights in a multiracial unitary state. While one-fifth of the respondents opt exclusively for a unitary state, approximately half of the respondents are prepared to accept a consociational formula.

The urban black population rejects an apartheid state in any conceivable form. It would prefer a dispensation on the model of British democracy, which ignores groups in politics. However, a considerable proportion of the respondents at least do not exclude compromises which would take into account the particular characteristics of a plural society.

6. *Political trends*

There are many well-established techniques for ascertaining political trends in an enfranchised population. One can ask people about the parties they prefer and belong to, without difficulty. And the 'Sunday question'—how respondents say they would vote if there were elections next Sunday—provides additional, if sometimes less reliable, information.

But such techniques are unsuitable when a population is excluded from the political system. The political parties of black South Africa which once commanded mass support and mass membership, viz., the African National Congress (ANC) and the Pan African Congress (PAC) have been prohibited for more than a decade and a half.

The Black Consciousness movement, not yet prohibited at the time of this study, is less a single organization than an état d'esprit of one generation—its constituent associations amounted to little more than a loose if intensively functioning communications network.

At present, the Inkatha movement alone is attempting to establish an

[30] Of those who *reject* black majority solutions 59 per cent have a higher education; support the idea of a qualified franchise (82 per cent); are democrats (46 per cent); are not peaceable (29 per cent); and are in favour of the Soweto protest (48 per cent). The comparable figures for the group which does *not* reject black majority solutions are: higher education (41 per cent); for qualified franchise (17 per cent); democrats (33 per cent); not peaceable (23 per cent); for protest (34 per cent).

organizational power base. But its systematically planned membership drive had not been running for long at the time of the inquiry.

Nevertheless, one general open question was asked, on organizational membership:

What organizations, trade-unions or clubs do you belong to?

As was to be expected, the answers were not very revealing about the political orientation of the black population. Over two-thirds of the respondents belong to no organization at all, and most of the remaining third belong to sports clubs (15 per cent).

Only 6 per cent of the respondents list membership in organizations with political relevance: one per cent carry trade-union membership cards, 3 per cent belong to Inkatha, 2 per cent belong to various organizations of the Black Consciousness movement. That few respondents listed membership in the ANC is less surprising than a sign of remarkable courage on their part, for the organization is prohibited.

It would certainly be a mistake to draw any conclusions from these data about political trends among the black population as a whole. But they do provide an indication of organized political developments. It is clear both that Inkatha has an organizational basis among broad sections of the population and that Black Consciousness is not *just* an état d'esprit. Further, that respondents acknowledge membership of the ANC may be taken as an indication that this party continues to exist illegally.

In order to identify broader streams of opinion, a further question was framed, that of a *preferred political leader*:

Thinking of African leaders here in South Africa, whom do you admire most?

The preliminary survey had shown that this question was answered without hesitation. Furthermore, it became evident in the numerous group interviews that admiration of a particular leader plainly coincides with support of a distinguishable political tendency. The results of the main survey confirmed this connection.

Who, then, are the political leaders of the urban blacks? Gatsha Buthelezi stands out among the rest, in being named by 44 per cent of all respondents. In second place come the leaders of the ANC, nominated by 22 per cent. Nelson Mandela is prominent among them—he is named by 19 per cent, while Oliver Tambo, Albert Luthuli, Walter Sisulu, Winnie Mandela, etc. are all mentioned by less than one per cent.

The homeland leaders, if taken as a group, follow in third place with the support of 18 per cent of all respondents. Cedric Phatudi does best with 6 per cent, followed by Prof. Hudson Ntsanwisi with 4 per cent.

Only 4 per cent of the respondents name Kaiser Matanzima, and 3 per cent Lukas Mangope.

On political leaders:

I am for Sobukwe and also for Gatsha Buthelezi. Buthelezi follows the same path as Sobukwe. He does not agree with the homelands. When he speaks you can hear that a proper leader is speaking.

I am for Mandela because he is one of the first who fought for the freedom of our people. Even if he is in prison we shall not forget him, because we know that his heart is still with us.

Mandela is our leader because he has said that South Africa is our country. He is not concerned with colour, he is not concerned with black or white. He says he likes everyone in Africa. That's why he is the best leader.

I like Tsietsi Mashinini. He has tried to fight drunkenness in our cities. That's why the beer halls were burnt down.

I would like to have Buthelezi as a leader. He doesn't care which ethnic group a black man belongs to. He now has an organization called Inkatha and everyone can belong to it, no matter from which nation he is. Inkatha is for the progress of all black people.

Anyone who wants nothing to do with colour can be our leader.

Buthelezi is against the bantustans, so he is the right man for us.

It wouldn't make any difference whether a leader is a Sotho or a Zulu. But the Zulus don't have a good reputation because they were always a strong nation.

Among all educated people, things are not what they were—so anyone from any nation could be a leader, provided he acts for the people. Nothing can be wrong with that.

Robert Sobukwe, the recently deceased PAC leader, is in fourth place with 7 per cent.

The fifth and last of the significant groups of politicians consists of the leaders of the Black Consciousness movement, who are named by 4 per cent of the respondents. Two per cent list Tsietsi Mashinini, one per cent Steve Biko—the inquiry took place before the occurrence of his death in detention. The results of this question do not reflect the real strength of the movement, since it never gave strong prominence to particular leaders. Further analysis shows that of respondents who did not name a particular leader 2–3 per cent must be reckoned as Black Consciousness supporters. These results are summarized in Table 11.5.

The fact that the ANC and PAC—both old parties—still have such a following, and above all the evidently uninterrupted popularity of Nelson Mandela and Robert Sobukwe—despite the duration of their

Table 11.5

Political leaders	
Gatsha Buthelezi	44%
Homeland leaders	18%
ANC leaders	22%
PAC leaders	7%
Black Consciousness leaders—approx.	6%

enforced absence from active politics—show that these ideas are still influential among almost one-third of urban blacks.

The Black Consciousness movement may appear numerically weak at first sight. If one takes into account, however, that it has only existed for five years, that its organizational development was continually impeded by government measures even before its final prohibition, and that it addresses itself almost exclusively to the younger generation, then the percentage achieved must be regarded as strikingly high. Three-quarters of its supporters are less than 29 years old; it is the 'youngest' of the political tendencies.

The homeland leaders are not without a following in the cities. Taken together, they enjoy almost the same degree of support as the ANC. There are, however, significant differences in popularity between those who have until now rejected the independence of their territories, like Phatudi and Ntsanwisi, and those who have accepted it, i.e., Matanzima and Mangope. The latter have hardly any political standing among urban blacks.

The outstanding political phenomenon in black urban politics is, without a doubt, Gatsha Buthelezi. The results of the inquiry show not only that he alone of all homeland leaders is a national political figure, but that over and above this he is *the* political figure of black South Africa. His following extends beyond the 44 per cent who cited him. For respondents who named neither Buthelezi nor another homeland politician as their preferred leader were asked an additional question:

Is there a homeland leader whom you consider a true political leader?

An additional 7 per cent of respondents then named Buthelezi, whereas no other achieved more than half a percent. This means that *more than half the respondents regard Buthelezi either as the best or at least as an acceptable political leader.*

Who are the supporters of the various political tendencies?

The central question concerning Buthelezi is whether his importance extends beyond his own ethnic group. Is he only a 'tribal leader', as his opponents often allege? The answer is that he is undoubtedly the leader of his own group, but that the support he enjoys goes far beyond it.

Forty per cent of his supporters among urban blacks are not Zulus. His supporters are an absolute majority among the Zulus in Durban and Soweto, and also among the Ndebele, a group traditionally allied with the Zulus. But as Figure 11.2 makes clear, he has a considerable following among other groups too.

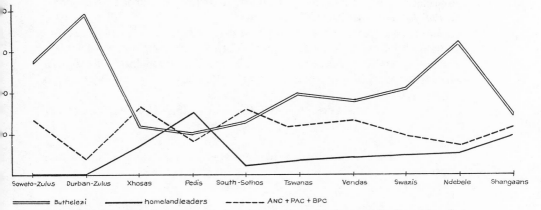

Table 11.6 displays the support for the various political tendencies among different ethnic groups. Among the Xhosas, the following of the ANC is marginally larger than Buthelezi's, and among the Pedis the homeland leader Phatudi is clearly ahead. But in all the remaining ethnic groups, Buthelezi comes out clearly on top.

Table 11.6

Ethnic group	Homeland leaders	Buthelezi	ANC	PAC	Black Consciousness	None, or others
	%	%	%	%	%	%
Soweto Zulu	—	54	24	3	—	18
Durban Zulu	1	78	8	1	—	13
Xhosa	15	23	25	6	5	27
Pedi	31	20	10	5	4	31
South Sotho	4	27	19	9	4	38
Tswana	8	39	19	3	2	29
Venda	9	37	17	—	10	27
Swazi	9	42	19	—	—	30
Ndebele	11	63	12	2	—	12
Shangaan	19	30	23	5	1	23

The picture might not have been quite so favourable to Buthelezi had it been possible to include the urban black population of the Eastern Cape in our survey. Even so, it is clearly the case that *the political approach advocated by Buthelezi represents a force in South Africa as a whole,* transcending regional and ethnic considerations.

All the homeland leaders besides Buthelezi have the support of only a minority of those city-dwellers from their own tribal groups. Phatudi, who has almost a third of the urban Pedis behind him, and Ntsanwisi, who commands the support of almost a fifth of the urban Shangaans, are relatively in the strongest positions.

The following of the ANC in the various ethnic groups is remarkably evenly distributed. Only Zulus in Durban name ANC leaders with less than average frequency. This is probably because Buthelezi, following in the footsteps of Luthuli, embodies the ANC tradition for many of its old supporters in Natal.

It is evident that the PAC and the Black Consciousness movement have little support among the Zulus in Durban.

How do the political tendencies differ in other respects? Table 11.7 shows differences with respect to a number of indicators of status and attitude.

Table 11.7

Characteristics	Preference for				
	Homeland leaders	Buthelezi	ANC	PAC	Black Consciousness
Upper strata/more educated	96*	92	116	125	111
Soweto	76	77	120	150	140
Durban	62	188	69	20	37
Pretoria	260	56	68	24	26
Strong identification with the city	61	87	116	188	91
No tribal bonds	106	87	97	131	97
No feelings of powerlessness	74	96	108	100	126
Not conservative	74	95	116	100	172
Religious	121	112	84	64	104
In favour of Soweto demonstrations	77	97	121	149	126
In favour of trade-unions	95	103	103	104	77
Not cautious	93	80	154	126	203
Not peaceable	56	78	140	186	177
In favour of free enterprise	101	93	98	104	100
Tolerant towards minorities	98	92	101	105	107
Democrats	107	95	83	160	117

*The figures give the deviation from the respective standard (= 100).

Social class and education have a significant effect. The PAC, ANC, and Black Consciousness draw support above their average levels from among the affluent and better-educated. By contrast, Buthelezi's support among the upper classes is below his average. But his supporters are still greater in number among the upper classes than those of the other tendencies: 38 per cent in Soweto, 68 per cent in Durban, and 42 per cent in Pretoria. The ANC following among the upper classes is 26 per cent in Soweto, 12 per cent in Durban, and 11 per cent in Pretoria.

Among the lower strata the support enjoyed by the various political tendencies differs markedly by region. Buthelezi is the preferred political leader for 38 per cent of lower-class members in Soweto, a figure which rises to 93 per cent in Durban, but drops to a relative low of 26 per cent in Pretoria. The ANC is supported by 20 per cent in Soweto, 10 per cent in Pretoria, and scarcely one per cent in Durban.

As a whole, the supporters of homeland leaders are clearly preponderant in Pretoria, those of Buthelezi in Durban. In Durban the ANC, the PAC and Black Consciousness draw their support almost entirely from the upper strata. Buthelezi enjoys equal support among the upper and the lower strata in Soweto. And in Pretoria homeland leaders do better than he does among the lower social strata.

The supporters of homeland leaders identify least with the city, while Buthelezi's followers do so to a below-average extent—the special character or urbanization in Durban analysed above is again evident here. The supporters of the ANC and particularly the PAC identify with the city to an above-average extent, while supporters of the Black Consciousness movement show by contrast a below-average level of identification. The latter may reflect the large number of students drawn from the rural areas.

The sense of social and political powerlessness is strongest among the supporters of homeland leaders. Followers of Buthelezi, the ANC and the PAC hardly deviate from the average in this respect, whereas Black Consciousness sympathizers feel least helpless of all.

A similar picture emerges with regard to conservatism. The followers of homeland leaders are the most conservative, supporters of Buthelezi and the PAC are average, and supporters of the Black Consciousness movement are the least conservative.

The religious differences among the supporters of the various political tendencies are particularly interesting. Followers of homeland leaders and Buthelezi are religious to an above-average extent, whereas followers of the ANC and especially the PAC are less religious than average. Representatives of Black Consciousness show an above-average level of religiousness; but closer analysis shows that this average conceals the existence of two juxtaposed groups within this movement, one hardly religious and one highly religious.

Followers of homeland leaders tend to disapprove of the Soweto demonstrations, and the reaction of Buthelezi supporters is average;

whereas most supporters of the ANC, the PAC, and Black Consciousness welcome them.

One is struck by the poor opinion which the Black Consciousness representatives have of trade-unions. This probably reflects the preponderance of intellectuals in the movement, and its lack of success among organized labour until now. Political caution is very widespread among Buthelezi's supporters, whereas such an attitude would be out of place among sympathizers of the PAC, the ANC, and above all the Black Consciousness movement. There are similar differences with respect to militancy and peaceableness. The ANC and above all the Black Consciousness and PAC followers are extremely militant; whereas those who favour homeland leaders are peaceably disposed to an extent far above the average, and those favouring Buthelezi to a slightly lesser degree.

It is noteworthy that the various political tendencies hardly differ in the extent to which they agree with the free enterprise system and with the principle of tolerating minorities.

Democrats are found especially often among the supporters of the PAC and Black Consciousness, relatively seldom among ANC supporters, and among adherents of Buthelezi and homeland leaders to a slightly below-average and above-average extent respectively.

Now what is the position of these political tendencies with regard to various conceptions of social change? Their differing political profiles emerge clearly from Table 11.8, which shows their deviations from the average (= 100).

Table 11.8

	Supporters of				
	Homeland leaders	Buthelezi	ANC	PAC	Black Consciousness
Partition	136	119	54	56	109
Unitary state *only*	60	101	115	124	129
Consociation	123	98	81	84	86

An above-average number of Buthelezi's supporters would accept a partition of the country—particularly a partition which allocated the larger area to the blacks. Their support for a unitary state and for consociation is average. The ANC and PAC supporters show no interest in partition, and also reject consociation more frequently. Most of them want equal political rights for all in a unitary state. A unitary state is also desired by the Black Consciousness movement to an extent far above average. But they are also prepared to consider partition, and equally something which applies to none of the other political tendencies—a system with qualified franchise.

358

The supporters of homeland leaders would accept partition more readily than other blacks. The ANC, PAC and Black Consciousness sympathizers tend more than the others to accept only a unitary state, while Buthelezi's followers are practically evenly divided on the suggested alternatives.

What is the relative support within the different political tendencies for the various conceptions?

Table 11.9

	Supporters of				
	Homeland leaders	Buthelezi	ANC	PAC	Black Consciousness
Prefer unitary state	78	88	81	81	69
Accept partition	27	23	11	11	21
Accept unitary state *only*	14	24	27	29	31
Accept consociational democracy	57	46	37	39	40

As Table 11.9 shows, a multiracial unitary state is the most popular conception in every case—even among the supporters of homeland leaders, and particularly so among supporters of Buthelezi.

Partition finds greatest support among followers of homeland leaders—but still from only one-quarter of them.

Almost a third of Black Consciousness and PAC supporters, and a quarter of Buthelezi and ANC supporters, will *only* accept a unitary state.

A consociational solution is approved of by a majority of the supporters of homeland leaders and slightly less than half of Buthelezi's following. Among the ANC, the PAC, and Black Consciousness between one-third and two-fifths agree with this proposal.

To sum up this aspect, all the tendencies would most welcome the unitary state. In none of them, however, is there more than a third who demand this solution under all circumstances and unconditionally. By contrast, at least a third of the following of each tendency accept a consociational solution. Buthelezi's supporters form not only the strongest by far of the existing tendencies, but are also least attached to any one specific conception. So it may depend on them, to a large extent, how opinions of these different conceptions develop in future.

Hence, the extent to which Inkatha can become an organization over and above Buthelezi's personal following is the crucial question. In other words, *Inkatha occupies a key role* in the future orientation of the urban black population.

On Inkatha: extracts from group interviews

Inkatha will make one nation of all blacks and conquer the country.

It can bring us to power. It is not only for Zulus but for all blacks and whites. It opens our eyes.

It unites the peoples and makes one nation of them. Like Verwoerd, when he said, 'Eendrag maak mag'.

It creates solidarity and, for the white man, fear.

To put it briefly, the organization prepares us to take power.

Inkatha? Isn't that a cinema? Oh, I'm sure it's a film.

I am against it. It's an organization like an army under Zulu leadership. Of the Zulus and for the Zulus.

Not for me. Their leader is paid by Pretoria. It's a dummy organization.

Sixty per cent of the respondents already knew of Inkatha, while 40 per cent had never heard of the organization. In Durban, where it was first built up, it was already known to all sections of the population at the time of the inquiry. In Soweto 59 per cent of the lower strata and 75 per cent of the upper strata were acquainted with Inkatha. In Pretoria, on the other hand, although almost half of the members of the upper strata knew of this organization, only 14 per cent of the lower strata did.

Wherever Inkatha is known, opinions are sharply divided about it. Support and rejection vary by region and strata. In Soweto, nearly one-fifth of the respondents react positively to the movement, with upper and lower strata being equally represented; and it is rejected by 29 per cent of the upper, but by only 13 per cent of the lower strata in Soweto. Attitudes in Durban also vary strongly according in this way. Twenty-four per cent of those from the upper strata express a negative opinion of Inkatha, while only 7 per cent from the lower strata do so; and it is supported by 41 per cent of the more affluent and by 52 per cent of those not so well-off. In Pretoria support and opposition are evenly balanced at about one-fifth each in the upper strata, whereas the majority of the lower strata are unaware of its existence.

The polarization of opinion on Inkatha also cuts across support for the various tendencies. Of course Buthelezi's supporters predominantly support Inkatha. One-third of the followers of the homeland leaders consider it a good thing, while one-tenth reject it. PAC and Black Consciousness sympathizers generally oppose it. Almost one-quarter of ANC supporters approve of the organization, while another quarter reject it—a reflection of the ambivalent relationship between the ANC tradition and Inkatha which also emerged during group discussions among political leaders.

The most important objection to Inkatha is based on the accusation that it is a Zulu tribal organization. This was mentioned by 6 per cent of the respondents. Two per cent also criticized Inkatha's involvement with the homelands policy. Yet the accusation of tribalism does not seem to correlate with acceptance or rejection of the organization. Among the Xhosas, for example, the balance of support is the same as among the Zulus in Soweto. What has already been said of Buthelezi's following as a political leader thus applies equally to Inkatha: support in Durban is especially strong, but also considerable in other regions and among non-Zulus.

Black solidarity is prominent among the reasons given for a positive attitude towards Inkatha—it was stressed by 8 per cent of the respondents. In addition, Inkatha's concern with self-help as a means to development, and its support for black emancipation without violence, was cited by 4 per cent and 3 per cent respectively.

Taken as a whole, 22 per cent of all respondents spoke favourably of Inkatha and 16 per cent unfavourably—a respectable result for an organization which had been active for only four years at the time of the inquiry. In the light of these results there can be no doubt that Inkatha represents *by far the strongest organized political tendency among urban blacks*. It is the organized core of Buthelezi's far larger personal following.

7. Priorities for change

What changes are particularly urgent and significant in the eyes of urban blacks? An open question was put on this subject:

Many people speak of improvements for Africans in South Africa. What changes and improvements would Africans like yourself see as being most needed for Africans in the future?

Economic changes or demands immediately connected with them take a clear first place in the list, being cited by over half of the respondents:

More jobs, better pay, same wages as the whites.	32%
Improvements of the infrastructure and living conditions, the right to own houses and property in the cities.	8%
To live like whites.	5%
The abolition of the pass laws, influx control, the freedom to settle anywhere	7%
	52%

13.4 per cent of the respondents give first priority to demands for changes or improvements in the *educational system*. These demands are causally related to hopes of economic advancement. Thus, approximately half of the references to educational issues involve general demands for more and better schools, often accompanied by the

361

statement that education is the major means of social and economic advancement. Almost a third of these replies concern the equality of black and white education—the same schools, multiracial education, education to an internationally recognized standard. Other demands include the abolition of school fees, more vocational training, and the opening of universities to all races.

On education

We need equal education, the same education for all races. No nation should be privileged. At the moment they have special education just for us, just for the blacks, and it is a bad education. We need the kind of education which doesn't make us more stupid than a white man's children. We want an international education which makes it possible for us to study wherever we want.

If these statements on the educational system are added to the statements referring directly to economic changes, then two-thirds of all demands can be regarded as being directed at economic changes in a wide sense.

In other words, inequalities in the economic conditions of life are stressed as the most pressing problem by a majority of the respondents.

Remarkably few of the respondents regard the issue of *social relations* between the race groups as urgent. Only 12 per cent cite the abolition of petty apartheid and social discrimination between the races as the most important change that they want.

Finally, 21 per cent of the respondents give priority to a fundamental change in *political relations*. Fifteen per cent name as their most urgent demand equal political rights, representation in parliament and government, and voting rights for all. A further 6 per cent emphasize the need for black solidarity and unity to achieve emancipation. They constitute the more militant wing of the group which gives priority to changes in political relations.

On priorities

What we need above all are better salaries. I want my children to be better off than I am now. What I would really like is my own business, to be able to provide for my children.

The most important thing is for our children to get the same education as the whites.

We have neither cattle, nor land, nor money. But even money would be no help; under this government we have no future. Our future will only improve when the government is totally changed. All South Africans must have a say in the government.

What kinds of people stress particular changes? Economic improvements in the narrow sense of the word are to the fore among the lower-income and less-educated groups. Those who feel powerless, mistrust other blacks, are cautious politically, disapprove of the Soweto demonstrations, and are peaceable and less democratic in outlook give priority especially often to more jobs and better salaries. In short, purely ecnomic demands take priority among the poor. Improvements in the education system are of prime importance for those people in the middle-income bracket who hope for peaceful change. It is also mainly members of the middle-income and education groups who demand the removal of social discrimination between the races. To put it simply, education and the abolition of petty apartheid are priorities for those who aim to ascend socially.

Political demands, on the other hand, are a priority of the educated and relatively affluent blacks. They are expressed in the first place by those who do not feel impotent, who have confidence in other blacks and are prepared to be politically active. To exaggerate slightly, an emphasis on political demands is the privilege of those in the economically subordinated black groups who are least badly-off and who therefore experience relative deprivation most strongly in non-economic areas. As we saw above, the structure of income and education varies considerably in the three regions examined. So it is not surprising that priorities vary between them.[31] In Pretoria economic demands predominate along with calls for better education, whereas political demands are less common. In Durban the wish for both economic and social change is frequently articulated. In Soweto the abolition of the pass laws is relatively prominent among the economic demands; for in Soweto live those people for whom the idea of homeland citizenship is an obvious fiction, and for whom a residence permit is accordingly of paramount importance. Finally, it is in Soweto that the abolition of social discrimination is relatively frequently demanded; and political rights are stressed by one-quarter of the respondents, as in Durban.

To sum úp, it can be said that *for the large majority* of urban blacks, and especially for the poorer among them, *economic improvements have priority*. Only one-tenth regard social discrimination as the central problem. One-fifth of the urban blacks, *the best-educated and most affluent section, stress the urgency of political changes*. But this issue is not yet a priority among the majority of respondents; they are peaceable because of a feeling of powerlessness in the face of the pressing economic problems of their daily lives. But a minority do already think in chiefly political terms, a minority who are prepared to welcome a democratic settlement but are also ready for conflict.

[31]	Economic priorities	Education	Social relations	Political demands
Soweto	46	14	16	25
Durban	49	14	11	26
Pretoria	66	18	5	12

PART FOUR

The Prospects of Consociation

In Part One of this book we discussed how conflict is regulated in contemporary South African society. In Parts Two and Three we considered how the conflict is perceived; the degree of change which the rulers are prepared to accept; and the expectations of change on the part of the ruled. We must now turn to the question of the prospects and practicability of an alternative way of regulating conflict—peacefully and democratically.

In the absence of large-scale foreign intervention, the present unilateral system of conflict regulation can undoubtedly survive for a considerable period. One should not under-estimate the power and repressive capacity of the existing state apparatus. It has, so far, never been seriously challenged.

Quite apart from the objective power relationships, the subjective prerequisites for a violent change of the present system are still largely absent. Most of the ruling whites are prepared to use force to defend the system against attack; but most members of the dominated groups are still quite peaceful, either out of conviction or out of a sense of powerlessness. However, few blacks believe that this mood will continue indefinitely. The social profiles of the groups which adopt militant attitudes confirm that they are likely to grow. No counter-revolutionary strategies will be able to contain them. For thirty years the South African government has tried to prevent the urbanization of blacks, separate white and black South Africans economically, reduce the dependence on black labour, engender a sense of tribal awareness amongst the younger generation by means of Bantu Education, and channel political ambitions into homeland politics. But although the government's efforts may have delayed change, they are failing to prevent it. Blacks are becoming increasingly urbanized, the dependence of the economy upon black labour and black consumers is growing, Bantu Education has generated Black Consciousness, and black politics—including the politics of the homeland leaders—hinges around the support of the urban blacks.

Urbanization, economic advancement, and youth: these are the factors which promote militancy. Cynical conflict management may be able to slow down the economic and educational advancement of the blacks, but only at a prohibitive economic cost. And even cynical conflict management cannot counter the effects of the urban environment and the changing outlook of a new generation; indeed, it probably reinforces them.

It would be a mistake to adduce a revolutionary situation from the militancy of any one section of the urban blacks; but it would be as mistaken to think that such a situation can be prevented from arising in the medium or long term.

At first glance, unilateral conflict regulation is more effective than the whites dare hope and the blacks concede. At the same time, however, this approach generates the social conditions which will guarantee its violent overthrow in the future.

How long such unilateral conflict regulation can be sustained or how it can best be overthrown are questions which we shall not dwell upon here. We are less interested in the prospects of counter-insurgency and revolution than in the prospects of peaceful and democratic conflict regulation. Crucial for such conflict regulation is the fact that a significant *potential for peaceful change* still survives among urban blacks. Just as crucial, however, is the fact that this potential will in all probability *diminish*.

In other words, *the peaceful and democratic regulation of conflict must be implemented quickly if it is to have any chance of success.* In the following chapters we shall investigate the possibility of this being realized. In Chapter 12 we shall contrast different views of the existing conflicts, analyse the seriousness of the conflicts, and discuss the extent to which they can in principle be regulated. In Chapter 13 we shall examine the specific prerequisites of a political dispensation in South Africa based on consociational democracy. Finally, in Chapter 14, we shall analyse the decisive role which the white political leadership plays, either in making possible the peaceful and democratic conflict regulation, or else in ensuring that it will fail.

366

'All or Nothing' or 'More or Less'?: the Perception and Severity of Conflict and the Extent to which it can be Regulated

How conflict is perceived by the parties involved in it has a decisive bearing on its seriousness. The more inclined the parties are to regard their respective interests as opposed, incompatible, or non-negotiable, the more serious is the conflict and the more difficult it will be to regulate it peacefully. The key question is thus: *Is the object of the conflict negotiable?*[1] Are the parties involved prepared to accept 'more or less' of something, or do they believe that they are faced with the alternative of 'all or nothing'?

Whether an object of conflict is negotiable or not depends upon its qualities, and these in turn depend on how they are perceived. It is easier to regulate a conflict by negotiation when the object of conflict is regarded as divisible; and conversely, it is more difficult when the object of conflict is regarded as an absolute value or a fundamental principle. Negotiation is easier when a gain for one side does not imply a loss for the other, in other words when it is not seen as a zero sum game. Further, it is easier to negotiate when public goods are at stake; when the parties involved feel they can calculate and assess the consequences of the process; and when the decisions made can be revised and corrected. By the same token, negotiation is extraordinarily difficult when private goods are at stake; when the parties feel uninformed about the consequences; and when the decisions taken are irreversible.[2]

---

[1] Cf. Richard Rose, *Governing without Consensus: An Irish Perspective* (London, 1971), p. 397.

[2] According to Rose, *op cit*, the negotiability of an object of conflict is determined by three characteristics: whether it is a zero-sum conflict or not; whether public or private goods are involved; and whether the demands are formulated as absolute values or in terms of more or less of something. In his study of the conflict in Northern Ireland Anthony Oberschall distinguishes among objects of conflict along five dimensions: are fundamental values or principles involved or not; is it a zero-sum conflict or not; is the

In his study of the conflict in Northern Ireland, Richard Rose established that economic conflicts such as, for example, class cleavages or urban/rural differences lend themselves to negotiation better than religious or national conflicts. The latter are seen particularly often as conflicts of identity involving absolute values, as zero sum conflict. So they are particularly difficult to regulate by consensus.[3]

What are the objects of conflict in South Africa? In simple terms, they are *prosperity, identity*, and *power*.

In the following sections we shall compare how the parties involved in the conflict perceive these objects and their features. This comparison will give us an indication of the severity of conflict in the economic, socio-cultural, and political dimensions, and will enable us to determine the prospects of regulating it non-unilaterally.

1. *Conflict about prosperity*

Three-quarters of the blacks we interviewed urgently desire economic improvement, and two-thirds gave this as their top priority. Increased prosperity is *the* priority of the urban black.

About four-fifths of the white electorate accept, in principle, higher wages and a better standard of living for blacks; two-thirds, both Afrikaners and English speakers, accept the principle of equal pay for equal work. While the majority of whites are not yet prepared to grant blacks full job equality, openness on this point grew steadily over the period of this study. In 1974, only 13 per cent of Afrikaners and 44 per cent of English speakers were prepared to work under a black; by 1977, this had risen to 24 per cent and 55 per cent respectively.

There is undoubtedly still a very wide gap between what the blacks demand and what the whites are prepared to grant them. However, it is quite apparent that neither group regards economic conflict as a fundamental cleavage, a cleavage of principle. Everyone perceives this issue in terms of 'more or less'. Most whites want to preserve their privileges, but are not in principle opposed to concessions, and, as the development over the four years of this study shows, growing numbers are prepared actually to make some concessions. Of prime importance for the negotiability of economic conflict is that the large majority of blacks

outcome of the conflict irreversible or not; are intangible goods involved or not; is the object of conflict calculable on the basis of common criteria or not? Cf. idem, 'Conflict and Conflict Regulation in Northern Ireland' (Paper for the Congress of the American Sociological Association, New York, 1973), here quoted from Maurice Pinard, 'The Moderation and Regulation of Communal Conflicts: A Critical Review of Current Theories' (Paper for the Joint Workshop of the European Consortium for Political Research and the Canadian Political Science Association, Louvain, 1976, duplicated), p. 38f.

[3] Richard Rose, *op cit*, pp. 398f.

accept a free market economy. What blacks want is a better and more appropriate position in the existing economic system. Were this not the case—if for instance the majority of blacks preferred some form of state economy or a socialist economic system—the econonic conflict could also become fundamental, and thus far more difficult to settle by negotiation. However, as long as the blacks seek to improve their situation within a free market system the conflict is not of a fundamental nature. On the contrary, if legal and administrative forms of discrimination were dismantled, the South African economic system would be freed from coercive elements, enabling the development of a genuine free market economy of greater potential.

Furthermore, conflict about prosperity need not be, or need not exclusively be, a zero sum game. This factor further reduces the seriousness of the economic conflict in South Africa and increases the prospects of its regulation. For in a country with good economic potential and corresponding possibilities of development the question of redistribution could be answered to a considerable extent by additional growth. The goods and additional incomes which should be channelled to blacks in terms of a peaceful regulation of economic conflict need not be taken away from the white population. It is far less painful to the privileged group to redistribute the benefits of additional growth than to have its income expropriated or reduced.

Of course, additional growth alone cannot provide for all the necessary redistribution; but it certainly facilitates the process. Within the white population the lower strata are least prepared to forego their privileges. However, the de facto abolition of job reservation has shown that they will in principle accept a loss of privilege provided that the leaders provide the political backing for it.

And the fact that one-third of whites were prepared by 1974 to accept the closing of the wage-gap between blacks and whites, even at the cost of additional inflation, illustrates that a mechanism of indirect redistribution is acceptable.

Blacks also do not regard the present economic conflict as a zero sum game. This is evidenced in the extraordinarily high tolerance which they show towards the economic role of the whites and Indians in a hypothetical future society. Direct questions and group interviews have established that the blacks are well aware of the whites' usefulness for the functioning of the South African economy. They do not want to expropriate white and Indian businesses; they rather want their own businesses and a share of the fruits of a booming economy.

In short, the conflict about prosperity need not be an 'all or nothing' matter, nor do the parties involved regard it as such.

The severity of economic conflict is further reduced, and the possibility of its regulation improved, by the fact that public goods are

369

initially affected far more than private goods. Many of the most urgent demands of the blacks affect public services and amenities: improved living conditions, the electrification of the townships, improved transport, a different and better educational system. It would have absolutely no direct effect upon the economic interests of individual whites if all these demands were met. This would require a redirection of public expenditure, and thereby the indirect dismantling of the collective privileges of the whites—but once again, this is a form of redistribution which lessens the possibility of conflict.

However, there is one instance in which private property is regarded as an object of economic conflict. About 50 per cent of blacks are opposed to whites' owning large farms in a future society. This is a manifestation of the feelings of a group which has over centuries been increasingly dispossessed of its traditional land, and which in the widespread practice of subsistence agriculture in the often barren homeland areas still experiences the problem of land scarcity. Even on this point, though, a peaceful and consensus solution to the conflict does not appear impossible, as long as sufficiently decisive political action is taken. Only a small part of the white population still lives on the land, and farming generally plays a secondary role within the framework of the whites' economic interests. The Kenyan experience demonstrated that generous compensation is a means of regulating a conflict about white farmland. However, the emotional force of this particular objective conflict in South Africa should not be under-estimated. The white rural population, primarily Afrikaans, have strong emotional ties to the land and their farms. They are also the most dependable supporters of the National Party. So one cannot be sanguine about white openness to compromise on this point. On the other hand, the current policy of so-called homeland consolidation—which involves the buying-up of white farms—shows that even on this sensitive issue partial compromises are not impossible.

A further object of conflict, and one which it may be more difficult to regulate in a way acceptable to all parties concerned, is recruitment to the civil service. At present this issue is necessarily hypothetical, and was therefore not included in the interviews of either the white electorate or the urban blacks. On the other hand, it often came up in the interviews with members of the leadership groups. Afrikaners predominate in the South African administration. As a simplification, one can say that one ethnic group governs and administers all the others.[4] Equality in the economic sphere should, naturally, also extend to the civil service—especially since in many societies previously disadvantaged groups have

[4] In 1960, 71 per cent of all whites employed by the state were Afrikaners. Cf. F. A. van Jaarsveld, *Van van Riebeeck tot Verwoerd: 'n Inleiding tot die Geskiedenis van die Republiek van Suid-Afrika* (Johannesburg, 1971), p. 275.

often advanced economically via the civil service. The advancement of the Afrikaners over the past decades was realized, to a considerable extent, precisely in this way. So opposition to change must be expected above all from those groups which, hitherto, have derived the greatest benefit from privileged entry to the administration. It is not accidental that civil servants belong to the most conservative groups in the white society. However it proceeds, the regulation of this conflict will be costly, whether it takes the form of compensation for early retirement, or salaries for extra administrative personnel—the more likely solution if this regulation is to enjoy white support. But it would probably be less expensive than the parallel administrations currently being created in all the homelands.

Our discussion of the different features of the objects of economic conflict and how they are perceived by both blacks and whites has skirted the extent and the complexity of economic conflict in South Africa. The whites' openness to change and the blacks' expectations of change are still a long way from coinciding.

But our discussion has shown that *economic conflicts* in South Africa, both as they are and as they are seen, *can in principle be solved.* To abolish administrative and legal discrimination, introduce equal opportunities, and dismantle inequality are goals of peaceful change which cause no fundamental conflict between blacks and whites. The conflict is one of the extent and speed of such changes, of 'more or less' and also 'now or later'. We could only touch on the difficulties of process and procedure. But the economic conflict concerns divisible goods, not absolute values; it is not regarded as a zero sum conflict; it affects public rather than private goods; and the effects of change can be calculated and corrected. All these features indicate that it is a conflict which can be regulated by negotiation. Thus the economic conflict *can* be regulated peacefully and democratically.

2. *Conflict about identity*

Rose's conclusions about the conflict in Northern Ireland are confirmed in South Africa. When a conflict is perceived as being about identity, it becomes particularly serious. It appears to be extremely difficult to regulate it peacefully and acceptably. A peculiarity of the socio-cultural dimension of conflict in South Africa is that conflict is generally determined by and arises from the one group's perceptions—from its self-awareness—whereas the other group feels that the conflict has been imposed upon them. The conflict derives its particular intensity from the fact that white identity manifests itself not only in cultural and social isolation from other South Africans, but also in administratively and legally enforced isolation.

371

Almost 60 per cent of whites are not amenable to any peaceful change in the field of social relations, and about 30 per cent are prepared to accept at best marginal changes. Only 10 per cent are ready to accept the abolition of enforced social segregation. These attitudes hardly changed between 1974 and 1977.

The attempts to promote and reinforce ethnic group awareness among urban blacks have all largely failed. Less than 15 per cent of them have strong tribal bonds; and little more than 20 per cent reveal varying degrees of 'tribal' group awareness. Over 60 per cent are unequivocally not oriented towards a group. Moreover, discrimination by the whites has not given rise to racism in reverse. The urban blacks show remarkable tolerance towards white and Indian minorities in a future society.

They regard institutionalized segregation as an insult. On the other hand, they accord a relatively low significance to conflict in the socio-cultural field. Only about 10 per cent regard the abolition of social discrimination as a matter of prime concern, whereas whites regard the social segregation of the races as extremely important.

The characteristics of this conflict about identity indicate that it will be particularly difficult. It is a fundamental conflict about absolute values. On the one hand there is the notion of a separate identity to be maintained at all costs; its roots are both racial and cultural. On the other hand there are the universal values of the equality and fraternity of all men. Likewise, against the conception of an ethnically, culturally, and historically established volk is set the conception of one nation in one country. The ruling minority regards these as zero sum conflicts, in which there can be no compromise and in which each and every concession is irreversible.

Distinctions between ethnic groups exist in many states, as well as the desire to defend ethnic identities against the concept of some transcending nationality; this is the classical problem of all ethnic and plural states, and of all ethnic minorities. In South Africa, however, ethnic identity is bound up with racial identity. In actual political practice, it is not the ethnic groups but the racial divisions which count, and form the basis of discrimination.

This raises the question of the connection between identity and privilege. Is identity only a rationalization of privilege, an ideology? Numerous authors support this view.[5] However, Schlemmer[6] has concluded on the basis of empirical studies, that some Afrikaners in par-

[5] E.g., Heribert Adam, 'Ideologies of Dedication versus Blueprints of Expedience', *Social Dynamics*, 2 (1976), pp. 84–5.

[6] Lawrence Schlemmer, 'The Devolution of Power in South Africa: Problems and Prospects', (Paper for the conference on 'Intergroup Accommodation in Plural Societies', organized by the Institute for Plural Societies of the University of Pretoria, Cape Town, 1977), p. 3f.

ticular have a strong and genuine sense of identity, largely unconnected with discriminatory attitudes; but this is true of less than 20 per cent of the group. For this section, identity involves primarily the preservation of the Afrikaans language and culture. The majority of the Afrikaner group, however, has a more racial than ethno-cultural awareness of identity. And this awareness is closely interwoven with the idea of maintaining economic and political privilege.

Surveys conducted within the framework of our own study confirm Schlemmer's earlier results. There are very clear relationships between Afrikaner identity, racial attitudes, and a determination to preserve privileges. However, the whites' wish to preserve their identity is not *only* an ideology serving the maintenance of privilege. This fact bears importantly on the severity of conflict and the possibilities of conflict regulation. For we have seen that the whites are far more open to concessions in the economic sphere than they are to initiating peaceful change in the sphere of social relations. This means that the whites' conception of their identity, whether basically ethno-cultural or racial, is a cause of conflict that is at least partially independent of the maintenance of privilege.

What, then, are the chances of a peaceful and generally acceptable regulation of this conflict?

Petty apartheid has been dismantled in peripheral ways without particular difficulty. The lifting of racial segregation in sport is an example of what decisive political action can achieve in this area. Over the course of a few years more and more loopholes were created in sport apartheid until finally all the administrative and legal measures enforcing it disappeared.[7] Sport may seem unimportant, but it has great symbolic and emotional significance in South Africa. It is now possible for a black boxer to defeat a white in accordance with the rules, without the whites' feeling that their identity is threatened—which would undoubtedly have been the case a few years ago. This success was due to the judicious, gradualist policies of the Minister responsible.

There is another, even more peripheral example of racial segregation which shows what political leadership can achieve. Apartheid in lifts was abolished in recent years. This change of official policy induced a change in the attitudes of the electorate. In 1974 only 28 per cent of Afrikaners approved of the abolition of lift apartheid; by 1977, this had risen to 49 per cent. Changes in attitudes did not facilitate a new policy—it worked the other way round.

It can therefore be assumed that peaceful change is possible on the periphery of social apartheid. But what is the situation at the core of racial segregation, apartheid in the more central concerns of life? The

[7] Cf. *Rand Daily Mail*, 23.2.1978, 'Koornhof Ends Sport Apartheid'.

attitudes of whites towards questions such as segregated residential areas and marriage across the colour bar hardly changed between 1974 and 1977. In 1974, 3 per cent of Afrikaners and 18 per cent of English speakers were in favour of integrated residential areas; in 1977, the figures were 6 per cent and 25 per cent respectively. On the question of mixed marriages, the figures did not change at all. In both 1974 and 1977, 4 per cent of Afrikaners and about 20 per cent of English speakers were in favour of abolishing the legal prohibitions. What are the chances of peaceful change in this respect?

There are some indications that a political leadership determined to repeal discriminatory laws and regulations would not necessarily lose the support of white voters. The results of the interviews show that individuals are more prepared to enter into social relationships with blacks and coloureds than to accept the repeal of discriminatory laws. This shows that a number of whites support the policy of social apartheid more out of a sense of political loyalty to government policies than out of personal conviction. This means that many whites do not approve of segregatory regulations because they think these are necessary for the preservation of their identity, but because political authorities they believe in have told them that the regulations are necessary. So if the authorities were to deem the segregatory regulations superfluous, and repeal them, the action is unlikely to be fiercely resisted by the electorate. The opposition of the electorate to peaceful change in the more central areas of social relations at present might well reflect the success of decades of opinion-formation by the party and the government, rather than genuine personal convictions.

Thus, as far as the core of social apartheid is concerned, peaceful change has to contend with two obstacles: white attitudes shaped by a sense of identity; and an ideology of identity which has been raised to a political doctrine, based on the will of the white leadership. To overcome the latter obstacle, a change in the politically determined ideology is necessary. This will be difficult, for the National Party has always emphasized the consistency and continuity of its doctrine—not only is the party always right, but it has always been right. Those members of the leadership group who seek to abolish legal apartheid go to great lengths to show that although it may once have been necessary to their identity, this is no longer the case. In other words, they argue that the administrative apparatus of petty apartheid is now superfluous. Are such arguments, which remain within the framework of the system, supported by the empirical data? It seems so. It has already been shown that within the white group there is widespread voluntary apartheid between the Afrikaners and the English speakers; only a small minority cultivate close social contact across the language barrier. The Afrikaner volk has been successful in preserving its cultural identity, even against a culture as self-confident and internationally prestigious as the English one—and it has done so without any enforced separation. So it is highly probable that voluntary social segregation between the white and black groups would persist after the abolition of legal measures. Indeed, in most plural societies there is a large social distance between the different population groups, on a purely voluntary basis. And social distance is not confined to plural societies. Even relatively homogeneous European societies disapprove, by and large, of close social contact with alien groups. In Germany for instance, although 22 per cent would consider marrying a Yugoslav, only 16 per cent would consider marriage with an Italian, 10 per cent with an African, and 10 per cent with a Turk. Similarly, 17 per cent of Britons would be prepared to marry a West Indian, and 15 per cent an Asian.[8] The social distance between South African whites and other groups is even larger. Eleven per cent of the English-speaking population would consider marrying a coloured, and 8 per cent a black—percentages which are fairly close to those of the Europeans. For the Afrikaners, however, the figures are 1 per cent and 0.4 per cent respectively.

These data show that the leaders' argument from within the system does hold: the preservation of white identity, be it understood in more cultural or more racial terms, does not require discriminatory laws. Similarly, the data show that the repeal of these laws would by no means lead to social integration, and that strong differences of a socio-cultural nature would continue to exist between the groups. The emergence of a homogeneous society would still be most unlikely. Finally, the data show that a policy which tried to go further by forcing social integration would meet with such resistance that it would hardly be possible to implement it peacefully.

However, a policy of integration is not at all what the blacks demand. They want discrimination to be abolished and social equality to be implemented, but they do not seek the disappearance of the whites as a cultural or ethnic group. They do not want social integration to be prohibited, but they do not want it to be enforced either. Thus it can be established that the peaceful resolution of conflict in the socio-cultural field, i.e., the abolition of enforced discrimination, will be exceptionally difficult to achieve. The *main obstacle* is not the whites' awareness of their identity as such, but the *political doctrine* that white identity must be maintained by means of discriminatory social segregation. To overcome this obstacle, it is not necessary for the whites fundamentally to change their attitude—that would be improbable—but for the leadership groups to change a political doctrine. This change is possible

[8] Cf. Projektgruppe Vorurteilsforschung, Deutsches Institut für Internale Pädagogische Forschung und Arnold-Bergstraesser-Institut, 'Einstellungen zu Fremdgruppen im internationalen Vergleich', *loc cit*.

in principle, if the leadership group has the will to do it.

The relatively low significance which the blacks attribute to this field of conflict helps to reduce the level of conflict. This factor is the most important condition for the success of peaceful change: thus far there is *no noticeable element of racism in reverse.* In other words, as far as the black majority is concerned, *peaceful change* in relations between the races *is still possible.*

3. *Conflict about power*

We have seen that the conflict about prosperity is fundamentally negotiable, and that the conflict about identity, although far more difficult, is not insoluble granted certain preconditions and reservations. What about the third field of conflict—conflict about power?

The features of the political struggle in South Africa make the peaceful and democratic regulation of conflict seem extremely difficult. The conflict about power is perceived by all the parties involved in a way that renders negotiation extraordinarily problematical.

The opposing ideological conceptions of blacks and whites have been shaped by absolute value conceptions; they are mutually exclusive. The dominant conception among the whites involves a political determination to use their might to safeguard their identity. It is immaterial whether this identity is defined primarily in terms of the Afrikaner people, or a white nation transcending the language groups or even including coloureds and Indians. The identity group whose core consists of the Afrikaners will not accept domination by other groups under any circumstances. If these other groups are no longer prepared to accept white or Afrikaner rule, then in the whites' view the only alternative is secession, i.e., partition of the country. Their future political self-determination is an indivisible good for the overwhelming majority of Afrikaners, and also for the other whites.

The basic political awareness which governs black politics in South Africa is based on other, equally absolute values. All who live in a country, regardless of their origin, race, religion, language, or culture, are members of one single indivisible nation. Equal rights should be enjoyed by all, and the majority should rule, whatever its composition.

Two visions thus stand opposed to one another: on the one hand, an ethnic vision of the nation-state, and on the other a vision of men choosing to live together within the same national boundaries. And each of these visions is bound up with a clear claim to power, by the whites and the blacks respectively. Thus not only are values mutually exclusive, but also claims to power. It is consequently not surprising that the political conflict is regarded by both sides as a zero sum game. Victory for the one side necessarily implies defeat for the other. Moreover, the whites regard each and every change in the existing power relationships as final and irreversible. Each side's perception of the political conflict shows all the features that would make it non-negotiable and serious. It appears to be a clear case of 'all or nothing'. This view of the conflict about power is particularly strong among the leaders on both sides.

So, the core of the white power-élite regards separate development as the only possible way to regulate conflict, whereas most black leaders believe that for it to be regulated, whites must be prepared to live as a minority within a multiracial unitary state, or in other words, to abandon all claim to power as a group.

Are separate development and partition on the one hand, and a multiracial unitary state on the other, feasible ways of democratically regulating conflict?

The experiences of other plural societies indicate that both ways must be treated with caution. History does provide a few examples of the peaceful partition of states: the dissolution of the union between Sweden and Norway, the secession of Belgium from the Netherlands, and the withdrawal of Singapore from the Malaysian Federation, among others. That these partitions were effected peacefully was undoubtedly largely because in all these cases ethnic, linguistic, or religious homogeneous subsystems were gaining their independence, and no resettlements of the population were necessary. The situation is quite different in the many territories in which there is no clear geographic distinction between the population groups involved in the conflict: Ireland, India and Pakistan, Palestine, Cyprus. These partitions were only effected after bloody conflicts, mass exodus, expulsion of large parts of the population, and international intervention. In all these cases, then, partition was far from peaceful. It was a means, after considerable violence, of forestalling further and possibly even worse violence.

If the strategy of partition offers only limited prospects for a regulation of conflict that is *peaceful*, the experiences of integrated unitary states in plural societies offer little hope of a regulation of conflict that is *democratic*. Democracy in a centralized plural state has seldom lasted long. At best, minorities have been mildly oppressed. But as a rule, authoritarian forms of government have taken over. As we saw in the first chapter, it was precisely the failure of numerous unitary democracies in plural societies which led many scientists to doubt whether democracy was possible in such societies at all. Even the school of 'democratic optimists' regards competitive democracy within a unitary state as a strategy of conflict management which, by and large, cannot be implemented in plural societies.[9]

The opposing attitudes which white and black South Africans have

[9] Cf. Gerhard Lehmbruch, 'Consociational Democracy in the International System', *loc cit*, p. 378.

377

towards the conceptions of separation or a unitary state respectively tend to confirm the view, based on the experiences of other societies, that neither of these conceptions can provide a peaceful and democratic regulation of conflict in South Africa.

The majority of white South Africans support the policy of 'separate development' and the creation of bantustans in the prescribed areas. Almost 90 per cent of Afrikaners and approximately 60 per cent of English speakers share this view—these percentages hardly changed between 1974 and 1977. About one-quarter of Afrikaners and a little more than one-third of English speakers are prepared to make concessions on the question of land and industrial areas. A fluctuating minority of each white group support a radical partition of the country into two parts. Among the Afrikaners, 12 per cent supported such a partition in 1974, as many as 24 per cent in October 1976 after the Soweto disturbances had broken out, but only 16 per cent in July 1977. Among the English speakers, 20 per cent supported a radical partition in 1974, 26 per cent late in 1976, and 20 per cent again in 1977. These fluctuations show that support for a partition of the country increases at traumatic times. However, graver events than the Soweto demonstrations are undoubtedly necessary before whites as a whole would accept a partition of the country. This confirms our assumption that partition would be acceptable only in the train of violent events, and then as the lesser evil.

In any case, partition could only be implemented peacefully if it enjoyed the support of the black majority. But this support is clearly lacking. Only one-fifth of urban blacks are in favour—less than the corresponding white figure. Even a solution which would grant the blacks more than half the country is approved by less than one-third.

Moreover, should a situation arise in which the majority of whites were indeed prepared to accept partition—if they felt that their group existence were threatened, for example—it is hardly likely that this same situation would make partition seem more attractive to blacks. The pressure under which whites would accept it might well incline blacks to push for a solution which better serves their own interests.[10]

In the light of these opposing perceptions of *partition* and its desirability, this solution appears conceivable only at the extreme, as a result either of fierce and violent struggles in which neither side can gain the upper hand, or of foreign intervention or arbitration after an armed struggle. *In neither case* would this be a *peaceful* way of regulating conflict.

The prospects of creating a multiracial unitary state by peaceful and

---

[10] A further complication for a radical partition of South Africa is the fact that within the white state the coloureds in the Cape Province would have to be incorporated into the political system in some or other way.

378

democratic means are hardly better. Although 80 per cent of the blacks desire such a state, the overwhelming majority of the whites are opposed to it. One must concede that the number of whites prepared to grant the blacks a qualified franchise rose significantly between 1974 and 1977: for the Afrikaners from 18 per cent to 40 per cent, and for the English speakers from 65 per cent to 76 per cent. But only one-fifth of the urban blacks accept a qualified franchise. On the other hand, full franchise for all South Africans is accepted by only 10 per cent of Afrikaners and approximately 20 per cent of English speakers. It would be impossible to institute political integration peacefully against this unambiguous expression of the will of the whites.

Our study among urban blacks has clearly shown that there would be real prospects for democracy in a multiracial unitary South African state if it were peacefully brought about. We have found that the democratic potential of the blacks is considerable, as is their tolerance towards the minority groups. Nevertheless, the data indicate that democratic stability in such a unitary state would be faced with many problems. The closer that urban blacks are tied to tribe or rural environment, the less likely they are to have democratic and tolerant attitudes, and the more likely they are to reveal tribal political preferences. Projected to possible voting behaviour, in a unitary state practising the British voting system of 'the winner takes all', this would lead to the ascendency of the strongest group and to the minorities' being deprived of all political say; that is, to the conditions which in numerous plural societies have typically led to the destruction of the democratic system. However, whether such considerations are plausible or not is purely hypothetical. Without the consent of the group which at present possesses power, *there can be no hope of peacefully erecting a unitary state in which a full franchise obtains*. And this consent is lacking.

It follows that the respective conceptions of political change preferred by the white and black groups cannot be implemented by peaceful means. Each conception is based on a zero sum strategy which benefits the group which supports it but is unacceptable to the other.

Does this mean that the conflict about power in South Africa cannot be settled in a peaceful and democratic way?

Let us examine the prospects of a third conceivable way of peaceful change in South Africa, viz., the sharing of power in a system based on consociational democracy. Now the ruling ideology of the white group is opposed to power-sharing; for in terms of this ideology power, like identity, is indivisible. If identity is non-negotiable, then by the same token so is power. In a study of the conflict in Northern Ireland—likewise an unsolved conflict in a plural society—Anthony Oberschall introduces a useful distinction between two different objects of the conflict about power. He maintains that in Northern Ireland there is on the one hand the national issue, which is the question of a Union with the Irish Republic or with Great Britain; and on the other hand there is the citizenship issue, which concerns the political and civil rights of the inhabitants of Northern Ireland. The national issue affects fundamental principles, i.e., it concerns indivisible goods and is therefore difficult to regulate. But the citizenship issue is less fundamental, and accordingly allows for compromise and negotiation.[11] Similarly, we must distinguish in South Africa between the political component of the identity conflict on the one hand, and the question of the division of power on the other. As long as both aspects are treated as one, the insoluble character of the identity issue will necessarily seem to preclude any solution to the issue of the division of power.

A peaceful and democratic regulation of political conflict is thus only possible when a political dispensation is chosen to provide political guarantees for those groups which regard themselves as identity groups. If a group has the assurance that its political identity is guaranteed, the question of the division of power can then be regarded as negotiable.

Now consociational democracy is a political system which pursues precisely this goal. Groups which want to maintain their identity are, as groups, regarded as elements of an overall political system in which power is shared between the groups and the division of power is negotiated.

How do white and black South Africans view power-sharing between groups? Among the whites, only a minority are in favour: only a fifth in 1974 and almost a third in 1977. The significant point is that support among Afrikaans voters rose considerably, from 13 per cent to 20 per cent, and that—unlike support for the idea of a radical partition—it did not drop again in 1977. As far as the English speakers are concerned, this notion now enjoys the support of a majority, 55 per cent.

In evaluating the attitudes of the Afrikaners, one must take into account that the concept of federalism as such has had negative overtones for them ever since the former United Party revealed its nebulous plans for a federation. Moreover, when one takes into account that Afrikaner support for a qualified franchise—a more 'understandable concept'— has in the meanwhile risen to over 40 per cent, it becomes clear that the idea of black participation in the South African political system has made considerable progress. If one further considers that no South African politicans have so far advocated a precise model of consociational democracy, the burgeoning of support among Afrikaner voters is astonishing. If an Afrikaner politician could successfully explain that the sharing of power in a consociational system would effectively preserve the Afrikaners' identity, one might expect that this

[11] Anthony Oberschall, 'Conflict and Conflict Regulation in Northern Ireland', *loc cit*, pp. 13–22.

380

system would gain widespread approval.

In brief, the idea of sharing power in a consociational democracy already enjoys the support of a majority of the English-speaking population; and although it is still far from enjoying the support of a majority of Afrikaners, it is approved by increasing numbers and seems capable of gaining further support. Thus, in contrast to a unitary state, it is not inconceivable that the white electorate would accept the solution of consociational democracy, as long as the white leadership shows the necessary political determination.

And among the blacks, a consociational solution is already supported by half of the urban blacks we interviewed.

To summarize: we have established that the conflict about power in South Africa, like the conflict about identity, raises considerable difficulties. The political dispensations supported by the whites and the blacks, i.e., partition and a unitary state respectively, are unable to command a consensus. They must therefore be excluded as peaceful and democratic means of regulating conflict. By contrast, the solution of some form of consociational democracy need not be completely excluded. Among the blacks, it is clearly a second-best but still an acceptable solution; among the whites it still lacks the decisive support of the political leaders.

We have thus established that in all three areas the severity of conflict is considerable, resulting from the different perceptions of the parties to the conflict. The conflict most likely to be resolved peacefully is the economic one, for the one group's openness to change is here closest to the expectations of the other group. The most serious conflict seems to be over socio-cultural identity and social relations between the groups; this conflict also makes the political conflict considerably more difficult to regulate. In no area, however, could we decisively conclude that the existing conflicts are insoluble in principle. We further established that the decisive factor for change in all the areas of conflict is the determination of the white leadership.

CHAPTER 13

Conflict Regulation by Consociational Democracy: Fulfilled and Unfulfilled Conditions

Our discussion of whether the conflicts in South Africa can in principle be regulated has led us to this conclusion: the concept of power-sharing is the only one of various possibilities of political change in South Africa that has any chance of obtaining the consensus of the parties involved. We shall construct a model of consociational democracy from the most important features of those political systems which democratically regulate conflict in plural societies. We can then use this model to establish which conditions exist, and which do not, for the regulation of conflict in South Africa by consociational means.

Over the last decade a great deal has been written on more or less successful consociational democracies, such as the Netherlands, Belgium, Switzerland, Austria, and the Lebanon before 1975.[1] The personal preferences of the various authors are clearly evident in their theoretical discussions; various details are disputed; and finally there is no lack of scepticism about the whole idea of consociational democracy, although few convincing counter-arguments have been presented so far.[2]

It would be beyond the scope of the present study to review this discussion in detail or engage in it. It is sufficient for our purposes to outline the basic characteristics of consociational conflict regulation, on which the leading authors of this school agree. This will be followed by an account of the conditions of consociational democracy mentioned in the literature, and a discussion of whether or not they are present in South Africa. The conditions are of four kinds: pertaining to the basic

[1] For surveys of the literature cf. Hans Daalder, 'The Consociational Democracy Theme', *loc cit*, and Brian Barry, 'Political Accommodation and Consociational Democracy', *British Journal of Political Science*, 5 (1975), pp. 477–505.

[2] Cf. Brian Barry, 'The Consociational Model and its Dangers', *European Journal of Political Research*, 3 (1975), pp. 393–412; cf. Lijphart's reply to this criticism in: idem, *Democracy in Plural Societies, op cit*, pp. 233f.

structural features of consociation in a society; to the political leadership; to the population as a whole; and to the relations between the leadership and the population.

1. The characteristics of consociational conflict regulation

Consociational democracy is defined as a political system in which conflict between sections of the population in a plural society is revolved by deliberate and, as a rule, institutionalized co-operation between the leadership groups or the élites of the different sections, in a manner which renders stable democratic government possible. In short, it is government by a cartel of élites. [3]

According to Lijphart, consociational democracy has four characteristics: government by a grand coalition, a mutual veto, the proportional representation of groups, and the autonomy of the various segments. In conjunction, these provide the mechanism of conflict regulation. [4]

Competitive democracy is based on the principle of narrow majorities. It gives the majority all the political rewards, and places the minority in opposition. Since majorities can change in homogeneous societies, nothing fundamental is at stake; the loser today can win tomorrow. In plural societies, by contrast, a great deal is at stake. If votes are cast according to group membership the majority is predetermined, i.e., the majority is built into the system. Given a competitive political system in a plural society, a change of government is improbable; the winner remains the winner, the loser always loses. The present political system in white South Africa is an excellent illustration of how this works out in a divided society. [5]

Consociational democracy, on the other hand, is based on the principle of a grand *coalition*. Every group participates in the exercise of power; none is excluded or relegated to perpetual opposition. No matter how different the basic ideological positions, or how contrary the interests of the different groups, government is a mutual responsibility. This means that compromises must be found. [6]

[3] Lijphart defines consociational democracy as 'Government by élite cartel designed to turn a democracy with a fragmented political culture into a stable democracy'. Cf. idem, 'Consociational Democracy', *loc cit,* p. 216. Lijphart has borrowed the concept of an élite cartel from Ralf Dahrendorf, who employs the concept in a less strict sense. Cf. Ralf Dahrendorf, *Gesellschaft und Demokratie in Deutschland* (Munich, 1965), pp. 296ff.

[4] Arend Lijphart, *Democracy in Plural Socieities, op cit*, pp. 25–52.

[5] Cf. above, Introduction to Chapter 6.

[6] Here only two of the numerous possible grand coalitions are mentioned, on account of the strongly institutionalized character. In *Switzerland* the Bundesrat is constituted on the basis of the 'magic formula', viz. two Liberals, two Social Democrats, two Christian Democrats, and one representative of the Farmers, Trades, and People's

A further factor in favour of compromise is the institutionalized *mutual veto*, which may be formal or informal. Important decisions cannot be made against the wishes of any of the groups, which provides a strong guarantee for minorities.[7] As a rule, the threat of veto is used sparingly; for if one group uses it, another group may be provoked to react in the same way. Moreover, compromises in one sphere can be made dependent on compromises in another.[8] Thus, the right of veto is an emergency measure which is employed only if one or other group fears that its most vital interests are seriously threatened.

The principle of 'proportionality' is the basis on which different sections of the population participate in the exercise of power. In most cases this applies not only to the legislature and the executive, but also to the civil service and the disbursement of public funds.[9] Thus, as far as the benefits of political power are concerned, the principle of 'the winner takes all' is replaced by 'to each his share'. In a number of consociational democracies the political institutions are not constituted in strict proportion; rather, *smaller groups are over-represented*,[10] so as to give them additional security.

In a few cases, especially when the population is divided into only two unequal sections, the divergence from proportional representation is greater, even to the extent of complete parity in the decision-making bodies.[11]

A further characteristic of consociational democracies is the far-reaching autonomy of the segments of the population. To reduce the possibilities of conflict, each group is entrusted with the administration

Party. At the same time due consideration is given to the variety of cantons and religious denominations. In the *Lebanon* every government is composed of the same number of Christians and Moslems; at the same time the strength of the different religious communities is taken into account (Maronite, Greek Orthodox, Greek Catholic, Sunnite, Shi'ite, and Druse).

[7] In the Lebanon, for example, the Christians and the Moslems each have a veto. A law can come into force only after it has been signed by both the State President and the Prime Minister; the former is always a Maronite, the latter always a Sunnite.

[8] Cf. the practices of 'linking' (linking of draft legislative measures in an attempt to force the enactment of one particular bill) and 'pacting' in the grand coalition in Austria. Cf. Gerhard Lehmbruch, *Proporzdemokratie, op cit*, pp. 26ff.

[9] In the Lebanon, for instance, there is parity between Christians and Moslems at all levels of the civil service. All religious communities are taken into account on the basis of their numerical strength.

[10] In the Swiss Bundesrat (Federal Parliament) the French and Italian-speaking Swiss are over-represented. They constitute 24.3 per cent of the population (1960), but have two or three of the seven members of the Bundesrat. Cf. Kurt B. Mayer, 'The Jura Problem: Ethnic Conflict in Switzerland', *Social Research*, 35 (1968), p. 718.

[11] E.g. in the Belgian Cabinet there is complete parity between Walloon and Flemish Ministers, although the Flemings constitute a majority in the population. There is also full parity in the Lebanon (cf. n. 6), whereas the respective strengths of the different religious communities is not known. The last census was held in 1932; it was decided to forego further censuses so as to preserve the principle of parity.

384

of those matters which directly affect it. This tends to lead to the emergence of numerous forms of organization which are specific to the population group or segment, not least in the cultural and educational fields.[12] The division into autonomous sections can be on territorial lines when the groups are geographically separated, or else on the basis of the key differentia, e.g., language or religion.[13]

Thus, group autonomy can be institutionally realized either through a geographic federation or through communities which are geographically integrated but socially or culturally distinct.

Consociational democracy also has its disadvantages. Decision-making is usually very slow; the system does not readily allow for innovation; and the implementation of proportionality is adminis-travively costly. The necessity for compromise between the leaderships groups reduces political participation, although this is partly com-pensated for by intensive participation in the institutions of the various sections.

However, the advocates of consociational democracy stress that the system can be very efficient in the long run, and that peaceful co-existence within a plural society is of the utmost importance.[14]

In sum, whatever the disadvantages of consociational democracy, *'in the unfavourable circumstance of sectional cleavages . . . it is the best form of democracy that one can reasonably expect'*.[15]

The school of consociational democracy broadly agrees on the schema as outlined above. However, there is considerable disagreement on the conditions which might facilitiate or hinder the emergence or main-tenance of such a system. Different authors list different conditions and rank their importance differently. In the following sections we shall consider only those conditions which have been held to be important by several authors. Our discussion will be largely based on an outstanding

---

[12] Cf. the practice of segmental autonomy in the Netherlands; the so-called 'Zuilen' have their own schools and universities, broadcasting networks, press, trade-unions, etc.

In the Lebanon the religious communities each have their own body of private law as well as their own courts to deal with matters pertaining to marriage and divorce, and their own educational systems and social welfare organizations.

[13] Segmental autonomy on the basis of the personality principle exists, e.g., in the Netherlands and the Lebanon; cf. the previous footnote. The Austrian socialist Karl Renner devised a particularly elaborate project of group autonomy on the basis of the personality principle for the former Austro-Hungarian Empire. Cf. Karl Renner (pseudonym: Rudolf Springer), *Der Kampf der österreichischen Nationen um den Staat* (Leipzig and Vienna, 1902); idem, *Grundlagen und Entwicklungsziele der österreichisch-ungarischen Monarchie* (Vienna and Leipzig, 1906); idem, *Das Selbst-bestimmungsrecht der Nationen in besonderer Anwendung auf Österreich, Part I, Nation und Staat* (Leipzig and Vienna, 1918).

[14] Cf. the discussion in Lijphart, *Democracy in Plural Societies, op cit*, pp. 47–52.

[15] *Ibid*, p. 48.

385

review of the current state of the argument presented by the Canadian sociologist, Maurice Pinard.[16]

However, we must first qualify the concept of a 'condition'. Lijphart emphasizes that his own set of conditions is neither necessary nor sufficient for consociational democracy. So even if all the conditions obtain, this does not guarantee the success of consociational democracy; and conversely, consociational democracy is by no means impossible even if the conditions are unfavourable.[17] There is a good reason for this qualification—the total number of successful consociational democracies is too small to allow for reliable conclusions. Accordingly, in the following sections a 'condition' will mean a factor which has proved to be either favourable or unfavourable for consociation in a number of cases.

2. Basic structural conditions of consociation

What basic structural conditions are conducive to the emergence or maintenance of a consociational democracy? Firstly, the *group structure* seems to be important. If there is a balance of power, i.e., if no one group is in a clear majority or a position of hegemony, and there are some different subcultures, even if there are not many, then the group structure is said to promote consociation.[18]

Secondly, it is an advantage if a country has a low international profile, i.e., if it is small and has little international significance.[19] Some authors maintain that an external threat is also conducive to consociation.

Finally, a political culture in which conflict regulation by amicable agreement is regarded as a fundamental norm is also a factor which promotes consociation.[20] A political culture of this kind often arises out of the experience of violence in a society. Or if armed conflict threatens between segments of the society, the political accommodation of all the parties involved may seem to be the lesser evil.

Do these basic conditions obtain in South Africa?

It is not easy to evaluate the group structure in South Africa in terms of a possible balance of power. If one goes by the numerical strength of

[16] Maurice Pinard, 'The Moderation and Regulation of Communal Conflicts: A Critical Review of Current Theories', *loc cit*.

[17] Arend Lijphart, *Democracy in Plural Societies, op cit*, p. 54.

[18] Cf. Gerhard Lehmbruch, 'Consociational Democracy in the International System', *loc cit*, p. 381.

[19] *Ibid*, pp. 381f.

[20] Lehmbruch in particular emphasizes the importance of a political culture which has developed over a lengthy period of time, and in which the élites have had the experience of a specific political socialization. Cf. idem, *Proporzdemokratie, op cit*; cf. also Kenneth McRae, 'Introduction', in idem, *Consociational Democracy: Political Accommodation in Segmented Societies, op cit*, pp. 1–26.

the respective racial groups, there is obviously a large imbalance. The numerical superiority of the blacks could be compared to that of the Greeks in Cyprus or the Protestants in Northern Ireland—comparisons that are hardly encouraging from the viewpoint of peaceful conflict regulation.[21]

However, can one describe 'the blacks' as a majority group without qualification? On the one hand, the white government takes great pains to emphasize that this is not the case, and insists on distinguishing numerous black ethnic groups. And South African blacks do exhibit great ethnic and linguistic diversity. However, earlier studies as well as our own data show that the urban blacks, at least, reject all forms of political organization based on ethnic distinctions.[22] The government's policy of 'divide and rule' has probably been the major cause of declining black ethno-political loyalty and growing black political unity.[23] There is no evidence that the blacks will accept ethno-political organizations in the future, so they may be excluded from consideration as a basis for a balance of power.

On the other hand, our data reveal that on non-ethnic criteria the urban blacks do not constitute a monolithic political majority—and it is the realm of the political that is our immediate concern. They form a coherent majority only in their rejection of the present system of domination. In other political respects, one can clearly distinguish different tendencies among them. There is no evidence to disprove the assumption that, given open democratic competition, black South Africa would manifest considerable political differentiation and even political cleavage. Black South Africa is also divided by differences between town and country, and *especially* by significant differences between regions. We have seen that the blacks in Soweto, Durban, and Pretoria form clear and distinct political cultures. There are numerous indications that this applies to the other regions of South Africa.

Thus, if one allows the hypothesis of free political organization, one can hardly expect that 'the blacks' will form a monolithic, hegemonic political whole.

It is above all the present oppression which has engendered the largely uniform political attitudes of the blacks; and even this has not hitherto fully eliminated the various political tendencies and different regional political cultures.

[21] Cf. Lawrence Schlemmer, 'The Devolution of Power in South Africa: Problems and Prospects, *loc cit*, p. 7.

[22] Cf. Philip Mayer, *Urban Africans and the Bantustans, op cit.*

[23] 'In fact, "multi-national development" has probably generated more unity among the unenfranchised groups than would otherwise have been the case'; Schlemmer, 'The Devolution of Power in South Africa', *loc cit*, p. 7.

Thus, if minority rule in South Africa were to cease it is likely that a multiple balance of power will emerge.

The crucial issue is surely the political structure. A Westminster system would most probably lead to one group establishing its hegemony. Proportional representation on its own would improve the prospects for political differentiation. Proportional representation within a federal system would be even more likely to promote the emergence of political checks and balances so as to ensure the equilibrium of power necessary for consociation. And this has not yet taken into account the innumerable possibilities of minority over-representation and the right of veto which consociational democracy allows for. In brief, *a multiple balance of power does seem possible in South Africa*.

It might also be possible to fulfil the condition of a *low international profile* in South Africa's case. South Africa is at present in the world's political limelight only because of its current racial policies. A low international profile has the advantage for consociational politics of minimizing some of the pressures which could lead to conflict between the sections of the population. Thus, small consociational democracies tend to adopt a neutral stance towards those disuptes between larger neighbouring states which could possibly provoke internal conflict. Now South Africa is not a small country, and it is of considerable interest to all industrial states because of its endowment of raw materials.[24] Moreover, for geopolitical and strategic reasons developments in South Africa are not unimportant, especially to the great powers.[25] Even so, a South Africa strengthened by a generally acceptable regulation of its internal conflict could avoid becoming an object of international disagreement; for it is undoubtedly strong enough to preserve its independence. Further, South Africa's geographical position makes it easier for the country not to get involved in inter-African conflicts. Finally, if internal conflict could be regulated in a generally acceptable way the mineral wealth of the country could become the basis of shared economic interests, which would in turn strengthen internal cohesion.

Some authors hold that external threats promote the internal cohesion of a plural society. But this may well only be true when a threat is perceived as such by all parts of the population, and to the same degree.[26] But this is by no means true of all existing consociational democracies,[27]

[24] On South Africa's raw materials cf. W. C. J. van Rensburg and D. A. Pretorius, *South Africa's Strategic Minerals* (Johannesburg, 1977). On the relative dependence of the Federal Republic of Germany upon South African raw materials, cf. Wolfgang Schneider-Barthold, *Die Beurteilung der Wirtschaftsbeziehungen der Bundesrepublik Deutschland zur Republik Süd-afrika und zu den OAU-Staaten aus deutscher Sicht* (Berlin, 1976).

[25] Cf. A. J. Cottrell, 'The Geo-Strategic Importance of Southern Africa', in Cas de Villiers (ed.), *Southern Africa: The Politics of Raw Materials* (Pretoria, 1977), pp. 9–19; cf. also Peter Janke, 'New Perspective to Strategic Studies', in Cas de Villiers (ed.), *op cit*, pp. 28–33.

388

and assuredly not in the case of South Africa. Under the current South African system, whites might well feel threatened by the possible intervention of other African states or by their support of guerilla movements, whereas it is unlikely that blacks do.[28] Thus, while an external threat must be eliminated as a favourable factor for consociation, it is quite possible that if South Africa were to adopt an acceptable form of conflict regulation it would achieve a low profile in international politics. This would considerably reduce the possibility of internal political conflicts developing out of foreign policy issues.

In this connection it may be noted that according to some authors the smaller the country the better the chances of consociational democracy, not only because of the international insignificance which this normally implies, but also for internal structural reasons. In a small country the political élite is also small, so its members often know one another personally, and are therefore in a better position to develop relationships coneducive to conflict regulation.[29] However, this argument applies more to demographic than to geographic size. South Africa is vast in geographic terms, but its population—approximately 22 million—is not so much larger than that of the Netherlands, a successful consociational democracy, that one could safely draw a qualitative distinction between them. Despite the enormous distances, the members of the leadership groups in South Africa, both black and white, know each other well. If personal relations between black and white political leaders are strained at the moment, it is hardly because of the technical difficulties of contact.

How does South Africa stand in respect of the third structural condition of consociation, viz., a *political culture* based on the *norm of amicable agreement?*

In many consociational democracies this norm has had decades, if not centuries, to develop. Generations of political leaders have grown up in the tradition of peaceful co-existence and have been taught that compromise is the greatest art in politics. In South Africa such a tradition is

[26] Thus Arend Lijphart, *Democracy in Plural Societies, op cit*, p. 67; cf. as well Gerhard Lehmbruch, 'Consociational Democracy in the International System', *loc cit*, p. 382.

[27] Cf. e.g. the fact that for Lebanese Christians the external threat is posed by the Arab states and particularly Syria, whereas for Lebanese Moslems it is posed by Israel. Cf. Theodor Hanf, 'Die drei Gesichter des Libanonkriegs', in Reiner Steinweg (ed.), *Friedensanalysen* (Frankfurt, 1978), pp. 64–122.

[28] 'The external threat, channelled through neighbouring black states, is not uniformly viewed in South Africa—many blacks have covert sympathies for the aims of militant expatriate organizations and for the black states ready to support them. Our external threat can cleave our society even more deeply'. Thus Lawrence Schlemmer, 'The Devolution of Power in South Africa', *loc cit*, p. 10.

Empirical evidence of this attitude is provided by the attitudes of urban blacks to Frelimo; cf. Chapter 11.

[29] Cf. Jürg Steiner, 'The Principles of Majority and Proportionality', *British Journal of Political Science*, 1 (1971), p. 65.

totally absent. The political style of the country has not been shaped out of amicable agreement but out of opposition, if not animosity. Political leaders are not expected to be flexible and able to compromise, but resolute and prepared to take uncompromising stands. The history of South Africa's political culture provides an almost perfect example of a 'love-hate' relationship, in both white politics and the political relationship between the race groups.

Given this tradition, is it conceivable that another political culture will emerge which is more conducive to consociational conflict regulation?

Pinard has pointed out that every political culture has certain structural features. Such features can be eroded, and may eventually disappear. When this happens, the corresponding political culture is also condemned to oblivion. Many of the crises in consociational democracies illustrate this point. Conversely, a political culture favourable to consociational democracy can emerge, if certain structural prerequisites exist.[30] What are these prerequisites? Compromise is the basis of consociational democracy. Consociational compromise has often been the outcome of the traumatic experience of violence within a society, for instance a civil war or revolution which neither party could win.[31] As soon as it becomes clear that there will be neither victor nor vanquished, but only sufferers, the parties settle for compromise. In more favourable situations, the possibility or probability of armed conflict is itself enough for consociation.[32] When the danger of armed conflict is perceived and the outcome is in doubt, when neither side is certain of carrying its cause, then the parties may conclude that sharing power is preferable to the risk of losing all of it, or of retaining it only at great cost. In other words, necessity, deriving from the recognition that one will not be able to achieve one's aims, can be transformed into a virtue—consociational democracy.

In recent years both black and white South Africans have become far more *aware of the possibility of armed struggle.* It is not impossible that precisely this awareness may form *the basis of a mutually acceptable settlement of conflict.*

[30] Maurice Pinard, 'The Moderation and Regulation of Communal Conflicts: A Critical Review of Current Theories', *loc cit,* pp. 9ff. Pinard refers to Daalder, who takes the view that consociational regulations arise from the existence of highly dispersed power structures. Cf. Hans Daalder, 'On Building Consociational Nations: The Cases of the Netherlands and Switzerland', *International Social Science Journal,* 23 (1971), p. 360. In this view, then, cultural patterns are based upon structural patterns. Pinard comes to the conclusion that a political culture with a tradition amenable to consociation is undoubtedly an asset, but not indispensable.

[31] Lehmbruch emphasizes the significance of the traumatic experience of violence, using as his examples Austria and the Lebanon. Cf. idem, *Proporzdemokratie, op cit.*

[32] Cf. Eric A. Nordlinger, *Conflict Regulation in Divided Societies* (Cambridge, Mass., 1977), Chapter 3. He suggests that, as a rule, in countries which have experienced sporadic unrest and violence the awareness of the real possibility of civil war is enough to promote the desire to avoid it.

To summarize, we may say that the basic conditions of the group structure in South Africa and the country's international profile are not unfavourable to the emergence of a consociational democracy. While the existing political culture clearly militates against it, the possibility exists that change may occur because serious conflict is recognized to be imminent.

3. Conditions pertaining to the political leadership

Political leadership groups, or as they are generally known in the literaturè, political élites, play a central role in the regulation of conflict in consociational democracies. The most important condition for such regulation is that political decisions are taken by the 'top leaders', the leading representatives of the different groups.[33]

The leaders must be both determined and able to take decisions. They must also combine the role of political leader with leadership roles in other spheres of society, communicate closely with each other across sub-cultural barriers, recognize the dangers inherent in the fragmentation of society, and be determined to keep the system intact.[34]

In South Africa they fulfil these conditions to varying degrees.

There can be little doubt that both white and black political leaders are willing and able to take decisions. There are political leaders on both sides who enjoy great prestige and command wide respect. And on both sides political and social leadership roles are closely combined. Thus, National Party leaders are also active in other Afrikaner organizations or rose to power through them—the Dutch Reformed Churches, cultural organizations, the universities, Afrikaans journalism and Afrikaans economic organizations. Similarly, leading political spokesmen of the black population usually exercise non-political functions as well: as church leaders, tribal chiefs, spokesmen for various professional organizations, trade-unionists and student leaders.

Unfortunately this exhausts the list of leadership requirements favourable to consociation that are to be found among both blacks and whites.

Take the danger of fragmenting South African society. Black leaders are quite aware of it. Within their own sphere of influence they have been

[33] All authors of the consociational school agree on this point. E.g. Daalder: 'Strongly divided societies can be stabilized by a conscious effort on the part of political élites, provided they deliberately seek to counteract the immobilizing and destabilizing effects of cultural fragmentation. Patterns of inter-élite accommodation therefore form an independent variable that may impede and reserve the centrifugal forces at the level of the masses.' Cf. idem, 'The Consociational Democracy Theme', op cit, p. 607.

[34] Cf. Arend Lijphart, Consociational Democracy, op cit, p. 216; cf. idem, 'Typologies of Democratic Systems', loc cit, p. 22f; cf. as well Jürg Steiner, Amicable Agreement Versus Majority Rule: Conflict Resolution in Switzerland, revised and expanded ed. (Chapel Hill, 1974), pp. 274f.

able to counter it with some success. Except for some homeland politicians, black leaders make a point of emphasizing not only the unity of the blacks, but the unity of all South Africans. Moreover, nearly all of them are determined to hold South Africa together within the framework of a single political system. However, among the white political élite only the leaders of the liberal opposition share the concern of the black leaders.

The leaders of the governing party, the real power-élite, do not see any danger in the fragmentation of the society; indeed, they try to promote it. They do not want to preserve the system as a whole; they want to take it apart. As we have seen, it is only a minority of the power-élite that doubts either that this policy of fragmentation serves their purposes or that it can be implemented.

Contacts between the leaders across group barriers are limited. Although the leaders of the white opposition have been cultivating contacts with moderate black politicians for some years, they lack the power to initiate change. Only in the last few years has there been any contact between the ruling white power-élite and black leaders. This is closely restricted to official contacts within the framework of the homelands policy, e.g., conferences between the South African Prime Minister and the homeland leaders. These official occasions are only used to promote the policies of the white power-élite, not to work out compromises with the demands of the majority of the population. Significantly, Chief Buthelezi boycotted such a conference at the beginning of 1978, on the grounds that it would not deal with relevant questions.

The possibility of reaching an acceptable resolution of conflict is rendered particularly difficult by the fact that the white power-élite recognizes only those black leaders who—whatever their reasons—either accept their policy or have accepted an official role within the framework of this policy. Black leaders who refuse to go along with this are not accepted as participants in discussion and negotiation. Worse, they are hampered in their political activities by police-state methods. The leaders of the previously large black parties—Nelson Mandela, the late Robert Sobukwe, and many other office-bearers of the ANC and the PAC—have been imprisoned or living under banning-orders for almost two decades. The leaders of the new black protest movement, the Black Consciousness movement—from Steve Biko, who was banned in 1973 and who was in detention when his death occurred in 1977, to detained members of the Soweto 'Committee of Ten'—have been subjected to similar repressive measures. In this way important political élites which according to our investigation enjoy the trust of large sections of the black population, are silenced.

Our political findings have shown that Gatsha Buthelezi is regarded as

392

the most important leader among the blacks. Yet the white power-élite seeks to confine his activities to his role as a homeland leader, in which official function he enjoys political immunity. At the end of 1977 the Minister of Justice seriously warned him not to expand his Inkatha movement beyond the Zulu ethnic group. In other words, the white power-élite is not interested in dialogue with the actual leaders of the majority, but only in contacts which are within the framework of, and serve, official policy.

Thus, certain of the conditions for consociation which pertain to political élites are clearly lacking. The most important requirement for the possible regulation of conflict by the élites is fulfilled—among both blacks and whites there are strong and representative leaders. But the attitude of the white power-élite prevents the process of regulation from getting under way. Indeed, *violent suppression of important sections of the black élite may well destroy one of the basic requirements of an acceptable solution; for one cannot negotiate with a group which has no leaders to fill the roles of negotiators.*

4. *Conditions pertaining to the population as a whole*

In some successful consociational democracies the structure of groups is such that the different groups overlap, or the various types of cleavage cut across one another. This has produced the hypothesis that the existence of such 'cross-cutting cleavages' is a condition of the success of consociational democracy.[35] In recent years, however, another view has gained increasing support, which is that whether cross-cutting cleavages are favourable or unfavourable to consociation depends on the nature of the cleavages themselves.[36]

It may well be that if different groups are well isolated from one another, areas of friction and the potential for conflict are reduced, and co-existence is thereby improved: 'good fences make good neighbours'. However, isolation between the groups could also be an obstacle to certain relations, i.e., those contacts across group barriers which would create a positive sense of community between the groups (e.g., in the case of common or complementary interests) and thereby help strengthen the cohesion of the society as a whole.

In South Africa the situation is that the nature of group segregation and of contact between the groups result in the *disadvantages* of group

[35] Lehmbruch, in particular, takes this view. Cf. idem, 'Segmented Pluralism and Political Strategies in Continental Europe: Internal and External Conditions of "Concordant Democracy"' (Paper for the Round-Table-Conference of the International Political Science Association, Turin, 1969).

[36] Cf. Maurice Pinard, 'The Moderation and Regulation of Communal Conflicts: A Critical Review of Current Theories', *loc cit*, p. 33, and Arend Lijphart, *Democracy in Plural Societies, op cit*, p. 81.

isolation and of contact between the groups reinforcing each other.[37]

On the one hand, blacks and whites are isolated from each other in many of those areas in which contact would have the effect of reducing conflict. There is hardly any contact between people who have the same status and similar professional interests, or between people with the same hobbies, and so on.

On the other hand, there is intense contact in those areas in which friction most easily occurs: in employer-employee relationships and in the economic and administrative spheres. In the hierarchies of professional life whites almost without exception give the orders and blacks carry them out. In the administrative sphere the people in charge are almost exclusively white; blacks nearly always find themselves being ordered about. To put it briefly, all the friction, anger, and irritation which arise in homogeneous societies in the sphere of work or interaction with administrative personnel, arise in South African society between black and white. This therefore leads almost automatically to friction and conflict between the two groups.

Furthermore, social apartheid eliminates most of those contacts which could moderate the perceptions of group conflict. That class and group cleavages coincide in South Africa, and that these cleavages are strengthened by the policy of social apartheid, jointly constitute one of the most unfavourable conditions for consociational democracy.[38] Only the elimination of racial discrimination in both the economic and social spheres could generate the conditions of group interaction among the whole population which are required for consociation.

On the other hand, an important condition noted in the previous chapter has already been met to a surprising extent—the perception of common economic interests. Despite all their economic conflicts, both blacks and whites are convinced that they inhabit a wealthy country with a very high potential for development. Each group realizes that the other contributes to the common good. Both groups are convinced of the advantages of a free market economy. But this perception of mutual interest can of course only survive to become a pillar in a system of consociational democracy if the economic position of the black population improves enormously.

With respect to the *conditions pertaining to the population as a whole*, we may conclude that they are in part favourable and in part un-favourable. They can be *adequately fulfilled only by incisive and peaceful change in the economic relations.*

---

[37] Cf. on this point and the next Lawrence Schlemmer, 'The Devolution of Power in South Africa: Problems and Prospects', *loc cit*, p. 9.

[38] Ibid.

5. *Conditions pertaining to relations between the leadership groups and the population as a whole*

What kind of relationships between political leaders and their supporters would facilitate the regulation of conflict within a consociational democracy?

Two important conditions can be inferred from the experiences of successful consociational democracies: firstly, there must be strong cohesion between the leadership group and the population within each of the various groups;[39] and secondly, the political leadership must be stable.[40]

What is the position in South Africa?

A strong affinity between leaders and their supporters can come about in various ways: by the mechanisms of a mass party; or by the great respect which certain leaders win even when the attitudes of the population are relatively a-political.[41]

The power of the white leadership derives from the well-organized mass party of an ethnic group. Party discipline is extraordinarily strong. The top leaders have a lot of latitude in decision-making and, even in the case of unexpected decisions, can count on the support of the entire party and its voters. A typical example was the development of the new constitutional plan in 1977. The plan was formulated by a small committee of party members drawn from the top leaders. It was first approved by the Cabinet and the parliamentary caucus, then made public, and only then presented to the provincial party congresses. The new plan proposed to include coloureds and Indians in the political system, in what until then had been an exclusively white power structure. This was obviously distasteful to large sections of the party; nevertheless, the plan was approved virtually unanimously at the congresses. Only one member of the parliamentary caucus criticized the plan in public. He was not put forward as a candidate in the following elections.

When the inner circle—the narrow power-élite—is united, it can clearly get its way whenever it wants. Just how strong the cohesion is between the National Party or its leadership and the Afrikaner population as a whole will be discussed more fully in the next chapter.

The cohesion between black leaders and their supporters is more

[39] Pinard regards this condition as of paramount importance. Cf. idem, *op cit*, p. 17; this condition was originally formulated by Arend Lijphart; cf. idem, *Consociational Democracy, op cit*, pp. 216ff.

[40] Nordlinger introduced the condition of political security for top leaders of the different conflicting segments. These leaders must be given the guarantee that their position is not undermined by politicians in the wings while they are trying to reach a compromise with leaders of other groups. Only leaders secure in their positions are able to negotiate and conclude difficult compromises which demand sacrifices. Cf. idem, *Conflict Regulation in Divided Societies, op cit*, pp. 65.

[41] Cf. Eric A. Nordlinger, *op cit*, Ch. 5.

complex. It is least pronounced in the Black Consciousness movement. The movement is represented by different spokesmen rather than by dominating leaders. Even someone like Steve Biko, who was a formative force, made a point of exercising his influence by stimulating people and arguing with them rather than by dominating them. So in this political movement decisions are not taken by any one leader. In the case of the older parties, the ANC and the PAC, it is now extremely difficult to determine the cohesion within them. It is a long time since these groups have had an organized structure on mass basis; they manifest their presence through a small underground movement on the one hand, and through strong but unorganized loyalty on the other. Yet their supporters are truly remarkable in the way in which they remain faithful to their imprisoned and banned leaders, and to a lesser extent to the leaders in exile. Even so, the question has to remain unanswered of the extent to which someone like Nelson Mandela, if he were free today, would be able to exercise effective leadership.

The support for the homeland leaders is quite different. As discussed above, they enjoy the respect of a reasonable number of supporters. However, this support is for the most part a-political and a matter of ethnic bonds.

Chief Buthelezi's support is the most interesting and, at the same time, the most complex phenomenon. On the one hand, he has an extraordinarily strong ethnic following—and, as the ethnic group involved is the Zulus, this is the largest of all ethnic followings in South Africa. But beyond this, he enjoys a personal prestige which reaches far into the ranks of other ethnic groups. In Natal he also seems to enjoy considerable support among adherents of the old ANC—a support which he carefully cultivates by means of various symbolic gestures. Finally, by resurrecting the Inkatha movement he has with considerable success created the organizational basis for a mass movement. All the evidence points to the fact that he not only has the greatest following in numerical terms, but also enjoys the highest personal standing of all the black leaders. He is without doubt the central figure in black politics in South Africa.

To summarize so far, we are looking at those conditions promoting consociation which pertain to the relations between leaders and the whole population. The first condition was that there be a strong affinity between the leaders and their supporters. This can be taken to be fulfilled for the white power-élite and for Buthelezi, and partially fulfilled for the other black leaders.

The same holds for the second condition, the stability of the political leadership. The succession of leaders is not rapid either in white or in black South Africa. In the National Party, Ministers and government leaders are not toppled or forced to retire. They remain in power until they themselves decide to step down, or they die in office. Despite all its formal internal party democracy, the National Party is characterized by its strong respect for hierarchy. The agonizing process by which Sir de Villiers Graaff retired as former Leader of the Opposition evidences a similar distaste for toppling leaders, even when virtually everyone is convinced of the necessity.

The leadership in black South Africa is also largely stable. With the important exception of the Black Consciousness movement, all the important names were already known a decade ago. The politically militant core of the urban blacks, especially the intellectuals, readily tend to question every leader who does not support the demands of the black population unequivocally and without compromise. As we have noted, it is this group which criticizes Buthelezi most strongly for his allegedly excessive moderation. Should this tendency increase, it is possible that the authority of the black leaders and their standing in negotiation will be weakened. For the moment, the overall strength of the Black Consciousness movement is confined to one stratum and one age-group. So the stability of the present black leaders will depend to a large extent on what they can achieve by way of peaceful change in the coming years. If the white leadership is so intransigent as to make success impossible, then the capacity to lead of the present leaders may well be decisively weakened, or else these leaders may be forced to become more intransigent themselves.

In other words, *the relations between the black leaders and their supporters are such that the majority group in South Africa is open to a policy of accommodation and consociation.* But whether this situation will persist is debatable.

CHAPTER 14

An Inadequate Readiness for Change: The Key Role of the White Power-Élite

We have examined whether the conflicts in South Africa can in principle be regulated by peaceful and democratic means, and we have discussed the specific conditions for doing so by means of consociation. We can now attempt to take stock.

What are the major obstacles to peaceful change in South Africa, and can they be overcome?

1. *General conditions of peaceful change: A reckoning*

The basic conditions for peaceful change were defined in Chapter 3. Have they been fulfilled?

The *first condition* was:

> The white political leadership must be convinced of the necessity for peaceful change, and must believe that the opinions and attitudes of the electorate are not inconsistent with such change.

Our analysis of the white political system has established that it is not the whole of the political leadership group which is decisive, but only the narrow power-élite. This power-élite consists of three groups which are roughly equally strong. The first unequivocally supports the status quo in all areas of conflict. The second is prepared to accept some changes, but not fundamental ones; essentially it too supports the status quo. The third group is convinced of the need for fundamental change. Its aspirations would fulfil most of the crucial requirements for peaceful change in the economic and social dimensions of conflict. Over the period during which this survey was conducted, the way this group came to conceive the political dimensions of conflict increasingly resembled a consociational form of regulation. Admittedly, there is an important qualification, namely that the sharing of power between the different racial groups would be possible only after some of the remaining homelands have become independent from the rest of South Africa.

The empirical data do not allow us to make any reliable predictions about the prospects of this group.

The second clause of the first condition has hardly begun to be fulfilled. The power-élite believes that the electorate is far more strongly oriented to the status quo than the empirical results show is actually the case.

The *second condition* was:

> The actual opinions and attitudes of the electorate must show a trend compatible with peaceful change, or at least not overwhelmingly opposed to it.

This condition has been fulfilled to a varying extent in the three dimensions of conflict. Our study has established that in the economic dimension the attitudes of the white electorate do allow in principle for an acceptable regulation of conflict. In the socio-cultural dimension the obstacles to change are considerable but not insurmountable, provided the political leadership acts with determination. In the political dimension of conflict the obstacles to a change towards a multiracial unitary state are insurmountable; however, the attitudes of the electorate do not preclude a change towards power-sharing, but this once again assumes that the leadership opts unequivocally for such a change.

Thus, the white electorate poses no insurmountable obstacles to change, provided the political leadership acts courageously and decisively.

The *third condition* was:

> The black leadership group must agree to the terms and guidelines governing peaceful change.

This condition is largely fulfilled. It is true that the black political leadership is unanimous in desiring a multiracial unitary state, and is not interested in discussing alternatives so long as these alternatives are not being seriously considered by the whites. However, the *black political leadership* has made it quite clear that it would be *seriously prepared to consider compromises* if these appear to be viable alternatives.

The *fourth condition* was:

> The urban blacks must show by their attitudes and behaviour that they are at least not opposed to the proposed course of peaceful change.

This condition has been fulfilled. Our survey has established that the majority of urban blacks are still peaceful. They are by and large good democrats, and supporters of a free market economy. They show a high level of economic, social, and cultural tolerance towards minority groups. Although a large majority desire a multiracial unitary state, approximately 50 per cent would also accept power-sharing under a consociational dispensation. Should they be seriously offered such a solution, *there can be little doubt that the majority of urban blacks would accept.*

Thus, the basic conditions for peaceful change are largely fulfilled with respect to the blacks. And the attitudes of the white electorate are, at least, not overwhelmingly opposed to such a change. *The real obstacle to change is the stand which the white power-élite has taken until now.*

2. *Specific conditions of consociational democracy: A reckoning*

We concluded from our consideration of the fundamental conditions and the fundamental regulability of political conflict that power-sharing on the basis of a consociational democracy is the only means of regulating conflict in South Africa which enjoys a consensus of support. Hence, we have to establish which of the specific conditions for a consociational democracy obtain in South Africa.

We found that provided all South Africans were allowed to exercise the right of political expression, there was a good prospect of fulfilling the various structural conditions of consociation—a multiple balance of power without the hegemony of any one group, a foreign policy which offers little cause for foreign intervention in internal conflicts, and the acceptance of a norm of amicable agreement based on the view that peaceful co-existence between the groups is preferable to armed conflict. The crucial obstacle to the fulfilment of these conditions is that the white power-élite generally believes that it can preserve its domination by means of unilateral conflict regulation.

Conditions favouring consociation with respect to the political leadership group are partly fulfilled. The political leaders of both white and black South Africans are sufficiently secure and determined to negotiate a sound resolution of conflict at an élite level. But the most crucial condition, an openness to compromise, is lacking on the part of the white power-élite. The current practice of this élite is to use repression on all black leaders who do not accept the framework of their bantustan policy. In effect, the white élite are hoisting themselves with their own petard; for even if the repression does not destroy the black élite, it will deprive them of precisely the power which is indispensable to their ability to participate in negotiating an acceptable regulation of conflict.

The conditions of consociation with respect to the whole population are fulfilled in part. Both sides perceive their shared economic interests. But without an enormous improvement in the economic position of the blacks, this situation can hardly be maintained indefinitely. And on the

400

other hand, the structure of group interaction has shown itself to be most unfavourable to consociational democracy. The effect of economic and social discrimination is that contacts between the groups are particularly intense in precisely those fields which promote conflict, viz., in hierarchic labour relations and in dealings with government officials; whereas drastic restrictions have been imposed on those contacts which could reduce conflict, viz., free social intercourse.

As for the conditions of consociation with respect to the relationship between the leadership groups and the masses, they have been fulfilled in a way which is, in principle, conducive to consociation. In both the black and the white groups the cohesion between political élites and their respective population groups is very strong and the positions of the leaders are quite stable. Thus, in principle, the requirements for making and implementing compromises exist on both sides. But once again, the white power-élite lacks the will seriously to consider such compromises.

Therefore, as was the case with respect to the general conditions for peaceful change, *the crucial obstacle to change as far as the specific conditions of consociational regulation are concerned is the current attitude of the white power-élite*, or more precisely, the current dominance of the group within this power-élite that is oriented towards the status quo.

3. *The scope for action of the white power-élite*

How do those members of the power-élite who do not in principle oppose peaceful change justify their inaction in this regard? They argue that the political leadership has only limited scope, because it is dependent upon the electorate, and that the electorate is extremely conservative and would be prepared to sanction only the most minor changes.

By contrast, our survey of the electorate's attitudes to peaceful change has shown that this is not true, at least in certain areas, and that the electorate is ahead of the leadership in some respects.

However, in view of the key role which the white power-élite will play in initiating change or preserving the status quo, this argument about limited scope becomes particularly important, and must therefore be more carefully analysed. How far do the electorate trust the leadership? How narrow is the leaders' scope for action? Could determined leadership promote peaceful change far more than it does at present?

In all four surveys the white voters were asked to agree or disagree with two statements:

Even if the leaders of my political party act in a way I don't understand, I will still trust them.

Even if my party takes political decisions of which I don't approve, I will still support my party.

401

To evaluate the answers, agreement in both cases was denoted as 'great trust' in the party leadership, agreement in one case as 'trust', and disagreement in both cases as 'no trust'.

Over the whole period of the survey, the trust which the National Party enjoys among its supporters remained extraordinarily and consistently high, as shown in Table 14.1.

Table 14.1

	April 1974	June 1976	October 1976	July 1977
Great trust	65	59	51	61
Trust	21	22	29	24
No trust	14	19	20	16

There were indeed some fluctuations: the results of the two surveys in 1976 reflect the reactions of National Party supporters to the Soweto events. As was also manifested in the interviews of white leadership groups, there was some doubt in 1976 about the ability of the power-élite to react appropriately to these events. Obviously, the broad basis of National Party support felt a similar doubt. But it is equally clear that this 'crisis of confidence' was restricted to a very small section of NP voters. Those who expressed 'no trust in the leadership' were only 6 per cent more numerous in the survey which produced the most unfavourable results for the leadership than in the one which produced the most favourable results. At its peak, this lack of trust was shared by only one-fifth of the total support of the National Party. Over 50 per cent of its supporters remained faithful to their leadership under all circumstances.

Just how steadfastly the National Party stands by its leaders emerges particularly clearly in a comparison with the opposition parties. In all our surveys, at least a third of the supporters of the United Party or its successors, the NRP and the SAP, had no confidence in the party leaders. And there is no question of blind loyalty from the followers of the Progressive Party or its successors, the PRP and the PFP: 60–70 per cent of their supporters disagreed with both statements, and only 10–15 per cent agreed with both.

These figures confirm the image of the NP as an extraordinarily leader-oriented movement—in clear contrast to the other parties, whose supporters are far more critical of their leaders. This is illustrated even more clearly in a comparison by language, between the respective degrees of trust placed in the National Party leadership by its Afrikaans-speaking and English-speaking supporters. Between one-quarter and one-third of the English-speaking NP supporters have no confidence in the party leaders, whereas this figure reaches a maximum of 18 per cent in the case of Afrikaans-speakers.

Who are the NP supporters who are not prepared blindly to support their party leaders?

They are mainly young and better-educated, and belong to the upper strata. Education is the most important of these criteria. Among supporters with not more than eight years of schooling, a maximum of 18 per cent have no confidence in the leadership, whereas among the more educated groups the figure varies between 23 per cent and 35 per cent.

We may also include among the more critical supporters of the NP those who, as indicated above, are more rather than less open to change. We shall return to this point below.

There can be no question that the loyalty on which the NP power-élite can rely is extremely great. This was borne out not by a single 'snapshot' poll, but by four separate surveys over several years, in times of crisis as well as political calm.

Can the leadership rely on this loyalty to obtain the approval of its supporters for unpopular and difficult decisions of extreme importance? In the last three surveys white voters were asked the following questions:

Imagine the following situation. The Prime Minister announces that in view of the serious situation it is necessary to make drastic changes in South Africa in the interests of the White nation. These changes will demand great sacrifice and concessions from the white community.
Which of the following statements do you agree with?
—I will support the Prime Minister unconditionally.
—I will support the Prime Minister only if I agree with his proposals.
—I will oppose any drastic change in our policies.

This question aimed at establishing the latitude available to the leadership in the area of 'great sacrifice and concessions'. The preselected answers offered, on the one hand, the possibility of unconditional agreement, i.e., the most difficult test of political support; and on the other, the option of opposing any significant change, i.e., the position which the government and the NP have consistently taken over the years.

The answers of NP supporters to this question are most enlightening. In June 1976 46.8 per cent gave their unconditional support to the Prime Minister, and in October 1976 and June 1977 the figure was 45.2 per cent. Percentages against any significant change in government policy were 7.6 per cent, 6.6 per cent and 5.6 per cent respectively. Amongst Afrikaans-speaking NP supporters, unconditional support for the Prime Minister is 2 per cent higher, whereas their support for the status quo fell to 4.3 per cent, 4.5 per cent and 3.5 per cent respectively.

Once again, it is the younger members and in particular the members of the better-educated strata who are least prepared to offer unconditional support. And the status quo position enjoys practically no support at all among the better-educated.

Finally, a remarkable result is the confidence which the Prime Minister enjoys among supporters of opposition parties: approximately one-third of the UP/NRP supporters, and even 10–15 per cent of the Progressive supporters.

There can therefore be absolutely no doubt that the white power-élite's latitude for action, especially in respect of 'great sacrifices and concessions', is extraordinarily wide.

We have already mentioned that it is those members of the NP who do not trust the leadership who would be most inclined towards peaceful change. This assumption was based on the social characteristics of the group. A further indication was that in answer to the question on the Prime Minister's scope for action, there was hardly any support for the status quo among members of the higher-income and better-educated strata.

This assumption is confirmed by a precise analysis of the respective groups who showed great, average, and no trust in the political leadership with respect to the different possibilities of political change. Among NP supporters who approve the division of power within the framework of a federal state, those who do not trust the leadership are about twice as numerous as those who do. This relationship between a critical attitude towards the leaders on the one hand, and openness to change on the other, is even more clearly evident with respect to the idea of a qualified franchise. It was approved by about 40 per cent of those supporters with 'great trust', about half of those with 'trust', and almost 60 per cent with 'no trust' in the leadership.

It has thus been confirmed that the white power-élite can place great reliance on the backing of its supporters, and others. This forms an especially sound basis on which to take decisions concerned with 'great sacrifice and concessions'. Almost half the NP supporters are prepared to support their party unconditionally, even when faced with such concessions. Further, it is precisely among those groups that are critical of the leadership and not prepared to grant it unconditional support that openness to change is at its greatest. Finally, the power-élite can also count on the backing of the opposition for moves in this direction.

There is an obvious conclusion to be drawn. *If the leadership is determined to introduce changes, those who support it unconditionally will accept its decisions because they accept them in any case; and those who are more critical of the leadership will also accept these decisions because they favour change. The white power-élite's scope for action is evidently considerable.*

4. *Is the peaceful and democratic regulation of conflict possible in South Africa?*

We can now answer this question. Black leaders and the black urban population are—still—open to peaceful change. They are also prepared to accept a means of regulating conflict to which the white electorate would not be opposed, if white political leaders were to take positive steps in this direction.

The *white power-élite* holds the key to the whole situation. In various respects it is also the crucial obstacle to change. This élite can *initiate change; it can also prevent it*. This is its unique, and perhaps its last, privilege.

Thus, the answer to the pivotal question of our study is: *a peaceful and democratic regulation of conflict in South Africa is not impossible.*

PART FIVE

Conjectures about the Immediate Future

A peaceful and democratic regulation of conflict in South Africa is not impossible. How likely is it?

There can be no reliable and scientifically substantiated answer to this question. Whether peaceful change can be initiated in South Africa depends on whether the attitudes and opinions of a very small group of people, the members of the white power-élite, can change; and then on how this power-élite acts.

As Lijphart has established:

'Élite behaviour seems to be more elusive and less susceptible to empirical generalisation than mass phenomena . . . to predict whether an unstable democracy can or will become stable by adopting consociational practices is much more difficult, because it entails a deliberate change in élite behaviour.'[1]

The question of how the white power-élite in South Africa will behave in the future, and whether or to what extent the influence of the different groupings within this élite will shift, cannot be answered by the methods at the disposal of empirical social research.

But we can in conclusion try to present some *conjectures* about the immediate future of South Africa. On the one hand these conjectures will be those of the authors, whose interest in the country goes back over a number of years. Our contacts have not been limited to empirical surveys and a study of the literature. In the course of innumerable, often night-long discussions with black and white South Africans, we have become concerned and sympathetic observers. On the other hand, the conjectures will be those of black as well as white South Africans—their fears and hopes and expectations of happiness and unhappiness over the coming decades.

[1] Arend Lijphart, *Democracy in Plural Societies, op cit*, p. 54.

CHAPTER 15

Sham Consociation: Unilateral Conflict Regulation in a New Guise

'Regardless of personal preferences, it is essential to discern what *is likely to occur*, rather than what *should happen.*'[2]

This warning by Heribert Adam against day-dreams should be kept in mind when conjecturing about the future of South Africa.

Prophecies of imminent revolution in South Africa are strewn about the literature of the last two decades. Nevertheless, what Max Gluckman wrote in 1958 still holds true today:

'The South African social system was then, and has become increasingly, a morally horrible one. But it worked and works, in toto and in its parts.'[3]

1. Unilateral conflict regulation: a continuing possibility

At the beginning of the book we stated our intention of restricting our study of the *possibilities* of peaceful change in South Africa to the internal situation in the country, *ceteris paribus*; i.e., we deliberately ignored all aspects of international politics. Although the whites are still firmly in the saddle, they could be toppled by large-scale intervention. So any discussion of *probable* future developments[4] must include a brief consideration of international aspects which could influence possible change.

[2] Heribert Adam, 'Three Perspectives on the Future of South Africa' (Unpubl. manuscript, 1977).

[3] Max Gluckman, *Analysis of a Social Situation in Modern Zululand* (Manchester, 1958), here quoted from Pierre L. van den Berghe, 'Pluralism', *loc cit*, p. 965.

[4] It is quite impossible to deal with the total body of speculative literature on South Africa; the authors have, thus, restricted themselves to thorough, well-substantiated works. Although published in 1971, Heribert Adam's book, *Modernizing Racial Domination, op cit*, particularly Chs. 5 and 6, is still one of the standard studies. Adam has further developed his basic thesis in two more recent works: 'Three Perspectives in the Future of South Africa', *op cit*, and 'When the Chips are Down, Confrontation and Accommodation in South Africa', *loc cit*. Christian P. Potholm has written nine scenarios of possible developments in Southern Africa; cf. idem, 'Towards the

Large-scale outside intervention is fairly improbable. It would require the agreement, if not the co-operation, of the two super powers, but they have no common interest in such a move. The possibility of one or other of them engineering a war by proxy, as in Angola, seems equally improbable; white South Africa cannot be equated with the FNLA or UNITA, or with the West Somalian Liberation Front, or even Somalia.

It is unlikely that Mozambique would be interested in an armed conflict with its mighty neighbour in the foreseeable future. And the approaching settlements in Rhodesia and Namibia are unlikely to turn these territories into militant front-line states, at least not immediately. In short, it is unlikely, at least for the time being, that Maputo, Salisbury, or Windhoek will play the role of Hanoi in a South African Vietnam.

The Republic's neighbours may well grant guerilla organizations the necessary facilities for their activities, or may not be in a position to refuse. Although guerilla warfare would be a constant irritation to South Africa, it would hardly constitute a serious threat to the existing system of domination. For geographical reasons alone, South Africa is not very suitable territory for unconventional warfare. But above all, not one white regime in Africa has been routed on the field of battle. Neither the French nor the Portuguese was ever decisively beaten; the people of Algeria, Angola, and Mozambique gained their victories less by force of arms in the colonies than politically in the metropoles. And South Africa's metropole is South Africa. In other words, a war of liberation in a situation of internal colonialism would probably be incomparably longer and more difficult than in a situation of external colonialism, precisely because it cannot be ended by the secession of the colony and its independence from the so-called mother-country. So there is little to support the view that white power in South Africa could be broken by outside intervention in the near future.

The situation with respect to the threat within the country itself is not very different. The demonstrations of recent years have undoubtedly been an expression of long-contained dissatisfaction, and the will of a new generation to emancipate themselves. However, they have not been able to weaken the foundations of white power.[5] However numerous

Millenium', in: idem and Richard Dale (eds), *Southern Africa in Perspective: Essays in Regional Politics, op cit*, pp. 321–31. An excellent collection of articles is: Leonard Thompson and Jeffrey Butler (eds), *Change in Contemporary South Africa, op cit*; for a consideration of possible future developments cf. in particular Leonard Thompson's resumé, 'White Over Black in South Africa: What of the Future?', *loc cit*, pp. 400–14. An analysis from the point of view of American political advisers is provided by John A. Marcum, 'Southern Africa after the Collapse of Portuguese Rule', in Helen Kitchen (ed.), *Africa: From Mystery to Maze, Critical Choices for Americans* (Lexington and Toronto, 1976), pp. 77–134. A most informative and extremely well-written work is R. W. Johnson's *How Long Will South Africa Survive?, op cit*.

[5] For an analysis of the prospects for revolution in a country like South Africa cf. the considerations of Crane Brinton, *The Anatomy of Revolution* (New York, 1938).

they might be, demonstrators who are unarmed or at best poorly armed have little chance against the monopoly of power enjoyed by the police force of a modern state, even without the military. The frustrations of non-violent and futile protest may drive a minority into becoming urban guerillas. This could well make life highly unpleasant for the whites. But there is no example anywhere of urban guerillas successfully overthrowing a regime—not even in countries offering more favourable conditions than South Africa.

A possibly serious threat to white power is a general strike. But this is unlikely to occur for a considerable time. Black workers have not forgotten the failures of the political strikes at the beginning of the 1960s. Pupils and students may be able to 'strike', given the financial support of their relatively prosperous parents. Workers, however, are not supported; they have to feed their families. For economic reasons, they simply cannot for the time being afford long strikes—and a long strike is necessary to force political change. Its recognition of this fact constrains organized black labour to avoid all political involvement.

To summarize, there is no serious threat to white political power in the immediate future, either external or internal. This means that *the maintenance of the present system of unilateral conflict regulation is as possible for the foreseeable future in South Africa, as peaceful change.*

2. Sham consociation: the consequences of preserving unity within the white power-élite

The proponents of the status quo within the white élite are therefore by no means the irrational fanatics they are often made out to be. They combine ideological confictions with the sober calculation that the whites of South Africa can preserve their privileged position for as long as the white government unswervingly and resolutely maintains its present political course. This may be difficult, and may demand financial as well as human sacrifices; but it is possible. So the verkrampte position does have a thoroughly rational basis, at least for the moment.

The chief difference between the 'verligte' and the 'verkrampte' positions lies in the more 'enlightened' view which the verligtes take of white or Afrikaner interests. This verligtheid consists above all in a long-term perspective on their interests. Like the verkramptes, they don't doubt that the present system can be maintained for a long time; but they do not believe that this can be done indefinitely. And in contrast to the verkramptes, they regard it as in the interests of the whites to eliminate the gross economic disparities between black and white in the medium term. In their view, social apartheid is a useless and redundant tradition which only makes political solutions more difficult. They are convinced that the bantustans in their present form hold no promise of becoming genuine states. Nor do they deceive themselves about the permanence of the urban blacks in 'white' South Africa, and about the fact that, in the last instance, South Africa must be their political homeland.

Their long-term view of developments and necessities has prompted the verligtes to consider the concept of consociational democracy in recent years. The verligte members of the power-élite have been supported by influential Afrikaner academics who openly advocate some kind of consociational solution.

However, they have so far only been able to implement their views in marginal matters. On crucial issues they have not succeeded against the preponderance of the verkrampte forces. Although the verkrampte bloc in the power-élite are not necessarily stronger, a specific mechanism works in their favour. In oligarchic leadership structures, 'the establishment need only sit tight'; one may recall the 'bunker' situation in Spain under Franco. The status quo, and especially the leaders who guide the social forces which support the privileges of the status quo, do not need any justification. Those who propose changes have to prove that the changes would bring an improvement. And when the leadership group operates on a principle of consensus—as in the case of the white power-élite in South Africa—then any innovation becomes extremely difficult. The mechanism which maintains an equilibrium between the groups in a consociational democracy also entrenches the status quo in South Africa's minority democracy.

In other words, under these circumstances the likelihood that the white power-élite will introduce changes is extremely small. There is no Franco in South Africa for whose death one can wait; there are several Francos, and for each that makes his exit there is a new one waiting in the wings. Nor is there a Juan Carlos in view.

To use a different analogy: South Africa has no de Gaulle to lead the way to internal decolonization.

Taking these facts about the structure and membership of the white power-élite into account, what changes are possible?

The power-élite act only when circumstances force them to do so. Their behaviour is like that of the Rhodesian Prime Minister over the last decade—always only the smallest step, and then at the last possible moment.

However, the pressures on the South African leadership have been pretty negligible so far. It has rather been the indirect effects of events in and around South Africa in recent years which have made their mark on the power-élite—economic factors, and the growing pressure of the Western powers. It has been recognized that although continuing outbreaks of unrest may not endanger the white élite, they do create a bad climate for foreign investment. And although Western influence in South Africa has so far been confined to diplomatic pressure and political

411

declarations, and is unlikely to rise to the level of effective coercion in the foreseeable future, even these actions could have damaging economic consequences via the encouragement they give the South African blacks.

What have been the effects of these perceptions and insights on the part of the white élite?

In some spheres outspokenly verkrampte politicians have been replaced, not by unequivocally verligte ones, but by intelligent technocrats belonging to the pragmatic centre of the power-élite. Some changes are being made which will genuinely improve the situation of the black population; but the crucial demands of the urban blacks are still unhesitatingly rejected.

Two developments clearly illustrate the nature of compromise within the power-élite: the new constitutional proposals, and—less important but equally characteristic—the re-naming of the Department of 'Bantu Administration and Development'.

The constitutional blueprint brings coloureds and Indians into the political system while guaranteeing the continued dominance of the whites. The blacks are still relegated to the homelands.[6] Meanwhile, the Department of 'Bantu Administration and Development' has been re-named the Department of 'Plural Relations and Development'.[7]

Both decisions conform to a basic pattern which will presumably characterize South Africa's immediate future. The proposed constitution is apparently similar to that of a possible consociational democracy, and the new designation of the Department has been borrowed from current terminology in the social sciences. In other words, some of the structural features of consociation have been adopted, as well as its vocabulary.[8] But its essence is missing: the regulation of conflict remains unilateral, rather than being worked out by all the parties concerned. Power remains in the hands of the white group. The way the recent changes were proposed was itself a typical example of the unilateral approach: the constitutional blueprint was drawn up exclusively by the whites, and then simply presented to the other groups.

Our conjecture about the immediate future is therefore that *the white power-élite will not opt for consociation, but for a sham consociation; that is, for a perpetuation of unilateral conflict regulation in forms which only resemble those of a consociational democracy.*

Sham consociation is the Afrikaner equivalent of the concept of qualified franchise. It is their version of a less harsh form of unilateral

---

[6] Cf. *Cape Times*, 13.9.1977, 'Constitutional Blueprint'; *Rand Daily Mail*, 18.9.1977 and 12.11.1977.

[7] Cf. *Rand Daily Mail*, 24.2.1978.

[8] E.g. the South African Foreign Minister R. F. Botha during a speech in parliament, quoted from an article by Arend Lijphart published in South Africa, 'Majority Rule versus Democracy in Deeply Divided Societies', *Politikon*, 4:2 (1977), pp. 113–16.

conflict regulation. Whereas enlightened English-speaking conservatives want to co-opt individuals into their system, enlightened Afrikaners want to co-opt groups; but neither party intends relinquishing the real power.[9]

This choice of sham consociation reflects divisions of opinion within the narrow power-élite. The verligte group is quite serious about genuine consociation, which the verkrampte group resists. The de facto compromise, espoused particularly by the representatives of the 'pragmatic' centre group of the power-élite, involves accepting the vocabulary and isolated elements of the verligte proposals, but without the essence of a generally acceptable means of regulating conflict.

The clearest formulation of the verligte position was contained in an important address by Minister Koornhof to an international conference on 'Accommodation in Plural Societies' in Cape Town on 23 May 1977.[10] This speech sets out clear directions for peaceful change in the economic and social dimensions of conflict. Each group should receive its due share of the goods and benefits of the whole society. All groups should have equal opportunities in the civil service and public sector. Civil rights should be restored.

Koornhof's solution to the political conflict qualifies as a form of consociational democracy: all groups should be involved in the central decision-making process. The urban blacks are expressly included—they should have an equal say in decisions where they live and work, 'that is, outside the bantustans'.

The political system it proposes is based on the Swiss example. Power would be decentralized. Within a federal or confederal system there would be geographically limited units, or cantons, some of which would have a white and others a black majority. Autonomous institutions would be created to allow for most decisions affecting people's daily lives to be taken within these units. This would ensure cultural pluralism. Each group would be able to take its own decisions about emotive cultural issues such as religion, language, and way of life.

These territorial units and groups would together form one nation. Decisions on matters of common interest would require a unanimous vote. There would be two different but complementary kinds of institution: on the one hand, group institutions with legislative and executive competence in all intra-canton affairs, and on the other hand national institutions with competence in affairs transcending group and territorial interests, and taking decisions on the basis of mutual agreement.

This speech is a veritable 'verligte manifesto'. Were it the government's policy, there would be no obstacle to its engendering peaceful change.

[9] Cf., e.g., W. J. de Klerk, 'South Africa's Domestic Politics: Key Questions and Options', *Politikon*, 4:2 (1977), pp. 178–89.

[10] Cf. *Cape Times*, 25.5.1977; *Rand Daily Mail*, 25.5.1977.

But the reactions to Koornhof's speech provide a clear illustration of the methods of policy-making in the power-élite. The verligte Afrikaans press greeted it with enthusiasm, followed by vehement denials on the part of Ministers oriented to the status quo. [11] After a few days the Prime Minister broke his silence: although he did not expressly reject his Minister's views, he declared that the inclusion of blacks in a plural political system would not become the 'effective policy of the government' in the foreseeable future. [12]

The new constitutional blueprint was presented a short time later: a quasi-consociational inclusion of coloureds and Indians to the exclusion of blacks; a sham, not a genuine, consociation.

One cannot doubt the sincerity of the verligte leaders' political stand. But one may be justified in doubting their prospects of success. It is by no means true that they want to provide an apology for the status quo— an accusation often levelled against them. However, the realities of the decision-making process within the white élite force them in fact into the role of apologists. This circumstance explains the frequent speculation, both in South Africa and overseas, on the possibility of the verligtes splitting away from the National Party.

This possibility need not be taken very seriously. A splinter group would have no chance of actually introducing verligte policies. A policy is only workable when it is supported by a majority within the National Party leadership; for only then would it have the whole party machine and the solid support of the NP voters behind it. Therefore, although they would never admit to it publicly, the verligtes in fact hope that the verkramptes will split away from the Party, thereby allowing the verligtes free rein. But this development is inhibited by the overwhelming desire of the power-élite to preserve the unity of the Afrikaner people. The secession of the HNP was a traumatic experience for the party. All the evidence suggests that the party is avoiding a new split at all costs.

The price is high. It clings obstinately to the status quo even where the pragmatic centre within the power-élite is in favour of changes.

In this respect Steve Biko commented: 'Because Vorster is afraid of causing a split in the party, he pays undue attention to the right wing. For this reason peaceful change is not very likely.' [13]

One can occasionally detect signs within the power-élite of impatience at its own immobility. For example, there are periodical rumours of an enlightened dictatorship, of a 'strong man' taking over the leadership. A leading member of the power-élite, himself not a politician, has stated: 'I really can't see any politician being in a position to take the necessary

[11] *Sunday Times*, 29.5.1977; *Rand Daily Mail*, 17.6.1977.
[12] *Rand Daily Mail*, 27.7.1977.
[13] Interview with Steve Biko, 17.4.1977.

steps. What we need is a political Tielman Roos.[14] The people of this country want leadership, and they are waiting for the man who can give it.'

Steve Biko's comments in this respect are again very acute: 'Should such a coup take place—and I don't think it will—then no coup in history will have been more discussed before it actually occurred. All this talk is evidence only of the leadership's inability to take decisions. And as people have no confidence in the leaders' ability to make innovations, they would like to see the generals force the leaders to make them.'[15]

A military coup is not very probable. There are relatively few professional soldiers in the South African army. Moreover, a strongly political vein runs through the army, and a putsch would run counter to all the political traditions of the Afrikaner community. A military government is only really conceivable in an unusually great state of emergency. So, all in all, it is unlikely that the verligte policies will be adopted. However, a purely verkrampte line is equally unlikely. The pragmatists within the power-élite are well aware that continuing racial unrest and confrontation are not in the interests of the whites. Consequently, they will make a few changes to remove some of the causes of black dissatisfaction, but without affecting the basic power structure. At the same time, they will try to refurbish the system's international appearance with trimmings cast in a verligte mould. What form might such a sham consociation in South Africa take in a few years' time? Some conjectures are in order.

3. Conjectures about the future of sham consociation

In the economic sphere some of the most immediate demands of the black majority in the cities will have been fulfilled. 'All their most urgent demands are demands which we can meet', one Minister has stated. And our survey supports him. Wage claims will be granted, at least to the extent which forestalls major strikes. A commission has already recommended major amendments to job reservation.[16] A start has been

[14] In 1931, during the Great Depression, England went off the Gold Standard; the South African government under General Hertzog did not follow suit, which precipitated a flight of capital from South Africa and a subsequent severe economic crisis. Tielman Roos, a Justice of the Appeal Court, founded a political movement with the aim of forming a 'national government' and abandoning the Gold Standard. Forced on to the defensive, the government decided to go off the Gold Standard. At the beginning of 1933 Hertzog and Smuts together formed a 'national government', and in 1934 fused their parties to form the 'United Party'. Here, thus, is an example of how someone outside political life can bring about spectacular changes in government policy and in party structures. Cf. D. W. Krüger, *The Making of a Nation* (London, 1969), pp. 154–63.

[15] Interview with Steve Biko, 17.4.1977.

[16] The Minister of Labour, S. P. Botha, set up a commission under the chairmanship of Prof. Wiehahn to examine all labour legislation.

made on large-scale improvements to the infrastructure in the black urban areas. The black middle class will be allowed greater economic freedom.

In the social sphere one can count on far-reaching measures to reduce racial discrimination. Petty apartheid is gradually being eliminated. The 'pragmatists' take an increasingly optimistic view of the positive effect of such measures on South Africa's foreign image. If the abolition of discrimination will exonerate the government in the eyes of the world, and if the power-élite regard this as worthwhile, they will not hesitate to cope with a little internal discontent to achieve it. Only the verkramptes doubt the élite's ability to cope with such a situation.

In the political sphere one can expect a 'modified application of apartheid', as Heribert Adam has termed it.[17] The homelands will be drastically enlarged to form consolidated territories.[18] It is probable that the offer of such arrangements will persuade black politicians in most of the homelands to accept independence. And since this will mean that most of the blacks living in the rest of the Republic will technically be foreign workers, it implies that the much reduced group of recognized urban blacks can then be incorporated into the political system of the Republic. The size of this group will have been manipulated in such a way that white numerical superiority is not endangered. Furthermore, the political institutions will be structured so that the whites will be able, if necessary, to achieve a majority on their own in the decision-making bodies. In addition, if the new constitutional proposal is any guide, only the majority parties of the various groups will be represented in the joint bodies. This is a precaution which would ensure that the Afrikaners in the National Party still have the final say. In effect, a political system will be erected in the remainder of the Republic in which coloureds, Indians, English-speaking whites and some blacks will indeed be represented, but in which the Afrikaners will remain the dominant group. In such a system, conflict can be regulated by consent whenever the other groups agree with the dominating group; otherwise, unilateral regulation will continue to apply. The Afrikaners' iron fist will be concealed in a velvet glove, but it will still be an iron fist.

Moreover, developments towards such a system of sham consociation will probably be gradual. They will occur in accordance with the principle of the smallest possible step at the last possible moment, and then only after extensive in-fighting within the power-élite, depending on the importance which they attach to internal or external pressures.

[17] Heribert Adam, 'When the Chips are Down', *op cit*, pp. 429ff.

[18] Cf. the plans drawn up by the South African Bureau of Race Relations (SABRA), a pro-government organization. Cf. Piet Bothma, 'Nog Grond na Swartes. Reuse-stede deel van Sabra-plan', *Beeld*, 10.8.1977. Cf. 'Ideën over deling van Zuid-Afrika', *Zuid-Afrika* (Amsterdam), 54:10 (1977), pp. 148f, and Tom Copeland, 'Partition: A Possible Solution for South Africa', *Cape Times*, 20.8.1977.

4. *Internal and external resistance*

Are there any serious obstacles to sham consociation? The most important may well be Buthelezi and his Inkatha movement. The whole achievement will be hollow unless KwaZulu accepts independence, for the Zulus on their own are more numerous than the whites. So one might surmise that the white power-élite will make every effort in the near future to promote the realization of an independent KwaZulu. On the one hand one might imagine that attempts will be made to replace Buthelezi by a more compliant political leader, but in view of his strength this is unlikely to succeed. On the other hand, it is not impossible that the white power-élite will finally bring itself to offer Buthelezi an independent Natal. Natal is not vital to the preservation of Afrikaner power and prosperity; its independence would remove from the Republic not only the Zulus, but also a strong section of the English-speaking white opposition. Such an offer would undoubtedly be very tempting for Buthelezi's Zulus: a viable state with a homogeneous black nation and co-operative white and Indian minorities, a kind of Kenya.

But if KwaZulu refused independence under any circumstances whatsoever, the issue would arise of a genuine consociational sharing of power between blacks and whites in South Africa. We must assume that this is the one, small remaining prospect for a democratic settlement of conflict in an undivided country. Let us surmise, however, that the white leadership is successful in removing this, the main obstacle to their policies by some other means. What are their prospects of imposing a settlement within the framework of a sham consociation?

The prospects are good. Independent homelands would not receive international recognition for a long time. But as the case of the German Democratic Republic shows, a state can emerge without international recognition. A neo-imperial system of states in Southern Africa would be able to function as smoothly without recognition as the neo-imperial system of states in Eastern Europe. Moreover, one may assume that in the course of time this system would be granted widespread de facto recognition. The attitudes of the important Western democracies will probably be decisive. Should they decide to put serious pressure on South Africa the development towards a genuine consociation is not impossible. The right amount of pressure must be exercised, and it must be selectively applied. Only the right amount will do, otherwise South Africa's whites will think in 'all or nothing' terms. They would then argue that all concessions are useless, and that total resistance to the outside world is the only way—a way which they could travel with success for a considerable time. Similarly, pressure should be applied selectively, to make it clear to the white élite that a genuine consociational solution is less harmful to their interests than the consequences of Western pressure.

417

However, one should not rely too heavily on selective and well-calculated Western influence.[19] Because the economic interests of the Western states vary, such pressure would require differing sacrifices from them. In such cases, it is customary to settle on the lowest common denominator. This could easily have the outcome that these states are satisfied by a few spectacular changes away from the more blatant aspects of racial discrimination, and quietly accept sham consociation.

If, as we have surmised, crude racial discrimination were gradually abolished in the Republic and blacks were allowed a voice in the political system, the Western states' most important objections would have been met. Most of these states are interested above all in smooth economic relations with South Africa. Should South Africa discard the most odious aspects of its present system and adopt a framework of sham consociation, they would have all the excuse that they need for far closer-co-operation with a welcome trading partner. They would hardly be more compromised by South Africa than they are by Brazil, Iran, or Indonesia. In sum, the evidence indicates that the introduction of a system of sham consociation would considerably reduce international pressure on South Africa.

5. Is a transition to genuine consociation conceivable?

Only one question remains: is there any prospect of sham consociation developing into genuine consociation in the long run? The experience of Belgium and the Netherlands would indicate so. The Flemings in the former and the Catholics in the latter were disadvantaged population groups for a long time. However, mainly as a result of their growing demographic importance, they were able to achieve equality by peaceful means within a system of consociational democracy. At first glance, Switzerland also seems to provide a precedent. The subjected cantons from the eighteenth century, which were jointly ruled by the old Swiss states, have subsequently been granted equal rights. But this was not brought about internally, but by the invasion of the French revolutionary army and the mediation of Napoleon. But there is no Napoleon in sight, or at least no statesmen in the Western democracies today, who could change the political face of South Africa.

Historical analogies are not decisive evidence. It is not impossible that sham consociation gradually develop into genuine consociation in South Africa, particularly if international pressure were applied. But if we are

[19] Moreover, Arnt Spandau has shown in a detailed economic work that a trade boycott of South Africa need not harm the country—at least in the medium term—and could, indeed, be beneficial in that South Africa would then be forced to manufacture a number of import-substitutes, especially in the capital goods sector, which would involve establishing a number of new industries. Cf. Arnt Spandau, *Wirtschaftsboykott gegen Südafrika* (Cape Town, 1977).

right in thinking that the latter is improbable, such a transition is then unlikely. What seems more likely is that some form of sham consociation will preserve white rule in South Africa in the medium term, but reduce the long-term prospect of genuine consociation. Changes of a purely decorative nature have taken place too often and for too long in South Africa. 'Apartheid' was re-named 'separate development' without any change of content at all. So we can assume that the majority of blacks will simply regard 'consociation' or 'plural democracy' as more new labels for apartheid, and that sham consociation will thereby destroy the prospect of a genuine and acceptable regulation of conflict in the future.[20]

Unilateral conflict regulation *in its present form* can be sustained for an indeterminate period of time. In his book 'How Long Will South Africa Survive?' Johnson concludes: 'To put it bluntly: if the Pretoria regime adopts a sufficiently ruthless and brutal policy at home it may well be able to suppress black rebellion well into the twenty-first century.'[21]

Now we have argued that Pretoria will not only rely on its present repressive strength, but will also disguise unilateral regulation *in new forms of sham consociation.* If we are right, its medium-term prospects of survival might well be even better.

[20] The concept of 'plural democracy' has become a synonym for apartheid, even among moderate blacks. Cf. G. Thula, 'The Process of Power Sharing', *loc cit*, p. 3: 'I will not dwell on the folly of homeland policies or separate development or *plural democracies.* It is like presenting a dud cheque. No one except the South African Government, the Transkei and Bophuthatswana will even try to cash it.'

[21] R. W. Johnson, *How Long Will South Africa Survive? op cit*, p. 314.

CHAPTER 16

White Fears and Black Hopes: How South Africans view the Immediate Future

'I feel uncertain and fearful about my future.' In 1977, half the whites and half the blacks we interviewed agreed with this statement. Three years previously, only a little over one-third of the whites had admitted to this feeling; now, however, the same proportion in each group was afraid. There may well be no better way of characterizing present-day South Africa than by the finding that the respect in which blacks and whites are in greatest correspondence is the extent of their fears about the future.

Both blacks and whites expect the future to bring considerable changes in their personal destinies. But what they expect of these changes is very different. The whites face them with trepidation, whereas the blacks have hopes of changes for the better.

More than half the whites today still regard themselves as 'very happy' or 'happy'. But only a little over one-third think that they will still be happy in ten years' time. Conversely, only one-tenth of the whites presently regard themselves as fairly unhappy or unhappy; one-quarter of them, however, think that they will be unhappy in ten years' time.

Black expectations are the other way round. Only one-fifth of them regard themselves as happy at the moment. But over 60 per cent of them think that they will be happy in ten years' time. And conversely, whereas at present over half the blacks feel unhappy or dissatisfied, only one-fifth think that this will still be the case in the future.

Thus, the whites' present fears are bound up with a very deep pessimism about their personal destiny. Blacks' fears, on the other hand, are closely bound up with great hopes.

In each group fear and hope are unevenly distributed. Who among the whites have the greatest fears, and who among the blacks have the greatest hopes? Among the *whites* the Afrikaners take a far more pessimistic view of future developments than English speakers. Almost one-third of Afrikaners as against less than one-fifth of English speakers think that they will be very unhappy in ten years' time. Members of the less-educated strata are far more pessimistic about the future than the better-educated. Among the better-educated twice as many people think they will be very unhappy in ten years' time as feel very unhappy today; among the less-educated, the figure is three times as high. It seems that those who have higher qualifications feel that a future in South Africa still holds some prospects for them, whereas the less-qualified fear for their privileges.

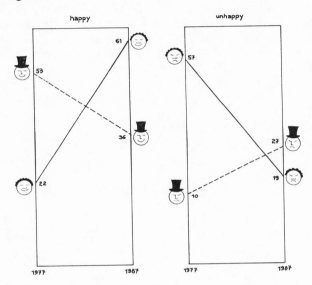

Finally, there are significant differences between the supporters of the different white parties. Among the PFP supporters, the assessments of present future happiness or unhappiness hardly differ. Evidently, this group still hopes that blacks and whites will be able to live together peacefully in the future. Some pessimism can be detected among supporters of the NRP; there is a slight increase in the proportion of those who think they will be very unhappy in ten years' time. By contrast, pessimism about the future is dramatic among supporters of the National Party. Although less than one-tenth regard themselves as very unhappy at present, three times as many think they will be unhappy in ten years' time.

This analysis of future expectations shows that fear among the whites is primarily fear among the Afrikaners—in particular, fear among Afrikaner supporters of the National Party.

How do *black* hopes vary?

421

Among blacks the degree of happiness and unhappiness also varies considerably according to stratum and education. One-third of the less-educated regard themselves as happy, whereas only one-tenth of the educated take this view. And about half of the members of the lower strata regard themselves as unhappy, whereas for the higher strata this figure is over 70 per cent. There are also differences on the basis of political orientation. One-third of the supporters of homeland leaders regard themselves as happy. By contrast, three-quarters of the supporters of Buthelezi, the ANC, and the PAC regard themselves as 'unhappy' and 'embittered'. But in their assessment of the future there are no significant differences at all, not on the basis of class, education, political orientation, or any other characteristic. Irrespective of their current situation and opinions, the vast majority of urban blacks have great hopes of a better future in the coming decade. The fears of the whites are the hopes of the blacks.

EPILOGUE

Are white fears less well founded than black hopes? An examination of internal and external power relationships warrants this conclusion. Fundamental changes in South Africa can hardly be expected in the coming decade, but rather around the turn of the century. One of the black leaders we interviewed remarked that twenty years was a very short interval in history, but a very long time in the life of an individual. Careful analysis inclines us to believe that 'a very long time' will probably pass before black hopes are realized.

But what presently seems probable is by no means inevitable. By equally careful analysis we have established that peaceful and democratic conflict regulation is still not impossible. And *what is not impossible can become a realistic goal of political endeavour both inside and outside South Africa.*

This book opened with quotations from Steve Biko and Alan Paton.

'Even if the prospects for peaceful change are extremely slim, they are worth investigating.' Our study has confirmed Biko's view. The realization that peaceful change is possible could itself increase the prospects of peaceful change.

'Do I have any hope? One doesn't need hope to act.' Alan Paton, and many black and white South Africans, may find it useful to learn that there are some grounds for hope. Despite our scepticism about what is most likely to happen, one must remember that all predictions of social and political developments are subject to the condition of *ceteris paribus*, i.e., that other factors remain constant. This is a condition which history honours as often in the breach as in the observance. Pessimistic predictions can serve as a warning, and perhaps thereby be proven wrong.

Postscript, August 1980
The Prospects of Peaceful Change Revisited

The world in 1980 is no better disposed towards the white minority regime in South Africa than when the German edition of this text appeared in 1978. As we expected,[1] one possible external inducement to peaceful change, pressure from the West, has barely been applied. It is true that the member states of the European Community drew up and attempted to impose a code of business practice upon European firms in South Africa. But this was done without much enthusiasm, and the measures advocated hardly go beyond those the South African government itself recommends to South African employers. The United States is currently more concerned with Iran, Afghanistan, and the Palestinian question than with South Africa. The indications are that once again, as during the Vietnam conflict, South Africa is about to enjoy a temporary respite from international attention.

However, South Africa will hardly escape the attention of African politics. 1980 brought the end of white supremacy in Rhodesia. Irrespective of the course adopted by the Zimbabwean Government, South Africa has lost a buffer state.

Between March and June 1980 assaults and acts of sabotage in South Africa occurred on an unprecedented scale: attacks on police-stations and on a bank in Silverton and, most importantly, the blowing up of oil tanks at the Sasol plant, the pride of South African industry and the symbol of economic independence.

One must allow that the change of power in Salisbury and incipient guerilla activity do not yet present a serious threat to white South African power. However, they are concrete evidence that, as we anticipated in 1978,[2] life for white South Africans is becoming considerably less pleasant. But more significant for the internal political climate are the hopes and expectations these events have raised among the black majority. Even if such expectations prove illusory in the short and medium term, the political repercussions will be considerable. By contrast, fear and a willingness to compromise have increased among the white population at large, as was also predicted.[3] As far as the white leadership is concerned however, it clearly perceives the future dangers but seems incapable of responding with a policy of preventative reforms.

1. *The limits on white pragmatism*

Without doubt the ruling white pligarchy's justifications for holding on

[1] See above, p. 418.
[2] See above, p. 410.
[3] See above, p. 236.

426

to power, and for the way in which it does so, are far more pragmatic than the ideological dogmatism prevalent as recently as two years ago. This change was neither intended nor planned, but was the consequence of a series of unwanted, unexpected, and indeed quite embarrassing events. The 'Information scandal'—financial and legal irregularities in the former Department of Information—forced the resignations first of the Minister of the Interior and of Information, Cornelius Mulder, and then of the Prime Minister, later State President, John Vorster. Vorster was succeeded as Prime Minister by P. W. Botha, who had long served as Minister of Defence and whose views were and are similar to those of his closest colleagues in the military: 'South Africa must change or perish.' As well as the armed forces, the new Prime Minister has the support of the Afrikaner business establishment, whose influence in the National Party has been on the increase since the 1960s at the expense of the interests of the reactionary, but shrinking, white working class. In his first six months of office Botha excited great hopes of reform, especially because he dispensed with the traditional rhetoric of slow and gradual change: 'Slow change? Nowadays only funeral processions are slow!'

With the support of the business community, which has long been demanding that central planning and state intervention be curtailed in the interests of a more efficient market economy, he has indeed brought about some substantial changes in the *economic field*. Black trade-unions have been granted the opportunity for formal recognition, albeit within fairly tight bureaucratic controls, something which many businessmen had long argued would bring greater labour stability. Moves are being made to reduce and rationalize the growth and complexity of the civil service. Urban blacks have been granted some recognition of their *de facto* permanency in so-called white areas by the granting of ninety-nine year leasehold rights to urban properties, and the intention to allow greater mobility for urban blacks within the influx control system has been announced.

Without doubt these measures indicate that repressive total control of the black labour force is giving way to a dual system. The aim is, on the one hand, to stabilize—in a controlled but relatively liberal, negotiated fashion—the permanent urban black labour force, which is the segment of the labour force likely to belong to effective trade-unions; and on the other hand to refine control—via official recruitment procedures and tougher influx restrictions—over the marginal working class of less-permanently employed, long-distance migrant workers, who are less likely to belong to attractive unions and to be protected by the new labour relations system.

Thus, although the changes in the economic sphere are not overwhelming, a new pragmatism is clearly discernible. In the field of *social relations* the situation is rather different. Initially the Prime Minister's remarks and statements served to raise expectations: he said that 'unnecessary discrimination' could and must disappear, and intimated that he considered both the Immorality Act and the Mixed Marriages Act to be 'unnecessary'. So far, however, fine words have had to suffice. No bills have been introduced to amend existing legislation, and at the level of petty apartheid no important administrative regulations have been aboliᵤhed.

In the *political* field, the South African government has set up an important new security council, which includes selected business leaders and professional and security advisors. According to Giliomee, this move towards the 'managerial approach to government and the political process'[4] can also be seen as a coalition of bourgeois interests in the governing party. However, the retention of exclusive power by Nationalist Afrikaners is still the primary objective, now to be achieved by more and more sophisticated means. Constitutional developments have been at best an anti-climax and at worst retrogressive. The elected Coloured Persons Representative Council was disbanded and in its purpose subsumed, after the tabling of the report of the Constitutional Commission under Minister Schlebusch, by a President's Council. This nominated body is to have solely advisory functions and, worse still, is to exclude Africans (who are supposed to be accommodated in a further black advisory council loosely related to the President's Council). A prominent Afrikaans academic, not known for his anti-government views, described such a development as akin to staging Shakespeare's 'Hamlet' without the prince. Predictably, no legitimate black or coloured leaders have been able to support the new Council, and the official opposition will also not serve on it.

The Prime Minister's other 'new input' was to announce the goal of a 'constellation of states'.[5] This is probably meant to amount to a loose confederation of Southern African states bound mainly by economic ties, presumably under an umbrella of military collaboration. It does not alter the principle of political independence for economically weak and dependent homelands and offers no prospect of an effective sharing of fiscal powers.[6]

In general, then, as far as the white leadership élite is concerned, it can

---

[4] Hermann Giliomee, *Structural Change and Political Options in the 1980s*, lecture given at the University of Natal, Centre for Applied Social Sciences and Extra Mural Studies Unit, 13 May 1980.

[5] This is in fact a fairly old idea, having been mooted by John Vorster several years ago.

[6] At best it represents some sharing of economic concerns and of responsibilities for development; at worst it represents a type of neo-imperialist economic and military control over newly 'independent' homelands, probably with all the economic distortions and development imbalances such a system has entailed for the Third World.

428

be expected that the rhetoric of limited reform, stability, unity and adaptation will become more and more prominent, but that signs of structural shifts in power are unlikely to appear soon. Heribert Adam states in his new book than 'an ethnic oligarchy . . . hardly anticipates the rising costs to its rule but instead mostly reacts to pressure only'.[7] A group within the oligarchy, including the Prime Minister himself, does appear to anticipate these costs and to fear the consequences. However, unless it is simply unable to draw the obvious conclusions from such insights, it must be unable to impose its view on the rest of the oligarchy.[8] The reason for the latter is to be found in the relative power of the different groups in the inner circle of the oligarchy, as analysed in Chapter 7. The events of the last two years have confirmed this analysis. The tensions between the widely differing viewpoints in the ruling party have recently erupted into open verbal confrontation between the Prime Minister and the highly conservative leader of the National Party in Transvaal, Andries Treurnicht. An uneasy compromise resulted which, if anything, turned out to be more of a retreat for the Prime Minister than for the right-wing faction. The influence of the traditional lobbies and their support in the National Party organization and in the parliamentary caucus is strong enough to hold the leadership to established National Party policies.

Pragmatism is thus confined within the narrow limits set by the workings of Afrikaner ethnic nationalism and of the inner circle of the power élite. Great pressure will be required to transgress these limits or establish new ones. 'So far, it is still cheaper to manage with traditional policy.'[9]

2. *The limits on black leadership*

In the past two years black politics in South Africa have been characterized on the one hand by renewed and widespread labour and student unrest after a period of relative apathy, and on the other hand by fierce and increasingly bitter factional rivalry among internal political leaders. Against this background, some of the problems of, and limits on, internal black leadership are more clearly discernible than previously.

While our surveys among the urban black populations were being analysed, the extended disturbances involving black youth and scholars which had commenced in June 1976 were coming to an end. In early 1980 the recovery of the economy started to make itself felt. Unemployment

[7] Heribert Adam and Hermann Giliomee, *Ethnic Power Mobilized: Can South Africa Change?* (New Haven and London 1979), p. 300.

[8] See above, pp. 410 ff.

[9] Adam and Giliomee, *op cit*, p. 4.

began to decline and South Africa's endemic problem, a shortage of skilled labour, reappeared. Restlessness among the black labour force has gradually become evident again, and to date there have been serious strikes in the Eastern Cape motor industry, among Western Cape meat workers, and in Natal and Transvaal, followed in late July by a strike of Johannesburg municipal workers. Pupils at black schools in Soweto began to voice protests of a socio-political kind once again (against the policy of excluding older, unsuccessful students and the employment of white servicemen as teachers). Soon afterwards, in February 1980, a coloured and black pupil boycott started in Cape Town and spread to other parts of the country, including the black universities.

Labour disturbances of a purely economic kind, the most common of the recent events, can be explained in terms of the high inflation rate and the lessening of job-insecurity which have coincided with the economic recovery. However, one major strike wave, which started at the Ford Motor Company plant in Port Elizabeth, had a more political flavour, since the strikes took place under the leadership of a voluntary community organization with political aims, PEBCO—the Port Elizabeth Black Civic Organization. A solidarity strike by black meat workers, and subsequent community support in Cape Town for attempts to gain recognition for a black workers' committee in one company, also had political overtones.

The boycotts by school and university students very soon acquired, or perhaps had from the outset, a political agenda which went beyond calls for equal education. In some places the boycotts seemed to assume the proportions of a pre-revolutionary mobilization.[10] Around the time of 16 June 1980—the anniversary of the onset of the 1976/77 disturbances—there were riots among non-student unemployed young adults in Cape Town, resulting in confrontations with the police and more than thirty deaths. At the same time the black newspaper *Post* launched a public campaign for the release of Nelson Mandela. These events followed several acts of sabotage and political assault between March and June, for which the ANC claimed responsibility. The funeral of one of the participants in the bank-siege killed by the police was attended by over 2,000 highly emotional black mourners and a minor confrontation with the police ensued.

Everything indicates, then, that the country experienced an upsurge of political unrest among blacks in early 1980, coinciding with the first results of an intensified underground campaign by exile organizations. The mood reached a high point round the anniversary of the 16 June outbreak of public demonstrations in 1976. Does all this indicate that the country has entered a period of heightened instability which is likely to

<hr />

[10] Hugh Robertson, 'The Schools Boycott is a Lesson in Protest', *Sunday Times*, 15 July 1980.

continue or escalate until there is a breakdown of the system? At this stage it is impossible to give a definite answer, but certain factors can be clarified in approaching the question.

Firstly, it is only to be expected that a period of heightened expectations should have accompanied Robert Mugabe's election campaign in January and February 1980, culminating in his victory at the polls in Zimbabwe at the end of February. Secondly, research conducted by the firm Markinor has shown that blacks responded with some anticipation to P. W. Botha's promises of reform and political progress after he assumed leadership. Thirdly, periods of economic recovery sometimes tend to create a sense of expectation since the more mundane preoccupations with material security and subsistence diminish. These factors combined with the absence of any really meaningful educational or social reform after 1976, a high inflation rate, and the more pervasive effects of rapidly growing numbers of pupils overloading limited educational facilities, could all have been expected to result in some manifestations of general political restlessness. Where might it lead?

One strong possibility is that once leaders in Zimbabwe have settled down to solving their numerous internal problems and become less visible to South African blacks, once disillusionment with the Prime Minister has developed into a quiet, helpless cynicism, and once the school boycotts are discovered to have been costlier for the participants than for the system, the black political climate will slowly revert to the apathetic compliance and limited verbal protest most generally typical of black political responses to apartheid since 1948. A fact supporting this view is that rank-and-file black adults have been relatively uninvolved in recent protests and demonstrations. As has been the case so often in the past, appeals by youthful protesters for stay-at-home strikes by adults have been largely unsuccessful.

However, one may expect that there will be an increase in labour disturbances as the economy improves but the inflation rate stays high. In that case there may be a response from black students once again. And if labour disturbances involve confrontations with the police, then protest strikes by adults could spread as a form of action in solidarity. Furthermore, an election campaign in Namibia and the release of political prisoners there could also create an upsurge in political consciousness, particularly if SWAPO enjoys a victory. Finally, if there is a particularly high level of effective underground action and sabotage, followed by public events like funerals or services, further reaction from the youth could be forthcoming. The situation is thus not likely to lose its potential for instability.

Since sustained labour action, elections in Namibia and a dramatic escalation of underground activity are probably some time off, however, it seems likely that there will be a period of relative calm, and that the

431

end of this current cycle of unrest will find the black political situation in South Africa relatively unchanged. The importance of institutional strategies would then reappear, and the white opposition, Inkatha and formal black political and church organizations would probably assume their former role and importance as the most visible agents for change and reform.

As in the 1976, there is one element in common to all the outbreaks of labour and student unrest in 1980: they are not the result of initiatives by internal political leaders. The unrest has not been organized by the homeland leaders or Gatsha Buthelezi or urban leadership groups such as the Committee of Ten in Soweto, and none of them has been able to prevent it or exercise significant influence upon its course. Nor is it likely that the liberation movements operating from beyond the country's borders have had greater influence, for they appear to be concentrating at the moment on well-planned, spectacular guerilla activities. All the available information suggests rather that the causes of the various outbreaks of unrest, although broadly similar, have in each case been local, and that they were led by, if not momentary, then occasional and local leaders.

In labour protests, where workers strike with concrete demands for higher wages, better working conditions, etc., this lack of influence on the part of the internal political leaders is, as it were, 'normal'. But protest as a means of general political expression—as in the case of the high school and university students—evidences a largely diffuse but considerable protest potential which is not under the control of the black political leadership.

This is the first limit on black leadership. A further limit results from the fierce struggle for influence between different political tendencies, as analysed in Chapter 10. The severity and bitterness of these conflicts have increased over the past two years. Has the standing of the different leadership groups changed significantly in this period? In the absence of the most reliable means of establishing this, viz., free elections, opinion polls can offer some information. They include research conducted for the Commission of Enquiry into the political future of the Ciskei, as well as a comparative study conducted in the Durban townships in 1979.[11] Although the data for 1979 are not fully comparable with those for 1977, they suffice for an analysis of general trends.[12] The results are shown in Table P.1.

[11] L. Schlemmer, 'Political Alternatives for the Ciskei: Political Attitudes and Values among Xhosa-speaking Africans of Ciskeian Origin or Residence', Appendix 12 in *The Quail Report*, 8.2.80, *Report of the Ciskei Commission* (Pretoria, Conference Associates, 1980). The comparative research in Durban has yet to be published but was undertaken by the centre for applied Social Sciences, University of Natal.

[12] In the question on black political leadership posed in the survey conducted for

432

Table P.1
Proportions of respondents giving scores of ten out of ten to various black political leaders: 1979

	Urban Xhosa in Tvl and W. Cape	Eastern Cape Xhosa	Urban Ciskei	Rural Ciskei	Xhosa migrant workers	Soweto Sotho	Soweto Zulu	Durban Zulu
	%	%	%	%	%	%	%	%
Chief Gatsha Buthelezi	18	26	27	22	25	23	48	45
Dr Motlana, Chairman, Soweto Committee of Ten	33	18	16	12	10	51	59	15
Bishop Tutu, Chairman, S.A. Council of Churches	30	22	19	11	7	29	31	12
Bishop Manas Buthelezi, Black Parents Assoc.	15	10	11	9	11	11	17	13
Mrs Winnie Mandela, Wife of Nelson Mandela	21	38	38	12	25	29	37	19
Chief Sebe, Chief Minister of Ciskei	24	47	48	60	53	NA	NA	NA
Dr Phatudi, Chief Minister of Lebowa	NA	NA	NA	NA	NA	44	NA	NA
Chief Matanzima, President of Transkei	5	27	33	26	18	12	5	5
n =	(100)	(218)	(199)	(100)	(83)	(75)	(75)	(150)

NA = not asked

433

A new dimension to the leadership picture has been added by the growing prominence since 1977 of the Committee of Ten in Soweto, under the chairmanship of Dr Nthato Motlana. In Soweto particularly, Dr Motlana emerges ahead of Chief Buthelezi, as he does among urban Xhosa. The support for Bishop Tutu and Bishop Manas Buthelezi are another sign of the strength of groupings opposed to Gatsha Buthelezi, again chiefly in Soweto and among the urban Xhosa-speakers.

The support for Winnie Mandela confirms the strength of the ANC trend observed in 1977.[13] Similarly confirmed is the finding that Chief Buthelezi's following cannot be dismissed as 'purely tribal'. Particularly interesting is the Eastern Cape sample, which is by no means anti-Buthelezi. Clearly, Buthelezi's support, like that of the ANC, is more evenly distributed across the country than that of the specifically Soweto or Witwatersrand-based leadership.

The 1979 results also show that homeland leaders like Chief Sebe and Dr Phatudi are not to be underestimated within their ethnic constituencies. In fact, it would seem that the Eastern Cape included in the sample used initially for this book, the homeland leader popularity would have been strengthened and Buthelezi would not have been markedly weakened.

The conclusion is obvious: both supporters and opponents of Buthelezi should recognize that their protagonists are not likely to disappear, that they cannot wish each other away; yet the animosity between them and the incompatibility of their strategy has not lessened. It is clear that this factionalism weakens organized black protest in South Africa: it represents the second important limit on black leadership potential.

This leadership potential is weakened by a third, and probably more important factor: the extent to which all the internal leaders depend on the fluctuating sentiments and protest activities of the black masses.

this book in 1977, respondents were asked to name the leader they admired most. In the study done for the Ciskei Commission in mid-1979, respondents were asked to think of the leader they admired most, give him a score of 10 out of 10, and then assign relative scores to a list of 9 leaders: Dr Motlana, Chairman of the Soweto Committee of Ten; Chief Gatsha Buthelezi; Mrs Winnie Mandela, wife of Nelson Mandela; Bishop Tutu, Chairman of the SA Council of Churches; Chief Sebe of the Ciskei; Mr Mabandla, leader of the Ciskei opposition; Bishop Manas Buthelezi, Chairman of the Black Parents Association in Soweto; Mr Thebahali, Chairman of the Soweto Community Council; and President Matanzima of Transkei. A similar procedure was followed in the Durban study conducted in October 1979. If one makes the assumption that a score of 10 our of 10 reflects the most popular leader, then the results for 1977 and 1979 are roughly comparable. The results for 1979 are given in Table P.1.

[13] This interpretation might appear to be somewhat debatable, since Mrs Mandela is, beyond any doubt, a political figure in her own right. However, since her scores are far higher in polls in which ANC leaders were not mentioned, there is some reason to interpret her support as a more general support for the ANC as well.

These fluctuations manifest themselves most clearly in Soweto and on the Witwatersrand, where black political leadership receives greatest publicity. For this reason it is interesting to look specifically at trends in the popularity of leaders in Soweto, as shown in Table P.2.

Table P.2
Rough trends in Leader popularity in Soweto and East Rand townships

Leader figures	Most popular leader-figure		Proportion giving 10 out of 10 to leader (scaled to 100%)	
	April 1977[14]	April 1978[15] (middle class)	Mid-1979[16]	Mid-1980[17]
	%	%	%	%
Dr. Motlana/Committee of Ten	0	(61)	28	26
Bishop Tutu	0	(NA)	17	33
Chief Buthelezi	28	(5)	19	12
Winnie Mandela/ANC leaders	27	(21)	19	18
Curtis Nkondo/other Black Consc. leaders	5	(7)	NA	11
PAC	11	(1)	NA	NA
Other homeland leaders	14	(3)	17	NA
Others/no answer	15	(2)	NA	NA
	100	(100)	100	100

NA = not asked

Again, the results are not strictly comparable from survey to survey (the middle class survey is explicitly unrepresentative) but broadly indicate a pattern which perhaps can be interpreted as follows.

The research in 1977 came at the end of the 1976/77 disturbances when urban leaders had been detained, banned, intimidated, or exiled, or else had proved to be ineffective in either controlling the situation or winning reforms. By April 1978 the government had started to announce or promise certain reforms, like the ninety-nine year leasehold system. This coincided with the emergence of the Committee of Ten under the

[14] Study conducted for this book: open-ended question.
[15] Study conducted by the Centre for Applied Social Sciences among 150 middle class Soweto males: simple question with response alternatives.
[16] Study conducted for Ciskei Commission: sample size for Soweto and other major Transvaal urban centres, n = 225.
[17] Study just being completed by Centre for Applied Social Sciences, preliminary figures hand-tabulated but roughly correct: sample size for Soweto and East Rand, n = 300.

leadership of Dr Motlana. This leadership filled a vacuum as regards the specific needs and interests of Soweto. Chief Buthelezi's support as we have seen, is more widely distributed and he obviously tends not to be seen specifically as a Soweto leader. These processes account for the dramatic increase in popularity of the Committee of Ten leadership in 1978, and for the lowered popularity of Buthelezi and also the ANC/PAC among the middle classes.

In 1979, the Committee of Ten leadership is still very prominent, but Bishop Tutu emerges clearly as a new spokesman. Gatsha Buthelezi features strongly, as do the ANC. In that year, no serious problems occurred to create disillusionment with internal leaders so all major tendencies made a strong showing, including the homeland leaders.

The most recent survey reflects a different picture. The support for the Committee of Ten seems to be falling, as for Chief Buthelezi. Bishop Tutu's position has strongly improved, probably because of his involvement in the efforts of the South African Council of Churches to meet the Prime Minister on the issue of educational and other black problems. Likewise, the support for the Black Consciousness position has strengthened slightly in the wake of school boycotts, even though Soweto was not itself affected by them in 1980.

In other words, what seems to be happening is that those leaders who are directly involved in the symbolic protest politics of the moment attract suddenly increased support at the expense of those who are not. Our own results obtained in 1977 suggest how short-lived the effects of disturbances on attitudes towards leadership might be: the adult organization which spoke on behalf of students at the time, the Black Parents Association, did not figure very prominently in leadership ratings, as it probably would have done a few months earlier.

Similarly, the Committee of Ten was extremely popular as long as it made the headlines. Then its popularity declined considerably as Bishop Tutu's ratings rose, to the extent that he and the South African Council of Churches spoke for black demands. The Survey of mid-1980 was carried out before Bishop Tutu's negotiations with the Prime Minister in August. These negotiations have not produced any concrete results. It should be interesting to observe the reactions of the population of Soweto in a few months time. For it is precisely there that unsuccessful initiatives result in a rapid loss of popularity, as the ratings of Dr Motlana indicate.

On the same basis, Gatsha Buthelezi's popularity always declines when his black opponents are involved in open confrontation with the government. And it has always risen when alternative strategies to his own appear to be relatively ineffective, as in 1977. It is particularly high when he opposes the government in a spectacular way, as for instance in the second half of 1978.[18] This probably explains his relatively strong position in 1979. At the beginning of August 1980 Buthelezi refused to take part in the Prime Minister's conference with the homeland leaders. It was his opposition which led the homeland leaders to reject the Government's proposal for a Consultative Black Council, and provoked the subsequent withdrawal of this proposal by the Government. This event has once again placed Buthelezi at the centre of black protest; future research will show whether this in turn strengthens his position in Soweto.

The surveys thus show that in Soweto—to a greater extent than in other parts of the country—hopes are quickly raised, and can be as quickly disappointed. The highly politicized population in Soweto is the barometer of the political climate in black South Africa, working in much the same way as the populations of the large cities in Western industrialized states.

These fluctuations over the last two years also show to what extent the influence of political leaders is affected by the movements of popular protest. Times of unrest bring instant, sometimes even anonymous, leaders to the fore; in the subsequent, relative calm the long-term political trends re-appear. The latter probably evidence the degree of organization of the various movements, which would explain the relative stability of Buthelezi's position.[19]

Be that as it may, what was established previously,[20] viz., that the black leaders are not so much leaders as protest spokesmen for the black masses, has been confirmed by the most recent data. If they cannot deliver the goods their position is quickly eroded. In the final instance the limits on the internal black leadership depend upon the willingness of the white power centre to negotiate. If those black leaders who are prepared to negotiate are not offered the opportunity to do so soon, then they will either no longer be prepared to negotiate or no longer be leaders.

3. *A silent majority for consociation*

At the time of the surveys among white voters and urban blacks the concept of a consociational policy of power-sharing was not yet established in South African politics. Since then, the Progressive Federal Party, particularly at the instigation of its present leader, Frederick van Zyl Slabbert, has put forward a constitutional proposal which is new in three respects: it presents a consociational solution for South Africa on

[18] See particularly his speech at the Grahamstown Conference, 'The Road Ahead', in August 1978.

[19] With approximately 300,000 members Inkatha is numerically the strongest political organization in the country.

[20] See above, p. 397.

a political rather than an academic platform; it directs the white opposition to more than the technical—and secondary—questions of the franchise and the ambiguities of semi-democratic solutions; and it traces a path for power-sharing without group domination that lies between the government policy, which is rejected by the black majority, and the idea of unitary state with majority rule, which is unacceptable to the dominant white minority.

The white opposition today is less hesitant and less vacillating than it was at the time the book was written. Nevertheless, its prospects of coming to power are as remote as ever. What have improved, however, are its opportunities and resources for encouraging the ruling minority and the still powerless majority to reflect on consociational conflict regulation[21] as a continuing possibility for peaceful change.

Among the leadership groups, the ruling party predictably rejected the opposition's proposals, while black political leaders have for the most part kept silent on the issue, or else been sceptical rather than dismissive. What of the attitudes of the black and white masses towards a policy of peaceful compromise?

Among *whites* the fear of unpleasant future developments has increased. Comparisons between nation-wide surveys in mid-1977 and early 1980 show that the proportions of white voters expecting that 'serious problems for whites' will arise out of the race situation in South Africa *within three years* has increased from 14 to 25% among Afrikaners and from 21 to 30% among English-speaking voters.[22]

As our previous analyses established, growing white fears give rise to only a limited 'right-wing back-lash'. Certainly, support for the right-wing opposition has increased to some extent, but mainly among rural, working-class and lower middle-class voters who in any case regarded the Prime Minister's new 'enlightened' terminology as a threat to their privileged position.[23] However, the possible growth of support to the right of the National Party has a clear ceiling—it has been estimated that right-wing opposition is unlikely to exceed 15 per cent of Afrikaans voters,[24] an estimation remarkably close to our previous assessment.[25]

[21] For a detailed discussion see Theodor Hanf and Heribert Weiland, 'Konkordanzdemokratie für Südafrika? Zur Bedeutung der neueren verfassungspolitischen Debatte', *Europa Archiv*, 23(1978) pp. 755–70.

[22] Lawrence Schlemmer, 'Modernization Tendencies and Reforms of White Minority Rule', paper presented to the Expert Discussion on Conflicts in South Africa: International Strategies and Internal Change, Friedrich Ebert Stiftung, Bonn, 29–30 May 1980.

[23] See L. Schlemmer, 'South Africans are Going to the Poles', *Sunday Tribune*, 18.5.1980.

[24] See Lawrence Schlemmer, 'No More than 15% of Nat Afrikaners Would Quit', a survey-based estimate which appeared in the *Sunday Tribune*, 11.5.80.

[25] See above, p. 125.

Recent research shows that while white attitudes to black abilities and characteristics, i.e. race prejudice as such, has not changed much over the period from 1974 through 1977 to 1980, whites have generally become more pragmatic and more tolerant of racial reform, due to the strategic necessity of achieving peace and stability in the country.[26] Although wide differences between the Afrikaans and English groups still persist, Afrikaners have shifted their attitudes more rapidly than English. Specifically on the issue of political options, the following item yielded interesting results. Whites were asked: *If the present government were to create a new legislative body on which coloured, Indian, homeland and other black leaders would (with whites) have a say over national affairs without one group being dominated by another, would you support/accept/oppose such a policy or withdraw support for the government?* The proportions supporting or accepting the idea rose between 1977 and 1980 from 47 to 56% for Afrikaners and from 69 to 78% for English-speakers.[27]

What about the *black* masses?

Research conducted since 1977 has tended to confirm the strong preference among blacks for the 'consociational' or 'concordance' option among political options for the future. In an April 1978 sample of 150 black men in Soweto with mid-high school education and above, subjects were asked:[28] *Think of people like yourself who live and work around you. What kind of government would such people (like yourself) be prepared to accept and be happy with in the future?* The alternatives offered were such as to force a clear choice between options. The outcome was as follows:

	Agree
—*Government of equal members of blacks and whites in Cabinet*	57%
—*Government in which blacks as the majority rule the whites*	35%
—*Blacks ruling half the country, whites the other half*	4%
—*Independent homelands with more land and towns added to them*	2%
—*Additional answers—diverse*	15%

The sample which provided this distribution of preferences was of quite 'radical' bent—over 70% gave answers suggesting that they were 'angry and impatient' or 'unhappy' with life in South Africa, 75% rejected Muzorewa internal settlement in Zimbabwe of that time in favour of options including the guerillas, and less than 10% gave as their

[26] Schlemmer, 'Modernization Tendencies . . .', *op cit.*
[27] *Ibid.*
[28] These results are reported more fully in L. Schlemmer, 'Change in South Africa: Opportunities and Constraints' in Robert M. Price and Carl G. Rosberg, The Apartheid Regime: *Political Power and Racial Domination*, (Berkeley, Institute of International Studies, University of California, 1980), pp. 236–280.

choice of leader any homeland leaders or others operating 'within the system'. One might expect that such a sample would overwhelmingly favour the black majority rule option. Some insight into the reasons for the substantial rejection of this option were obtained when the sample was asked: *What problems do you think might arise in the future if black people should rule South Africa?* The question was open-ended and the answers showed that 37% envisaged the possibility of black ethnic tensions, 29% mentioned economic problems or inefficiency, 19% feared the possibility of losing or alienating whites, while only some 20% stated that no problems would exist. The author of the original article concluded that 'There is some evidence, therefore, that in a group of highly politicized and discontented black South Africans, a preference for consociational rule is based to some extent on an awareness of major socio-political problems characteristic of a highly diversified society.' [29]

Interesting and somewhat similar results were obtained in the research undertaken for the Ciskei Commission. [30] In that mid-1979 study, the samples were presented with a wider range of political options for the future and asked for any number which they would be happy to accept. Three out of eight possibilities emerged as the most 'acceptable' choices: unitary state, multiracial democracy; completely self-governing homelands enlarged to include more land, towns and factories; and consociational rule involving homeland leaders, black elected urban leaders and white leaders (or the latter two groups). For different groups the order of preference between the *three most popular* options was as shown below. It should be borne in mind, however, that the percentage preferences are very close and the order of choice is not necessary statistically significant: [31]

Urban Xhosa: unitary democracy (94%), consociation of white and black elected leaders (78%), consociation of white, black and homeland leaders (73%).

Eastern Cape Xhosa: unitary democracy (92%), enlarged homelands (90%), consociation of white, black and homeland leaders (84%).

Urban Ciskei: enlarged homeland (91%), unitary democracy (88%), consociation of white, black and homeland leaders (86%).

Rural Ciskei: enlarged homeland (89%), unitary democracy (89%), consociation of white, black and homeland leaders (84%).

Xhosa Migrant Workers: enlarged homeland (90%), unitary democracy (88%), consociation of white, black and homeland leaders (87%).

Soweto Zulu: unitary democracy (92%), consociation of white, black and homeland leaders (85%), enlarged homeland (79%).

[29] *Ibid.*
[30] Lawrence Schlemmer, 'Political Alternatives for the Ciskei . . .' *op cit.*
[31] Sample size: Urban Xhosa 100, Eastern Cape 218, Urban Ciskei 199, rural Ciskei 100, Xhosa migrants 83, Soweto Zulu 75, Durban Zulu 150, Soweto Pedi 75.

Durban Zulu: unitary democracy (95%), consociation of white, black and homeland leaders (87%), consociation of white and homeland leaders (73%).

Soweto Pedi: unitary democracy (97%), enlarged homeland (85%), consociation of white, black and homeland leaders (79%).

In these results the multiracial unitary democracy option (which incidentally is not necessarily understood as black majority rule, to judge from the results mentioned earlier) clearly has the edge on other options, but the preferences are very close. One could reasonably conclude that the black population is open to any alternative which contains the elements of political legitimacy and socio-economic justice. The inflexible insistence by some black spokesmen on the unitary state majority-rule option does not reflect popular black preferences as surveyed above.

It would be fair to accept, then, that the basic attitudes required among the white and black populations at large for genuine political compromise in South Africa have improved during the last years. Clearly, there is a majority on both sides in favour of, or at least prepared to accept, some kind of consociational solution. Yet it is a silent majority.

4. *Mounting black anger*

The observed trends in white and black opinion should not lull one into thinking that a reassuring process of evolutionary change is under way, which will have meliorative results in the long term. For one of the most dramatic trends observed subsequent to the first publication of this book relates to overall political consciousness among blacks. In 1977 a test of political discontent was employed using thumbnail sketches of five faces with matching statements expressing degrees of overall contentment or discontent with the situation, ranging from *very happy with life as it is for Africans in South Africa today* through to *angry and impatient with life.* Subsequent results, using the same test and the same interviewing team yield the comparisons given in Table P.3 [32]

The results show what can only be described as a dramatic increase in discontent since 1977. Whatever one may feel about the absolute validity of the test, the trend over time cannot easily be discounted. As we indicated earlier, the present situation of unrest may be one in which blacks are experiencing a temporary state of heightened expectations and political consciousness. While it may not continue now, the anger and

---

[32] Table P.3 is taken directly from Lawrence Schlemmer, Valerie Moller and Peter Stopforth, *Black Urban Communities, Socio-Political Reform and the Future* (Durban, Centre for Applied Social Sciences, Document and Memorandum Series, March 1980) p. 10.

Table P.3
Trends in socio-political consciousness among urban black men, 1977–1979: responses to scale item on happiness-anger with present situation of blacks in South Africa

	April 1977 (Hanf et al.)	March 1978 (Schlemmer)	August 1979 (Schlemmer)	October 1979 (Schlemmer)
	%	%	%	%
Reef/Soweto/Tvl; all ethnic groups	(n = 592)		(n = 422)[1]	
Happy/neutral	36		38	
Unhappy	25		17	
Angry	39		44	
Reef/Soweto; Xhosa-speaking	(n = 70)		(n = 700)[1,2]	
Happy/neutral	29		27	
Unhappy	33		15	
Angry	38		57	
Reef/Soweto/Durban; Zulu	(n = 378)		(n = 225)	
Happy/neutral	34		22	
Unhappy	26		21	
Angry	39		56	
Durban; Zulu	(n = 191)			(n = 88)
Happy/neutral	30			19
Unhappy	26			25
Angry	44			55
All areas; all ethnic groups; middle-class white-collar/professional/ std 8 +	(n = 395)	(n = 150)	(n = 72)[1]	
Happy/neutral	29	28	24	
Unhappy	26	32	17	
Angry	45	40	58	

[1] Includes a minority of Western Cape respondents.
[2] Includes men and women.

discontent reflected in these results can arise again in any number of situations of social uncertainty. At such times the stability of the society is extremely tenuous. Or to put it another way, black anger is like a bush-fire. It can sometimes be rapidly controlled and extinguished. But if the wind changes suddenly it can easily become a conflagration.

5. The politics of the tortoise

This analysis of political developments in South Africa and of the political attitudes of the white and the black populations accords with our original conclusion that the main obstacle to peaceful change is the

442

white power élite in all its divisions, antagonisms and inner contradictions.

Given the facts of black political consciousness, and given the opportunities for compromise solutions which popular attitudes still allow, this élite is surely not doing enough to overcome the constraints on responsible policy action imposed by its own structure and by the lobbies and pressure groups. In a recent BBC television documentary on 'Africa's White Tribe', Dr Koornhof, Minister of Co-operation and Development, referred to one of the more powerful of these pressure groups—civil servants in the apartheid bureaucracies—as being akin to a tortoise. A tortoise moves slowly, and if you try to push it, it simply stops and pulls in its head. The excuse is shallow, however, since the white power élite is apparently quite happy to keep the tortoises well fed and secure, at the cost of peace, welfare and security for the rest of South Africa's peoples, white and black, who are not protected by thick shells.

Thus, notwithstanding the change of government in Zimbabwe, sharpening world criticism, the lessons of the student disturbances in 1976/77 and 1980, and the clear evidence of latent internal strain, the only significant changes of policy in the period since the book appeared are firstly adaptations in the labour policy reflecting a shift in class interests within the National Party, and secondly a little increased pragmatism *vis-à-vis* urban blacks. The rest is, as described in Chapter 15, 'sham consociation' at its most obvious. The centre does not intend to devolve or share an iota of real power at this stage. Any use of the term consociationalism with reference to the present South African situation does the concept a monumental disservice—'fake consociationalism' has become even more blatant in recent versions of government policy, without the policy itself being significantly changed.

Will the government respond to its opportunities and move away from this 'Scheinkonkordanz' towards less feigned attempts at compromise? The internal pressures on it are increasing as much as the external ones. All the important Afrikaans newspapers in the Transvaal constantly call for meaningful policy reform. The Afrikaanse Studentebond has just split, partly on the issue of the exclusion of blacks from the New President's Council. It is very difficult today to find a competent Afrikaans academic, scientist or business leader who supports the policy choices of the government unquestioningly. Even the staunchly pro-apartheid South African Bureau of Racial Affairs has declared its lack of confidence in the viability of the status quo by absurdly proposing a homeland for whites in the Northern Cape/Free State. The government is thus experiencing what one may call a flight of its own intellectuals, mainly to the left but also to the right. Its majority is still safe, and it will win further elections by trading on insecurity and by making promises; but politically and ideologically it is increasingly isolated and under attack. The central question at the moment is whether or not a government can maintain its own morale, coherence and unity in the face of continuous reminders of its shortsightedness from its own people as well as from the rest of South Africa and the world. For when a tortoise is caught in a bush-fire, even pulling its head in won't help it.

APPENDIX

Questionnaire for the White Electorate

INTERVIEW SCHEDULE

Interviewer's Introduction:

A group of European and South African scientists wish to improve their knowledge and understanding of South African society. Therefore they have undertaken a joint study project. They have commissioned IMSA to interview a scientifically selected cross-section of South Africans on a number of social, economic, political and cultural issues.

You are one of the many people who have been selected randomly, and your opinions and co-operation in this regard will be appreciated.

This study is completely confidential. No answers of individuals will be made known. Your answers are grouped together with those of others in a computer to produce statistics.

There are no right or wrong answers. We are interested in how you personally feel about these issues.

FORMAAT VAN ONDERHOUDE

Ondervraers se Inleiding:

'n Groep Europese en Suid-Afrikaanse wetenskaplikes wil graag hul begrip en insig van die Suid-Afrikaanse gemeenskap verbreed. Hulle het IMSA versoek om 'n wetenskaplik-goedgekeurde deursnee van Suid-Afrikaners, oor 'n aantal sosiale, ekonomiese, politieke en kulturele aangeleenthede te ondervra.

U is een van 'n groot aantal persone wat toevallig gekies is. U menings en saamwerking oor hierdie sake sal hoog op prys gestel word.

Die studie is geheel-en-al vertroulik. Die antwoord van geen enkele individu sal bekend gemaak word nie. Alle inligting word anoniem deur 'n komper verwerk om statistiese gegewens te verkry.

Daar is geen korrekte of verkeerde antwoorde nie. Ons stel slegs belang in u eie menings en hoe u persoonlik oor hierdie verskillende kwessies voel.

Respondent is: Male   Female

Q.1a   What is your home language, that is the language you speak most often at home?

Wat is u huistaal, d.w.s. die taal wat u meeste tuis gebruik?

445

Afrikaans
Afrikaans

English
Engels

Both
Beide

Other (specify)
Ander (spesifiseer)

IF BOTH: Which of the two is spoken most?
INDIEN BEIDE: Watter een van die twee word die meeste gepraat?

Afrikaans
Afrikaans

English
Engels

Q.1b   What is or was the home language of your parents?
Wat is, of was, die huistaal van u ouers?

Afrikaans
Afrikaans

English
Engels

Both
Beide

Other (specify)
Ander (spesifiseer)

IF BOTH: Which of the two is/was spoken most?
INDIEN BEIDE: Watter een van die twee word, of was die meeste gepraat?

Afrikaans
Afrikaans

English
Engels

Q. 2.   Could you mention what you feel are the two major problems facing
South Africa at the moment?
Wat sou u sê is die twee belangrikste probleme waarmee Suid-Afrika
tans te kampe het?

1. _____

2. _____

Q. 3   As we know, among Whites, there are Afrikaans and English speaking
people. Could you tell me for each of the following statements whether it
is, *for you, very important, fairly important, rather unimportant,* or *not
important at all.*
Soos ons weet, bestaan die Blankes uit Afrikaans- en Engelssprekende
mense. Sal u asseblief vir my ten opsigte van elkeen van die volgende
stellinge sê of dit *vir u, baie belangrik, taamlik belangrik, ietwat on-
belangrik* of *hoegenaamd nie belangrik is nie.*

446

STATEMENT/STELLING A:

Feeling that you belong fully to your language group—The Afrikaners/English speakers (DELETE INAPPLICABLE)

Die gevoel dat u ten volle aan u taalgroep behoort. (Afrikaans, Engels) (LAAT WEG WAT NIE VAN TOEPASSING IS NIE).

STATEMENT/STELLING B:

Having as much close contact as possible with other language group—the English speakers/Afrikaners (DELETE INAPPLICABLE)

Om soveel nou kontak as moontlik met die ander taalgroep te hê. (LAAT WEG WAT NIE VAN TOEPASSING IS NIE).

STATEMENT/STELLING C:

Sharing the opinions and thinking of most people in your group—the Afrikaners/English speakers. (DELETE INAPPLICABLE)

Om die menings en denke van meeste mense in u groep te deel. (LAAT WEG WAT NIE VAN TOEPASSING IS NIE).

STATEMENT/STELLING D:

The language groups drawing closer together and losing some group feeling.

Dat die taalgroepe nader aanmekaar beweeg en daardeur 'n mate van groeps-gevoel verloor.

STATEMENT/STELLING E:

Your children marrying into your own group only—the Afrikaners/English speakers. (DELETE INAPPLICABLE)

Dat u kinders slegs binne u eie groep trou. (LAAT WEG WAT NIE VAN TOEPASSING IS NIE).

Q. 4   Do you regularly visit close, personal friends who are members of the other language group or not?

Besoek u gereeld intieme vriende wat Engelssprekend is of nie?

Yes   No

Q. 5   Do you ever discuss politics seriously with members of the other language group or not?

Bespreek u ooit die politiek, ernstig met lede van die ander taalgroep of nie?

Yes   No

Q. 6   What proportion of your life have you lived in or very near to any of the following big cities: Johannesburg, Pretoria, Durban, Cape Town, Port Elizabeth, Bloemfontein, East London, Kimberley, Pietermaritzburg, or the Witwatersrand-Vereeniging area?

Watter gedeelte van u lewe het u in of baie naby aan die volgende groot stede gewoon: Johannesburg, Pretoria, Durban, Kaapstad, Port Elizabeth, Bloemfontein, Oos Londen, Kimberley, Pietermaritzburg of die Witwatersrand-Vereeniging gebied?

All my life
My hele lewe

447

More than half
Meer as helfte
Less than half
Minder as helfte
Never
Nooit

Q. 7   Where did your parents live during most of your school years? SPECIFY
Waar het u ouers gewoon gedurende die grootste gedeelte van u skooljare? SPESIFISEER.

_____

_____

Q. 8   About official policy regarding the separation of the races in South Africa: do you think official policy should separate the races or not in each of the following:
Betreffende die amptelike beleid van rasseskeiding in Suid-Afrika: dink u dat die amptelike beleid die rasse behoort te skei of nie, in elkeen van die volgende:

	SEPARATION/ SKEIDING	NO SEPARATION/ GEEN SKEIDING
Lifts in buildings Hysers in geboue		
Busses and trains Busse en treine		
Residential areas Woongebiede		
Ordinary friendship and visiting Gewone vriendskap en besoeke		
Intimate friendship between sexes Intieme vriendskap tussen die geslagte		
Church Kerk		
Marriage Huwelik		

Q. 9   About Bantu and jobs: which level should official policy allow Bantu to reach *in White areas*? Please tell me whether you *agree* or *disagree* with each of the following:
Betreffende die Bantoe en hul werk: tot watter vlak behoort amptelike beleid die Bantoes toe te laat *in Blanke gebiede*? Sê my asseblief met watter van die volgende stellinge u saamstem of verskil:

AGREE   DISAGREE

Bantu should be allowed in all occupations in White areas
Bantoe behoort in enige beroep in Blanke gebiede toegelaat te word

Bantu should be allowed in jobs of great importance and high prestige; like senior officials in companies
Bantoes behoort in belangrike beroepe met hoë aansien toegelaat te word; soos senior beamptes in maatskappye

448

Bantu should be allowed in jobs where Bantu may be in charge of Whites
Bantoes behoort in posisies toegelaat te word waar hulle in bevel van Blankes mag wees

Bantu should be allowed in clerical jobs at the same level as Whites in offices
Bantoe behoort in klerikale werk op dieselfde vlak as Blankes in kantore toegelaat te word

Bantu should be allowed in skilled jobs if economically necessary even if some White workers' jobs are threatened
Bantoes behoort in geskoolde werk toegelaat te word as dit ekonomies genoodsaak is, selfs al word sommige Blanke werknemers se dienste bedreig

Bantu should be allowed in skilled jobs if economically necessary but no White worker's job is threatened
Bantoes behoort in geskoolde werk toegelaat te word as dit ekonomies genoodsaak is, mits geen Blanke werknemer se werk daardeur bedreig word nie

Q. 10a Do you think a Bantu, if properly trained, could work:
Dink u 'n Bantoe kon, indien behoorlik opgelei,

Just as well as a White man
Net so goed soos 'n Blanke man werk

Nearly as well
Amper so goed

Not as well
Nie so goed nie

Q. 10b About Bantu wages; please tell me whether you agree or disagree with each of the following statements.

Betreffende Bantoe lone; sê my asseblief of u saamstem of nie, met elk van die stellinge.

	AGREE	DISAGREE

The wage gap between Blacks and Whites should be closed even if it leads to increased prices.
Die loongaping tussen Swartes en Wit behoort verwyder te word, selfs al lei dit tot verhoogde pryse.

Bantu wages should be increased to gradually close the wage gap between Blacks and Whites.
Bantoelone behoort verhoog te word ten einde die loongaping tussen Swart and Wit geleidelik te verwyder.

Bantu wages should be increased to allow the Bantu a higher standard of living.
Bantoelone behoort verhoog te word ten einde die Bantoe 'n hoër lewensstandaard te bied.

Bantu wages should only increase to meet the rising prices
Bantoelone behoort slegs verhoog te word om die stygende pryse die hoof te bied

Bantu wages should remain just as they are.
Bantoelone behoort net so te bly.

Q.11   The policy of separate development is supposed to lead eventually to the independence of the Bantustans. Could you tell me for each of the following statements whether you agree or disagree?

Die beleid van afsonderlike ontwikkeling is veronderstel om uiteindelik tot die onafhanklikheid van die Bantoe tuislande te lei. Sê my asseblief of u saamstem of verskil met elk van die volgende stellinge:

> We should be prepared to give up half of South Africa to make separate development succeed.
> Ons behoort bereid to wees om die helfte van Suid-Afrika prys te gee om Afsonderlike Ontwikkeling te laat slaag.

> We should be prepared to give a great deal of financial aid to independent Bantu homelands to make separate development succeed.
> Ons behoort bereid te wees om grootskaalse finansiële steun aan onafhanklike Bantoetuislande te verleen ten einde Afsonderlike Ontwikkeling te laat slaag.

> There should be independent Bantustans with more land and some of our industrial areas.
> Daar behoort onafhanklike Bantoetuislande te wees met meer grond en 'n gedeelte van ons nywerheidsgebiede.

> There should be independent Bantustans as they are planned at the moment.
> Daar behoort onafhanklike Bantoetuislande te wees soos hulle tans beplan is.

> I am not in favour of the separation of the racial groups.
> Ek is nie ten gunste van die skeiding van rassegroepe nie.

> The Bantu groups should remain under the control of a White government.
> Die Bantoegroepe behoort onder die beheer van 'n Blanke regering te bly.

Q. 12   Here are two things people often say. Do you agree with A or B even a little more than the other?

Hier is twee stellinge wat mense dikwels maak: Stem u met A of met B saam, al is dit net effens meer as die ander?

> A. Some say: Separating races and protecting group culture is important above all.
> Sommige sê: Die skeiding van rasse en die beskerming van groepskultuur is belangrik bowe alles.

> B. Others say: Separating races should not be too important if it is impractical for us.
> Ander sê: Die skeiding van rasse behoort nie te belangrik te wees as dit onprakties vir ons is nie.

Q. 13a People have different personal feelings about contact with non-Whites. Think of *Coloureds* in a *similar position* in life as yourself. What kind of contact would you personally accept with *Coloureds*? Give me just your personal feeling about each of the following types of contact.

Mense het verskillende persoonlike gevoelens betreffende kontak met nie-Blankes. Dink aan *Kleurlinge* in 'n *soortgelyke posisie* in die samelewing as uself. Watter soort kontak met *Kleurlinge* sou u per-

450

soonlik aanvaar? Gee my net u eie gevoel ontrent elkeen van die volgende kontaksituasies.

Yes/Ja   No/Nee

Would sit next to such a Coloured on a bus
Sou langs so 'n Kleurling in 'n bus sit

Would invite such a Coloured to dine in my house
Sou so 'n Kleurling vir ete na my huis nooi

Would accept such a Coloured as my neighbour
Sou so 'n Kleurling as my buurman/vrou aanvaar

Would dance with such a Coloured at a party
Sou met so 'n Kleurling by 'n partytjie dans

Would marry such a Coloured if allowed
Sou met so 'n Kleurling trou—indien toegelaat

Would accept such a Coloured worshipping at my church
Sou dit aanvaar dat so 'n Kleurling dienste in my kerk bywoon

Would shake hands with such a Coloured
Sou met so 'n Kleurling handskud

Q. 13b Now think of a *Bantu* in a *similar position* in life as yourself. What kind of contact would you personally accept with *Bantu*? Give me just your personal feeling about each of the following types of contact.

Dink nou aan die *Bantoe* in 'n *soortgelyke posisie* as uself. Watter soort kontak met *Bantoes* sou u persoonlik aanvaar. Gee my net u eie gevoel omtrent elkeen van die volgende kontaksituasies.

Yes/Ja   No/Nee

Would sit next to such a Bantu on a bus
Sou langs so 'n Bantoe in 'n bus sit

Would invite such a Bantu to dine in my house
Sou so 'n Bantoe vir ete na my huis nooi

Would accept such a Bantu as my neighbour
Sou so 'n Bantoe as my buurman/vrou aanvaar

Would dance with such a Bantu at a party
Sou met so 'n Bantoe by 'n partytjie dans

Would marry such a Bantu if allowed
Sou met so 'n Bantoe trou—indien toegelaat

Would accept such a Bantu worshiping at my church
Sou dit aanvaar dat so 'n Bantoe dienste in my kerk bywoon

Would shake hands with such a Bantu
Sou met so 'n Bantoe handskud

Q. 14a Some political leaders want South Africa to become a Federal State. That is a state with some sharing of power between White and non-White groups and areas. Could you tell me for each of the following statements whether you agree or disagree?

Sommige politieke leiers wil hê Suid-Afrika moet 'n Federale Staat word. Dit is 'n staat waarin sekere magte tussen Blanke en nie-Blanke groepe en gebiede gedeel word. Sê my asseblief of u saamstem of verskil met elk van die volgende?

AGREE   DISAGREE
STEM SAAM   VERSKIL

451

A federal state in which power should be shared between White and non-White groups and areas so that no one group dominates.

'n federale staat waarin magte gelykop tussen Blanke en nie-Blanke groepe en gebiede gedeel behoort te word sodat geen enkele groep oorheers nie.

A federal state in which non-White groups and areas take some part in nation-wide government decisions but the White group has the final say in government.

Nie-Blanke groepe en gebiede in 'n mate deelneem in landswye regeringsbesluite, maar die Blanke groep het die finale seggenskap in die regering.

A federal state in which non-White groups and areas should not take part at all in nation-wide government decisions but just run their own group affairs under a central White government.

Nie-Blanke groepe en gebiede hoegenaamd nie behoort deel te neem in landswye regeringsbesluite nie, maar slegs hulle eie groepsake onder beheer van 'n Blanke sentrale regering hanteer

Q. 14b When do you think a Federal System should be introduced in South Africa?

Wanneer dink u behoort 'n Federale Stelsel in Suid-Afrika ingestel te word?

Right now
Onmiddellik

After about 10 years
Na ongeveer 10 jaar

After about 30 years
Na ongeveer 30 jaar

Never
Nooit

Q. 15 Here is a list of words. Can you please read through them quickly and tick those words which you personally feel *should* be very important in our government policy?

Hier is 'n lysie woorde. Sal u hulle asseblief vinnig deurlees en 'n merkie langs daardie woorde maak wat u persoonlik voel baie belangrik *behoort* te wees in ons regeringsbeleid.

TICK/MERK

Honesty
Eerlikheid

Authority
Gesag

Flexibility
Buigsaamheid

Strength
Kragtigheid

Tolerance
Verdraagsaamheid

Tradition
Tradisie

452

Enlightenment
Verligtheid
Order
Orde
Gentleness
Sagtheid

Q. 16   Here is a set of cards. They are things people say about many issues.
Please read through a statement and then rate it on the card E where you
think it should be, i.e. agree, partly agree, partly disagree, disagree.

Hier is 'n stel kaarte. Daarop staan dinge wat mense omtrent 'n aantal
sake sê. Lees asseblief deur elke stelling en plaas dit op Kaart E waar u
dink dit moet wees, d.w.s. stem saam, stem gedeeltelik saam, verskil
gedeeltelik, verskil.

Agree/ Stem saam	Partly Agree/ Stem Gedeeltelik saam	Partly disagree/ Verskil Gedeeltelik	Disagree/ Verskil

A.   No matter what the future holds, I feel we will manage.
Ongeag wat die toekoms inhou, voel ek ons sal deurkom.

B.   White babies are cleverer than Black babies.
Blanke babas is slimmer as Swart babas.

C.   Racial separation in this country is necessary to prevent racial disturbances.
Rasseskeiding in hierdie land is noodsaaklik om rasseonluste te voorkom.

D.   Whites and non-Whites should get equal pay for equal work.
Blankes en nie-Blankes behoort gelyke betaling vir gelyke werk te kry.

E.   I believe in life after death.
Ek glo in 'n lewe hiernamaals.

F.   Friendship and close social contact between the races is a bad thing in
itself.
Vriendskap en noue sosiale verkeer tussen die rasse is op sigself sleg.

G.   Political rights in White areas should be given to educated successful
urban Bantu.
Politieke regte in Blanke gebiede behoort aan geleerde, suksesvolle
stedelike Bantoes gegee te word.

H.   I feel uncertain and fearful about my future.
Ek voel onseker en bevrees omtrent my toekoms.

I.   Any concessions to non-Whites will endanger the Whites' position in the
long run.
Enige toegewings aan nie-Blankes sal op die lange duur die Blankes se
posisie in gevaar stel.

J.   I believe that there is an almighty God.
Ek glo dat daar 'n Almagtige God is.

K.   Despite statements of some Blacks, the Black people are satisfied with
things as they are.
Ondanks uitlatinge van sommige Swartes, is die Swartmense tevrede
met die huidige verloop van sake.

L.   Given the opportunity, the Bantu could have the same ability and reach
the same standards as Whites.
Indien die geleentheid gegun, kan die Bantoe dieselfde bekwaamheid hê
en dieselfde standaarde as Blankes bereik.

453

M.	We should consider strengthening our position by accepting Coloureds as equal citizens.
Ons behoort dit te oorweeg om ons posisie te versterk deur die Kleurlinge as gelyke burgers te aanvaar.

N.	One should know that something really works, before taking a chance on it.
Mens behoort te weet dat iets wel sal slaag voordat mens dit waag.

O.	Most non-Whites are as much in favour of keeping to their own group as most Whites.
Meeste nie-Blankes is net so ten gunste daarvan om by hulle eie groep te hou soos die meeste Blankes.

P.	We should be prepared to pay more in taxes to develop the Bantu homelands.
Ons behoort bereid te wees om hoër belasting te betaal ten einde die Bantoetuislande te ontwikkel.

Q.	It is a great pity that some Afrikaners prefer to speak English rather than their own language.
Dit is uiters jammer dat sommige Afrikaners verkies om Engels eerder as hulle eie taal te praat.

R.	Afrikaners and Afrikaans-speaking Coloureds need not really be separate social and cultural groups.
Afrikaners en Afrikaanssprekende Kleurlinge hoef inderdaad nie afsonderlike sosiale en kulturele groepe te wees nie.

S.	Even if the leaders of my political party act in a way I don't understand, I would still trust them.
Selfs al sou die leiers van my politieke party op 'n manier optree wat ek nie verstaan nie, sal ek hulle nogtans vertrou.

T.	Most poorer Whites, English and Afrikaans, have only themselves to blame for their circumstances.
Meeste armer Blankes, Engels en Afrikaans, kan slegs hulself blameer vir hul omstandighede.

U.	I can look forward to my future with confidence.
Ek kan met vertroue na my toekoms uitsien.

V.	The basis of any policy should be the interests of the needy ordinary White voter.
Die grondslag van enige beleid behoort die belange van die behoeftige gewone Blanke stemgeregtigde te wees.

W.	I believe in all the age-old basic teachings of my church.
Ek glo in al die eeue-oue basiese leerstellinge van my kerk.

X.	Despite present differences, the inborn intelligence of Whites and Bantu is the same.
Ondanks huidige verskille, is die ingebore intelligensie van Blankes en Bantoes dieselfde.

Y.	We can make many concessions to non-Whites as long as Whites have the main say in politics.
Ons kan baie toegewings aan nie-Blankes maak solank Blankes die hoofseggenskap in die politiek het.

Z.	Most Bantu are becoming increasingly bitter toward the Whites.
Meeste Bantoes word meer en meer verbitterd teenoor die Blankes.

AA. If you start trying to change things, you usually make them worse.
Wanneer mens dinge begin probeer verander, vererger mens dit gewoonlik.

BB. Bantu should be allowed trade-unions to push for higher wages even if it means White wage increases are slower.
Bantoes behoort vakbonde toegelaat te word wat op hoër lone kan aandring, selfs al sou dit stadige loonverhogings vir Blankes beteken.

CC. Whites should not have to pay higher taxes to develop the Bantu homelands.
Blankes behoort nie hoër belastings te betaal om die Bantoetuislande te ontwikkel nie.

DD. It seems that threats to our position will become serious in the future.
Dit skyn asof bedreigings van ons posisie ernstig in die toekoms sal word.

EE. Our prosperity and economic growth should be the main basis of our race policy.
Ons voorspoed en ekonomiese groei behoort die vernaamste grondslag van ons rassebeleid te wees.

FF. I believe in some form of existence after death.
Ek glo in een of ander vorm van voortbestaan na die dood.

GG. The changes are that eventually there will be a Black uprising in South Africa.
Dit is waarskynlik dat daar uiteindelik 'n Swart opstand in Suid-Afrika sal wees.

HH. Most ordinary Bantu do not want political rights, perhaps just better wages and living conditions.
Meeste gewone Bantoes verlang nie politieke regte nie, moontlik slegs beter lone en lewensomstandighede.

II. Only somebody who believes in God can be a good South African.
Slegs 'n persoon wat in God glo, kan 'n goeie Suid-Afrikaner wees.

JJ. The church should be concerned with the souls of people rather than social issues and poverty.
Die kerk behoort begaan te wees oor die siele van mense, eerder as oor sosiale kwessies en armoede.

KK. In general, policy should be decided by those who have high education, culture and have proved their success in life.
In die algemeen behoort beleid bepaal te word deur diegene met hoë opvoeding en kultuur en wat reeds hulself in die lewe bewys het.

LL. Even if my party takes political decisions of which I don't approve, I will still support my party.
Selfs al sou my party politieke besluite neem wat nie my goedkeuring wegdra nie, sal ek nog steeds my party ondersteun.

MM. I am afraid that our children might never enjoy as high a standard of living as we have now.
Ek is bevrees ons kinders mag nooit so 'n hoë lewenspeil geniet as wat ons nou het nie.

Q. 17 What would life be like for Whites in some country or another where Bantu have the main say in government? Here is a list of words. Please read through this list *quickly* and pick any number of words: Words you

feel could fit life in a country under a mainly Bantu government *in the long run.*
Hoe sou die lewe vir Blankes in een of ander land wees waar die Bantoe die hoofseggenskap in die regering het NADAT DINGE BEDAAR HET? Hier is 'n lysie woorde. Lees asseblief vinnig deur die lys en kies enige aantal woorde uit: Woorde wat u voel moontlik van toepassing kon wees ten opsigte van die lewe OP DIE LANGE DUUR in 'n land onder 'n hoofsaaklik Bantoe-regering.

LIFE UNDER A MAINLY BANTU GOVERNMENT IN THE LONG RUN/
LEWE ONDER HOOFSAAKLIK BANTOE-REGERING OP DIE LANGE DUUR

TICK/MERK

Prosperous/Welvarend
Uncertain/Onseker
Whites needed/Blankes nodig
Bad administration/Swak administrasie
Peaceful/Vreedsaam
White unemployment/Blanke werkloosheid
Much the same/Min of meer dieselfde
Dirty/Vuil
Intermarriage/Ondertrouery
Shortages/Tekorte
Fairness/Regverdigheid
Chaotic/Chaoties
World Acceptance/Deur die wêreld aanvaar
Frustrating/Frustrerend
Racial co-operation/Rassesamewerking
Whites poorer/Blankes armer
Social justice/Sosiale regverdigheid
Terrifying/Vreeswekkend
Stronger country/Sterker land
Immoral/Onsedelik
Economic growth/Ekonomiese groei
Communist/Kommunisties
Breakdown/Ineenstorting
Safe future/Veilige toekoms
Undemocratic/Ondemokraties
Friendly/Vriendelik
Our culture weakened/Ons kultuur verswak
Unreliable/Onbetroubaar
Honest and dependable/Eerlik en betroubaar
Cruelty/Wreedheid
Unchristian/OnChristelik
Rule of law/Regsorde

Q. 18   Some political leaders suggest that non-Whites take part *in our politics,* not only in the homelands. Could you tell me for each of the following statements whether you agree or disagree?
Sommige politieke leiers stel voor dat nie-Blankes *in ons politiek* moet deelneem—nie slegs in die tuislande nie. Sê my asseblief of u saamstem of verskil ten opsigte van elk van die volgende stellinge.

Non-Whites should be allowed to be elected as members of our parliament.
Nie-Blankes behoort toegelaat te word on as lede van ons parlement verkies te word.

All Whites and non-Whites should have the right to an equal vote in our country.
Alle Blankes en nie-Blankes in ons land behoort op 'n gelyke stem geregtig te wees.

Well educated non-Whites with decent jobs should vote in our country no matter what their numbers.
Welontwikkelde nie-Blankes wat goeie poste beklee, behoort ongeag hul getalle stemreg te hê in ons land.

Well educated non-Whites should be allowed to vote in our country but the Whites should retain control.
Welontwikkelde nie-Blankes behoort toegelaat te word om in ons land te stem, maar die Blankes behoort die beheer te behou.

No non-White should vote in our White political system.
Geen nie-Blanke behoort in ons Blanke politieke stelsel te stem nie.

Q. 19 Let us just imagine that anger, discontent and unrest among *urban Bantu* were to become so serious in future as to threaten peace. *What should policy be?* Answer Yes or No in each case.
Laat ons net veronderstel dat woede, ontevredenheid en onrus onder *stedelike Bantoes* in die toekoms so ernstig sou word, dat dit die vrede bedreig. *Wat behoort die beleid te wese?* Antwoord asseblief Ja of Nee in elke geval.

Only strong action to keep order.
Slegs sterk optrede om orde te handhaaf.

Sending urban Bantu to homelands even if it means a labour shortage.
Die stedelike Bantoe na die tuislande stuur selfs al sou dit tot 'n arbeitstekort lei.

Enlarging or developing of homelands even if white South Africa has to sacrifice.
Vergroting of ontwikkeling van tuislande selfs al moet Blanke Suid-Afrika opoffer.

Strong action but also gradual voting rights for urban Bantu in White politics.
Sterk optrede maar ook geleidelike stemreg vir die stedelike Bantoe in Blanke politiek.

Acceptance of urban Bantu as equal citizens.
Aanvaarding van stedelike Bantoe as gelyke burgers.

Strong action but also better wages and better conditions for urban Bantu.
Sterk optrede maar ook beter lone en beter omstandighede vir die stedelike Bantoe.

Lastly, just a few questions about yourself which we need in order to place people in groups for computerization.

Laastens, slegs 'n paar vrae omtrent uself wat ons nodig het om mense vir komper doeleindes te groepeer.

457

Q. 20　What is your age?
Wat is u ouderdom?

Q. 21　What is your religious denomination or church?
(RESPONDENT'S OWN DENOMINATION).
Wat is u geloof of kerkverband?
(RESPONDENT SE EIE KERKVERBAND).

N.G.K.	Methodist
N.G.K.	Metodis
G.K.	Presbyterian
G.K.	Presbiteriaan
H.K.	Other Christian, spec:
H.K.	Ander Christelike, spes:
Lutheran	Jewish
Luthers	Joods
Catholic	Other, spec:
Katoliek	Ander, spes:
Anglican	Atheist/Agnostic/None
Anglikaans	Ateis/Agnostiek/Geen

Q. 22　How often do you:
(a) attend religious services?
(b) read the Bible?

Hoe dikwels woon u:
(a) kerkdienste by
(b) lees u die Bybel?

	(a) Church	(b) Bible
Never Nooit		
Hardly ever Omtrent nooit		
On special religious occasions Op spesiale godsdienstige geleenthede		
About 2–3 times a month Omtrent twee tot drie keer per maand		
About 2–3 times a month Omtrent twee tot drie keer per maand		
Once a week or more Eeen keer per week of meer		
Daily Daagliks		

Q. 22c　*ASK AFRIKAANS-SPEAKING RESPONDENTS ONLY:*
Word Huisgodsdiens in die huisgesin waar u woonagtig is gehou?
JA　　　NEE

Q. 23　What is your education?
Wat is u onderwyspeil?
Less than Standard 5
Minder as Standerd 5

458

Standard 5/6
Standerd 5/6

Junior Certificate (Standard 8)
Junior Sertifikaat (Std. 8)

Senior Certificate/Matric (Standard 10)
Senior Sertifikaat/Matriek (Std. 10)

Technical College/Technical Ticket (specify fully)
Tegniese Kollege/Tegniese Kwalifikasie (Spesifiseer ten volle)

Post-school diploma (specify)
Na-skoolse diploma (spesifiseer)

University Degree (Specify)
Universiteitsgraad (spesifiseer)

Post-Graduate Degree(s) (specify)
Ná-graadse Graad of Grade (spesifiseer);

Q. 24 What is your present occupation? Please give details of position, type of
industry/organization and size of organization.

Wat is u huidige beroep/betrekking? Gee asseblief besonderhede van
posisie, aard van industrie/organisasies en grootte van organisasie.

Details of Position
Besonderhede van pos

Type of industry or organization
Tipe organisasie

Size of organization
Grootte van organisasie

IF RETIRED/UNEMPLOYED:
What was your last permanent or full-time occupation?
INDIEN AFGETREE/WERKLOOS:
Wat was u laaste permanente of voltydse beroep of betrekking?

Details of position
Besonderhede van pos

Type of Industry or organization
Tipe organisasie

Size of organization
Grootte van organisasie

Q. 25 *ASK MARRIED/DIVORCED/WIDOWED WOMEN:*
What is/was your *husband's* occupation?
VROUE: GETROUD/GESKEI/WEDUWEE:
Wat is/was u man' se beroep?

Details of position
Besonderhede van pos
Type of industry or organization
Tipe organisasie
Size of organization
Grootte van organisasie

Q. 26 How many children do you have, if any?
Hoeveel kinders het u, indien enige?

459

Q. 27 *ASK ALL:*
What was your *father*'s highest position/occupation?
VRA ALMAL:
Wat was u *vader* se hoogste beroep/betrekking/pos?

Details of position
Besonderhede van pos

Industry
Industrie

Size of organization
Grootte van organisasie

Q. 28 What is the total amount of money contributed to this household monthly?
Wat is die totale som geld wat maandelike tot hierdie huishouding bygedra word?

TICK/MERK

Less than R200.00 per month
Minder as R200.00 per maand

R200.00–R299.00 per month
R200.00–R299.00 per maand

R300.00–R399.00 per month
R300.00–R399.00 per maand

R400.00–R499.00 per month
R400.00–R499.00 per maand

R500.00–R599.00 per month
R500.00–R599.00 per maand

R600.00–R799.00 per month
R600.00–R799.00 per maand

R800.00–R999.00 per month
R800.00–R999.00 per maand

R1,000.00–R1,199.00 per month
R1,000.00–R1,199.00 per maand

R1,200.00–R1,399.00 per month
R1,200.00–R1,399.00 per month

R1,400.00 or more
R1,400.00 or meer

Q. 29 Which political party in South Africa in general best represents your political feelings?
Watter politieke party in Suid-Afrika verteenwoordig in die algemeen u politieke gevoelens die beste?
NP/NP UP/VP PP/PP HNP/HNP DEM.P/DEM.P NONE/GEEN

Q.30a Did you vote in the last general election?
Het u in die jongste algemene verkiesing gestem?
Yes/Ja   No/Nee

Q.30b IF YES: For which party did you vote?
INDIEN JA: Vir watter party het u gestem?
NP/NP UP/VP PP/PP HNP/HNP DEM.P/DEM.P

460

Q. 30c Have you ever voted for another party?

Het u al ooit vir 'n ander politieke party gestem?

Yes/Ja   No/Nee

Q. 30d IF YES: Which one?

INDIEN JA: Vir watter een?

NP/NP   UP/VP   PP/PP   HNP/NHP   DEM.P/DEM.P

Q. 31a IF NO TO Q.30a: Why not?

INDIEN NEE VIR V. 30a: Waarom nie?

Uncontested seat
Onbestrede setel

My party not represented
My party nie verteenwoordig nie

Other (specify)
Ander (spesifiseer)

Q. 31b How *would you* have voted if all parties had been represented in your constituency?

Hoe *sou u* gestem het as alle partye in u kiesafdeling verteenwoordig was?

NP/NP   UP/VP   PP/PP   HNP/HNP   DEM.P/DEM.P
NONE/GEEN

Q. 31c The *last time* you voted, for which party did you vote?

Die *laaste keer* wat u gestem het, vir watter party het u gestem?

NP/NP   UP/VP   PP/PP   HNP/HNP   DEM.P/DEM.P

Q. 32 Sometimes people are dissatisfied with their political party. If you were, would you vote for another political party, not vote at all, or still vote for your own party?

Mense is soms ontevrede met hul politieke party. As u ontevrede sou wees, sou u vir 'n ander party stem, buite stemming bly, of nog steeds vir u eie party stem?

Another party
Ander party

Not at all
Buite stemming bly

Same party
Dieselfde party

Other answer, specify:
Ander antwoord, spesifiseer:

Q. 33 Did or does your father generally vote for the same party as you do or not?

Stem of het u vader gewoonlik vir dieselfde party gestem as u of nie?

Same party
Dieselfde party

Other party (sp.)   NP/NP
Ander party (sp.)   UP/VP
                             PP/PP
                             HNP/HNP
                             Dem.P/Dem.P

461

Other answers (specify)
Ander antwoorde (spes.)

Do not know
Weet nie

Q. 34a Are you a paid-up member of a political party?
Is u 'n volop-betaalde lid van 'n politieke party?

Yes/Ja   No/Nee

Q.34b IF YES: which one?
INDIEN JA: Watter een?
NP/NP UP/UP PP/PP HNP/HNP DEM.P/DEM.P

Q. 35a Have you done any of the following in the past year?
We do not wish to know the party.
Het u enigeen van die volgende gedurende die afgelope jaar gedoen?
Ons wil nie weet watter party ter sake is nie.

Attended a political meeting
'n Politieke vergadering bygewoon

Did some active work for a political party
Aktief vir 'n politieke party gewerk

Given money to a political party
Geld gegee/geskenk aan 'n politieke party

Held any office in a political party
Enige amp in 'n politieké party beklee

Q. 35b IF YES TO OFFICE-HOLDING: What type of office and at what level of the party?
INDIEN JA: Watter amp en op watter vlak van die party?

Q. 36a Which voluntary social, cultural or political organizations are you a member of—for example, Rapportryers, Round Table, Vrouefederasie, Housewives League, etc.
Aan watter vrywillige maatskaplike kulturele of politieke organisasies behoort u—byvoorbeeld, Rapportryers, Round Table, Vrouefederasie, Housewives League, ens.

Q.36b ASK FOR EACH MENTIONED:
Do you hold any office in:
TEN OPSIGTE VAN ELKE ORGANISASIE GENOEM:
Beklee u enige amp daarin:

36a Organization/Organisasie	Member of	36b Yes/Ja	Office No/Nee
Rapportryers			
Round Table			
Vrouefederasie			
Housewives League			
Lions			
Rotary			
Others specify Ander spesifiseer			

Interviewer Instructions

Towns:

The name and addresses of the *individual to be interviewed* has been recorded on your questionnaire. *Nobody else* at this address may be interviewed unless this particular individual is no longer resident at this address or will not be available for a period of four weeks or longer. Two calls must be made before substitution takes place. Substitutes in all cases *must* be registered voters.

Substitutes must be of the *same sex* as the individual previously required at that address. If it was a male, you may only substitute with a male; if it was a female, you may only substitute with a female.

If there is no person of the same sex who is a registered voter at that address, substitute at the next address, that is next door.

These respondents have been randomly selected from the voters roll, therefore, these instructions *must not be deviated from*. Should you be in any doubt about what action to take, contact this office Johannesburg 725–2324.

Rural:

You will be assigned a number of farms between specified towns where you will interview either a male or female registered voter as instructed.

Work done in towns must be returned to this office or the branch office in the area in which you are working at least twice a week. The office must be contacted twice a week by people working in smaller towns and travelling in rural areas.

The questionnaire has been designed after extensive preliminary testing. Under no circumstances may interviewers enter into discussions or explanations of the questions. You may only read the question again as written, if the respondent wishes.

USE THE EXACT WORDING OF THE QUESTIONNAIRE AT ALL TIMES. PRACTISE READING THE QUESTIONS ALOUD.

ORIGINAL   SUBSTITUTE

Name
Address
Tel. No.
Home Suburb
Constituency
Area

Reason for substitution:
Moved
Unavailable 4 + weeks
Other (specify)

THIS WILL BE STRICTLY BACK-CHECKED

Checked
Back-Checked

Questionnaire for the Urban Blacks

Introduction

Good Morning/Afternoon/Evening. My name is .... I am from IMSA, a company that interviews people to find out about products and what people think about problems (show identity card). At the moment a study is being done in a number of African countries to find out what their opinions about their countries are. In South Africa IMSA is doing this study to find out how African people feel about their lives at the moment. We are speaking to over 1,000 different people and we would be very happy for you to talk to us.

Your answers will not be shown to anyone — We do not even want to know your name. There are no right or wrong answers. We just want your opinions.

Thank you for giving us your time.

Q. 1   First, which language should we use during this interview?

_____

Q. 2   Speaking about languages: What language do you speak most when
       talking to different people, e.g.:
       — to your parents (when you were a child)
       — to other African people at work
       — to your children
       Zulu
       Xhosa
       N. Sotho
       S. Sotho
       Setswana
       Venda
       Seswati
       Ndebele
       Shangaan
       English
       other specify:

Q. 3   How old are you? Yrs. ....

Q. 4   What is/was your father's highest occupation?

_____

Q. 5   What is your occupation? Spontaneous reply

_____

       (*IF VAGUE:* What sort of work do you do in your job? Probe for details —
       'labourer' too vague)

Q. 6   What sort of place do you work at?
                                          Big   Medium   Small
       A factory
       A construction company
       An office
       In government service
       In a shop/wholesaler
       Transport
       Mining
       Domestic
       Other

Q. 6a How long have you worked there? Yrs. ...... Month ......

Q. 7   What place do you feel in your heart to be your home? (If respondent
       mentions church or work probe: a place for living in?)

_____

Q. 8   What kind of a job would you prefer:
       (a) A job in a factory or an office with a good salary you can rely on
           or
       (b) Your own business where you can win a lot or lose a lot?

465

Q. 9   Here are a number of things we have heard African people all over Africa say. Tell me whether an African like yourself in .... (township) would agree with the things said or not?

There is very little that somebody like yourself can do to improve the life of African people in South Africa.

Agree
Don't Know
Disagree
Refuse

Q. 10   An African's child should marry into its own tribal group only.

Q. 11   African, Coloured and India people should be one black people compared with the Whites.

Q. 12   I prefer to be with people who speak my own language.

Q. 13   I don't care whether my neighbour belongs to my own tribal group or to another.

Q. 14   If you try to change things you usually make them worse.

Q. 15   One should know that something really works before taking a chance on it.

Q. 16   I feel uncertain and fearful about my future.

Q. 17   I believe in Christ the son of God, the heavenly father.

Q. 18a The religion of our ancestors and witchcraft is stronger than Christian religion.

Q. 18b African workers could be very strong if they would stand together against the bosses they have now.

Q. 19a I can be happy and enjoy life without believing in God or any god.

Q. 19b If Africans governed themselves there would be no improvements because they would fight amongst themselves.

Q. 20a An educated African who has been to university should not earn more than an ordinary African factory worker.

Q. 20b It is wise for Africans in town to be careful in politics and not lose what they have.

Q. 21a I believe in a life after death, where good people will be rewarded and bad people will be punished.

Q. 21b One must be very cautious with people — you cannot trust the African people who live and work around you.

Q. 22a I try hard to live my daily life according to the teachings of my religion.

Q. 22b When I see what the Whites have I feel envious and feel it is right that I should have the same.

Q. 23a There is a great deal to learn from the knowledge and skills of the Whites.

466

Q. 23b The Whites are strict but also honest and fair—we would not be happier under our own people.

Q. 24a A successful and educated African should not live as the Whites but follow a true African way of life.

Q. 24b No matter what Africans try to do to improve their lives they will not succeed against the power of the Whites.

Q. 25a The most important thing is to respect and follow the ways and beliefs of our ancestry.

Q. 25b Africans who support trade-unions cause a lot of trouble and bring no progress.

Q. 26   Here is a picture of how African people can feel about life for Africans in South Africa.
(READ AND POINT TO FACES):

(a) The face at the top is of African people who are *very happy* with life as it is in South Africa.

(b) The next face is of African people who are *just happy but not very happy* with life as it is in South Africa.

(c) The next face is of people who are *not happy but also not unhappy*—they are in the middle.

(d) The next face is of people who are *unhappy* with life in South Africa.

(e) The last face is of people who are *angry and impatient* with life as it is in South Africa.

Which face shows the way most African people like yourself in .... (mention township) feel about life in South Africa *now?*
(RECORD BELOW UNDER):

1. Very happy
2. Happy
3. Neutral
4. Unhappy
5. Angry and impatient
6. Refuse

Q. 27   Which face shows the way most African people like yourself in .... (mention township) will most probably feel like in *ten (10) years from now?*
(RECORD BELOW UNDER):

467

1. Very happy
2. Happy
3. Neutral
4. Unhappy
5. Angry and impatient
6. Refuse

(If answer to Q.27 differs from Q.26 ask):

Why do you think your feelings will change?

Q. 28 Many people speak of improvements in South Africa for Africans. What changes and improvements would Africans like yourself see as being most needed for Africans in the future?

_____
_____

(PROBE:) What else?

_____
_____

THINKING OF AN INDEPENDENT AFRICAN COUNTRY RULED BY AFRICANS—SUCH AS TANZANIA, ZAMBIA, BOTSWANA OR ANY OTHER INDEPENDENT AFRICAN COUNTRY:

Q. 29 What do you think is best for such an African country
(a) One political party only with one single plan for the country's future,
or
(b) More than one party each with its own plan for the country's future.

Uncertain/Don't know
Refuse

Q. 30 (a) Factories and businesses should be owned by private African businessmen who will work hard to make their businesses grow,
or
(b) Factories and businesses should be owned by the African government so that the representatives of the people decide how the businesses should be run.

Uncertain/Don't know
Refuse

Q. 31 What would be best for such an African country?
(a) A government which listens to criticisms and tries to satisfy people who disagree with it,
or
(b) A government which does not allow too much criticism for the sake of order and unity.

Uncertain/Don't know
Refuse

Q. 32 What would you think is best for such an African country
(a) An opposition party which is able to criticise government plans,
or

468

(b) No opposition party because opposition can divide the country —

Uncertain/Don't know
Refuse

Q. 33 Now let us think of what kind of leader would be good for such an African country. Choose between the following leaders.

(a) A leader who decides after getting guidance from many assistants and followers,

or

(b) A leader who makes his own decisions and guides his assistants and followers.

Q. 34 Think of Africans, Indians, Coloureds and Whites who have all had exactly the same education, who would be the most intelligent, next intelligent and who would be the least intelligent?

(INDICATE BY NUMBER THE ORDER OF CLEVERNESS)

	MOST	NEXT	LEAST
Africans			
Indians			
Coloureds			
Whites			
All people the same			
Don't know			
Decline/Refuse			

Q.35–
Q. 47 We would like you to think of Kenya which is an independent African country ruled by Africans. Kenya has two big groups of African people and some smaller groups and also has many Whites and Indians. Kenya is busy deciding on plans for the people of Kenya. We would like you to think of what would be best for Kenya.

I. *ABOUT AFRICAN GROUPS*

There is one big powerful group (called the Kikuyu). There is another group also big but smaller (than the Kikuyu called the Luo) as well as some smaller groups.

READ OUT THE ALTERNATIVES. THEN ASK INDIVIDUALLY

Agree	Disagree	Don't know	Refuse

(a) Should most of the political leaders be from the biggest group (the Kikuyu)?

(b) Should all groups each have the same number of leaders?

(c) Should people be allowed to vote for whoever they like, even if some groups have more leaders than others?

II. *ABOUT THE INDIANS*

(a) Should Indians be allowed to stay in Kenya?

(b) Should Indians be allowed to vote?

(c) Should Indians be allowed to have businesses?

(d) Should Indians be allowed to have African girlfriends?

III. Some other African countries have Coloureds, like South Africa. What do you think about them?

(a) Should Coloureds be allowed to stay?

(b) Should Coloureds be allowed to vote?

(c) Should Coloureds be allowed to have their own schools?

IV. *ABOUT THE WHITES*

(a) Should Whites be allowed to stay in Kenya?

(b) Should Whites be allowed to vote?

(c) Should Whites be allowed to have businesses?

(d) Should Whites be allowed to have big farms?

(e) Should Whites be allowed to have African girlfriends?

Q.48–
Q. 54   About plans for Africans in the future.

Which of the following plans would Africans who live and work around you — Africans like yourself — be happy to accept?

(a) Some say: Africans should get independent states for themselves in South Africa — independent states bigger and richer than the present homelands and including some industrial areas.

> Yes   Don't know   No   Refuse

(b) Some say: South Africa should be divided into two halves, one half for Blacks and the other half for Whites, that is Blacks ruled by Blacks and Whites ruled by Whites.

(c) South Africa should be divided, but the Blacks sbould get the bigger part and the Whites the smaller one.

(d) In South Africa there should be Black provinces where Blacks vote for their leaders, and White provinces where Whites vote for their leaders, and Black and White leaders should have equal power in a main South African government.

(e) Blacks should be the strongest in the main government, but Whites should be allowed to run their own affairs in their own areas.

(f) South Africa should be one country for Blacks and Whites together but only those with decent jobs and better education should be allowed to vote.

(g) South Africa should be one place for all people. All people — that is Blacks and Whites, rich and poor, educated and illiterates — should be allowed to vote.

Q. 55–
Q. 59   Now we would like you to think of Rhodesia. (Rhodesia) is a country with many Africans ruled by a much smaller number of Whites. In this country (Rhodesia) Africans do not have the same political rights as Whites and they also get lower wages and cannot live where they like.

There are Africans in (Rhodesia) this country who want to change things, but they have different ideas on how to bring about changes. I will read you some of the things that Africans in (Rhodesia) this country think.

Do you agree or disagree with the following statements?

> Agree   Disagree   Don't Know   Refuse

(a) Improvements for Africans will come through patient negotiations between White and Black leaders.

(b) The only way of bringing improvements for Africans is by making trouble in public and by strikes.

470

(c) Africans will never get improvements without fighting and violent action.

(d) Fighting and violence will harm the Africans very much more than the Whites because the Whites are very strong.

(e) Africans in (Rhodesia) this country should never think of fighting and violence because hurting anybody, even Whites is very bad.

Q60–Q.63 Mozambique used to be ruled by Portugal. After years of fighting, Africans have become leaders in Mozambique—they are called Frelimo. Would most people like yourself here in .... (mention township) agree or disagree with the following statements?

Agree   Don't know   Disagree   Refuse

a) Frelimo won only because of the help it got from other African countries.

b) Frelimo won because of its own strength and struggle.

c) Frelimo won only because of the weakness of the Portuguese.

d) Frelimo would never have won if the South African Whites had been in place of the Whites in Mozambique.

Q. 64 Some say that the demonstration by young people in Soweto and other places were a good thing for the future of African people. Others say no good can come out of such actions:
What do you feel?
Why?

Q. 65 There is an organization in the African areas called Inkatha. Do you know about it?

Yes   No

IF YES:
What can such an organization do for Africans like you in the future?

Q. 66 Thinking of African leaders here in South Africa, Whom do you admire most?
Whom else?

Q. 67 (INTERVIEWER: IF Q.66 NO HOMELAND LEADER IS MENTIONED ASK FOLLOWING QUESTIONS):
Is there a homeland leader whom you consider a true political leader?

Q. 68 IF YES: Who?

Q. 69 Which Church or religion do you belong to?

Anglican
Catholic
Methodist
Other Established Christian
(DRC, Presbyterian,
Lutheran)
African Sep. Churches (Zion,
Ethiopian, Non-European
Sects).
European Sects (Apostolic/
Baptist/Full Gospel, etc.)

471

Other (STATE)
None

Q. 70 Do you go to religious services?

Yes, regularly
Yes, sometimes
No

Q. 71 Have you any close relatives or people dependent on you who live in a homeland?

Yes   No

Q. 72 Which homeland?

Q. 73 Do you have any of the following in a homeland?

Rights to use land
Cattle
House

Q. 74 In general, how often do you travel to a homeland?

Q. 75 How many people live in this household?
Number   Number 1
                                       2
                                       3–4
                                       5–6
                                       7–8
                                       9–10
                                       11 +

Q. 76 Who is the main breadwinner of this household?

Respondent
Father
Other Relative
Landlord
Other

(IF BREADWINNER IS NOT THE RESPONDENT, ASK:)
What is the breadwinner's occupation? (Details)

Q. 77 What is the breadwinner's total income?
(INTERVIEWER: RECORD IN WEEKLY OR MONTHLY RATE)
Week: R ....   Month: R ....

Q. 78 Can you read:

English
Afrikaans
An African Language

Q.79 If any, which newspaper do you read regularly?

Q. 80 Did you ever go to school or follow a correspondence college course?

Yes   No

IF YES:

What was the highest standard you passed at school?

> Sub Standard 1 + 2
> Standard 1 + 2
> Standard 3 + 4
> Standard 5 + 6
> Form 1 + 2
> Form 3 + 4
> Form 5
> Higher but no degree
> Degree

Q. 81 For how many years have you lived in a large city or town?
Number of years ....

Q. 82 Are you   married?
single?
divorced/separated

Q. 83 How many children do you have? (That is in total no matter where they are living at present)
Number of children ......

Q. 84 What organizations, trade-unions or clubs do you belong to?

Q. 85 What ethnic group appears on your Reference Book?

Q. 86 *(INTERVIEWER NOTES):*

	Good Condition	Poor Condition	None
Describe furniture			
Lounge suite			
Dining Room suite			
Fridge			

ASK ALL: EVEN IF NOT DONE IN HOME

	Yes	No
Do you have a motor car?		
Radiogram		
Kind of pictures — portraits		
religious		
other		
none		
Garden with lawn		
Garden with flowers		
Mealies in back garden		
Fruit trees in garden		
China cups and plates		
Tin cups and plates		
Both		

473

Enjoyed the interview:

_____

_____

Done in respondent's house
Not done in Respondent's house

(RECORD): Area—Soweto
              Durban
              Pretoria

Selected Bibliography

Adam, Heribert, *Südafrika—Soziologie einer Rassengesellschaft* (Frankfurt, 1969).

Adam, Heribert, *Modernizing Racial Domination: The Dynamics of South African Politics* (Berkeley, 1971).

Adam, Heribert, 'The South African Power-Elite: A Survey of Ideological Commitment', in Heribert Adam (ed.), *South Africa—Sociological Perspectives* (London, 1971), pp. 73–102.

Adam, Heribert, 'Kultureller Pluralismus als politischer Konflikt', *Die Dritte Welt*, 2:1 (1973), pp. 44–58.

Adam, Heribert, 'The Rise of Black Consciousness in South Africa', *Race*, 15:2 (1973), pp. 149–65.

Adam, Heribert, 'Three Perspectives on the Future of South Africa' (Unpublished manuscript, 1977).

Adam, Heribert, 'When the Chips are Down: Confrontation and Accommodation in South Africa', *Contemporary Crises*, 1 (1977), pp. 417–35.

Albrecht, Gisela, *Soweto oder der Aufstand der Vorstädte: Gespräche mit Südafrikanern* (Reinbek, 1977).

Almond, Gabriel A. and S. Verba, *The Civic Culture: Political Attitudes and Democracy in Five Nations* (Princeton, 1963).

Amnesty International, *Politische Inhaftierung in Südafrika* (Baden-Baden, 1978).

Bagley, Christopher, 'Racialism and Pluralism: A Dimensional Analysis of Forty-Eight Countries', *Race*, 13:3 (1972), pp. 347–54.

Barratt, John *et al* (eds), *Accelerated Development in Southern Africa* (London and Basingstoke, 1974).

Barry, Brian, 'The Consociational Model and its Dangers', *European Journal of Political Research*, 3:4 (1975), pp. 393–412.

Beinart, W., 'The Policy of Industrial Decentralisation in South Africa', Study Project Paper No. 12, in *Foreign Investment in South Africa, The Conditions of the Black Worker* (Uppsala, 1975), pp. 85–125.

Bekker, Simon, 'The Plural Society and the Problem of Order' (Ph D dissertation, University of Cape Town, 1974).

Benson, Mary, *South Africa, The Struggle for a Birthright* (Harmondsworth, 1966).

Biesheuvel, S., 'The Influence of Social Circumstances on the Attitudes of Educated Africans', *South African Journal of Science*, Vol. 53, pp. 309–14.

Biko, Steve, 'White Racism and Black Consciousness', in H. W. van der Merwe and David Welsh (eds), *Student Perspectives on South Africa* (Cape Town, 1972), pp. 190–202.

Biko, Steve, 'Black Consciousness and the Quest for a True Humanity', in Basil Moore (ed.), *Black Theology: The South African Voice* (London, 1973), pp. 36–47.

Bilger, Harald R., *Südafrika in Geschichte und Gegenwart* (Konstanz, 1976).

Blenck, Jürgen and Klaus von der Ropp, 'Republik Südafrika: Teilung als Ausweg?' *Außenpolitik*, 27:3 (1976), pp. 308–24.

Bluhm, William T., *Theories of the Political System: Classics of Political Thought and Modern Political Analysis* (Englewood Cliffs, 1965).

Brett, E. A., *African Attitudes—A Study of the Social, Racial, and Political Attitudes of some Middle Class Africans* (Johannesburg, SAIRR, 1963).

Brookes, E. H., *Apartheid, A Documentary Study of Modern South Africa* (London, 1968).

Brückner, Reinhard, *Südafrikas schwarze Zukunft* (Frankfurt, 1977).

Bunting, Brian, *The Rise of the South African Reich* (Harmondsworth, 1969).

Buthelezi, Gatsha, *White and Black Nationalism, Ethnicity and the Future of the Homelands* (Johannesburg, SAIRR, 1974).

Butler, Jeffrey, 'The Significance of Recent Changes within the White Ruling Caste', in Leonard Thompson and Jeffrey Butler (eds), *Change in Contemporary South Africa* (Berkeley and Los Angeles, 1975), pp. 79–103.

Butler, Jeffrey, Robert I. Rotberg, and John Adams, *The Black Homelands of South Africa—The Political and Economic Development of Bophuthatswana and KwaZulu* (Berkeley and London, 1977).

Carter, Gwendolen M., 'African Concepts of Nationalism in South Africa', in Heribert Adam (ed.), *South Africa: Sociological Perspectives* (London, 1971), pp. 103–20.

Christian Institute of Southern Africa, *Torture in South Africa* (Cape Town, 1977).

Coleman, James S. and Carl G. Rosberg (eds), *Political Parties and National Integration in Tropical Africa* (Berkeley, 1964).

Crijns, A. G. J., *Race Relations and Race Attitudes in South Africa* (Nijmegen, 1959).

Cronjé, G., *Kerk en Huisgesin: die Huidige Kerklike en Godsdienstige Lewe van die Afrikaner* (Cape Town, 1958).

Daalder, Hans, 'The Consociational Democracy Theme', *World Politics*, 26 (1973/4), pp. 604–21.

Davenport, T. R. H., *South Africa: A Modern History* (London and

Basingstoke, 1977).

De Kiewiet, C. W., *A History of South Africa—Social and Economic* (London, 1957).

De Klerk, W. A., *The Puritans in Africa: A Story of Afrikanerdom* (London, 1975).

De Klerk, W. J., 'The Concepts "Verkramp" and "Verlig"', in N. Rhoodie (ed.), *South African Dialogue* (Johannesburg, 1972), pp. 519-31.

De Klerk, W. J., 'South Africa's Domestic Politics: Key Questions and Options', *Politikon*, 4:2 (1977), pp. 178-89.

Deutsch, Karl W., *Nationalism and Social Communication* (Cambridge, Mass., 1953).

Deutsches Institut für Internationale Pädagogische Forschung/Arnold-Bergstraesser-Institut: Projektgruppe Vorurteilsforschung, 'Einstellungen zu Fremdgruppen in der Bundesrepublik Deutschland, Großbritannien, den Niederlanden und Südafrika' (Unpublished manuscript, Frankfurt/Freiburg, 1976).

De Villiers, Cas (ed.), *Southern Africa: The Politics of Raw Materials* (Pretoria, 1977).

De Villiers, René, 'Afrikaner Nationalism', in Monica Wilson and Leonard Thompson (eds), *The Oxford History of South Africa*, Vol. II (Oxford, 1971), pp. 365-423.

Douwes-Dekker, L., D. Hemson, J. S. Kane-Berman, J. Lever, and L. Schlemmer, 'Case Studies in African Labour Action in South and South West Africa, *The African Review*, 4:2 (1974), pp. 205-36.

Doxey, G. V., *The Industrial Colour Bar in South Africa* (Cape Town, 1961).

Du Preez, A. B., *Eiesoortige Ontwikkeling tot Volksdiens* (Cape Town, 1959).

Du Toit, M. A., *South African Trade Unions: History, Legislation, Policy* (Johannesburg, 1976).

Du Toit, S., *Holy Scripture and Race Relations* (Potchefstroom, 1960).

Duve, Freimut (ed.), *Kap ohne Hoffnung oder die Politik der Apartheid* (Hamburg, 1965).

Edelstein, Joel C., 'Pluralist and Marxist Perspectives on Ethnicity and Nation-Building', in Wendell Bell and Walter E. Freeman (eds), *Ethnicity and Nation-Building: Comparative, International and Historical Perspectives* (London, 1974), pp. 45-57.

Edelstein, M. L., *What do Young Africans Think?* (Johannesburg, 1972).

Etzioni, A., *Political Unification: A Comparative Study of Leaders and Forces* (New York, 1965).

Feit, Edward, *African Opposition in South Africa—The Failure of Passive Resistance* (Stanford, 1967).

Feit, Edward, *Workers without Weapons, The South African Congress of Trade Unions and the Organization of the African Workers* (Hamden/Conn., 1975).

Feit, Edward and Randall G. Stokes, 'Racial Prejudice and Economic Pragmatism: A South African Case-Study', *The Journal of Modern African Studies*, 14:3 (1976), pp. 487–506.

Furnivall, J. S., *Colonial Policy and Practice: A Comparative Study of Burma and Netherlands India* (Cambridge, 1948).

Furnivall, J. S., *Netherlands India: A Study of Plural Economy* (Cambridge, 1939).

Geertz, Clifford, (ed.), *Old Societies and New States: The Quest for Modernity in Asia and Africa* (New York, 1963).

Giliomee, Hermann, 'Die Ontwikkeling van die Afrikaner se Selfkonsepsies' (Working paper for conference on 'Die Afrikaner Vandag', Cape Town, March 1974).

Gluckman, Max, *Analysis of a Social Situation in Modern Zululand* (Manchester, 1958).

Grey Coetzee, J. A., *Industrial Relations in South Africa* (Cape Town, 1976).

Halbach, Axel J., *Die südafrikanischen Bantu-Homelands: Konzeption—Struktur—Entwicklungsperspektiven* (München, 1976).

Hammond-Tooke, W. D., 'Tribal Cohesion and the Incorporative Process in the Transkei, South Africa', in R. Cohen and J. Middleton (eds), *From Tribe to Nation in Africa* (Philadelphia, 1970).

Hampel, R. and B. Krupp, 'The Cultural and Political Framework of Prejudice in South Africa and Great Britain', *Journal of Social Psychology*, 103 (1977), pp. 193–202.

Hanf, Theodor, *Erziehungswesen in Gesellschaft und Politik des Libanon* (Bielefeld, 1969).

Hanf, Theodor, 'Liberale Demokratie in einem Entwicklungsland: Libanon' (Working paper for the study group on 'Übertragbarkeit westlicher Demokratievorstellungen auf Entwicklungsländer', Conference of the German Association for Political Science, Berlin, October 1969).

Hanf, Theodor and Gerda Vierdag, *'People's College'—'The World''s Educational Supplement* (Deutsches Institut für Internationale Pädagogische Forschung, Frankfurt, 1977).

Harding, Leonhard, *Afrikanische Politik im Südlichen Afrika* (Mainz, 1975).

Harding, Leonhard, *Die Politik der Republik Südafrika* (Mainz, 1975).

Heimer, Franz-Wilhelm, 'Begriffe und Theorien der politischen Entwicklung', in Dieter Oberndörfer (ed.), *Systemtheorie, Systemanalyse und Entwicklungsländerforschung* (Berlin, 1971), pp. 449–515.

Heimer, Franz-Wilhelm, 'The Decolonisation Conflict in Angola 1974–1976', An Essay in Political Sociology' (Mimeograph, Arnold-Bergstraesser-Institute, Freiburg, 1977).

Hirschmann, David, 'Southern Africa: Détente?', *The Journal of Modern African Studies*, 14:1 (1976), pp. 107–26.

Hoagland, Jim, *South Africa—Civilizations in Conflict* (London, 1973).

Horrell, Muriel, *Legislation and Race Relations* (Johannesburg, SAIRR, 1971).

Horrell, M. *et al, A Survey of Race Relations in South Africa* (Johannesburg, 1970ff).

Horwitz, Ralph, *The Political Economy of South Africa* (London, 1967).

Hudson, W., G. F. Jacobs, and S. Biesheuvel, *Anatomy of South Africa—A Scientific Study of Present Day Attitudes* (Cape Town, 1966).

Huntington, Samuel P., *Political Order in Changing Societies* (New Haven, 1969).

Huntington, Samuel P., 'The Change to Change: Modernization, Development and Politics', *Comparative Politics*, 3:3 (1971), pp. 283–322.

Johnson, R. W., *How Long Will South Africa Survive?* (London and Basingstoke, 1977).

Johnstone, Frederick A., *Class, Race and Gold: A Study of Class Relations and Racial Discrimination in South Africa* (London, 1976).

Karis, Thomas and Gwendolen M. Carter (eds), *From Protest to Challenge, A Documentary History of African Politics in South Africa, 1882–1964* (Stanford, 1972).

Keet, B. B., *Die Etiek van Apartheid* (Johannesburg, 1957).

Kleynhans, W. A., 'Political Parties in South Africa', *Politikon*, 2:1 (1975), pp. 6–32.

Kotzé, J. C. G., *Principle and Practice in Race Relations* (Stellenbosch, 1962).

Kraft, Robert, 'Labour: South Africa's Challenge of the Seventies', *Optima*, 20:1 (1970), pp. 2–11.

Krause, O., 'Trends in Afrikaner Race Attitudes', in N. J. Rhoodie (ed.), *South African Dialogue* (Johannesburg, 1972), pp. 532–9.

Krüger, D. W., *The Making of a Nation* (London, 1969).

Kuper, Leo, 'Political Change in White Settler Societies: The Possibility of Peaceful Democratization', in Leo Kuper and M. G. Smith (eds), *Pluralism in Africa* (Berkeley and Los Angeles, 1969), pp. 169–94.

Landman, W., *A Plea for Understanding* (Cape Town, 1968).

Laurence, P., *The Transkei: South Africa's Politics of Partition* (Johannesburg, 1976).

Leftwich, Adrian, 'The Constitution and Continuity of South African Inequality: Some Conceptual Questions', in Adrian Leftwich (ed.), *South Africa: Economic Growth and Political Change* (London, 1974), pp. 125–85.

Legassick, Martin, 'South Africa: Capital Accumulation and Violence', *Economy and Society*, 3:3 (1974), pp. 253–91.

Legassick, Martin and Harold Wolpe, 'The Bantustans and Capital Accumulation in South Africa', *Review of African Political Economy*, 7 (1976), pp. 87–107.

Lehmbruch, Gerhard, *Proporzdemokratie: Politisches System und politische Kultur in der Schweiz und in Österreich* (Tübingen, 1967).

Lehmbruch, Gerhard, 'Konkordanzdemokratie im politischen System der Schweiz', *Politische Vierteljahresschrift*, 9:4 (1968), pp. 443–59.

Lehmbruch, Gerhard, 'Consociational Democracy in the International System', *European Journal of Political Research*, 3:4 (1975), pp. 377–91.

Lemon, Anthony, *Apartheid, A Geography of Separation* (Westmead, Farnborough, 1976).

Lever, H., 'A Comparative Study of Social Distance Among Various Groups in the White High School Population of Johannesburg' (Ph D dissertation, University of the Witwatersrand, Johannesburg, 1966).

Lever, H. and O. J. M. Wagner, 'Ethnic Preferences of Jewish Youth in Johannesburg', *Jewish Journal of Sociology*, 9 (1967), pp. 34–67.

Lever, H., *Ethnic Attitudes of Johannesburg Youth* (Johannesburg, 1968).

Lever, H., 'Ethnic Preferences of White Residents in Johannesburg', *Sociology and Social Research*, 52 (1968), pp. 157–73.

Lever, H., *The South African Voter—Some Aspects of Voting Behaviour* (Cape Town, 1972).

Lijphart, Arend, 'Typologies of Democratic Systems', *Comparative Political Studies,* 1:1 (1968), pp. 3–44.

Lijphart, Arend, 'Consociational Democracy', *World Politics*, 21 (1969), pp. 207–25.

Lijphart, Arend, *Democracy in Plural Societies, A Comparative Exploration* (New Haven and London, 1977).

Lijphart, Arend, 'Majority Rule versus Democracy in Deeply Divided Societies', *Politikon*, 4:2 (1977), pp. 113–26.

Lipset, Seymour Martin, *Political Man: The Social Bases of Politics* (Garden City, 1963).

MacCrone, I. D., 'A Comparative Study of European and Non-European Differences in Race Preferences', *South African Journal of Science*, 35 (1938), pp. 412–16.

MacCrone, I. D., 'Reaction to Domination in a Colour-Caste Society: A Preliminary Study of the Race Attitudes of a Dominated Group', *Journal of Social Psychology*, 26 (1947), pp. 69–98.

MacCrone, I. D., *Race Attitudes in South Africa* (Johannesburg, 1957).

Malherbe, E. G., *Race Attitudes and Education* (Johannesburg, 1946).

Marcum, John A., 'Southern Africa after the Collapse of Portuguese Rule', in Helen Kitchen (ed.), *Africa: From Mystery to Maze, Critical Choices for Americans*, Vol. VI (Lexington and Toronto, 1976), pp. 77–134.

Marquard, Leo, *South Africa's Colonial Policy* (Johannesburg, 1957).

Marquard, Leo, *A Federation of Southern Africa* (London, 1971).

Mayer, Philip, *Urban Africans and the Bantustans* (Johannesburg, SAIRR, 1972).

Mbanjwa, Thoko (ed.), *Black Review 1974/75*.

McRae, Kenneth (ed.), *Consociational Democracy: Political Accommodation in Segmented Societies* (Toronto, 1974).

Meer, Fatima, 'African Nationalism: Some Inhibiting Factors', in H. Adam, *South Africa: Sociological Perspectives* (London 1971), pp. 121–57.

Moodie, T. D., *The Rise of Afrikanerdom: Power, Apartheid, and the Afrikaner Civil Religion* (Berkeley and Los Angeles, 1975).

Moore, Basil (ed.), *Black Theology: The South African Voice* (London, 1973).

Morse, Stanley J. and Christopher Orpen (eds), *Contemporary South Africa: Social Psychological Perspectives* (Cape Town, 1975).

Muller, C. F. J., *Die Oorsprong van die Groot Trek* (Cape Town, 1974).

Nengwekhulu, Ranwedzi, 'The Meaning of Black Consciousness in the Struggle for Liberation in South Africa', *Notes and Documents of the United Nations Centre Against Apartheid*, No. 16/76 (July 1976).

Nordlinger, Eric A., *Conflict Regulation in Divided Societies* (Cambridge, Mass., 1977).

Oberschall, Anthony, 'Conflict and Conflict Regulation in Northern Ireland' (Congress paper to the American Sociological Association, New York, 1973).

O'Dowd, Michael, 'South Africa in the Light of the Stages of Economic Growth', in Adrian Leftwich (ed.), *South Africa: Economic Growth and Political Change* (New York, 1974), pp. 29–43.

Orpen, C., 'Authoritarian and Racial Attitudes Among English-Speaking South Africans', *Journal of Social Psychology*, 84 (1971), pp. 301–2.

Pauw, B. A., *The Second Generation: A Study of the Family among Urbanized Bantu in East London* (Cape Town, 1963).

Pettigrew, T. F., 'Social Distance Attitudes of South African Students', *Social Forces*, 38 (1960), pp. 246–53.

Pettigrew, T. F., 'Racially Separate or Together?', *Journal of Social Issues*, 25:1 (1969), pp. 43–69.

Pinard, M., 'The Moderation and Regulation of Communal Conflicts: A Critical Review of Current Theories' (Duplicated conference paper, Louvain, 1976).

Pityana, Nyameko, 'What is Black Consciousness?' in Basil Moore (ed.), *Black Theology: The South African Voice* (London 1973), pp. 58–63.

Pogrund, Benjamin, 'Constraints on Black Workers and White Employers in South Africa', Study Project Paper No. 14, in *Foreign Investment in South Africa, the Conditions of the Black Worker* (Uppsala, 1975), pp. 127–60.

Potholm, C. P. and Richard Dale (eds), *Southern Africa in Perspective, Essays in Regional Politics* (New York and London, 1972).

Rabushka, Alvin and Kenneth A. Shepsle, *Politics in Plural Societies, A Theory of Democratic Instability* (Columbus, Ohio, 1972).

Randall, Peter (ed.), *South Africa's Minorities*, SPRO-CAS Publication No. 2 (Johannesburg, 1971).

Randall, Peter (ed.), *Towards Social Change*, SPRO-CAS Publication No. 6 (Johannesburg, 1971).

Randall, Peter (ed.), *Apartheid and the Church*, SPRO-CAS Publication No. 8 (Johannesburg, 1972).

Randall, Peter (ed.), *South Africa's Political Alternatives*, SPRO-CAS Publication No. 10 (Johannesburg, 1973).

Rex, John, 'The Plural Society: The South African Case', *Race*, 12:4 (1970/71), pp. 401–13.

Rhoodie, N. J., *Apartheid and Racial Partnership in Southern Africa*, (Pretoria and Cape Town, 1969).

Rhoodie, N. J. (ed.), *South African Dialogue: Contrasts in South African Thinking on Basic Race Issues* (Johannesburg, 1972).

Rich, Paul, 'Ideology in a Plural Society: The Case of South African Segregation', *Social Dynamics*, 1 (1975), pp. 167–80.

Ripken, Peter and Gottfried Wellmer (eds), *Wanderarbeit im südlichen Afrika*, ISSA, Vol. 5 (Bonn, 1976).

Roberts, M. and A. E. G. Trollip, *The South African Opposition 1939–1945* (London, 1947).

Rokkan, Stein, *Citizens, Elections, Parties: Approaches to the Comparative Study of the Processes of Development* (Oslo, 1970).

Rose, Richard, *Governing without Consensus: An Irish Perspective* (London, 1971).

Runge, Erika, *Südafrika—Rassendiktatur zwischen Elend und Widerstand. Protokolle und Dokumente zur Apartheid* (Reinbek, 1974).

Sadie, J. L., 'Population and Economic Development in South Africa', *The South African Journal of Economics*, 39:3 (1971), pp. 200–22.

Schermerhorn, R. A., *Comparative Ethnic Relations* (New York, 1970).

Schlemmer, L., *Privilege, Prejudice and Parties—A Study of Patterns of Political Motivation Among White Voters in Durban* (Johannesburg, 1973).

Schlemmer, L., 'The Afrikaners: Youth and Change', *Optima*, 24:2 (1974), pp. 56–65.

Schlemmer, L., *Black Attitudes: Reaction and Adaptation* (Centre for Applied Social Sciences, Durban, 1975).

Schlemmer, L. and Tim J. Muil, 'Social and Political Change in the African Areas: A Case Study of KwaZulu', in Leonard Thompson and Jeffrey Butler (eds), *Change in Contemporary South Africa* (Berkeley and Los Angeles, 1975), pp. 107–37.

Schlemmer, L., 'The Devolution of Power in South Africa: Problems and Prospects' (Duplicated conference paper, Cape Town, 1977).

Schlemmer, L., 'Theories of the Plural Society and Change in South Africa', *Social Dynamics*, 3:1 (1977), pp. 3–16.

Schlemmer, L. and Eddie Webster (eds), *Change, Reform and Economic Growth in South Africa* (Johannesburg, 1978).

Seiler, John, 'South African Perspectives and Responses to External Pressures', *Journal of Modern African Studies*, 13:3 (1975), pp. 447–68.

Serfontein, J. H. P., *Die Verkrampte Aanslag* (Cape Town and Pretoria, 1970).

Serfontein, J. H. P., *Brotherhood of Power: An Exposé of the Secret Afrikaner Broederbond* (London, 1979).

482

Simpson, G. Eaton and J. Milton Yinger, *Racial and Cultural Minorities: An Analysis of Prejudice and Discrimination* (New York, 1965), Ch. 6: 'The Consequences of Prejudice and Discrimination: The Responses of Minority-Group Members', pp. 130–57.

Smith, M. G., 'Social and Cultural Pluralism', in *Annals of the New York Academy of Sciences*, 83 (1960), pp. 763–77.

Smith, M. G., 'Institutional and Political Conditions of Pluralism', in Leo Kuper and M. G. Smith (eds), *Pluralism in Africa* (Berkeley and Los Angeles, 1969), pp. 27–66.

Smith, M. G., 'Some Developments in the Analytic Framework of Pluralism', in Leo Kuper and M. G. Smith (eds), *Pluralism in Africa* (Berkeley and Los Angeles, 1969), pp. 415–58.

Smooha, Sammy, 'Pluralism and Conflict: A Theoretical Exploration', *Plural Societies*, 6:3 (1975), pp. 69–89.

Spandau, Arnt, 'Einkommensverteilung in Südafrika', in Heinz D. Ortlieb and Arnt Spandau (eds), *Südafrika: Revolution oder Evolution?* (Hamburg, 1977), pp. 129–50.

Spandau, Arnt, *Wirtschaftsboykott gegen Südafrika* (Cape Town, 1977).

Staub, Hans O., *Südafrikareport: Rassentrennung, Wunschtraum, Wahn und Wirklichkeit* (Wien, 1975).

Steiner, Jürg, 'The Principles of Majority and Proportionality', *British Journal of Political Science*, 1:1 (1971), pp. 63–70.

Steiner, Jürg, *Amicable Agreement versus Majority Rule: Conflict Resolution in Switzerland* (Chapel Hill, 1974).

Stephan, Klaus, *Südafrika—Weg in die Tragödie* (Munich, 1977).

Sundermeier, Theo (ed.), *Church and Nationalism in South Africa* (Johannesburg, 1975).

Thompson, Leonard, 'The Subjection of the African Chiefdoms', in Monica Wilson and Leonard Thompson (eds), *The Oxford History of South Africa*, Vol. II (Oxford, 1971), pp. 245–84.

Thompson, Leonard and Jeffrey Butler (eds), *Change in Contemporary South Africa* (Berkeley and Los Angeles, 1975).

Thula: Gibson, 'The Process of Power Sharing' (South African Institute of Race Relations, Doc. RR 178/77 of 20.12.1977).

Trapido, Stanley, 'South Africa in a Comparative Study of Industrialization', *Journal of Development Studies*, 7 (1971), pp. 309–20.

Troup, F., *Forbidden Pastures—Education under Apartheid* (London, 1976).

van den Berghe, Pierre L., 'Race Attitudes in Durban, South Africa', *Journal of Social Psychology*, 57 (1962), pp. 55–72.

van den Berghe, Pierre L., *South Africa: A Study in Conflict* (Middletown, 1965).

van den Berghe, Pierre L., *Race and Racism: A Comparative Perspective* (New York, 1967).

van den Berghe, Pierre L., 'Pluralism', in John J. Honigmann (ed.), *Handbook of Social and Cultural Anthropology* (Chicago, 1973), pp. 959–77.

483

van der Horst, S. T., *Progress and Retrogression in South Africa: A Personal Appraisal* (Johannesburg, SAIRR, 1971).

van der Horst, S. T. (ed.), *The Theron Commission Report: A Summary* (Johannesburg, 1976).

van der Merwe, C. J. and Ben Piek, *Die Houding van Blanke Kiesers Jeens die Kleurlinge* (Johannesburg, 1976).

van der Merwe, Hendrik W., M. J. Ashley, Nancy C. J. Charton, and Bettina J. Huber, *White South African Elites—A Study of Incumbents of Top Positions in the Republic of South Africa* (Cape Town, 1974).

van der Merwe, P. J., 'Labour Policy', in J. A. Lombard (ed.), *Economic Policy in South Africa* (Cape Town, n.d.), pp. 158–99.

van Jaarsveld, F. A., *The Afrikaner's Interpretation of South African History* (Cape Town, 1964).

van Rensburg, W. C. J. and D. A. Pretorius, *South Africa's Strategic Minerals* (Johannesburg, 1977).

van Zyl Slabbert, F., 'Afrikaner Nationalism, White Politics, and Political Change in South Africa', in L. Thompson and J. Butler (eds), *Change in Contemporary South Africa* (Berkeley and Los Angeles, 1975), pp. 3–18.

Vergnani, T., 'A Survey of Empirical Attitude Studies Conducted in South Africa' (Duplicated manuscript, Arnold-Bergstraesser-Institute, Freiburg, 1971).

Vorster, J. D., 'Etniese Verskeidenheid, Kerklike Pluriformiteit en die Ekumene', in *Grense, 'n Simposium oor Rasse en ander Verhoudinge* (Stellenbosch, 1961), pp. 65–80.

Walshe, Peter, *The Rise of African Nationalism in South Africa* (Berkeley, 1971).

Warren, Neil and Maria Jahoda (eds), *Attitudes* (Harmondsworth, 1973).

Wellmer, Gottfried, *Südafrikas Bantustans: Geschichte, Ideologie und Wirklichkeit* (Bonn, 1976).

Welsh, D., *The Roots of Segregation: Native Policy in Colonial Natal, 1845–1910* (Cape Town and London, 1971).

Welsh, D., 'The Political Economy of Afrikaner Nationalism', in A. Leftwich (ed.), *South Africa: Economic Growth and Political Change* (London, 1974), pp. 249–85.

Welsh, D., The Politics of White Supremacy, in L. Thompson and J. Butler (eds), *Change in Contemporary South Africa* (Berkeley and Los Angeles, 1975), pp. 51–78.

Wilson, Francis, *Migrant Labour* (Johannesburg, 1972).

Wilson, Monica and Archie Mafeje, *Langa: A Study of Social Groups in an African Township* (Cape Town, 1963).

Wilson, Monica and Leonard Thompson (eds), *The Oxford History of South Africa*, 2 Vols (Oxford, 1969 and 1971).

Wolpe, Harold, 'Industrialism and Race in South Africa', in S. Zubaida (ed.), *Race and Racialism* (London, 1970), pp. 151–79.

Wolpe, Harold, 'The Theory of Internal Colonialism: The South

African Case', in Ivar Oxaal, Tony Barnett, and David Booth (eds), *Beyond the Sociology of Development—Economy and Society in Latin America and Africa* (London and Boston, 1975), pp. 229–52.

Woods, D. J. (ed.), 'Conference at Bulugha, South Africa's First All Race Assembly, 9–11 November 1973' (Daily Dispatch, East London).

Worrall, D. (ed.), *South Africa—Government and Politics* (Pretoria, 1971).

Wright, Harrison M., *The Burden of the Present: Liberal-Radical Controversy over Southern African History* (Cape Town, 1977).

Index of Names

Index of Subjects

489

492